BLACK LITERARY MARKETPLACE
—2008 / 2009—

BAPWD

BLACK AUTHORS
——— & ———
PUBLISHED WRITERS DIRECTORY

A Grace Company Publication

BLACK LITERARY MARKETPLACE
2008 / 2009

Edited by Grace Adams

BAPWD

BLACK AUTHORS
&
PUBLISHED WRITERS DIRECTORY

BLACK LITERARY MARKETPLACE
2008 / 2009

BAPWD

BLACK AUTHORS

&

PUBLISHED WRITERS DIRECTORY

EDITED BY GRACE ADAMS

A Grace Company Publication

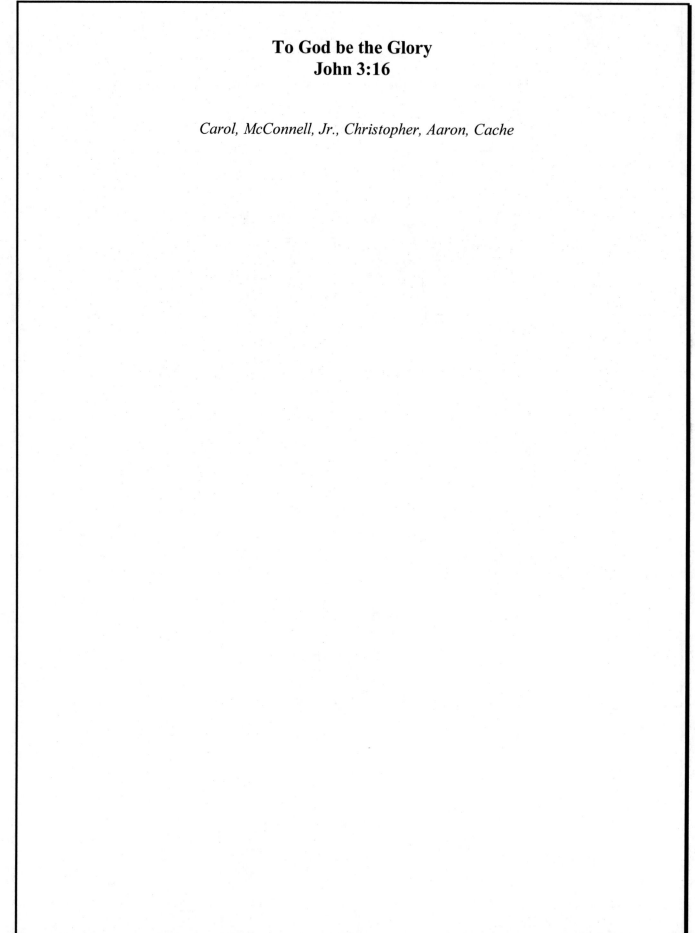

To God be the Glory
John 3:16

Carol, McConnell, Jr., Christopher, Aaron, Cache

Introduction

The purpose of the Black Authors and Published Writers Directory is to save you time in your marketing and research efforts! All the resources for Black authors, publishers, producers, agents, services, suppliers and speakers you are likely to ever need are listed here.

During the process of compiling and verifying the information for this directory notices and questionnaires were mailed to over 10,000 Black professionals in the literary industry. The tremendous response and completion of the questionnaires by the Black literary marketplace serves as the basis for the successful completion of this directory. If a Black author or literary firm is not listed in this directory, it may be due to insufficient information for a complete listing, or they requested deletion from the directory.

Literary professionals currently listed in this directory are encouraged to keep us up-to-date with any changes in information appearing in this directory. All additions, changes, or deletions for this directory should be sent to the address indicated below.

The Grace Publishing Company

829 Langdon Court, #45

Rochester Hills, Michigan 48307 USA

E-mail: **info@bapwd.com** - Website: **www.bapwd.com**

This book is dedicated to Black authors and the thousands of published writers working to effect a change in the world by eliminating illiteracy. May your wonderful works and deeds – as captured on these pages – help others to learn faster and enjoy "the journey" more . . .

- Grace Adams

Foreword

Black Authors and Published Writers Directory is ultimate marketing tool for authors, writers, publishers, producers, agents, booksellers, librarians, print media services, and others. It is guaranteed to save you from long hours of literary research. The time you save can be used toward other aspects of your business. However, the information contained in this directory should not be interpreted as an indication that a publisher, producer or agent accepts unsolicited material.

If you are searching for a publisher, producer or agent for publication of your literary material, you should first investigate the type of material the company publishes before submitting your material. Send a query letter, and always enclose a self-addressed stamped envelope with your submission. A sample query letter may be found at the end this book.

If your material is accepted by a publisher, producer or agent, you may be requested to send additional material. Other additional information may include your biography (brief profile), a description of your material, review copies, press releases, press kits, or articles previously written about your literary work.

If you are seeking publicity for your book or work — e-mail, fax, phone, and mail your news release, flyer, available for interview/tip sheet with teaser questions, mock-up review, book, and sales letter to appropriate media contacts. But, don't waste your time and money trying to get interviews on a show or in a newspaper section where your book doesn't fit.

To court media coverage most effectively, authors should first understand that newspapers, magazines, newsletters, radio programs, and television news are all driven by common needs. They have a need to fill time and space, to be special, to be first, and to provide information of value to readers, viewers, and listeners.

Newspaper and magazine editors look for stories that inform or entertain their viewers. Demonstrate to a newspaper editior or radio and TV talk show hosts, or producers, that you will be a good interview subject and that your book will interest and benefit their audience and they will interview you.

"The Ability To Read Awoke In Me A Long Dormant Craving To Be Mentally Alive."

-Malcolm X

About The Editor

Grace Adams
Editor * Publisher * Signatory Agent

In 1990-92, Adams impressed with the vast pool of Black talent in the media, began to compile a listing for her publication, <u>Black Authors and Published Writers Directory.</u> Over 1,000 Black authors, publishers, producers, distributors, song, film, and playwrights, agents, librarians, talk show hosts, consultants, advertising agents and other marketing resources were listed in the book. In 2003, Adams created and founded BAPWDcom the official website of the <u>Black Authors & Published Writers Directory</u>. Like the book, the website is a "must" for anyone interested in networking with major Black media professionals and services.

Native Greenville, Mississippian, Adams is the first Black signatory agent (*Writers Guild of America*). She has assisted and represented several major talents with book publishing projects, including legendary Mrs. Rosa Parks, <u>Quiet Strength</u> (1995, Zondervan Publishing Company), <u>Dear Mrs. Parks</u> (1996, Lee & Low Publishing), producer, songwriter, and Gospel recording artist, Fred Hammond, TV Judge and author, Greg Mathis, <u>Inner City Miracle</u> (2002, Warner Books), entertainment attorney and author, Gregory J. Reed, Esq., <u>Economic Empowerment Through The Church</u> (1994, Zondervan Publishing Company) and others.

Adams is editor and publisher of <u>Black Literary Players *(BLP),*</u> an on-line newsletter update for the <u>Black Authors and Published Writers Directory</u>. Published monthly, the *BLP* newsletter update features Black authors and published writers, profiles and literary and media professional services. Her Rochester, Michigan firm, **The Grace Company,** also acts as a distribution agent for several publishing entities that provide material that meet the needs of business.

What others are saying about . . .

Black Authors and Published Writers Directory

". . . A book that should be on the shelf of any person who is interested in African-American literature and arts."

Lenard D. Moore, author, <u>Desert Storm: A Brief History</u>, Staff Reviewer For Library Journal

"This ground-breaking publication is <u>"the doorway"</u> to the extraordinary world of African creativity. Along with its contents, the book's easy-to-read and well organized format makes it a must resource for anyone interested in the Black writers' market."

Steven Whitehurst, author, <u>Words From An Unchained Mind</u>

"A major resource directory for years to come. . . unleashes the hidden treasure chest of the finest African-American writers, publishers and griots the world over..."

Deborah Ray-Sims, president, Diasporic Communications

Contents

Profiles

Agents

Janell Walden Agyeman Agent, Janell Walden. Contact Ms. Janell Walden, Marie Brown & Associates, 990 North East 82nd Terrace, Miami, Florida 33138 Phone: (305) 759-4849 Fax: (305) 754-8081

Barrett Books Agency Agent, Audra Barrett. Since, 1999. Submission guidelines: Submit original query, book proposal, and resume. Audra Barrett, Barrett Books Agency, 12138 Central Avenue, Suite 183, Mitchellville, Maryland 20721 E-mail: **audra@barrettbooksagency.com** Website: **www.barrettbooksagency.com**

Marie Brown & Associates Agent, Marie Brown. Literary agent. 40-year veteran of the book business. Since 1984, has represented over 100 authors. Contact Ms. Marie Brown, Marie Brown & Associates, 412 West 154th Street, New York, New York 10032 Phone: (212) 939-9725 Fax: (212) 939-9728 E-mail: **mbrownlit@aol.com**

Connor Literary Agency Agent, Marlene Connor Lynch. Literary agent for books; also handles TV and film rights, general and non-fiction books - popular audience, mystery, thrillers, romance, self-help, how-to, cookbooks and general. Special ability to work with illustrated books. We do some packaging and book producing. The agency negotiates the terms of the publishing agreement, in complete consultation with the author, and handles all subsidiary rights retained by the author including first serial, movie/TV rights, and foreign rights in major countries throughout the world. The agency represents books being published by Crown, HarperCollins, John Wiley and Sons, Penguin Putnam, Simon and Schuster, Sourcebooks, Warner Books, and others. The Agency has also served as a consultant and agent for such corporations as Essence Communications, publishers of Essence Magazine and the Simplicity Pattern Company. "Query with SASE, Outline." Marlene Connor Lynch, Connor Literary Agency, 2911 West 71st Street, Minneapolis, Minnesota 55423 Phone: (612) 866-1486 E-mail: **connoragency@aol.com**

Crichton & Associates, Inc., Literary Agency Agent, Sha-Shana N.L. Crichton. Crichton & Associates represents writers of fiction and non-fiction works, including materials with African, African-American, Caribbean and Latin American themes. Currently seeking non-fiction by expert authors, contemporary fiction, commercial fiction, chick-lit, and romance novels (contemporary, inspirational, African-American and multicultural). Contact Crichton, Crichton & Associates, Inc., 6940 Carroll Avenue, Takoma Park, Maryland 20912 Phone: (301) 495-9663 Fax: (202) 318-0050 E-mail: **cricht1@aol.com** Website: **www.crichton-associates.com**

Grace Company Literary Agency Agent, Grace Adams. First Black Signatory Agent (Writers Guild of America), since 1994. Especially interested in Christian, and non-fiction books, plays, songs and films. Contact Ms. Grace Adams, The Grace Company, 829 Langdon Court, #45, Rochester Hills, Michigan 48307 E-mail: **query@bapwd.com** Website: **www.bapwd.com**

Lawrence Jordan Literary Agency Agent, Lawrence Jordan. Lawrence Jordan Literary Agency, 68 West 120th Street, #1517, New York, New York 10027 Phone: (212) 865-7170 E-mail: **LJLAgency@aol.com** Website: **www.Morningstar-communications.com**

Karen E. Quinones Miller Associate Agent. Karen is author of the Essence Bestselling novels, Satin Doll; I'm Telling; Using What You Got; Ida B., and Satin Nights. A former newspaper reporter, Miller also owns a small publishing company and recently became an associate agent with Liza Dawson Associates. Karen E. Quinones Miller, 1039 East Durham Street, Philadelphia, Philadelphia 19150 Phone: (215) 381-0645 Fax: (801) 881-2472 E-mail: **kmiller@lizadawsonassociates.com** Website: **www.karenequinonesmiller.com**

Milligan Literary Agency Agent, Dr. Rosie Milligan. Editorial consultant and book agent. Ghost writing, book evaluation, book rewriting for mainstream publishing submission. Dr. Rosie Milligan, Milligan Literary Agency, 1425 West Manchester Avenue, Suite C, Los Angeles, California 90047 Phone: (323) 750-3592 Fax: (323) 750-2886 E-mail: **DrRosie@aol.com** Website: **www.milliganbooks.com**

Nelson Literary Agency, LLC Agent, Kristin Nelson. An up-and-coming young agency, the Nelson Literary Agency specializes in representing commercial fiction (with a particular interest in romance and women's fiction) and high caliber literary fiction. The agency also represents a select few nonfiction projects that tend to be story-based, such as memoir or narrative nonfiction. Kristin Nelson, Nelson Literary Agency, LLC, 1020 15th Street, Suite 26L, Denver, Colorado 80202 E-mail: **query@nelsonagency.com** Website: **www.nelsonagency.com**

Serendipity Literary Agency LLC Agent, Regina Brooks. Contact Ms. Regina Brooks, Serendipity Literary Agency LLC., 732 Fulton Street, Suite 3, Brooklyn, New York 11238 E-mail: **rbrooks@serendipitylit.com** Website: **www.serendipitylit.com**

Tracy Sherrod Literary Services Agent, Tracy Sherrod. With partners Beverly Williams and Tony Clark, formerly in marketing at Holt, Sherrod offers clients everything from marketing to author career counseling, typing, editing, and inputting services. Accept e-mail queries. Contact Tracy Sherrod, Tracy Sherrod Literary Services, Inc., 2034 5th Avenue, Suite 2A, New York, New York 10035 Phone: (212) 369-6785 E-mail: **tracysherrod10027@yahoo.com**

Nichole L. Shields Associate Agent. Nichole L. Shields, Connor Literary Agency, 1645 West Ogden Avenue, Suite 309, Chicago, Illinois 60612 E-mail: **nicholelshields@yahoo.com**

Stinson Literary Agency Agent, Denise Stinson. Also, publisher and editor of contemporary Christian books at her company, Walk Worthy Press. Contact Ms. Denise L. Stinson, Stinson Literary Agency, 33290 West Fourteen Mile Road #482, West Bloomfield, Michigan 48301 E-mail: **editor@walkworthypress.net** Website: **www.walkworthypress.net**

Thompson's Literary Agency Agent, Maxine E. Thompson. Works with ebooks, fictional books, non-fictional books, short story collections, memoirs or autobiographies. Maxine E. Thompson, Black Butterfly Press, Post Office Box 25279, Philadelphia Pennsylvania, 19119 E-mail: **maxtho@aol.com** Website: **www.maxinethompson.com**

Artists/Illustrators

James Eugene Albert Digital Artist. Exhibitions: Permanent Gallery Artist at World Fine Art, Inc., 2002 - 2004, New York; Permanentt Gallery Artist at ARTWorks Gallery, 1997- 2004. Honors and Awards: "First runner up to First Place" Encyclopedia of Living Artists, 9th Edition, 1995; Academic Associate Art Institute, Verbano, Italy, 2001. Juried Shows: "The Best Contemporary Art Juried Collection" CD, Art Communications International, 1996, New York; "Out of the Internet", Sharon Arts Center, Peterborough, New Hampshire, 1995. Education: 1971 - 1985, University of California at Los Angeles and Berkeley. Contact Mr. James Eugene Albert, 601 Van Ness, Suite E 3518, SanFrancisco, California 94102 Phone: (415) 776-6632 E-mail: **jamesealbert@email.msn.com** Website: **www.jameseugenealbert.com**

Rashida Aisha Ali Author, poet, artist, educator and philanthropist, Rashida lectures nationwide, and conducts workshops, seminars, and symposiums on women related topics. Rashida Aisha Ali, House of Ra Publishing Company, 44 North East 51st Street, Miami, Florida 33137 E-mail: **venusra@bellsouth.net**

Paul Alleyne A published writer, (poetry and fiction), as well as a visual artist, Mr. Alleyne is author of Whatever It Takes (2005), and These Are Our Stories (2007). Contact Mr. Paul Alleyne, 2643 Bridgewater Drive, Grand Prairie, Texas 75054 Phone: (323) 230-9336 Website: **www.redbubble.com/people/bambooo**

Ron Anderson Visual Artist and art consultant for Ron Anderson Studio, LLC., Mr. Anderson is an oil painter and an art educator and has been a successful working artist for more than 20 years. He has earned many awards for his oil paintings and was a nominee for the 2005 Governor's Awards for the Arts in Ohio in the Individual Artist category. Ron's biographical information/photograph was included in the 2004 edition, the 2006 edition, and the 2007 edition of Who's Who in Black Columbus. My paintings are included in the permanent art collections of corporate and private art collectors. I completed six oil paintings for the Supreme Court of Ohio depicting the "The History of the Rule of Law," that are on display on the 11th floor of the Ohio Judicial Center. I was commissioned to create two portraits in oil of George Washington Williams. The paintings are on display in the "George Washington Williams Memorial Room" at the Ohio Statehouse. Three of my oil paintings were added to the permanent art collection of The King Arts Complex in a permanent interactive installation entitled "Cargo: The Middle Passage." The King Arts Complex was the recipient of the Greater Columbus Arts Council "Artistic Excellence" Award for the "Cargo" art exhibit in 2006, and received an award of $10,000.00. Panel three of "Cargo" was included in a hard cover Scholastic book for elementary students entitled The African American Story by author Joy Masoff. Original oil paintings for corporate and personal art collections. Fine art for public art projects, and for art licensing. Paintings include landscapes and figurative artwork. Contact Mrs. Robin Anderson, Ron Anderson Studio, LLC, Post Office Box 340241, Columbus, Ohio 43234 E-mail: **admin@ronandersonstudio.com** Website: **www.ronandersonstudio.com**

Michele Barkley Artist, writer, and poet, her visual art is an expression of a need to give voice to a world beyond words, as exhibited in her abstract and figurative paintings. She is author of Wayfaring Stranger-Poems, producer of the video poem - In View Of A Cup Half-Full, and author of a recently completed novel manuscript, Still A Blue Sky. Michele Barkley, PMB 88, 3703 South Edmunds Street, Seattle, Washington 98118   Phone: (206) 818-1091 E-mail: **michelebarkley@artuncommon.com** Website: **www.artuncommon.com**

Donald S. Benjamin Nationally acclaimed visual artist by training with a talent for literary and proposal writing. Masters in Fine Art, Howard University. Thirty-year career as an exhibiting artist and in visual communications art. Contact Mr. Donald S. Benjamin, 3525 16th Street, North West Washington, DC 20010   Phone: (202) 387-4495 E-mail: **dsben@mindspring.com**

Michael Billups Artist. Paintings, watercolors, graphite drawings, giclee's and poems. My paintings, pay homage to the diverse beauty of the Black Woman. Michael Billups, 702 15th Street South East, Washington, DC 20003 Phone: (202) 544-7285 Fax: (630) 214-2225 E-mail: **michaelbillups@hotmail.com** Website: **www.billupsstudio.com**

Vonetta Booker-Brown Writer, editor, virtual assistant, web designer and graphic artist, Ms. Brown's client roster includes CB Commercial, UBS Warburg, Pitney Bowes, Weekly Reader Corporation, Essence Communications, Daymon Worldwide and PH Factor Productions. An accomplished journalist and writer she is also designer, creator and editor of Triscene.com, an online magazine that covers the New York and Connecticut area. Vonetta Booker-Brown, Right Hand Concepts, 2020 Pennsylvania Avenue, North West, #341, Washington, DC 20006 E-mail: **chiefelement@gmail.com** Website: **www.righthandconcepts.com**

Ron Clowney Founder of Ron Clowney Designs; offers both traditional art services in addition to computer graphics design work in the areas of print and animation, pencil or painted portraits, pencil drawings of notable homes that the owner wants drawn and any type of commissioned artwork. Contact Mr. Ron Clowney, Ron Clowney Designs, 5513 Adode Falls Road, Unit 10, San Diego, California 92120 Phone: (619) 501-5740 E-mail: **rclowney@cox.net** Website: **www.rclowney.com**

Maurice Copeland Artist, author and poet, Maurice Copelands' poems have appeared in National publications, Frontier Report and The Secular Humanist. Contact Mr. Maurice Copeland, 8415 East 56th Street, Kansas City, Missouri 64129 Phone: (816) 550-9563 Website: **www.africanartwholesale.com**

Anna W. Edwards Fine Artist. Contact Ms. Anna W. Edwards, 237 East 14th Street, San Leandro, California 94577 Phone: (510) 636-1721 E-mail: **anna@annawedwards.com** Website: **www.annawedwards.com**

Conrad E. Gardner Self taught artist who grew up in Bronx, New York. Art work inspired by love of history and predominantly depicts African/African Americans in roles in which they are not traditionally seen. Contact Conrad Gardner, Hotep Creations, 2776 Parkview Terrace, Suite 1L, Bronx, New York 10468 Phone: (646) 391-0401 E-mail: **hotepcreations@yahoo.com** Website: **www.hotepart.com**

J. Lee Cooper-Giles Author of The Hypocrites. Lifelong political and social activist, he has three under-graduate college degrees from the Ohio State University, a BA in Black Studies and English, BA in Journalism, BFA in Painting and Drawing. J. Lee Cooper-Giles, 1761 Clifton Avenue #10, Columbus, Ohio 43203 Phone: (614) 251-1829 E-mail: **leegiles78@hotmail.com**

Cassandra Gillens A self-taught artist, Cassandra's art can be found from all parts of the Low country, and various states throughout America and featured in dozens of newspapers and magazines such as Southern Living Magazine. She won the accolades of United Airlines, and was proudly featured in that magazine's February edition. Her participation in PICCOLO SPOLETO ART EXHIBIT resulted in a sell out. Cassandra is a member of Beaufort Arts Association. Benjamin Gillens, Studio Manager. Cassandra Gillens Studio, Post Office Box 884 Beaufort, South Carolina 29901 Phone: (843) 592-0944 E-mail: **gillensart@hargray.com** Website: **www.cassandragillens.com**

Tania Guerrera Artist, and author of "Thoughts and Transformations." Contact Ms. Tania Guerrera, 311 North Avenue #11, New Rochelle, New York 10801 Phone: (917) 578-4264 E-mail: **TheArtist@taniaGuerrera.com** Website: **www.TaniaGuerrera.com**

Akua Lezli Hope A third generation New Yorker, firstborn, Akua Lezli Hope has won two Artists Fellowships from the New York Foundation for the Arts (1987, 2003), a Ragdale U.S.-Africa Fellowship (1993), and a Creative Writing Fellowship from The National Endowment for The Arts (1990). She received an Artists Crossroads Grant (2003) from The Arts of the Southern FingerLakes for her project, Words on Motion. She is published in numerous literary magazines and national anthologies including: The Yearπs Best Writing, Writerπs Digest Guides, 2003; DARK MATTER, (the first!) anthology of African American Science Fiction, Time Warner Books, 2000; THE BLUELIGHT CORNER, black women writing on passion, sex, and romantic love, edited by Rosemarie Robotham, Three Rivers Press, 1999. She holds a B.A. in psychology from Williams College, a M.B.A. in marketing from Columbia University Graduate School of Business, and a M.S.J. in broadcast journalism from Columbia University Graduate School of Journalism. She is a founding section leader in the Poetry Forum on Compuserve. She co-authored a biweekly column on social, political, and cultural issues for the Star Gazette in 1995. Her manuscript, The Prize is the Journey, was a finalist in the 1983 Walt Whitman contest. She is a founding member of the Black Writers Union and the New Renaissance Writers Guild whose alumni include Baron James Ashanti and Terri McMillan. Akua Lezli Hope, Post Office Box 33, Corning, New York 14830 E-mail: **akua@artfarm.com** Website: **www.artfarm.com**

Adin Kachisi Visionary, social critic, writer and an artist, his writings deal with societal issues like values, development, politics, economics, education, identity, spirituality and societal transformation. Mr. Adin Kachisi, 4049 Broadway, Box #190, New York, New York 10032 Fax: (360) 406-9287 E-mail: **akachisi@yahoo.com**

Roxann Latimer Writer, poet, journalist, artist, and entrepreneur, Roxann works as a television producer with her company WIM Media and as Publisher and Editor in Chief of Women In Motion magazine. She has published 2 romance novels and 1 book of poetry. Roxann Latimer, 3900 West 22nd Lane #10G, Yuma, Arizona 85364 Phone: (928) 343-9729 E-mail: **wimmedia@yahoo.com** Website: **www.roxannlatimer.com**

James Hiram Malone   Author, journalist, columnist, graphic and visual artist. African-American subjects in a flat, graphic style; medium most often used is pen and ink suitable for silkscreen or offset processes. Mr. Malone is author/illustrator, a writer and journalist he has written articles and contributed to Michigan Chronicle Newspaper (Contributor); Lighthouse and Guide; Atlanta Journal/Constitution Newspaper; Ebony (Contributor) and Negro Digest (Contributor). He is listed in Who's Who Among Black Americans; Contemporary Authors, and Who's Who in America. He is also winner of the Carnegie's National Art Award, and others. Mr. James Hiram Malone, 1796 North Avenue, North West, Atlanta, Georgia 30318 Phone: (404) 794-0948 E-mail: **j.l.t.malone@att.net** Website: **www.j.l.t.malone.home.att.net**

Gary Maynard Innovative interactive graphics designer, skilled animator and web designer. Gary Marynard, Maynard Graphics, Post Office Box 1545, Royal Oak, Michigan 48068 E-mail: **Gary@MaynardG.nu**

Janie McGee   A professional artist for 27 years, Janie creates commission art prints and is a published writer with a Christian base and reflection of black history. Contact Ms. Janie McGee, Vintage Coffee Press, 2406 Forest Edge Court, Suite 302B, Odenton, Maryland 21113 E-mail: **vintagecoffeepress@hotmail.com** Website: **www.sundaymorninz.com**

Charlotte Riley-Webb Educated in the public school system of Cleveland, Ohio, Charlotte Riley-Webb earned her B.F.A. degree from The Cleveland Institute of Art. She began her M.F.A. at Georgia State University, screen printing at The Atlanta College of Art, mono-printing and abstract art at Tougaloo College, Mississippi. She visually documented the essence of her culture in her three year traveling exhibition, From Stories of My America and used it as a springboard for The High Museum workshop where she was asked to compare her work to that of Jacob Lawrence. Gullah Rhythms, a painting from the tour, was also displayed as a part of the Kente' exhibition at The Marco Carlos Museum in Atlanta. Webb's work is included in numerous, private, business and corporate collections. Charlotte Riley-Webb was recently voted into the oldest most prestigious organization of women artists, The National Association of Women Artists, New in York. She received a September 2005 fellowship to The Hambidge Art Center and the Women's Studio Workshop, New York in January 2006. Contact Ms. Charlotte Riley-Webb, 120 Sandy Drive, Stockbridge, Georgia 30281 Phone: (678) 284-1770 E-mail: **cwebbart@bellsouth.net** Website: **www.charlotterileywebb.com**

Leo D. Sullivan Artist/Animator, writer, publisher and producer of videos and books. Contact Mr. Leo D. Sullivan, Owner, Vignette Multimedia, 1800 South Robertson Boulevard, Suite 286, Los Angeles, California 90035 Phone: (323) 939-4174 E-mail: **vignmulti@aol.com** Website: **www.afrokids.com**

George Edward Tait Multi-talented artist, musician, educator, and activist. Editor/ Publisher: Cosmic Colors (A Black Music Magazine) 1974. Curator and featured artist for The Black Solar Art Gallery (1973). Chairman, Pan-Alkebu-Lan Rhythm Association which produced programs honoring Marcus Garvey, Kwame Nkrumah, Nat Turner, Harriet Tubman, and Carlos Cooks (1973). Composer, sound editor, and actor for film Oh! My God! (1972). Faculty Member, Queens College S.E.E.K. Program. George Edward Tait, Post Office Box 1305, New York, New York 10035 E-mail: **georgeedwardtait@msn.com** Website: **www.georgeedwardtait.org**

C. A. Webb Visual artist, radio and television talk show host, weekly newspaper columnists, and poet. He has been involved with the arts since 1991, using his talent to encourage the youth in public schools in Mississippi to be active with their gifts. In 1999 he was recognized by the city of Jackson, Mississippi as a Hometown Hero and continues to participate with programs geared at assisting the arts and education. C. A. Webb, C.A. Webb Enterprises, 105 McCornell Circle, Brandon, Mississippi 39042 Phone: (601) 201-8139 E-mail: **cawebb@eastman.com** Website: **www.notthetate.co.uk/cawebb/index.html**

Fredrick Woodard Visual artist and poet. Contact Mr. Fredrick Woodard, 2905 Prairie du Chien Road, North East, Iowa City, Iowa 52240 E-mail: **fredrick-woodard@uiowa.edu**

Molefi Kete Asante
Author * Educator * Painter * Poet

Molefi Kete Asante is Professor, Department of African American Studies at Temple University. He is also a Guest Professor, Zhejiang University in Hangzhou, China. Asante has published 67 books, among the most recent are Afrocentric Manifesto (2008); The History of Africa: The Quest for Eternal Harmony (2007); Global Intercultural Communication (2007); Cheikh Anta Diop: An Intellectual Portrait (2006); Spear Masters: An Introduction to African Religion (2006), co-authored with Emeka Nwadiora; Handbook of Black Studies, (2005), co-edited with Maulana Karenga; Encyclopedia of Black Studies, (2004), co-edited with Ama Mazama; Race, Rhetoric, and Identity: The Architecton of Soul (2005); Erasing Racism: The Survival of the American Nation, (2003); Ancient Egyptian Philosophers (2000); Scattered to the Wind, Custom and Culture of Egypt, and 100 Greatest African Americans. He has recently been recognized as one of the most widely cited scholars. In the 1990s, he was recognized as one of the most influential leaders in American education.

Dr. Molefi Kete Asante completed his M.A. at Pepperdine and received his Ph.D. from the University of California, Los Angeles, at the age of 26, and was appointed a full professor at the age of 30 at the State University of New York at Buffalo. At Temple University he created the first Ph.D. Program in African American Studies in 1987. He has directed more than 130 Ph.D. dissertations. He has written more than 300 articles for journals and magazines and is the founder of the theory of Afrocentricity. Dr. Asante was born in Valdosta, Georgia in the United States, of Sudanese and Nigerian heritage, one of sixteen children. He is a poet, dramatist, and a painter. His work on African language, multiculturalism, and human culture and philosophy has been cited by journals such as the Africalogical Perspectives, Quarterly Journal of Speech, Journal of Black Studies, Journal of Communication, American Scholar, Daedalus, Western Journal of Black Studies, and Africaological Perspectives. The Utne Reader called him one of the "100 Leading Thinkers" in America. In 2002 he received the distinguished Douglas Ehninger Award for Rhetorical Scholarship from the National Communication Association. He regularly consults with the African Union. In 2004 he was asked to give one of the keynote addresses at the Conference of Intellectuals of Africa and the Diaspora in Dakar, Senegal. He was inducted into the Literary Hall of Fame for Writers of African Descent at the Gwendolyn Brooks Center at Chicago State University in 2004 and is the recipient of more than 100 national and international awards, including three honorary degrees.

Dr. Asante is the founding editor of the Journal of Black Studies (1969) and was the President of the Civil Rights organization, the Student Non-Violent Coordinating Committee chapter at UCLA in the 1960's. In 1995 he was made a traditional king, Nana Okru Asante Peasah, Kyidomhene of Tafo, Akyem, Ghana.

Associations

Afrocentric Homeschoolers Association   Non-profit resource for homeschooling families which are engaging in Afrocentric, African American or pro-Black education.   AHA was founded by Cheryl Edwards in 1996.   Contact Cheryl Edwards, AHA, 266 Charlotte Street, #292, Peterborough, Ontario K9J 2V4 Canada   Group E-mail: **blackhomeschool@yahoo.com** Website: **www.geocities.com/blackhomeschool**

Arizona Association of Black Journalists   A chapter of the National Association of Black Journalists.   President, Michelle Fitzhugh-Craig.   Contact Shades Magazine, Post Office Box, 865, Phoenix, Arizona 85001 Phone: (602) 435-8524 E-mail: **aabj@azblackjournalists.com** Website: **www.azblackjournalists.com**

Association For The Study Of African-American Life And History Foundation date 1915. ASALH is a national association "committed to education, research, and publishing African American history and culture."   ASALH, Howard University, CB Powell Building, 525 Bryant Street, Suite C142, Washington, DC 20059 Phone: (202) 865-0053 Fax: (202) 265-7920 E-mail: **executivedirector@asalh.net** Website: **www.asalh.com**

Association Of African American Web Designers   AAWDD is an index of black professional web developers located through out the United States.   In our listing, you will find web and graphic designers, programmers, writers, system administrators, marketers, e-commerce, flash and network specialist, and other web professionals.   AAWDD, Post Office Box 146, Malone, New York 12953 Website: **www.africanamericanwebdesigners.com**

Association Of African American Web Developers   The Association of African American Web Developers is a vehicle for promoting camaraderie, collaboration, and professional growth among men and women of color in all phases of web development and design, and to demonstrate their talents, skills, creativity, and contributions to the growth of the industry. Wiley Pompey-Kulia, Founder.   Website: **www.aaawd.net**

Bay Area Black Journalists Association   Bob Butler, president.   BABJA, 484 Lake Park Avenue, Post Office Box 61, Oakland, California 94610 E-mail: **bobbutler7@comcast.net** Website: **www.babja.org**

Black Caucus Of The American Library Association (BCALA)   National association of Black librarians serves as an advocate for the development, promotion, and improvement of library services and resources to the nation's African American community.   The BCALA publishes a monthly newsletter and librarians list on labels.   Contact Mr. Andrew P. Jackson, (Sekou Molefi Baako), President.   BCALA, Virginia State Library, Richmond, Virginia 23219 Phone: (804) 786-2332 Fax: (804) 786-5855 E-mail: **andrew.p.jackson@queenslibrary.org** Website: **www.bcala.org**

Black Entertainment & Music Association Bob Lott, 1501 Christian Street, Suite 200, Philadelphia, Pennsylvania 19146 Phone: (215) 545-5850 Fax: (215) 609-4425 E-mail: **blott@bemanow.org** Website: **www.bemanow.org**

Black Entertainment & Sports Lawyers Association (BESLA) Members represent leading celebrities and professionals in the entertainment and sports industries. Denis E. Kellman, Esq. President. Ms. Phyllicia M. Hatton, Administrative Director. Contact BESLA, Post Office Box 441485, Fort Washington, Maryland 20749 Phone: (301) 248-1818 Fax: (301) 248-0700 E-mail: **BESLAmailbox@aol.com** Website: **www.besla.org**

Black Journalists Association of Southern California A chapter of the National Association of Black Journalists. Lois Pitter Bruce, President. BJASC, Post Office Box 75129, Los Angeles, California 90075 Phone: (213) 427-8246 E-mail: **info@bjasc.org** Website: **www.bjasc.org**

Black Storytellers Association Of San Diego Our primary focus is to preserve and celebrate the unique culture of African Americans through an art form that reaches back thousands of years to the tribal ancestors of Africa. Black Storytellers Association of San Diego, 110 Orange Drive, Chula Vista, California 91911 Phone: (619) 422-7053 E-mail: **mcfarlin@cox.net**

Columbus Association of Black Journalists Professional media organization committed to fair and accurate coverage and portrayals of the African-American community. Contact CABJ, Post Office Box 1924, Columbus, Ohio 43216 E-mail: **cabjcolumbus@yahoogroups.com** Website: **www.cabjcolumbus.org**

Dallas/Fort Worth Association of Black Communicators Stephen Wright, Acting President. Stephen is also assignments manager at KXAS/NBC 5 Dallas/Ft Worth. Contact Stephen Wright, FW/ABC, A.H. Belo Building, Communications Center, Lock Box 11, Dallas, Texas 75265 E-mail: **info@dfwabc.org** Website: **www.dfwabc.org**

Michigan Black Independent Publishers Association Resource for authors, writers, companies, supplies, publishers and has trainings and events that are focused on the literary community. We are nationwide organization and a regional affiliate of PMA. Contact Ms. Tanya R. Bates, MBIPA, Post.Office Box 14304, Lansing, Michigan 48901 Phone: (517) 204-4197 E-mail: **info@tanyabates.com** Website: **www.tanyabates.com**

Motown Alumni Association, Inc. Helps artists, performers, and or musicians to move forward as professional entertainers. Most of our consulting services are free. We deal with amateurs, semi-professionals (wedding bands, and bar bands), and professional entertainers. Billy J. Wilson, Motown Alumni Association, Inc. 621 Orleans # 65, Detroit, Michigan 48207 Phone: (734) 972-7582 E-mail: **Billy_j_Wilson@Yahoo.com** Website: **www.motownalumni.com**

National Association For Multi-Ethnicity in Cable Educates the industry on marketing approaches, programming interests and operations strategies for our nation's ever-changing population, and guides industry understanding of these complex issues. Kathy Johnson, President. NAMIC, Inc., 336 West 37th Street, Suite 302, New York, New York 10018 Phone: (212) 594-5985 Fax: (212) 594-8391 E-mail: **info@namic.com** Website: **www.namic.com**

National Association For The Study and Performance Of African American Music (NASPAAM) Newsletter/Professional Organization. The organization serves its members and others by increasing the awareness of Black Music and its contribution to the arts, culture, and society. Also host the NASPAAM Professional Music Conference. Frank Suggs, President. NASPAAM, 1201 Mary Jane, Memphis, Tennessee 38116 Phone: (901) 396-2913 E-mail: **fsuggs@midsouth.rr.com**   Website: **www.naspaam.org**

National Association Of African American Studies & Affiliates Seeks to further research and promote interest in African American studies. The association provides a forum for research and artistic endeavors; provides information and contact resources for its members, and conducts educational programs. NAAAS, Post Office Box 325, Biddeford, Maine 04005 Phone: (207) 839-8004 Fax: (207) 839-3776 E-mail: **naaasgrp@webcom.com** Website: **www.naaas.org**

National Association Of Black Accountants (NABA) Represents the interests of over 100,000 African-Americans and other minorities participating in the fields of accounting, auditing, business, consulting, finance, and information technology. Host annual conventions. Publishes newsletters and video tapes. Ms. Rose Elder Harper, Chief. Contact NABA, 7249-A Hanover Parkway, Greenbelt, Maryland 20770 Phone: (301) 474-6222 Fax: (301) 474-3114 E-mail: **rharper-elder@nabainc.org** Website: **www.nabainc.org**

National Association of Black Female Executives in Music & Entertainment, Inc. A 501 (c) (6) nonprofit professional organization led by volunteer entertainment executives, NABFEME was launched in February 1999 with a mission to raise the profile and elevate the awareness of Black women in music and entertainment. Former DreamWorks Records Head of Urban Promotion, Johnnie Walker, founded NABFEME in 1998. Before taking the reins at DreamWorks, Walker had previously served as Senior Vice President of R&B Promotion at the Island Def Jam Music Group, having joined the staff of Def Jam Recordings in 1990 at the personal invitation of label founder Russell Simmons. During her 14-year tenure at the Island Def Jam Music Group, Walker was instrumental in developing the careers of some of the biggest names in recorded music including Jay-Z, Ja Rule, Ashanti, Ludacris, DMX, LL Cool J, Musiq, Dru Hill, Foxy Brown, Method Man, Case, Onyx and Montell Jordan, as well as fostering the success of the "Rush Hour" and "The Nutty Professor" soundtracks, among numerous other projects. The Executive Board of NABFEME is comprised of women from many different sectors of the business world and the entertainment industry. The organization's COO and annual Women's Leadership Summit Executive Director is Elektra Entertainment Vice President, Michelle Madison. Ramona Harrison serves as CFO, while veteran radio announcer/Program Director, Pam Wells serves as the organization's Vice President. NABFEME, Offices of Padell Nadell Fine Weinberger, 59 Maiden Lane, 27th Floor, New York, New York 10038 Phone: (212) 424-9568 E-mail: **johnnie_walker1@msn.com**   Website: **www.nabfeme.org**

National Association of Black Journalist (NABJ) Organization of journalists, students and media-related professionals that provide quality programs and services to and advocates on behalf of black journalists worldwide. NABJ seeks to strengthen ties among African-American journalists and promote diversity in newsrooms. Karen W. Freeman, NABJ, University of Maryland, 8701-A Adelphi Road, Adelphia, Maryland 20783 Phone: (301) 445-7100 Fax: (301) 445-7101 E-mail: **kfreeman@nabj.org** Website: **www.nabj.org**

National Association Of Black Owned Broadcasters (NABOB) Since 1976, the first and largest trade organization representing the interests of African-American owners of radio and television stations across the country to establish a voice and a viable presence in the industry. Contact NABOB, 1155 Connecticut Avenue, North West, Suite 200, Washington, DC 20036 Phone: (202) 463-8970 E-mail: **info@nabob.org** Website: **www.nabob.org**

National Association of Negro Musicians The National Association of Negro Musicians, Inc., is an organization that had its beginning May 3, 1919 in Washington, DC, at a temporary initial conference of Negro Musicians under the leadership of Henry Grant and Nora Holt. Members. Contact NANM, Post Office Box 43053, Chicago, Illinois 60643 Phone: (773) 568-3818 Fax: (773) 568-3818 E-mail: **organdiva@earthlink.net**

National Black MBA Association (NBMBA) Professional organization. Members. Publishes a monthly magazine. Also publishes a newsletter. Robin Melton, NBMBA, 180 North Michigan Avenue, #1400, Chicago, Illinois 60601 Phone: (312) 236-2622 Fax: (312) 236-0390 E-mail: **mail@nbmbaa.org** Website: **www.nbmbaa.org**

National Newspaper Publishers Association (NNPA) Also known as the Black Press of America, The NNPA is a 62-year-old federation of more than 200 Black community newspapers from across the United States. Since World War II, it has also served as the industry's news service, a position that it has held without peer or competitor since the Associated Negro Press dissolved by 1970. George Curry, Publisher. NNPA, 3200 13th Street, North, Washington, DC 20010 Phone: (202) 319-1291 E-mail: **news@nnpa.org** Website: **www.nnpa.org**

New Orleans Association of Black Journalists Freddie Willis Jr., president. Contact NOABJ, Post Office Box 51222, New Orleans, Louisiana 70151 E-mail: **fwillis@timespicayune.com** Website: **www.noabj.org**

South Florida Black Journalists Association Annual awards competition and conference. Terence Shepherd, President. SFBJA, Post Office Box 260807, Pembroke Pines, Florida 33026 E-mail: **tshepherd@miamiherald.com** Website: **www.sfbja.org**

Tampa Bay Association of Black Journalists Chapter President, Eric Deggans. Contact Tampa Bay NABJ, Post Office Box 172092, Tampa, Florida 33672 Fax: (727) 892-2327 E-mail: **NABJ@aol.com** Website: **www.freewebs.com**

Unity: Journalists of Color, Inc. Representing 7,000 journalists of color comprised of four national associations: Asian-American Journalists Association, National Association of Black Journalists, National Association of Hispanic Journalists, and the Native American Journalists Association. Unity, 1601 North Kent Street, Suite 1003, Arlington, Virginia 22209 E-mail: **info@unityjournalists.org** Website: **www.unityjournalists.org**

The Warwick Valley Writers' Association Founder and Director L. Guy Burton, through this local writers' group has been able to polish, complete and promote several Works in various genres, as well as help others to do the same. L. Guy Burton, The Warwick Valley Writers' Association, 12 Burton Lane, Warwick, New York 10990 E-mail: **booknook1@hotmail.com**

Attorneys

Abdul-Jalil al-Hakim President/CEO of Superstar Management world renowned for unprecedented services for Muhammed Ali, Brian Taylor, U.S. Rep. J.C. Watts, Warner Bros. Records, Deion Sanders, Delvin Williams, Giant Records, Kareem Abdul-Jabbar, M.C. Hammer, Capitol Records, Lyman Bostock, Evander Holyfield, Spencer Haywood, Cliff Robinson, Abbey Lincoln, EMI Records, Emanuel Stewart (Lennox Lewis, Prince Naseem Hamed, Oscar DeLa Hoya), Pebbles, John Carlos, Reggie White, and Marvin Gaye to name a few. He has a tremendous wealth of experience in all aspects of business and personal management negotiates and drafts all agreements for all publishing, merchandising and licensing; commercial advertisements and product endorsements; corporate sponsorships and affiliations; motion picture, television, radio and personal appearances; professional personal services contracts; electronic multimedia, literary, publishing, merchandising, licensing, concerts, tours, broadcasting, and video. He was the first African-American in the field and has taught and lectured Entertainment Law for 30 years. He has produced shows for Disney, ABC-TV and ESPN, events in Japan, Russia, Egypt, Romania, Paris, Europe, Brunei, U.S.; consulted BBDO Worldwide Advertising, Royal Family of Saudi Arabia, Arthur Ashe Foundation, Rare Multimedia, Capcom, Comspan, National Medical Association, Apex 1, The ESPY'S, "90210", Black Entertainment Television (BET), Sega, Sultan of Brunei, Nike, Pepsi, Screen Actors Guild (SAG), Producers Guild of America (PGA), Broadcast Music Inc. (BMI). Contact Mr. Abdul-Jalil al-Hakim, Superstar Management, 7633 Sunkist Drive, Oakland California 94605 E-mail: (510) 638-0808 Fax: (510) 638-8889 E-mail: **jalil@superstarmanagement.com** Website: **www.superstarmanagement.com**

Corey D. Boddie Entertainment attorney specializing in copyright/trademark litigation in the areas of music, fashion, and film, Mr. Boddie is a summa cum laude graduate of the University of Virginia, and a graduate of Southern University Law Center. His legal career include his 2001 appointment to the General Counsel for the Manhattan Short Film Festival-considered to be one of the largest short film festivals in the world. In 2003, Corey was profiled on "Celebrity Justice" and "Entertainment Tonight" with regards to a highly publicized multimillion-dollar copyright/trademark infringement case against the "Osbourne Family" and Sony Music Entertainment. In 2006, he was apart of the legal team regarding copyright infringement against Beyonce Knowles. In addition, Corey has appeared as a panelist on a number of entertainment education conferences as a specialist in the field of entertainment law. His client roster includes: the clothing company- Meoshe, KING and RIDE Magazine, Todd 1 and Visionary Media, LLC, Nokio of R&B group, Dru Hill, Lady Bug Mecca, formerly of Grammy Award Winning group, Digable Planets, musical icon, KOOL & THE GANG, chart-topping reggae artists Wayne Wonder, Bad Boy recording artists Black Rob and MTV's "Da Band" E. Ness, Grammy nominated songwriter "Taj" Jackson, and many other stars in the entertainment world. Mr. Corey D. Boddie, Esq., Boddie & Associates, 2040 Exchange Place, Suite 1800, New York, New York 10005 Phone: (212) 480-7652 Fax: (212) 480-6581 E-mail: **C.Boddie@earthlink.net** Website: **www.boddieassoc.com**

Sha-Shana N.L. Crichton, Esq. Author and entertainment attorney, Sha-Shana N.L. Crichton frequently lectures on negotiating publishing contracts and author-editor-agent relationships. She counsels artists, authors, musicians, photographers, and other creative entities regarding drafting, and negotiating contracts, copyrights, wills, small business management, permits and employment issues relating to intellectual property, such as work-for-hire and non-competition clauses. She is author of Distinguishing Between Direct and Consequential Damages Under New York Law in Breach of Service Contract Cases, Howard Law Journal 2002. She is a graduate of Howard University School of Law (J.D. cum laude); the University of the West Indies (B.A. Honors); and the Instituto Benjamin de Tudela, Navarra, Spain. She is a former managing editor of the Howard Law Journal and has edited several articles and books, including Constitutional Law: Analysis and Cases by Ziyad Motala and Cyril Ramaphosa (Oxford University Press, 2002).   She is licensed to practice in New York, New Jersey and the District of Columbia, and is a member of the Litigation and Arts, Entertainment and Sports Sections of the DC Bar. Contact Sha-Shana N.L. Crichton, Esq. Crichton & Associates, Inc., 6940 Carroll Avenue, Takoma Park, Maryland 20912 Phone: (301) 495-9663 Fax: (202) 318-0050 E-mail: **cricht1@aol.com** Website: **www.crichton-associates.com**

Dedra S. Davis One of the most highly sought after speakers in the nation on entertainment law issues including, but not limited to, music publishing, sampling, and independent labels, Entertainment Attorney Dedra Davis represents platinum, gold, as well as uncertified artists, producers, writers, record labels, managers and publishing companies from all over the world. In addition to reading, writing, and negotiating entertainment contracts, placing tracks, and placing music in movies and TV, she provides worldwide entertainment business consulting services, and has strong relationships with major records labels, publishing, production, movie, and television companies all over the world. She is also CEO of Dedra's Entertainment Group, a marketing and promotion company which successfully produced events such as Black Cinema Cafe-Houston, Producer's Panel, NABFEME "Living Your Dream" event, and BESLA fundraiser, etc. She received her Bachelor's Degree from Texas Tech University and her Doctor of Jurisprudence from South Texas College of Law, an affiliate of Texas A&M University. Law Offices of Dedra S. Davis, 26 Broadway, Suite 400, New York, New York 10004 Texas: 7322 Southwest Freeway, Suite 1100, Houston, Texas, 77242 Phone: (713) 981-3861 Fax: (713) 981-3862 E-mail: **DEDRADAVIS@musiclw.com** Website: **www.musiclw.com**

Teresa R Martin, Esq. Although a full service practice firm, our office is especially able to serve clients in the following areas: Entertainment (copyright and trademark, Business, Contract, Real Estate, Collections and Bankruptcy matters. A graduate of Touro Law School in Huntington, New York, Teresa received her JD in 1997. In December 2001, Martin cut the ribbon on Smith Martin, LLP with offices located in the Bronx and West Babylon, New York, where she is managing partner. Teresa R. Martin, Teresa R Martin, P.C., 67 Wall Street, Suite #2211, New York, New York 10005 Phone: (212) 709-8224 E-mail: **info@martinlegal.com** Website: **www.martinlegal.com**

Darrell D. Miller, Esq. Film. Entertainment Attorney. Member of the Black Entertainment and Sports Lawyers Association. Contact Mr. Darrell D. Miller, Esq., Mason Miller, LLP, 2121 Avenue of the Stars, Suite 2580, Los Angeles, California 90067 Phone: (310) 424-1120 Fax: (310) 424-1121 E-mail: **ddm@masonmillerllp.com** Website: **www.masonmillerllp.com**

Gregory J. Reed, Esq. Author, agent, entertainment attorney and producer, Reed's experiences are diverse and he is the only attorney to represent six (6) world champion boxers: Thomas Hearns, Hilmer Kenty, Leon Spinks, Pipino Cuvas, and Tony Tucker. He was instrumental in negotiating one of the largest contracts in boxing history in excess of 30 million dollars involving Thomas Hearns and Sugar Ray Leonard. Reed negotiated the unification of all boxing titles involving Mike Tyson and Tony Tucker. He was the chief lead counsel involving the first historical multi-million dollar lawsuit case, Miss Carole Gist (first black Miss USA 1990) v. Miss Universe, Inc., Pageant, settled (Jan. 1992). Reed was selected to be the legal counsel for Nelson Mandela's tour committee of Michigan. Civil Rights Legend, Mrs. Rosa Parks' attorney for the last 15 years he recently represented her in her case against rappers OutKast/BMI Records, settled (2005). He founded the Parks Legacy and Museum. Reed has lectured in foreign countries and nationwide on sports and entertainment law. He is used as an expert witness in contract, trademark and entertainment cases throughout the United States. He is one of the founders Vice President board member of The Black Entertainment Sports Lawyers Association and has been a professor of taxation in the School of Business at Wayne State University. Reed is the first African American Board Member of Michigan State University Foundation $40 million entity and was the first African American lawyer to be a member of the Internal Revenue Service Advisory Board of the United States. Contract areas include The Statue of Liberty restoration projects; radio announcers; movie contracts; TV project syndication; corporate clients; and attorneys. Education: B.S., Michigan State University (Engineering); M.S., Michigan State University (Management Science); J.D., Wayne State University; L.L.M., Wayne State University (Master Of Taxation Law). Gregory J. Reed, Esq., Gregory J. Reed & Associates, 1201 Bagley, Detroit, Michigan 48226 Phone: (313) 961-3580 Fax: (313) 961-3582 E-mail: **gjrassoc@aol.com** Website: **www.gjreedlaw.com**

Gary A. Watson Film. Entertainment attorney, Gary has lectured at numerous events, including the Black Entertainment and Sports Lawyers Association's Annual Conferences. As well as Annual Meetings for the American Bar Association's Forum on the Entertainment and Sports Industries. He has addressed Northwestern University's prestigious Kellogg School of Business in Evanston, Illinois. He taught an entertainment law and business class at Stanford University; and a course entitled Music Production, Business & Legal Aspects at the Law Center of the University of Southern California; and a feature film financing class for Whittier Law School's Inaugural Summer Abroad Program in Santander, Spain. He obtained his AB in 1980 from Stanford University, and his law degree from the University of California at Berkeley in 1984. He served as lead attorney for Universal Pictures on "The Guardian," a film by the director of "The Exorcist" William Friedkin; two pictures by Spike Lee, "Mo' Better Blues" and "Jungle Fever;" "Childs Play 3;" Wes Craven's and Shep Gordon's "People Under The Stairs;" the John Goodman starrer, "The Babe;" the film featuring Goldie Hawn, Bruce Willis and Meryl Streep, directed by Robert Zemekis, entitled "Death Becomes Her;" and the Oscar Award winning picture starring Al Pacino titled "Scent of a Woman." He is Chair Elect and a Governing Committee Member of the American Bar Association's Forum on Entertainment and Sports Industries. He served as Division Chair of the Motion Pictures, Television, Cable and Radio Division and as Celebration of Black Cinema Committee Member for The 35th Chicago International Film Festival. Gary Watson, Esq., Gary A. Watson & Associates, 1875 Century Park East, Suite 1000, Los Angeles, California 90067 Phone: (310) 203-8022 Fax: (310) 203-8028 E-mail: **gwatson@garywatsonlaw.com** Website: **www.garywatsonlaw.com**

Tonya M. Evans-Walls Visiting Professor of Law at Widener University School of Law (Harrisburg campus) and an attorney specializing in the areas of entertainment law (literary, music and film), intellectual property (copyright and trademark), estate planning, and municipal finance. Ms. Evans-Walls will be joining the tenure track faculty as Assistant Professor of Law at Widener beginning July 2008. She is the Chair of the Pennsylvania Bar Association Sports, Entertainment and Art Law Committee, and has served as an adjunct professor of copyright, publishing and licensing at York College of Pennsylvania. She is a nationally recognized speaker who presents to various audiences regularly on publishing and intellectual property law and estate planning issues. Tonya, known affectionately as "Lawyer by Day, Poet by Night" is also a performance poet and writer, and the author of numerous books, including Contracts Companion for Writers, Copyright Companion for Writers, Literary Law Guide for Authors: Copyright, Trademark, and Contracts in Plain Language, Seasons of Her and SHINE! Forthcoming titles include Contracts Companion for Writers (Spring 2007). Her short story, Not Tonight appears in an anthology titled Proverbs for the People, published by Kensington. Tonya attended Northwestern University on a four-year tennis scholarship, and thereafter she competed on the women's professional tennis circuit and played most notably in the US Open, Virginia Slims of Philadelphia, and Lipton in 1993. Thereafter, she attended Howard University School of Law on an academic scholarship, served as Editor-in-Chief of the Howard Law Journal and graduated with honors. Tonya now lives in Philadelphia with her husband, O. Russel Walls, III, and is a member of Alpha Kappa Alpha Sorority, Inc. Tonya M. Evans-Walls, TME Law, LLC, 6703 Germantown Avenue, Suite 200, Philadelphia, Pennsylvania 19119 Phone: (215) 438-0468 Fax: (215) 438-0469 E-mail: **tme@tmelaw.net** Website: **www.tmelaw.net**

Authors

Stacy Hawkins Adams Authors, journalist, motivational and inspirational speaker, Stacy has been putting pen to paper for as long as she can remember. Her debut novel, Speak To My Heart, was voted 2004 Best New Multicultural Christian Fiction, and Stacy was named 2004 Best New Multicultural Christian Fiction Author by Shades of Romance Magazine. Black Expressions Book Club dubbed her a literary "Rising Star." In her novels, Stacy enjoys creating plots that keep readers turning pages and characters that compel readers to examine the role faith plays in their lives. As a public speaker, she shares motivational, inspirational or spiritual messages that leave her corporate, civic or religious audiences desiring to lead lives of excellence. She is a former board member of The READ Center, a program that teaches adults to read, and now assists with the Richmond affiliate of Reach Out and Read. Stacy lives in a suburb of Richmond with her husband and two children. Contact Mrs. Stacy Hawkins Adams, Post Office Box 25985 Richmond, Virginia 23260 Phone: (804) 768-1292 E-mail: **stacy@stacyhawkinsadams.com** Website: **www.stacyhawkinsadams.com**

Jacques Sotero Agboton Author of the book Philosophy of Engagement, (An Ideological Basis for the Liberation of African People) Jacques was born in Senagal. His published works in fiction include Mistress of the Fish Trading Post, Lord Berkley's Wife, the Death of a Battered Woman. Jacques Sotero Agboton, JSA Publishing, Post Office Box 776, Fort Lauderdale, Florida 33302 E-mail: **jsagboton@jsapublishing.com** Website: **www.jsapublishing.com**

Darlene Aiken Author of "How to Be A Young Lady: Your Total Guide for Being the Best Possible You! Aikens is President/CEO of Inner Beauty Solutions. Contact Ms. Darlene Aiken, MPS, Post Office Box 313, Central Islip, New York 11722 Phone: (631) 561-8006 E-mail: **innerbeautysolutions@hotmail.com** Website: **www.innerbeautysolutions.net**

Curtis L Alcutt Author of the novel, "Dyme Hit List," an erotic, urban love story based in Oakland, California. Curtis L Alcutt, Post Office Box 5351, Sacramento, California 95817 E-mail: **blackauthor@yahoo.com**

Vincent R. Alexandria Author, actor, producer, director, composer, lyricist, screenwriter, vocalist, and musician. He holds a Masters degree in literature from Baker University and holds a Bachelor's degree in Psychology from Rockhurst College. He is the founder of the Brother 2 Brother African-American Male Literary Symposium. He has completed a book of poetry From the Bottom of My Heart and three murder detective mystery novels, "Postal Blues," "Black Rain," and his first novel, "If Walls Could Talk. Vincent Alexandria also wrote the movie script, Walls of Deception. He's received numerous awards for outstanding service as a volunteer with the Boys and Girls Club of America. He has written, produced and directed three musical stage plays, "His Eyes Are On The Sparrow", "The Changing of an Uncle Tom," and "If She Only Knew." Contact Mr. Vincent R. Alexandria, c/o We Must X-L, Inc., 10900 Fuller, Kansas City, Missouri 64134 E-mail: **raychone1@yahoo.com** Website: **www.vincentalexandria.com**

Humza al-Hafeez Author of Some Things To Think About (2003), a collection of speeches and letters concerning the state of the black men and woman experience in America, and documenting one of the most important life giving philosophies of our time, which is the message given to us by the Honorable Elijah Muhammad. He has lectured at universities and correctional institutes through out the country. In 1959, Mr. Hafeez entered the New York Police Department (NYPD) where he worked as Narcotic Bureau Investigator, and as: Special Investigator (Undercover) U.S. DEA, NAAP Commission Investigator, Manhattan and Brooklyn New York, D.A. Offices. He worked as a consultant, U.S. Justice Department, Director of Security: Uganda Mission, Inner City Broadcasting Corporation, Boys Choir of Harlem and Iran Mission, Administrative Minister, Temple of Islam, Inc., and as Personal Security to Minister Louis Farrakhan. He is Founder and Past President of the National Society of Afro-American Policemen, Inc., and also former Editor in-chief of Your Muhammad Speaks newspaper. Minister Humza al-Hafeez, 1211 Atlantic Avenue, Brooklyn, New York 11216 Phone: (718) 789-7747 E-mail: **alhafeez@earthlink.net**

David E. Alston Author of books: (Release Your Glory), (Know Pain......Know Gain), (The Rough Road to Destiny), and (The Ten Commandments for Surviving Children with Behavioral Problems). David Alston, 66 Mt. Pleasant Church Road, Manson, North Carolina 27553 Phone: (252) 915-7339 Fax: (252) 456-9977 E-mail: **bishop@strengtheningthebody.org**

Karima Amin Performing storyteller and a children's author who provides programming for adults and children in a variety of venues. She is the author of The Adventures of Brer Rabbit and Friends and several of her stories have appeared in publications produced by Publications International of Lincolnwood, Illinois. Karima is also author of You Can Say That Again! which includes six of her favorite stories plus commentary on CD. Karima Amin, Do Tell Productions, Post Office Box 273, Buffalo, New York 14212 E-mail: **karimatells@yahoo.com**

Claud Anderson Author of the books, Black Labor, White Wealth: A Search for Power and Economic Justice and PowerNomics: The National Plan to Empower Black America. He is also founder of The Harvest Institute, a research educational, policy and advocacy organization. Claud Anderson, The Harvest Institute, 623 Florida Avenue, North West, Washington, DC 20001 Phone: (202) 518-2465 Fax: (301) 564-1997 E-mail: **info@harvestinstitute.org** Website: **www.harvestinstitute.org**

Monica Anderson Motivational speaker, dentist, and author her latest release is, I stand accused. Her debut novel, "When A Sistah's FED UP," was an Essence, Dallas Morning News, and Booking Matters Best Seller for paperback fiction, 2006. She has also authored two non-fiction books: Black English Vernacular and Mom, Are We There Yet? Her short stories and poetry are included in several anthologies. She earned her Bachelor of Arts degree from Baylor University, and her doctorate from the University of Minnesota School of Dentistry. In 1996, she became the first African-American columnist for the Arlington Star-Telegram, writing over four-hundred columns while practicing dentistry full-time. Awards: Outstanding Young Women of America, the Distinguished Black Alumni Award from the Baylor Black Alumni Association, and the Millennium Award for Medicine from Altrusa International, Inc. Monica "Dr. Moe" Anderson, Post Office Box 14115, Arlington, Texas 76094 Phone: (817) 446-6636 E-mail: **drmoeanderson@sbcglobal.net** Website: **www.drmoeanderson.com**

Stanice Anderson　Author, Inspirational Speaker, and Freelance Writer.　Author of, I Say A Prayer For Me: One Woman's Life of Faith and Triumph (Walk Worthy Press/Warner Books) and 12-Step Programs: A Resource Guide.　Stanice Anderson, Shout Glory, LLC, 9605 Muirkirk Road, Suite D-160, Laurel, Maryland 20708　E-mail: **stanice@stanice.com**　Website: **www.stanice.com**

Vinton R Anderson　Retired Bishop in the African Methodist Episcopal Church.　Author of My Soul Shouts! (Judson Press).　Bishop Vinton R. Anderson, 22 West Sherwood Drive, Overland, Missouri 63114　Fax: (314) 427-2794　E-mail: **vander2201@aol.com**

Artist C. Arthur　Author of contemporary African American romance.　Contact Mr. Artist C. Arthur, 5404 Addington Road, Baltimore, Maryland 21229　E-mail: **acarthur22@yahoo.com**

Molefi Kete Asante　Professor, Department of African American Studies at Temple University. Considered by his peers to be one of the most distinguished contemporary scholars, Asante has written 60 books, among the most recent are Encyclopedia of Black Studies, (2004), co-edited with Ama Mazama, Race, Rhetoric, and Identity.　The Architecton of Soul, Erasing Racism: The Survival of the American Nation, (2003), Ancient Egyptian Philosophers (2003), Scattered to the Wind, Custom and Culture of Egypt, and 100 Greatest African Americans. The second edition of his high school text, African American History: Journey of Liberation, 2nd Edition, (2001), is used widely throughout North America.　He has published more scholarly books than any contemporary African author and has recently been recognized as one of the ten most widely cited African Americans.　Ana Yenenga, Post Office Box 30004, Elkins Park, Pennsylvania 19027　Phone: (215) 782-3214　E-mail: **masante@temple.edu**　Website: **www.asante.net**

Jabari Asim　Author of Not Guilty: Twelve Black Men Speak Out on Life, Justice and the Law and The Road to Freedom: A Novel of the Reconstruction.　Deputy Editor, Washington Post Book World.　Columnist, washingtonpost.com.　Mr. Jabari Asim, 1150 15th Street, North West, Washington, DC 20071　E-mail: **asimj@washpost.com**　Website: **www.washingtonpost.com**

Keidi Awadu　Author of 18 published books including the latest "The Road to Power: Seven Steps to an African Global Order."　Host of a daily talk radio show The Conscious Rasta Report on LIBRadio.com and LIBtv.com.　Featured regularly on radio stations and spoken around the world on subjects covering health and biology, HIV/AIDS solutions, politics, technology, culture, transformation, global business development, media communications and metaphysics. Keidi Obi Awadu, 664 West Arbor Vitae Street, Suite 5, Inglewood, California 90301　Phone: (661) 526-4787　E-mail: **keidi@libradio.net**　Website: **www.Keidi.biz**

Azarel　A native of North Carolina, her first novel, A Life to Remember provides the opportunity to show her readers everyone can change.　Azarel, Post Office Box 423, Brandywine, Maryland 20613　E-mail: **Tressa428@cs.com**　Website: **www.lifechangingbooks.net**

Shonell Bacon　Co-author of Luv Alwayz and Draw Me with Your Love.　Currently working on her MFA in Creative Writing at McNeese University, as well as teaching English courses at McNeese.　Shonell Bacon, 605 Division Street, Lake Charles, Louisiana 70601　Phone: (337) 433-9728　E-mail: **sdb6812@hotmail.com**　Website: **www.intothespotlight-inc.com**

Michael Baisden From best-selling author to drive-time radio host in New York City, Michael Baisden can be heard each weekday afternoon on 98.7 KISS FM. A Chicago native Michael redefined marketing in the book industry when he self-published his first book, Never Satisfied: How and Why Men Cheat. The controversial book of short stories about infidelity sold over 400,000 copies nationally. His latest novel, "Gods Gift to Women" was released on October 1, 2002. In 1999, he self-published his third book, The Maintenance Man, which was adapted into a stage play by I'm Ready Productions and toured 25 cities in early 2003. His second book entitled Men Cry in the Dark (1997) was also adapted to a stage play by I'm Ready Productions in 2002. Contact Gina Philip, Personal Manager, Post Office Box 372, Riverdale, New York 10471 E-mail: **GPhilip@michaelbaisden.com** Website: **www.michaelbaisden.com**

Sharonda Baker Ghostwriter, radio personality and mentor, Sharonda "Mecca" Baker is author of Heat: Code of the Streets Book Series Part 1, 2, 3. She is CEO of S. Baker Publishing and S. Baker Media Group. Sharonda "Mecca" Baker, S. Baker Media Group, Post Office Box 7537, Newark New Jersey 07107 E-mail: **sbakerpublishing@gmail.com**

Michele Barkley Artist, writer, and poet, Michele Barkley lives in Seattle, Washington. She is author of Wayfaring Stranger-Poems, producer of the video poem - In View Of A Cup Half-Full, and author of a recently completed novel manuscript, Still A Blue Sky. Michele Barkley, PMB 88, 3703 South Edmunds Street, Seattle, Washington 98118 Phone: (206) 818-1091 E-mail: **michelebarkley@aruncommon.com** Website: **www.artuncommon.com**

Lindamichelle Baron Drawing on 20 years of hands-on literacy instruction, Dr. Baron creates fun, educationally sound, literacy-based books that encourage critical thinking through strategies based on Best Practice and State Standards. Her publishing company Harlin Jacque Publications has sold more than a quarter million books to school systems, libraries, churches, and literacy organizations across the nation. Contact Dr. Lindamichelle Baron, Harlin Jacque Publications, Post Office Box 336, Garden City, New York 11530 Phone: (516) 489-0120 Fax: (516) 292-9120 E-mail: **harlinjacquepub@aol.com** Website: **www.lindamichellebaron.com**

Tanya R. Bates   Author of the book One Day's Peace: A Woman's Journey Through Life, Ms. Bates is a graduate of Fisk University and Davenport University. Tanya R. Bates, Black Pearl Enterprises, Post Office Box 14304, Lansing, Michigan 48901 Phone: (517) 204-4197 E-mail: **anyarbates@hotmail.com** Website: **www.tanyabates.com**

Rose Jackson-Beavers Author, and Chief Executive Officer of Prioritybooks Publications. Received her Bachelor and Master degrees from Illinois State and Southern Illinois Universities. She is a Program Director and a motivational speaker who has worked in the Social Work industry for seventeen years. She has worked as a Freelance writer for the A-Magazine, a Saint Louis Publication and as an Opinion Shaper for the North County Journal Newspaper. She currently writes as a columnist for the Spanish Word, a local community newspaper. She completed Back Room Confessions, released in early 2004 and her first book, Summin to Say is a book of poems and essays about everyday life was published in 2001-2002. Her second book, Quilt Designs, and her book Poetry Rhymes was co-written with nationally known fabric artist, Edna Patterson-Petty. Rose Jackson-Beavers, Post Office Box 2535, Florissant, Missouri 63032 Phone: (314) 741-6789 E-mail: **rosbeav03@yahoo.com** Website: **www.priortybooks.com**

Wayne Beckles Baltimore based divorced father of three, college professor and author of Crossing the Desert. Crossing the Desert is part autobiography, part instruction manual, and all of a riveting tale of one man transformation to compassion. Wayne Beckles, Post Office Box 3633, Baltimore, Maryland 21214 E-mail: **musicforwayne@yahoo.com**

Cassandra Darden Bell As a graduate of East Carolina University in 1992, Cassandra took her first job with WNCT-TV9 as a part-time Production Assistant andwent on to be a News Reporter and News Anchor. It was during one of her Newscast, that Cassandra asked the question you see above, "Why am I here", and that is when the spark of a dream got re-ignited. Cassandra left her career in News Broadcasting to become a stay-at-home mom and full-time writer. In May 2002 she self-published her first book The Color of Love and completed her second manuscript, "Mississippi Blues" a few months later, which landed her a two-book deal with BET/Kensington Publishing Company. Cassandra is represented by Crichton and Associates Literary Agency. She is a member of the Southeast Black Writer's Group. Her book The Color of Love is included on a reading list at East Carolina University. Her new book After the Storm was released in 2005. Cassandra Darden Bell, Post Office Box 1395, Winterville, North Carolina 28590 E-mail: **cdbell@cassandrabell.com** Website: **www.cassandrabell.com**

Kenda Bell Author and motivational speaker, Kenda's two books are My Soul Craves A Touch and a new book titled, For Every Love There Is a Reason. She has been published in Baltimore Magazine and Honey Magazine. She is a member of the Baltimore Urban League and is active in various community-based activities for women and children. Currently she is an online columnist at mahoganybutterfly.com. Contact Ms. Kenda Bell, 2360 Eutaw Place, Unit #2, Baltimore, Maryland 21217 Phone: (410) 900-7601 E-mail: **kb621@aol.com** Website: **www.myspace.com/foreverylove**

LaVerne A. Smith-Bell Author of The Newlyweds' Promises To Keep Manual, LaVerne A. Smith-Bell holds a Masters of Science in Education, Guidance and Counseling Degree and a Bachelors of Science Degree in Psychology. She has worked as a program supervisor and therapeutic clinician in the mental health field dealing with various aspects of individual and family crisis intervention. She is the mother of four adult children, grandmother of seven and owner of two adorable Shih Tzu puppies. Mrs. Bell has been married for 39 years and is an avid gardener. LaVerne and her husband, Charlie, were former guests on the Oprah Winfrey Show discussing the seven levels of marriage. Mrs. LaVerne A. Smith-Bell, 9043 South Greenwood Avenue, Chicago, Illinois 60619 Phone: (773) 731-0118 Fax: (773) 731-3162 E-mail: **laverne@amongfriendsfamily.com** Website: **www.amongfriendsfamily.com**

Kendra Norman-Bellamy Full-time writer and part-time fitness instructor, Kendra is a native of West Palm Beach, Florida. The BET and Moody Publishers author is also president of KNB Publications, LLC, and has authored several poems, short stories and novels highlighting love for family and for Christ. She is a motivational speaker and facilitator. Also a contributing staff writer for an online Christian magazine, Divine Eloquence Ezine. She also serves as an editorial consultant for Booking Matters Magazine. Kendra graduated with honors from Valdosta Technical College with an Associates in Applied Science, Valdosta, Georgia. Kendra Norman-Bellamy, KNB Publications, LLC, Post Office Box 54491, Atlanta, Georgia 30308 Phone: (937) 304-9473 E-mail: **kendra_bellamy@hotmail.com** Website: **www.knb-publications.com**

Donald S. Benjamin   Nationally acclaimed visual artist by training with a talent for literary and proposal writing. Masters in Fine Art, Howard University. Thirty-year career as an exhibiting artist and in visual communications art. The author is also Artist, and Culturalist committed to re-vitalizing the near defunct 1919 National Memorial Association, Inc., and it's 1936 spin-off The National Memorial to the Progress of the Colored Race in America, Inc. He is also associated with an effort to recognize the existence of the longest lived Visual Arts Tradition in the African American Experience, and New Orleans as the Cradle of African American Life, Culture and Civilization. He is particularly interested in the role Africans in the Diaspora, played in the discovery of this nation. Much of which dated back to the San Miguel De Graudalupe Settlement in 1524-26. Contact Mr. Donald S. Benjamin, 3525 16th Street, North West Washington, DC 20010   Phone: (202) 387-4495 E-mail: **dsben@mindspring.com**

T. Garrott Benjamin Jr.   Author, and senior pastor of the historic 3,000 member Light of the World Christian Church in Indianapolis, Indiana. Contact Pastor T. Garrott Benjamin Jr., Heaven on Earth Publishing, Post Office Box 18088, Indianapolis, Indiana 46218 Phone: (317) 254-5922 E-mail: **ahord@lightoftheworld.org** Website: **www.lightoftheworld.org**

Carolyn Ladelle Bennett   Author. Listed in: Who's Who in the South and Southwest, 1997-98. Who's Who of American Women, 1979-80. Phi Kappa Phi Honor Society, MSU, 1976. Memberships: Association for Education in Journalism and Mass Communication, American Journalism Historians Association, Society of Professional Journalists, Association for the Study of African American Life and History, National Association of Women Writers, Women's International League for Peace and Freedom, Women's Institute for Freedom of the Press, National Writer's Union. Assistant Professor in Education: Fayetteville State University, North Carolina. Assistant Professor in Education: Paine College, Augusta, Ga. Founding Editor and Publisher: Network of North Carolina Women Newspaper [501(c)(3)], Fayetteville, North Carolina. Contact Ms. Carolyn L. Bennett, 221 Greystone Lane-16, Rochester, New York 14618 E-mail: **cwriter@aol.com** Website: **www.hometown.aol.com/cwriter85/index.html**

O. H. Bennett   Author, writer, The Colored Garden is O.H. Bennett's first novel. Mr. Bennett received a degree in Journalism from the University of Evansville (Indiana) and is a graduate of the George Mason University Creative Writing program in Fairfax, Virginia where he earned his master of Fine Arts degree. Currently, I am a technical writer for a software developer. Contact O.H. Bennett, Laughing Owl Publishing, 12610 Highway 90 West, Grand Bay, Alabama 36541 Phone: (888) 865-4884 E-mail: **bennetto@erols.com** Website: **www.laughingowl.com**

Tiffany L. Benton   Author, Gospel recording artist and songwriter, Tiffany's single title "God Is On Our Side" was released May 10, 2005. Tiffany L. Benton, Totally Blessed Music Ministries, 174 Seven Pines Road Collierville, Tennessee 38017 Phone: (901) 351-1031 E-mail: **memphisgospel@hotmail.com** Website: **www.memphisgospelmusic.com**

David Valentine Bernard   Author of three novels: How To Kill Your Boyfriend (In Ten Easy Steps) (2006); God In The Image Of A Woman (2004); The Last Dream Before Dawn (2003); and coming in the Fall of 2007, Intimate Relations With Strangers. I'm originally from Grenada, living in New York City (Brooklyn). David Valentine Bernard, 454 East 48th Street, Brooklyn, New York 11203 E-mail: **dv@dvbernard.com**

Bertice Berry Best-selling author of an inspirational memoir, I'm On My Way, But Your Foot Is On My Head, and the hilarious bestsellers Sckraight From the Ghetto, You Might Be Ghetto If and the sequel You STILL Ghetto. Her first work of fiction, Redemption Song, published by Double Day in 2000, is also a Best Seller and has been praised by critics for it's ability to entertain, inspire and educate. Berry followed Redemption Song, with another bestseller, The Haunting of Hip Hop. In August 2002, she released her most passionate work ever with Jim & Louella Homemade Heart-fix Remedy. Dr. Berry graduated magna cum laude from Jacksonville where she was awarded the President's Cup for leadership. She subsequently earned a Ph.D. in sociology from Kent State University at the age of 26. Contact Bertice Berry, Bertice Berry Productions, 31 Abercorn Street, Savannah, Georgia 31401 Website: **www.berticeberry.com**

Wanda Shiryl Miller-Berry Born in Boley, Oklahoma, a historically affluent African-American Township and raised in Oklahoma City, Oklahoma, Miller-Berry is a graduate of Oklahoma Baptist University and a graduate student at the University of Central Oklahoma. She is also a Cushcity.com 2007 Best New Author Award Nominee, an honorary member of the 2006/2007 Manchester's Who's Who Among Executive and Professional Women "Honors Edition" of the Registry and author of the novel, BUCK. She is currently working on her second novel and a collection of poems. Contact Wanda Shiryl Miller-Berry, 1000 NE 14th Street, Oklahoma City, Oklahoma 73117 Phone: (405) 525-9249 Fax: (405) 601-0774 E-mail: **wandasb2002@cox.net** Web: **www.authorsden.com/wandasmillerberry**

Venise Berry Associate professor of Journalism and Mass Communication at the University of Iowa in Iowa City. She is the author of three national bestselling novels; So Good, An African American Love Story (1996), All of Me, A Voluptuous Tale (2000) and Colored Sugar Water (2002). Her fourth novel, Pockets of Sanity is expected in 2008. In 2003, she received the "Creative Contribution to Literature" award from the Zora Neale Hurston Society. All of Me received a 2001 Honor Book Award from the Black Caucus of the American Library Association. She is published widely in academic circles with numerous articles based on her research in the area of media, youth and popular culture. Her current non-fiction project based on current research, I Used to be a Rap Music Fan: Racialism and the Media, is due out in 2009. She has co-authored two non-fiction resource books with S. Torriano Berry, an associate professor in Film at Howard University, The Historical Dictionary of African American Cinema (Scarecrow Press, 2007) and The 50 Most Influential Black Films (Citadel 2001). Mediated Messages and African-American Culture: Contemporary Issues (Sage, 1996), a co-edited, a non-fiction project, won the Meyers Center Award for the Study of Human Rights in North America in 1997. A second edited book, What do you believe? Essays on faith, spirituality and divine intervention, featuring prominent authors such as: Tina McElroy Ansa, Marita Golden, Steven Barnes, Tananarive Due, Jewell Parker Rhodes, Breena Clark, Sands Hall and Victor Villaneuva will be released in 2008. Venise Berry, BerryBooks, Post Office Box 5411, Coralville, Iowa 52241 Phone: (319) 335-3361 Fax: (319) 335-3502 E-mail: **sogood@mchsi.com** Website: **www.veniseberry.com**

Janie P. Bess Author, her first book a memoir is titled VISIONS. Janie also founded a non-profit writing organization Writers Resource Center. Jamie P. Bess, Writers Resource Center, 1500 Oliver Road, Suite K, PMB 265, Fairfield, California 94534 Phone: (707) 399-9169 E-mail: **janie@Janiepbess.com** Website: **www.janiepbess.com**

Daryl E. Smith-Bey A native of Detroit, where he bases his debut novel, The Glass Key. Several years ago Daryl wrote a semi autobiography and anti gang/crime manual, HARD TALK. The book is a tool for law enforcement, social workers as well as youth in deterring criminal and gang acticity. Currently incarcerated for the past 17 years, for a non-violent offense, Daryl is a changed man from when he was first imprisoned. Daryl has become a minister who counsels on right living and making the transition from prison to payroll, and prosperity once outside of prison. Daryl Smith-Bey, WIM Media, 3900 West 22nd Lane, Suite 10G, Yuma, Arizona 85364 E-mail: **desbey@msn.com**

ReShonda Tate Billingsley Author, of My Brother's Keeper, #1 Essence Magazine Bestselling Book, Let the Church Say Amen and the national bestseller, I Know I've Been Changed. She has five more books coming in the next two years. ReShonda's latest projects include the sequel to Let the Church Say Amen, Everybody Say Amen and her teen inspirational novels, Nothing But Drama, Blessings in Disguise (which was voted a #1 pick by Ebony Magazine) and With Friends Like These, as well as her non-fiction title, Help! I've Turned into my Mother. She is a general assignment reporter for KRIV-TV, the Fox affliate in Houston, Texas, and a 1991 graduate of The University of Texas at Austin, where she majored in Broadcast Journalism. Ms. ReShonda Billingsley E-mail: **ReShondaT@aol.com** Website: **www.reshondatatebillingsley.com**

Sabrina D. Black National and international speaker Sabrina is contributing author to the Soul Care Bible (Thomas Nelson, 2001). She is co-author of Prone to Wander: A Woman's Struggle with Sexual Sin and Addiction, (Infinity 2002, rev. PriorityONE 2003); co-editor of Counseling in African American Communities, (Zondervan 2002); the author of Can Two Walk Together? Encouragement for Spitually Unbalanced Marriages (Moody Press 2002), co-author of HELP! For Your Leadership, (PriorityONE Publications 2003), and contributing author for two soon to be released Bibles through NIA Publishing. She is a national and international speaker for conferences, retreats and workshops. Counselor, Life Coach, Mentor and Nationally Syndicated Radio Host of "IT'S RELATIONAL" which airs Wednesdays at 8amCST or 9amEST on rejoice-now.com.   Dr. Sabrina D. Black, L.L.P.C., C.A.C.-1, is the CEO and Clinical Director of Abundant Life Counseling Center, which emphasizes spiritual values. Dr. Sabrina D. Black, Abundant Life Counseling Center, 20700 Civic Center Drive #170, Southfield, Michigan 48076 Phone: (313) 201-6286 E-mail: **jadebooks@aol.com** Website: **www.sabrinablack.com**

Andrea Blackstone Author of the novel Schemin, Confessions of a Gold Digger, Andrea Blackstone was born in Long Island, New York, and moved to Annapolis, Maryland, at the age of two. She majored in English and minored in Spanish at Morgan State University where she was recipient of The Zora Neale Hurston Scholarship. She earned an M.A. from St. John's College in Annapolis, Maryland. Contact Ms. Andrea Blackstone, Dream Weaver Press, Post Office Box 3402, Annapolis, Maryland 21403 E-mail: **Andrea@dreamweaverpress.net** Website: **www.dreamweaverpress.net**

Tonya Bolden Caldecott Honor-winning author of Maritcha, and the soon-to-be published photobiography of Martin Luther King, Jr. Ms. Tonya Bolden, Harry N. Abrams, 115 West 18th Street, New York, New York 10011 E-mail: **freepub@abramsbooks.com** Website: **www.hnabooks.com**

Gwyneth Bolton   The author was born and raised in Paterson, New Jersey. She currently lives in Syracuse, New York with her husband Cedric. She has a BA and an MA in creative writing and a Ph.D. in English. She teaches classes in writing and women' s studies at the college level. Gwyneth Bolton, Post Office Box 9388, Carousel Center, Syracuse, New York 13290 E-mail: **gwynethbolton@prodigy.net** Website: **www.gwynethbolton.com**

Kola Boof   In 2004, three of her best books were released, "Nile River" a collection of her best and most controversial poems, "Train to the Redeeming Sin", her acclaimed bestselling short story collection and the English translation (by Said Musa) of her provocatively erotic Black American historical romance, "Flesh and the Devil." Ms. Kola Boof c/o Door of Kush, 324 South Diamond Bar Boulevard, Suite 504, Diamond Bar, California 91765 E-mail: **kolaboof_email@yahoo.com** Website: **www.kolaboof.com**

Angela Boone   Author, business owner of my own construction firm for seven years, and a motivational and inspirational speaker. My first book "Faith Cometh By Hearing." is primarily nonfiction in the areas of business, education, personal development and relationships. Contact Ms. Angela Boone, Boone International, Post Office Box 211144, Detroit, Michigan 48221 E-mail: **aboone@angelaboone.com** Website: **www.angelaboone.com**

Kenneth Bowens   Born in Paris, Texas, Kenneth (Kanko) Bowens is author of the new book Dirtied Brown Leaves, the story of African American rage personified through its main character, Baby. Kenneth Bowens, 1208 North West 106th Street, Oklahoma City, Oklahoma 73114 E-mail: **kennethbowens1@cox.net** Website: **www.kanko.us**

Sheritha Bowman   New, up and coming writer who is staking her claim in the Christian fiction and non-fiction writing field. In her debut, "Soul Inspiration For Women Married To Unbelievers," (February 1998). Bowman lives with her husband and three kids in Maryland, where she is at work on a Christian romance novel.   Contact Ms. Sheritha Bowman, Post Office Box 817, Germantown, Maryland 20875 E-mail: **gvhmthnks@aol.com** Website: **www.members.aol.com/bobowsb/intro.htm**

Nicole Rouse Bradley Contradictions" is Ms. Bradley's first novel, about relationships. She is a graduate of Indiana University, where she was a member and president of the theater group, SWAV which performed her original play entitled; "Unforgotten Memories." She is a member of Zeta Phi Beta Sorority Inc, and Authors For Charity. She currently teaches high school in Gary, Indiana and is currently working on her second novel. Contact Ms. Nicole Bradley. Post Office Box 2916, Gary, Indiana 46403 E-mail: **n-bradley@sbcglobal.net** Website: **www.nicolebradley.com**

Demetria Brandon Native New Orleanian, novelist and author of fiction with hundreds of stories and poetry pieces. Her fiction includes, Dark Echoes, Bedside Fairy Tales and Brandon's Chamber of Amazing Tales. As a poet, Demetria has performed in various venues and is the founder of VisualVoices Poetry Society based in Atlanta, Georgia.   She has conducted writers groups and lectures all ages on topics of book and poetry writing, how to get a literary agent and how to get published. Contact Ms. Demetria Brandon, Post Office Box 491197, Atlanta, Georgia 30349 E-mail: **db@demetriabrandon.com**

Donna L. Brazile Well known political commentator, activist, and author of the book Cooking with Grease (June 2004, Simon & Schuster), an intimate account of Donna Brazile's thirty years in politics. Her stories of the leaders and activists who have helped shape America's future. Her book Cooking with Grease follows Donna's rise to greater and greater political and personal accomplishments: lobbying for student financial aide, organizaing demonstrations to make Martin Luther King Jr.'s birthday a national holiday and working on the Jesse Jackson, Dick Gephardt, Michael Dukakis and Bill Clinton presidential campaigns. But each new career success came with its own kind of heartache, especially in her greatest challenge: leading Al Gore's 2000 campaign, making her the first African American to lead a major presidential campaign. Prior to joining the Gore campaign, Brazile was Chief of Staff and Press Secretary to Congresswoman Eleanor Holmes Norton of the District of Columbia where she helped guide the District's budget and local legislation on Capitol Hill. Contact Ms. Donna L. Braziles, Brazile and Associates, LLC, Post Office Box 15369, Washington, DC 20003 E-mail: **info@brazileassociates.com** Website: **www.brazileassociates.com**

Alice Talbert Breaux Completed her first novel titled, "I'll Make Them All Pay!" in 2003. Alice Talbert Breaux, 1410 Sumner Street, New Orleans, Louisiana 70114 Phone: (504) 368-0543 E-mail: **bigmamaal1@aol.com**

Magdalene Breaux The author of supernatural/paranormal erotic literature; The Family Curse, Imaginary Playmate, John E. Calico, ChD, and Family Secrets. A TV host and producer, she is a native of New Orleans and graduate of the University of New Orleans. Magdalene Breaux, Post Office Box 67, Fairburn, Georgia 30213 Phone: (770) 842-4792 E-mail: **magbreaux@mindspring.com** Website: **www.familycurse.com**

Kim Marshella Brewer Author of the newly released book Grief: The REAL Deal: A Realist Perspective was released in January, 2006 (PriorityOne Publications) equips people from all walks of life to prepare for grief when it hits home. Missionary Kim M. Brewer, Real Life Ministries, 18452 Washburn, Detroit, Michigan 48221 E-mail: **KimMBrewer@Yahoo.com** Website: **www.kimmbrewer.com**

Wilbur Lee Brower Educational consultant and trainer, Dr. Brower is also a certified teacher high school and founder and president of the Institute for Youth Development & Educational Resources (IYDER), Inc. Dr. Brower earned an undergraduate degree in English Education, an MBA in Management and a Doctoral Degree in Business Administration, with a concentration in Human and Organizational Development. He is the author of A Little Book Big Principles— Values and Virtues for a More Successful Life (1998) and Me Teacher, Me…Please! (2002). He also has been published in Harvard Business Review (Nov.-Dec. 1996) Cultural Diversity at Work (January, 1997) and Vital Speeches of the Day (Feb. 15, 2000). Wilbur Lee Brower, Ph.D., Post Office Box 1719, Fayetteville, North Carolina 28302 Phone: (910) 483-5943 E-mail: **brower311@aol.com**

Brian Christopher Brown Author of the book Think About It: A Write and Reflect Book, is about major issues that young people have to face on a day to day basis. Brian Christopher Brown, RAP Publishing, Inc., 19785 West 12. Mile Road, Suite #303, Southfield, Michigan 49076 E-mail: **Blackprince006@aol.com**

Bertrand E. Brown Author of The Heart is a Lonely Hunter. A former elementary and middle school teacher, social worker, program director, and sports editor for The Challenger newspaper, Mr. Brown just returned from a two year hiatus in London, England where he put the finishing touches on his first novel and worked as a private tutor. He is currently on tour and promoting his novel. Bertrand E. Brown, 1706 Kay Street, Greensboro, North Carolina 27405 E-mail: **berttheveran@yahoo.com**

Clayton F. Brown Author, Under The Green Tree. Founder, Charlotte African-American Writers Group (CAAW). Clayton F. Brown, Post Office Box 29155, Charlotte, North Carolina 28229 E-mail: **claytonfbrown@msn.com**

Crystal C. Brown Author of Caramel and Cream. Also she is CEO and President of Crystal Clear Communications-an award winning public relations and marketing firm in Houston, Texas. Contact Ms. Crystal C. Brown, 2470 S. Dairy Ashford #252, Houston, Texas 77077 E-mail: **cbrown5530@aol.com** Website: **www.crystalcommunicates.com**

Delores Tyler Brown Author, Gospel Artist, Visionary Founder Inspirations of Hope Global Ministries. Contact Ms. Deloris Tyler Brown, Post Office Box 330806, Houston, Texas 77233 E-mail: **b3mg@houston.rr.com**

Kimberly R. Brown I am a new author who has just written a book called Spiritual Advisor that has been published by Publish America. Spiritual Advisor is a phenomenal book about Christianity and one's purpose in life. I am a Christian who resides in Sanford, Florida with my husband and son. Kimberly R. Brown, 128 Sterling Pine Street, Sanford, Florida 32773 Phone: (407) 461-1333 E-mail: **kimrbrown@bellsouth.net**

Les Brown Internationally recognized speaker, author and television personality, Les Brown has risen to national prominence by delivering a high energy message which tells people how to shake off mediocrity and live up to their greatness. Les is author of Live Your Dreams, and newly released book, It's Not Over Until You Win. Former host of The Les Brown Show, a nationally syndicated daily television talk show he is one of the nation's leading authorities in understanding and stimulating human potential and can be heard on Les live on V103.com every Sunday morning from 6-8 AM CST. Les Brown, Les Brown Enterprises, Inc., 233 North Michigan Avenue, Suite 2800, Chicago, Illinois 60601 Phone: (800) 733-4226 E-mail: **lesbrown@lesbrown.com** Website: **www.v103.com/main.html**

Lillian Ojetta Brown MSW, CSW Author, poet, and photographer. Ms. Ojetta Brown was born in Greenwood, South Carolina and received her Bachelor of Science Degree in Psychology from South Carolina State College. She moved to Detroit, Michigan in 1985 and received her Master of Social Work Degree with a concentration in Occupational Psychology and Mental Health from Wayne State University in 1993. She is the author of the 2005 publication, Remembering My Father, published by The Rochester Hills, Michigan, Public Library under the auspices of the Write From Life Series. She is a Psychotherapist, Ordained Minister, and Reiki Practioner. Contact Ms. L. Ojetta Brown, Founder/CEO of the Center for Peace and Holistic Healing, 34 Village Circle Drive, Rochester Hills, Michigan 48307 Phone: (248) 703-3990 Fax: (248) 844-1892 E-mail: **center4peace@aol.com**

Lovely T. Brown Author of the book Time Will Reveal, Lovely T. Brown "Black Coffee" was born in Mississippi, raised in the Dirty South and schooled on life, in New Orleans. She takes the name Black Coffee for her literary work. She is an accomplished author of both literature, spoken word and music. She is CEO of her own company, Thug Related Publishing & Records founded in 2002. Lovely T. Brown, 2613 West Steven Circle, Gulfport, Mississippi 39503 Phone: (228) 326-2476 E-mail: **blackdollone@blackdollone.com**

Luther Brown, Jr. B.S. in English from North Carolina A&T State University (1969) where he became the school's first Woodrow Wilson Fellow, and a juris doctorate degree from Georgetown University (1988). He attended graduate school in English at Rutgers University before going to work for CBS News in 1972. Later he moved to NBC News, where he was an editor, reporter and producer during a 14-year tenure. A divorced single-father of two, Brown published (in 2006) his memoir about the experience. The book is titled "Raising My Best Friends," and subtitled "Meeting the Challenge of Being a Single Parent." Brown is a contributor to Harvard University's African American National Biography and he has written for many magazines, including Essence, the NAACP's Crisis, the Smithsonian's American Visions, Black Enterprise, Modern Black Men, Ebony Man and Intermission. Luther Brown, Jr., 918 14th Street, South East, Washington, DC 20003 E-mail: **nikmar@pacbell.net**

Misherald L Brown Author, CEO/Publisher, Reality Press. Contact Misherald L. Brown, Reality Press LLC, 2684 Ranger Drive, North Charleston, South Carolina 29405 E-mail: **missy@realitypressllc.com** Website: **www.realitypressllc.com**

Tony Brown TV Journalist/Commentator, radio talk show host, keynote speaker, self-empowerment advocate and bestselling author. Contact Tony Brown, Producer, Tony Brown Productions, Inc., 2214 Frederick Douglass Boulevard, Suite 124, New York, New York E-mail: **mail@tbol.net** Website: **www.tonybrown.com**

Renee Jones-Brown Author of the book, Silent Fear, released August 2006. Renee Jones-Brown, 69-10A 188th Street, #1A, Fresh Meadows, New York 11365 Phone: (347) 622-3444 E-mail: **reneejonesbrown@yahoo.com** Website: **www.reneejonesbrown.com**

Beverly A. Browning CEO of BBA, Inc., and author of nearly two dozen grants-related publications, including audio and video products, including Fundraising with the Corporate Letter, Grant Writing For Dummies™ (2001 and 2005, Wiley) and Grant Writing for Educators (2004, NES). Contact Dr. Beverly A. Browning, BBA, Inc., 25650 West Northern Lights Way, Buckeye, Arizona 85326 Phone: (480) 768-7400 Fax: (800) 859-2330 E-mail: **grantsconsulting@aol.com**

Monique Miles Bruner BA and MA degrees in Public Administration and a Masters of Human Relations, University of Oklahoma. Monique has also completed the requirements for her doctoral degree in Adult Education from Oklahoma State University. She has several publications including a textbook, Strategies that Empower People for Success in College and Life (Houghton Mifflin). She was the co-editor of Delta Girls: Stories of Sisterhood, and is featured in a book of poetry entitled Violets. Monique Miles Bruner, 6409 Braniff Drive, Oklahoma City, Oklahoma 73105 Phone: (405) 615-6711 E-mail: **n2delta@yahoo.com**

Troy Buckner A songwriter/lyricist and literary writer, Ms. Buckner released her first 300 page novel, entitled "A Bird In Flight" in July 2004. She has written two other novels entitled, "A Forbidden Love" and "Chocolate Cravings. She graduated from Southern University holding a Bachelor's Degree in Accounting and a Minor in Business Law and Administration. She the Chief Executive Officer for her company, Hy'Tara Entertainment. Ms. Buckner was the Producer and Executive Producer for the thought provoking and soul searching theatrical production, 'Tell Hell I Aint Comin', starring Tommy Ford from the successful sitcom, 'Martin & New York Undercover' and Tony Grant from the Grammy nominated R & B Group, 'Az Yet' on the La Face Record label. Buckner is currently writing, managing, and producing several upcoming artists. Troy Buckner, Hy'tara Entertainment, Post Office Box 19049, Anaheim, California 92817 Phone: (714) 227-5000 E-mail: **birdinflight@aol.com** Website: **www.abirdinflight.com**

Ed Bullins Author, playwright, Ed Bullins's latest book is ED BULLINS: 12 Plays and Selected Writings (U of Michigan Press, 2006). Distinguished Artist-in-Residence, Northeastern University. Mr. Bullins is the author of seven books, including Five Plays By Ed Bullins, The Duplex, The Hungered One, Four Dynamite Plays, The Theme is Blackness, and The Reluctant Rapist. He wrote and produced for the theatre several commission works, including *Rainin' Down Stairs* for the 1992 San Francisco Theatre Artaud, and has been editor for a number of theatre magazines and publications. He was producer of *Circles of Times,* Boston's Lyric Theatre in August 2003. Among his awards and grants is three Obie Awards, four Rockefeller Foundation Playwriting Grants, two Guffenheim Playwriting Fellowships, an NEA Playwriting Grant, the AUDELCO Award, the New York Drama Critics Circle Award for Best American Play of 1974 -75, the National Black Theatre Festival Living Legend Award, and the OTTO Award in 2004. The Ed Bullins Reader will soon be published by Michigan University Press. It will contain plays, prose, interviews, etc. by Mr. Bullins. Editor is Mike Sells. Contact Mr. Ed Bullins, 37 Vine Street #1, Roxbury, Massachusetts 02119 Phone: (617) 442-6627 E-mail: **rct9@verizon.net** Website: **www.edbullins.com**

Anita Bunkley Multi-published author of African American women's fiction, writing coach, and inventor. Author of nine book-length works of fiction, two novellas, and one work of non-fiction. Anita's latest releases include: Relative Interest (Dafina 2004); Mirrired Life (Dafina 2003), Black Expressions Book Club Main selection. Her upcoming new book is You Only Get Better (Mira, July 2006). Contact Anita Bunkley, Post Office Box 821248, Houston, Texas 77282 E-mail: **arbun@sbcglobal.net** Website: **www.anitabunkley.com**

L. Guy Burton Published writer of a non-fiction book Follow The Right Leader published by Quill Publishers, copyright, 1991, novels Jack In The Pulpit, Xlibris, copyright 2004, and Come Die With Me, PublishAmerica, copyright 2006, magazine articles, poetry, and a movie script. My articles and poetry have appeared in Interrace magazine, and my screenplay Latent Blood—which won honorable mention in a Writer's Digest contest—was represented by The Berzon Agency of Glendale, California. As founder and Director of The Warwick Valley Writers' Association, I have, through this local writers' group, been able to polish, complete and promote several works in various genres, as well as help others to do the same. L. Guy Burton, The Warwick Valley Writers' Association, 12 Burton Lane, Warwick, New York 10990 E-mail: **booknook1@hotmail.com**

Nickcole Byrd Co-author with LaTrice Martin of the new book Girls From The Hood, The Delivery. Nickcole and LaTrice are the founders of Hebrew Women Ministries, a spiritually inspired quest to reach those who have been abused and are desperately seeking a way back through holy biblical teachings and continued growth in faith. Ms. Byrd is program administrator at Rice University. Contact Ms. Nickey Byrd, 4605 West Columbary, Rosenberg, Texas 77471 E-mail: **nickcolebyrd@aol.com**

Ivette Cambridge Author of the new book "Hanging Without A Noose" a real life book of poems (June 1, 2006, Semaj Publications of Denver). Ivette poetically speaks on child abuse, domestic violence and the drug addiction that nearly killed her every being. Contact Ms. Ivette Cambridge, 13918 East Mississippi Avenue, #506, Aurora, Colorado 80012 Phone: (303) 325-5155 E-mail: **poetivette@yahoo.com**

Emory S. Campbell   Executive Director Emeritus of Penn Center, a National Historic Landmark District on Saint Helena Island, South Carolina. President of Gullah Heritage Consulting where he conducts an institute on the Gullah culture through lectures, short courses, and the Gullah Heritage Trail Tours on Hilton Head Island. Author and self-publisher of the guidebook, Gullah Cultural Legacies: A Synopsis of Traditions, Customary Beliefs, Artforms and Speech on Hilton Head and vicinal Sea Islands in South Carolina and Georgia (2002). In 2005 he published the Second Edition of Gullah Cultural Legacies that includes monographs on two Gullah celebrations. Contact Mr. Emory S. Campbell, Gullah Heritage Consulting Service, Post Office Box 22136, Hilton Head Island, South Carolina 29925 Phone: (843) 681-3069 E-mail: **esc@gullaheritage.com** Website: **www.gullaheritage.com**

Carla Rowser Canty Author, air personality at WTQT 89.9FM and producer and host of "Sayword" an entertainment television show. Interviews authors, artists. Ms. Carla Rowser Canty is the self-published author of Diary of A Blackgurl. Contact Ms. Carla Rowser Canty, A Blackgurl Production, Post Office. Box 843, Hartford, Connecticut 06143 Phone: (860) 983-3257 E-mail: **BlackGurrl@aol.com** Website: **www.wqtqfm.com/wqtq**

Bil Carpenter In 2005, Carpenter's first book Uncloudy Days: The Gospel Music Encyclopedia (Backbeat Books) was published and the companion compilation CD Uncloudy Days (Artemis Gospel) was released. He resides in Washington, D.C. where he runs Capital Entertainment, a small public relations company that has worked extensively with gospel artists such as Vickie Winans, Bishop T.D. Jakes, CeCe Winans, and Donald Lawrence & the Tri-City Singers, among many others. Bil Carpenter, Capital Entertainment, 217 Seaton Place North East, Washington, D.C. 20002 Phone: (202) 636-7028 E-mail: **carpbil@aol.com** Website: **www.bilcarpenter.com**

Monica P. Carter Freelance corporate writer, motivational speaker and author of two books, Monica is a columnist for The Times Newspaper in Shreveport, Louisiana., as well as for the website soulsistasunite.com. She grew up in Jackson, Mississipi and received a degree in journalism from the University of Southern Mississippi. She is author of As If Nothing Happened which was her first novel and her second novel, Sacrifice the One was released in 2004. Monica Carter, Post Office Box 52482, Shreveport, Lousiana 71115 E-mail: **mpcarter7@aol.com** Website: **www.monicapcarter.com**

Jonnathein Chambers Co-Author of "Come Join e! Under the Apple Tree!" Jonnathein (7) has made headlines. He recently passed the Gifted And Talented Education (G.A.T.E.) Examination. Hobbies - playing video games, writing and creating. Among the first African-American Youth (his age) to become a published author this year, and make appearances at libraries, schools, trade shows, hospitals and churches. Jonnatheim Chambers, 15555 Main Street, Suite D-4, PMB #523, Hesperia, California 92345 Phone: (951) 532-4177 E-mail: **YouthAuthors@AchieveLifeSuccess.com** Website: **www.AchieveLifeSuccess.com**

Jonnetta Chambers Author of Success Does Not Come On a Silver Platter: 71 'Must Know' Strategies of 21st Century Successful People, and a contributor to the books, Cases in Organizational Behavior by Teri C. Tompkins, Ph.D., and Modern Day Heroes: In Defense of America by Pete Mitchell & Bill Perkins. She serves on the Advisory Council at the California State University, San Bernardino, College of Extended Learning and for the Moreno Valley Black Chamber of Commerce. She works as an adjunct faculty member for the California State University CEL Department, San Bernardino and has written for Professional Business Journals, Magazines and Newspapers. Jonnetta Chambers, 15555 Main Street, Suite D-4, PMB #523, Hesperia, California 92345 Phone: (951) 532-4177 E-mail: **jc@AchieveLifeSuccess.com** Website: **www.AchieveLifeSuccess.com**

Lareece Chambers Co-Author of "Come Join e! Under the Apple Tree!" Lareece (9) and her brother Jonnathein (8) coauthored the book. Lareece is a very motivated, competitive, and active youth. She is an "Accelerated," Award-Winning reader and is talented in the areas of writing, math and spelling. She has been among top students in her class mastering Math Facts in a Flash, an accelerated math learning module at school. She is a member of Women in Focus Forum. Ms. Lareece Chambers, 15555 Main Street, Suite D-4, PMB #523, Hesperia, California 92345 Phone: (951) 532-4177 E-mail: **YouthAuthors@AchieveLifeSuccess.com** Website: **www.AchieveLifeSuccess.com**

Cliff Chandler Award winning author of three mystery novels: "The Paragons, Vengeance Is mine, and Devastated." Devastated was chosen as "Mystery Novel of the Year" by JADA Press. Former host of "Art With A Capital" WGNM TV64, Macon, Georgia. He worked as a professional photographer - German School of Photography, Jazz Musician - The Muse, and as an editorial writer for a local newspaper. Poetry Awards, Short Story Awards, Marquis Who's Who In The East, and the JADA Award Mystery Novel Of The Year 2004. Education: BFA, Pratt Institute, Brooklyn, New York, Masters Writing courses at New York University, and editing classes at The New School. Cliff Chandler, 2492 Tredway Drive, Macon, Georgia 31211 E-mail: **CDuke23@aol.com** Website: **http://theparagons.homestead.com/paragons2.html**

Frank Chase Jr. Author of False Roads to Manhood, subtitled, What Women Need To Know, What Men Need to Understand is the author's seven journey of adventure, suspense and intrigue into the heart and soul of the secret life of manhood. Frank has served as a teacher, counselor, mentor and leader in men's ministry, and as a lay minister for twenty years. He earned a Bachelor of Arts Degree in Communications and a minor in Sociology from Washington State University. Currently works as a writer for an Army Magazine on Redstone Arsenal at LOGSA. Frank Chase Jr., FC Publishing, LLC, Post Office Box 5675, Huntsville, Alabama 35814 E-mail: **fchase@fcpublishing.com** Website: **www.fcpublishing.com**

Orean D. Chatman The Time is Wright is his first novel. Mr. Chatman grew up in Houston, Texas. He received a B.S. in Business Services from the University of Houston Downtown and a Masters of Public Administration from Long Island University, Brooklyn, New York. He has worked in the Health Care Support Services industry for eight years. Contact Mr. Orean D. Chatman, 2833 Smith Avenue, #238, Baltimore, Maryland 21209 Phone: (443) 844-1360 E-mail: **odc@oreandchatman.com**

Bernice Gorham Cherry Author of "The Onion You Are Eating Is Someone Else's Water Lily," Cherry, is currently working on her second book, as well as assisting others in achieving their dream of becoming published. Ms. Bernice Cherry, 2110 Sir Raleigh Court, Greenville, North Carolina 27858 Phone: (252) 355-8970 E-mail: **zoe4u2c@suddenlink.net**

Charles W. Cherry II Author, attorney, Vice-President/General Counsel Board Secretary and principal shareholder of Tama Broadcasting, Inc., the largest black owned media company in the Southeast, Mr. Cherry is publisher of his family-owned weekly newspaper. He has served as the General Manager of WPUL-AM since 2000, and as General Manager of WCSZ-AM from 1998 to 2000. He earned his undergraduate degree in Journalism from Morehouse College in 1978, and the Master of Business Administration and Juris Doctor degrees from the University of Florida in 1982. He is the author of Excellence Without Excuse: The Black Student's Guide to Academic Excellence (International Scholastic Press, 1994). Contact Charles W. Cherry II, Esq., Tama Broadcasting, Inc., 5207 Washington Boulevard, Tampa, Florida 33619 Phone: (813) 620-1300 E-mail: **info@tamabroadcasting.com** Website: **www.tamabroadcasting.com**

Mamadou Chinyelu A career writer, Chinyelu is the author of three books, including Harlem Ain't Nothin' But A Third World Country: The Global Economy, Empowerment Zones and the Colonial Status of Africans in America; Sons of the Prophets: 9 Inspirational Stories About African men and Boys in the Land of Captivity; and Debunking The Bell Curve and Scientific Racism. His most recently published book is Motive, Means and Opportunity: Probable Cause for Indicting George W. Bush, his Sponsors and Aides for the Attack of September 11, 2001 (Mustard Seed Press, 2004). His writings have been published as chapters in seven other books, two of which are history anthologies edited by the distinguished historian Prof. Ivan Van Sertima — Golden Age of the Moor and Great Black Leader: Ancient and Modern, which includes his biography of nineteenth century freedom fighter Frederick Douglass. In 1977, Chinyelu became a working journalist and since has been a staff writer for publications. He has also published innumerable freelance articles. Chinyelu is the founder and president of the David Walker College for Writing & Publishing, named in honor of the nineteenth century author and publisher of David Walker's Appeal. Contact Mamadou Chinyelu, Post Office Box 32406 Charleston, South Carolina 29417 E-mail: **mchinyelu99@hotmail.com**

Hope C. Clarke Author of five best selling books: Vengeance Is Mine, Carring Mama's Baggage, Not With My Son, April 2003, Best Seller, 2003, and Shadow Lover, 2004. She is the eldest daughter of seven siblings who reside in Brooklyn, New York. Hope is a single mom who divides her time between being a full-time mom, employee of JP Morgan Chase and a devoted entrepreneur. Contact Ms. Hope C. Clarke, A New Hope Publishing, Post Office Box 1746, New York, New York 10017 Phone: (718) 498-2408 E-mail: **hopeclarke@aol.com** Website: **www.anewhopepublishing.com**

Stanley Bennett Clay Author of the novel "Looker." Stanley Bennett Clay, c/o Simon and Schuester, Adult Division, 1230 Avenue of the Americas, New York, New York 10020 Phone: (212) 698-1257 E-mail: **sbcpublishers@earthlink.net**

Blondie L.Clayton My writing began to take on a life of its own after I was faced with a husband who had two days to live. At that moment I began to seek the meaning of life and ended up receiving a spiritual revelation which altered the course of my life. The three books I authored: There in the Midst The Mysterious Exposed; Why Money Isn't Your Problem- Making the Right Connection; You Write You Publish. Blondie L.Clayton, Post Office Box 132, Sharpes, Florida 32959 Phone: (321) 637-1128 E-mail: **blondie48@bellsouth.net**

Nanci Clayton Miami based performance poet. Ms. Clayton is the author of I'm Every Woman (February 2000), a motivational speaker, educator, performing artist and model. Her studies in broadcast journalism were completed at the University of Miami, Florida. Contact Ms. Nanci Clayton, Nu-B Du-B Expressions, Post Office Box 531134, Miami Shores, Florida 33153 E-mail: **nubdub@aol.com** Website: **www.nanciclayton.com**

Black Coffee Self-published author of two novels; Time Will Reveal Part 1 & 2. Black Coffee Phone: (228) 326-2476 Fax: (228) 831-9086 E-mail: **blackdollone@cableone.net** Website: **www.blackdollone.com**

Bernadene High Coleman Born in rural Louisiana the author grew up in Los Angeles. She received her MS from Loyola-Marymount, and her BA from California State University, Los Angeles. She has also attended UCLA School of Writing. She has been presented at The Library of Congress and has appeared at many universities, colleges and high schools with her historical-factional-literary work. Mrs. Coleman is the author of two novels, Mama Rose and I leave You My Dreams. She has just completed a third novel, Beyond Color. She has also written a fourth book, Listen My Children, a collection of poetry. Coleman has read her work across the United States including at the Library of Congress in Washington, D.C. Mrs. Coleman is a widow, mother of three, grandmother of eight and continues to write. She is also a retired school teacher who taught in the Los Angeles Unified School District and the Pasadena School System for nearly 30 years. Contact Bernadene High Coleman, Post Office Box 4372, Culver City, California 90231 Phone: (310) 641-0106 E-mail: **bernhicole@sbcglobal.net** Website: **www.mamarose.com**

Monica A. Coleman Author of the book The Dinah Project: A Handbook For Congregational Response To Sexual Violence, Coleman is an ordained elder of the African Methodist Episcopal Church (AMEC). She earned her undergraduate degree in Afro-American Studies at Harvard University.   At Vanderbilt University, she obtained the master's of divinity degree and Certificate in the Study of Religion, Gender and Sexuality. She earned her doctorate in Philosophy of Religion and Theology at Claremont Graduate University, Claremont, California. She is currently the Director of Womanist Religious Studies and Assistant Professor of Religion at Bennett College for Women in Greensboro, North Carolina. Reverand Monica A. Coleman, Ph.D., Director, Womanist Religious Studies, Assistant Professor of Religion, Bennett College for Women, 900 Eeast Washington Street, Box 104, Greensboro, North Carolina 27401 Phone: (336) 517-1534 E-mail: **revmonica@worldnet.att.net**

Valerie L. Coleman Author and Publisher, contributor, editor and compiler of Blended Families An Anthology. Contributor to KNB Publications' The Midnight Clear, a Christian fiction anthology. Contributor to Chicken Soup for the Stepfamily Soul. Valerie L. Coleman, Pen Of The Writer, LLC, PMB 175, 5523 Salem Avenue, Dayton, Ohio 45426 Phone: (937) 307-0760 E-mail: **info@penofthewriter.com** Website: **www.penofthewriter.com**

Danny Colton A native of Detroit, Michigan. Husband and father of 5. Education: Northern Michigan University, University of Michigan: Masters in Public Health, Wayne State University: Medical Degree. Doctor Colton is currently a general surgeon and aspires to be a Heart Surgeon. Author of the motivational and inspirational book: From Hard Life to Heart Surgeon. Danny M. Colton, MD, 1282 Stabler Lane, Suite 630 #108, Yuba City, California 95993 E-mail: **dannycolton@aol.com** Website: **www.dannycolton.com**

Donna Conger Born and raised in Kansas, Ms. Conger studied Sociology at Gordon College in Wenham, Massachusetts. She is the published author over 100 articles, short stories and poems in small and large magazines. She is also the author of 4 romances: "Forgotten", an interracial Christian romance, "VetCop", a murder mystery and romance, "The Last Lesson," a murder mystery and romance, and "The Green Moon", a Native American futuristic romance and a nonfiction book, "Don't Call Me African American." She is awaiting the release of her first children's book, for ages 9-12, Jared's Adventure. Orlis Bonk. Donna Conger, 1316 North 630 West, Clinton, Utah 84015 E-mail: **treszure7@yahoo.com** Website: **www.donnaconger.com**

Vivi Monroe Congress The author of The Bankrupt Spirit Principles for Turning Setbacks into Comebacks, The McMillon Family cookbook: Something to Shout About! and newly released, Manna for Mamma: Wisdom for Women in the Wilderness. She hold a Bachelor of Arts degree in Human Relations, a Master of Theological Studies and a Doctor of Ministry degree in Christan Counseling. Dr. Vivi Monroe Congress, Little Light Productions, LLC, Post Office Box 540741, Grand Prairie, Texas 75054 E-mail: **Littlelightprod@aol.com** Website: **www.drvivimonroecongress.com**

Marlene Kim Connor Author of WELCOME TO THE FAMILY: Memories of the Past for a Bright Future, published January 2006 by Broadway/Doubleday. Marlene is also author of, WHAT IS COOL? Understanding Black Manhood in America (AGATE and Crown publishers for paperback and hardcover respectively). She is also an accomplished literary agent for books; handles TV and film rights, general and non-fiction books. Marlene Connor Lynch, Connor Literary Agency, 2911 West 71st Street, Minneapolis, Minnesota 55423 Phone: (612) 866-1486 Fax: (612) 869-4074 E-mail: **connoragency@aol.com**

William Alfred Council Author of Heroic Visions - a Super Hero Role Playing Adventure Game. William Alfred Council, Post Office Box 105, Albuquerque, New Mexico 87103 E-mail: **NewVisionPublications@juno.com**

William Richard Craft Author of the book The Booker T. Washington Chronicles. Coming: The Black Man's Burden, The Liberia Chronicles, and Character Building. Contact Mr. William Richard Craft, Phoenix Publications, Post Office Box 683, Bronx, New York 10475 E-mail: **phoenixpublications@yahoo.com** Website: **www.phoenixpublications.net**

Sha-Shana N.L. Crichton   Author of Distinguishing Between Direct and Consequential Damages Under New York Law in Breach of Service Contract Cases, Howard Law Journal 2002. Sha-Shana, an entertainment attorney, frequently lectures on negotiating publishing contracts and author-editor-agent relationships. She is a graduate of Howard University School of Law (J.D. cum laude); the University of the West Indies (B.A. Honors); and the Instituto Benjamin de Tudela, Navarra, Spain. She is a former managing editor of the Howard Law Journal and has edited several articles and books, including Constitutional Law: Analysis and Cases by Ziyad Motala and Cyril Ramaphosa (Oxford University Press, 2002). Contact Crichton & Associates, Inc., 6940 Carroll Avenue, Takoma Park, Maryland 20912 Phone: (301) 495-9663 Fax: (202) 318-0050 E-mail: **cricht1@aol.com** Website: **www.crichton-associates.com**

Alice T. Crowe New York Attorney and author of the new book Real Dads Stand Up! A legal guide to help single fathers in family court. She is a partner in the law firm of Crowe & Crowe with her identical twin sister and author Alicia Crowe. Contact Ms. Alice T. Crowe, Crowe & Crowe, 99 Main Street, Suite 321, Nyack, New York 10960 Phone: (845) 348-1160 E-mail: **theurbanevoice@yahoo.com**

Alicia M. Crowe Attorney/Author of the new book, Real Dads Stand Up! What Every Single Father Should Know About Child Support. Rights and Custody (Blue Peacock Press). A guide for fathers about how to navigate the legal system and maintain access to their children. Alicia M. Crowe, Post Office Box 1011, Nyack, New York 10960 Phone: (845) 348-1160 Fax: (845) 348-1964 E-mail: **thefatherfriendlyguide@yahoo.com** Website: **www.realdadsstandup.com**

George Curry Author, journalist and nationally acclaimed columnist, and radio commentary host, Mr. Curry is former editor-in-chief of the National Newspaper Publishers Association News Service and BlackPressUSA. His weekly column is syndicated by NNPA to more than 200 African-American newspapers, with a combined readership of 15 million. George is the author/editor of three books, Best of Emerge Magazine Edited by George E. Curry, The Affirmative Action Debate edited by George Curry, and Jake Gaither: America's Most Famous Black Coach. Contact Mr. George E. Curry, NNPA, 3200 13th Street, North West, Washington, DC 20010 E-mail: **george@georgecurry.com** Website: **www.georgecurry.com**

J. Daniels Author of "Serpent in My Corner." She's also the co-author of "Luv Alwayz" and "Draw Me with Your Love." She is working on the completion of the third novel of the Luvalwayz trilogy "If You Asked Me To," along with Shonell Bacon. And also, 'Shades of a Chameleon,' the sequel to 'Serpent in My Corner'. Writing as A.J. White, JD's her novel 'Ballad of a Ghetto Poet' was published in 2003 by Strebor Books. J. Daniels, Post Office Box 518, Aylett, Virginia 23009 E-mail: **Jd@jdanielsonline.com** Website: **www.jdanielsonline.com**

Natalie L. Darden Voted Best New Self-Published Author 2003, Mahogany Book Club and Awarded Afro-American Author of Excellence 2003 by Dare 2 Dream Book Club, for her book All about Me. Also author of a novel "Single as a Dollar Bill: Love Yourself First, the Rest Is Easy," (2004). Natalie is a graduate of Rutgers University, where she obtained a BA in English and Communications. Natalie L. Darden, Naldar Publishing Group, Post Office Box 1501, Bloomfield, New Jersey 07003 Phone: (973) 454-1214 E-mail: **naldarpub@yahoo.com** Website: **www.nataliedarden.com**

Brooklyn Darkchild Author of This Ain't No Hearts and Flowers Love Story. Owner of Brooklyn Dreams Publishing (through Lulu.com). Brooklyn Darkchild,1886 Windmill Way, Cincinnati, Ohio 45240 Phone: (513) 238-6898 E-mail: **BKDarkchild@cinci.rr.com**

Deanne Renee Davis Author of the book Unforgiveness the Unnoticeable Sin, Deanne serves as a minister of Saint Johns Full Gospel Ministries located in Bloomfield, Connecticut, a ministry she has had the privilege of being born and raised in. Deanne Davis, 55 Marguerite Avenue, Bloomfield, Connecticut 06002 E-mail: **deannedavis_7@hotmail.com**

Floyd B. Davis The author lives and works in New York City. He spent two years in the Peace Corps in Ethiopia from 1963 to 1965 where he taught at the secondary school in Gore, Illubabor. He has also traveled extensively throughout East Africa. "1896" is his first work of fiction. Mr. Floyd B. Davis, 324 West 84th Street, #72, New York, New York 10024 Phone: (212) 501-9187 E-mail: **fbdav@earthlink.net**

Tony Darnell Davis Teaches a community theatre class at the Essex Studios and has been an actor for 35 years. He has written 11 books of poetry and won recognition for his work as an actor, poet, director, and arts administrator. For 21 years he has been an educator at the University of Cincinnati, teaching Black Drama and Acting Workshops. He is founding president of Theatre Inc., and Program Coordinator for the Free Theatre, Cincinnati's oldest Black theatre company. He is past board chairperson of the Cincinnati Black Theatre Company and board member of Why Not D.A.N.C.E. Contact Mr. Tony Darnell Davis, Essex Studios, 2511 Essex Place, Cincinnati, Ohio 45206 Phone: (513) 363-7797 Fax: (513) 363-7765 E-mail: **davisad@email.uc.edu**

Wayne Dawkins Author, "Black Journalists: The NABJ Story," August Press, 199, "Rugged Waters: Black Journalists Swim the Mainstream," August Press, 2003. Editor and contributing author, "Black Voices in Commentary: The Trotter Group," August Press, 2006. Contributing writer [four entries], "Encyclopedia of American Journalism," Routledge, 2007. Contributing writer, "African American National Biography," Oxford University Press, 2008. Editor and founder, Black Alumni Network newsletter, Columbia University Journalism, 1980-present. Wayne Dawkins, Post Office Box 6693, Newport News, Virginia 23606 Phone: (800) 268-4338 Fax: (757) 591-2371 E-mail: **wdawk69643@aol.com** Website: **www.augustpress.net**

Deborah Day President of Ashay by the Bay, a publishing and marketing company that she founded in 1997. Poet, author and publisher of the book (s) Mindful Messages. In 2002 she wrote and published Mindful Messages and the Mindful Messages Mentoring Workbook. Currently she is working on the Mindful Messages Teachers Guide. Deborah Day, Ashay by the Bay, Post Office Box 2394, Union City, California 94587 Phone: (510) 520-2742 Fax: (510) 441-0498 E-mail: **dday@ashaybythebay.com** Website: **www.ashaybythebay.com**

Cedric Lamonte Dean Author of "For The Love of the Streets," "Best Friends for What," "This Ain't Living," "Pimping in the Name of the Lord," and "How to Stop Your Children From Going to Prison." Dean took his life experience and knowledge of the streets to create these non-fictional stories. Cedric Lamonte Dean, Kreative Konsepts, Inc., 25422 Trabuco Road #105, Lake Forest, California 92630 E-mail: **KreativeKonsepts@aol.com**

Montez DeCarlo A Detroit native and co-author/editor of Our Sacred Identity: The Book of American Indian Names and Their Meanings, makes his Novel debut with Black Chameleon Memoirs. As a graduate of the streets and school of hard knocks, Montez has climbed the corporate ladder to Director of Global Networks and IT Security for an international pharmaceutical company. He currently mentors troubled teens by sharing his experiences and allowing them to shadow him on the job. Montez DeCarlo, Post Office Box 141, Wake Forest, North Carolina 27588 E-mail: **mdecarlo@blackchameleonmemoirs.com**

Janie DeCoster Author of Man of My Dreams? and Love on the Wrong Side of Town. Contact Janie DeCoster, Post Office Box 733, Timmonsville South Carolina 29161 E-mail: **sweetsmells2003@yahoo.com**

Ruby Dee Author, actor, playwright, and activist, Ms. Dee is author of children's books, Tower to Heaven and Two Ways to Count to Ten; a book of poetry and short stories, My One Good Nerve (which she has adapted into a solo performance piece); and With Ossie and Ruby: In This Life Together, a joint autobiography co-authored with her late husband. Ms. Ruby Dee, c/o Author Mail, Little, Brown and Company, 237 Park Avenue, New York, New York 10017 Website: **www.hachettebookgroupusa.com**

Anita Davis-DeFoe Author of the book, "A Woman's Guide to Soulful Living…Seven Keys to Life and Work Success." She is an Associate Editor with the Caribbean Voice, a South Florida newspaper. In addition, she is the television host of caribbeanwomentoday, a segment on Caribbean Weekly; an informational and community affairs program. Dr. Anita Davis-DeFoe, Defoe Group, Post Office Box 451973, Sunrise, Florida 33345 Phone: (954) 816-9462 E-mail: **dranitadavisdefoe@hotmail.com** Website: **www.dranitadavisdefoe.com**

Anna Dennis Author of Who Will Hear My Screams, The Purest of Pain, and On the Line, is her third novel. She has written several children's short stories and has had commentary published in Essence Magazine. She was a presenter at the 1997 Sisters Circle Book Club Awards in San Francisco and formerly co-owned Black Spring Books in Vallejo, California. She is co-founder of The Bay Area Book Writers Guild and a book reviewer for The LineUp's Bookworm Column. Also co-host of The DR BookChat Radio Show, 97.7 and 88.1 FM (KECG/More Public Radio). Anna Dennis, Apex Publishing, Post Office Box 5077, South San Francisco, California 94083 E-mail: **apexpublishing@aol.com**

Christina Dixon Contributing writer in the Wisdom and Grace Devotional Bible for Young Women of Color, by Nia Publishing and HELP! for Your Leadership by PriorityONE Publications and she has written articles for WOW! Women's Magazine by Joy2BHizz.com, Just for You Ministries, and TRUTH magazine. In January, 2005 she revised her first book entitled, How to Respect an Irresponsible Man by PriorityONE Publications. Active member of the Writer's Resources and Accountability in Publishing (WRAP), American Christian Writers-Detroit Chapter, the National Biblical Counseling Association (NBCA), and the Lydia Circle of Business and Professional Women and United Christian Women's Ministries. Adjunct instructor for Christian Research and Development. Contact Mrs. Christina Dixon, PriorityONE Ministries, Post Office Box 725, Farmington, Michigan 48332 Phone: (313) 283-3596 E-mail: **info@christinadixon.net** Website: **www.christinadixon.net**

Norris Dorsey Author of the book, The Art of Inclusion: Success Stories of African American in the Nonprofit Sector (2006), Dr. Dorsey is a college professor currently at California State University and Los Angeles Mission College. He earned his Doctoral degree in Education from the University of La Verne. He teaches various business classes such as: accounting, business, management, marketing, and supervision. He also consults nonprofits and small business owners on issues related to management, networking, leadership, accounting, and how to motivate employees. Norris (Rashe) Dorsey, 11024 Balboa Boulevard., Suite #328, Granada Hills, California 91344 Phone: (818) 402-5050 E-mail: **ndorsey@socal.rr.com**

Celise Downs Author. Contact Ms. Celise Downs, Gemini Mojo Press, 2343 West Claremont Street, Phoenix, Arizona 85015 Phone: (888) 354-5794 E-mail: **celise@geminimojopress.com** Website: **www.GeminiMojoPress.com**

Janet Carr-Dudley Author of Mama's Last Chance, a fiction novel that deals with domestic violence. Contact Ms. Janet Carr-Dudley, 960 Ellis Mill Road, Glassboro, New Jersey 08028 E-mail: **janetdud_57@yahoo.com**

Kia DuPree Author of Robbing Peter and a native of Washington, DC., Ms. DuPree is a public relations specialist, college English instructor and a freelance copy writer. She is a graduate of Hampton University and Old Dominion University. Like Holding A Butterfly, a novel is her next release. Kia DuPree, Prism Pages, Post Office Box 7189, Hampton, Virginia 23666 Phone: (757) 218-8587 E-mail: **info@prismpages.com** Website: **www.prismpages.com**

Sherry Sherrod Dupree Teacher, historian, research specialist, former librarian, Sherry Sherrod Dupress is author of Displays for Schools, which is based on materials collected while working as a media specialist. The book was featured in several American and Canadian publications. DuPree is also author of The African-American Holiness Pentecostal Movement, an annotated bibliography guide to the Afro-American Pentecostal churches in the U.S., serving as both a reference text and as a general introduction to the religious movement. Contact Mrs. Sherry Sherrod Dupree, Santa Fe Community College, 3000 North West 83rd Street, Building S-212, Gainesville, Florida 32606 Phone: (352) 395-5407 Fax: (352) 395-4475 E-mail: **sherry.dupree@sfcc.edu**

Michelle Dunn In 1998, Dunn opened M.A.D Collection Agency and published her first book, How to Make Money Collecting Money - Starting a Collection Agency, in 2002. She is now publishing Become the Squeaky Wheel, A Credit and Collections Guide for everyone and a book of 7 short stories. Michelle Dunn, Never Dunn Publishing, Post Office Box 40, Plymouth, New Hampshire 03264 E-mail: **michelle@michelledunn.com** Website: **www.michelledunn.com**

Amanda Easton Author of The Last Love Letter, the raw, provocative and humbling story of a heartbreaking relationship involving a young African-American couple that begins with a one-night stand. Additionally, she is launching Dirty Laundry Ink, an independent publishing company based in Des Moines, Iowa that publishes autobiographies, memoirs, and confessional-style fiction depicting the more honest aspects of intimate relationships. Amanda Easton, c/o Dirty Laundry Ink, Post Office Box 65862, West Des Moines, Iowa 50265 Phone: (515) 314-0812 E-mail: **amanda@thelastloveletter.com**

Gloria Taylor Edwards Mystery writer/women's issues. Inspirational Speaker; radio talk show host on wclmradiocom Author of The Proclamation, published in 1992; Stories From Ancient Africa, published in 1995; Death Will Pay The Debt, published in 2000; and, Sins Of The Parents, release date January 2004. Gloria Taylor Edwards, Voices from the Drum, Post Office Box 27504, Richmond, Virginia 23261 Phone: (804) 323-6441 E-mail: **vftdgte@aol.com** Website: **www.gloriatayloredwards.com**

Jefferson D. Edwards, Jr. The author of 6 books. Books written: "Where Are All the Fathers," "Purging Racism From Christianity," subtitled (Freedom and Purpose Through Identity). "Gifted - Discovering Your Hidden Greatness," "The Call of God," subtitled (Since I've Been Called to Preach - Now What?). "Liberated: No Longer Bound," subtitled (What Really is Freedom). "Chosen - Not Cursed," subtitled (The Destiny of the Spiritual Ethiopian). Contat Dr. Jefferson D. Edwards, Jr., Jeff Edwards Ministries International, Post Office Box 300873, Kansas City, Missouri 64130 Phone: (816) 363-6633 Fax: (816) 822-9998 E-mail: **jemikcmo@aol.com** Website: **www.jeffedwards.org**

Dorothy G. Elliott Author, writer, Afro-American children books. Contact Ms. Dorothy G. Elliott, Hosanna Productions, Post Office Box 3011, Petersburg, Virginia 23805 E-mail: **elliottoge2003@yahoo.com**

K. Elliott A native of Charlotte, North Carolina, K. Elliott attended Central Piedmont Community College in the early nineties. Elliott placed in a competition and later earned a scholarship to the North Carolina Writer's Conference in 2001 the same year in which he began working on his first Novel entitled "Entangled." Contact K. Elliott, Urban Lifestyle Press, Post Office. Box 12714, Charlotte, North Carolina 28205 E-mail: **kelliott11@carolina.rr.com**

Marvie Ellis Received her Bachelor of Science degree in Communicative Disorders from Jackson State University in Jackson, Mississippi and her Master of Science degree from the University of North Carolina at Chapel Hill (1996). She owns a private pediatric speech-language and occupational therapy practice (Speech Kids, P.C.) in Round Rock, Texas. Marvie has specialized training in working with the birth to five population, children with autism spectrum disorders, speech-language delays, oral motor therapy, play based therapy, sensory therapy, and behavior modification techniques. Marvie Ellis, Speech Kids Texas Press, Inc., 3802 Beaconsdale Drive, Austin, Texas 78727 Phone: (512) 426-0163 E-mail: **marvie_ellis@yahoo.com** Website: **www.speechkidstexaspress.com**

Nishawnda Ellis Author of the new book Snowed, A Lesson In Love. After, graduating from Boston Latin Academy with honors, Nishawnda attended Hampton University in Hampton Virginia where, she earned a Bachelors of Science degree and went on to practice as a Registered Nurse. Ms. Nishawnda Ellis, Post Office Box 692092, Quincy, Massachusetts 02269 E-mail: **nishawnda@kindleeyesbooks.com** Website: **www.kindleeyesbooks.com**

Shawn Ellis Derrick Hicks, aka Shawn Ellis, has a Associates Degree in Video Arts Technology from the Borough of Manhattan Community College. He has finished one novel, called The Youngblood of Babylon. Shawn Ellis, 998 Williams Avenue, #3D, Brooklyn, New York 11207 E-mail: **rabbitshawn@hotmail.com**

CC Fann The author has written several books. Last year she released Part one of "Can't Let Go." Part two of "Can't Let Go: The Hidden Agenda" will be released in November. Her latest release is "Common Sense Do Not Play The Game With An Inmate." She has been featured in Booking Matter Magazine for Black Authors. She also conducts workshops at the Corrections Academy for the Georgia Department of Corrections. She is a member of Buckeye Baptist Church of Dublin GA, Southern States Correction Association, Peace Officers Association, and Phi Beta Lambda. She is retired from the Department of Corrections with 14 years. Contact Ms. CC Fann, Post Office Box 81, Wrightsville, Georgia 31096 Phone: (478) 278-7956 E-mail: **jabspub@yahoo.com** Website: **www.ccfanncommonsense.com**

Holly K. Ferguson Author of "Getting Deep with God", "Spring Cleaning", "Encouragements from the Heart," and "Where Is The Church." Holly K. Ferguson, Now U No Publishing Company, Post Office Box 9501, Cincinnati Ohio 45209 Phone: (513) 226-6450 E-mail: **carla.sams@nowuno-enterprises.com** Website: **www.nowunopublishingco.com**

Peggy M Fisher   Author of "Lifting Voices:Voices of the Collective Struggle." Her poems have appeared in several anthologies. Her lastest book, "Search Lights for My Soul," just received the Readers View 2007 Award in the category of Self Help. She is one of the featured authors in an anthology of essays, "The Story That Must Be Told," published by Loving Healing Press in June 2007. Contact Ms. Peggy M Fisher, Pyramid Collections, Post Office Box 2775, Camden, New Jersey 08101 Phone: (856) 964-4284 E-mail: **pyramidcl@cs.com** Website: **www.pmmfisher.com**

Valdez V. Fisher, Jr. Author of the self-help/motivational book I Ain't Bitin' My Tongue. Valdez V. Fisher, Jr., Post Office Box 23951, Baltimore, Maryland 21203 Phone: (410) 456-3660 E-mail: **booksbyvaldez@aol.com**

Pansie Hart Flood Children's author and educator Mrs. Flood grew up in Wilmington, North Carolina as the youngest of seven children.   Fond memories of summer visits to her grandmother's gave her the inspiration and vivid setting for her first book, Sylvia & Miz Lula Maye. Two sequels followed. Secret Holes was released in 2003 and September Smiles was released in 2004 and a young readers series called Tiger Turcotte is forthcoming. She earned her bachelor's degree from East Carolina University in Greenville, North Carolina. She teaches at E. B. Aycock Middle School. Member of the Society of Children's Book Writers and Illustrators, North Carolina Writer's Network and North Carolina Association of Educators. Pansie H. Flood, Post Office Box 20614, Greenville, North Carolina 27858 E-mail: **floodpan@earthlink.net**

Nancey Flowers Editor-In-Chief of Game Sports Magazine and publisher of Flowers In Bloom Publishing, Inc., Nancey attended Morgan State University in Baltimore, Maryland, where she received her bachelor's degree in mass communications with a minor in journalism. She is author of the #1 Essence Bestselling novel Shattered Vessels, and No Strings Attached. She paid tribute to her parents by using their native Jamaica, West Indies, as the setting for her first novel, A Fool's Paradise. Contributing author in the erotica sensation Twilight Moods, and the anthology Proverbs For The People. Nancey Flowers, Flowers In Bloom Publishing, Inc., Post Office Box 473106, Brooklyn, New York 11247 E-mail: **nanceyflowers@msn.com** Website: **www.flowersinbloompublishing.com**

Penelope Flynn Author and Screenwriter of Erotica, Science Fiction, Fantasy, Sensual Romance, Paranormal Romance, Legal comedy and drama and Horror. Penelope Flynn, 824 North Marsalis Avenue, Suite C, Dallas, Texas 75203 Phone: (214) 371-7366 Fax: (214) 942-0980 E-mail: **penelope@penelopeflynn.com**

Dawn Fobbs Born September 24, 1972 in Houston Texas. Writer, Creative Publisher of Stand Magazine since 2004.   Entrepreneur, Mentor, Author of 7-Days of Networking, a book for the serious networkers taking the initiative to take their business and branding to the next level. Contact Ms. Dawn Fobbs, Stand Magazine, Post Office Box 6667, Katy, Texas 77491 Phone: (281) 587-4054 E-mail: **msdawwn@sbcglobal.net** Website: **www.standmagazine.biz**

Gyasi A. Foluke Nontraditional Minister (Cosmic Christian), and part-time CEO, Minister (Dr.) Gyasi A. Foluke has been an activist-scholar-author in the struggle for human rights and dignity for over 50 years, beginning at age 16 when he established the first Youth Council of the NAACP in his hometown of Columbia, South Carolina. Author of The Real-Holocaust: A Wholistic Analysis of the African American Experience, 1441-1994 (1995), The "Old Time Religion": A Wholistic Challenge to the Black Church (1997), The Crisis and Challenge of Black Mis-education in America: Confronting the Destruction of African People Through Euro-centric Public Schools, (2001), The Scoundrel Syndrome: Essays on the African American Experience, 1996-2003, Revisiting The Real-Holocaust (2004) and A Wholistic Freedom Agenda: Practical Remedies for Racial Justice, Beyond Empty Rhetoric, With a Special Focus on Charlotte-Mecklenburg North Carolina (2007). Graduate of Howard University, Washington, D. C., 1958 (BA Political Science/Economics, Magna Cum Laude) and American University, Washington, D.C., 1960 (MA Public Administration). Earned a Doctor of Divinity Degree from the Neotarian College of Philosophy, Kansas City, Missouri, 1980. Dr. Gyasi A. Foluke, The Kushite Institute for Wholistic Development, 4215 Colonial Drive, Columbia, South Carolina 29203 Phone: (803) 754-8317 E-mail: **gflack1@bellsouth.net** Website: **http://tkifwd.tripod.com/**

Michael Fontaine Writer and author, his mainstream fiction novel titled: "Yesterday I Could Sing", was inspired by society's incredible failure at juvenile delinquent rehabilitation. He served as a juvenile probation officer with the Lake County Superior Court System, in Gary, Indiana from 1973 through 1978 where he had an active caseload of more than 200 delinquents involved in crimes against person and property.   Michael Fontaine, #34 Queensbrook Place, Saint Louis, Missouri 63132 Phone: (314) 994-9927 E-mail: **drfontaine303@sbcglobal.net**

Darnella Ford Author of the novel Rising (St. Martin's Press, Jan. 2003), a raw tale of incest and redemption hailed by Ebony Magazine as the "Survival anthem of the year." She is author of four other novels: Crave (March 2004); Choke (2005); 19 Floors (2006); Naked (2007). Upcoming projects include the screenplay adaptation of Rising, Salvaged, a non-fiction book 2007, Skin (Kensington) 2008, Crack'd (Feature Film), and Intercept (Feature Film). Darnella Ford Phone: (818) 458-2062 E-mail: **dapoet@aol.com** Website: **www.darnella.com**

Roger A. Forsyth Author of Black Flight, the story of the three flights of Albert Forsythe and Al Anderson (later the chief instructor for the Tuskegee Airmen). Mr. Forsyth details their three exciting flights. Contact Mr. Roger Forsyth, Allcourt Publishing, Post Office Box 491122, Los Angeles, California 90049 E-mail: **allcourtpublishing@yahoo.com**

Gwendoline Y. Fortune A former "Corporate wife" with strong social and environmental interests, Family Lines is Ms. Fortunes' second novel. Her first novel, Growing Up Nigger Rich, received rave endorsements and was a regional best seller. Gwen has been a classical soprano and has traveled on five continents. Active in several writers organizations, education has always been a high priority. She holds degrees in education and social science. Before her second career as a writer, she was an elementary school teacher and professor of history and social science. Ms. Fortune is active in the alumni associations of Bennett College, J. C. Smith, Roosevelt, and Nova Southeastern Universities. Gwendoline Y. Fortune, 8620 NW 13th, Suite #71, Gainesville, Florida 32653　Phone: (352) 372-0021　E-mail: **gyfort@earthlink.net** Website: **www.zenarts.com**

Rebera Elliott Foston Author, poet, Dr. Rebera Elliott Foston was the valedictorian of Gary Roosevelt High School in 1966. She was a Phi Beta Kappa, Magna Cum Laude 1970 graduate of Fisk University in Nashville, Tennessee, and a 1974 graduate of Meharry Medical College, also in Nashville. In 1981, she received her masters' degree in Public Health from the University of North Carolina, Chapel Hill, where she was elected to Delta Omega, the honor society for Public Health. She completed a Post Doctoral fellowship in teaching Family Medicine at Michigan State University in East Lansing, Michigan, 1984. That same year she completed her residency in Family Practice and became Board Certified. Dr. Foston has published an inspirational journal entitled Peace on Earth, and 20 books of poetry which include You Don't Live On My Street, No Stoppin' Sense, The Parade and In God's Time. Her signature poems are You Don't Live On My Street, Annie's Baby and Not My Chile. Dr. Rebera Elliott Foston, M.D., DMin, Post Office Box 726, Clarksville, Tennessee 37041　Phone: (800) 418-0374　Fax: (931) 645-3500　E-mail: **minfoston@aol.com**　Website: **www.drfoston.com**

Antoinette V. Franklin Author, poet and educator. Native of San Antonio, Texas, Ms. Franklin has served on various enhancement boards of the arts. She has written six chap books of poetry. The titles being These Rainy Days, An Untouched Song, My Rock And My Salvation, A New Beginning, Going Home, Sisterly Love (a chap book of children's poetry and short stories). Her latest book of poetry will debut in January 2005, In The Mist Of Struggle, Authors House Press. She has been published in over 100 anthologies. The latest being Violets and Delta Girl Stories and Poets Along The River. Her new book released in 2007, Hot Woman Needing a Man, a play and other stories. Contact Ms. Antoinette V. Franklin, Author House, 550 Crestway Drive, San Antonio, Texas　Phone: (210) 264-1518　E-mail: **franklin_antoinette@hotmail.com**　Website: **www.antoinettefranklin.com**

Mike Frazier Author of Surviving the Storm: Finding life after death, about a torrential storm ravaged Dallas, Texas, on May 5, 1995, devastating the life of Mike Frazier forever. Using his talent as a bass guitarist and drummer, Mike Frazier has toured with artist such as Kirk Franklin, R. Kelly, Stevie Wonder, La Shun Pace and Ann Nesby. He has appeared on live recordings of Bishop T.D. Jakes and gospel great James Moore. For the past several years he has been touring the country with Tyler Perry Gospel Stage plays, I know I've been changed, I can do Bad All By Myself, The Diary of a Mad Black Woman, Madea's Family Reunion, Madea's Class Reunion and currently Mike is the Musical Director for Tyler Perry, Meet the Browns. Mike Frazier, Post Office Box 201571, Arlington, Texas 76006　E-mail: **mike@survivingthestorm.com**　Website: **www.survivingthestorm.com**

Walter Fredericks Author and Entrepreneur. Walter Fredericks writes under the pen name T.F. Walters. He is the author of the critically acclaimed urban literary work, My Brothers Keeper. He vividly tells the story of two brothers growing up in poverty as they face death and betrayal as each ascends to fame and fortune in two opposites manners. Founder and CEO of Walter Fredericks Enterprises, Inc., a multimedia company that specializes in the production and marketing of urban literature (also known as Street Lit). Contact Walter Fredericks Enterprises, Inc, 644 Saint Anns Avenue, Suite #1, Bronx, New York 10455 Phone: (917) 664-4070 Fax: (718) 401-8450 E-mail: **wenterprisesinc@yahoo.com** Website: **www.walterfredericks.com**

Harrine Freeman Author of the book, How to Get out of Debt: Get an "A" Credit Rating for Free Using the System I've Used Successfully with Thousands of Clients (2006, Adept Publishers). Freeman is a member of the American Association of Daily Money Managers, the National Association of Women Writers, IEEE and Women In Technology. She has a B.S. degree in Computer Science and is currently pursuing a Master's degree in Information Technology. She writes frequently and has written technical documentation for the IEEE Instrumentation and Measurement Magazine, as well as written several ezine on personal finance. As a panelist she participated in a number of national and local conferences. She has appeared in Market Watch, Essence Magazine, Pink Magazine, the Prince Georges Gazette, Bankrate.com, Creditcards.com, and Yahoo.com. She is a member of the American Association of Daily Money Managers, Credit Professionals International, the National Association of Women Writers, and Toastmasters. Harrine Freeman, H.E. Freeman Enterprsies, 3 Bethesda Metro Center, Suite 700, Bethesda, Maryland 20814 Phone: (301) 280-5923   E-mail: **hfreeman@hefreemanenterprises.com** Website: **www.hefreemanenterprises.com**

Charlotte A. Clark-Frieson Aside from being the "Matriarch" of her own Mortuary Company and the CEO of her own Company, Wilkie Clark's Daughter Enterprises, LLC, Charlotte A. Clark-Frieson is a new author of the soul stirring biography of her late father, entitled Chief Cook & Bottle-Washer, The Unconquerable Soul of Wilkie Clark. The story is about Wilkie Clark, who during the 20th century, rose to the occasion of racism and economic oppression in Alabama. Charlotte A. Clark-Frieson, Wilkie Clark's Daughter Enterprises, LLC, 322 Wilkie Clark Drive, Roanoke, Alabama 36274 Phone: (334) 863-4885 Fax: (334) 863-6062 E-mail: **caclarkfrieson@msn.com** Website: **www.wilkieclarksdaughter.net**

Dr. Lisa H. Fuller Practicing psychiatrist, Community Chaplain, and author of the book, "You Already Have All of the Tools that You Need" tells us how one can transform their life based on Biblical truth. Dr. Fuller obtained her medical degree from the West Virginia School of Osteopathic Medicine. Her field of specialty is psychiatry. She is the executive director of LRHF Mental Health Consultants and president of Learn Realistic Habits for the Future Publishing. Dr. Lisa H. Fuller, 15565 Northland Drive, Suite 206E, Southfield, Michigan 48075 Phone: (313) 645-1596 E-mail: **drlisahfuller@aol.com** Website: **www.drlisahfuller.com**

Sandra Peoples-Gates Author of the book 'No More Drama' and founder of BlackBerry Literary Services, a company whose mission is to teach authors the correct way to self publish a book. Her company provides proofreading, editing, and marketing services as well. Sandra Peoples-Gates, BlackBerry Literary Services, 2956 Mackin Road, Flint, Michigan 48504 Phone: (810) 240-4372 E-mail: **bblit@hotmail.com**

Kyra Gaunt Author of The Games Black Girls Play: Learning the Ropes from Double-Dutch to Hip-hop (NYU Press, 2006), Kyra a.k.a. "Professor G" is a singer-songwriter and an associate professor of ethnomusicology at New York University who lectures nationally and internationally on African American music and issues of race, gender and the musical body. Kyra Gaunt, 1 Washington Square Village, #5-H, New York, New York 10012 Phone: (646) 831-0615 E-mail: **kyraocity@yahoo.com**

Carol Gee Author, Carol Gee has been an educator for over twenty years. She trained as a Gestalt Therapist counseling adults and children in a mental health center for several years. However her first love has always been writing. Contact Ms. Carol Gee, Post Office Box 832004, Stone Mountain, Georgia 30083 E-mail: **VenusChronicles@aol.com**

Carolyn Gibson A native of Boston, Massachusetts, and a Simmons College graduate, Gibson is author of a novel, "Repairman Jones" and a collection of 60 poems titled "Urban Poetry." Carolyn Gibson, Carolyn's Corner, Post Office Box 300160, Jamaica Plain, Massachusetts 02130 Phone: (617) 298-7484 Fax: (617) 298-1018 E-mail: **Carolynscorner@aol.com** Website: **www.Carolynscorner.com**

Richard Charles Gibson The author's first book of short stories Life Lessons was published in 2003. Contact Richard C. Gibson, 2517 West Harrison Street, Chicago, Illinois 60612 Phone: (312) 243-5343 E-mail: **gibsonsnoopy@aol.com**

Gladys "Nyagus" Gikiri Nyagus is creator of a new children's book series called My Malaika. The author was inspired to start writing by her grandmother who told her the most amazing African folk stories when she was a child. Nyagus has a BBA and an MBA and for many years she worked as a Finance Professional. When she quit her job to spend more time with her young children she discovered her true calling: writing children's books. Nyagus enjoys visiting schools and motivating children to read. Nyagus lives in Florida with her husband (a math professor) and their two children. Ms. Gladys Nyagus Gikiri, My Malaika Children's Books, 5413 Whistler Drive, Tallahassee, Florida 32317 Phone: (850) 878-7741 E-mail: **gladys@mymalaika.com** Website: **www.mymalaika.com**

J. Lee Cooper-Giles Author of The Hypocrites. Lifelong political and social activist, he has three under-graduate college degrees from the Ohio State University, a BA in Black Studies and English, BA in Journalism, BFA in Painting and Drawing. J. Lee Cooper-Giles, 1761 Clifton Avenue #10, Columbus, Ohio 43203 Phone: (614) 251-1829 E-mail: **leegiles78@hotmail.com**

Thomas Gist Author of You Too, Can Have, The Fruits of Life! Without "White Folks" BS (Business Suck-ins). Thomas Gist, 112 South Lavergne Avenue, Chicago, Illinois 60644 Phone: (773) 261-4005 E-mail: **thomas@hannibalisatthegates.com**

Sheronde Glover Business consultant, speaker and co-author of Sipping Tea and Doing Business: A Holistic Journey to Business Success, a guide for starting and growing your business written specifically for women entrepreneurs. Contact Ms. Sheronde Glover, Glover Enterprise, Attn: Sipping Tea and Doing Business, Post Office Box 870354, Morrow, Georgia 30287 E-mail: **sheronde@sippingteaonline.com** Website: **www.sippingteaonline.com**

Beverly T. Gooden Author of the book, Confessions of a Church Girl. Confessions outlines the true story of a young woman's secret five-year struggle with sexual addiction. Faced with infection and rape, she races to uncover the truth about her faith, and hear the voice of the God. This emotional, yet empowering story is an autobiographic journey entailing love, lies, sex, and drugs, teaching one young woman the true meaning of forgiveness. Ms. Beverly T. Gooden, 1754 Woodruff Road, #121, Greenville, South Carolina 29607 Phone: (864) 417-2540 E-mail: **info@beverlyt.com** Website: **www.BeverlyT.com**

Maurice M. Gray, Jr. Author and owner/operator of Write The Vision, Inc., a Christian publishing company committed to assisting writers to bring forth their creative visions and to prepare them for publication. He is the author of To Whom Much Is Given (fiction), I Really Didn't Mean To Get HIV by Livingston N. Lee, Jr. as told to Maurice M. Gray, Jr. (nonfiction) and All Things Work Together (fiction). Maurice M. Gray, Write The Vision, Inc., Box 12926, Wilmington, Delaware 19850 Phone: (302) 778-2407 E-mail: **writevision2000@yahoo.com** Website: **www.writethevision.biz**

Carmen Green Author of more than twenty novels and novellas. Her most recent novel is FLIRT, a romance novel (Kensington Dafina). Her first collaboration novel with Victor McGlothlin and Tracey Price Thompson is entitled Indecent Exposure (February, 2006). Her next comedy What A Fool Believes (August, 2006). Carmen Green, 325 Wildcat Lake Drive, Lawrenceville, Georgia 30043 E-mail: **carmengreen1201@yahoo.com**

Kisha Green Author. Kisha Green, Divabook, Inc., 2 Evergreen Drive, Wayside, New Jersey 07712 Phone: (732) 695-0082 Fax: (732) 695-0422 E-mail: **kisha@divabooksinconline.com** Website: **www.divabooksinconline.com**

Thomas Green, Jr. Ex athlete and ex sports reporter, Thomas now writes love stories involving pro athletes. He has self published four such novels, Courting Miss Thang, Love's Home Run, Player No More, When It Hurts So Bad and Ice Thug Blues (October 2004). Contact Mr. Thomas Green Jr., 3371 Adkins Road, Atlanta, Georgia 30331 E-mail: **tjverde05@yahoo.com** Website: **www.CourtingMissThang.com**

Thomas J. Greene Children's book author and publisher. Thomas J. Greene, Greene Bark Press Inc, Post Office Box 1108, Bridgeport, Connecticut 06601 Phone: (610) 434-2802 Fax: (610) 434-2803 E-mail: **greenebark@aol.com** Website: **www.greenebarkpress.com**

Evelyn Gresham Author of Brown Little Babies, a children's picture book honoring African American babies contains beautiful photos of African American babies, illustrations and inspiring poems. Evelyn has also designed her first ethnic doll, a look-a-like doll of the author. She has been writing poetry and children's stories ever since she was young. She attended Cincinnati State College for Early Childhood Education. Evelyn has taught children's Sunday school, regular children's bible class and vacation bible school for preschoolers. She worked in the medical field for twenty one years as a nursing assistant and telemetry tech. and has volunteered in variuos daycare centers including the YMCA. Evelyn Gresham, Elg Books and Collectibles, Otter Branch Drive, Apt. #8, Magnolia, New Jersey 08049 Phone: (856) 292-6565 E-mail: **laurine11@hotmail.com** Website: **www.elgbooksanddolls.com**

Neisha Brown Grice   Author of the book, F.A.M.I.L.Y - Fathers And Mothers In Loving Youth group. Contact Ms. Neisha Brown Grice, 700 West Center Street, Suite #297, Duncanville, Texas 75116 Phone: (972) 283-8153 E-mail: **neishabrown31@yahoo.com**

Vanessa Davis Griggs Author of three novels: Destiny Unlimited, The Rose of Jericho and the latest book: Promises Beyond Jordan published by BET Books/New Spirit, Vanessa's new release from BET Books Wings of Grace was published in February 2005. She is the recipient of numerous recognitions including finalist for the BWA 2002 Gold Pen Award for Christian Fiction, named 2002 Self-published African American Author Book of the Year Award as well as the self-published version of Promises Beyond Jordan winning Best Christian Fiction. Vanessa Davis Griggs, Post Office Box 101328, Birmingham, Alabama 35210 E-mail: **Vanessa@VanessaDavisGriggs.com** Website: **www.vanessaDavisGriggs.com**

Tania Guerrera Artist. Author of the book Thoughts and Transformations. The book contains poetry, art and essays all dealing with love, social issues, justice and spirituality. Tania Guerrera, 311 North Avenue #11, New Rochelle, New York 10801 Phone: (917) 578-4264 E-mail: **TheArtist@taniaGuerrera.com** Website: **www.TaniaGuerrera.com**

Shirley Hailstock Award-winning novelist, Shirley Hailstock holds a bachelors degree in Chemistry from Howard University in Washington, DC, and an MBA in Chemical Marketing from Fairleigh Dickinson University in Teaneck, New Jersey. Whispers of Love, Shirley's debut novel, was published in September, 1994. The romantic suspense received critical acclaim from the Gothic Journal, Romantic Times Magazine, Affaire de Couer, Rendezvous and Booklist. Whispers of Love, winner of the Holt Medallion from the Virginia Romance Writers, is now in its 4th printing and recently was optioned for a television movie of the week. Clara's Promise, Shirley's first historical romance, won the Utah Romance Writers Heart of the West Award. White Diamonds, (August 1996) was nominated for a Romantic Times Award as the Best Multicultural Romance of 1996. Additionally, Romantic Times presented Shirley with a Career Achievement Award and her novel, Legacy, received the Waldenbooks Award for Bestselling Multicultural Romance. The author of 17 novels and novellas, her next book, You Made Me Love was released in April 2005. She has been an Adjunct Professor of Accounting at Rutgers University, New Brunswick campus and taught Novel Writing at Middlesex County College. Contact Shirley T. Hailstock, Post Office 513, Plainsboro, New Jersey 08536 Phone: (609) 275-8323 E-mail: **shirley.hailstock@comcast.net**

Alex Hairston An Essence best-selling author and nurse originally from Baltimore. Alex Hairston now resides in Randallstown, Maryland with his wife and three kids. He is the author of two books, "If Only You Knew" and Love Don't Come Easy, A Novel. Alex Hairston, Post Office Box 1138, Randallstown, Maryland 21133 E-mail: **alexhairston@yahoo.com** Website: **www.alexhairston.com**

Forest Hairston   Author of the book "Spirit Ran Free", Forest Hairston is a Detroit, Michigan, native. His successful career as a songwriter-music producer, screenwriter and poet, extends his talents a step further as a great author with a definite voice. Forest Hairston, ForGen Productions, 3654 Barham Boulevard, Suite Q301, Los Angeles, California Phone: (323) 851-1225 E-mail: **fgprod@forgen.com** Website: **www.forgen.com**

William Hairston Author, playwright and poet Mr. Hairston's books include: "The World of Carlos" (novel) "Sex and Conflict" (novel) "History of The National Capital Area Council/Boy Scouts of America" "Spaced Out" (space adventure) "Showdown At Sundown" (western novel)" Ira Frederick Aldridge" (The London Conflict) (Play, non-fiction), "Swan Song" (novel), "It's Human Nature" (short story collection), "Passion And Politics" (novel) and "Poetry And Prose Of Passion And Compassion" (poetry). Contact Mr. William Hairston, 5501 Seminary Road, Falls Church, Virginia 22041 Phone: (703) 845-1281 E-mail: **WilliamRHairston1@msn.com**

Patricia Haley Author and motivational speaker. National bestselling author of Nobody's Perfect, Blind Faith, and No Regrets is a trailblazer. She self-published Nobody's Perfect in 1998 and her faith-based debut novel was the first of its kind to repeatedly make numerous bestselling lists, including #1 on the Essence list. With her engineering degree from Stanford University and M.B.A. in marketing and finance from the University of Chicago, she works part-time as a project manager. Patricia is also a member of Delta Sigma Theta Sorority. Ms. Patricia Haley, Anointed Vision, Post Office Box 80735 Valley Forge, Pennsylvania 19484 Phone: (610) 935-0413 E-mail: **info@patriciahaley.com**   Website: **www.patriciahaley.com**

Evelyn D. Hall Self-published author, residing in, Atlanta, Georgia. The author has published three books, Enter Eve's Poetic Paradise, Dontay's Poetic Playground and Dontay's Alphabet Book of Color. Contact Evelyn D. Hall, Post Office Box 1775, Mableton, Georgia 30126 E-mail: **lilpoet2you@aol.com** Website: **www.poeticparadise.ipfox.com**

Hallema A Miami native, Hallema is the author of two books, Mass Deceptions (2003) and a new novel, True Intentions (2004). Hallema discovered her writing talent as a senior in high school. Her undergraduate education prepared her for a career in law. She holds dual Bachelor of Science degrees in Criminology and Political Science from Florida State University. Upon graduating from FSU, she was awarded a full scholarship to Stetson University College of Law, where she continued to nurture her writer's voice. Following law school, Hallema returned to her roots in Miami. She became a local favorite as a spoken word artist in South Florida by reciting her original and dramatic poetry. Building on her celebrity status, Hallema founded Just us Girls, a book club for inner-city teenage girls. Community service has been a guiding principle throughout her life. Member: Dade County Alumnae Chapter of Delta Sigma Theta Sorority, Inc, The Universal Truth Center and The Black Alumni Association of Florida State University. Completed Mass Deception", August, 2003. Hallema, Mahogany Publishing, Post Office Box 170952, Hialeah, Florida 33017 E-mail: **Hallemawrites@aol.com** Website: **www.hallema.net**

Sandra Hamer Author of the book Glory...the Hair. Contact Ms. Sandra Hamer, 1779 Kirby Parkway #1-PMB161, Memphis, Tennessee 38138 Phone: (901) 272-2031   E-mail: **glorythehair@yahoo.com**

John Hamilton Educator, consultant and author of two books, The Elevator is Broken and Vainglorious: How Today's Black Men Graduate, Dr. Hamilton founded Hamilton and Associates Consulting, a Los Angeles based consulting firm, since 2004. Contact Mr. John P. Hamilton, Hamilton & Associates Consulting, Post Office Box 2627, Gardena, California 90247 Phone: (323) 309-2502 Fax: (310) 538-0760 E-mail: **Johnphamilton@aol.com** Website: **www.hamiltonandassociatesconsulting.org**

Robyn Maria Hamlin   Author and Screenwriter.   Novels, "The Zone of Danger Test" is my breakout novel.   "Shades of Gray" and "Zone of Danger" are my only two registered screenplays to date.   Poetry, "The Red Flag," "Bread Crumbs," "The Teamplayer," "A Hand for ME," and "There Is A River" are a few of my poems that have been published to date.   My writings have also been featured in both EBONY (October 2005) and ESSENCE (January 2006) magazines.   Contact Ms. Robyn Maria Hamlin, 1900 Wesleyan Drive, #2807, Macon, Georgia 31210 Phone: (478) 476-8776 E-mail: **weeda5weeda@aol.com**

Julian Vaughan Hampton An author of adult and children's fiction, poetry, commentary, and an award winning songwriter. His first published book, a crime drama titled, The Contradiction, was an underground hit. Julian's second book, a thriller titled, Limbus received rave reviews, setting the stage for the release of a book of spoken word poetry titled Love, Life and Kingdom. He is the founder and CEO of Vaughanworks, a literary empowerment and publishing company designed to assist emerging writers, and assist in community building. Julian Vaughan Hampton, Vaughanworks, Post Office Box 18511-0511, Milwaukee, Wisconsin 53218 Phone: (877) 829-6757 E-mail: **Vaughanworks1@mfire.com**

Daniel D. Hardman Christian writer and author of the book titled Essays from Church: Volume One. Writes a column, The Other Side at theblackmarketcom. Daniel D Hardman, Post Office Box 1886, Cedar Hill, Texas 75106 E-mail: **essaysfromchurch@edincorporated.com**

P. Stephen Hardy Co-author with Sheila Jackson Hardy, M.Ed., of Extraordinary People of the Harlem Renaissance (Scholastic). P. Stephen Hardy, 6125 South LaCienega Boulevard, Los Angeles, California 90056 E-mail: **thenewnegro@hotmail.com**

Sheila Jackson Hardy Co-author with P. Stephen Hardy, of Extraordinary People of the Harlem Renaissance, winner of 2001 New York Public Library Best Books for the Teen Age 2001 and the Children's Book Council/National Council for Social Studies Notable Social Studies Trade Book for Young People - published by Scholastic Inc. Their recently completed Extraordinary People of the Civil Rights Movement, was released in September 2006. Sheila Jackson Hardy, M.Ed., 6125 South LaCienega Boulevard, Los Angeles, California 90056 E-mail: **thenewnegro@hotmail.com**

Julia Hare   Nationally acclaimed speaker and master teacher, Dr. Julia Hare was named Educator of The Year by American University, World Book Encyclopedia, and the Junior Chamber Of Commerce. Contact Dr. Julia Hare, 1801 Bush Street, Suite 118, San Francisco, California 94109 Phone: (415) 474-1707 Fax: (415) 771-3485

Nathan Hare Born: 04-09-33. First person hired to coordinate a Black studies program in the United States, Dr. Hare coined the term "Ethnic Studies," which initially was being called "Minority Studies." Co-winner with Harold Cruse, of the National Award for Distinguished Scholarly Contributions to Black studies, National Council for Black Studies; 1990 winner of the Marcus and Amy Garvey Award from the Institute of Pan-African Studies. United Negro Distinguished Scholar. Contact Dr. Nathan Hare, The Black Think Tank, 1801 Bush Street, Suite 118, San Francisco, California 94109 Phone: (415) 474-1707 Fax: (415) 771-3485 E-mail: **nhare@pacbell.net**

CaNon Harper Writer. Grown Man Publishing, LLC, Post Office Box 205, Jeffersonville, Indiana 47131 Phone: (502) 994-9344 E-mail: **canon@grownmanpublishing.com** Website: **www.grownmanpublishing.com**

Keith Harrell Dynamic coach and highly acclaimed and innovative professional speaker, Keith is the author of Attitude is Everything: Ten Life Changing Steps to Turning Attitude into Action. Keith Harrell, Harrell Performance Systems, Inc., Post Office Box 81268, Atlanta, Georgia 30366 Phone: (770) 451-3190 Fax: (770) 451-7232 E-mail: **info@keithharrell.com** Website: **www.keithharrell.com**

A. C. Jones-Harris Holiness Priest, living with HIV/AIDS. The title of his work is, Which Road Should I Take? Learning To Live With AIDS, published by PublishAmerica. He is the president and founder of Greater Deliverance Ministries, Inc., a keynote speaker about AIDS prevention, paralegal and peer counselor. Apostle has received his significant education from Troy State University, Darton College, Georgia State University, and University of Georgia. Contact Apostle A.C. Jones-Harris, Greater Deliverance Ministries, Inc., Post Office Box 911, Blakely, Georgia 39823 Phone: (229) 309-0083 E-mail: **greater@alltel.net**

Ardara Harris Born the youngest of four siblings, raised in a very stable home in a very unstable environment on the Northeast side of Houston, Texas in Studewood, his first Novel titled Foolish Men, Harris says that it was looking into his son's eyes that inspired him to write this very insightful book. His second Novel, Whoa-Man (Because Men Just Don't Give a Damn!), was birthed due to his personal experience of marriage and the struggles of life and being able to gain an understanding of the another side of the coin. After the tragic loss of his brother, Harris pushed through a place where no one should have to go and through his pain, his passion was once again rekindled which produced yet a third book titled, Skin Games (Is Success Measured by Tint?). An active member of the Alpha Phi Alpha Fraternity and a self-proclaimed idealist, Ardara strives to further educate himself by working on his Masters at the University of St. Thomas and delivering motivational speeches on the subjects of Self-Reliance and Self Motivation. He continues to write as well as educate. His life's goal is to make a difference in at least one person's life and to follow the footsteps that God has laid before him. Contact Ardara Harris, 7422 Gatecraft Drive, Missouri City, Texas 77489 Phone: (281) 437-0434 E-mail: **thetalentedharris@sbcglobal.net** Website: **www.ardaraharris.com**

Kathy Harris Author, motivational speaker, publisher & CEO, Angels Press, Post Office Box 870849, Stone Mountain, Georgia 30087 Phone: (770) 873-2072 Fax: (678) 254-5018 E-mail: **info@angelspress.com** Website: **www.angelspress.com**

Latasha S. Harris Editor and publisher of non fiction. Latasha S. Harris, 805 Anvil Road, Fredericksburg, Virginia 22405 Phone: (540) 373-7007 E-mail: **tasha.harris@sbcglobal.net**

Saundra E. Harris Born in Maryland, Saundra is author of the book, THE PARTY (2003). Her company Saphari books re-released the book in 2006. She holds a Bachelors Degree in Business Management, from the University of Phoenix. Contact Ms. Saundra E. Harris, Saphari Books, Inc., Post Office Box 232, Pasadena, Maryland 21123 Phone: (443) 517-7196 E-mail: **sapharibooks@yahoo.com** Website: **www.sapharibooks.com**

Sonya Harris Resides in Boston, Massachusetts where she is an educator, a licensed General Securities Representative (Series 7 & 63), a State Examination Proctor, a Promising Pen Pal, an organizer of Emerging-Authors Writers' Group, and a member of several online writers' groups as well. Topics covered in her novel Guilty Pleasures: attire influence abstinence, safe sex, education, and maintaining a positive attitude. Sonya graduated from Boston Technical High School, and graduated with honors from Emmanuel College with a BS degree in Business Administration. Sonya Harris, Sayha Pub, Post Office Box 260274, Boston, Massachusetts 02126 E-mail: **sh@sonyaharris.com** Website: **www.sonyaharris.com**

Natasha Brooks-Harris Author of Panache, a contemporary romance novel, Ms. Harris' two latest projects are novellas published in the books, Summer of Love (2004), and Can I Get An Amen? (2005). Her sophomore romance novel, In Perfect Harmony, is in the revision stages. She is a full-service copy editor, line editor, and proofreader of novel and short fiction manuscripts. She has worked in the publishing field since 1987. Nathasha is the editor of Black Romance and Bronze Thrills magazines. She is also co-owner of Write On! Literary Consortium, a company that provides literary consulting services and more. Natasha Brooks-Harris, 297 7th Street, Brooklyn, New York 11215 E-mail: **nabrooks@aol.com**

Shelia Dansby Harvey A native Houstonian, Mrs. Shelia Harvey was inspired to write Illegal Affairs when she returned to her alma mater, Thurgood Marshall School of Law at Texas Southern University, as an adjunct professor. She received her law degree from Texas Southern University, a HBCU. She is a practicing attorney and has taught at Texas Southern's law school and at Rice University's graduate school of business. Among her many accomplishments, she and her husband Henry were the publisher of Black Tie, an African American lifestyle magazine. Shelia and Henry reside in Houston, where she is at work on the sequel to Illegal Affairs. Mrs. Shelia Dansby Harvey, S & H Productions, LLC, Post Office Box 42257, Houston, Texas 77242 E-mail: **info@illegal-affairs.com** Website: **www.illegal-affairs.com**

Cynthia L. Hatcher Author of the following books: The Abuser's Daughter, Bewitched in the Local Church, Choosing to Dream, and A Man and His Wife. Cynthia L. Hatcher, Dare to Dream Ministries Inc., Post Office Box 494, Genesee, Michigan 48437 Phone: (810) 394-8612 E-mail: **clynn@truevine.net**

Lorenzo L. Heard Author of the book Stuck In A Storm and Missing Your Calm: Discovering God's Purpose for Your Life. Contact Lorenzo L. Heard, Senior Pastor Albany Greater Second Mount Olive Missionary Baptist Church, 302 Adkins Street, Albany, Georgia 31701 Phone: (229) 435-9961 E-mail: **llheard@bellsouth.net**

Michelle Heath Author of the book 7 Principles to Become Your Own Superhero. In her twenty years as a nurse, Michelle Heath witnessed an incredible amount of pain and suffering. Overweight, with uncontrolled high blood pressure and unhappy, Heath believed she had nothing to do with the mess her life was in. It wasn't until she realized that she wasn't simply an innocent bystander in her own life that she began to take control. Written as part of Heath's own healing and as a means to help others on their own path to inner freedom and peace, the book is a real-life book that explains how to find—and love—the Superhero inside of you. Michelle L. Heath, 167 Benziger Avenue, Staten Island, New York 10301 E-mail: **Msouli7@yahoo.com**

Janet Marlene Henderson   Author of LUNCH WITH CASSIE (2005), about a preacher's daughter-in-law who has an affair with a billionaire when her marriage hits the skids, will be releasing another book soon. THE ASSASSIN WHO LOVED HER, a romance novel about a journalist who is stalked by a serial killer she once wrote about, will be released in Summer 2008. Dr. Janet M. Henderson lives in Chicago and teaches English at Malcolm X College. She has a Ph.D in Biblical Studies, an M.A. in English Composition and an M.A. in Education. Contact Janet Marlene Henderson, 7837 South Ada Street, Chicago, Illinois 60620 Phone: (773) 620-2778 E-mail: **jhendalert2@yahoo.com** Website**: www.janethenderson.net**

Kenneth R. Henry Jr.   Owner of Real Ink Publishing and author of a poetry book entitled Tears That Grip A Whole Nation. Real Ink specializes in poetry, self help, and youth centered books. Kenneth R. Henry Jrs., Real Ink Publishing, Post Office Box 496, League City, Texas 77574 Phone: (409) 641-2320 E-mail: **realinkpub@yahoo.com**

Ernestine L. Hill   Female mystery writer. Two novels, The Sable Night, tradionally published 1988, If You Die Before You Wake (2002), and If You Live Another Day (in the hands of an agent). Contact Ernestine L. Hill, 4907 East Laureldale Drive, Houston, Texas 77041 E-mail: **elh11@prodigy.net**

Ida Byrd-Hill   Author of the book, Breakin' Out of Your Financial Funk! She is the President of Uplift, Inc., a 501(c)3 Idea Incubator. She has spent 15 years as a financial advisor and mortgage lender attempting to educate people to view their mortgage as a part of an integrated financial plan and not the plan alone. She believes when property values increased double and triple fold, Americans were baited into the false sense this boom would continue forever. It did not. Ida Byrd-Hill, Post Office Box 241488, Detroit, Michigan 48224 Phone: 313-483-2126 Fax: (313) 899-7091 E-mail: **breakinout@upliftinc.org**   Website: **www.upliftinc.org**

Jessica Holter   Founder of The Punany Poets, of HBO notoriety, Ms. Holter self-published 6 titles before signing to Zane's Strebor Books in 2006. Simon & Schuster will publish her controversial book of erotic poetry and HIV/AIDS awareness entitled Verbal Penetration, April 17th, 2007. Ms. Jessica Holter, 3133 Maxwell Avenue, Oakland, California 94619 E-mail: **ghettogirlblue@yahoo.com** Website: **www.JessicaHolter.com**

Joe C. Hopkins Attorney, since 1982, and publisher of The Pasadena/San Gabriel Valley Journal News since 1989, serving Altadena, Pasadena, Monrovia and Duarte and surrounding cities in the west San Gabriel Valley, California area. Author of "I WILL NOT APOLOGIZE - Uncompromising Solutions to Black America's Dilemma in the 21st Century." Mr. Joe C. Hopkins, 1541 North Lake Avenue, Suite A, Pasadena, California 91104 Phone: (626) 398-1194 Fax: (626) 798-3972 E-mail: **pasjour@pacbell.net**

Renda Horne Best-selling author of "Seven Years in Egypt: Recognizing Your Setbacks as Set-Ups for Your comeback!" and highly sought-after conference speaker, Renda Horne, is wailing for hurting people to come out of darkness and be totally free and delivered from ALL bondage – forever! She is founder/overseer and president of Woman at the Wail Ministries, Renda Horne Ministries, and Wailing Enterprises. Renda Horne, Post Office Box 401479, Redford, Michigan 48240 E-mail: **renda@rendahorne.com** Website: **www.rendahorne.com**

Marlin L. Houser Author of the award winning series The Adventures of Little Fox Book One: "Generations" (two awards) Book Two: The Secret of Squirrel Meadow (two awards). Winner of the USABOOKNEWS Best Book Award 2005 for The Adventures of Little Fox, Book One Generations. I'm also a two time winner of the FPA President Children's Fiction Award 2006 & 2007. My books are chapter books for children 7 - 11 years of age (3 grade - 5 grade). Martin L. Houser, Marhouse Inc., Post Office Box 150605, Altamonte Springs, Florida. 32714 Phone: (407) 599-5307 E-mail: **marlin@adventurefox.com** Website: **www.adventurefox.com**

Elbert Howard One of the 6 original members of the Black Panther Party: Positions Held: Deputy Minister of Information, First Editor of the BPP Newspaper, Member of the BPP Central Committee, Coordinator of National and International Support Committee, BPP Spokesman Community Activist: Positions Held: 2003 Coordinator of All of Us or None Ex-Offender Re-Entry Program; Vice President African American People Organization - Memphis, Tennessee; 2004 Board of Directors - Muumbi Charter School-Memphis, Tennessee; 2004 Board of Directors - Childrens' Institute for Higher Learning & Development, Inc.; Commitee Member - Millions for Reparations - Memphis, Tennessee. Books Published: "Panther on the Prowl (self-published, 2003); College Peer Counseling Handbook (Merritt College, Oakland, California, 1967); Each One Teach One (Merritt College, Oakland, California ,1967). He recently wrote the foreword for the book Up Against the Wall by Curtis J. Austin (2006). Elbert "Big Man" Howard, Post Office Box 130, Forestville, California 95436 E-mail: **bigman0138@aol.com**

Sylvia Hubbard Native Detroiter, Sylvia is the published author of two novels, "Dreams of Reality, and Stone's Revenge." She also lectures on writing and journalism. She is owner of HubBooks Literary Service and co-founder of Essence of Motown Writers Alliance Literary Conference. She is moderator of Detroit Writers Galore and Lulu's Romance Writers. Sylvia Hubbard, Post Office Box 27310, Detroit, Michigan 48227 Phone: (313) 289-8614 E-mail: **motownwriters@yahoo.com** Website: **www.MotownWriters.homestead.com**

Cheryl Willis Hudson Publisher and co-founder of Just Us Books. Began career in publishing in 1970 with Houghton Mifflin; worked for Macmillan Publishing Company, as design manager and Arete Publishing Company as assistant art director. Free-lance consultant; has designed or art directed projects for Waldenbooks' Longmeadow Press, Angel Entertainment, Hayden Company, Grosset & Dunlap, Grolier and Three Continents Press. Mrs. Cheryl Willis Hudson, Just Us Books, 356 Glenwood Avenue, 3rd Floor, East Orange, New Jersey 07017 Phone: (973) 676-4345 E-mail: **justusbooks@aol.com** Website: **www.justusbooks.com**

Wade Hudson President and CEO, of Just Us Books, Mr. Hudson is the author of nearly 20 books for young people including the picture books *Jamal's Busy Day, Pass It On: African American Poetry for Children* and his latest title for young adults, *Powerful Words*. An advocate of diversity in literature, he conducts workshops and presentations on topics such as "Building a Curriculum of Diversity," and serves on the board of many organizations, including the Langston Hughes Library at the Alex Haley Farm, operated by the Children's Defense Fund. A 2003 inductee into the International Literary Hall of Fame for Writers of African Descent, Mr. Hudson lives in New Jersey with his family. Contact Mr. Wade Hudson, Just Us Books, 356 Glenwood Avenue, East Orange, New Jersey 07017 Phone: (973) 676-4345 Fax: (973) 677-7701 E-mail: **justusbooks@aol.com** Website: **www.justusbooks.com**

Wanda D. Hudson Author of Wait for Love: A Black Girl's Story. Comedian - Miss WandaLuv. Wanda D. Hudson, 2284 Grand Avenue 1J, Bronx New York 10468 Phone: (347) 589-5857 E-mail: **wanda_d_hudson@yahoo.com** Website: **www.wandadhudson.com**

Gloria P. Humes Author of the book Divorced: Marriage Over!...But God! (2002) and two short stories, "A Gift of Faith" (2004), and "The Christmas Daddy Moved" (2007). Certified in Family and Consumer Sciences, Certified Christian Counselor, Certified Behavioral Consultant, Newsletter Editor for FEFACS (Florida Educators of Family and Consumer Sciences), 2003-present. Gloria P. Humes, 18865 North West 54th Court, Miami Gardens, Florida 33055 Phone: (305) 625-6371 E-mail: **gloriahumes@bellsouth.net**

Earl Ofari Hutchinson Nationally acclaimed speaker and journalist, radio host and TV commentator, Dr. Earl Ofari Hutchinson is the author of nine books about the African-American experience in America. His numerous published articles appear in newspapers and magazines across the country. He has received numerous awards for his writings. He holds a Bachelor's degree in Humanities from California State University, Dominguez Hills, and a Doctorate in Social Sciences from Pacific Western University. He is host of L.A.s popular public issues weekly talk show, On Target With Earl Ofari Hutchinson on L.A. Citywide Channel 36. Contact Dr. Earl Ofari Hutchinson, Hutchinson Communications, 614 East Manchester Boulevard, Suite 204, Inglewood, California 90301   Phone: (323) 296-6331 Fax: (323) 291-6324   E-mail: **ehutchinson@thehutchinsonreport.com**   Website: **www.thehutchinsonreport.com**

C.F. Jackson Author of the book Won't Be Denied, C.F. Jackson is a poet, and mentor. She has been featured on one Atlanta's largest radio station, WVEE 103.3 FM, and spotlighted on Atlanta's UPN69 Community Calendar. Currently, she is working on her second novel, set in the author's birth place, St. Petersburg, Florida. She obtained a B.S. degree in Criminal Justice from Georgia Southern University. Ms. C.F. Jackson, Organized Thoughts Publishing, Post Office Box 920622, Norcross, Georgia 30010 Phone: (678) 421-1684 E-mail: **info@cfjackson.us** Website: **www.cfjackson.us**

Edwardo Jackson Originally from Seattle, Washington, Jackson is an author, actor and screenwriter. He is a graduate of Morehouse College ('97; B.A. Drama/English) in Atlanta, Georgia, and the University of Phoenix ('02, M.B.A.) in Gardena, California. Previously published in the anthologies Proverbs for the People (Kensington, 2003) and Intimacy (Plume, 2004), he is author of several screenplays, as well as the prequels to I Do? (February 2006,), Ever After and Neva Hafta (Random House/Villard). Edwardo Jackson, JCM Books, 15228-B Hawthorne Boulevard., Suite 203, Lawndale, California 90260 Phone: (310) 349-3309 Fax: (310) 370-6098 E-mail: **EverAfterANovel@aol.com**

Sibyl Avery Jackson It was through Sibyl's position as spokesperson for a large wireless service provider that inspired the writing of her book Degree of Caution (2003 Books and Authors.net Award for Literary Excellence; 2002 Sistah Circle Book Club Self-Publishing Award for Best Mystery. Sibyl has a B.A. degree in English from Spellman College in Atlanta, Georgia. She is currently at work on a new Special Agent Monica Sinclair novel. Contact Ms. Sibyl Avery Jackson, 1101 Heights Boulevard., Houston, Texas, 77008 E-mail: **SibylAJackson@aol.com** Website: **www.sibylaveryjackson.net**

Jahzara Author of the novel Luv Don't Live Here Anymore. Jahzara, Tranquil Moments LLC, Post Office Box 2916, Gary, Indiana 46403 E-mail: **jahzara2007-books@yahoo.com**

Roland S. Jefferson A graduate of Howard University Medical College, Mr. Jefferson has been writing literary fiction since the early 70's. His first novel, the still controversial political thriller, THE SCHOOL ON 103RD STREET was self published and released to critical acclaim. Twenty five years later it was republished by mainstream publisher WW Norton & Co and ultimately was listed in The Guide To Literary Los Angeles 2000 by the Los Angeles Times Book Review. This first work was followed by novels: A CARD FOR THE PLAYERS and 559 TO DAMASCUS; In 2004 under the banner of Simon & Schus-ter's imprint Atria Books, he published the exciting heist thriller DAMAGED GOODS and in 2006 the current sensual crime noir mystery ONE NIGHT STAND. Roland S. Jefferson, 3870 Crenshaw Blvd. #771, Los Angeles, California 90008 Phone: (310) 281-6023 E-mail: **rsjeff@hotmail.com**

Jovita Jenkins Success strategist, and author of the highly acclaimed book, Get Out Of Your Own Way – Create The Next Chapter Of Your Life. Jovita brings a wealth of experience from her 30-year career in aerospace where she rose through the ranks from software engineer to the executive level before creating her own next chapter as a author, leadership coach, lecturer, and business owner. She is founder and president of Ajides International, Inc., a management consulting, leadership training, and executive coaching firm. Contact Ms. Jovita Jenkins, 5875 Doverwood Drive, Suite 211, Culver City, California 90230 Phone: (310) 337-7343 E-mail: **Jovita@jovitajenkins.com** Website: **www.jovitajenkins.com**

K.B. Jenkins Author of four books An Epidemic of Singleness, Royal Moments of A King's Daughter, Pacifying The Flesh: Sexual Alternatives?, and Collegebound on Higher Ground. K.B. is a graduate of the State University of New Jersey, and currently in pursuit of her Masters of Divinity. She is founder/president of S.O.L.O. 4 Christ c/o The King's Daughters Ministries, Inc., and Messianic Music, as well as the RestPress Publishing Company. Minister K.B. Jenkins, RestPress Publishing, Post Office Box 244086 Atlanta, Georgia 30324 Phone: (800) 630-4813 E-mail: **info@restpresspublishing.org** Website: **www.restpresspublishing.org**

Tony Jenkins Author of "Exposing Racism & Sexism in the American Arts." (How the Federal Courts covered up racism & sexism for the Metropolitan Opera). He attended Duquense University, The Univerity of Pittsburg, USC Opera Workshop, and he holds a BA and MS from City College in New York City. Tony Jenkins, Walls Tumbling Down Publishing, Manhattanville Station, Post Office Box 871, New York, New York 10027 Phone: (212) 865-6008 E-mail: **Antonioj365@aol.com**

King Jewel Author of the book, Thirteen and a half, a gripping story about friendship, trust and taking responsibility for one's action. Co-owner of New World Publishing. King Jewel, New World Publishing, Submission Department, Post Office Box 660, Randallstown, Maryland 21133 Phone: (410) 948-8088 E-mail: **Newworldpublishing@hotmail.com**

Siddeeq Jihad Accomplished author and lecturer, Qur'aanic Arabic Teacher, Imam Jihad is also the publisher of The Good New Journal. Siddeeq Jihad, Good News Journal, Post Office Box 43474, Detroit Michigan 48243 Fax: (313) 532-5246 E-mail: **siddeeq@msn.com**

Yolanda Joe Prolific writer and author, journalist, former producer and writer for CBS news, Chicago, Yolanda Joe is author of nine best selling books, Falling Leaves of Ivy, The Hatwearer's Lesson, He Say, She Say, Bebe's By Golly Wow, This Just In, Details at Ten, Hit Time and My Fine Lady. Yolanda earned her B.A. in English literature from Yale University; and her M.A., Journalism, Columbia University. E-mail: **yolandajoe416@aol.com** Website: **www.yolandajoe.com**

Beverly Black Johnson The first in our series of publications is "Gumbo For The Soul: the Recipe for Literacy in the Black Community". Gumbo For The Soul is a savory blend of anthologies that focus on humanitarian issues effecting communities worldwide! From education to adoption and everything in between, we will bring inspirational and informative publications that promise to spark change, heighten awareness and offer resources and resolutions to the issues we outline. Beverly Black Johnson, GFTS, Post Office Box 5193, San Jose, California 95150 Phone: (209) 947-4743 E-mail: **gumboforthesoul@yahoo.com**

Charlotte Russell Johnson Founder of Reaching Beyond, Inc. and Reaching Beyond the Breaks Ministries. Dedicated to enhancing lives, she is a writer, motivational speaker, and Christian evangelist. Ms. Johnson is as fascinating and inspiring as the messages she shares. She gained national fame following the release of her first novel A Journey to Hell and Back. In the past four years, she has penned four additional books: Daddy's Hugs, Grace Under Fire: The Journey Never Ends, The Flipside: A Journey to Hell and Back, and Mama May I. Gifted, she delivers a message that is both timely and challenging. Ms. Charlotte Johnson, Reaching Beyond, Inc., Post Office Box 12364, Columbus, Georgia 31917 Phone: (706) 573-5942 E-mail: **admin@reachingbeyond.net** Website: **www.reachingbeyond.net**

Keith Lee Johnson A native of Toledo, Ohio, Keith Lee Johnson begin writing purely by accident when a literature professor unwittingly challenged his ability to tell a credible story in class one day. He picked up a pen that very day, and has been writing ever since. Upon graduating from high school, Keith joined the United States Air Force the following September, and attained a Top Secret security clearance. Keith has written four books and is currently working on his fifth. Author of two books; Sugar and Spice, November 2003 and Pretenses, June 2004. He is currently working on SCARECROW another Phoenix Perry novel. Coming soon, The Whirlwind and Mama Said. Mr. Keith Lee Johnson, 1013 Marmion Avenue, Toledo, Ohio 43607 E-mail: **keithleejohnson1@aol.com** Website: **www.keithleejohnson.com**

Kevin Wayne Johnson Author of the book series, Give God the Glory! Kevin graduated from Virginia Commonwealth University earning a BS degree in Business Administration. Kevin is a 2002 graduate of the True Disciple Ministries Bible Institute, Somerville, New Jersey. Kevin Wayne Johnson, Writing For The Lord Ministries, 6400 Shannon Court, Clarksville, Maryland 21029 Phone: (443) 535-0475 Fax: (443) 535-0476 E-mail: **kevin@writingforthelord.com** Website: **www.writingforthelord.com**

Rayford L. Johnson Author of Thug Mentality Exposed-Journal of a Correctional Counselor & Photojournalist. Contact Rayford L. Johnson, 7119 Elk Grove Boulevard, Suite 121-PMB#162, Elk Grove, California 95758 Phone: (916) 714-5840 E-mail: **rayfordjohnson@mac.com** Website: **www.thugexposed.com**

Vanessa Alexander Johnson   Author of When Death Comes a Knockin', a self-help, inspirational book about loss and the grief process (2005). She is also contributing author in the following anthologies: Down The Cereal Aisle, (Daniels House Publications, 2003) Living by Faith, (Obadiah Press, 2004) Celebrations Anthologies, (Adassa Prendergast Publishers, 2004) and beyond with 35 Titles in Series), and the soon to released anthologies, Second Chances, The Anthology, Gumbo For the Soul Anthology, and The Purple Pen Anthology of Short Stories. Vanessa Alexander Johnson, Post Office Box 9, Ama, Louisiana 70031 Phone: (504) 431-7360 E-mail: **vjohns1@bellsouth.net** Website: **www.vanessaajohnson.com**

Yolanda M. Johnson   Author of the novel My Daughter's Keeper (2004). She is currently obtaining her IT degree at the University of Phoenix and will be transferring to the University of North Texas to major in Literary Sciences. Yolanda M. Johnson, Prosperity Enterprises, Post Office Box 821473, Dallas, Texas 75382 E-mail: **yolanda@awarenessmagazine.net**

Patricia Jonea Author of the book, Healing Hurts. It gives a fascinating account of the healing process from any hurt to freedom through the power of God. Contact Ms. Patricia Jonea, Post Office Box 13756, Oklahoma City, Oklahoma 73113 E-mail: **imblessed4@cox.net** Website: **www.healinghurtsbook.com**

Frank A. Jones Author of the groundbreaking book, What Have We Done To Our Children? He has written several books: poetry, a novel, collections of social essays and some religious discussions. Educated at San Francisco City College, University of California, Berkeley, University of San Francisco, and The Union Institute and University, Cincinnati, Ohio, he earned his BA, MA, and PhD degrees. He is also publisher of Mirror-Gibbs Publications. Frank A. Jones, Mirror-Gibbs Publication, Post Office Box 6573, Oakland, California 94603 Phone: (510) 409-9571 E-mail: **pinoquit@hotmail.com** Website: **www.gibbsmagazine.com**

Franklin Jones Author / Self-Publisher of the book entitled: The Black Matrix: The Modern Mental and Social Suppression of African American Under National Interest (2006, 2008). Franklin G. Jones, 2045 Mount Zion Road, No 233, Morrow, Georgia 30260 Phone: (678) 895-5216 E-mail: **thanubian2@yahoomail.com**

Jusbee Jones Author of Confessions of the Twelfth Man: A Different Game Played Off The Field. Under the pseudonym of Jusbee Jones, sports publicist LaShirl Smith has been associated with sports most of her life. She has worked with professional athletes for over fifteen years in the capacity of sports public relations and marketing. Jusbee Jones, 15030 Ventura Boulevard, Suite 525, Sherman Oaks, California 91403 E-mail: **JusbeeJones@aol.com** Website: **www.confessionsofthe12thman.com**

Marsha Jones   In 2005, her debut novel, Love Begins With Truth, and Slices of Soul, a compilation book of celebrity interviews, was published by St. Vincent's Press. Currently, Marsha is working on two novels, Win-Win and Shorts. Her short stories have been published in the books, Visions and Viewpoints: Voices of The Genesee Valley and COMPEER's The Healing Power of Friends and she has edited three books, Shadow of Dreams and Who's Who in Black Rochester, Volumes One and Two. Marsha Jones, 411 Communications, 97 Culver Parkway, Rochester, New York 14609 E-mail: **defdefyingmj@yahoo.com**

Rashun Jones Author of Healthy Attitudes Smart Choices: Living the Life You Choose, Power of Life: Use It or Lose It You Decide and Blueprints A Way of Life. Rashun is the owner of Nushape Publication, a publishing company that provides books and speaker services. Rashun Jones, Nushape Publication, Post Office Box 36651, Oklahoma City, Oklahoma 73136 Phone: (405) 424-5445 Fax: (800) 550-9718 E-mail: **rashun@nushapepublication.com** Website: **www.nushapepublication.com**

Sophie Jones Author of the novels Twisted Lies, A Mother's Love, and Twisted Lies 2: The Lies Untwisted. Sophie Jones, 19703 B Eastex Freeway #126, Humble, Texas 77338 Phone: (713) 560-5708 E-mail: **sophie@sophieswords.com** Website: **www.sophieswords.com**

Twana Bond-Jones Author of "When It's Right, It's Right", an urban love story, Mrs. Twana Bond-Jones is a native New Yorker, residing in Birmingham, Alabama. She has held a passion for the written word since her first poem at age 12. She has published a volume of poetry "Treasures from the Deep" and a children's book, "The Big Big Waterfall." She founded the S.T.A.Y Coalition (Supporting Teens and Youth) and the Po'Art Literary Foundation to help promote literacy in school age children through poetic art. Editor in Chief of the Po'Art Press. Twana Bond-Jones, Po'Art Press, Post Office Box 611510, Birmingham, Alabama 35261 E-mail: **tbondjones@poartpress.com** Website: **www.poartpress.com**

Joylynn M. Jossel A Graduate of Columbus State Community College's Associates Degree program and Capital University's Bachelor Degree program, Joy is a full-time multi-genre writer who, in addition to her debut title, Please Tell Me If The Grass Is Greener, has completed three diaries of poetry. Joy completed her first self-published novel The Root of All Evil, which St. Martin's Press picked up and re-released in June 2004. In addition, they have signed Joy to a three book deal (When Souls Mate, the sequel to The Root of All Evil and Harlem's Blues). They also signed Joy to a novella deal titled An All Night Man in which Joy's contribution is titled Cream. Joy's triumphing street novel Dollar Bill, which was published by Triple Crown Publications, was on the Essence Magazine best-sellers list for April 2004. Her latest two books are, Mama, I'm in Love …with a gangsta (2006, Urban Books) and Wet (2007). She is currently working on her next novel titled Thicker Than Water. Joylynn M. Jossel, Post Office Box 298238, Columbus, Ohio 43229 Phone: (614) 284-7933 E-mail: **joylynnjossel@aol.com** Website: **www.joylynnjossel.com**

Ella Joyce Author of Kink Phobia, Journey Through A Black Woman's Hair, Ella Joyce is an accomplished actress of stage, TV and film, most remembered for her role as "Eleanor" on Fox TV's sitcom "Roc." She is also the author of "A Rose Among Thorns," a one-woman, one-act, dramatic tribute to Civil Rights icon Rosa Parks. She is married to actor/photographer, Dan Martin, and lives in southern California. Ella Joyce, c/o Landmark Artists Management, 4116 West Magnolia Boulevard., Suite 101, Burbank, California 91505 Phone: (818) 848 9800 Fax: (818) 848 9821 E-mail: **ellajoyce@mymailstation.com** Website: **www.ellajoyce.com**

Carmen D. Julious Fiction, short stories, some sci fi. Nonfiction, women's issues, public health, literature, entertainment. Grant writing, research and editing. Carmen D. Julious, Julious & Associates, 9 Brookmist, Columbia, South Carolina 29229 Phone: (803) 318-4707 Fax: (803) 699-0263 E-mail: **cjulious@aol.com**

Adin Kachisi A visionary, social critic, writer, artist, and author of three books, Beyond the Talented Tenth, Tears of Ether and Depths of Melancholy. Mr. Adin Kachisi, 4049 Broadway, Box #190, New York, New York 10032 Phone: (212) 862-5027 Fax: (360) 406-9287 E-mail: **akachisi@yahoo.com**

Baruti K. Kafele Author and publisher of two best seller books, A Black Parent's Handbook to Educating Your Children (Outside of the Classroom) and A Handbook for Teachers of African-American Children (May, 2004).   Baruti K. Kafele, Post Office Box 4088, Jersey City, New Jersey 07304 Phone: (201) 433-9484 E-mail: **bkafele@earthlink.net**

Djehuti wa Kamau Cultural journalist, author of the book Warrior Song, an Africentric exposition of Black music and the international music industry. Djehuti wa Kamau, First Scribe Books, Box 62, Fort Lauderdale, Florida 33302 E-mail: **firstscribebooks@yahoo.com** Website: **www.firstscribebooks.com**

Prince M. Kaywood Jr. Author of the books, Self Publish: By Starting Your Own Company, and Katrina That Bitch! The Drama Continues. Contact Mr. Prince M. Kaywood, Jr., Parallel View Publishing, Post Office Box 741353, New Orleans, Louisiana 70174 E-mail: **godsight2@yahoo.com** Website: **www.parallelviewpublishing.com**

Janis F. Kearney Former presidential diarist to President William Jefferson Clinton, Janet Kearney debuted her first book, Cotton Field of Dreams, a Memoir, about her journey from a sharecropper's environment in the south Arkansas delta, to the most revered address in America: 1600 Pennsylvania Avenue, in January 2005. Kearney's second book, Conversations: William Jefferson Clinton...from Hope to Harlem, is an oral and pictorial biography (2006). Janis F. Kearney, Writing our World Press, 1507 East 53rd Street #278, Chicago, Illinois 60615 Phone: (773) 493-2007 E-mail: **janisfk@aol.com** Website: **www.writingourworldpress.com**

Jennifer Keitt Author of the book, "The Power Of Being A Real Woman," Host of the nationally syndicated radio show. Jennifer Kreitt, The Today's Black Woman Corporation, Post Office Box 440981, Kennesaw, Georgia 30160 Phone: (678) 569-2407 Fax: (678) 354-4334 E-mail: **tbwoman@bellsouth.net** Website: **www.todaysblackwomanradio.com**

Lewis V. Kelley Author of the novel Auslander, Lewis was born in Kansas City Missouri. He has been a Denver Firefighter for nearly 15 years. Lewis Kelley, 705 South Florence Street, Denver, Colorado 80247 E-mail: **lkwriter@comcast.net**

Janice Kenyatta Co-Author of The Truth About Black Hairstyles: The Whole Story Revealed. Janice Kenyatta, 1471 Indian Mountain Lake, Albrightsville, Pennsylvania 18210 Phone: (215) 325-1893 Fax: (570) 643-4162 E-mail: **donedeal8@earthlink.net** Website: **www.black-hairstyles-truth.com/black-hair-book.html**

Kamau Kenyatta Co-Author of The Truth About Black Hairstyles: The Whole Story Revealed. Kamau Kenyatta, 1471 Indian Mountain Lake, Albrightsville, Pennsylvania 18210 Phone: (215) 325-1893 Fax: (570) 643-4162 E-mail: **donedeal8@earthlink.net** Website: **www.black-hairstyles-truth.com/black-hair-book.html**

Tanya Kersey Black State of the Arts: A Guide to Developing a Successful Career as a Black Performing Artist, considered by many to be the "Bible" for blacks in the performing arts. She also authors two annual publications -- The Black Film Report, a comprehensive report on the financial performance of black films; and The Urban Hollywood Resource Directory, a "yellow pages" of urban entertainment contacts and resources. Tanya has appeared on news and entertainment programs on countless television and cable networks including CNN, NBC, FOX-11, KTLA, BET and Reelz Channel, to name just a few. Her most recent endeavors are as the host and producer of "Inside Urban Hollywood" on BlogTalkRadio and the CEO of BlackHollywoodUniversity.com. Ms. Tanya Kersey, 8306 Wilshire Blvd. Suite 2057, Beverly Hills, California 90211 Phone: (310) 203-1336 E-mail: **tanya@tanyakersey.com** Website: **www.tanyakersey.com**

Dorothy Jackson-Kimble Self-published author of her debut memoir "A Mighty Long Way." Dorothy Kimble, 19200 Archer, Detroit, Michigan 48219 Phone: (313) 532-3624 E-mail: **dotkimble@comcast.net**

Dr. Willie J. Kimmons One of America's leading authorities on higher education, leadership, parental involvement and health related issues, Dr. Kimmons holds a Bachelor of Science Degree in Health Education and Psychology; a Master of Science Degree in Curriculum and Instruction and a Doctorate in Educational Administration and Supervision in Higher Education. His current book is, A Parenting Guidebook. Contact Dr. Willie J. Kimmons, 1653 Lawrence Circle, Daytona Beach, Florida 32117 Phone: (386) 253-4920 E-mail: **wjkimmons@aol.com** Website: **www.savechildrensaveschools.com**

Kimani Kinyua Author of The Brotherhood of Man (Strebor International/Simon & Schuster). Kimani Kinyua has lived in the Washington, D.C. area for more than fifteen years. He graduated from Howard University in 1995 with a bachelor's degree in journalism. He is currently an independent project manager and web site contractor and consultant project manager in the Washington D.C. Metropolitan area. He has written a number of technology-related articles for trade magazines. Kimani Kinyua, 6253 Fernwood Terrace, Riverdale, Maryland 20737 Phone: (301) 326.3917 E-mail: **author@kimanikinyua.com** Website: **www.kimanikinyua.com**

Y. N. Kly Author of five books. The Invisible War: The African Anti-Slavery Resistance from the Stono Rebellion Through the Seminole Wars; International Law and the Black Minority in the US; The Anti-Social Contract: The Black Book: The True Political Philosophy of Malcolm X; Societal Development and Minority Rights and A Popular Guide to Minority Rights. Editor of: In Pursuit of the Right to Self-determination and In Pursuit of an International Civil Tribunal. Dr. Kly holds a Ph.D. in Political Science, with specialty in International Law from Laval University, an Int. LPD from the College of Law of England and Wales and the International Bar Association, a Masters degree from the University of Montreal, a D.E.S. from the University of Algiers, B.A. from the University of Iowa, and a JD from the NCBL Community College of Law and International Diplomacy Chicago. He has conducted two years of post-doctoral research in human rights law at The Hague Academy of International Law in The Netherlands, and was selected to take the exam for the Diploma of the Hague Academy of International Law. Dr. Y. N. Kly, Clarity Press, Inc., 3277 Roswell Road, Suite. 469, North East, Atlanta, Georgia 30305 E-mail: **yussuf.kly@uregina.ca** Website: **www.claritypress.com**

Jawanza Kunjufu Author, publisher, and renowned educator, Dr. Kunjufu is the president of African American Images, a communications company. Contact Dr. Jawanza Kunjufu, African American Images, 1909 West 95th Street, Chicago, Illinois 60643 Phone: (773) 445-0322 **aarcher@africanamericanimages.com** Website: **www.africanamericanimages.com**

Anita Hackley Lambert Biographer, researcher, genealogist and author of the book F.H.M. MURRAY: First Biography of a Forgotten Pioneer for Civil Justice. Murray, who happens to be Ms. Lamberts' great-grandfather, left an inspiring and dynamic legacy to his African American race, to U.S. history, and to his family. Contact Anita Lambert, HLE Publishing, 13001 Jackson Drive, Fort Washington, Maryland 20744 Phone: (301) 292-7960 E-mail: **author@anitahackleylambert.com** Website: **www.AnitaHackleyLambert.com**

Rena Deloris Canady Laster Founder of Omega Sherhawabeth Associates, a business dedicated to the upbuilding of family and faith. Publisher of P. J. and Friends Christian Alphabet, an interactive coloring/Activity Book for Children. Rena Deloris Canady Laster, Omega Sherhawabeth and Associates, 300 Northfield Drive, Warner Robins, Georgia 31093 Phone: (478) 929-8585 Fax: (478) 929-0055 E-mail: **renacanadylaster@aol.com**

Roxann Latimer Writer, poet, journalist, artist, and entrepreneur, Roxann has published 2 romance novels and 1 book of poetry. Murder Most Mystic, a romance mystery is her second novel in a series of mysteries written by Roxann. She works as a television producer with her company WIM Media. She is also Publisher and Editor in Chief of the award winning multicultural magazine, Women In Motion. Ms. Roxann Latimer, WIM, 3900 West 22nd Lane #10G, Yuma, Arizona 85364 Phone: (928) 343-9729 E-mail: **wimmedia@yahoo.com** Website: **www.roxannlatimer.com**

Kristin Hunter Lattany Author of eleven books. Four of her titles are for young people; the others are for adults. Her latest books are Breaking Away (One World/Ballantine, 2003) and The Lakestown Rebellion (Coffee House Press 2003). Kristin Hunter Lattany, c/o Dystel & Goderich Literary Management, One Union Square West, New York, New York 10003 E-mail: **klattany@comcast.net**

Jacqueline Lawrence Christian fiction author of Single & Waiting, Prosperity Planning God's Way, The Hidden Mysteries for Hearers are TOP SECRET and Won't Somebody Come Correct?, includes real, down-to-earth poems in her works. A doctor of Christian Counseling, her writing style is inspirational, witty and humorous. Two of her books, Single & Waiting and Won't Somebody Come Correct? are published by Harlequin, formerly BET Books, and the other two are self-published (Xlibris). Dr. Jacqueline Lawrence, 212 Kittery Point Santa Rosa, California 95403 Phone: (707) 566-9778 E-mail: **drjministries@yahoo.com**

Clara Baldwin Leake An active member of the NAACP and a Parish Nurse, Clara is the author of "The Love Inside" (Iuniverse, 2003), and the sequel, "A Brand New Life" (2006). Served in the United States Women's Army Corp from 1959-1961. Retired from her full time job and worked part time as a Home Health Registered Nurse. Contact Mr. Clara Baldwin Leake, 631 Franks Street Asheboro, North Carolina 27203 Phone: (336) 625-9174 E-mail: **nightengalehh@embarqmail.com**

Charles E. Lee, II Born 12-30-1953. Mr. Lee is a 1973 Graduate of Rutgers University - Newark, New Jersey with a degree in liberal arts. Mr. Lee is an Ordained Minister-Motivational Speaker-Seer-Spiritual Advisor/Teacher-Author-Publisher and a certified master celebrity protection specialist instructor with Executive Protection Academy International in Atlanta, Georgia, Plus: Certified by the New York State Security Guard Advisory Council. He provided personal protection for: Michael Jackson, and The Jackson's - Whitney Houston - Bobby Brown - Natalie Cole - Colonel Abrams - Stephanie Mills – Usher –Madonna - People's Court - Curtis Court - John Edward of Crossing Over With John Edward. Inducted into the: Grand Master Don Nagel 2000 American-Okinawa Martial Arts "Hall of Fame." He was given the silver award for (30) yrs., and given the golden award for over (40) yrs. in the Martial Arts, and inducted into the: 2001 American Karate-Do Organization "Hall of Fame" for martial arts pioneer award. Books Authored: Know Thyself: Start to Reclaim Your Life-1998, Know Thyself: The Essence of Truth Workshop Hand Book Pamphlet-2003; Know Thyself: The Prophecy of Truth-2003, SKIF/Know Thyself: Empower Children to Think Successfully-2005, The Black descendants of General Robert E. Lee and Mary Elizabeth Lee - 2006, Bodyguarding: The Art of Personal Protection Executives, Dignitaries, Celebrities and Clergy - 2006, The Essence of Truth: The Holy Spirit Thy God, Excuses-less Handbook – 2007. Charles E. Lee, II, Post Office Box 2052, Hiram, Georgia 30141 Phone: (770) 443-9957 Fax: (770) 505-2839 E-mail: **SKIF2PPIC@aol.com**

Dante Lee The 24-year old president and CEO of Diversity City Media, a very successful multicultural marketing and public relations firm based in Columbus, Ohio, is author of the new book, How To Think Big...When You're Small. Contact Mr. Dante Lee, Diversity City Media, 750-Q Cross Pointe Road, Columbus, Ohio 43213 E-mail: **dante@diversitycity.com** Website: **www.HowToThinkBig.com**

Harold Leffall Author of Brother CEO: A Business Success Guide for African-American Men which has been featured in Black Enterprise and Entrepreneur magazines. With no experience and very little money, he turned his dream of owning his own business into a multi-million dollar reality in four years. He travels all over sharing his message of perseverance and success in workshops and seminars. He has been featured in Black Enterprise, Essence, and Entrepreneur magazines. Harold Leffall, 2175 Boulder Forest Drive, Ellenwood, Georgia 30294 Phone: (404) 381-0423 E-mail: **leffall@aol.com** Website: **www.brotherceo.com**

Sylvia Willis Lett Born in the small town of Rusk, Texas, Ms. Sylvia Willis Lett is a 1982 graduate of Rusk High School and a 1984 graduate of Tyler Junior College with a Computer Science Degree, Ms. Lett has been writing romance novels since the age of 18. Her love for reading shines through in her writing. For Christina's Sake has made the Dallas Best Seller List. Ms. Lett is a member of Romance Writers of America. Ms. Sylvia Willis Lett, Letts Dream Big Publishing, Post Office Box 472172, Garland, Texas 75047 Phone: (972) 271-2072 E-mail: **smlett@comcast.net** Website: **www.lettsdreambigpublishing.com**

Elliott Lewis Author of "Fade: My Journeys in Multiracial America," (Carroll & Graf). The book weaves his memoirs as a black-and-white biracial American with the voices of dozens of multiracial people who are challenging how we think and speak about race today. Elliott Lewis, Post Office Box 2247, Rockville, Maryland 20847 E-mail: **FadeAuthor@aol.com**

Jakeshia Monique Lewis Author/Novelist of the book, I Found One, the first in a series. Her next book, Not Work Related, is due to be released in 2008. Jakeshia Monique Lewis, 505 Cypress Station Drive, Apt. 5010, Houston, Texas 77090 Phone: (832) 882-9944 Fax: (281) 895-0446 E-mail: **jakeshialewis320@sbcglobal.net** Website: **www.jakeshialewis.com**

Natosha Gale Lewis Author of the book Only Fools Gamble Twice, Natosha Gale Lewis recently released her children's books series, entitled, The adventures of Squally Squirrel which discuss child safety issues. Natasha is a graduate of Rosemont College. She holds a Bachelor of Arts in Business Communications and is an active member of the Wilmington Delaware Alumni Chapter, Delta Sigma Theta Sorority. Ms. Natosha Gale Lewis, Post Office Box 12723, Wilmington Delaware 19850 Website: **www.natoshagalelewis.com**

Shelia E. Lipsey Christian fiction author of Into Each Life (Kensington, 2007), Sinsatiable (Kensington/Urban Christian, August 2007). Lipsey is an avid reader, inspirational speaker and a full time writer. Sheila E. Lipsey, 436 Bonita Drive, Memphis, Tennessee 38109 Phone: (901) 348-2511 E-mail: **shelialipsey@yahoo.com** Website: **www.shelialipsey.com**

C. McGhee Livers Author, college instructor, ordained minister and lecturer, C Mcghee Livers translates the original Greek and Hebrew text of the Old and New Testament of the Bible. She is the author of Biblical History of Black Mankind translated from the original Hebrew and Greek text of the Bible. A sought after teacher and translator of the Greek and Hebrew Biblical languages, C. McGhee has taught these languages at several colleges. As she began translating the 4000 year old Hebrew manuscripts of the Old Testament into English, she found astounding truth concerning the origin, heritage, and destiny of mankind. "The Black man's heritage and history did not begin with slavery. It began in the Garden of Eden nearly 8,000 years ago." Contact Ms. C. McGhee Livers, Shahar Publishing, 8605 Allisonville Road #283, Indianapolis, Indiana 46250 Phone: (317) 577-0392 Fax: (317) 570-0620 E-mail: **shaharpublishing@hotmail.com**   Website: **www.blackmankind.com**

Julius R. Lockett Author of "Urban Essentials 101: Unleashing the Academic Potential in Urban Underperforming Schools, " Julius holds a Bachelor's and Master's of Science in Public and Urban Affairs from Georgia State University, and in 1997 completed work on his California Teaching Credential at Fresno Pacific University. He was a history and language arts teacher with the Fresno County Office of Education, working at the Elkhorn Correctional (Boot Camp) facility, and he has worked as a social sciences teacher in underperforming school settings in San Diego. Julius received a Professional Clear California Teaching Credential in Social Sciences, and he obtained a Cross-Cultural, Language and Academic Development Certificate from the University of California San Diego. He is currently employed as Dean of Student Success at Samuel Gompers High School in San Diego, California. Julius R. Lockett, 5026-1/2 Field Street, San Diego, California 92110 Phone: (619) 276-4987 E-mail: **thelocketts@peoplepc.com** Website: **www.ue101.com**

Nancy Ann Long Author of "The Life and Legacy of Mary McLeod Bethune", a 128 page biography and first-hand accounts of Dr. Bethune with photos (September, 2004). Dr. Nancy Ann Long, 1967 Red Cedar Circle, South Daytona, Florida 32119 Phone: (386) 767-6163 E-mail: **bethunelegacy@earthlink.net**

Vicky Spring Love Author of the book Stop Robbing Peter To Pay Paul, foreword by Dr. Myles Munroe, a dynamic pastor and best selling author, Vicky Spring Love is an associate minister at Family Victory Fellowship (FVF) in Southfield, Michigan under the dynamic leadership of Pastors Larry and Sylvia Jordan. Vicky is founder and president of Victory Financial Corporation, a residential mortgage company. She has worked for 12 years in the mortgage field where she not only provides mortgage financing but also counsels people on how to get their finances in order. She holds a Bachelor of Arts degree from the University of Detroit and a Master of Business Administration degree in Finance from Oakland University. Contact Ms. Vicky Spring Love, Post Office Box 3286, Southfield, Michigan 48037 Phone: (248) 354-3686 E-mail: **service@StopRobbingPeter.com** Website: **www.StopRobbingPeter.com**

Matthew Lynch Professional educator, grant reviewer, grant writer, and author. He is currently employed as an Exceptional Education Teacher at Sykes Elementary School and is the CEO of Lynch Consulting Group, LLC. Lynch Consulting Group, LLC, is a comprehensive consulting firm that provides innovative educational & business consulting solutions to K-12 & Higher Education institutions, nonprofit organizations, various levels of government, as well as members of the business sector. He is also a Doctoral Candidate at Jackson State University majoring in Early Childhood Education, with a cognate in Educational Administration. He is also the author of Closing the Racial Academic Achievement Gap, and a children's book, entitled Matthew and the Money Tree. Mr. Lynch is a contributing columnist for several publications including the Mississippi Link, Emerging Minds Magazine, an online magazine devoted to uplifting the African American community, Renaissance Men Magazine, Bahiyah Women Magazine, etc. He is also the founder of Project E.P.I.P.H.A.N.Y, a research based mentoring program. Matthew Lynch, 2324 Princess Pine Drive, Jackson, Mississippi 39212 Phone: (601) 373-1552 E-mail: **lynch39083@aol.com**

C. Lynn Author of the new book, "The Abuser's Daughter." This gripping novel shares the story of one woman's struggle with domestic violence, sexual abuse, promiscuity and drug addiction. C. Lynn, HATCHBACK Publishing, Post Office Box 480, Genesee, Michigan 48437 Phone: (810) 394-8612 E-mail: **clynn@truevine.net** Website: **www.hatchbackpub.com**

Kelly Starling Lyons A children's book author and award-winning journalist. Her first book, NEATE: Eddie's Ordeal (Just Us Books), is title #4 in the middle-grade series NEATE and has won praise for exploring the relationship between a 13-year-old student athlete and his civil rights veteran father. Her picture book, One Million Men and Me (Just Us Books), debuts February 2007. Lyons is also a story contributor to Chicken Soup for the African American Woman's Soul. Contact Kelly Starling Lyons, Post Office Box 1341, Durham, North Carolina 27702 E-mail: **email@kellystarlinglyons.com** Website: **www.kellystarlinglyons.com**

Cassandra Mack Native New Yorker, Cassandra is president of Strategies for Empowered Living Inc., a company that provides corporate coaching, workplace seminars and consultation to nonprofits, private companies and governmental agencies. Author of three books, Her Rite of Passage: How to Design and Deliver A Rites of Passage Program for Girls, Cool, Confident and Strong: 52 Power Moves for Girls, and Young, Gifted and Doing It: 52 Power Moves for Teens. Cassandra Mack, Strategies for Empowered Living, 333 Madison Street, New York, New York 10002 E-mail: **empoweredliving4u@yahoo.com** Website: **www.empoweredliving.net**

Haki R. Madhubuti Best-selling author of poetry and non-fiction, Mr. Madhubui is publisher and editor of Third World Press. Some of his published books are Think Black: Don't Cry, Scream (1970), We Walk The Way of The New World (1970); Directionscore: Selected and New poems (1971); and To Gwen, With Love (1971). He is president of the African American Book Centers also located in Chicago and editor of Black Books Bulletin. He is president and founding member of the African-American Booksellers, Publishers and Writers Association. Professor of English Literature and director of the Gwendolyn Brooks Center at Chicago State University, he received the 1991 American Book Award and was named Author of the Year by the Illinois Association of Teachers of English in 1991. Haki R. Madhubuti, Third World Press, 7822 South Dobson Street, Chicago, Illinois 60619 Phone: (773) 651-0700 Fax: (773) 651-7286 E-mail: **twpress3@aol.com** Website: **www.thirdworldpressinc.com**

Beverly Mahone Best Selling Author of Whatever! A Baby Boomer's Journey Into Middle Age. The Ohio University graduate has now put her expertise to work by establishing her own media coaching and consulting business called Soul Solutions/Talk2Bev where she teaches her clients the mechanics of preparing for media interviews. As a result of the book's success, she has been featured as a baby boomer expert on MSNBC-TV and written about in the recently released book, Talk Radio for Authors by Francine Silverman. Contact Ms. Beverly Mahone, Post Office Box 11037, Durham, North Carolina 27703 Phone: (301) 356-6280 E-mail: **beverly@talktobev.com** Website: **www.thebabyboomerdiva.com**

Makenzi Author of two fiction novels, That's How I Like It! and the follow-up Dangerously (2006). Makenzi, Xpress Yourself Publishing, Post Office Box 1615, Upper Marlboro, Maryland 20773 Phone: (202) 528-0450 E-mail: **Authormakenzi@yahoo.com**

Gloria Mallette Began her true literary journey by self-publishing her second novel Shades of Jade in April of 2000. By July, and 13,000 sold copies later, Gloria signed on with Random House who re-released Shades of Jade in 2001. Shades of Jade made several best sellers lists, including Black Board and Essence Magazine Along with numerous reviews in national magazines and newspapers, Gloria has been featured in The New York Daily News, USAToday, ToDay's Black Woman, Upscale Magazine, and The Pocono Record. She also has a featured novella, Come Tomorrow, on the USAToday website. To her credit, Gloria now has several published titles: If There Be Pain, What's Done in the Dark, Distant Lover, The Honey Well, Promises to Keep, Weeping Willows Dance, Shades of Jade, When We Practice to Deceive and Living, Breathing Lies. Gloria Mallette, Post Office Box 488, Bartonsville, Pennsylvania 18321 E-mail: **gloriamallette@aol.com** Website: **www.gloriamallette.com**

James Hiram Malone Columnist, commercial illustrator, fine artist, cartoonist, Mr. Malone is author/illustrator of No-Job Dad, Blues Poetry, Here and There Poetry, Grandma Sarah's Closet, Brother (Author/illustrator), His soon to be released novel, "If I Live", chronicles the life of the hard working rural Afro-American Wheeler family. Other books written and illustrated by the author include, "Say" literacy guide, Y'all Come Back (Author/illustrator), Atlanta, The Democrats are Coming (Author/illustrator). Writer and journalist, Mr. Malone has written articles and contributed to the Atlanta Journal Consititution. James Hiram Malone, Laughing Trees Association, 1796 North Avenue, North West, Atlanta, Georgia 30318 Phone: (404) 794-0948 E-mail: **j.l.t.malone@att.net** Website: **www.j.l.t.malone.home.att.net**

Julianne Malveaux Author, economist and commentator, Dr. Malveaux is the President and CEO of Last Word Productions, Inc, a multimedia production company. She is an accomplished author and editor. Her academic work is included in numerous papers, studies, and publications. She is the editor of Voices of Vision: African American Women on the Issues (1996); the co-editor of Slipping Through the Cracks: The Status of Black Women (1986), and recently co-edited The Paradox of Loyalty: An African American Response to the War on Terrorism (2002). She is the author of two column anthologies: Sex, Lies, and Stereotypes: Perspectives of a Mad Economist (1994), Wall Street, Main Street, and the Side Street: A Mad Economist Takes a Stroll (1999). She is the co-author of Unfinished Business: A Democrat and A Republican Take On the 10 Most Important Issues Women Face (2002). Most recently, her co-edited volume, The Paradox of Loyalty: An African American Response to the War on Terrorism (2002) was released in paperback in October, 2004. A committed activist and civic leader, Dr. Malveaux serves on the boards of the Economic Policy Institute, and The National Committee for Responsive Philanthropy, Women Building for the Future - Future PAC. Contact Dr. Julianne Malveaux, Last Word Productions, 1318 Corcoran Street, North West, Washington, DC 20009 Phone: (202) 462-1932 Fax: (202) 462-6612 E-mail: **lastwordprod@aol.com** Website: **www.juliannemalveaux.com**

Traci Marquis Author, book and film critic. She writes biographies on women, true crimes, fiction and nonfiction, etc. First novel, I Can't Cry was a 2003 Finalist in the ABC Entertainment Group, New Talent Program. Book and Film Critic for The Grand' Manner Magazine of Connecticut and New York. Ms. Traci Marquis, 1333 Baecher Lane, Norfolk, Virginia 23509 Phone: (757) 353-5450 E-mail: **Tbmarquis@hotmail.com**

Kathy J Marsh Born and raised in Wilmington, North Carolina, Ms. Marsh attended several North Carolina colleges and graduated with honors from Johnson C Smith University in Charlotte. Writing is a recently discovered passion and as with everything about which Kathy is passionate, she devoted many hours to learning her craft and writing her first novel, The Aura of Love, while working at a local university. Kathy is hard at work on her second novel, Suddenly Younger. Kathy J Marsh, Post Office Box 7874, Charlotte, North Carolina 28241 Phone: (704) 996-0482 Fax: (704) 337-2238 E-mail: **kathyjmarsh@aol.com** Website: **www.kathyjmarsh.com**

Cheryl Martin The author walked away from a successful full-time career as a broadcast journalist in 2002 to pursue her greatest passion…speaking to audiences about living with purpose… and succeeding in their relationships and careers. Since then, more than 50,000 women have experienced Cheryl using the ABCs of Accuracy, Boldness, and Clarity in her presentations. She has worked as a reporter and producer for the NBC-owned and ABC affiliate television stations in Washington, D.C. For nine years, Cheryl was a popular News Anchor and Host on the national cable network, BET. In 1996, she became the moderator of the network's signature Sunday news analysis show, "Lead Story," interviewing some of the nation's top newsmakers, including former president Bill Clinton, General Colin Powell, and Condoleezza Rice. Cheryl is the author of 1st Class Single: Rules for Dating and Waiting God's Way. She also writes the column, "Successfully Single," in GOSPEL TODAY magazine. Ms. Cheryl Martin, Post Office Box 15285, Chevy Chase, Maryland 20825 Phone: (301) 907-8215 E-mail: **info@cherylmartin.org** Website: **www.cherylmartin.org**

Roland S. Martin Author, nationally award- winning journalist and syndicated columnist with Creators Syndicate, Roland S. Martin is the founding editor of BlackAmericaweb.com and currently the executive editor of The Chicago Defender, is a frequent commentator on TV-One, CNN, MSNBC, FOX, and Black Entertainment Television (BET). He is also author of Speak, Brother! A Black Man's View of America. Additionally, he is a member of the National Association of Black Journalists (NABJ), the American Society of Newspapers Editors and the Alpha Phi Alpha Fraternity, Inc. Contact Ms. Monique Smith, WVON 1690 AM, 3350 South Kedzie, Chicago, Illinois 60623 Phone: (773) 247-6200 E-mail: **roland@rolandsmartin.com** Website: **www.rolandsmartin.com**

Dallas Maxwell Author of "DREAMIN" the first of three novels to follow. Contact Dallas Maxwell, Post Office Box 153, Buffalo, New York 14213 Phone: (716) 603-6806

Rych McCain Author of the new book Black Afrikan Hair and The Insanity of the Black Blonde Psych!, Mr. Rych McCain is an international/nationally syndicated Urban Entertainment Newspaper/Magazine Columnist with 3.5 Million readers. His interviews and print features reads like a who's who of the urban film, TV, stage and recording arenas. McCain's print features and famous photo spreads include Hollywood Red Carpet Movie Premieres, Major Awards Shows, Press Junkets, Exclusive One to One interview/photo shoots, Concerts, Club Promotional Parties, Forums, Conferences, Private Celebrity Parties to you name it. McCain is M.P.A.A. (Motion Picture Association of America) Accredited and is a graduate of The University of Nebraska-Lincoln, with a BA Degree in Psychology with post graduate work completed as well. He also does Afro-Centric, visual screen presentations and lectures on college campuses, particularly during Black History Month and conducts Self Esteem Workshop/Presentations geared strictly for Black Afrikan Youth Self Esteem. Rych McCain, Post Office Box 2272, Beverly Hills, California 90213 Phone: (213) 387-3493 E-mail: **rychmccain@sbcglobal.net**

Gary McCants The author of Challenges of Faith and Family & Challenges of Relationships, Gary McCants is a former contributing writer to Ebony and Jet Magazines. He is a relational & community building consultant. Gary McCants, 1398 East 20th Avenue, Columbus, Ohio 43211 Fax: (802) 609-2715 E-mail: **garymccants@excite.com**

Sylvia McClain Author of "Skipping Through Life, the Reason I Am," Ms. McClain holds a Bachelor of General Studies: Communications, English, and Art History degree from the University of Michigan and an Associates of Arts in Accounting from Wayne County Community College. She is a contributing writer for Equal Opportunity Publications and Braids World. Ms. Sylvia McClain, 7287 Vaughan, Detroit, Michigan 48228 Phone: (734) 326-3341 E-mail: **sylmcclain@juno.com** Website: **www.scribalpress.com**

DeWayne McCulley An ex-diabetic who survived a near-death, diabetic coma and lived to tell about it. He credits his recovery to God, his mother, and his daughter Cynthia. DeWayne used his 30 years of experience in engineering and biochemistry to beat his diabetes and write the acclaimed book, Death to Diabetes. Contact Mr. DeWayne McCulley, Death to Diabetes, 1170 Ridge Road, Suite #190, Webster, New York 14580 Phone: (800) 813-1927 E-mail: **engineer@deathtodiabetes.com** Website: **www.deathtodiabetes.com**

Brian McClellan Cofounder and CEO of BAMSTRONG Presentations, a career consulting firm, and the author of The Real Bling: How to Get the Only Thing You Need. Prior to becoming an entrepreneur, he served as a vice president of sales with Georgia-Pacific Corporation, a Fortune 100 company at the time. A graduate of Princeton University and the Columbia Business School, Brian is a powerful motivational speaker that has mentored countless fellow professionals seeking to improve their personal and professional lives. Brian is also a former rap singer, which is evident in hip-hop sensibility with which he offers his message of self-discovery and self-determination. Brian McClellan, 2700 Braselton Highway, Suite 10-390, Dacula, Georgia 30019 Phone: (888) 276-6730 Fax: (888) 209-8212 E-mail: **bam@bamstrong.com** Website: **www.bamstrong.com**

Charles E McClinon African-American author and playwright in Cincinnati, Ohio. Enjoy writing fiction, drama and musicals. I am also a singer and songwriter and prefer to use mostly original music in the musicals that I write. Charles E. McClinon, 8307 Mayfair Street, Cincinnati, Ohio E-mail: **cmcclinon@yahoo.com**

Tia McCollors Author, Tia McCollors joined the literary scene with her Essence best-seller, book A Heart of Devotion (Moody Publishers, Jan 2005). In addition to writing novels for the adult market, Tia is penning a series of children's early chapter books targeted towards girls, ages 7-9. A new novel Zora's Cry will be released in the Spring, 2006. She is a native of Greensboro, North Carolina and a graduate of the University of North Carolina at Chapel Hill. Over the years, she has built a career as a public relations professional and currently works for a private institution. She resides in Atlanta, Georgia with her husband. Contact Mrs. Tia McCollors, 3653 Slakes Mill Road, Decatur, Georgia 30034 Phone: (770) 598-9599 E-mail: **Tia@TiaMcCollors.com** Website: **www.TiaWrites.com**

Jacquelin Salvatto McCord A high school teacher in the Chicago Public Schools, Ms. McCord is also author and publisher of four books. Born in Meherrin, Virginia, raised in Yonkers, New York, she graduated from Fordham University with a Bachelor of Science in Education, received a Master of Arts from Spertus College and a Doctor of Naprapathy from Chicago National College of Naprapathy. She has taught on various levels from day care to college. She was a consultant for the School Improvement Network whereby she conducted teacher training workshops throughout the Midwest. Prior to going back into education, Dr. McCord maintained a successful private practice as a Naprapathic physician. Naprapathy is very similar to Chiropractic Therapy. She has been written about in several books and magazines relating to health care issues such as Hands On Healing by the publisher of Prevention Magazine. She is the founder and CEO of T. Joy Andrea Publishers which has published four of her books. One is for adults: "When We Get Straight"; and three are for children: "A Molehill Is A Mountain", "Miss America and the Silver Medal" and "Fur Coats In My Closet." She is the contributing writer for several magazines, newspapers and books. Some of the publications in which one can find her articles: NASABA Magazine, The Gospel Scene Magazine, and Wisdom, Grace Devotional Bible for Young Women of Color. She is a member of Delta Sigma Theta Sorority, Inc., Delta Authors on Tour (DAOT), Black Literary Umbrella (BLU), and the Society of Children's Book Writers and Illustrators. Contact Jacquelin S. McCord, Post Office Box 167054, Chicago, Illinois 60616 Phone: (733) 363-6613 Fax: (773) 363-6650 E-mail: **jsmc45@aol.com** Website: **www.jsmccord.com**

Tiffany S. McCullers Author. Contact Ms. Tiffany S. McCullers, 1979 Greenleaf Drive, Norfolk, Virginia 23523 E-mail: **tmayababy@yahoo**

Trevy A. McDonald College professor, radio announcer/producer and writer, Trevy A. McDonald's passion for writing developed during her childhood when she and her friends spent their summer afternoons writing plays which included current popular music. She went on to compete in the Illinois Junior Academy of Writer's Young Writer's competition while in sixth grade where her book "Drama" which she wrote and illustrated received recognition. A graduate of the University of Wisconsin-Oshkosh and the University of North Carolina at Chapel Hill, this Chicago native has taught courses in speech and broadcasting at North Carolina State University and North Carolina Central University. She is the co-editor of Nature of a Sistuh: Black Women's Lived Experiences in Contemporary Culture which was released by Carolina Academic Press in December of 1998 as well as Time Will Tell and How We Got Over: Testimonies of Faith, Hope, and Courage edited by Trevy A. McDonald and Bettye J. Allen. Trevy A. McDonald, Reyomi Publishing Company, Post Office Box 43255, Chicago, Illinois 60643 E-mail: **Time_Will_Tell@reyomi.com** Website: **www.reyomi.com**

Lurea C. McFadden Born in 1960 in Harlem, New York, Ms. McFadden is now a native of Trenton, New Jersey where she works for the State of New Jersey. She attended Jacksonville University where she received a Bachelors of Arts Degree in History. Laura has spent many years working in the public school system as a Social Studies Teacher. She now enjoys riding motorcycles in her spare time and is currently working on a third novel entitled Female Traits II. Lurea C. McFadden, Bruce Publishing, 947 Carteret Avenue, Trenton, New Jersey E-mail: **brucepublishing@hotmail.com** Website: **www.lureamcfadden.com**

Anthony Ellis McGee In October 2007, Mr. McGee's debut novel "Under the Same Roof" received the Black Excellence Award for Outstanding Achievement in Literature (Fiction) from the African American Arts Alliance. Mr. Anthony McGee, 621 East 84th Street, Suite 3W, Chicago, Illinois 60619 Phone: (773) 488-9561 E-mail: **anthony.mcgee@sbcglobal.net** Website: **www.anthonyellismcgee.com**

Valerie CJ McGee Writing since 1968 and currently learning Braille, Valerie CJ McGee, lived in four of NYC's boroughs. She retired after a combined 37 years with the military and Civil Service. Her time is devoted to her son and daughter's education. Valerie is finishing her next book (of 36) and enjoying life. Valerie C J McGee, Post Office Box 5324, Williamsburg, Virginia 23188 E-mail: **AuthorOfINSIGHT@yahoo.com**

Victor McGlothin Essence and National best-selling author Victor Mcglothin almost lost an athletic scholarship due to poor reading skills. Ultimately, he overcame that obstacle and later completed a Masters degree in Human Relations & Business. After he developed a love for the written word, Victor left a vice president position with a local bank to pursue a career in literature. His published books are: Autumn Leaves (2003), Every Sistah Wants It (2004), What's a Woman to Do? (2003), Sinful (2007) Borrow Trouble (2006) Down on My Knees (2006), Indecent Exposure (2006), Whispers between the Sheets (2005). Victor McGlothin, Post Office Box 864198, Plano, Texas 75086 E-mail: **Thewritebrother@hotmail.com** Website: **www.victormcglothin.com**

Michelle McGriff A storyteller since three years of age Ms. McGriff now has ten grown up novels under her pen and still continues to entertain readers with fresh tales taken from the world around her. Her latest book is The Legend of Morning (2004) with co author, T.L. Gardner. With an MBA in Marketing she hopes to offer new and established writers ideas in thinking out of the box as well as getting their books out of the boxes and onto the shelves of bookstores. Michelle McGriff, Wet Post Office Box 2216, Gresham, Oregon 97030 E-mail: **Wetaugustbooks@aol.com** Website: **www.wetaugust.com**

Joel Eli McIver A graduate of Winston Salem State University where he earned a Bachelor of Arts degree is Mass Communications, Joel Eli McIver has worked in television production, in an art gallery, education and in the legal field. His debut novel is What Is Forever? He is currently working on his next two books, Dancing With My Shadow and Love Is. Mr. McIver lives in Winston Salem, North Carolina with his wife and three children. Contact Mr. Joel McIver, 4Unity Publishing, Post Office Box 548, Pfafftown, North Carolina 27040 E-mail: **mciverjoel@4unitypublishing.com**

Gracie C. McKeever A native New Yorker, Gracie C. McKeever has authored several novels, among them the Siren Top Sellers, Terms of Surrender, Guardian Seductress, and Bouncer's Folly. She has been writing since the ripe old age of seven when two younger brothers were among her earliest, captive audience for various short story readings and performances. It wasn't until 2001, however, when Gracie caught the erotic romance bug that produced an instant affinity for the genre and spawned her own first erotic romance, Beneath the Surface, published in 2006 by Siren Publishing, Inc. Contact Ms. Gracie C. McKeever, Post Office Box 1074, New York, New York 10116 E-mail: **gwiz10@optonline.net** Website: **www.graciecmckeever.com**

Tina Brooks McKinney Best Selling author of All That Drama (Strebor Books, December, 2004). Its sequel Lawd Mo Drama was released in November, 2005. Tina is working and finalizing the finishing touches to the third and final part of the "Drama" series "Fool Stop Trippin'," scheduled to be published in 2008. Contact Tina Brooks McKinney, 425 Princeton Way, Covington, Georgia 30016 Phone: (678) 625-9261 E-mail: **tybrooks2@yahoo.com** Website: **www.tinamckinney.com**

Leslie Hope McMurray Author. Leslie Hope McMurray, 1523 Virginia Street, Lancaster, South Carolina 29720 E-mail: **ah6575@yahoo.com**

Angela Shelf Medearis Children's book author, Mrs. Medearis was noted as "one of the most influential writers of children's literature", by Texas Monthly magazine. Angela's desire to write books for children who had difficulty reading has blossomed into an award-winning career that spans over a decade includes over 90 children's books and three cookbooks, with sales exceeding 10 million copies worldwide. She founded and is host of The Kitchen Diva! cooking show that airs nationwide on public television as well as several educational video series including the popular and award-winning animated and bilingual "Storyteller's Series", narrated by Medearis. Contact Ms. Angela Shelf Medearis, Diva Productions, Inc., Post Office Box 91625, Austin, Texas 78709 Phone: (512) 444-3482 Fax: (512) 444-3399 E-mail: **medearis@medearis.com** Website: **www.medearis.com**

Cherlyn Michaels Born and raised in St. Louis, Missouri, Cherlyn Michael's first writing experiences were in grade school where she wrote, produced, and starred in her first play, "Cindy: The Black Cinderella," — a comedic version of the Cinderella fairy tale. She continued to write sporadically over the years and has accumulated a small collection of short stories and poems. Ms. Michaels graduated with a Bachelor's in Chemical Engineering from the University of Missouri. at Rolla pursuing her dream of completing her first novel. In June of 2002, she began her pursuit by studying writing, attended conferences, taking writing courses, and attending UCLA Extension and other workshops. She attended the Voices of Our Nations Arts Master's Workshop with Terry McMillan in June of 2003 after which Ms. McMillan inscribed in her book, "Cheryl, you can write your butt off…" Cherlyn drafted nine story lines and in January of 2003, she chose to begin her writing career with one of them: "Counting Raindrops through a Stained Glass Window." In the first three months of publication, Counting Raindrops was selected by several book clubs as their Book of the Month selection and held a bestseller spot at Cushicity.com, a Houston based African American bookstore, for five months. Contact Ms. Cherlyn Michaels, 11220 West Florissant Avenue, #298, Florissant, Missouri 63033 Website: **www.cherlynmichaels.com**

J.J. Michael Lifelong student and teacher of Metaphysics and healing principles, Ms. Michael is the founder/publisher of Pathtotruth.com, an ezine that promotes spiritual awareness, self-development and world peace. She is the author of Path to Truth: a Spiritual Guide to Higher Consciousness, iUniverse.com, 2000, a non-fiction book that brings together a wide variety of metaphysical and spiritual principles. Her first novel, Life is Never as It Seems, published by Genesis Press Inc., will guide you through the complexities and the controversies of spirituality and religion, women's rights, and love relationships, all seen through the life of Lindy Lee, a young women coming of age in the late sixties. Besides her writings, Ms. Michael conducts workshops on numerology, energy anatomy, and the Chios Healing Modality and gives book readings and lectures. She is a founding member of the Rays of Healing Team of Falls Church, Virginia, and a Chios Master Healer and Teacher of the Chios Institute of Santa Rosa, California. She has appeared on the local Virginia Cable Television and has been featured on National Public Radio (NPR). A renowned numerologist, Ms. Michael appeared in CNN's segment, "A Wrinkle in Time." Her formal education includes a BA from Howard University and a MLS from the University of Maryland. For over thirty years, Ms. Michael worked as an administrative librarian for the District of Columbia Public Library System. She is a member of Delta Sigma Theta Sorority. Her second novel is It's Not Over Yet, and she is currently working on another non-fiction novel, Sacred Light. J.J. Michael, Post Office Box 55804, Washington, D.C. 20040 Phone: (202) 487-1165 E-mail: **jj@jjmichael.org** Website: **www.jjmichael.org**

David C. Miller Co-founder and Chief Visionary Officer for the Urban Leadership Institute, LLC, David C. Miller is a nationally recognized speaker and program developer working with African American males. A sought after lecturer and advocate for youth of color, David has over 13 years of hands on practical experience working with African American males and is author of, Lessons I Learned From My Father: A Collection of Quotes From Men of African Descent. Miller designed the Dare To Be King Training Program for African American males, which is a 240 page life skills curriculum for boys ages 10-17. Contact David Miller, Urban Leadership Institute, 28 Allegheny Avenue, Suite 503, Towson, Maryland 21204 Phone: (877) 339-4300 E-mail: **dmiller@urbanleadershipinstitute.com** Website: **www.urbanyouth.org**

Karen E. Quinones Miller Author of Essence bestselling novels, "Satin Doll," "I'm Telling," and "Using What You Got," and also "Ida B." In October 2000, Oshun Publishing Company, Inc., the company Karen created to publish Satin Doll, published Yo Yo Love, by a 23-year-old Temple University student named Daaaimah S. Poole. "Yo Yo Love" went on to become an Essence Bestseller, and Kensington Publishing Company purchased the rights in 2001. Satin Doll was released in hardcover by Simon & Schuster in July 2001, and once again hit the Essence Bestseller's List. Her second book, "I'm Telling" was published by Simon & Schuster in July 2002, and also landed on the Essence Bestseller's List. Her third novel, "Using What You Got," was published by Simon Schuster in July 2003 and her latest release "Ida B." was published by Simon & Schuster in August 2004. Contact Ms. Karen E. Quinones Miller, 1039 East Durham Street, Philadelphia, Philadelphia 19150 Phone: (215) 381-0645 Fax: (801) 881-2472 E-mail: **authorkeqm@aol.com** Website: **www.KarenEQuinonesMiller.com**

Minnie E Miller Fiction author and native of Chicago, though she has lived in many cities over the past thirty years. She is an activist and has worked in politics since the age of eighteen. Ms. Miller bravely served as secretary to an attorney for the Black Panther Party when it wasn't the safest job for a young lady, and worked as office manager in the State Appellant Defender's Chicago office. Her journals—in many boxes in her closet—contain essays on her evolution from "colored," "black," and "African American." Even today, her stories touch on all these issues in metaphor—yes, even the vampire short stories in Catharsis. Her novel, The Seduction of Mr. Bradley, published November 2006, is another political statement as well as a spiritual view of love for humankind. Minnie E. Miller, 4700 South Lake Park Avenue, Suite 2104, Chicago, Illinois 60615. Phone: (773) 538-9902 E-mail: **minnie247@sbcglobal.net** Website: **www.millerscribs.com**

Moses Miller Award winning author, journalist and co-founder of Mind Candy, LLC, which is a company focused on book publishing and the development of creative and thought provoking screenplays. A native New Yorker, Moses exhibits the uncanny ability to capture the pulse of the streets with intelligence, strong character development and well thought out storylines. In the past, he has contributed articles and written for various websites and publications including The Voice, Newsday and 88HIPHOP.COM where he is currently the Editor in Chief of content. He holds a Bachelors degree in Business Management and a Masters of Science degree in Technology Management obtained from Polytechnic University. His first novel, Nan: The Trifling Times of Nathan Jones has received awards and critical acclaim from critics, readers and book clubs around the world. After selling thousands of copies of his first novel, Mr. Miller cemented a deal with F.E.D.S. magazine resulting in a joint venture to publish his second release, Once Upon A Time in Harlem in September of 2007. The highly anticipated second installment in the Nan series, The Game of Trife, will be released through his company Mind Candy, LLC in the summer of 2008. Mr. Miller is a socially conscious individual that strives to play a key role in helping to improve the literacy rates amongst African American and Hispanic teens. Awards and Accomplishments: Most Outstanding Rising Urban Novelist YOUnity Guild 2007; Best New Author Infini Awards 2008; Most Underrated Author's List Urban Book Source 2008; Nan: The Trifling Times of Nathan Jones; 5 out of 5 Top Shelf Rating UrbanReviews.com, Best Characters Infini Awards 2008; Best Street/Urban Fiction Novel Afr'Am Fest's Literary Awards 2008. Moses Miller, Mind Candy, Post Office Box 2185, Garden City, New York 11531 Phone: (516) 318-4433 Fax: (516) 379-7749 E-mail: **Moses@MindCandyMedia.com**

Rosie Milligan Registered nurse, counselor/health consultant, author, and Ph.D. in Business Administration, Dr. Rosie Milligan lectures nationally on economic empowerment, managing diversity in the workplace, and male/female relationships. Author of 14 books. Owner of Milligan Books, Inc., largest and fasting growing African-American female publisher in the nation. She is founder of Black Writers On Tour. Have publisher 150 plus authors and helped to launch 10 publishing companies. I am a literary agent and have sold books to some of the most prestigous New York publishing houses. Her books, Starting a Business Made Simple and Getting Out of Debt Made Simple have helped many across the country. Her most recent release, Creating A New You In Six Weeks Made Simple, is a must read. Dr. Rosie Milligan, Milligan Books, 1425 West Manchester Avenue, Suite C, Los Angeles, California 90047 Phone: (323) 750-3592 Fax: (323) 750-2886 E-mail: **DrRosie@aol.com** Website: **www.milliganbooks.com**

Sydney Molare A veterinarian by profession and Mississippi native, Sydney Molare is the author of four books, Somewhere In America: Situations of XX and XY, a collection of short stories is a comedic and controversial look at life in these United States, Changing Places, Grandmama's Mojo Still Working, and Small Packages. Her book, Somewhere In America, was chosen as a "Cream of the Crop" selection receiving 5/5. Her latest novel, is Devil's Orchestra. Dr. Sydney Molare, Post Office Box 362, Roxie, Mississippi 39661 Phone: (601) 384-0219 Fax: (601) 384-1667 E-mail: **sydney@sydneymolare.com** Website: **www.sydneymolare.com**

Baba Evans Moore Author of five fiction novels: Choice of a Lifetime (2000), The Pastor's Letter (2001), While the Village Sleeps (2003), Just a Picture in A Frame (2006) and An Extra Ordinary Affair (2008). Baba has received awards from Disigold Publications and C&B Book Distributors, Inc. He resides in Temple Hills, Maryland and when not writing historical fiction novels, teaches adults in the Toyota Family Literacy Program. Baba is also CEO of the Ward 8 Mentoring Project, a parenting agency that conduct workshops promoting responsible fatherhood. Baba Evans Moore, Post Office Box 30311, Washington, DC 20030 Phone: (301) 275-0474 E-mail: **evansmoore@hotmail.com** Website: **www.babaevans.com**

Carman Moore Composer, Author, Music Critic. A dedicated educator, Moore has taught at the Yale University Graduate School of Music, Queens and Brooklyn Colleges, Carnegie-Mellon University, Manhattanville College, and The New School for Social Research. Particularly interested in reaching out to children, he spent several years in the 1960's, 70's and 80's as a teaching artist for Lincoln Center and Jazzmobile and at The Dalton School. Moore conducted his work and lectured in New York public schools with the Lincoln Center Institute, which commissioned his The Magic Turn Around Town and Save the Dragon. In 1995 he served as consultant to Wynton Marsalis on his popular PBS-broadcast home video series for children, Marsalis On Music. Moore is also the author of two youth-oriented books: Somebody's Angel Child: The Story of Bessie Smith (Dell), and Rock-It (a music history and theory book for Alfred Music Publishers). He has served as Board member and adjudicator for several major organizations, including Composers Forum, the Society of Black Composers, the N.Y. State Council on the Arts, and the National Endowment for the Arts. In addition he has been music critic and columnist for the Village Voice and has contributed to The New York Times, The Saturday Review of Literature, Vogue, and Essence among others. Contact Mr. Carman Moore, 152 Columbus Avenue, New York, New York 10023 Phone: (212) 580-0825 E-mail: **skycarmuse@mindspring.com**

E. Joyce Moore The authors writings is included in the Bestfriends Anthology (2003) and she is a contributor to Chicken Soup for the African American Soul. She has also expressed her creativity on film, directing a cable television show in Indiana back in 1984, creating an infomercial for AT&T products in 1988 and producing a video introducing African American Fine Artists for the 2001 National Black Fine Arts Show in Manhattan. She is also developing several television scripts, freelances and has just completed her first ghostwriting project. E. Joyce Moore, Post Office Box 88403, Indianapolis, Indiana 46208 E-mail: **jemiltd@aol.com**

Katherine Bell Moore A former college professor and national award winning business woman who served for fourteen years as the Mayor Pro Tem of the Wilmington, North Carolina City Council. While a member of the Council, Moore wrote and published a book entitled, "Memoirs of An Honest Politician." The book exposed many of the City's "dirty little secrets." The book alluded to political corruption, misuse of federal funds that were targeted for the poor, ongoing cases of police brutality, and law enforcement's negligence in prosecuting child molesters. As the problems continue and intensify, Moore is writing another book entitled, "Sex, Drugs, and My City." Katherine Moore, 3530 Mystic Pointe Drive Tower 500, #1204, Aventura, Florida 33180 Phone: (954) 673-2709 Fax: (305) 933-8914 E-mail: **saintfrancisdes@yahoo.com**

Toi Moore Author of the book, Unbreakable, An Understanding to Marriage and Relationships (2005). This book was written with her husband, Gregory Moore. Mind Games, the sequel to her first self-published novel Momma, Please Forgive Me! is a mystery thriller. The book has been endorsed by celebrities such as; Vivica A. Fox, James Ingram, Patrice Rushen, and TC Carson to name a few. Toi also writes for other publications such as Billboard, Upscale, The Cause and Saludos Hispanos Magazines to name a few, where she has over 200 published articles in various newspaper and magazines throughout the United States and Canada. She has written several short stories, four novels and two screenplays. She has also worn the hat of publisher, by publishing her own magazine titled "Mini Romances." She has several bylines to her credit in which she has authored and interviewed a variety of well-known celebrities such as: Oprah Winfrey, Laila Ali, James Ingram, Vivica A. Fox, Kweisi Mfume, Lisa "Left Eye" Lopez, Patti LaBelle, Boney James, B2K, Jaheim, and Patrice Rushen to name a small few. Her experience, faith and hard work make her an experienced and well-rounded writer. Today, she continues her writings, while realizing and accepting her gift from God. Toi Moore, Post Office Box 2099, Sun City, California 92586 Phone: (951) 231-1633 E-mail: **toimoore@aol.com** Website: **www.toimoore.com**

Wanda Moorman Dynamic writer, poet, songwriter and speaker, Ms. Moorman is a native West Virginian but now resides in Washington, DC. She holds graduate and undergraduate degrees in Business Administration, and has worked in the Federal and Washington, DC, city governments as a Contracts Manager. She has written song lyrics for several Hollywood record companies and poetry for the International Library of Poetry. Her first novel, In His Ex-Wife's Shadow, was released in March 2000 and her sophomore novel, Corporate Sponsor, in Fall 2000. She is a member of the Black Writers Alliance, Romance Writers of America and the New Jersey Romance Writers. She is a contributing writer for The Washington Informer newspaper. She is currently at work on her third novel. Wanda Moorman, Story Book Productions, Post Office Box 60096, Washington, DC 20039 E-mail: **wandamoorman@storytale.com** Website: **www.storytale.com**

Gwendolyn R. Morris Romantic of 'old world' proportions, Ms. Morris knows that African-American women can be strong, but feminine and educated at the same time. Thus were the beginning concepts for her sensual romance books, Angels, Nubian Passion, and Vampire. Gwen has also written 6 custom-made children's books. Contact Ms. Gwendolyn R. Morris, 542 Berlin-Cross Keys Road, Suite 3-255, Sicklerville, New Jersey 08081. E-mail: **kazi22@msn.com**

Mary B. Morrison National bestselling author of "When Somebody Loves You Back," and "She Ain't the One." Mary's first book of poetry Justice Just Us Just Me was self-published, August 23, 1999. Mary was born in Aurora, Illinois, reared in New Orleans, Louisiana, and currently resides in the Oakland, California. She is president and founder of Booga Bear Publishing and The RaW Advantage. Her books, Nothing Has Ever Felt like This, When Somebody Loves you Back, and Our Little Secret were published in 2005, 2006, and 2007, respectively. Contact Ms. Mary "HoneyB" Morrison, ELR Entertainment, 2318 25th Avenue, Oakland, California 94601 Phone: (510) 261-5306 E-mail: **MaryBMorrison@aol.com** Website: **www.marymorrison.com**

Gloria Morrow Licensed Clinical Psychologist and author of the book, Too Broken to be Fixed? A Spiritual Guide to Inner Healing, Dr. Morrow specializes in treating adults and adolescents who suffer from depression, anxiety, PTSD, as well as grief and loss issues. Her other new books to be released are "Strengthening the Ties that Bind: A Guide to a Healthy Marriage" and "The Things that Make Men Cry." Contact Dr. Gloria Morrow, Ph.D., GM Psychological Services, 308 North 2nd Avenue, Suite B, Upland, California 91786 Phone: (909) 985-3773 E-mail: **Dr_Gloria_Morrow@msn.com** Website: **www.gloriamorrow.com**

Talib A. Muhammad A Houston, Texas native, Talib has release his new autobiography, "Fire 722 The Spiritual Journey of Talib Muhammad." Chronicled in this engaging story Talib, son of an ingenious mathematician, outlines his family history connecting him to General Robert E. Lee, Former Texas State Senator Friench Simpson and The Legendary Apache Warrior Geronimo. In this tell-all book Talib shares his life's journey with vivid photographs and raw experiences as: 1) a soldier in the United States Army; 2) a former firefighter in Houston, Texas; Inglewood, California; and Montgomery County, Maryland; 3) a member of The Nation of Islam, where he became the Chief of Security for Dr. Khallid A. Muhammad (former National Spokesman for The N.O.I.) and interacted directly with The Honorable Louis Farrakhan; 4) the current Chief of Security for the R&B music phenomenon Maze featuring Frankie Beverly. Contact Mr. Talib A. Muhammad, Fire Seven Twenty Two Unlimited, Post Office Box 88191 Houston, Texas 77288 E-mail: **talib@fire722.com** Website: **www.fire722.com**

Leah Yvonne Mullen Author, writer, Leah is originally from Chester County, Pennsylvania, the fictional setting for her debut novel, Again and Again. A prolific journalist, Leah has penned hundreds of essays, articles, reviews, and profiles which have appeared in over twenty publications and websites including: Mosaic and African American Literature Book Club (aalbc.com). She has a BA in print journalism from the Pennsylvania State University. Leah Mullen, Post Office Box 7047, JAF Station, New York, New York 10116 E-mail: **leahmullen@yahoo.com**   Website: **www.leahmullen.com**

Anthony Jerome Mungin Published a book of poetry called "Conceptions of the Heart and Mind," and completed a novel called "Same Sins Separate Paths." He has started another novel "Ungodly Promises." He holds a bachelors degree in Business as well as a M.B.A., both of which he considers major accomplishments, given the many obstacles. Mr. Anthony J. Mungin, Post Office Box 42087, Houston, Texas 77242 E-mail: **ajmungin@houston.rr.com** Website: **www.conceptionsoftheheartandmind.com**

Daphne Muse Award-winning author of four books, her most recent The Entrance Place of Wonders: Poems of the Harlem Renaissance (Abrams 2006) was selected by Black Issues in Book Reviews as one of the best collections of poetry for children. She is also a New Frontiers Radio Essayist and her social commentaries have been published in major newspapers and air on public radio and commercial stations across the country, including NPR and Radio. Daphne Muse, 2429 East 23rd Street, Oakland, California 94601 Phone: (510) 436-4716 Fax: (510) 261-6064 E-mail: **msmusewriter@sbcglobal.net** Website: **www.daphnemuse.com**

MWALIM Writer/Director/Producer. He is a published author of one book, A Mixed Medicine Bag: 7 Original Black Wampanoag Folk-tales, several poems and short stories appearing in numerous anthologies. Mwalim is a three-time recipient of the Ira Aldridge Fellowship. He is a professor of English and African/African American Studies at University of Massachusetts, Dartmouth. Mwalim (Professor MJ Peters), English Department, University of Massachusetts, Dartmouth, 285 Old Westport Road, North Dartmouth, Massachusetts 02747 Phone: (508) 999-8304 Fax: (508) 999-9235 E-mail: **mwalim@gmail.com**

P. Durrell Nathan Author of 666 The New World Order and Secret Societies Of The New World Order. P. Durrell Nathan, 1885 Forest Maple Lane, Apt-C, Columbus, Ohio 43229 Phone: (614) 256-3343 E-mail: **Diamondjewlz77@yahoo.com**

Charleszine Nelson Special collection and community resource manager for the Blair-Caldwell African American Research Library. She is also the co-author (with Bonnie F. McCune) of Recruiting and Managing Volunteers in Libraries, which has become a valuable manual for managers of volunteer programs throughout the nation. Born and raised in Denver, Nelson attended Manual High School, earned a bachelor's degree in Sociology and Psychology from the University of Colorado at Boulder, and a master's degree in Information Technology and Library Science from Emporia State College. She is a current candidate for a master's degree in History and Preservation at the University of Colorado at Denver. Contact Ms. Charleszine Nelson, Blair-Caldwell African American Research Library, 2401 Welton Street Denver, Colorado 80205 Phone: (720) 865-2401 E-mail: **tnelson@denverlibrary.org** Website: **www.aarl.denverlibrary.org**

Paula Newberry Author of the biographical novel, "Someone Noticed" (Author House Books) and Opera Singer, Ms. Newberry has toured with her own "Evening of Opera" and "Spirit Moving Spirituals" concerts throughout the United States. She has appeared at Carnegie Hall (Weill Recital Hall) and concert auditoriums such as The Germantown Performing Arts Center. Her awards and honors include The Chancellor's List. Ms. Paula Newberry, Post Office Box 753446, Memphis, Tennessee 38175 Phone: (901) 216-6593 E-mail: **newdivaof2005@yahoo.com** Website: **www.classicalsinger.net**

Fred Newman Born in the South Bronx, New York City in 1935, Newman was the first in his family to attend college, at City College of New York. After serving in the U.S. Army in Korea, he received his doctorate in the philosophy of science from Stanford University in 1962. He is also the Artistic Director of the Castillo Theatre, where he has gained recognition, over the last decade, as a leading voice in the world of avant-garde and political theatre. Newman has written numerous books exploring performance and human development including: Performance of a Lifetime: A Practical-Philosophical Guide to the Joyous Life and Let's Develop! A Guide to Continuous Personal Growth. He is co-author with Dr. Lois Holzman of Lev Vygotsky: Revolutionary Scientist (Routledge, 1993); Unscientific Psychology: A Cultural Performatory Approach to Understanding Human Life (Praeger Press); and The End of Knowing: A New Developmental Way of Learning (Routledge, 1997). Newman is a frequent lecturer on social, psychological and political topics and has been featured on CNN, PBS, WNBC-TV and in the pages of the New York Times, Newsweek, and The Christian Science Monitor. Mr. Fred Newman, Castillo Theatre, c/o All Stars Project Inc., 543 West 42nd Street, New York, New York 10036 Phone: (212) 941-9400 Website: **www.castillo.org**

Lisa Nichols Co-author of the 2004 Black Book Award Winner, Chicken Soup for the African American Soul: Celebrating and Sharing Our Culture One Story at a Time, by Lisa Nichols, Tom Joyner, Jack Canfield and Mark Victor Hansen. Lisa Nichols has been a personal coach to CEO's, entrepreneurs, investors, principals, professionals, pastors, and parents. She is the Founder and CEO of Motivating the Teen Spirit, LLC which is recognized by many as the most comprehensive empowerment skills program available today for teen self-development. Ms. Nichols has been recognized for her work and dedication by receiving the 2003 Trail Blazers Entrepreneurs award, Lego Land Heart of Learning award, Emotional Literacy award and having November 20th proclaimed by the Mayor of Henderson Nevada as Motivating the Teen Spirit Day. Contact Ms. Lisa Nichols, Teen Spirit, LLC, Post Office Box 943, Puunene, Hawaii 96784 Fax: (808) 879-8201 E-mail: **Lisa@AfricanAmericanSoul.com** Website: **www.africanamericansoul.com**

Nikki Nicole Published Author. Nikki Nicole, G Dot Media, Post Office Box 152979, San Diego, California 92195 E-mail: **thagstands4@yahoo.com**

Kwame Frimpong Nyanor Founder of Christ To The Nations Ministries, and Pastor of All Nations Fellowship Church, Kwame is author of two book, "Overcoming offenses" and "It's not your fault." He is currently working on his third book. He speaks regularly in churches about pain, hurt and rejections. He is also a powerful revival speaker with signs and wonders following. He is a Bible teacher, motivational speaker and has a passion to see believers discover and fulfill their individual callings. Also he has a desire to help believers recognize and defeat the enemy in their personal lives and in their churches. Kwame Frimpong attended Bible College in the year 1992-1993 at Action Faith Bible College, Accra –Ghana, where the chancellor is Bishop Nicholas Duncan-Williams. Since 1989, he has been in full time ministry teaching extensively in Africa, Europe and the United States. His teaching ministry has also included radio broadcasts on spiritual warfare on WWGB radio station in Maryland. Kwame Frimpong Nyanor, Christ To The Nations Ministries, 145 Village Green Trail, Garner, North Carolina 27529 Phone: (919) 971-6691 E-mail: **pastor@pastorkwame.com**

Oasis Entrepreneur by nature and author by trade. He was born and raised in Cleveland, Ohio. His journey in the arts began as a Spoken Word Artist. He is a writing mentor and a government-certified creative-writing instructor who has been teaching the craft for years. His novels include Push Comes To Shove, (Urban Lifestyle Press, 2007) and Duplicity, (Oasis Publishing Group, 2007) which is offered free from his website. Oasis is busy working on other novels. Oasis, Post Office Box 19101, Cleveland, Ohio 44119 E-mail: **oasisreader@oasisnovels.com** Website: **www.oasisnovels.com**.

Omowale Self-published author of several books, including A Taste of Africa, Aisha, Expect A Miracle, A Lack of Knowledge, Sun People of the Nile and I Sing Because I'm Happy, several poems and songs. Contact Omowale, Omowale's Herb Garden, Livonia Mall, 29522 West 7 Mile Road, Livonia, Michigan 48152 Phone: (248) 474-8806 Fax: (248) 474-8836 E-mail: **mz_omowale@yahoo.com** Website: **www.A1StopOnlineShop.com**

Chika Onyeani Author of the explosive and internationally acclaimed No.1 bestselling book, "Capitalist Nigger: The Road to Success," and the blockbuster novel "The Broederbond Conspiracy. Contact Chika Onyeani, Timbuktu Publishers, 463 North Arlington Avenue, East Orange, New Jersey 07017 Phone: (973) 675-9919 Fax: (973) 675-5704 E-mail: **timbuktupublishers@yahoo.com** Website: **www.thebroederbondconspiracy.com**

Travis Otey 42 year old networks operations support specialist by education, his newest book is One Man's Soul: Lessons of a Lifetime, a non-fiction work of Inspirational self-help essays. Contact Mr. Travis Otey, Diligent Publishing Company, Post Office Box 390605, Snellville, Georgia 30039 Phone: (404) 409-6025 E-mail: **Travis@OneMansSoul.com** Website: **www.OneMansSoul.com**

Renea Overstreet Author of Desire, Duty & Destiny. Always a Bridesmaid is her first work of fiction. Contact Ms. Renea Overstreet, 201 Oak Park Drive, Suite #202, Alvin, Texas 77511 E-mail: **mlordolove@yahoo.com**

Madge D. Owens A native Atlantan and graduate of Clark College. She began her career in Georgia government as a legislative aide, before being appointed to the Tours and Special Events Program at the Georgia State Capitol, where she worked for nine years. She is presently on the legislative staff of the Georgia House of Representatives. She also serves as president and primary consultant of Write Page Literary Service, Inc., an Atlanta-based business and creative writing firm. Her first novel,"To Silence Her Memory," was published by AuthorHouse. Madge D. Owens, Write Page Literary Service Inc., Post Office Box 38288, Atlanta, Georgia 30334 Phone: (404) 280-5029 Fax: (404) 656-0238 E-mail: **writepagemo@yahoo.com**

Vivian Owens Author of three books, Parenting For Education, Create A Math Environment, and Nadanda The Wordmaker, a Writer's Digest Best Book Award Winner. Her newspaper articles have appeared in over 200 newspapers across the country, and her magazine articles have appeared in such publications as Upscale Magazine, About…Time Magazine, and The Virginia Science Journal. Her latest book release is How Oswa Came to Own All Music. Vivian Owens, Eschar Publications, Post Office Box 1194, Mount Dora, Florida 32756 Fax: (352) 357-9695 E-mail: **escharpub@earthlink.net** Website: **www.vivianowens.com**

Deadria Farmer-Paellmann Excerpt of "Black Exodus: The Ex-Slave Pension Movement Reader" published in "Should America Pay: Slavery and the Raging Debate on Reparations" by Raymond Winbush, Ph D. Lawyer, Activist, Adjunct Professor. Restitution Study Group, Executive Director. Organization of Tribal Unity, Chair. Deadria Farmer-Paellmann, Post Office Box 1228, New York, New York 10009 Phone: (917) 365-3007 Fax: (201) 656-1981 E-mail: **Paellmann@rcn.com**

Margaret D. Pagan Author of the book, More Than A Slave: The Life of Katherine Ferguson. The book was a finalist in the 2004 Atlanta Daily World Choice Awards. She has published articles in newspapers, magazines, journals, and newsletters since graduating from Morgan State University. Margaret D. Pagan, 3809 Juniper Road, Baltimore, Maryland 21218 E-mail: **mdpagan@verizon.net** Website: **www.margaretpagan.com**

Evelyn Palfrey Author of four novels, the current hit Everything In Its Place, the romantic thriller Dangerous Dilemmas, the best-selling Price of Passion and the classic Three Perfect Men, Ms. Palfrey is a contributor to two books in the Chicken Soup series. She is currently at work on her fifth novel. Ms. Palfrey grew up in East Texas. She is a graduate of Southern Methodist University and the University of Texas Law School. she is active with the Austin Writers League, the Austin Romance Writers of America, the Travis County Bar Association and the Links Inc Evelyn was nominated for Career Achievement Award, Romantic Times Magazine. Evelyn Palfrey, Post Office Box 142495, Austin, Texas 78714 Phone: (512) 773-8776 E-mail: **evelyn@evelynpalfrey.com**   Website: **www.evelynpalfrey.com**

Lincoln Park Author of Sculptured Nails and Nappy Hair, and The Brevity of the Selves. Contact Lincoln Park, 4465 PReSS, 610-A East Battlefield Road, Suite 279, Springfield, Missouri 65807 Phone: (866) 842-1042 Fax: (775) 257-1286 E-mail: **press4465@yahoo.com** Website: **www.4465press.com**

Electa Rome Parks Author of the best-selling novels The Ties That Bind and Loose Ends, Almost Doesn't Count (August, 2005, Penguin/NAL) and Almost Doesn't Count was also released in 2004. With a BA degree in marketing and a minor in sociology, she is presently following her true passion and working on a fourth novel. Her company Novel Ideal Editorial Services is a full service editorial service offering copy editing, content editing and proofreading services. Electa Rome Parks, 2274 Salem Road, Suite 106, Post Office Box 173, Conyers, Georgia 30013 E-mail: **novelideal@yahoo.com** Website: **www.electaromeparks.com**

Pearl Jr. Author of three books, the most recent is Black Women Need Love, too! This is a manual that gives advice, techniques, and strategies as to how to get the man you want. Pearl Jr., Elbow Grease Productions, 5632 Van Nuys Boulevard #195, Van Nuys, California 91401 E-mail: **pearljr@trutalk.us** Website: **www.BlackWomenNeedLoveToo.com**

Suzetta M. Perkins Author of Behind the Veil, A Love So Deep, and EX-terminator, Life After Marriage. Contributing author of My Soul to His Spirit, an anthology of short stories that was featured in Ebony magazine (2005) and winner of the 2006 Fresh Voices Award. Cofounder and president of the Sistahs Book Club. Suzetta M. Perkins, Post Office Box 64424, Fayetteville, North Carolina 28306 E-mail: **nubianqe2@aol.com** Website: **www.suzettaperkins.com**

M. LaVora Perry   Author of Taneesha's Treasures of the Heart released in June 2003. "Taneesha Never Disparaging" Middle Grade Realistic Fiction, 2008, Wisdom Publications and "Teen Sisters Health--A Body, Mind, & Spirit Wellness Guide for Girls of Color" (Co-Author, Linda Bradley, MD). M. LaVora Perry has performed in stage and film productions in New York and Europe. In 1995 she graduated from Cleveland State University cum laude with a Bachelor of Science degree in Elementary Education. That same year she became the first African-American staff card writer in the world's largest publicly-owned greeting card company - American Greetings. Since then, her words have appeared on gift items in the U.S, U.K., Canada, Australia, New Zealand and in Spanish translation in Mexico. LaVora edited AG's 2003 Day-at-a-Time 365 Days of Healthy Living and 2003 and 2004 African-American Almanac desktop calendars. She received AG Creative Excellence awards in 1999 (Juvenile and Conventional Writing) and 2000 (Concept Innovation In Rhythm). Awards in fiction contests held by the Cleveland Free Times newspaper and Ohio Writer Magazine for her short story, "Forgiving." (1990). M. LaVora Perry, 13200 Forest Hill Avenue, East Cleveland, Ohio 44112 E-mail: **mlavoraperry@mlavoraperry.com** Website: **www.mlavoraperry.com**

Naresha S. Perry Author. Also founder and publisher of Publishing Company. Better Day Publishing is dedicated to children with different learning abilities. Contact Ms. Naresha S. Perry, 1152 Westheimer #341, Houston, Texas 77042 Phone: (713) 548-4048 E-mail: **contact@betterdaypublishing.com** Website: **www.betterdaypublishing.com**

Roy L. Pickering Author, photographer, poet, and freelance writer his debut novel is Patches of Grey, a gallery of his photographs, and much more. Roy's monthly column covering prevalent issues in the world of pro sports can be found at suite101.com. In 2003, Roy's prose was featured in two anthologies. Kensington Books put out Proverbs for the People, which includes his short story, Lessons. Later that Summer, The Game...Short Stories About the Life was published by Triple Crown Publications. This book of gangster/hip hop literature contains two of Mr. Pickering's tales packaged under a single title - "Mama's Boy". Additionally, an anthology consisting entirely of his own stories Enigmas of Desire was epubbed by Free-Fiction.com. Roy L. Pickering, 1185 Avenue of the Americas, 26th Floor, New York, New York 10036 E-mail: **RoyLPickering@aol.com** Website: **www.RoyPickering.net**

Adriene Pickett Originally from Passaic, New Jersey, Adriene Pickett is the author of Never Forget The Bridge That Crossed You Over. She is a graduate of William Paterson University and has been writing fiction for many years. She learned the art of storytelling firsthand in her home, which was filled with relatives who told stories of the south, her family's history, and African Americans' meaningful experiences.   She lives in Los Angeles, California. Adriene Pickett, Post Office Box 643062, Los Angeles, California 90064 Phone: (310) 351-0378 E-mail: **adrienepickett@aol.com** Website: **www.adrienepickett.com**

Naiomi Pitre Author of two books, Broken Vows, and a second book newly released in January 2007, entitled In The Panty Drawer - Journey Into The Mind of a Sexual Woman. This steamy collection of stories offers a uniquely dark view of women thrust into precarious situations. Contact Ms. Naiomi Pitre, 39070 South Angelle Court, Gonzales, Louisiana 70737 Phone: (225) 673-8395 Fax: (225) 296-8858 E-mail: **naiomipitre@hotmail.com** Website: **www.NaiomiPitre.4t.com**

Darlene Pitts Author of Haunted Revenge, a novel about a psychic artist who seeks the ultimate revenge on a longtime enemy only to have it backfire in the form of an apparition. She is also the author of Discover Your Intuition & Let's Talk Intuition. Darlene Pitts, Inspiration & Intuition, Post Office Box 391, Smyrna, Georgia 30081 Phone: (770) 434-5240 E-mail: **dpitts@inspirationandintuition.com** Website: **www.inspirationandintuition.com**

D.T. Pollard Born in Henderson, Texas, He earned an academic scholarship to the School of Business and Industry at Florida A & M University in Tallahassee, Florida. His first novel The Trophy Wife Network was published in April 2006 followed by Rooftop Diva-A Novel of Triumph After Katrina in September 2006. D. T. Pollard, Post Office Box 541651, Grand Prairie, Texas 75054 E-mail: **dtpollard@dtpollard.com** Website: **www.dtpollard.com**

Cheryl Lynn Pope Parenting author of '25 Ways To Make Your Child(ren) Feel Special.' She is currently working on a children's book series that is targeted towards towards black girls ages 5-9. Cheryl Pope, 6340 Devereaux, Detroit, Michigan 48210 Phone: (313) 598-2710 E-mail: **mylilbratz@hotmail.com**

M. Quinn Writer, Lecturer and Author of the book Removing the Veil. M. Quinn, Post Office Box 411, Mountain. View, California 94042 E-mail: **twentyfirstcentury_writer@yahoo.com**

Francis Ray Author of 31 best-seller books and native Texan, Ms. Francis Ray lives in Dallas, Texas and is a graduate of Texas Woman's University. Her titles consistently make bestseller's lists such as Blackboard and Essence Magazine. Incognito, her sixth title, was the first made-for-TV movie for Black Entertainment Television (BET). She has written fourteen single titles and eight anthologies. The Turning Point, her first mainstream, was a finalist for the prestigious HOLT Medallion Award. At the release event for Turning Point in May 2001, she established The Turning Point Legal defense Fund to assist women of domestic violence to help restructure their lives. With the release of her second mainstream, I Know Who Holds Tomorrow in May 2002, Ms. Ray has pledged to continue the effort. Her book I Know Who Holds Tomorrow made the bestseller's list of The Dallas Morning News, Blackboard, Black Expressions Book Club, and Essence Magazine. The book was selected as Book Club Favorites for Black Issues Book Review Best of 2002. Somebody's Knocking At My Door, her third mainstream, made bestseller's list across the country. Her fourth mainstream is Like The First Time, (May 2004). Other releases include To Love Me December 2003, Trouble Don't Last Always January 2004, First Touch, February 2004, Whole Lotta Love, February 2004, Love At Leo's July 2004, The Falcon Saga, August 2004, You And No Other, December 2004, Any Rich Man Will Do, October 2005/St. Martin's Press, Chocolate Kisses, January, 2006/NAL and Dreaming of You, September 2006. Francis Ray, Post Office Box 764651, Dallas, Texas 75276 Phone: (214) 375-8627 E-mail: **francisray@aol.com**

Gene T. Reed Author of Here's to My Lady a must-have for men looking to improve their relationships and know what to do and say in almost every situation. Mr. Reed was born and raised in Baltimore, Maryland, where he enjoyed a long and successful career in sales and as a sales trainer. Today, Reed lives in the Los Angeles area and pursues his longtime love of music. Gene T. Reed, 1833 Raleo Avenue, Rowland Heights, California 91748 Phone: (626) 965-8327 Fax: (626) 839-2422 E-mail: **genereed7@msn.com** Website: **www.HerestoMyLady.com**

Gregory J. Reed Author, agent, producer, attorney and specialist in tax and entertainment law, Gregory J. Reed is the author of twelve books: Tax Planning and Contract Negotiating Techniques for Creative Persons, Professional Athletes and Entertainers (1979), This Business of Boxing and and Its Secrets (1981), This Business of Entertainment and Its Secrets (1985); Negotiations Behind Closed Doors (1992); Economic Empowerment Through The Church (Zondervan, 1994, American Book Award Winner) and This Business of Celebrity Estates. Reed is co-author of the book Quiet Strength, with Mrs. Rosa Parks (Zondervan, 1995), and Dear Mrs. Parks (Lee & Low, 1996). Education: B.S., Michigan State University (Engineering); M.S., Michigan State University (Management Science); J.D., Wayne State University (Master of Taxation Law). He is a recipient of the John Hensel Award for significant contributions to the arts. Gregory J. Reed & Associates, PC, 1201 Bagley, Detroit, Michigan 48226 Phone: (313) 961-3580 Fax: (313) 961-3582 E-mail: **gjrassoc@aol.com** Website: **www.gjreedlaw.com**

Taryn Reed Author, his first novel was "The Other Side of Da Court", and the latest release is "The Calm Before The Storm," both published by Publish America. Contact Taryn Reed, 410 Farmington Avenue, Unit L5, New Britain, Connecticut 06053 Phone: (914) 420-8838 E-mail: **tarynr@sbcglobal.net**

Tom Reed Writer, Black music documentaries, Wattstax Revisited and Ray Charles: Words and Music, etc. Producer/host of 'For Members Only' TV, L.A.'s longest running locally produced Black cultural entertainment & information television program. Awards, commendations and plaques grace his walls, given to him because of his competitive spirit and his concern for his fellow man. He holds a B.S. & M.S. Honorary Doctorate in Education (Communications) from City Unit, Los Angeles, 1982. Tom Reed, Post Office Box 27487, Los Angeles, California 90027 Phone: (818) 894-8880

James Reedom Author of The Pro se Attorney Manual: Layman Strategies In The Law. He is a former Pre-Law Professor, Public Administration and Economic and Community Development strategist. He has worked at such universities as Grambling State University and The State University of New York. He ia a former Instructor at TCU Off Campus Continuing Education Program in Political Science Public Administration, Whitehouse Empowerment Conference Participant 1999-2000 and several distinguished community colleges. Contact Mr. James Reedom, Post Office Box 8221, Fort Worth, Texas 76112 E-mail: **preed230@netscape.net** Website: **www.authorhouse.com**

Barbara A. Reynolds Award winning journalist and author of 3 books, No I Won't Shut Up: 30 Years of Telling It Like It Is, Out of Hell and Living Well, and Jesse Jackson: America's David. Born in Columbus, Ohio, Dr. Reynolds received her BA in journalism from The Ohio State University, her Masters Degree from Howard University School of Divinity in 1991, and her doctorate in Ministry from the United Theological Seminary in Dayton, Ohio in 1998. She was awarded an honorary doctorates from Shenandoah University and her alma mater, The Ohio State University. As a professor, she has held the Jessie Ball Dupont Chair in Journalism at Shenandoah University in Winchester, Virginia and was a Freedom Forum Scholar for the 1998 school year in journalism at Florida A&M University. Dr. Barbara A. Reynolds, JFJ Publishing, 4806 Saint Barnabas Road, Suite 598, Temple Hills, Maryland 20757 Phone: (301) 899-1341 E-mail: **reynew@aol.com** Website: **www.reynoldsworldnews.com**

Evie Rhodes Fiction author, Evie Rhode's first novel Expired, a psychological thriller set in Harlem was published in 2005. She is a novelist, award-winning songwriter and award-winning music video scriptwriter. She is the writer for the "Standing In Da Sprit" album, which won a Canadian Music Award for Best Gospel Album, and the scriptwriter for Changed, which won for Best Gospel Music Video. Evie Rhodes, Post Office Box 320503, Hartford, Connecticut 06132 Phone: (212) 633-3315 E-mail: **evierhodes@evierhodes.com** Website: **www.evierhodes.com**

Patricia Richardson Author of A Place For Ida and A Time For Jonathan. Patricia Richardson, Leap Of Faith Publishing, Post Office Box 957705, Duluth, Georgia 30095 Phone: (770) 689-6924 E-mail: **richprch@aol.com** Website: **www.leapoffaithpublishing.bravehost.com**

Naomi Roberson Author of After Daddy Died, a shocking true story of how a family was affected by their father's psychotic behavior. Dr. Naomi Roberson is an organizational psychologist and a motivational speaker. For the past fifteen years, she has been a volunteer talk show host for Access Television. Dr. Roberson is also a producer, director, and camera operator and has produced and directed documentaries, award shows, public service announcements, and interviews for local television and the outlying areas. Dr. Roberson has an associate degree in accounting, a bachelor's degree in behavioral science, a master's degree in management and human resources, a doctorate in organizational psychology, and a doctorate in divinity. She is a licensed and ordained minister. Dr. Naomi Roberson, GEM, Inc., Post Office Box 557533, Chicago, Illinois 60655 Phone: (312) 458-9812 E-mail: **ncroberson@comcast.net**

Janeen Robichaud Author of two published erotic novels Candy and Candy2, The Sequel; one teen novel about bullying at school and the effects it has on one particular student, Laura Wellington entitled They Killed Me. Janeen has also written numerous poems and short stories; featured in anthologies, Messages from the Universe and Wounds of War (soon to be released). Contact Ms. Janeen Robichaud, 7000 Donald Street, Millville, New Jersey 08332 E-mail: **candyjaneen@aol.com**

Brenetia Adams-Robinson Entrepreneur, trainer, motivational speaker and author, Brenetia Adams-Robinson is the President of Epitome' Consulting Services, a consulting firm specializing in training and development and Founder / Executive Director of Proverbial Peace Revived Ministries. She is a contributing writer of the acclaimed "100 Words of Wisdom for Women: A 31-Day Exercise in Empowerment", as well as contributor for "Entertaining Secrets", an e-book for Christian event planners. Brenetia Adams-Robinson, Epitome' Consulting Services, Post Office Box 743, Jonesboro, Georgia 30237 E-mail: **epitomeconsult@yahoo.com**

C. Kelly Robinson A graduate of Howard University and Washington University in St. Louis, CK self-published his first novel, Not All Dogs while still working in corporate America. In October 2001 Not All Dogs was re-released by Random House/Villard, under the new title Between Brothers. It has been a bestseller on CushCity.com and been favorably reviewed in publications including Essence, Publishers Weekly, and the Chicago Sun-Times. His 2002 release of the romantic comedy No More Mr. Nice Guy also went on to top the April 2003 Essence Best-Seller list. CK is at work on the sequel to Nice Guy, The Perfect Blend. C. Kelly Robinson, Against the Grain Communications, Post Office Box 58, Clayton, Ohio 45315 E-mail: **ckrob7071@aol.com** Website: **www.ckellyrobinson.com**

Cheryl Robinson Author, and host of Just About Books Talk Show, an internet radio talk show with a worldwide audience featuring authors, book reviews, book clubs, and literary events for African American book lovers.   Cheryl Robinson, Just About Books Talk Show, 1282 Smallwood Drive, West, Suite 116, Waldorf, Maryland 20603 Phone: (301) 643-2077 E-mail: **JustAboutBooks@yahoo.com** Website: **www.JustAboutBookTalkShow.com**

Christine Young-Robinson Raised in New York, Christine now resides in her place of birth, Columbia, South Carolina. Isra the Butterfly Gets Caught for Show and Tell, her first children's book, was inspired by her granddaughter and put into print to share with other children. She has now released her second children's book, Chicken Wing. She is the recipient of the Carrie Allen McCray Award, "Honorable Mention" for Juvenile Fiction given by the South Carolina Writer's Workshop. She is also presently working on a chapter book and an adult fiction novel. Christine Young-Robinson, Yoroson Publishing, 10120 Two Notch Road, #143, Columbia, South Carolina 29223 Phone: (803) 419-5890 Fax: (803) 865-9001 E-mail: **miraclewriter4u@aol.com** Website: **www.christineyoungrobinson.com**

Lynda Davis Robinson Author, conference speaker, educator, entepreneuer facilitator, mentor, motivator, pastor, psalmist, trainer, and teacher. CEO of Whiteshoes Communications & Publishing and PowerSerge News Publications. Rev. Dr. Lynda Davis Robinson, 3697 Mint Street, Clearlake, California 95422 E-mail: **lcdavisrob@aol.com**

Michelle Janine Robinson Studied Journalism at New York University. Erotic short story Mi Destino is included in the anxiously awaited Zane anthology, Caramel Flava. Currently working on two novels, You Created a Monster and Pleasure Principle. Ms. Michelle Janine Robinson, 148 East 150th Street, Bronx, New York 10451 E-mail: **Robinson_201@hotmail.com**

Sabra A. Robinson A writer of both children's literature and non-fiction with plans to write in all age groups. She is the author of the multicultural picture book, Micky, Ticky, Boo! Says Hello and founder of the African-American Children's Writers and Illustrators online group AACBWI.com. a collective information-sharing forum for children's authors and illustrators, young and old. Sabra received her bachelor's degree in Sociology from Morgan State University and currently works in corporate America. Her vision and proposal to animate her characters for film and television allowed her to become recognized as a finalist out of over 300 applicants for the ABC/Disney New Talent Development program for 2003. Sabra A. Robinson, Post Office Box 620324, Charlotte, North Carolina 28262 E-mail: **sabra@sabrarobinson.com** Website: **www.sabrarobinson.com**

Gayle Rogers Founder and co-paster of L.I.F.E. Outreach Ministries International, Inc., Dr. Rogers has authored several books including the recently released Healing the Traumatized Soul. She is a teacher/trainer, teaching on such subjects as Effective Leadership, Discovering Your Potential as a Woman, Walking in Your Authority, Overcoming Sexual Trauma, God's Purpose for Your Life, and much more. She received her Ph.D. in Women's Studies from Trinity Theological Seminary and certification by the American Society of Development and Training (ASTD) through the University of Oklahoma. Contact Dr. Gayle Rogers, Forever Free, Inc., Post Office Box 390475, Snellville, Georgia 30039 Phone: (678) 344-8638 E-mail: **drgayleforhelp@comcast.net** Website: **www.bforeverfree.org**

Carla Sams Author. Contact Ms. Carla Sams, Now U No Publishing Company, Post Office Box 9501, Cincinnati Ohio 45209 Phone: (513) 226-6450 E-mail: **holly.ferguson@nowuno-enterprises.com** Website: **www.nowunopublishingco.com**

Deon C. Sanders (Deno Sandz) embraces and turns southern myths and religion into his second published supernatural/horror novel. Contact Publicist, Dawn Sanders, 2259 West Adams, Chicago, Illinois 60612 Phone: (708) 539-7827 E-mail: **dsanders4119@yahoo.com**

Carolyn Chambers-Sanders A registered stockbroker and financial planner, Carolyn is author of the book Sins, Secrets & Success. She has a BS from Florida A&M University and a MBA from Texas Southern University. Currently, working on her next novels, "The Games We Play" and "Young Divas in Training. Ms. Carolyn Chambers, C. Chambers Publishing Group, 4100 Morris Road. Suite 1027, Flower Mound, Texas 75028 E-mail: **carolyn@carolynsanders.com** Website: **www.carolynsanders.com**

Marsha D. Jenkins-Sanders Born in Detroit, Michigan, Marsha D. Jenkins-Sanders is a writer of novels and songs. She received acclaim in the music industry for lyrics written for Keith Washington's freshmen album project, Make Time for Love. Both "Kissing You" and "Closer" introduced her writing talent and she received award-winning recognition from ASCAP for Writer and Publisher in the R & B genre. "Kissing You" was certified gold and went on to be featured as the background music for love scenes on ABC's soap, General Hospital. "The Other Side of Through", her debut novel was released in February 2007, on the Strebor/Simon & Schuster label. "Jealousy: A Strange Company Keeper" will follow in 2008. Marsha D. Jenkins-Sanders, Markei Publishing, 18455 Miramar Parkway, #162, Miramar, Florida 33029 E-mail: **mrcsdno@yahoo.com**

Vince Sanders Author of the book, can't get HERE from THERE (1st Books) and That's Not Funny! (Booksurge), Vince is former chief operator of the broadcast division of National Black Network. Vince is a retired veteran of the broadcast industry. During more than 35 years of professional radio and television, his assignments included Vice President and General Manager of radio station WWRL in New York City, from 1983 thru 1995; Vice President of Broadcast Operations at the National Black Network from 1973 thru 1983--Anchor/Reporter for NBC news from 1971 thru 1973. In addition, Vince did on-air stints in the Chicago area at WMAQ-AM radio and TV, WBEE-AM radio, WMPP-AM radio and WCIU-TV. In 1968, he was also special correspondent for KPOI radio in Honolulu, Hawaii. As an actor, Sanders traveled with the American Negro Opera Guild and served as Theatrical Consultant to the Chicago Emancipation Centennial Authority in the early 1960's. He is a founding member of the National Association of Black Journalists and was inducted into its Hall Of Fame (Region IV) in 2005. Vince Sanders, Post Office Box 917358, Longwood, Florida 32791 Phone: (321) 277-7214 Fax: (407) 786-0709 E-mail: **vincnet@cfl.rr.com** Website: **www.vincesanders.com**

Viola Sanders Owner and founder of Vii's Services, Inc., an African American Educational company providing seven traveling exhibits. Published in 1995, AFRICAN AMERICAN INVENTORS book and in 2003 published, An African American Tea Ceremony book. Contact Ms. Viola Sanders, Post Office Box 181, Blythewood, South Carolina 29016 Phone: (803) 754-5620 E-mail: **vii@viiservices.com**

Luticia Santipriya Psychopathologist, psychologist theoretician, book editor-publisher. Born in Oakland, California. Specialist in psycho-archeology and the slave trade. Author of The Ipuwer Chronicles (2005), A Bluejay's Eye: Notes on Our Time from a Psychologist's Daybook (in press 2007) and Rebel Sunrise with a Twist of Sour: A Memoir (in press 2008). Currently shopping these works for the stage and screen and to academia as textbooks. Ardent public speaker and former university professor (New York Hospital Medical Center in Queens, The City University of New York, The College of Mount Saint Vincent). Honored by The New York Association of Black Psychologists for valuable lifetime contribution to the field of psychology and numerous plaque and gavel awards from students for excellence in teaching clinical, abnormal, forensic and industrial psychology. Educated at Stanford University, New York University, The California Institute of Asian (Integral) Studies, and trained under the renowned Black clinician Dr. Guy O. Seymour at Boston Medical Center, and at his behest is distinguished as a joint Clinical Fellow of Harvard Medical School and Teaching Fellow of Boston University School of Medicine. Dr. Luticia Santipriya, Post Office Box 136, Brooklyn, New York 11231 Phone: (212) 715-6873 E-mail: **santipriya@hotmail.com**

Yolanda Brunson-Sarrabo A native of Brooklyn, New York, Yolanda Brunson-Sarrabo has worked at various levels of the fashion industry. Along with writing The Ins and Outs of the Fashion Industry she also co-writes a popular monthly newsletter, The Laundry Source. Yolanda's entrepreneurial spirit has led her to form Spitfir Productions, a literary home for authors who want to display their talents in writing. She is currently working on a second novel based on the epidemic of AIDS in the Black community, and lives in Brooklyn with her husband. Yolanda Brunson-Sarrabo, Spitfir Productions,1454 Rockaway Parkway, Brooklyn, New York 11236 E-mail: **blackwriternew@yahoo.com** Website: **www.ybrunson.com**

Rodney Saulsberry One of the top voice-over talents in the country, Mr. Saulsberry is a new author of the book You Can Bank on Your Voice: Your Guide to a Successful Career in Voice-Overs. (August 2004, Tondor). As one of the top trailer voices in the business, movie fans have heard Rodney's voice promoting some of their favorites:Tupac Resurrection, How Stella Got Her Groove Back, Drumline, Undercover Brother, Dumb & Dumberer, Finding Forrester, and many more. In March 2003 he announced the NAACP Image Awards and the Essence Awards specials on FOX Television. Rodney Saulsberry, Tomdor Publishing, LLC, Post Office Box 1735, Agoura Hills, California 91376 Phone: (818) 207-2682 E-mail: **rodtalks@aol.com** Website: **www.rodneysaulsberry.com**

Deirdre Savoy Native New Yorker Deirdre Savoy spent her summers on the shores of Martha's Vineyard, soaking up the sun and scribbling in one of her many notebooks. It was here that she first started writing romance as a teenager. The island proved to be the perfect setting for her first novel, SPELLBOUND, published by BET in 1999. Since then Deirdre has published more than a dozen books and two novellas, all of which have garnered critical acclaim and honors. She has won two prestigious Emma awards. Her work has been featured in a variety of publications, including Black Issues Book Review, Romantic Times, Affaire de Coeur and Blackboard Bestsellers List. Deirdre lives in Bronx, New York with her husband and their two children. She enjoys reading, dancing, calligraphy and "wicked" crossword puzzles. Deirdre Savoy, Post Office Box 233, Bronx, New York 10469 Phone: (646) 418-1257 Fax: (718) 994-7343 E-mail: **deesavoy@gmail.com** Website: **www.deesavoy.com**

Beatrice Lee Scott Graduated from Norfolk State University with a degree in Social Work. Author of The Cracked Door (2006, Tate Publishing). Contact Bea Lee, 1310 Holly Avenue, Chesapeake Virginia 23324 Phone: (757) 543-2443 E-mail: **beatricescott_334@msn.com**

Devon Scott Author of Unfaithful, published in May, 2008 by Kensington. Mr. Devon Scott,. c/o Kensington Publishing Corp, Dafina Books, 850 Third Avenue, New York, New York 10022 E-mail: **info@devonscott.com** Website: **www.devonscott.com**

Gloria Dean Randle-Scott Author, Ph.D., Indiana University; Retired President Bennett College 1987-2001; Former Executive Vice President Clark College 1978-1987; President of G. Randle Services - Organizational and Leadership Development Firm 1975-present; Former Board Member United Negro College Fund; National Urban League; National President of Girl Scouts USA 1975-1978; Chair of the 50th Anniversary Celebration of UNCF - 1994; authored the book The Golden Book of Excellence, 1994, a description and dialogue about the 41 private HBCUS of the United Negro College Fund. Vice Chair of National Advisory Board on Historically Black Colleges and Universities to Presidents Jimmy Carter, 1976-1982 and Member of National Advisory Board on HBCUs to President George H. Bush, 1989-1994. Dr. Gloria Scott, Post Office Box 9174, Corpus Christi, Texas 78469 E-mail: **randle@rivnet.com**

Sandra J. Scott Founder and executive director of Y.E.S., Inc., Ms. Scott is also the author of three published books: Lord, Let There Be Light, Becoming Whole Before Becoming One, and Baggage Handlers: My road to letting go of life's painful luggage. Sandra Scott, 630 Minnesota Avenue, Suite 206, Kansas City, Kansas 66101 E-mail: **becomingwhole@hotmail.com**

Harley A. Searcy Honored as an Outstanding Young American and in Who's Who In California, Mr. Searcy received a B.A. degree from UCLA, in English and a Juris Doctorate from Stanford Law School. He has been writing creatively for over twenty years. His literary accomplishments include: "In The Eye of the Midnite Pearl," a collection of his poetry. His works are included in "Black Light", an African-American poetry anthology by Hallmark Press and "NOMMO", the UCLA Black Students' publication where he served as both Poetry Editor and Managing Editor. He was also Co-Producer and writer for "The Cotton Club Revue', a song/dance/drama/musical annual show for five consecutive years at the Wilshire Ebell Theatre in Los Angeles. He has released a CD collaboration with Don Whitehead (formerly of Earth, Wind & Fire) of words and music. He is currently an attorney specializing in public and private real estate development. Harley A. Searcy, 27802 Audrey Court, Canyon Country, California 91351 Phone: (323) 595-0105 Fax: (661) 299-5747 E-mail: **harleysearcy@myway.com**

Janet West Sellars Writing has been Janet's most enduring passion for as long as she can remember. The embodiment of her passion is impressively revealed in her first novel, Quiet As It's Kept. Janet was born in the Washington, DC, area to the late Leola and Willie West. The oldest of their three children, her creative spirit was cultivated and nurtured by her mother's love of the arts. She has lived and traveled extensively throughout the US and Europe. She has had careers in the armed forces, academia, and public service. Janet holds a Bachelor's degree in Sociology and a Master's degree in Human Relations. Mrs. Janet West Sellars, 908 Bellgate Court, Newport News, Virginia 23602 Phone: (757) 897-1015   E-mail: **jsellars@cox.net** Website: **www.janetwestsellars.com**

Earl Sewell Has authored such titles as The Good Got To Suffer With the Bad, Taken For Granted and You're Making Me Wet. When not writing Earl Sewell spends his time training to complete an Ironman Triathlon. Earl resides in Palatine, Illinois, and is currently working on his next title A Hot Mess. Through Thick and Thin is Earl's second BET novel. Earl Sewell, Kicheko Driggins, One BET Plaza West, Washington, DC 20018 E-mail: **earl@earlsewell.com** Website: **www.earlsewell.com**

Ntozake Shange Award winning author, poet, playwright and novelist. Contact Author Appearance Coordinator, Simon & Schuster, 1230 Avenue of the Americas, New York, New York 10020 Phone: (212) 698-2808 Fax: (212) 698-4350 Website: **www.SimonSaysKids.com**

Anesha A. Sharp Director of Charles Martin Ministries, Author, Multi-gifted Motivational Speaker and Youth Minister. Anesha is the author of "Unlocking the Doors to Destiny" an inspirational book of deliverance, healing, and restoration of identity and purpose. Mrs. Anesha Sharp, 4501 North Meridian, Oklahoma City, Oklahoma 73112 Phone: (405) 822-6090 E-mail: **asharpauthor06@sbcglobal.net**

Jesse Sharpe Writer and self publisher of adult fiction and non-fiction books as well as educational books for children and adults. Books include poetry, short story, short novel, workbooks, and educational reference. Jesse Sharpe, 6629 Adrian Street, New Carrollton, Maryland 20784 Phone: (240) 375-6033 E-mail: **sharpesolutions@comcast.net** Website: **www.sharpebooksonline.com**

Kali Shirah Author, my work includes non-fiction, career and fiction books, Start Your Own Transcription Business (1-3rd Editions), Real Estate Agent's Yearly Planner/Organizer, and A Dieting Diva's Diary. Fiction, inspirational romance & general romance includes, Romancin' the Reverend, and In Cahoots with the Choir. Kali Shirah, Post Office Box 1088, Tioga, Louisiana 71477 Website: **www.kaliannah.com**

Yasmin Shiraz Author of The Blueprint for My Girls, (Rolling Hills Press) a motivational guidebook for teens and young women, Yasmin is Chief Executive Officer of Rolling Hills Press, an independent publishing company. Yasmin Shiraz, Post Office Box 220053, Chantilly, Virginia 20153 Phone: (703) 542-5072 Fax: (703) 542-5073 E-mail: **yasminshiraz@aol.com**

Margie Gosa Shivers Voted 2003 Best Self-Published Author, Mahogany Book Club. She also received the Disilgold Mystery Novelist Award of Excellence 2004 and the YOUnity Reviewers Guild Most Sought Book of the Year 2004. Margie Gosa Shivers, 16781 Torrence Avenue #294, Lansing, Illinois 60438 Phone: (708) 889-9886 E-mail: **margegosa@aol.com**

Della Faye Showunmi Pen name, Della Faye, she is author of the inspirational book, Always Try Just One More Time. Della Faye Showunmi, Post Office Box 743842, Dallas, Texas 75374 E-mail: **della@dellafaye.com** Website: **www.dellafaye.com**

Lura Sutton-Sims An author/publisher of "Step by Step Travel Guide for Corporate and Leisure Travel." Lura Sutton-Sims, 5910 Purple Sage, Houston, Texas 77049 Phone: (281) 458-2972 E-mail: **luras@houston.rr.com**

Nea Anna Simone Author of Reaching BACK her debut work was selected by Borders Bookstores as an "Original Voice of Fiction," chosen for "Readers Choice Fiction Award", Atlanta Daily World. The sequel, ReBorn is number 6 on the Essence Magazine Best Seller list and was nominated for the "Hurston-Wright Legacy Award," and was also chosen as Book of The Year by Relaxing Sisters Book Club, New Jersey. Nea Anna Simone Phone: (404) 630-1622 E-mail: **nea@neasimone.com** Website: **www.neasimone.com**

Irene Smalls Author, storyteller, historian. Award winning author of 15 books for children and 3 storytelling CDs, Ms. Smalls is a graduate of Cornell University and has an MBA from New York University. Irene Smalls, Post Office Box 990441, Prudential Center, Boston, Massachusetts 02199 Fax: (617) 266-3308 E-mail: **ISmalls107@aol.com**

Andrea Smith Her debut novel received outstanding reviews and is quickly gaining bestseller status. Her book Friday Nights At Honeybee's was chosen by Barnes and Noble as a "Discover Great New Writers" selection for Winter 2003, Borders, February 2003 "Original Voices" title and spotlighted on the cover of Black Expressions Book Club's Spring 2003 catalog as special feature. Andrea is currently working on her second novel, due to be released by Random House/The Dial Press and is tentatively titled "Canaan Creek. She now lives in Atlanta, Georgia with her eight year old son. Andrea Smith, c/o Julia Shaw, Shaw Literary Group, 295 Madison Avenue, 21st Floor, New York, New York 10017 E-mail: **shawlit@aol.com** Website: **www.andreamsmith.com**

Gina Johnson-Smith Author of 100 Important Life Lessons for Everyone, Life Lessons for Youth, and Life Lessons for Women. Publisher of the Rancho Cucamonga/Ontario community News, Carson/South Bay community News, and Las Vegas community News. Gina Johnson-Smith, Smith Publishing & Media Group, #385 South Lemon Avenue, #E236, Walnut, California 91789 E-mail: **ginajohnsonsmith@sbcglobal.net**

Horane Smith Award-winning author of six published novels. He's the recipient of the BURLA Award for outstanding contribution to African North American and Caribbean literature. Having worked in radio, television and the print media for nearly twenty years, he took on creative writing seriously in 1999, when his first novel Lover's Leap, based on the Jamaican Legend, was published to international acclaim. He has since written Port Royal, Underground to Freedom, The Lynching Stream, Reggae Silver, and Dawn at Lover's Leap, the sequel to Lover's Leap. Horane Smith, 36 Pinedale Gate, Vaughan, Ontario L4L 8W9, Canada E-mail: **Horane_Smith@hotmail.com** Website: **www.horanesmith.com**

Katherine Smith The Naked Author - Exposing the Myths of Publishing. Formerly co-host of the morning radio show on ABC Radio Networks, Inc., "Classic Soul Hits" format, Ms. Smith is an internationally published writer and the author of The Book Seller's List and Love the Vicious Cycle. She is presently a member of The Writer's Block, Inc. writers group, Small Publishers Association of North America (S.P.A.N.), the National Association of Women Writers (NAWW) and North Dallas Writes critique group. In 1996, Kat started a writing service, K. S. & Associates. In 1998 it became a "paper communications" service, and in 2001 added publishing to its services. Katherine "Kat" Smith, Post Office Box 701478, Dallas, Texas 75370 E-mail: **kat@kat-smith.biz** Website: **www.tomkatproductions.com**

Linda Hudson-Smith Currently has 23 titles to her credit, Linda is the award winning author of Ice Under Fire her debut Arabesque novel, which has received rave reviews and won the 2000 Gold Pen Award. Her book Soulful Serenade, released in August 2000, was selected by Romance In Color as the Best Cover for August 2000. Desperate Deceptions was released in March 2001. Fire Beneath the Ice, a sequel to Ice Under Fire was a November 2001 release. Linda's first mainstream novel, Ladies In Waiting was released August 2002. In February 2006 Linda's anthology novel, Thicker Than Water/The Devil's Advocate was #7 on the Essence Best Seller's list, capturing her the title of national best selling author. Linda is a member and a national spokeswoman for the Lupus Foundation of America, Romance Writers of America, and The Black Writer's Alliance. Linda was also recently awarded the key to the city by the mayor of Crestview, Florida for the contributions she's made to educating others about lupus. Contact Ms. Linda Hudson-Smith, 16516 El Camino Real, Box 174, Houston, Texas 77062 Phone: (281) 804- 9092 E-mail: **lhs4romance@yahoo.com** Website: **www.lindahudsonsmith.com**

Peaches Smith Storyteller and author of 13 childrens books. Ms. Smith is also founder of Bullets to Books turning trigger-pullers into page-turners. Contact Ms. Peaches Smith, 108 Ridgewood Street, Hot Springs, Arkansas 71901 E-mail: **peachessmith@sbcglobal.net**

Swanzetta Smith Author of the romance novel, Private Passions. A fiction writer since 1996, Ms. Swanzetta Smith is a member of The Black Writers Alliance, and Romance Writer's of America. She is currently working on her second novel. Swanzetta Smith, 231 East Alessandro Boulevard, #A-107, Riverside California 92507 E-mail: **mszetta@earthlink.net** Website: **www.swanzettasmith.com**

M. Lavonte Stanley Syracuse, New York author of the book, The Makings of a Superwoman" by Red Bull. I currently reside in the Tampa, Florida area. M. Lavonte Stanley, Authorhouse Publishing, 1663 Liberty Drive, Suite 200, Bloomington, Indiana 47403 Phone: (888) 519-5121 E-mail: **truthshespeaks@yahoo.com** Website: **www.themakingsofasuperwoman.com**

Crystal Perkins-Stell An educator and author, Crystal was raised in Detroit, Michigan, and is a three-time Who's Who inductee. She completed her undergraduate degree at Langston University with scholastic honors and obtained her Master's degree from the University of Oklahoma in Human Relations, where she graduated Summa Cum Laude. She is a member of Delta Sigma Theta Sorority Inc., a 2004 honorary inductee of Tau Beta Sigma Band Sorority, and an affiliate of several professional literary and educational organizations. She is also an advocate for HIV and AIDS Awareness, which led to her participating in a project with former NFL Players Kenny Blair and Ron Fellows. Crystal, wrote and performed a song entitled, "The Magic Touch," which was dedicated to Magic Johnson. She worked with the Oklahoma State Senate Election for the first black female federal judge currently serving in the United States, the Honorable Vickie Miles-Lagrange. In 2001, Crystal was inspired by Tom Joyner during a commencement address to give back to individuals less fortunate. She sold her car, gave up her 2001 Tax return, and organized Crystell Publications, Marketing and Distributions, Inc. Stell has three novels, Soiled Pillowcases, Hood Rich, and Never Knew a Father's Love. Crystal Perkins Stells, Crystell Publications, Post Office Box 8044, Edmond, Oklahoma 73083 Phone: (405) 414-3991 E-mail: **cleva@crystalstell.com** Website: **www.crystalstell.com**

Timothy N. Stelly, Sr. Author of three novels: "Tempest In The Stone," "The Malice of Cain," and "Like A Straight-Up Sucka." He is also a frequent contributor to e-zines useless-knowledge.com and e-zinearticles.com. Mr. Stelly has penned more than thirty screenplays, including "Twangbangers." Timothy N. Stelly, Sr., Post Office Box 1264, Pittsburg, California 94565 Phone: (925) 473-0741 E-mail: **stellbread@yahoo.com**

Torrance Stephens His work has appeared in print and publications such as NOMMO, Creative Loafing, Rolling Out, Talking Drum, the North Avenue Review and other periodicals. He graduated from Hamilton High School in Memphis and attended Morehouse College where he studied, psychology, biology and chemistry. He received a master's degree in Educational Psychology and Measurement from Atlanta University and a Ph.D. in Counseling from Clark Atlanta University. Torrance Stephens, Post Office Box 1331, Palmetto, Georgia 30268 Phone: (404) 354-1449 E-mail: **torrance_stephens@yahoo.com**

Johnnie P. Stevenson Author, BA, MS, Retired Teacher of English with special interest in writing, drama, and interpreting poetry including Fathers of my Fathers, Dream Crasher, Children of a Far Country, etc. and The Lynching of Laura, novel. Contact Johnnie P. Stevenson, 12720 Nelson Avenue, Spencer, Oklahoma 73084 Phone: (405) 769-3748 E-mail: **johnniepstevenson@sbcglobal.com**

Lisa St. Hill The author dived into the world of the Entertainment Industry as a Fashion & Makeup Stylist. Her trek from the melting pot of Brooklyn into the high-profiled world of glitz and glamour, allowed a titillating voyeuristic peek into some of the most exciting experiences that every author lives to write of. Rubbing elbows and being the "right hand" woman to many top leading executives led her to pen one of the most insightful, knee-slapping and jaw-dropping accounts of what it really takes to make a movie in Hollywood. Lisa St. Hill, 28 Hazelplace, Irvington, New Jersey 07111 Phone: (718) 812-1327 E-mail: **Lisa_sthill@yahoo.com**

Michelle Stimpson Author, Public Teacher. Publications: Boaz Brown (Christian fiction), and 2 upcoming novels with Warner/Walk Worthy Press. Michelle also serves on the writing/editing team for Heartbeat, the official quarterly magazine of the Oak Cliff Bible Fellowship Church, Dr. Tony Evans, Pastor. Work in progress: Divas of Damascus Road. Michelle Stimpson, Post Office Box 2195, Cedar Hill, Texas 75106 E-mail: **michelle@michellestimpson.com** Website: **www.michellestimpson.com**

Rosalind Stormer Author, Christian Fiction. Ms. Stormer's debut novel entitled Healing The Breach is BlackRefer.com's best pick for Christian Fiction in 2004. Her second book is In The Wrong Hands (2005). Contact Ms. Rosalind Stormer, Heavenly Bound Publishing Company, Post Office Box 12106, Cincinnati, Ohio 45212 Website: **www.heavenlybound.org** E-mail: **rosalind@heavenlybound.org**

Cheryl Samuel Stover Author of From the Inside Out: How to Transform Your School to Increase Student Achievement, Elementary Basic Skills Through Black History; and Walk Out of the Shadows: Poetry to Inspire and Encourage Youth in the 21st Century. Dr. Cheryl Samuel Stover, 3516 John G. Richards Road, Post Office Box 153, Liberty Hill, South Carolina 29074 Phone: (803) 273-3772 E-mail: **chrylstover@yahoo.com** Website: **www.wastelandpress.net**

Vickie Stringer CEO of Triple Crown Publications, the world leader of urban literature publishing, and the author of the best selling books "Let That Be The Reason" and the sequel "Imagine This," and a third book, Dirty Red. "Let That Be the Reason," is a novel based on the author's real-life experiences. Contact Ms. Vickie Stringer, Triple Crown Publications, 4449 Easton Way, 2nd Floor, Columbus, Ohio 43219 Phone: (614) 934-1233 Fax: (614) 934-1593 E-mail: **manager@triplecrownpublications.com** Website: **www.triplecrownpublications.com**

Carol A. Taylor Former Random House book editor and the editor of the bestselling 4 book series, Brown Sugar. She has been in the book publishing business for over 10 years and is a published author, a freelance writer, book editor and an editorial consultant who has worked with book publishers, agents, best selling authors and up and coming writers. For book editing or consulting queries send an e-mail. Contact Ms. Carol A. Taylor, Black Star Consulting, 295 Clinton Avenue #E3, Brooklyn, New York 11205 E-mail: **carol@brownsugarbooks.com** Website: **www.BrownSugarBooks.com**

Marlene Taylor Author, Life Is What You Make It, Darlin', and A Silver Tongue, Marlene has created a booksigning event that is sweeping the nation called 3rd Thursdays Book Celebration!™ Working in collaboration with African American booksellers., Ms. Taylor is working to offset the potentially devastating drop in literacy levels among black American families. She visits prisons and shelters to speak up about the importance of literacy and how it can affect the overall quality of a person's life. Her book was the first book chosen for the Philadelphia Prison System's inmate reading group and was nominated for an NAACP Image Award for best fiction writing. Graduate of the University of Pennsylvania, Wharton School; publisher of Radio TV Interviews Media Magazine (RTIMM); founder of million dollar corporation, Accura Business Forms and Mailing Services. The company was formally recognized as one of the Philadelphia Business Journal's "Top One Hundred Fastest Growing Companies" for two consecutive years. Marlene Taylor, 633 West Rittenhouse Street, Suite B823, Philadelphia, Pennsylvania 19144 Phone: (215) 438-5283 E-mail: **mttw@msn.com**

Michael Taylor Author, publisher, personal development coach and entrepreneur, Michael Taylor is author of the book Brothers, Are You Listening: A Success Guide For The New Millennium. He is a motivational speaker who has overcome many of the obstacles facing black Americans. His workshops and seminars are designed to help men embrace the changing roles of manhood and to provide guidance and support for men who want to create balance and connection in their lives. The workshop covers relationships, health and fitness, fatherhood, spirituality and community service. Contact Mr. Michael Taylor, Creation Publishing Group, 1219 Nikki Lane, Stafford, Texas 77477 Phone: (713) 303-2067 E-mail: **mtaylor@creationpublishing.com** Website: **www.creationpublishing.com**

Ruby L. Taylor Author of Aunt Ruby, Do I Look Like God?, a thought provoking story for young readers. Taylor also became an entrepreneur and formed Connected 2 The Father Publishing, which distributes children's books, DVDs and merchandise that help children build spiritual relationships. She is also author of Love Don't Come Easy and If Only You Knew. Contact Ruby L. Taylor, M.S.W., Connected 2 The Father Publishing, 3203 Grace Avenue, Bronx, New York 10469 Phone: (718) 813-3363 E-mail: **RLT@connected2theFather.com** Website: **connected2theFather.com**

Willie Tee Author of The Winds of Destiny a nonfiction memoir about his families tragedies and triumphs on a small farm in the rural south from the 1950s to present. Born at Pender County, North Carolina during the 1950's. Retired US Army Staff Sergeant. Bachelors Degree in Criminal Justice. Member of American Legion and Prince George Rotary. Alumni of Virginia Commonwealth University and John Tyler Community College. Contact Mr. Willie Tee, Post Office Box 5171, Midlothian, Virginia 23112 Phone: (804) 739-8073 E-mail: **dwindsofdestiny@aol.com**

The Black Dot Author, writer, poet and emcee, his debut book entitled "HIP HOP DECODED" takes its readers from Hip Hop's ancient origin, to its modern day Matrix. The foreword to the book was written by legend and Live Rhyme Master Grandmaster Caz, and the illustrations were drawn by the legendary Graffiti Writer. The Black Dot,1461 First Avenue, Suite 291, New York, New York 10021 Phone: (212) 252-2270 E-mail: **blackdot16@matrixofhiphop.com** Website: **www.matrixofhiphop.com**

Brenda L Thomas Essence best selling author of THREESOME, FOURPLAY and the anthology FOUR DEGREES OF HEAT fame, Brenda L. Thomas released her third novel on January 4, 2005, THE VELVET ROPE. Ms. Thomas is a Philadelphia-based marketing professional who has made numerous appearances on national television in the wake of the Kobe Bryant case including CNN, Entertainment Tonight, ESPN and Dateline as an expert on the culture surrounding athletes. She also worked as the personal assistant to NBA All-Star Stephon X. Marbury. She also signed on to pen a novel with rapper Lil Kim and was featured in the Philadelphia Daily News as one of the Top 21 people to watch for in 2004. Contact Ms. Brenda Thomas, Admin Ink, Post Office Box 39111, Philadelphia, Pennsylvania 19136 Phone: (215) 331-4554 Fax: (215) 333-8053 E-mail: **brenda@phillywriter.com** Website: **www.phillywriter.com**

Jacquelin Thomas Award winning author with twenty-nine titles in print. Her books have garnered several awards, including two EMMA awards, the Romance In Color Reviewers Award, Readers Choice Award and the Atlanta Choice Award in the Religious & Spiritual category. Her other credits include contributions to the Women of Color Devotional Bible and Brides Noir magazine. Her current BET Books/New Spirit release is titled Soul Journey. Jacquelin is the founder and producer of the Faith-Based Fiction Lovers Weekend, a three-day conference designed to showcase the talents of a wide-ranging spectrum of gifted authors currently publishing in Christian/Inspirational Fiction. Ms. Jacquelin Thomas, Post Office Box 99374, Raleigh, North Carolina 27624 Website: **www.jacquelinthomas.com**

Carla Thompson An award-winning freelance writer, is the author of "Bearing Witness: Not So Crazy in Alabama" (May 2005, August Press) which chronicles the Harlem native's nearly six years of adventures while living in Montgomery, Alabama. Carla Thompson, 872 Pacific Street, Brooklyn, New York 11238 Phone: (718) 857-9574 E-mail: **cwrite@earthlink.net**

Carlyle Van Thompson Author of Tragic Black Buck: Racial Masquerading in the American Literary Imagination. Mr. Thompson is also Associate Professor of English at Medgar Evers College. Carlyle Thompson, PhD., Medgar Evers College, CUNY, 1650 Bedford Avenue, Brooklyn, New York 11225 E-mail: **kj190@juno.com**

Maxine E. Thompson An award-winning writer, Dr. Maxine E. Thompson has self-published 2 novels, The Ebony Tree and No Pockets in a Shroud and 2 ebooks, her short story collection, A Place Called Home and Second Chances. She has also written The Hush Hush Secrets of Creating a Life You Love, and How To Promote, Market, and Sell Your Book Via eBook Publishing. In May 2002, she edited and published her anthology, Saturday Morning. In February 2003, she published an ebook, The Hush Hush Secrets of Writing Fiction That Sells. In December 1998, she created On The Same Page, her website ezine column for new and self-published writers. She has written a monthly column on self-publishing on careermag.com. She has written a monthly column on bwip.org and a column on TheBlackMarket.com, regarding self-publishing. She had a published short story, "Dance of The DNA," on the Moondance website in the Summer '99 issue. She had an article on LA Woman Magazine's website. called, "Burn Out or Divine Discontent?" In June 2003, her short story, Valley Of The Shadow, was published in Kensington's Proverbs For The People. Maxine E. Thompson, Black Butterfly Press, Post Office Box 25279, Philadelphia Pennsylvania, 19119 E-mail: **maxtho@aol.com** Website: **www.maxinethompson.com**

Delores Thornton Author of "Ida Mae", "Babe", "Anybody Seen Junebug?", and "Divine Appointment: A Caregiver's Guide." She belongs to several organizations, including her own Marguerite Press (margueritepress.com), founded in 1996, Marguerite Press Promo, founded in 2003, and Black Writers On Tour. She is the host of "A Round 2 It" and "BookNook" Internet radio shows on artistfirst.com. Thornton is a columnist for the Indiana Herald newspaper, and for the HYPE Magazine. Additionally, she is the "Literary Expert" on blackrefer.com and she writes articles at doenetwork.com and for Oneswan Productions (an Internet site). Voted the "Literary Queen/2003" by C&B Books Distribution (of New York). Contact Delores Thornton, Marguerite Press, Post Office Box 53941, Indianapolis, Indiana 46253 Phone: (317) 626-6885 Fax: (317) 298-8889 E-mail: **dthorn4047@aol.com**   Website: **margueritepress.com**

Jessica Tilles Author, Jessica Tilles is a writer who specializes in all genres of fiction. She has several novels in print, In My Sister's Corner, Apple Tree, Sweet Revenge, the sequel to her debut, Anything Goes, and Fatal Desire. She is a recipient of the 2003 Memphis Black Writer's Conference Rising Star Award and The Jackson Mississippi Readers Club's Contribution to African American Literature Award. She has been featured in Booking Matters Magazine, Memphis VIP Magazine, and The Clarion-Ledger. Founder, The Writer's Assistant. Staff Writer, AMAG! Online. Contact Jessica Tilles, Xpress Yourself Publishing, Post Office Box 1615, Upper Marlboro, Maryland 20773 Phone: (301) 404-5615 Fax: (530) 685-5346 E-mail: **XYPublishing@AOL.com** Website: **www.jessicatilles.com**

G.C. Tobias Author. Crime novel entitled, Murder By Dawn. Contact G.C. Tobia, GLC International Book Company, Post Office Box 21225, White Hall, Arkansas 71612 E-mail: **gctobiasnovels@yahoo.com** Website: **www.gctobias.9k.com**

Pia Townes Author of the novel, Bloodless Affairs: A Tale of Necrophilia (2006). Johnson C. Smith University, 1988 BS in Biology; East Carolina School of Medicine, 1993 Medical Doctorate; Residency/ Psychiatric Medicine, Pitt County Memorial Hospital. Pia Townes, MD, Post Office Box 668034, Charlotte, North Carolina 28266 Phone: (704) 763-7810 E-mail: **pia@piatownes.net** Website: **www.piatownes.com**

Dempsey J. Travis Born: 02-25-20. Best Selling Author of twenty four books including I Refuse to Learn to Fail, Views from the Back of the Bus During WWII and Beyond, The Duke Ellington Primer, and The Louis Armstrong Odyssey. Mr. Travis is President of Travis Realty Company (1949-present). He is President of Travis Insurance Company (1951-present) and President/Publisher of Urban Research Press (1969-present). Contact Mr. Dempsey J. Travis, Urban Research Press, 840 East 87th Street, Chicago, Illinois 60619 Phone: (773) 994-7200 Fax: (773) 994-5191 E-mail: **travisdt88@sbcglobal.net** Website: **www.dempseytravis.com**

Martha Tucker Author of the suspense thriller The Mayor's Wife Wore Sapphires (Urban Classic Books). Martha (Marty) is the wife of the late Mayor Walter R. Tucker who served as Compton, California's Mayor for 12 years. Martha Tucker, Urban Classic Books, 6245 Bristol Parkway, # 265, Culver City, California 90230 E-mail: **writelink3@yahoo.com** Website: **www.urbanclassicbooks.com**

Brenda C. Turner Adjunct Professor, University of Phoenix-VA Campus, Senior Education Program Specialist, U.S. Department of Education, Researcher, Evangelist and Inspirational Speaker, Published Books: Tithing: Need or Greed Part I and II (2004, 2006, respectively). Dr. Brenda C. Turner, M.Ed., D.D., Post Office Box 44967, Fort Washington, Maryland 20749 Phone: (301) 292-5555 Fax: (301) 229-6876 E-mail: **jbtre2006@verizon.net**

Denise Turney Author of Portia, Love Has Many Faces and the book Spiral. Editor of The Book Lover's Haven. Denise Turney, c/o Chistell Publishing, 2500 Knights Road, Suite 19-01 Bensalem, Pennsylvania 19020 E-mail: **soulfar@aol.com** Website: **www.chistell.com**

Omar Tyree New York Times bestselling author, Omar Tyree is the winner of the 2001 NAACP Image Award for Outstanding Fiction. His books include Boss Lady, Diary of a Groupie, Leslie, Just Say No!, For the Love of Money, Sweet St. Louis, Single Mom, A Do Right Man and Flyy Girl. Omar Tyree, Post Office Box 562296, Charlotte, North Carolina 28256 E-mail: **Omar8Tyree@aol.com** Website: **www.omartyree.com**

Robert Upton Author of Racism@Work: Among the LORD's People, Mr. Upton is a gifted public speaker, community leader and evangelist. Robert Upton, Upton Consulting, 1407 Laurel Avenue, South East, Grand Rapids, Michigan 49501 Phone: (616) 243-5129 E-mail: **rsuptongr@sbcglobal.net** Website: **www.robertupton.com**

Valdez V. Fisher, Jr. The young Baltimore author who just won't quit. His book, I Ain't Bitin' My Tongue is one of the most unconventional books of its genre. Although pregnant with truth and delivering vital points, it manages to remain absolutely hilarious all throughout. His favorite pass-time is shooting pool, and hanging out in the Moose Lodge where he is a member. Valdez Vincent Fisher, Jr., Post Office Box 23951, Baltimore, Maryland 21203 Phone: (410) 456-3660 E-mail: **BooksByValdez@aol.com**

Eric Velasquez The authors latest book Le Mozart Noir tells the remarkable story of the Chevalier de Saint George, one of the most famous men in 18th Century France. Contact Mr. Eric Velasquez, Harry N. Abrams, 115 West 18th Street, New York, New York 10011 E-mail: **freepub@abramsbooks.com** Website: **www.hnabooks.com**

Carmel S. Victor Author of award-winning novel: "Facing Our Skeletons" and Best Work of Poetry for 2005 "Every Day Again: Real Life through Poetry and Short Stories." Carmel S. Victor, Post Office Box 1132, Union, New Jersey 07083 Phone: (908) 206-0828 E-mail: **carmel@carmelsvictor.com** Website: **www.carmelsvictor.com**

Frank X. Walker Author and librarian. Contact Mr. Frank X. Walker, 2197 Curtiswood Drive, Lexington, Kentucky 40505 Phone: (513) 375-7221 E-mail: **affrilachia@aol.com** Website: **www.frankxwalker.com**

Jacquelyn Dupont-Walker Co-author of the book A Model Of A Servant Bishop (The Ministry of Vinton Randolph Anderson) with Reverands Lee P. Washington, Ronald E. Braxton, Barbara Y. Glenn, and William D. Watley. Contact Ms. Jacquelyn Dupont-Walker, VRA Book Fund, 22 West Sherwood Drive, Overland, Missouri 63114 E-mail: **jdupontw@aol.com**

Tonya M. Evans-Walls Poet and author, Ms. Evans-Walls the author of Literary Law Guide for Authors: Copyright, Trademark, and Contracts in Plain Language, Seasons of Her and SHINE! Her short story, Not Tonight appears in a new anthology titled Proverbs for the People, published by Kensington. Tonya M. Evans-Walls, Esq., TME Law, 6703 Germantown Avenue, Suite 200, Philadelphia, Pennsylvania 19119 Phone: (215) 438-0468 Fax: (215) 438-0469 E-mail: **tme@tmelaw.net** Website: **www.tmelaw.net**

S. Courtney Walton Columnist, Author, and Editor of "FUNgasa: Free Oneself! The Magazine for African-American Home Educators" and homeschooling columnist for The Good News Herald in Saint Louis, Missouri, "Real Living...Real Learning with S. Courtney Walton." Founder of African-American Unschoolers, a national network of Black Homeschooling families. Courtney Walton, 7549 West Cactus Road #104-340, Peoria, Arizona 85381 Phone: (623) 205-9883 E-mail: **Editor@afamunschool.com** Website: **www.afamunschool.com**

Karen R. Ward CEO of Gracious Hands Literary Company. Author of "The King's Men," and the educational book entitled, "It's All About School," Ms. Ward also teaches educational course to both youth and adults. Contact Ms. Karen R. Ward, Gracious Hands Literary Company, Post Office Box 20167, Rochester, New York 14602 Phone: (585) 235-2976 E-mail: **kwgracioushands@yahoo.com** Website: **www.Gracioushandsliterary.com**

Vicki Ward Writer, publisher and CEO of Nubian Images Publishing which published Life's Spices From Seasoned Sistahs, A Collection of Life Stories From Mature Women of Color in 2005. The book garnered three awards including Book of the Year, Best Anthology, and Honorable Mention. Contact Ms. Vicki Ward, Publisher, Nubian Images Publishing, Post Office Box 1332, El Cerrito, California 94532 E-mail: **vicki@nubianimagespublishing.com** Website: **www.nubianimagespublishing.com**

Shellie R. Warren Full-time writer in Nashville, Tennessee, published in over 40 publications. An entertainment columnist for a local Gannett publication (All The Rage), a co-host on Freestyle, a local talk show, and the author of "Inside of Me: Lessons of Lust, Love and Redemption" (Relevant Books). Shellie Warren, 3840 Augusta Drive, Nashville, Tennessee 37207 E-mail: **shellie@shellierwarren.com** Website: **www.shellierwarren.com**

Cecil Washington The author writes science fiction, fantasy and horror, in addition to poetry. Some of his published books include Alien Erotica, A collection of short stories and verses, Walkware, A techno-thriller, Seeing Red---SF short story, sold to Alienskinmag.com, July 2003 issue, Asspitality"---song lyrics written for the "Avenue X" movie soundtrack (lyrics written in September 2003), and Badlands: An Underground Science Fiction Novel. Mr. Washington graduated from Bowie State University in 1993 with a degree in Business Administration, and minors in Marketing, Music, Communications and Economics. He works as a QA Test Analyst in the private sector. He is also the founder of Creative Brother's Sci-Fi Magazine. Cecil Washington, 5701 Galloway Drive, Oxon Hill, Maryland 20745 Phone: (301) 749-1505 E-mail: **cecilwashington@yahoo.com** Website: **www.cecilwashington.com**

Mason Weaver   Author of It's OK to Leave the Plantation, The Rope, and Diamond in the Rough, which discusses the social issues that affect us all and that bind us together. With a degree in Political Science from U.C. Berkeley and experience as a Congressional Aid, Federal Contract Specialist, teacher and entrepreneur, Mason is gifted with an extraordinary view of government and business. He is a noted conference speaker and guest lecture and has appeared on national TV, cable and news programs. He is often contacted by national news organizations to comment on breaking stories. Mason Weaver, Mason Media Company, 8301 Rio San Diego Drive, #10, San Diego, California 92108 E-mail: **masonweaver@masonweaver.com** Website: **www.masonweaver.com**

Nancy Weaver Recipient of Blackrefer.com Reviewer's Choice Award Outstanding Read for 2004 for her work In Her Presence: A Husband's Dirty Secret. Native Mississippian, Weaver was born and reared in the small town of Marks, Mississippi. She was valedictorian of State University of New York Empire State College. During her studies at Empire State College, Nancy won several scholastic awards, including the Cecil Cohen award for Black Studies. Nancy Weaver, Time & Chance Publishing, 149 Freedom Avenue, Staten Island, New York 10314   Phone: (718) 370-3655 E-mail: **contact@timeandchancepublishing.com**   Website: **www.timeandchancepublishing.com**

Kevin M. Weeks Author of The Street Life Series, a collection of crime fiction novels. The series chronicles main character Teco Jackson's action packed life as Teco chooses exciting careers and emerges as a strong male figure. Weeks is a 2007 New York Book Festival Award Winning Author and MosaicBooks.com 2007 Bestselling Author. His published works include: The Street Life Series: Is It Passion or Revenge? (Xlibris, 2008), and The Street Life Series: Is It Suicide or Murder? (Xlibris, 2006). Born on the rough side of West Philadelphia, Pennsylvania, the author has seen a lot on the streets, which is what brought about his debut novel. He is currently serving time at the Georgia Department of Corrections in Atlanta, Georgia. Kevin M. Weeks, 3961 Floyd Road; Suite 300, PMB 178, Austell, Georgia 30106 Phone: (404) 806-9542 E-mail: **thestreetlifeseries@yahoo.com** Website: **www.thestreetlifeseries.com**

Theressa Gunnels Wesley Author, Ms. Wesley edited Published Black American Writers Past and present: A Biographical and Bibliographical Directory (Scare Crow Press: Meteuchen New Jersey, 1975), a two-volume directory listing complete bibliographies and biographies of over 2000 writers. Contact Ms. Theressa G. Wesley, 14508 Sara Lynn Drive, Little Rock, Arkansas 72206 E-mail: **twesley@aol.com**

Sandra L. West The author has made many contributions in the area of academic writing. She wrote Encyclopedia of The Harlem Renaissance, published by Facts on File, Inc. 2003 (with co-author) which has captured a significant number of awards: Choice Library Journal Award for Best Reference Text, 2004; New Jersey Notable Book for 1995-2005, New Jersey Center for the Book; and, Best Historical Text Award from Memphis TN Black Writers Guild, 2005. In addition, the encyclopedia was adopted for Harlem at Its Zenith, course given at Thompson Middle School, Richmond, VA, 2006. West wrote about playwrights Mary Burrill, Joseph Seamon Cotter, Sr., and Joseph Seamon Cotter, Jr., for the on-line Black Drama Database, published by Alexander Street Press, 2002. She completed an entry about Maya Angelou for Contemporary American Women Poets: An A-Z Guide, Published by Greenwood 2002; and, she wrote the entry on Angelou for the Student's guide To Literature, published by Facts on File, 2008. West authored two entries for the 2008 Greenwood Encyclopedia of Hip Hop Literature (Black Book Clubs and Triple Crown Publishers). West wrote A Shared Joy of Reading for Emerge Magazine (1992) and Entrusted To Our Keeping for African Voices Magazine (2004). Outside of encyclopedias, Sandra L. West has written for on-line journals. From 2005 to 2007, she wrote several essays for Chickenbones: A Journal of Literary and African American Themes -- Badge of Honor (growing up in 1960s Newark New Jersey), We Are a Dancing People (black dance as documented in Harlem Renaissance literature), and Missing in Action: Leslie Garland Bolling's Witness to Humanity and Dignity (the life and work of 1930s folk artist Leslie Garland Bolling). For on-line journal The Newark Metro, in 2006 West contributed the essay Rich in Grace, memoir of an urban bibliphile. As a poet, West's "Wendy, Stand up With Your Proud Hair" was anthologized in Say That The River Turns: The Impact of Gwendolyn Brooks (Third World Press, 1987). Contact Ms. Sandra L. West, 177 Camden Street, Newark, New Jersey 07103 Phone: (973) 424-0538 E-mail: **slwest@andromeda.rutgers.edu**

Carole E. Wharton Author. Carole Wharton, 1015 Morning View Drive, #210, Escondido, California 92026 Phone: (323) 244-5579 E-mail: **wadeinthebluewater@sbcglobal.net**

Dorrie Williams-Wheeler Entertainment journalist, screenwriter, educator, web designer and author of three books, Sparkledoll Always Into Something, Be My Sorority Sister-Under Pressure and The Unplanned Pregnancy Handbook. She has worked as an educator, curriculum developer and as a computer specialist Intranet/Internet for the Department of Defense. Completed her Masters of Science in Education Degree in Curriculum & Instruction with a major in Instructional Technology and her undergraduate course work at Southern Illinois University at Carbondale. Dorrie Williams-Wheeler, Post Office Box 56173, Virginia Beach, Virginia 23454 E-mail: **dorrie@sparkledoll.com** Website: **www.dorrieinteractive.com**

D. S. White Author of Age is Just a Number: Adventures in Online Dating (Vol I). D.S. White, Divine Truth Press, Post Office Box 145, Whitehall, Pennsylvania 18052 Fax: (530) 504-7094 E-mail: **dee@deeswhite.com** Website: **www.deeswhite.com**

Tanya White Editor/Writer of Tanya's Tips weekly international e-newsletter and author of Relationship Reruns: How To Break The Cycle of Choosing The Wrong People For The Right Relationships (August, 2008), and How To Deal With A Difficult Woman. Tanya White, Post Office Box #16635, Louisville, Kentucky 40256 Phone: (502) 449-0157 Fax: (502) 449-0157 E-mail: **tanya@tanyawhite.com** Website: **www.tanyawhite.com**

Crystal E. Wilkinson Born in Hamilton, Ohio, in 1962 and raised in Indian Creek, Kentucky, Crystal graduated from Eastern Kentucky University and worked for many years as a public relations professional. She became assistant director of the Carnegie Center for Literacy and Learning in Lexington, where she served as writing mentor and taught creative writing classes for the center. She is a former chair of the creative writing department for the Kentucky Governor School for the Arts and has taught creative writing at the University of Kentucky. She was recently Writer in Residence/Visiting Professor at Eastern Kentucky University and is now an assistant professor of Creative Writing in Indiana University's MFA program. Crystal is the 2002 recipient of the Chaffin Award for Appalachian Literature and is a member of a Lexington-based writing collective, The Affrilachian Poets. She is the author of two books, Blackberries, Blackberries (July 2000), and Water Street, recently a long-list finalist for the prestigious Orange Prize and short-listed for a Zora Neal Hurston/Richard Wright Foundation Legacy Award in fiction (September 2002), both published by Toby Press. In 2001 Blackberries was named Best Debut Fiction by Today's Librarian Magazine. She has been published in the anthologies Confronting Appalachian Stereotypes: Back Talk from an American Region (University of Kentucky Press 1999); Gifts From Our Grandmothers (Crown Publishers, a Division of Random House, May 2000); Home and Beyond: A Half-Century of Short Stories by Kentucky Writers (University Press of Kentucky 2001); A Kentucky Christmas (University Press of Kentucky 2003) and Gumbo: Stories by Black Writers (Doubleday, Harlem Moon Press Fall 2002). Crystal E. Wilkinson, c/o Indiana University, English Department, 442 Ballantine Hall, 1020 Kirkwood Avenue, Bloomington, Indiana. E-mail: **WilkinsonCrystal@aol.com**

Barbara Joe-Williams Author/Publisher. Contact Barbara Joe-Williams, Amani Publishing, Post Office Box 12045, Tallahassee, Florida 32317 Phone: (850) 264-3341   E-mail: **Amanipublishing@aol.com** Website: **www.amanipublishing.net**

DWe Williams Accomplished storyteller, playwright, performer and educator. DWe, a graduate of North Carolina A&T State University and SIU Carbondale holds a Master's degree with a double major in Speech and Theater. DWe has seven children and resides in Oklahoma City, Oklahoma. DWeLo Publications is a joint venture between DWe Williams and Loretta Ford. These two talented women have combined their talents to create a series of children's books entitled "We Were Always There." This series focuses on the contributions and accomplishments of African American heroes. The first book in this series is Bridget "Biddy" Mason: A Walking Sensation. DWe Williams, 2609 North West 38th Street, Oklahoma City, Oklahoma 73112 E-mail: **ewdwms@sbcglobal.net**

Helen E. Williams Author and librarian; B.A., Morris College, 1954, English/Social Studies; M.S.L.S., Atlanta, University, 1960; Library Science; C.A.S., University of Illinois-Urbana, 1968; Library Science; Ph.D., University of Wisconsin -Madison, 1983, Library Science. State Certifications for New York and Arizona, School Librarian. 1981-83, Lecturer, College of LIS and the College of Education, University of MD, 1983-1991, Assistant Professor, College of Library and Information Services and the College of Education, University of Maryland. Summer 1991, Associate Professor, School of LIS, University of Hawaii. Also a National University of Lesotho Professor of librarianship/reviewer. Ms. Helen E. Williams, National University of Lesotho, Naseru, Lesotho, South Africa, 8404 Cathedral Avenue, New Carrollton, Maryland 20784 E-mail: **helen.williams@pgcps.org**

Hubert P. Williams, Jr. An anointed singer, songwriter, and producer that also writes poetry and inspirarional messages to uplift the Name of the Lord and the children of the Lord. Mr. Williams also writes songs and instrumental music for other artists. Contact Minister Hubert P. Williams, Jr., Trinity Music Group, 2907 Kingfisher Drive, Fayetteville, North Carolina Phone: (910) 977-7354 E-mail: **willi526@earthlink.net**

Kim Williams The authors debut novel, 40 Hours And An Unwritten Rule: The Diary of a Nigger, Negro, Colored, Black, African-American Woman, was released, July 2004. Kim graduated from the University of North Texas with a degree in Radio-TV-Film in 1996. She currently is writing her second novel. Kim Williams, Butterfly Ink Publishing, Post Office Box 56874, Sherman Oaks, California 91413 E-mail: **kim@butterflyinkpublishing.com** Website: **www.butterflyinkpublishing.com**

Jennifer L. Williams Author of the book My Bowl of Cherries is All Pitts. Her company Gentle Touch Design and Publications also designs greeting cards. Contact Ms. Jennifer Williams, Gentle Touch Design & Publications, Post Office Box 1757, Clinton, Maryland 20735 E-mail: **info@phraseology.net** Website: **gentleto@gentletouchdesigns.com**

Laura Williams The authors' debut work, Lead Us Not Into Temptation, is a novel depicting the life of a desperate and lonely young woman who's desire for love is so strong that she crosses and destroys all moral boundaries. Contact Ms. Laura Williams, 5121 Kenwood Road, Durham, North Carolina 27712 Phone: (919) 471-5121 E-mail: **Godzfavor2@yahoo.com** Website: **www.Godzfavor.com**

Maiya Williams Began her career as a children's author with the publication of her middle-grade novel The Golden Hour in 2005. Her inclusion of African-American main characters is a rarity in this genre and her skill and sense of adventure is deeply felt in each title she writes. The sequel, The Hour of The Cobra, is her second novel. Maiya Williams, Harry N. Abrams, 115 West 18th Street, New York, New York 10010 E-mail: **freepub@abramsbooks.com**

Patricia H. Williams Author of No Longer Will I Hide The Stranger In My Bed based on a true story of an 18 year Domestic Violence situation. Contact Ms. Patricia H. Williams, RAPHA, Inc, Post Office Box 1184, Groton, Connecticut 06340 Phone: (860) 449-1374 E-mail: **joyindamornin@earthlink.net**

Richard Williams An author and health educator, Dr. Williams' emphasis of study includes psychology, religion, and health. Consultant, he conducts workshops and seminars on the family and on health. He speaks on issues affecting African-Americans, including problems facing the black male, problems facing the black female, effectively educating the black child. He explains why African-Americans must determine their destiny by themselves and for themselves. He is the author of They Stole It But You Must Return It, as a young classic, and Torches On The Road Of Passage is particularly helpful to the growth of the young male's development into manhood and father hood. He has appeared on more that 70 different radio and TV talk shows including The Oprah Winfrey Show and Black Entertainment Network (BET). Dr. Richard Williams, 56 Wildbriar Road, Rochester, New York 14623 Phone: (419) 297-6636 E-mail: **aym@blackfamilysite.com** Website: **blackfamilysite.com**

Rozalia Williams Author, Educator, Publisher, President of Hidden Curriculum Education, Inc. Author of the College FAQ Book: Over 5,000 Not Frequently Asked Questions About College!, Rozalia Williams holds an Ed.D. from Harvard University. A college administrator for over twenty years, she has devoted her professional career to creating, implementing and evaluating student development programs. She is founder and president of Hidden Curriculum Education, Inc., where she teaches the two-day intensive College Life Skills Course. Her experiences as a sixteen-year old college student, retention counselor, pre-college program director, assistant to the vice president of student affairs, branch campus director, assistant dean and instructor of first year experience courses at two-and four-year institutions frame the questions for the book and the course. Contact Dr. Rozalia Williams, Post Office Box 222041, Hollywood, Florida 33022 Phone: (954) 457-8098 Fax: (954) 457-3331 E-mail: **hiddencurriculum@aol.com**

Sonja T. Williams Author of the children's book, "Aloma and the Red Suitcase." Sonja T. Williams, STP Publishing, Post Office Box 291712, Columbia, South Carolina 29229 E-mail: **sonii_t@yahoo.com**

Terrie Williams Author and President / Founder of The Terrie Williams Agency and The Stay Strong Foundation, Terrie Williams' first book The Personal Touch: What You Really Need to Succeed in Today's Fast-Paced Business World (1994 Warner Books) is a best-selling book on developing business practices and includes a foreword by Bill Cosby and a preface by Jonathan M. Tisch, the president and CEO of Loews Hotels. Another of her books is Stay Strong: Life Lessons for Teens (Scholastic 2001), and another is a inspirational, self-help book called A Plentiful Harvest: Creating Balance and Harmony Through Seven Living Virtues (2001 Warner Books). She is a social worker by training and a public relations professional by her own design and is a most sought-after lecturer, dealmaker, a mentor, an executive coach, and a community activist. She has shared her own brand of success and personal development strategies with numerous Fortune 500 companies, and organizations such as New York University's Continuing Education Program, the New School for Social Research, and The National Hockey League, The National Basketball Association, among others. Terrie Williams Agency, 382 Central Park West, Suite 7R, New York, New York 10023 Phone: (212) 316-0305 Fax: (212) 749-8867 E-mail: **tmwms@terriewilliams.com** Website: **terriewilliams.com**

Ann E. Williamson A professional coach, Dr. Ann E. Williamson specializes in assisting individuals make changes in their personal and professional lives. She is co-author of the Survival Skills for African American Women (2007). She is also the founder and executive director of the Butterfly House Inc. Ms. Ann E. Williamson, Ph.D., 321 North Cottonwood Drive, Gilbert, Arizona 85234 Phone: (480) 892-7756 E-mail: **dranelwi@aol.com** Website: **www.annewilliamson.com**

Ramon Williamson Author of "Six Simple Things That Can Change Your Life," is a successful entrepreneur, television personality, motivational speaker and life coach to the stars. Because of his unique ability to consistently deliver the strategic advice, coaching and systems needed to advance personal and business goals, he is a trusted advisor to CEOs, celebrities, businesses large and small, and everyday people at all levels of success. Ramon Williamson, Ramon Williamson Coaching, Post Office Box 778, Leesburg, Virginia 20178 Phone: (800) 811-1577 E-mail: **support@ramonwilliamson.com** Website: **www.ramonwilliamson.com**

Emily Means-Willis Educator, author, literary reviewer, columnist. After 37 years as an instructor in secondary education, Emily Means-Willis, recently retired and has published a novel entitled "Looking for that Silver Spoon". She also writes for various magazines. A second novel "Flip Side of the Coin" will be released in 2007. Emily Means-Willis, We, Us and Company, International, 419 Douglas Street, Park Forest, Illinois 60466 Phone: (708) 769-4116 E-mail: **pamemi@comcast.net** Website: **www.weusandcompany.com**

Jessica Nyel Willis Author, writer of articles for magazines, short stories, film script, teleplays, sitcom and drama scripts, as well as novels for young adults and adults. Contact Jessica Nyel Willis, 8629 144th Street, #2, Jamaica, New York 11435 Phone: (646) 207-1877 E-mail: **JessicaNyelWillis@hotmail.com**

Anita L. Wills Lecturer, and Historian, Anita's specialty is Free Persons of Color, in Colonial Virginia. Author of numerous articles and a book, Notes And Documents of Free Persons of Color: Four Hundred Years of An American Family History (Lulu Press, 2003). Anita Wills, 2041 Miramonte Avenue, #12, San Leandro, California 94578 E-mail: **alani2@yahoo.com**

Raymond A. Winbush Director of the Institute for Urban Research at Morgan State University in Baltimore, Maryland. Author of The Warrior Method: A Program for Rearing Healthy Black Boys (2001) and Should America Pay?: Slavery and the Raging Debate on Reparations (2003), both published by Amistad/HarperCollins. Received his Ph.D. from the University of Chicago in psychology and is considered a scholar-activist on issues involving African-centered education, reparations and developmental issues affecting Black boys. He has taught at Alabama A & M, Fisk and Vanderbilt Universities. Raymond A. Winbush, PhD., 1190 West Northern Parkway, Suite 717, Baltimore Maryland 21210 Phone: (410) 532-2252 Fax: (410) 988-3018 E-mail: **rwinbush@usit.net** Website: **www.raymondwinbush.com**

Shakeeta Winfrey A native of Nashville, Tennessee, Shakeeta A. Winfrey now makes her home in the metropolitan Atlanta community. She is graciously utilizing her life's journey as a testimony to women who are seeking to overcome the obstacles that may be hindering their success. As such, her journey is chronicled in her just-released book, The Other Winfrey, wherein she candidly shares her story of what it is to live in the shadow of one of the world's most admired celebrities, her cousin Oprah Winfrey. Shakeeta Winfrey, The Other Winfrey, 400 Colony Square, Suite 200, Atlanta, Georgia 30361 Phone: (770) 323-3114 Fax: (770) 593-7840 E-mail: **winfreyinc@gmail.com**

Laureen Wishom Nationally known guest speaker and author of five how to business books, The Greater Houston Resource Guide, The Source Newsletter, The Entrepreneur and Career Professionals Newsletter, and The 501(c)3 Newsletter. Her articles have appeared in numerous newspapers, magazines, and online publications. She holds a Bachelor's degree in General Education, a Master's degree in Psychology/Sociology and a Ph.D. in Psychology/Christian Counseling. She holds a Board Goverance and Leadership certification, and certificate for Productivity Education from the Academy of Human Potential. She is a certified hospice volunteer and a commissioned lay Chaplain. Dr. Laureen Wishom, Masterpiece Solutions, LLC, Post Office Box 441234, Houston, Texas 77244 Phone: (281) 584-0348 Fax: (281) 584-0355 E-mail: **drlaureen@drlaureen.com** Website: **www.masterpiecesolutions.biz**

L. Marie Wood Author of the Bram Stoker Award recommended novel "Crescendo." Her short stories can be found in anthologies such as The Black Spiral and Chimeraworld, as well as in her collection of 35 tales, "Caliginy," also recommended for a Stoker Award in 2003. Editor with Cyber-Pulp Publishing. Ms. L. Marie Woods E-mail: **author@lmariewood.com** Website: **www.lmariewood.com**

Petra E. Woodard An educator, author, poet and inspirational speaker, and certified counselor, Petra also speaks on school organization & advisement and career guidance. Her debut novel INcomPLETE DENIAL, a suspenseful romance, was published in 2004. Her plays have been performed in various communities for over ten years. Petra Woodard, Post Office Box 273, Arcadia, Oklahoma 73007 Phone: (405) 370-1604 Fax: (405) 396-2290 E-mail: **mwoodard@ionet.net**

Alice G. Wootson The author of ten contemporary romance novels. Her 10th novel, Ready to Take a Chance, was released by Kimani/Arabesque in 2006. All of her novels, including her latest, Perfect Wedding, have been published by BET Books/Arabesque. Alice G. Wootson, Post Office Box 18832, Philadelphia, Pennsylvania 19119 E-mail: **agwwriter@email.com** Website: **www.alicewootson.net**

Frances Faye Ward-Worthy Graduated from the Art Institute of Atlanta (music business and video); had classes at Cranbrook Institute (film & video); scriptwriting with Tim Jeffrey. I've been Production Assistant on music videos, documentaries and TV productions. given lectures and workshops on rap/hip hop and the Black Madonna. Ms. Frances Faye Ward-Worthy, 242 Chalmers, Detroit, Michigan 48215 E-mail: **worth23karat@yahoo.com**

Sankofa Camille Yarbrough Author of several young adult and children's books, Yarbrough, is a multi-talented veteran of theater, film, dance, and song. Vanguard Records recorded her first album of original songs and poetry, "The Iron Pot Cooker" in 1975 and re-released it in 2000. Community activist, writer, teacher, composer, singer, dancer, radio talk show host, and lecturer, her work as an actress can be heard on the cast album of Lorrain Hansberry's Play, "To Be Young, Gifted and Black." She was a faculty member of the Black Studies Department of City College of New York for twelve years and has contributed articles to the Journal of African Civilizations and the New York Times" Drama Section. Sankofa Camille Yarbrough, African American Traditions Workshop, 80 Saint Nicholas Avenue Suite 4G, New York, New York 10026 Phone: (212) 865-7460 E-mail: **Yarbroughchosan@aol.com** Website: **www.ancestorhouse.net**

Francine A. Yates Born in Jacksonville, Florida, Francine's hometown was the setting for her first book, Carrie O and Me (What A Woman God Made). In 2002, Fran founded her own publishing company, Yates Publishing, LLC which produced the sequel, Faith Holds the Key (2004). Fran has been a mentor at an Indianapolis public school. She created a book club at the Wheelers Boys & Girls Club of Indianapolis. She studied Business at Indiana University/Purdue University in Indianapolis. Memberships include: Urban Arts Consortium of Indianapolis Writer's Group, Authors Supporting Authors Positively (ASAP), Women in Networking (W.I.N.) Francine, A. Yates, Yates Publishing, LLC, Post Office Box 18982, Indianapolis, Indiana 46218 E-mail: **fran3214@yahoo.com** Website: **www.franyates.net**

Samuel F. Yette Born in Harriman, Tennessee, in 1929. Mr. Samuel F. Yette attended Morristown (Tennessee) college; B.A. Tennessee State University; MA Indiana University. He is the author of "The Choice: The Issue of Black Survival in America" (1971), and "Washington and Two Marches: The Third American Revolution" (1984). He is also a photo-journalist whose works have appeared in National Geographic, People Magazine, Jet Magazine and the movie, "Kiss the Girls" (Paramount), starring Morgan Freeman. He worked as a reporter for the Afro-American and Dayton Journal Herald newspapers; associate editor of Ebony: information director at Tuskegee institute; executive secretary of Peace Corps; Washington correspondent for Newsweek, and professor of journalism at Howard University where, in 1977, he was designated a University Scholar. He worked in the documentation of the 1984 and 1988 presidential campaigns of the Reverand Jesse L. Jackson. Contact Mr. Samuel F. Yette, Cottage Books, 4000 Deerfield Road, Knoxville, Tennessee 37921 Phone: (865) 584-9735 Fax: (865) 766-0546 E-mail: **cottagebooks@comcast.net**

Roxanne Marie Zeigler Author of "Are You Looking Through The Window of My Soul?" Roxanne Marie Zeigler, 9401 NE 45th Street, Spencer, Oklahoma 73084 Phone: (405) 761-6869 E-mail: **roxanneswindow2003@hotmail.com**

Zhana Author of Success Strategies for Black People and Black Success Stories. Zhana is an African American woman living in London, and has been writing for many years. Her first major work, Sojourn, a collection of writings by Black women in Britain about Black mother/daughter relationships, sisterhood and friendships, was published by Methuen London Ltd. in 1988. Her new book Black Success Stories will be available in the autumn. Contact Zhana, Zhana Books, Post Office Box 12156, London SE5 8ZJ United Kingdom E-mail: **zhana2002@hotmail.com** Website: **www.blacksuccess1.com**

Gary A. Watson, Esq.
Attorney * Lecturer

Gary A. Watson was an attorney in the Law Department of Universal Pictures at MCA, Inc., in Universal City, California, before establishing his own law firm. He handled a broad range of legal matters for clients. Specifically he negotiated, arranged and prepared contracts for the financing, development, production and exploitation of motion pictures, television programs, books, plays and musical recordings. He served as lead attorney for Universal Pictures on "The Guardian," a film by the director of "The Exorcist" and "The French Connection," William Friedkin; two pictures by Spike Lee, "Mo' Better Blues" and "Jungle Fever;" "Childs Play 3;" Wes Craven's and Shep Gordon's "People Under The Stairs;" the John Goodman starrer, "The Babe;" the film featuring Goldie Hawn, Bruce Willis and Meryl Streep, directed by Robert Zemekis, entitled "Death Becomes Her;" and the Oscar Award winning picture starring Al Pacino titled "Scent of a Woman." His music industry clients have included Motown Records, Def Jam Records, Tommy Boy Records, and Dr. Dre. In the motion picture industry he represented BET Pictures, II and the producers of the feature film, "Get On The Bus," which was executive produced by Spike Lee and starred Ossie Davis and Charles Dutton. Television industry clients included BET, actresses Lisa Gay Hamilton from "The Practice" and Suzzanne Douglas from the series, "The Parenthood," consulting producer, Kathleen McGhee Anderson on the series, "Soul Food" and "Any Day Now" and the producer of the movie "Free of Eden," which stars Sidney Poitier.

Before joining Universal Pictures' Law Department, Gary was an associate with the law firm of Dern, Mason and Floum located in Century City, California. There he was responsible for drafting, commenting on and negotiating rights acquisition, writers, producers, directors, actors, composers, distribution and sales agency agreements and completion bonds for a wide range of clients in the television and motion picture industries. He handled matters for clients who are well established in their respective fields, such as Dustin Hoffman, Warren Beatty, Nicole Kidman, Michael Jackson, Oliver Stone, Gene Hackman and others.

Mr. Watson is Chair Elect and a Governing Committee Member of the American Bar Association's Forum on Entertainment and Sports Industries and served as the Division Chair of the Motion Pictures, Television, Cable and Radio Division. He also serves on the Board of Trustees of the American Cinematheque, and is a member of the Beverly Hills and Los Angeles County Bar Associations, as well as, the State Bar of California.

He is an active member of the Black Entertainment and Sports Lawyers Association (BESLA) and has served as a member of the Board of Directors as well as Chair of the Public Relations Committee and has been inducted into the BESLA Hall of Fame.

Book Clubs

African American Book Club Summit (AABCS) Annual. Contact Pamela Walker-Williams, Pageturner.net, PMB-120, 2951 Marina Bay Drive, #130, League City, Texas 77573 Phone: (866) 875-1044 E-mail: **pwsquare@pageturner.net** Website: **www.pageturner.net**

African American Literature Book Club Founded in 1997 by Troy Johnson, the AALBC website features author profiles, book excerpts, poetry, online discussion boards, chat sessions, contests, and information about upcoming events. AALBC, 55 West 116th Street #195, Harlem, New York 10026 Phone: (866) 603-8394 E-mail: **troy@aalbc.com** Website: **www.aalbc.com**

Apooo Information regarding African American Literature. Features upcoming literary events, book reviews, forthcoming books, bookstore. Contact Ms. Yasmin Coleman, A Place of Our Own, 4426 Pinewood Court, Harrisburg, Pennsylvania 17112 Website: **www.apooo.org**

Between the Covers Book Club The first WVON radio station book club launched by award-winning air personality, Sharon K. McGhee who is also News Director at WVON. Contact Monique Smith, WVON 1690 AM, 3350 South Kedzie, Chicago, Illinois 60623 Phone: (773) 247-6200 E-mail: **monews74@hotmail.com** Website: **www.wvon.com**

Black Expressions African American book club. Also on-line book seller. Contact Diversity City Media, 225 West 3rd Street, Suite 203, Long Beach, California 90802 Phone: (562) 209-0616 Website: **www.blackexpressions.com**

BookClubEtc. A group of 15+ African American men and women who meet on a monthly basis to discuss books by and about our people. We have been together for five years. We also host book signings and poetry readings. Jennifer Belfield, 217 Union Street, Hampton, Virginia 23669 E-Mail: **BookClubEtc@aol.com**

Escapade 'A Soulful Circle' Book Club We read books by African American authors of fiction and non-fiction literature. We meet on the fourth Saturday of each month. Escapade Book Club, Post Office Box 3581, San Leandro, California 94578 Phone: (510) 332-9997 E-mail: **escapadebookclub@yahoo.com** Website: **www.escapadebookclub.com**

Grits Online Reading Club On-line book club for men and women who love reading and discussing classic and contemporary African American Literature! Club Managers: Marlive Harris, aka MsGRITS and Loretta Brown, aka MsLo. The Grits, Post Office Box 118154, Carrollton, Texas 75011 E-mail: **clubmanagers@thegrits.com** Website: **www.thegrits.com**

Imani Book Club Diverse group of African-American women who enjoy reading. Contact Imani Book Club, c/o Cashana, Post Office Box 240063, Montgomery, Alabama 36124 E-mail: **imanivoices@aol.com** Website: **www.imanivoices.com**

Kindred Spirits Book Club African-American women meet to discuss a variety of literary accomplishments with a focus on Black authors. Contact Ms. Sharon Hollis, Kindred Spirits Book Club, 11024 Balboa Boulevard. Suite #634, Granada Hills, California 91344 E-mail: **contact@kindredspiritsbookclub.org** Website: **www.kindredspiritsbookclub.org**

Mindful Thinker's Bookclub We consist of (6) members and live throughout the Dallas, Texas Metroplex. Kemmerly Beckham, Mindful Thinker's Bookclub, 5214 Banting Way, Dallas, Texas 75227 E-mail: **members@mindfulthinkers.org** Website: **www.mindfulthinkers.org**

MWG Book Club Multicultural Writers Guild, Inc. aka (MWG, Inc.) is a literary and small press company dedicated to creative writers and readers looking for all sorts of resources. Contact Ms. Mikki Ealey, Founder. MWG Book Club, Post Office Box 6259 Bronx, New York 10451 E-mail: **mwgnews@mdenterp.com** Website: **www.mdenterp.com**

OOSA Online Book Club Online book club and reviewing team that focuses on African American authors. OOSA Online Book Club, Midwest Chapter, Post Office Box 220336, Saint. Louis, Missouri 63122 E-mail: **oosaonlinebookclub@yahoo.com**

Q.U.E.E.N.S. Book Club of Atlanta (Quality Unique Elegance Exquisite & Naturally Sophisticated) is a group who possess a genuine passion in reading thought-provoking novels and having a good time. Contact Q.U.E.E.N.S. Book Club of Atlanta, 2884 Pearl Street, East Point, Georgia 30344 Phone: (404) 543-7183 E-mail: **queensbookclubofatlanta@yahoo.com**

Rawsistaz Founded in September 2000 by Tee C. Royal with a focus on reading and writing (RAW). RAWSISTAZ Reviewers, Post Office Box 1362, Duluth, Georgia 30096 Phone: (775) 363-8683 Fax: (775) 416-4540 E-mail: **tee@rawsistaz.com** Website: **www.rawsistaz.com**

Sistah Circle Book Club, Inc. (The) Founded,1999. Group of avid African American women readers which seeks to promote reading among African American women and their families. The Sistah Circle Book Club, Post Office Box 41035, Dallas, Texas 75241 E-mail: **thesistahcircle@thesistahcircle.com** Website: **www.thesistahcircle.com**

Sistahs Book Club Suzetta M. Perkins, cofounder and president. Sistahs Book Club, Post Office Box 64424, Fayetteville, North Carolina 28306 **nubianqe2@aol.com** Website: **www.suzettaperkins.com**

SistahFriend Book Club Book club for all women who share a love and respect for African-American Literature. SistahFriend Book Club, PMB #351, 4611 Hardscrabble Road, Columbia, South Carolina 29229 E-mail: **admin@sistahfriend.com**

Thumper's Corner Reading group. Thumper's Corner, AALBC, 55 West 116th Street, #195, Harlem, New York 10026 Phone: (866) 603-8394 Website: **www.thumperscorner.com**

UC His Glory Book Club Online book club supporting Urban Christian authors. Sheila E. Lipsey, President. UC His Glory Book Club, Post Office Box 128, Reynoldsburg, Ohio 43068 E-mail: **urbanchristianinfo@yahoo.com** Website: **www.urbanchristianonline.net**

Bookstores

A & B Distributors Wholesaler specializing in Afro-American books, tapes and gifts. Contact A & B Distributors, 223 Duffield, Brooklyn, New York 11201 Phone: (718) 783-7808 Fax: (718) 783-7267 E-mail: **ericgift2002@yahoo.com** Website: **www.anbbooks.com**

African American Books Online Guide To African-American books. AABooks, 5036 Switch Grass, Naperville, Illinois 60564 E-mail: **info@aabooks.com** Website: **www.aabooks.com**

African American Images We have one of the largest Black-owned bookstores in the country, with over 10,000 square feet of space and over 4,000 titles. Mr. Jawanza Kunjufu, African-American Images, 1909 West 95th Street, Chicago, Illinois 60643 Phone: (773) 445-0322 E-mail: **aarcher@africanamericanimages.com** Website: **www.africanamericanimages.com**

African Imports Since 1990. Operates two super stores in Dallas and Fort Worth, Texas. Raymond and Blessing Odimegwu, Managers. African Imports, South West Center Mall, 3662 West Camp Wisdom, #1045, Dallas, Texas 75237 Phone: (877) 8-AFRICA Fax: (972) 296-9550 E-mail: **sales@africanimportsusa.com** Website: **www.africanimportsusa.com**

Afro-American Book Stop Sells books written by and about or relevant to African Americans. Large selection. Two locations. Afro-American Book Shop, 7056 Read Boulevard, New Orleans, Louisiana 70127 Phone: (504) 243-2436 E-mail: **afrobooks2@aol.com** Website: **www.theafroamericanbookstop.com**

Afro Books Bookstore. Book sellers. Afro Books, 871 Ralph D. Abernathy Boulevard, Atlanta, Georgia 30310 Phone: (404) 755-0095 Fax: (404) 755-0756

Afrocentric Books II African American bookstore. Book Signings. Afrocentric Books, 4655 South Martin Luther King Drive, Chicago, Illinois 60653 Phone: (773) 924-3966 E-mail: **afrocentricbst@sbcglobal.net**

A Good Book Located in the heart of Woodlawn Village, sells new/used books and related novelty gifts. We specialize in providing self-help titles that promote a better living spiritually, financially and emotionally. We offer free space for bookclub meetings and workshops and we support and promote local authors. We host a monthly poetry night every last Sunday of each month. Julie Williamson, 2101 Gwynn Oak Avenue, Baltimore, Maryland 21207 Phone: (410) 944-5565 Fax: (443) 267-0113 E-mail: **info@agoodbook.biz** Website: **www.agoodbook.biz**

Alkebu-lan Images Bookstore, book club, African American art and educational materials; positive Black apparel; importer; wholesaler, bookseller. Contact Alkebu-lan Images, 2721 Jefferson Street, Nashville, Tennessee 37203 Phone: (615) 321-4111 Fax: (615) 627-0018 E-mail: **kenyatta36@aol.com** Website: **www.alkebulanimages.homestead.com**

Anointed Creation We offer a variety of high quality African figurines, sculptures, fine art, faith based books, bibles and African home decor. Contact Manager, Town & Country Plaza, 1816 Frink Street, Cayce, South Carolina 29033   E-mail: **owner@anointedcreation.com** Website: **www.anointedcreation.com**

Ashay by the Bay On-line Bookstore. Established in 1997. On-line reseller of African American Children's Books and Educational Products. We have a huge selection of books for children Pre School to High School and some great books for adults. Ashay by the Bay, Post Office Box 2394, Union City, California 94587 Phone: (510) 520-2742 Fax: (510) 498-4459 E-mail: **poetashay@aol.com** Website: **www.ashaybythebay.com**

Biashara.Biz Ltd Online store. Sells books. Contact Pauline Omolo, Biashara.Biz Ltd, Post Office Box 4282, 00506, Nyayo Stadium, Nairobi, Kenya Phone: 254 20 2727632 Fax: 254 20 2727269 E-mail: **biashara@africaonline.co.ke** Website: **www.biashara.biz**

Black Book Plus An African-American Bookstore. Online bookseller. Contact Black Book Plus, Post Office Box 030064, Elmont, New York 11003   Phone: (877) 227-6977   E-mail: **blackbookplus@verizon.net** Website: **www.blackbookplus.com**

Black Bookworm Bookseller. Contact Black Bookworm, 605 East Berry Street, Suite #110, Fort Worth, Texas 76110 Phone: (817) 923-9661 E-mail: **bookdreamer@aol.com** Website: **www.theblackbookworm.com**

Black Classics Books & Gifts Specializes in Black Literature for children and adults. We sell all sorts of fiction and non-fiction books. We also sell Black figurines, sorority, fraternity, Masonic, Girlfriends and Black Chef merchandise, Black Art Tapestries, Collectibles from Africa, greeting cards, calendars and other Black novelty items. Black Classics Books & Gifts, 140 S. Sage Avenue, Suite B, Mobile, Alabama 36606 Phone: (251) 476-1060 Fax: (251) 476-4642 E-mail: **blackbkgft@aol.com**

Black Library Booksellers Founded in 1993 by Kevin L. Fisher and Lloyd E. Hart, Jr. Contact The Black Library Booksellers, 325 Huntington Avenue, Suite 83, Boston, Massachusetts 02115 Phone: (617) 442-2400 Fax: (617) 442-6526 E-mail: **blacklib@theblacklibrary.com** Website: **www.theblacklibrary.com**

Black Start Books African American Bookstore. Omari, Manager, Black Star Books, 19410 Livernois, Detroit, Michigan 48221 Phone: (313) 863-2665

Bookladder.com Online internet bookseller. We offer thousands of quality African American interest books from all publishers. Vernon Hamilton, Bookladder, Post Office Box 557 Nyack, New York 10960 E-mail: **info@bookladder.com** Website: **www.bookladder.com**

Books For Thought, Inc. Specializing in books by and about African Americans. Gift items including greeting cards, collectibles, puzzles, games, art, wedding invitations, journals, stationery and figurines. Books For Thought, Inc., 10910 North 56th Street, Tampa, Florida 33617 Phone: (813) 988-6363 Fax: (813) 988-6866 E-mail: **books4thought@aol.com**

Brownstone Books African American bookstore. Brownstone Books, 409 Lewis Avenue, Brooklyn, New York 11233 Phone: (718) 953-7328 E-mail: **info@brownstonebooks.com** Website: **www.brownstonebooks.com**

B.Y.O.B., Inc. (Beyond Your Ordinary Bookstore) We are a book store that caters predominately to the African American. We offer a wide range of books, from fiction to non-fiction. Open mic/spoken word every Thursday from 7-9:30 p.m. Tonette & David Washington, B.Y.O.B., 312 Auburn Avenue, Suite A, Atlanta, Georgia 30303 Phone: (404) 389-0538 Fax: (404) 389-0733 E-mail: **beyondyourordinarybookstore@yahoo.com**

C & B Books Distribution We offer our books for less than the major distributors. We stock titles in all categories, fiction, nonfiction, spiritual and inspirational etc. We support self-published and first time authors by providing various services. Caroline Rogers, C & B Books Distribution, 65-77 160th. Street, #3A, Flushing, New York 11365 Phone: (718) 591-4525 E-mail: **cbbookdist@aol.com** Website: **www.cbbooksdistribution.com**

Charis Books & More Poetry and book signings. Charis Books & More, 1189 Euclid Avenue, North East Atlanta, Georgia Phone: (404) 524-0304

Christian Living Books Publishes and distributes Christian books. Contact Christian Living Books, Post Office Box 7584, Largo, Maryland 20792 Phone: (301) 218-9092 Fax: (301) 218-4943 E-mail: **info@ChristianLivingBooks.com** Website: **www.christianlivingbooks.com**

Cushcity Online African-American selection of DVDs, videos, books, art and more. Cushcity, 13533 Bammel North Houston Road., Houston, Texas 77066 Phone: (281) 444-4265 Fax: (281) 583-9534 E-mail: **GRichardson@cushcity.com** Website: **www.cushcity.com**

DC Bookman Lounge Bookstore, booksignings, promotions, publishing. Contact DC Bookman Lounge, 3705 Rhode Island Avenue, Mount Rainier, Maryland 20712 Phone: (301) 760-7362 E-mail: **sales@dcbookman.com**

Dynasty Books Hosts Book Signing & Receptions. Dynasty Books, Eastland Mall, 5471 Central Avenue, Charlotte, North Carolina 28212

Esowon Bookstore Bookstore/Bookseller. Esowon Bookstore, 4331 Debnan Boulevard, Los Angeles, California 90008 Phone: (323) 290-1048 E-mail: **esowonbooks@aol.com**

GEL Enterprizes Provides a full line of apparel, gift items, school supplies, college textbooks at reasonable prices. Lecture Serries and Poetry Readings. Gregory E. Lewis, GEL Enterprizes, Post Office Box 190049, Atlanta, Georgia 31119 Phone: (404) 846-2420 Fax: (404) 846-8444 E-mail: **glewis@gel-enterprizes.com** Website: **www.gel-enterprizes.com**

Hakims Bookstore and Giftshop Family owned and operated for over 40 years. African-American titles, black doll collectibles, wall tapestry, posters and postcards. Hakims Bookstore and Giftshop, 210 South 52nd Street, Philadelphia, Pennsyvania 19139 Phone: (215) 474-9495 Fax: (215) 471-7177 E-mail: **hakims@critpath.org** Website: **www.hakimsbookstore.com**

Heritage Bookstore and More, Inc. Bookstore. Heritage Bookstore and More, Inc., 1430 West 7th Street, Oakland, California 91786 Phone: (909) 484-8411 Fax: (909) 484-8405 E-mail: **heritageandmore@aol.com** Website: **www.heritagebookstoreandmore.com**

Howard University Bookstore University bookstore. Contact Manager, Howard University Bookstore, 2225 Georgia Avenue, North West, Washington, DC 20059 Phone: (202) 238-2640 E-mail: **customerservice@hubookstore.com** Website: **www.hubookstore.com**

Hueman Bookstore & Cafe African-American books. Author signings. Hueman Bookstore & Cafe, 2319 Frederick Douglass Boulevard, New York, New York 10027 Phone: (212) 665-7400 E-mail: **info@hueman-bookstore.com** Website: **www.huemanbookstore.com**

Jokae's African American Books. Readings, signings & aspiring authors workshop. Contact Jokae's Bookstore, 3223 West Camp Wisdom, Dallas, Texas 75237 Phone: (214) 331-8100 Fax: (214) 331-8400 E-mail: **mstil0372@aol.com** Website: **www.jokaes.com**

LittleAfrica.com, LLC Online Bookseller. LittleAfrica.com, LLC, 8192 Misty Shore Drive, West Chester, Ohio 45069 Phone: (513) 870-9337 E-mail: **Market@LittleAfrica.com** Website: **www.LittleAfrica.com**

Lushena Books, Inc. Publish and distribute literary items written for, by and/or about African Americans. Lushena Books Inc., 607 Country Club Drive, Unit E, Bensenville, Illinois 60106 Phone: (630) 238-8708 E-mail: **lushenabks@yahoo.com** Website: **www.lushenabks.com**

Marcus Books Books by and about Black people everywhere. Contact Karen, Marcus Books, 1712 Fillmore Street, San Francisco, California 94115 Phone: (415) 346-4222

Marcus Books Books by and about Black people everywhere. Contact Karen, Marcus Books, 3900 Martin Luther King Jr. Way, Oakland, California 94609 Phone: (510) 652-2344

Medu Books Established in 1993. Stocks books by, about, and relevant to people of African descent. Medu Books, Greenbriar Mall, 2841 Greenbriar Parkway, Atlanta, Georgia 30331 Phone: (404) 346-3263 E-mail: **medu@bellsouth.net** Website: **www.medubooks.com**

Milligan Books Bookstore Contact Dr. Rosie Milligan, Milligan Books, 1425 W. Manchester Avenue, Suite C, Los Angeles, California 90047 Phone: (323) 750-3592 Fax: (323) 750-2886 E-mail: **DrRosie@aol.com** Website: **www.milliganbooks.com**

Nghosi Books Bookseller. Founded in 2002. Provides forum where artists can display, submit and promote their work. Nghosi Books, Post Office Box 1908, Stone Mountain, Georgia 30086 Phone: (866) 464-4674 E-mail: **info@nghosibooks.com** Web site: **www.nghosibooks.com**

Precious Memories Reading & Collectibles Bookstore Poetry Night. Events, Booksignings. Contact Ms. Linda Pate, Precious Memories Reading & Collectibles Bookstore, 3229 Idlewood Avenue, Richmond, Virginia 23221 Phone: (804) 726-8501 Fax: (804) 726-8502 E-mail: **lpate@preciousmemoriesreading.com** Website: **www.preciousmemoriesreading.com**

The Shrine Bookstore Sells African-American books. Contact The Shrine Bookstore, 946 Ralph David Abernathy Boulevard South West., Atlanta, Georgia 30310 Phone: (404) 752-6125 Fax: (404) 753-4884 Website: **www.shrinebookstore.com**

The Shrine Bookstore Cultural Center and bookstore. Sells African-American books. The Shrine Bookstore, 13535 Livernois Avenue, Detroit, Michigan 48238 Phone: (313) 491-0777 Website: **www.shrinebookstore.com**

The Shrine Bookstore Large selection of Black books. Contact The Shrine Bookstore, 5309 Martin L. King Boulevard, Houston, Texas 77021 Phone: (713) 645-1071 Fax: (713) 645-2469 Website: **www.shrinebookstore.com**

Sisterspace and Books African-American Bookstore and online bookseller. Sisterspace and Books, 1515 U Street, North West, Washington, DC 20009 Phone: (202) 332-3433 E-mail: **sistersp@covad.net** Website: **www.sisterspace.com**

Sister's Uptown Bookstore African American Bookstore. Sisters Uptown Bookstore, 1942 Amsterdam Avenue, New York, New York 10027 Phone: 212-862-3680

Smiley's Bookstore Mecca of Information. Smiley's Bookstore, 20220 S. Avalon Boulevard, Suite D, Carson, California 90746 Phone: (310) 324-9444 E-mail: **info@smileysbooks.org** E-mail: **info@smileysbooks.org**

Soul On Wheels Books Internet based retailer of Black literature, art and body care products. Hubert Toussaint, President. Contact Kenny, Soul On Wheels Books, 294 Sumpter Street, #2F, Brooklyn, New York 11233 Phone: (718) 453-6017 E-mail: **soulonwheels@optonline.net** Website: **www.soulonwheels.com**

TimBookTu On-line bookseller we also publish a newsletter. Memphis Vaughan, Jr., is editor and publisher. Contact TimBookTu, Post Office Box 933, Mobile, Alabama 36601 E-mail: **editor@TimBookTu.com** Website: **www.TimBookTu.com**

Truth Bookstore African American books and Booksignings. Located in the Northland Mall. Truth Bookstore, 21500 Northwestern Highway, Southfield, Michigan 48075 Phone: (248) 557-4824 E-mail: **truthbookstore@sbcglobal.net**

Umoja Books & Products Sells books. Asante Sana, Umoja Books & Products, 1006 Surrey Street, Lafayette, Lousiana 70501 Phone: (337) 593-8665 E-mail: **gjm3768@louisiana.edu**

Underground Railroad Reading Station Bookstore African specialty store. We sell books, gifts and fine collectables. Ann King, Underground Railroad Reading Station Bookstore, 4878 Chambers Road, Denver, Colorado 80239 Phone: (303) 375-9343

Williams Books and Church Supplies Sells books and Church supplies. Roy Williams owner. Williams Books and Church Supplies, 1409-B Kathy Lane South West, Decatur, Alabama 35601 Phone: (256) 351-6531

Winston Salem State University Bookstore Store Manager, John Ray. Contact Winston Salem State University Bookstore, 601 South Martin Luther King Boulevard, Winston-Salem, New Carolina 27110 Phone: (336) 750-2780 Fax: (336) 750-2781 E-mail: **wssu@bkstr.com** Website: **www.wssu.edu**

Xavier University of Louisiana Bookstore Thaddeus Delay, store manager. Contact XULB, University Center, 4980 Dixon Street, New Orleans, Louisiana 70125 Phone: (504) 520-7300 Fax: (504) 520-7932 E-mail: **bksxula@bncollege.com** Website: **www.xula.bkstore.com**

Zahra's Books-N-Things Bookstore. Host author signings. Zahra's Books-N-Things, 900 North LaBrea Boulevard, Inglewood, California 90302 Phone: (310) 330-1300 E-mail: zarasbooksnthings@sbcglobal.net Website: **www.zarasbooksandthings.com**

Zawadi Books, Inc. Black owned and operated company and North America's largest seller of black themed books. We have everything you need right here, with over 40,000 items in stock! And with our outstanding service, you can be sure that when you shop here, you will get nothing but the best. Tressa Sanders, Publisher. Zawadi Books, Inc., 1068 Chrisler Avenue, Schenectady, New York 12303 Phone: (518) 831-9073 E-mail: **contactus@zawadibooks.com** Website: **www.zawadibooks.com**

Columnists

Stacy Hawkins Adams Professional journalist and speaker, Ms. Hawkins is a nationally acclaimed author of several Christian fiction novels - "Watercolored Pearls," "Nothing But the Right Thing" and "Speak To My Heart." Stacy Hawkins Adams, Post Office Box 25985, Richmond, Virginia 23260 Phone: (804) 768-1292 E-mail: **stacy@stacyhawkinsadams.com** Website: **www.stacyhawkinsadams.com**

Keith Alexander Reporter. Keith Alexander, The Washington Post, 1150 15th Street, North West, Washington, DC 20071 Phone: (202) 334-7796 E-mail: **Alexanderk@washpost.com**

Melissa A. Allen Self-syndicated columnist. Melissa writes a fitness column that is published in several local San Diego newspapers as well as online. She is a member of the San Diego Press Club as well as the National Society of Newspaper Columnists (NSNC). Contact Ms. Melissa Allen, Post Office Box 1957, El Cajon, California 92022 Phone: (619) 252-4993 Fax: (619) 447-6689 E-mail: **opticondit@aol.com** Website: **www.optimumcondition.com**

Tracy Allen Journalist, writer and reporter. Contact Ms. Tracy Allen, Kansas City Call, 1715 East 18th Street, Kansas City, Missouri 64108 E-mail: **tracyKccall@hotmail.com**

Adrienne Anderson A music journalist with credentials in academic journals, magazines and online journalism. A freelance writer, Adrienne is a fourth-generation San Franciscan, and has been writing for more than 15 years. Adrienne Anderson Fax: 415-680-2413 (no unrelated faxes, please). E-mail: **me@adrienneanderson.com** Website: **www.adrienneanderson.com**

Jabari Asim Author, columnist, and Deputy Editor of Washington Post Book World. Columnist, washingtonpost.com. Jbari Asim, 1150 15th Street, North West, Washington, DC 20071 E-mail: **asimj@washpost.com** Website: **www.washingtonpost.com**

Alicia Banks Columnist, renowned radio personality, radio producer, host, educator, scholar, rebel public intellectual. Contact Alicia Banks, Post Office Box 55596, Little Rock, Arkansas 72215 E-mail: **ambwww@yahoo.com**

Jillina "J-Bax" Baxter Website Journalist – The Hive/Blaze 1 Radio at blaze1graphixs.com in Atlanta, Georgia. J-Bax has written a catalog close to 300 consisting of Rap & R&B songs and poetry pieces. Jillina "J-Bax" Baxter, 184 Second Avenue, Albany, New York 12202 Phone: (518) 210-3518 E-mail: **jbmeow@yahoo.com**

Rose Jackson-Beavers Columnist, Ms. Beavers currently writes as a columnist for the Spanish Word, a local community newspaper. Rose Jackson-Beavers, Chief Executive Officer, of Prioritybooks Publications, Post Office Box 2535, Florissant, Missouri 63032 Phone: (314) 741-6789 E-mail: **rosbeav03@yahoo.com** Website: **www.priortybooks.com**

Carolyn L. Bennett Writer-journalist, educator, public affairs columnist since the 1970s, Dr. Bennetts teaching areas and interests: editorial, opinion, feature writing, news writing and reporting, magazine article writing, ethics in journalism, minorities in media, etc. Carolyn L. Bennett, 221 Greystone Lane-16, Rochester, New York 14618 E-mail: **cwriter85@aol.com** Website: **www.hometown.aol.com/cwriter85/index.html**

Edith Billups Free-lance writer for The Black-owned Washington Informer Newspaper. Reviews theater, music and film and also writes regularly for a travel column, "Pack Your Bags." Ms. Edith Billips, The Gabriel Group, 8720 Georgia Avenue, Suite 906, Silver Spring, Maryland 20910 Phone: (301) 562-5460 Fax: (240) 562-5468 E-mail: **eybillups@aol.com**

Aminisha Black Columnist - two columns - The Parents Notebook in Our Time Press newspaper, Brooklyn, NY and Spirited Parent in Single Parent: Raising our Children news magazine. Aminisha Black, The Parents Notebook, Post Office Box 755, Brooklyn, New York 11238 Phone: (718) 783-4432 E-mail: **parentsnotebook@yahoo.com**

Jennifer Elaine Black Author of several poetry books including "Issues of Life" and "The Healing Tree for all Nations." She is a speaker and instructor for The End Times Arts Movement International founded by herself. She teaches youth to be empowered through the use of their own creativity. She teaches acting, praise dance, writing, and music workshops. She is also a writer for Gatekeeper magazine and Virtuous Woman magazine. Jennifer Elaine Black, The End Times Arts Movement International, Inc., Post Office Box 56394, Little Rock, Arkansas 72215 Phone: (501) 859-0841 E-mail: **booking@thepropheticartist.com**

Herb Boyd National editor of The Black World Today (TBWT). An award-winning journalist, Boyd is the author of nine books, including Brotherman: The Odyssey of Black Men in America--An Anthology that he co-edited with Robert Allen which received the 1995 American Book Award. He has taught Black Studies for almost 30 years at various universities and currently teaches African and African American history, College of New Rochelle in Manhattan. Herb Boyd, The Black World Today, Post Office Box #328, Randallstown, Maryland, 21133 Phone: (410) 659-8298 Fax: (410) 521-9993 E-mail: **HBoyd@tbwt.com** Website: **www.tbwt.org**

Marion Boykin Sports Editor, The Black World Today. Boykin is a highly acclaimed authority on boxing and a versatile communicator on a wide range of sports activities. His commentaries have earned him several national prizes and he has appeared as a guest on a number of television and radio sports shows. Contact Mr. Marion Boykins, The Black World Today, Post Office Box 328, Randallstown, Maryland 21133 Phone: (410) 659-8298 Fax: (410) 521-9993 E-mail: **MBoykin@tbwt.com** Website: **www.tbwt.org**

Donna L. Brazile Author of the book Cooking with Grease (June 2004, Simon & Schuster), an intimate account of Donna Brazile's thirty years in politics. She is a weekly contributor and political commentator on CNN's Inside Politics and American Morning. In addition, Ms. Brazile is a columnist for Roll Call Newspaper and appears regularly on MSNBC's Hardball and Fox's Hannity and Colmes. Ms. Donna L. Brazile, Brazile and Associates, LLC, 1001 G Street, North West, Suite 1001, Washington, DC 20001 E-mail: **donna@cookingwithgrease.com** Website: **www.cookingwithgrease.com**

Crystal C. Brown Freelance journalist-published author of "I can see clearly now", "Life is Crystal Clear" and " Survivor: Tales of a broken and mended heart." She is also the CEO and President of Crystal Clear Communications-an award winning public relations and marketing firm. Crystal C. Brown, 2470 S. Dairy Ashford #252, Houston, Texas 77077 Phone: (281) 589-2007 E-mail: **cbrown5530@aol.com** Website: **www.crystalcommunicates.com**

Vonetta Booker Brown An accomplished journalist and writer who has contributed to various publications including Stamford Advocate, Fairfield County Weekly, New Haven Register, MediaBistro.com, HealthQuest, Essence, Vibe, Honey and XXL. Vonetta Brown, Right Hand Concepts, 2020 Pennsylvania Avenue, North West, #341, Washington, DC 20006 Phone: (646) 234-9443 E-mail: **chiefelement@gmail.com** Website: **www.righthandconcepts.com**

Lisa-Anne Ray-Byers Licensed and certified speech-language pathologist and educational consultant who has worked in education for over two decades. She holds graduate degrees in speech-language pathology and multicultural education. She also holds certification in educational administration. She is the author of the book, "They Say I Have ADHD, I Say Life Sucks!" Thoughts From Nicholas. She is currently employed in the Hempstead School District in Hempstead, New York. In addition to her duties to her students, she also writes a weekly educational column entitled, Ask Lisa-Anne. Her column appears in four local newspapers throughout New York. Her column covers topics in education, education law, special education, and many other related issues to better equip parents and teachers with resources and information for their students. Lisa-Anne Ray-Byers, 41 East Woodbine Drive, Freeport, New York 11520 Phone: (516) 770-2972 E-mail: **speechlrb@yahoo.com** Website: **www.asklisaanne.com**

Monica P. Carter A most sought-after speaker and award winning columnist for The Times newspaper in Shreveport, Louisiana, Monica is president and chief copywriter at RootSky Publishing. She is a seasoned writer, with nearly 10 years of professional writing experience. She is also an author and freelance writer and conducts publishing and writing workshops. She is also a columnist for the soulsistasunite.com. Contact Ms. Monica Carter, RootSky Publishing, Post Office Box 52482, Shreveport, Louisiana 71115 Phone: (318) 617-3267 E-mail: **mpcarter7@aol.com** Website: **www.monicapcarter.com**

TonyaSue Carther Associate editor, romance columnist, movie / DVD review specialist and book editor of Black Noir Magazine. A native New Yorker, TonyaSue currently lives in New Jersey, where she is pursing a career in film. TonyaSue Carther, Black Noir Magazine, 100 Park Avenue South, Suite 1600, New York, New York 10017 Phone: (201) 408-4306 E-mail: **Gigone2112@cs.com** Website: **www.floanthonysblacknoir.com**

Mamadou Chinyelu Working journalist since 1977. Contact Mamadou Chinyelu, Post Office Box 32406 Charleston, South Carolina 29417 E-mail: **mchinyelu99@hotmail.com**

Rick Christie Assistant Managing Editor. Palm Beach Post, Post Office Box 24700, West Palm Beach, Florida 33416 Phone: (561) 820-4476 E-mail: **rchristie@pbpost.com**

Denise Clay Education Writer. Denise Clay, The Bucks County Courier Times, 8400 Route 13, Levittown, Pennsylvania 19057 Phone: (215) 949-4195 E-mail: **dclay@phillyBurbs.com**

Floyd A. Cray III Writes a Holy CD review column monthly for The Tri State Voice Christian Newspaper. Floyd is also alternative Gospel music director at 89.1 WFDU-FM. Contact Floyd A. Cray III, Gospel Vibrations Inc, 114 Shepard Avenue, Teaneck, New Jersey 07666 Phone: (201) 833-0694 E-mail: **GospelVibrations@aol.com** Website: **www.wfdu.fm**

George E. Curry Former editor-in-chief of the National Newspaper Publishers Association News Service (NNPA). His weekly newspaper column is syndicated by NNPA to more than 200 African-American newspapers. Mr. George E. Curry, NNPA, 3200 13th Street, North West, Washington, DC 20010 E-mail: **george@georgecurry.com** Website: **www.georgecurry.com**

Wayne Dawkins Editor of the Black Alumni Network Newsletter. Contact Wayne Dawkins, Post Office Box 6693, Newport News, Virginia 23606 Phone: (800) 268-4338 Fax: (757) 591-2371 E-mail: **wdawk69643@aol.com** Website: **www.augustpress.net**

Anita Davis-DeFoe Author, journalist, and television host of caribbeanwomentoday, a segment on Caribbean Weekly; an informational and community affairs program produced by the Duke of Earle Media Group (Florida/Jamaica). Dr. DeFoe is also resident advice guru for She-Caribbean, a St. Lucian magazine that is sold in 16 islands, New York, Atlanta, New Jersey, South Florida, Canada and London. Her articles have appeared in the Saturday Edition (Miami) Carib Life (New York), and others. Anita Davis-DeFoe, She Advice Guru-Straight Talk Column, Contributing Writer, The Mobay Group, The Defoe Group, Post Office Box 451973, Sunrise, Florida 33345 Phone: (954) 816-9462 E-mail: **dranitadavisdefoe@hotmail.com** Website: **www.dranitadavisdefoe.com**

Eric Deggans Writer. Contact Mr. Eric Deggans, The Saint Petersburg Times, 490 1st Avenue, South, Saint Petersburg, Florida 33701 Phone: (727) 893-8521 Fax: (727) 892-2327 E-mail: **deggans@sptimes.com**

Angela P. Dodson Free-lance editor and writer for magazines, online services, individual authors and book publishers. She is a senior editor of NeWorld Review, a literary magazine and blog and an online editor for DIVERSE Issues in Higher Education. She is the former executive editor of Black Issues Book Review and has been a journalist for more than 30 years. Angela is a former senior editor and Style editor for the New York Times. Dodson has also done writing and editing for various other magazines and newspapers. She has been a consultant, instructor in media studies and public speaking and is the host of a weekly radio program about black Roman Catholics. She is a journalism graduate of Marshall University and has a master's degree in journalism and public affairs from the American University in Washington, D.C. She has led workshops on writing and editing for many organizations. Angela P. Dodson, 324 Hamilton Avenue, Trenton, New Jersey 08609 Phone: (609) 394-7632 Fax: (609) 396-7808 E-mail: **angela4bibr@aol.com**

Sean Drakes Writer/Correspondent. Drakes specializes in documenting the Caribbean region for inflight magazines like BWIA Caribbean Beat and Air Jamaica's Skywritings. Drakes is a contributor to the lifestyle section of Black Enterprise and MACO magazines and a regular freelance photojournalist with the Atlanta Journal-Constitution, a leading daily newspaper. Travel, daily life, and style are his areas of concentration. E-mail: **contactcoty@hotmail.com**

Ervin Dyer Staff Reporter. Contact Mr. Ervin Dyer, Pittsburgh Post-Gazette, 34 Boulevard of the Allies, Pittsburgh, Pennsylvania, 15222 Phone: (412) 263-1410 Fax: (412) 263-1706 E-mail: **edyer@post-gazette.com**

Tannette Johnson-Elie Writer. Ms. Tannette Johnson-Elie, Milwaukee Journal Sentinel, 333 West State Street, Milwaukee, Wisconsin 53201 Phone: (414) 223-5172 Fax: (414) 223-5528 E-mail: **telie@journalsentinel.com** Website: **www.journalsentinel.com**

Deborah Gabriel A multi - skilled journalist with international experience in the UK, Jamaica and Africa, across the mediums of print, TV, radio and online. She is currently the editor of an online news publication and founder and director of Imani Media Ltd, an organization that works closely with social enterprises and voluntary organizations. Contact Ms. Deborah Gabriel, Imani Media Ltd, (Registered Office) 2nd Floor, 145-157 Saint John Street, London EC1V 4PY E-mail: **deborahgabriel@layersofblackness.com** Website: **www.imani-media.com**

Daniel Garrett Writer of journalism, fiction, poetry, and drama. Recently Mr. Garrett has written a series of in-depth film essays for the web magazine Offscreen.com, essays that focus on international cultures, philosophy, history, and politics. Daniel Garrett, 05-63 135th Street, Richmond Hill, New York 11419 E-mail: **dgarrett31@hotmail.com**

Michelle R. Gipson Publisher of Written Magazine, the former Director of Advertising for Black Issues Book Review and Managing Editor of the Atlanta Daily World's Celebration of Books. Earned her B.A. in Mass Media and her M.A. in Counseling from Hampton University. Published in Jane, the Atlanta Daily World and Chicken Soup for the African American Soul. Michelle R. Gipson, Written Magazine, Post Office Box 250504, Atlanta, Georgia 30310 Phone: (404) 753-8315 E-mail: **michelle.gipson@writtenmag.com** Website: **www.writtenmag.com**

C.D. Grant Journalist, essayist, poet and short story writer, nationally published since 1970, Essence Magazine, Soul, etc. Co-founder of Blind Beggar Press, based in the Bronx in New York City, since 1977. TV show host, Mr. Grant interviews authors, and other guests. Mr. C.D. Grant, Publisher, Blind Beggar Press, Post Office Box 437, Bronx, New York 10467 Phone: (914) 683-6792 E-mail: **blindbeggar1@juno.com** Website: **www.blindbeggarpress.com**

Vanessa Davis Griggs Award winning author and motivational speaker Vanessa Davis Griggs pens a column A Peace of My Mind and periodically writes articles for various magazines and newspapers. Vanessa is the recipient of numerous recognitions including: March 2006 recipient of The Greater Birmingham Millennium Section National Council of Negro Women Inspiration Award. Ms. Vanessa Davis Griggs, Post Office Box 101328, Birmingham, Alabama 35210 E-mail: **Vanessa@VanessaDavisGriggs.com** Website: **www.vanessaDavisGriggs.com**

Bernice L. Guity Seasoned award winning journalist with more than nine years experience as reporter and writer, Ms. Guity has written numerous front-page stories on issues involving education, health care, real estate, social services and manufacturing for the New York Times Newspaper Group, Knight-Ridder Newspapers and the American City Business Journals. Bernice L. Guity, P & G Communications, Inc., Post Office Box 715, Avondale Estates, Georgia 30002 Phone: (404) 298-7799 Fax: (404) 298-0059 E-mail: **pgcommuns@aol.com**

Nathasha Brooks Harris Editor of Black Romance and Bronze Thrills magazines. Co-owner of Write On! Literary Consortium, a literary consulting services. Ms. Natasha Brooks Harris, 297 7th Street, Brooklyn, New York 11215 E-mail: **nabrooks@aol.com**

Adele Hodge A seasoned media communications professional with a solid reputation for strong people management skills, consistency and creative presentation of ideas and concepts in print, electronic and live media started her television career at WXYZ-TV/ABC in Detroit. She moved to the NBC-TV affiliate, before taking a position as newswriter-producer at the NBC owned and operated WMAQ-TV in Chicago. Adele Hodge, Post Office Box 3584, Phoeniz, Arizona 85030 Phone: (602) 274-7842 E-mail: **writers@earthlink.net**

Eugene Holley Arts and music critic with particular emphasis on Jazz musicians. The Black World Today, Post Office Box #328, Randallstown, Maryland 21133 Phone: (410) 659-8298 Fax: (410) 521-9993 Website: **www.tbwt.org**

Earl Ofari Hutchinson Nationally acclaimed author and journalist, his writings have appeared in such publications as the Los Angeles Times, Ebony, Newsday, Black Scholar, Los Angeles Herald, Harpers and many others. He is a radio host and TV commentator and has received numerous awards for his writings. Earl Ofari Hutchinson, Hutchinson Communications, 614 East Manchester Boulevard, Suite 204, Inglewood, California 90301 Phone: (323) 296-6331 E-mail: **ehutchinson@thehutchinsonreport.com** Website: **www.thehutchinsonreport.com**

Kevin Wayne Johnson Author, writer, television and radio talk show host, Keith is author of a nine-book series entitled Give God the Glory! and the recipient of multiple literary awards. Columnist, The Joys of Fatherhood, for The Church Guide of Detroit. Kevin Wayne Johnson, Writing for the Lord Ministries, 6400 Shannon Court, Clarksville, Maryland 21029 Phone: (410) 340-8633 E-mail: **kevin@writingforthelord.com** Website: **www.writingforthelord.com**

Tonisha Johnson New York freelance writer, editor and publisher of Gesica Magazine. Tonisha Johnson, Gesica Magazine, Post Office. Box 30231, Staten Island, New York 10303 Phone: (718) 216-3530 E-mail: **TonishaJohnson@gmail.com** Website: **www.gesicaonline.com**

Jusbee Jones Worked with professional athletes for over fifteen years in the capacity of sports public relations and marketing. Jones is currently President of a sports entertainment publicity firm and contributes to a monthly sports entertainment column. Contact Jusbee Jones, Adnor Books, 15030 Ventura Boulevard., Suite 525, Sherman Oaks, California 91403 E-mail: **JusbeeJones@aol.com** Website: **www.confessionsofthe12thman.com**

Marsha Jones A graduate of Purdue University, Marshas' works have appeared in such regional publications as about..time magazine, Rochester Business Magazine, Business Strategies, and her weekly 411 column in The Buffalo Challenger. She has interviewed such notables as filmmaker Spike Lee, poets Nikki Giovanni and Sonia Sanchez, musicians Miriam Makeba, Bobby McFerrin, The Brothers Johnson, and Wynton, Branford, and Ellis Marsalis, authors Maya Angelou and Antowne Fisher, comedians Bernie Mac and Chris Rock, and actors Malik Yoba and Danny Glover. Marsha Jones, 411 Communications, 97 Culver Parkway, Rochester, New York 14609 E-mail: **defdefyingmj@yahoo.com**

Eugene Kane Journalist. Writer/ columnist. Contact Mr. Eugene Kane, Milwaukee Journal-Sentinel, 333 West State Street, Milwaukee, Wisconsin 53201 Phone: (414) 223-5521 E-mail: **ekane@journalsentinel.com**

Tanya Kersey As one of Hollywood's most respected and well-regarded entertainment journalists and commentators, Tanya has her finger on the pulse of what's happening in the world of urban entertainment. Throughout her career, Tanya has developed and earned a reputation for covering the entertainment industry, focusing on celebrities, film, television, music, fashion, award shows, special events and the business of entertainment in a trend-setting, groundbreaking format. Kersey is perhaps best known as the Founder, Publisher and Editor-in-Chief of the online entertainment trade publication, BlackTalentNews.com, and as the Founder and Executive Director of the Hollywood Black Film Festival. Among the many books and publications she has authored are Black State of the Arts: A Guide to Developing a Successful Career as a Black Performing Artist, the Black Film Report, the Urban Hollywood Resource Directory, and The Performer's Plan. Tanya Kersey, 8306 Wilshire Boulevard, Suite 2057, Beverly Hills, California 90211 Phone: (310) 203-1336 E-mail: **tanya@tanyakersey.com** Website: **www.tanyakersey.com**

Russell LaCour Journalist. Copy Editor. Contact Mr. Russell LaCour, Tulsa World, 315 South Boulder Avenue, Tulsa, Oklahoma 74103 Phone: (918) 581-8327 Fax: (918) 581-8353 E-mail: **russell.lacour@tulsaworld.com**

Matthew Lynch Author of the book Closing the Racial Academic Achievement Gap and an upcoming children's book entitled Matthew and the Money Tree. Also a contributing columnist for the Mississippi Link, and Emerging Minds, an online magazine devoted to uplifting the African American community. He is founder of Project E.P.I.P.H.A.N.Y, a research based mentoring program. Matthew Lynch, 2324 Princess Pine Drive, Jackson, Mississippi 39212 Phone: (601) 373-1552 E-mail: **lynch39083@aol.com**

Beverly Mahone Veteran journalist who has spent more than 25 years in radio and television. The Ohio University graduate has now put her expertise to work by establishing her own media coaching and consulting business called Soul Solutions/Talk2Bev. Ms. Mahone is also the author of the book Whatever! A Baby Boomer's Journey Into Middle Age. As a result of the book's success, she has been featured as a baby boomer expert on MSNBC-TV and written about in the recently released book, Talk Radio for Authors by Francine Silverman. Contact Ms. Beverly Mahone, Post Office Box 11037, Durham, North Carolina 27703 Phone: (301) 356-6280 E-mail: **bmahone@nc.rr.com** Website: **www.thebabyboomerdiva.com**

James Hiram Malone Columnist, book reviewer and author, Mr. Malone worked as a graphic designer for Atlanta Journal/Constitution Newspapers and wrote a weekly column in Atlanta News, weekly newspaper. He has also written articles and contributed to the Michigan Chronicle and Atlanta Journal/Constitution Newspapers; Ebony and Negro Digest. He is author/illustrator of No-Job Dad, Blues Poetry, Here and There Poetry, Grandma Sarah's Closet, and Brother (Author/illustrator). Mr. James Hiram Malone, 1796 North Avenue North West, Atlanta, Georgia 30318 Phone: (404) 794-0948 E-mail: **j.l.t.malone@att.net** Website: **www.j.l.t.malone.home.att.net**

Julianne Malveaux As a writer and columnist, her work appears regularly in USA Today, Black Issues in Higher Education, Ms. Magazine, Essence magazine, and the Progressive. Her weekly columns, syndicated by King Features, appeared in numerous newspapers across the country from 1990 until 2002. Well-known for appearances on national network programs, she is a charismatic and popular guest on CNN, BET, as well as on Howard University's Television show, Evening Exchange. She has appeared on ABC's Politically Incorrect, Fox News Channel's O'Reilly Factor and stations such as C-SPAN, MSNBC and CNBC. She has also hosted talk radio programs in Washington, San Francisco, and New York. Currently, she has a show in development, The Malveaux Report: An Economic Perspective, that will be presented on PBS through Howard University's WHUT-TV. Contact Dr. Julianne Malveaux, Last Word Productions, 1318 Corcoran Street, North West, Washington, DC 20009 Phone: (202) 462-1932 E-mail: **lastwordprod@aol.com**

Traci Marquis Published writer. Book and Film Critic for The Grand' Manner Magazine of Connecticut and New York. Contact Ms. Traci Marquis, 1333 Baecher Lane, Norfolk, Virginia 23509 Phone: (757) 353-5450 E-mail: **Tbmarquis@hotmail.com**

Roland S. Martin Nationally award winning journalist and syndicated columnist with Creators Syndicate, the founding editor of BlackAmericaweb.com and currently the executive editor of The Chicago Defender, is a frequent commentator on TV-One, CNN, MSNBC, FOX, and Black Entertainment Television (BET). He is also the author of Speak, Brother! A Black Man's View of America. Additionally, he is a member of the National Association of Black Journalists (NABJ), the American Society of Newspapers Editors and the Alpha Phi Alpha Fraternity, Inc. Contact Monique Smith, WVON 1690AM, 3350 South Kedzie, Chicago, Illinois 60623 Phone: (773) 247-6200 E-mail: **roland@wvon.com** Website: **www.wvon.com**

Rych McCain Author of the new book Black Afrikan Hair and The Insanity of the Black Blonde Psych!, Mr. Rych McCain is an international/nationally syndicated Urban Entertainment Newspaper/Magazine Columnist with 3.5 Million readers. His interviews and print features reads like a who's who of the urban film, TV, stage and recording arenas. McCain's print features and famous photo spreads include Hollywood Red Carpet Movie Premieres, Major Awards Shows, Press Junkets, Exclusive One to One interview/photo shoots, Concerts, Club Promotional Parties, Forums, Conferences, Private Celebrity Parties to you name it. McCain is M.P.A.A. (Motion Picture Association of America) Accredited and is a graduate of The University of Nebraska-Lincoln, with a BA Degree in Psychology with post graduate work completed as well. He also does Afro-Centric, visual screen presentation/lectures on college campuses, particularly during Black History Month and conducts Self Esteem Workshop/Presentations geared strictly for Black Afrikan Youth Self Esteem. Rych McCain, Post Office Box 2272, Beverly Hills, California 90213 Phone: (213) 387-3493 E-mail: **rychmccain@sbcglobal.net**

Sylvia McClain Contributing writer for Equal Opportunity Publications and Braids World. Wrote a monthly column on-line in The Essence E-Zine, Straight Up Talking. Featured in The Writer's Digest on-line Speak Out section, guest columnist and a contributing writer for the Michigan Chronicle, and regularly quoted in The Detroit Free Press and Detroit News as a subject matter expert. Sylvia McClain, 7287 Vaughan, Detroit, Michigan 48228 Phone: (734) 326-3341 E-mail: **sylmcclain@juno.com** Website: **www.scribalpress.com**

Cedric McClester Award winning journalist, turned author. He wrote, Kwanzaa, Everything You Always Wanted To Know, But Didn't Know Where To Ask, and his latest childrens book, The Legend of Nia Umoja. Additionally, Mr. McClester is a prolific lyricist who has written over a thousand songs. He is a motivational speaker who speaks to various groups across the country. He has a Masters of Science in Education and has written for national and international publications, including the New York Times, Daily News and their Sunday Magazine, Black Enterprise, Modern Black Men, Amsterdam News, The Connection Newspaper and Big Red Newspaper, among others. Cedric McClester, 1966 First Ave. # 12-K, New York, New York 10029 E-mail: **Gandpadamis@aol.com**

Jacquelin Salvatto McCord A muti-talented individual with a varied professional background: Naprapath, Educator and Writer, currently, Ms. McCord is a high school teacher in the Chicago Public Schools. She is the author and publisher of four books. She is the contributing writer for several magazines, newspapers and books. These are just some of the publications in which one can find her articles: NASABA Magazine, The Gospel Scene Magazine, Saints newspaper and the Cross and the Crown Newsletter, How I Got Over: A Testimony of Faith, and Hope and Courage; The Women of Color Devotional Bible, and Wisdom, Grace Devotional Bible for Young Women of Color. She is a member of many professional organizations, among them includes: Delta Sigma Theta Sorority, Inc., Delta Authors on Tour (DAOT), Black Literary Umbrella (BLU), the Society of Children's Book Writers and Illustrators. Ms. McCord is also an active member of the Apostolic Church of God. Contact Ms. Jacquelin S. McCord, Post Office Box 167054, Chicago, Illinois 60616 Phone: (733) 363-6613 Fax: (773) 363-6650 E-mail: **jsmc45@aol.com** Website: **www.jsmccord.com**

Sharon K. McGhee Award-winning personality, Sharon K. McGhee, born in St. Louis, has found a new home and exciting challenges in Chicago as news director for WVON radio. She hosted the top rated morning talk show, "Good Morning St. Louis," for five years. Sharon won the prestigious AIR Award on KATZ radio for a series on the death of Emmitt Till. By all accounts, talk radio is a format made for Sharon McGhee. During her short time in Chicago, Sharon has won the prestigious AIR Award for a five-part series on Breast Cancer. Sharon also launched the first WVON book club, "Between the Covers." Sharon's wealth of talent has been recognized by WVON management and was rewarded by opening an early morning time slot and creating a program especially for her, titled First Light. Sharon brings her world views, intelligence, and wit to listeners Monday through Fridays beginning at 5am - 6am. Sharon's professional affiliations include, the Association of Black Journalists (ABJ), the Chicago Chapter of the Urban League, and Sharon participates in the yearly Cook County Annual Youth Summit. Sharon has traveled to Africa six times; South America; Europe; and the Caribbean islands. Sharon McGhee is an aspiring writer and currently working on her first project. Contact Monique Smith, WVON 1690AM, 3350 South Kedzie, Chicago, Illinois 60623 Phone: (773) 247-6200 E-mail: **monews74@hotmail.com** Website: **www.wvon.com**

Michelle Mellon Freelance writer and editor and has had articles published in Imprint and Blue Planet Quarterly, poetry in journals and anthologies such as Hodgepodge and Seasons of the Heart, and was co-author of a book chapter on professional mentoring. Contact Ms. Michelle Mellon, 2416 Casa Way, Walnut Creek, California 94597 Phone: (925) 937-1947 E-mail: **michelle@mpmellon.com** Website: **www.mpmellon.com**

Denise Meridith A New York City native Ms. Meridith has a BS from Cornell University and a MPA from the University of Southern California. She was the first female professional hired by the US Bureau of Land Management, a natural resource agency, and went on to an illustrious 29 career that took her to six states and the District of Columbia, where she served as the Deputy Director of the agency of 200 offices and 10,000 employees. She retired early in 2002 and has her own public and community relations firm. Since 1998, she has been a regular columnist with the Phoenix Business Journal and was a finalist in the 2004 National Association of Black Journalists' excellence awards. Denise Meridith Consultants Inc, 5515 North 7th Street, Suite 5, Phoenix, Arizona 85014 Phone: (602) 763-9900 E-mail: **denisemeridithconsultants@cox.net**

S. Renee Mitchell Author, writer, playwright, poet, columnist, novelist, Renee is an award-winning newspaper columnist. She also is a powerful public speaker, who uses poetry and personal experiences to bring audiences to their feet, as well as touch their hearts. Renee, a survivor of domestic violence and sexual assault, experienced decades of low self-esteem and feelings of unworthiness. Her tireless and creative work in the last few years to support other survivors of domestic violence resulted in her being selected as one of 2006's 21 Leaders of the 21st Century by New York City-based Women eNews, which bestowed Renee with the international Ida B. Wells Award for Bravery in Journalism. She was also nominated for the 2005 Pulitzer Prize for commentary. S. Renee Mitchell, 6835 SW Capitol Hill Road #34, Portland, Oregon 97219 Phone: (503) 803-0864 E-mail: **reneemitchellspeaks@yahoo.com** Website: **www.reneemitchellspeaks.com**

Melissa Monroe Reporter/Writer. Contact Melissa Monroe, San Antonio Express-News, Post Office Box 2171, San Antonio, Texas 78297 Phone: (210) 250-3329 Fax: (210) 250-3232 E-mail: **mmonroe@express-news.net**

Spencer Moon Authored articles published by: American Writer: Journal of the National Writers Union; Cinezine; Release Print; Media Review; Black Film Bulletin of the British Film Institute 1980 - Now. Co-authored, co-published, co-marketed with George Hill, PhD, Blacks in Hollywood: Five Favorable Years, 1987-1991 (Daystar Press, Los Angeles, California 1991). Authored - Reel Black Talk: A Sourcebook of 50 American Filmmakers (Greenwood Press, Westport, Connecticut, 1997}. Education: Master of Arts, Film & Television Production, Columbia Pacific University, San Rafael, California. Bachelor of Arts, Filmmaking, Antioch College, San Francisco, California program. Awards: Service Award, 1984; Media Award, 1997; Lifetime Member Award, 1997. Spencer Moon, Post Office Box 4510, Atlanta, Georgia 30302 E-mail: **moonrye@aol.com**

Toi Moore Freelance writer for publications such as Billboard, Upscale, The Cause and Saludos Hispanos Magazines to name a few, where she has over 200 published articles in various newspaper and magazines throughout the United States and Canada. She has written several short stories, four novels and two screenplays and published her own magazine titled "Mini Romances." Toi also has several bylines to her credit in which she has authored and interviewed a variety of well-known celebrities such as: Oprah Winfrey, Laila Ali, James Ingram, Vivica A. Fox, Kweisi Mfume, Lisa "Left Eye" Lopez, Patti LaBelle, Boney James, B2K, Jaheim, and Patrice Rushen to name a small few. Toi Moore, Post Office Box 2099, Sun City, California 92586 Phone: (951) 231-1633 E-mail: **toimoore@aol.com**

Shanté Morgan Writer, editor, educator, Shanté Morgan, founder of Morgan Communications, a full-service communications company. She is also currently editor of Turning Point Magazine, freelances as a copyeditor and proofreader. In addition she has also worked as a college instructor teaching journalism. Shanté Morgan, 1710 North Moorpark Road #163, Thousand Oaks, California 91360 Phone: 310-594-9890 E-mail: **ShanteMorgan@aol.com**

Maidstone Mulenga Global Editor. Contact Maidstone Mulenga, Democrat and Chronicle, 55 Exchange Boulevard, Rochester, New York 14614 E-mail: **bamulenga@aol.com**

Daphne Muse Writer, social commentator, and poet, Daphne's commentaries and radio essays have been featured on KTOP-FM, KPFA-FM, KQED-FM and NPR. She is also a New Frontiers Radio Essayist and her social commentaries have been published in major newspapers and air on public radio and commercial stations across the country. She has written more than 300 feature articles, essays, reviews and op-ed pieces for major newspapers, academic journals and on-line zines. Daphne Muse, 2429 East 23rd Street, Oakland, California 94601 Phone: (510) 436-4716 Fax: (510) 261-6064 E-mail: **msmusewriter@sbcglobal.net** Website: **www.daphnemuse.com**

Darren Nichols Reporter. Darren Nichols, Detroit News, 615 West Lafayette Avenue, Detroit, Michigan 48226 Phone: (734) 462-2190 Fax: (734) 462-6771 E-mail: **dnichols@detnews.com**

Tom Marion Noble Writer. Poetry, Fiction short stories and most notably, non-fiction accounts of the War in Iraq. Tom Marion Noble, 1st Armored Division, CMR 467 BOX 143, APO AE 09096, 011-49-174-571-5390 E-mail: **tom.noble@us.army.mil**

Greg Patterson Editor. Reporter. Contact Greg Patterson, Star Tribune, 425 Portland Avenue, Minneapolis, Minnesota 55488 Phone: (612) 673-7287 E-mail: **gpatterson@startribune.com**

Gwendolyn King Perry Rreligious Christian writer. Communications Specialist II, Southern University Alumni Affairs Office and Advisor, Southern University Digest. Contact Gwendolyn King Perry, 2330 Jacock Road, Slaughter, Louisiana 70777

William Pleasant Among America's most provocative journalists, Mr. William Pleasant's groundbreaking independent arts journal Stono and the weekly New York City Liberator won fiercely loyal audiences in the U.S. and Europe. As deputy editor of NYC's Daily Challenge, Pleasant's hardball reporting on local political corruption, criminal police activities and human rights abuses in Africa were widely praised. He and his wife, the attorney Kellie Gasink, went on to found the Coalition Against Slavery in Africa (CASIA). Pleasant wrote the U.N. Human Rights Commission indictment against the Government of Sudan on behalf of the Nubian People in 1997. William Pleasant, 22 West Bryan Street, Suite 172, Savannah, Georgia 31401 Phone: (866) 237-7563 E-mail: **yamacrawpress@lycos.com**

William Raspberry Columnist. Contact The Washington Post, 1150 15th Street, North West, Washington, DC 20071 Phone: (202) 334-6000 E-mail: **willrasp@washpost.com**

Rashida Rawls Copy Editor/Designer. Rashida Rawls, The Macon Telegraph, 120 Broadway, Macon, Georgia 31201 Phone: (478) 744-4420 E-mail: **miss_rawls19@hotmail.com**

Barbara A. Reynolds Author and an award winning journalist, her syndicated newspapers columns have reached an estimated 10 million people weekly. She has appeared on such major television shows as the "Oprah Winfrey Show," "Politically Incorrect," and "CNN." Dr. Barbara A. Reynolds, JFJ Publishing, 4806 Saint Barnabas Road, Suite 598, Temple Hills, Maryland 20757 Phone: (301) 899-1341 E-mail: **reynew@aol.com** Website: **www.reynoldsnews.com**

Evie Rhodes Fiction Author. Writes feature short stories for The Gospel Magazine, Inc. Evie is also the writer for the "Standing In Da Sprit" album, which won a Canadian Music Award for Best Gospel Album, and the scriptwriter for Changed, which won for Best Gospel Music Video. Contact Evie Rhodes, Post OfficeBox 320503, Hartford, Connecticut 06132 Phone: (212) 633-3315 E-mail: **evierhodes@evierhodes.com** Website: **www.evierhodes.com**

Wanda Sabir Columnist and Arts Editor, at the San Francisco Bay View Newspaper. Contact Ms. Wanda Sabir, Post Office Box 30756, Oakland, California 94604 Phone: (510) 261-8436 E-mail: **wsab1@aol.com** Website: **www.wandaspicks.com**

Yolanda Brunson-Sarrabo A native of Brooklyn, New York, Ms. Yolanda Brunson-Sarrabo has worked at various levels of the fashion industry. Along with writing The Ins and Outs of the Fashion Industry—From a Fashion Insider she also co-writes a popular monthly newsletter, The Laundry Source. Yolanda form Spitfir Productions, a literary home for authors who want to display their talents in writing. Yolanda Brunson-Sarrabo, Spitfir Productions,1454 Rockaway Parkway, Brooklyn, New York 11236 E-mail: **blackwriternew@yahoo.com** Website: **www.ybrunson.com**

Matthew Scott Personal Finance Editor. Contact Matthew Scott, Black Enterprise Magazine, 130 Fifth Avenue, New York, New York 10011 Phone: (212) 886-9589 Fax: (212) 886-9610 E-mail: **scottm@blackenterprise.com**

Terence Shepherd Weekend Business Editor, The Miami Herald. President of the South Florida Black Journalists Association. Contact Mr. Terence Shepherd, The Miami Herald, One Herald Plaza, Miami, Florida 33132 Phone: (305) 376-3596 Phone: (954) 764-7026 Fax: (305) 376-5287 E-mail: **tshepherd@herald.com**

Stan Simpson Columnist. The Hartford Courant, 285 Broad Street, Hartford, Connecticut 06115 Phone: (860) 241-6521 Fax: (860) 241-3865 E-mail: **simpson@courant.com**

Erma Somerville Wrote Negotiating For Love, also wrote short stories in Black Romance magazines for Sterling MacFadden publications. Erma Somerville, 2000 Lee Road, Suite 100, Cleveland Heights., Ohio 44118 Fax: (216) 397-0645 E-mail: **Lermaj@aol.com**

Larry D. Starks Sports Editor, St. Louis Post-Dispatch, 900 North Tucker Boulevard, Saint Louis, Missouri 63101 Phone: (314) 340-8000 E-mail: **lstarks@post-dispatch.com**

Torrance Stephens Writer and Author. Currently, senior Op-Ed writer for Rolling Out Urban weekly. Contact Mr. Torrance Stephens, Post Office Box 1331, Palmetto, Georgia 30268 E-mail: **torrance_stephens@yshoo.com**

Juanita Torrence-Thompson   Nationally acclaimed poet, author, and freelance writer. Publishes a weekly poetry column in New York Voice, New York. Contact Ms. Juanita Torrence-Thompson, New York Voice, Post Office Box 751205, Forest Hills, New York 11375 E-mail: **poetrytown@earthlink.net**   Website: **www.poetrytown.com**

Richard Thompson Business Writer. The Commercial Appeal, 495 Union Avenue, Memphis, Tennessee 38103 Phone: (901) 333-2011 E-mail: **spkyjuice@bellsouth.com**

Delores Thornton Columnist for the Indiana Herald newspaper, and for the HYPE Magazine. Additionally, she is the "Literary Expert" on blackrefer.com. Delores Thornton, Marguerite Press, Post Office Box 53941, Indianapolis, Indiana 46253 Phone: (317) 626-6885 Fax: (317) 298-8889 E-mail: **dthorn4047@aol.com**   Website: **margueritepress.com**

Mark J. Tuggle Freelance Writer. Contact Mr. Mark J. Tuggle, 102 West 109th Street, Apartment #1B, New York, New York 10025 E-mail: **mjt579@msn.com**

Ismail Turay, Jr. Journalist, writer and reporter. Ismail Turay, Jr., Dayton Daily News, 45 South Ludlow Street, Dayton, Ohio 45402 E-mail: **liberian_1@man.com**

Raymond Tyler Columnist, Freelance writer-photographer, Essence, The Source, and Vibe Magazine. Contact Mrs. Raymond Tyler, Atlantic City Shines, 6701 Black Horse Pike, Suite A-4, EHT, New Jersey 08234 Phone: (609) 677-0168 E-mail: **acshines2004@aol.com**

Monica Z. Utsey Freelance writer & editor, Ms. Utseys work has appeared in national publications, including Heart & Soul and Upscale Magazines. Ms. Monica Z. Utsey, 201 I Street South West, #531, Washington, DC 20024 Phone: (202) 479-9222 Fax: (202) 484-5680 E-mail: **MONICAUTSEY@aol.com** Website: **www.southerndcmochamoms.com**

Denise T. Ward Sports Writer. Denise T. Ward, San Diego Union Tribune, 350 Camino De La Reina, San Diego, California 92108 Phone: (619) 718-5304 Fax: (619) 293-2443 E-mail: **denise.ward@uniontrib.com**

Jerry W. Ward, Jr. Professor of English at Dillard University, Ward is a poet, literary critic, and editor. Contact Jerry W. Ward, Jr., Department of English, Dillard University, 2601 Gentilly Boulevard, New Orleans, Louisiana 70122 E-mail: **jerryward31@hotmail.com**

Tamika Washington Writer. Contact Ms. Tamika Washington, 2201 Hayes Road, Suite #4215, Houston, Texas 77077 E-mail: **markusmond@hotmail.com**

Rod Watson Urban affairs editor and columnist. Contact Rod Watson, The Buffalo News, One News Plaza, Post Office Box 100, Buffalo, New York 14240 Phone: (716) 849-5598 Fax: (716) 847-0207 E-mail: **lcoles@njn.org**

C. A. Webb Writer for the Arts/Entertainment section of The Mississippi Link newspaper. Contact C. A. Webb, C.A. Webb Enterprises, 105 McCornell Circle, Brandon, Mississippi 39042 Phone: (601) 201-8139 E-mail: **cawebb@cawebb.com** Website: **www.cawebb.com**

Sandra L. West A journalist with credits in Urban Profile and Black Masks magazines, and is currently a Staff Writer for Positive Community Magazine and New Jersey Forum newspaper. She was Assistant Editor of The Savannah Tribune during the 1990s; and a Journalist for Information News for the City of Newark during the late 1970s. Ms. West is a member of Harlem Writers Guild and Carolina African-American Writers Collective. Contact Ms. Sandra L. West, 177 Camden Street, Newark, New Jersey 07103 Phone: (973) 424-0538 E-mail: **slwest@andromeda.rutgers.edu**

George White Vice President (print) of The Black Journalist Association of Southern California (BJASC). Contact Mr. George White, UCLA Center for Communications, 3701 Stocker Street, Suite 204, Los Angeles, California 90008 Phone: (310) 206-2189 Fax: (310) 206-2972 E-mail: **geowhite@ucla.edu** Website: **www.uclaccc.ucla.edu**

Dera R. Williams Published writer of short stories, articles and essays free lance writer-travel and contributor to literature manual. Also a literary columnist at Dera's Den. Contact Ms. Dera R. Williams, CocoWriter Book & Tea Parlor, 4316 Rilea Way Suite 2, Oakland, California 94605 E-mail: **dwillautho@aol.com** Website: **www.apooo.org**

Emily Means-Willis Educator, literary reviewer, columnist. Recently retired and has published a novel entitled "Looking for that Silver Spoon." She is involved in doing numerous literary reviews and critiques for noted authors and poets. She also writes for various magazines. A second novel "Flip Side of the Coin" will be released in 2007. Emily Means-Willis, We, Us and Company, International, 419 Douglas Street, Park Forest, Illinois 60466 Phone: (708) 769-4116 E-mail: **pamemi@comcast.net** Website: **www.weusandcompany.com**

Freddie Willis Sports Copy Editor, The Times Picayune, 3800 Howard Avenue, New Orleans, Louisiana 70140 Phone: (504) 826-3405 E-mail: **fwillis@timespicayune.com**

Gloria Dulan-Wilson Freelance writer/photographer, screenwriter and public speaker who has covered the Black political arena of New York and Northern New Jersey. Has interviewed and profiled such luminaries as Ossie Davis, Min. Louis Farrakhan, Cong. Charles Rangel, Floyd Flake, Kweisi Mfume, interviewed Diana Ross, Don King, the late Johnnie Cochran, Rosa Parks, the late Mrs. Coretta Scott King, and Maynard Jackson among others. She recently formed NYNJAA NEWS(c) (an acronym for New York New Jersey African American News) to provide greater services for print and electronic media. Many of her exclusive photos have been utilized by other publications, as well as accompanying her own articles. Ms. Dulan-Wilson has hosted call-in talk shows, including Kaleidoscope, in California; has 12 appearances on DONAHUE and 4 appearances on GERALDO. Gloria has written for the Daily Challenge News, New York Beacon, Positive Community Magazine, About. Time Magazine, the African Sun Times, The African Observer, Today's Black World, and special editions for the Amsterdam News. Ms. Gloria Dulan-Wilson, 90 Church Street, Suite 3343, New York City, New York 10008 E-mail: **geemomadee@yahoo.com**

Alecia Goodlow-Young Author, columnist, and a freelance writer. Alecia Goodlow-Young, 28490 Tavistock Trail, Southfield, Michigan 48034 Phone: (313) 796-7949 Fax: (313) 541-6638 E-mail: **aleciawrites@sbcglobal.net**

Competitions/Awards

Black Filmmakers Hall Of Fame Inc. Features film presentations and festivals of works by independent black filmmakers. Annual film, video and screenplay competition. BFHFI also publishes an annual catalogue featuring biographical material about filmmakers being inducted into the Black filmmakers Hall Of Fame. Felix Curtis, Executive Director, BFHFI, 410 14th Street, Oakland, California 94612 E-mail: **bfhfinc@aol.com**

The Black Caucus Literature Awards Recognize excellence in adult fiction and nonfiction by African American authors published in the previous year, recognition of a first novelist, as well as a citation for Outstanding Contribution to Publishing. Deadline for nominations is December 31. Contact BCALA Literary Awards Committee Chair, John S. Page, BCALA Awards, 3003 Van Ness Street, North West, W522, Washington, DC 20008 Phone: (202) 274-6030 Fax: (202) 274-6012 Website: **www.literature-awards.com/black_caucus_awards.htm**

Candace Award The National Coalition Of One Hundred Black Women host the Annual Candace Award ceremony which recognizes the outstanding achievements of Black women, and men who have demonstrated unique support of Black women and their initiatives in numerous fields of endeavor. Contact NCBW, 38 West 32nd Street, Suite 1610, New York, New York 10001 E-mail: **NC100BW@aol.com** Website: **www.ncbw.org**

The Coretta Scott King Award Presented annually by the Coretta Scott King Task Force of the American Library Association's Ethnic Multicultural Information Exchange Round Table (EMIERT). Recipients are authors and illustrators of African descent whose distinguished books promote an understanding and appreciation of the "American Dream." Contact Tanga Morris, ALA, Office of Literacy and Outreach Services, 50 East Huron Street, Chicago, Illinois 60611 Phone: (800) 545-2433 Website: **www.ala.org/ala/srrt/corettascottking/corettascott.htm**

Film Life Movie Awards Established in 1997, by Jeff Friday, President and CEO of Film Life, Inc., the Film Life Movie Awards is a star-studded awards ceremony celebrating Black cinema. It is held as the culminating event of the American Black Film Festival (ABFF). The awards were created to recognize the achievement of persons of African descent in Hollywood, as well as to showcase and reward the work of the independent filmmaker. Contact Jana Elise Taylor, Film Life, Inc., Post Office Box 688, New York, New York 10012 Phone: (212) 966-2411 Fax: (212) 966-2411 E-mail: **info@thefilmlife.com** Website: **www.thefilmlife.com**

Hurston/Wright LEGACY Award The first national award presented to published writers of African descent by the national community of Black writers. This award, underwritten by Borders Books & Music, consists of prizes for the highest quality writing in the categories of Fiction, Debut Fiction, Nonfiction, and Contemporary Fiction. The Hurston/Wright Foundation, 6525 Belcrest Road, Suite 531, Hyattsville, Maryland 20782 Phone: (301) 683-2134 Fax: (301) 277-1262 E-mail: **info@hurstonwright.org** Website: **www.hurstonwright.org**

International Black Writers & Artists (IBWA/LA) Annual conference features an awards dinner dance banquet. Linda A. Hughes, Board Member and Co-conference Planner. Contact IBWA/LA, Post Office Box 43576, Los Angeles, California 90043 Phone: (323) 964-3721 E-mail: **lahughes@ibwala.org** Website: **www.ibwala.org**

NAACP Image Award Event celebrating the outstanding achievements and performances of people of color in the arts as well as those individuals or groups who promote social justice/ NAACP Image Awards, 4929 Wilshire Boulevard, Suite 310, Los Angeles, California 90010 Phone: (323) 938-5268   Fax: (323) 938-5045 E-mail: **imageawards@naacpnet.org** Website: **www.naacpimageawards.net/main.html**

OBS Pilot Competition Competition features cash awards for winning pilot scripts to be read by major production companies and top talent agencies (UTA, Edmonds Entertainment, UPN, Disney, Fox TV). Winners in each genre will receive a Professional Table Reading. Contact OBS Pilot Competition, The Organization of Black Screenwriters, Inc., 1968 Adams Boulevard, Los Angeles, California 90018 Phone: (323) 735-2050 E-mail: **sfranklin@obswriter.com** Website: **www.obswriter.com**

Philadelphia Writers' Conference, Inc. Contest. Submit manuscripts in advance for criticism by the workshop leaders. About a dozen contest categories. Cash prizes and certificates are given to first and second place winners, plus full tuition for the following year's conference to first place winners. Contact PWC Registrar, D. O. Haggerty, 535 Fairview Road, Medford, New Jersey 08055 E-mail: **info@pwcwriters.org** Website: **www.pwcwriters.org**

Romance Slam Jam Competition Awards Ema Rogers Award. Annaual conference.recognize the authors of this remarkable genre, and to celebrate their craft with their avid fans - from just a few to several hundred, and has welcomed writers and fans from more than twenty-five cities and four countries." Romance Slam Jam, 90-06 Merrick Boulevard, Jamaica, New York 11432 E-mail: **romanceslamjam2005@yahoo.com** Website: **www.romanceslamjam.com**

Composers/Songwriters

Michael Antonio The primary writer for Cultivatedflix Productions L.L.C., an independent media company that creates entertainment for the black/urban community. Michael Antonio, Cultivatedflix, 27111 167th Place South East, Suite 105-16, Covington, Washington 98042 E-mail: **admin@cultivatedflix.com** Website: **www.cultivatedflix.com**

Tiffany L. Benton-Bailey Songwriter and publisher. Provides music production and promotion services to various artists and businesses. Conduct workshops, conferences, musical eventsTiffany Benton-Bailey, Totally Blessed Productions, 9913 Maury Cove, Olive Branch, Mississippi 38654 Phone: (662) 893-0760 E-mail: **totallyblessedgospel@hotmail.com**

Jillina "J-Bax" Baxter Website Journalist – The Hive/Blaze 1 Radio at blaze1graphixs.com in Atlanta, Georgia. J-Bax has written a catalog close to 300 consisting of Rap & R&B songs and poetry pieces. Other projects include working on a number of books (poetry "Vision Though Verses", semi-autobiography "Web Celeb", a fictional novel "The Strangers We Call Friends" and a coffee table book "A Pictorial Purpose". Jillina "J-Bax" Baxter, 184 Second Avenue, Albany, New York 12202 Phone: (518) 210-3518 E-mail: **jbmeow@yahoo.com**

Troy Buckner A songwriter/lyricist and literary writer, Ms. Buckner was the Producer and Executive Producer for the theatrical production, 'Tell Hell I Aint Comin', starring Tommy Ford from the sitcom, 'Martin & New York Undercover' and Tony Grant from the Grammy nominated R & B Group, 'Az Yet' on the La Face Record label. Ms. Buckner has managed and co-produced Gospel Renown Artist and Stella Award Winner, Kenny Smith and Vernessa Mitchell from the Motown's Grammy Award winning R & B Group, 'Hi-Energy. Ms. Troy Buckner, Hy'tara Entertainment, Post Office Box 19049, Anaheim, California 92817 Phone: (714) 227-5000 E-mail: **birdinflight@aol.com** Website: **www.abirdinflight.com**

Mary Kathryn Cannon Published poet/writer/author/songwriter. The song Hold On was recorded in 2002. I am a member of ASCAP music Industry. I began writing in 1988 have publications in many news papers, school newsletters public schools and colleges, have written articles in the Sussex Countain, Milford Chronicle, the Shore Times, Harrington Journal and the Delaware State News. Contributed poems to the Save Our Children Coalition, Boys Town, The Del-Tec College Newsletter, The Child Inc, The Covenant House in New York The community Drumbeat paper, The Correctional Institutions state wide, the Montel Williams Show and the White House. Nominated Who's Who in poetry 2004 by the International Library of Poetry and published in Eternal Portraits in 2004. Listed in The American Biographical Institution as Thousand Notable Women in 192, and nominated Five Thousand Personalities of The World in 1994. I received The Dr Martin Luther King Jr Literary Award and a certificate from the Youth and Families Child Inc Of Delaware. Golden Poet Award in 1989, Silver Poet in 1992 and was awarded a certificate in 1988 by The International World of Poetry. Mary Kathryn Cannon,19643 Donovans Road, Georgetown Delaware 19947 E-mail: **kittymaryq@aol.com**

Bil Carpenter A songwriter, Carpenter's songs have been recorded by Grammy nominees David "Pop" Winans and Candi Staton, among others. In 2005, Carpenter's first book Uncloudy Days: The Gospel Music Encyclopedia (Backbeat Books) was published and the companion compilation CD Uncloudy Days (Artemis Gospel) was released. Bill Carpenter holds a B.A. in history from the American University in Washington, D.C. He also studied at the University of Bourgogne in France. Over the last decade, he has worked both as a music journalist and a record label publicist. He was a contributing editor to the first edition of the All Music Guide and has written hundreds of articles for publications such as People magazine, the Washington Post, Goldmine and Living Blues. He has also written liner note essays for various CD compilations for Sony/BMG Music, Malaco, Warner Bros, and EMI Records. He resides in Washington, D.C. where he runs Capital Entertainment, a small public relations company that has worked extensively with gospel artists such as Vickie Winans, Bishop T.D. Jakes, CeCe Winans, and Donald Lawrence & the Tri-City Singers, among many others. Carpenter's "Did You Know" trivia segments can also be heard weekly on "The BeBe Winans Radio Show" that is syndicated to over 100 radio stations throughout the USA. In the fall 2006, Carpenter released "An Uncloudy Christmas" CD of new collection of holiday songs recorded by Candi Staton, Pookie Hudson & the Spaniels, and others. Contact Bil Carpenter, Capital Entertainment, 217 Seaton Place North East, Washington, D.C. 20002 Phone: (202) 636-7028 E-mail: **carpbil@aol.com** Website: **www.bilcarpenter.com**

Gordon Chambers Grammy Award winner currently signed to L.A. Reid's prestigious Hitco Music publishing company where he has written for over 60 recording artists, including household names, Aretha Franklin, Queen Latifah, Brandy, Gladys Knight, Chaka Khan and Marc Anthony. He is best known for his 1994 Grammy winning hit "I Apologize" for Anita Baker and his 1995 #1 Grammy-nominated smash "If You Love Me" for the trio Brownstone (which was later featured as the theme song of the film "Living Out Loud"). More recently, the eight-time ASCAP winner has written for superstars Patti Labelle and Ron Isley ("Gotta Go Solo"), as well as penned tunes for superstars Whitney Houston and Bobby Brown ("My Love"), R&B crooner Carl Thomas ("My Valentine"), breakthrough soul singer Angie Stone "No More Rain (In This Cloud)" and pop sensation Beyonce ("After All Is Said And Done"). Over the years, his compositions have been performed at the ESSENCE awards, the American Music Awards and the Goodwill Games as well as six major motion pictures. He has received community service awards from the New York youth organizations Boys Harbor and the Bay Shore Schools Arts Education Fund. Gordon has just finished and released his debut album "Introducing Gordon Chambers" which features special guests Carl Thomas, Glenn Lewis, Roy Hargrove and Mike Phillips. Produced by Chambers with Troy Taylor (B2K), Barry Eastmond (Anita Baker) and Brian Bacchus (Norah Jones), the album is classic R&B with hints of his first love: jazz. Awards for I Apologize: Grammy Winner, Best R&B Performance, Female, 1995 If You Love Me: Grammy Nomination, Best R&B Performance, Duo or Group, 1995 Missing You: Grammy Nomination, Best Pop Collaboration with Vocals, 1996, No More Rain: Lady of Soul Winner, Best R&B Song, Female, 2001, If You Love Me: ASCAP Winner, Top 50 Pop Songs of the Year, 1995, If You Love Me: ASCAP Winner, Top 50 R&B Songs of the Year, 1995, I Apologize: ASCAP Winner, Top 50 R&B Songs of the Year, 1995, No More Rain, ASCAP Winerr Top 50 R&B Songs of the Year, 2001. Contact Mr. Gordon Chambers, 171 Adelphi Street, Brooklyn, New York 11205 Phone: (212) 696-6774 Fax: (718) 852-1886 E-mail: **gordon@gordonchambers.com** Website: **www.gordonchambers.com**

Harry Walter Cooper, Jr. Lyricist and composer. Most well know song "ON The Other Side of Through." The song was recorded by James Bignon and reached #17 on the gospel billboard charts. Number one in Atlanta for 3 weeks in 1998. Harry Walter Cooper, Jr., 210 South Euclid Avenue, San Diego, California 92114 Fax: (619) 264-9049 E-mail: **sepastor@yahoo.com**

Kolade Daniel Poet, Songwriter, Scriptwriter. Kolade Daniel, 17 Igun Street, Itire Surulere, Lagos 23401 Nigeria Phone: 234 806650672 E-mail: **koladedaniel@praize.com**

Arthur Douse Vice President, writer, and HipHop artist. Publishing company. Arthur Douse, Fat Boy Hits Music Group, 1244 Herkamer, Brooklyn, New York 11233 Phone: (718) 216-5334 E-mail: **celsiusbk@aol.com**

Kenneth Gamble Co-founder/Chairman of Gamble-Huff Music. Legends Kenny Gamble and Leon Huff were songwriting and producing partners for 30 years. Born in Philadelphia on August 11, 1943, Mr. Gamble first teamed with Leon Huff during the late '50s while a member of the harmony group the Romeos, which also included another aspiring area musician named Thom Bell, who would become crucial to Gamble's later success. "The 81," a 1964 single by the little-known Candy & the Kisses, was the inaugural Gamble-Huff co-production, and three years later the duo scored their first Top Five pop hit with the Soul Survivors' "Expressway to Your Heart." Soon recruiting the aforementioned Bell as arranger, they subsequently scored with several smash hits. He and partner Kenny Gamble wrote or co-wrote over 3,000 songs in 35 years including R and B #1 hits, pop #1 hits, gold and platinum records, Grammy winners and BMI songwriters awards honorees. Contact Mr. Kenneth Gamble, Gamble-Huff Music, 309 South Broad Street, Philadelphia, Pennsylvania 19107 Phone: (215) 985-0900 E-mail: **chuckgamblepir@aol.com** Website: **www.gamble-huffmusic.com**

Kyra Gaunt Kyra a.k.a. "Professor G" is a singer-songwriter and an associate professor of ethnomusicology at New York University who lectures nationally and internationally on African American music and issues of race, gender and the musical body. Her 2006 book The Games Black Girls Play: Learning the Ropes from Double-Dutch to Hip-hop (NYU Press, 2006) creates a new way of thinking about how black musical style and taste is learned and developed through interactions between the sexes and between genres. Kyra Gaunt, 1 Washington Square Village #5-H, New York, New York 10012 Phone: (646) 831-0615 E-mail: **kyraocity@yahoo.com**

Forest Garfield Hairston Poet, script and songwriter, Forest Garfield Hairston is author of the book "Spirit Ran Free", an emotional saga about love and courage. Poems from the book include Caged Soul, Even Further, Ever America, Truth, and Across This Land. Here in this superb work, Forest brings his personal experience as an author avidly aware of our Black history. His successful career as a songwriter-music producer, screenwriter and poet, extends his talents a step further as a great author with a definite voice. Contact Mr. Forest Hairston, Producer, ForGen Productions, 3654 Barham Boulevard, Suite Q301, Los Angeles, California Phone: (323) 851-1225 E-mail: **fgprod@forgen.com** Website: **www.blackvillage.com**

Vernon Hairston Composer, jazz pianist. Original Compositions. Composer for hire. Music Transcription services. Contact Vernon Hairston, Hairstonning Music, Post Office Box 91194, Columbus, Ohio 43209 E-mail: **vh@vernonhairston.com** Website: **www.vernonhairston.com**

Fred Hammond Songwriter, bassist and vocalist, and gifted musical arranger and producer. But, his work with Face to Face Productions Corporation, the company for which he is both founder and CEO, has earned him the title the "Babyface" of gospel. Few gospel artists can boast of the consistency of sales, radio airplay and concert appearances which Hammond has achieved over the course of his career. As a solo artist and member of the pioneering urban group, Commissioned, he has sold nearly 2 million albums. Since retiring from that group in 1995, his work with Radical for Christ has made him a mainstay on Billboard's Gospel Chart top 10, along with frequent appearances on the magazine's Heatseekers and Music Video Sales charts. In addition, as if that were not enough, Hammond's work as a producer has landed him in the #1 spot among gospel producers according to the Gospel Music Round-up. His projects have received and been nominated for every major award including the Grammy, and the N.A.A.C.P. Image, Stellar, Dove, and GMWA Excellence Awards. Contact Mr. Kevin Wilson, Face To Face, Inc., 501 North Loop, Cedar Hill, Texas 75104 Phone: (972) 293-2885 Fax: (972) 293-6866 E-mail: **kwilson@fredhammondmusic.com** Website: **www.fredhammondmusic.com**

Leslie Harris Born and raised in Detroit, Michigan. Married with two children. Received B.S. from Michigan State University and J.D. from University of Detroit Mercy School of Law. Author of 18 manuscripts of poetry. Individual works have been publsihed in various magazines and ezines (Facets Magazine, FRESH!). Also a songwriter (in various genres). Member of the songwriting team known as Infectious Grooves. E-mail: **quality6287@aol.com**

Joseph Harrison Songwriter. Demo production/multimedia packages using our original music. Contact Mr. Joseph Harrison, Post Office Box 2742, Prairie View, Texas 77446 E-mail: **Joseph_Harrison@pvamu.edu** Website: **www.GrooveDepot.com**

Leon Huff Co-founder and Vice Chairman of Gamble-Huff Music Company, Mr. Leon Huff helped to bring the genre of Philadelphia soul music to the world. He and partner Kenny Gamble wrote or co-wrote over 3,000 songs in 35 years including R and B #1 hits, pop #1 hits, gold and platinum records, Grammy winners and BMI songwriters awards honorees. Songs they have written and co-produced "Backstabbers," Cowboys to Girls, Don't Leave Me This Way, For the Love of Money, Love Train, If You Don't Know Me By Now and many others. In February 1999, Kenny and Leon were honored by the National Academy and Recording Arts and Science with the coveted Trustees Award. On May 31, 1995 they were inducted in the National Academy of Songwriters' Hall of Fame. Contact Mr. Leon Huff, Gamble-Huff Music, 309 South Broad Street, Philadelphia, Pennsylvania 19107 Phone: (215) 985-0900 E-mail: **chuckgamblepir@aol.com** Website: **www.gamble-huffmusic.com**

K.B. Jenkins A graduate of the State University of New Jersey, Minister K.B. Jenkins is currently in pursuit of her Masters of Divinity. She is the founder/president of S.O.L.O. 4 Christ c/o The King's Daughters Ministries, Inc., and Messianic Music, as well as the RestPress Publishing Co. This psalmist/preacher/teacher/songwriter and now acclaimed author has had the opportunity of serving as an associate minister and worship leader under the leadership and tutelage of the honorable Bishop Donald Hilliard, Jr. c/o The Cathedral International of New Jersey for several years. Minister K.B. Jenkin, RestPress Publishing, Post Office Box 244086 Atlanta, Georgia 30324 Phone: (800) 630-4813 E-mail: **info@restpresspublishing.org** Website: **www.restpresspublishing.org**

Rodney Jenkins Musician, songwriter, producer, and savvy businessman, Rodney Jenkins is President/CEO of Dark Child, Inc., a music and song production company. Dubbed "Hitman" by the music industry, Rodney is one of the most sought after pop, R&B and Gospel music producers in the industry. Grammy (s) Award winner, he has written, produced and co-wrote songs for such artists as Michael Jackson, Whitney Houston, Britney Spears, N'Sync, Backstreet Boys, Mark Anthony, Kenneth "Babyface" Edmunds, to name a few. Contact Mr. Rodney Jenkins, Dark Child, Inc. E-mail: **info@darkchild.com** Website: **www.darkchild.com**

Darryl D. Lassiter Composer, Writer, Producer-Director/Filmmaker. A musician since 1975, Darryl has played nearly every instrument in the brass family, including trombone, baritone, and french horn. But it is the trumpet that he is most familiar. Concentrating on music along with television, radio, and print media as a student at Alabama State University; the 1986 grad began laying the foundation of the story for what would become PAY THE PRICE! Darryl played first chair in every band at Alabama State University (ASU) including the marching, jazz, symphonic, brass ensemble, and trumpet quartet. He won every major award in the 'school of music.' He wrote the entire band a cappella songs in the movie as well as composed and performed on three of the songs on the soundtrack. Using his experiences in the marching band and speaking with former band members, he came up with the idea to tell the never-before-told story of the price one pays to be in a Black College Marching Band. Working tirelessly on this project since August 1, 1991 (currently in $450 Million litigation against 20th Century Fox for DRUMLINE). Darryl used all of his connections as a newspaper editor, magazine writer, television and video producer, radio programmer and filmmaker to get the word out that he needed funds to make his movie dream come true. It began to come true upon producing/directing a music video for David Gough (Executive Producer) in 1999, and the rest is history. He recently was given a proclamation from the mayor of his hometown, inducted into the National Black College Alumni Distinction Hall Of Fame a Lifetime Achievement Literacy Classic Award 2003 and the coveted Stellar Award 2004 for "Video Of The Year." Contact Mr. Darryl D'Wayne Lassiter, Post Office Box 50374, Atlanta, Georgia 30302 E-mail: **darryl@ddlentertainment.net** Website: **www.ddlentertainment.net**

Charles E. McClinon African-American author, singer, songwriter and playwright. Enjoy writing fiction, drama and musicals. Charles E. McClinon, 8307 Mayfair Street, Cincinnati, Ohio Phone: (513) 417-9465 E-mail: **cmcclinon@yahoo.com**

Roy Dennis Merriwether   A contemporary, classic composer Mr. Merriwethers' music is rooted in a strong gospel tradition, infused with jazz, blues, and rock elements, all intertwined with classical influences. His compositions range from jazz ballads to big band arrangements to folk operas (scored for vocal chorus, orchestra and dances) to compositions orchestrated for an 85-piece orchestra. He started playing piano at age three; turned professional with his own group at age 18 and has devoted himself to both composing and performing ever since. His earlier works include: "The Alma Mater," a ballad, "March Tempo," for Thomas Edison State College, Trenton, NJ, "The All Nighter," jazz/funk, 1984 and "Sister City, Let It Be Done," inspirational and commissioned for the celebration of sister cities, Trenton, New Jersey and The Lenin District of Moscow, Russia, 1985. He wrote "A Song For Sarah," a ballad, co-written by Blaine Collins, 1986. His latest work is a love ballad written in Meriwether's classical jazz style titled, "This One's On Me." E-mail: **info@roymeriwether.com** Website: **www.roymeriwether.com**

Carman Moore Composer, Author, Music Critic. Born in Lorain, Ohio, Carman earned his Bachelor of Music Degree at Ohio State University before moving to New York City, where he studied composition privately with Hall Overton and at the Juilliard School with Luciano Berio and Vincent Persichetti where he earned his Masters Degree with distinction. He began composing for symphony and chamber ensembles while writing lyrics for pop songs, gradually adding opera, theatre, dance and film scores to his body of work. His work in popular music included lyrics and arrangements for ex-Rascals leader Felix Cavaliere. Among his early commissioned symphonic works were Wildfires and Field Songs for the New York Philharmonic conducted by Pierre Boulez and Gospel Fuse for the San Francisco Symphony with Seiji Ozawa conducting and Cissy Houston the vocal soloist. Among other of his works for symphony orchestra have been Concerto for Blues Piano and Orchestra (for Jay McShann); Four Movements for A Five-Toed Dragon, conducted by Isaiah Jackson with the American Symphony Orchestra and Orchestra of the Sorbonne (Paris); Hit; A Concerto for Percussion and Orchestra (Jackson and the Rochester Philharmonic); and Concerto for Flute, Pi'pa, and Orchestra (premiere pending). In 1980 he founded the innovative electro-acoustic SKYMUSIC ENSEMBLE, which since has performed in America, Europe and Asia, including at La Scala in Milan, Geneva's Made-In-America Festival, and at the 9th Hong Kong Ready-to-Wear (fashion) Show. Based in New York City, SKYMUSIC ENSEMBLE, for which Moore acts as conductor and principal composer, appears at venues ranging from the Lincoln Center Out-Of-Doors Festival (where they performed on August 15, 2007) to the Cathedral of St. John the Divine, where Moore and the Ensemble were Artists-in-Residence for many years. Carman Moore's intermedia MASS FOR THE 21st CENTURY was commissioned by Lincoln Center, where, at its enthusiastically-received 1994 outdoor performances conducted by the composer, the Mass attracted one of the largest audiences in Lincoln Center history. In December of 1999 it was performed at the Parliament of the World's Religions in Cape Town, South Africa and in New York at the Winter Garden on the World Financial Center's Millennium Series. Moore's music theatre work includes "Distraughter, or the Great Panda Scanda" and "Paradise Re-Lost," collaborations with the distinguished playwright Charles "Oyamo" Gordon. In 1998 he scored a libretto by Ishmael Reed for the gospel opera, Gethsemane Park, which played in San Francisco's Elaine Hansbury Theatre and at New York's Nuyorican Poets' Cafe during the summer of 2000. A previous collaboration of Moore, Reed, and poet Colleen McElroy, the musical Wild Gardens of The Loup Garou, was commissioned by the Music Theare Group/Lenox Arts Centre and subsequently produced both at New York's Judson Memorial Church and at the Bayview Opera House in San Francisco. Moore's comic opera The Last Chance Planet received over 70 performances in 1994 by the Dayton Opera Company during Moore's year as Composer-in-Residence to the City of Dayton. Among Moore's scores for theatre have been Yale Rep's production of Shakespeare's Timon of Athens (starring James Earl Jones and directed by Lloyd Richards) and When The Bough Breaks at LaMama E.T.C., directed by Lawrence Sacharow. Carman Moore, 152 Columbus Avenue, New York, New York 10023 Phone: (212) 580-0825 E-mail: **skycarmuse@mindspring.com**

Kevin Neal Pastor, singer and BMI registered songwriter. Kevin Neal, 4173 Wellington Hills Drive, Snellville, Georgia 30039 Phone: (770) 972-9632 E-mail: **1kdneal@bellsouth.net**

Dariel Raye Author, composer, editor. Dariel Raye, 655 Welworth Street, Mobile, Alabama 36617 Phone: (251) 661-3464 E-mail: **darielraye@yahoo.com**

Marsha D. Jenkins-Sanders Writer of novels and songs. Marsha received acclaim in the music industry for lyrics written for Keith Washington's freshmen album project, Make Time for Love. Both "Kissing You" and "Closer" introduced her writing talent and she received award-winning recognition from ASCAP for Writer and Publisher in the R & B genre. "Kissing You" was certified gold and went on to be featured as the background music for love scenes on ABC's soap, General Hospital. "The Other Side of Through", her debut novel will be released in February 2007 on the Strebor/Simon & Schuster label. "Jealousy: A Strange Company Keeper" will follow in 2008. Marsha D. Jenkins-Sanders, Markei Publishing, 18455 Miramar Parkway, #162, Miramar, Florida 33029 Phone: (734) 334-3645 E-mail: **mrcsdno@yahoo.com**

James Tatum Composer, Jazz concert pianist, teacher, performer and recording artist, Mr. James Tatum presents a unique lecture program designed to enhance music appreciation in the educational setting with special emphasis on jazz music, one of America's richest forms of cultural heritage. His jazz lecture seminar/performance covers such topics as *Jaxx-What Is It?*, *The History of Jazz, Jazz Artists and Their Styles, and Listening To Jazz Throughout Its History*. The series is designed to encourage audience participation throughout the lecture and appeals to audiences in K-12 and university and adult level. He has composed major jazz works; the Contemporary Jazz Mass, Return of Joshua, and many others. He is listed in Who's Who Among African-Americans 2003. Contact Mr. James Tatum, James Tatum Trio, Inc., Post Office Box 32240, Detroit, Michigan 48232 Phone: (313) 537-1265 Fax: (313) 255-9014 E-mail: **office@jamestatum.com** Website: **www.jamestatum.com**

Roosevelt "Rozie" Turner IV By the age of 5, Rozie was already singing lead vocals and traveling with his church youth choir, the Voices of Love, across the country. He was briefly a member of the gospel group All or Nothing, where he wrote and arranged most of the music. He is now a member of the Holy Hip-Hop movement, the Mobster's of Light. By far one of the most versatile up and coming artists in the music and entertainment industry –singer, emcee, songwriter, producer and actor- this Oklahoma City native fully accepted his calling of ministry through music. Roosevelt Turner, Post Office Box 32713, Oklahoma City, Oklahoma 73123 Phone: (405) 255-6716 E-mail: **rozieturner@cox.net**

Narada Michael Walden Producer, composer, singer, songwriter, musician, Narada Michael Walden was born in 1952 and grew up in Plainwell, Michigan, near Kalamazoo, situated strategically between Detroit and Chicago. Walden has been honored by his colleagues with a Grammy Award for Best R&B Song in 1985 (*Freeway of Love*), co-writing and producing two smash hits for Franklin, *Freeway* and *Who's Zoomin' Who?*, which opened the way for Franklin to garner her first platinum record in thirty years of record making. Walden cites the wealth of great soul music emanating from Detroit's Motown Records and Chicago's Chess Records as the catalyst that spurred his decision to pick up the drums and eventually write and produce "Lil Brother" and "Look What We'd Have (If You Were Mine) by T.E.V.I.N.; singles, "Never In My Life:, "Still In Love," "Nothing's Ever Gonna Stop Us Now," and "Gee Whiz" by Cherrelle; film soundtrack, "All The Way" from Dying Young by Jeffrey Osborne; "So Intense" and "Save Me" by Lisa Fischer; "There's Got To Be A Way," by Brenda Russell; "Glad To Be Alive" by Teddy Pendergrass. Contact Mr. Narada Michael Walden, Tarpan Studios, 1925 East Francisco Boulevard, Suite L, San Rafael, California 94901 Phone: (415) 485-1999 Fax: (415) 459-3234 E-mail: **inquiries@tarpanstudios.com** Website: **tarpanstudios.com**

Hubert P. Williams, Jr. Singer/songwriter/producer/poet. Mr. Hubert P. Williams, Jr., Trinity Music Group, 2907 Kingfisher Drive, Fayetteville, North Carolina Phone: (910) 977-7354 E-mail: **min.hpwilliams@yahoo.com** Website: **www.geocities.com/trinitymusicgroup2004**

Kenneth Wilson An accomplished writer, keyboardist, director, producer, publisher, minister of the gospel and businessman who is now making an awesome, new impact within gospel music made his debut over twenty seven years ago as a writer with his number one selling hit song titled "Prepare To Meet Him" recorded by the late Rev. James Cleveland and the Southern California Choir selling over 500,000 records, also recorded by Kenneth Wilson and the Greater Grace Temple Celestial Voices of Detroit, Michigan. Ken's new CD project is titled "Lifestyles of Worship." Kenneth Wilson and the Kenneth Wilson Chorale a local yet nationally known music group through their TV program Late Night Praise & Worship formerly aired nationwide on cable TV for over 8 years. Ken won the Bobby Jones Gospel Diamond Festival three years in a row for most outstanding gospel music TV production, which was also nominated for a Cable ACE Award. Their new CD project "Lifestyles of Worship" is sure to take them to their next level in gospel music. Ken, whose roots are in Detroit, Michigan, was inspired to write music by his mother the late Orpha Wilson and the late Bishop David L. Ellis, pastor of Greater Grace Temple where he was raised and recorded his first LP titled Prepare to Meet Him in 1979. Ken is now experiencing yet another level of music ministry as he is now becoming one of the most fruitful and anointed songwriters of our time, producing over 100 new gospel songs ready for any Sunday morning praise and worship service. Kenneth Wilson & the Kenneth Wilson Chorale, Post Office Box 21100, Detroit, Michigan 48221 Phone: (313) 496 3999 E-mail: **kennethwilson2@netzero.com**

Conferences/Expos

African American Arts Festival Annual county-wide celebration of African American Arts, Culture and Heritage. Atelier provides an environment for visual exposure, educational exchange and a showcase for African American art and artists. African American Atelier, 200 North Davie Street, Box 14, Greensboro, North Carolina 27401 Phone: (336) 333-6885 E-mail: **info@africanamericanatelier.org** Website: **www.africanamericanatelier.org**

African American Book Club Summit Annual, the AABCS is an excellent opportunity for book clubs to gather to discuss books, exchange ideas, develop strategies, and meet some of the country's finest authors. Contact Ms. Pamela Walker-Williams, AABCS, Pageturner, PMB-120, 2951 Marina Bay Drive, Suite #130, League City, Texas 77573 Phone: (866) 875-1044 E-mail: E-mail: **pwsquare@pageturner.net** Website: **www.pageturner.net**

African American Heritage Festival Annual festival celebration of African American culture. AAHF is a week of educational and cultural programs culminates with a weekend of social and recreational activities. Arican American Heritage Festival, The Multicultural Center, 4th Floor, Ohio Union, 1739 North High Street, Columbus, Ohio 43210 Phone: (614) 688-8449 E-mail: **multiculturalcenter@osu.edu** Website: **www.multiculturalcenter.osu.edu/afam**

African American Publisher's Pavilion Annual Conference. Founded in 2004 by Niani Colom, Associate Publisher, Genesis Press; Adrienne Ingrum, Associate Publisher, Black Issues Book Review, and Tony Rose, Publisher/CEO, Amber Communications Group, Inc. Contact Tony Rose, Publisher. Amber Communications Group, Inc., 1334 East Chandler Boulevard, Suite 5-D67, Phoenix, Arizona 85048 Phone: (480) 460-1660 Fax: (480) 283-0991 E-mail: **amberbk@aol.com** Website: **www.amberbooks.com**

African World Festival (AWF) The largest public outreach program of the year with attendance topping one million, this festival is a dynamic, colorful mix of people and cultures of the African Diaspora. Contact AWF, The Museum Of African American History, 315 East Warren Avenue, Detroit, Michigan 48201 Phone: (313) 494-5824 Fax: (313) 494-5855 E-mail: **dhamm@maah-detroit.org** Website: **www.maah-detroit.org**

Afro-American Historical and Genealogical Society, Inc. Host annual authors' luncheon held in different cities each year. Focus is on authors of Black history or genealogical books. Contact AAHGS, Post Office Box 73067, Washington, DC 20056 Phone: (202) 234-5350 E-mail: **khadmatin@earthlink.net** Website: **www.aahgs.org**

American Black Film Festival Annual. Founded in 1997 by Jeff Friday, President and CEO of Film Life, Inc. Showcases the cinematic work of independent artists of vision and emerging talent. Contact Mr. Jeff Friday, ABFF c/o of Film Life, Post Office Box 688, New York, New York 10012 E-mail: **abff@thefilmlife.com** Website: **www.abff.com**

The Arizona Black Film Showcase   Annual, competitive film showcase dedicated to supporting, celebrating and promoting the dynamic works of Black filmmakers locally and nationally.   Contact The Arizona Black Film Showcase, 68 West Buffalo Street, Suite 230 Chandler, Arizona 85225   Phone: (602) 304-0830   E-mail: **info@azblackfilm.com**

ASALH   Annual convention to celebrate and study Africana life and history hosted by The Association for the Study of African American Life and History (ASALH).   Also hosts an annual Black History Month Luncheon and co-sponsors with the National Education Association the annual Carter G. Woodson Award.   Sylvia Cyrus, ASALH, CB Powell Building, 525 Bryant Street, North West, Suite C142, Washington, DC 20059   Phone: (202) 865-0053   Fax: (202) 265-7920   E-mail: **executivedirector@asalh.net**   Website: **www.asalh.org**

Birmingham Civil Rights Institute   Host annual events, exhibitions, archives, and online resource gallery.   Serves as a depository for civil rights archives and documents.   Contact BCRI, 520 Sixteenth Street North, Birmingham, Alabama 35203   Phone: (205) 328-9696   Fax: (205) 251-6104   E-mail: **award@bcri.org**   Website: **www.bcri.org**

Black Business Professionals and Entrepreneurs Conference   Annual BBPE national conference whose mission is to service the minority business community.   Jewel Daniels, BBPE, Post Office Box 60561, Savannah, Georgia 31420   Phone: (912) 354-7400   E-mail: **jewel@blackbusinessprofessionals.com** Website: **www.blackbusinessprofessionals.com**

Black Caucus of the American Library Association (BCALA)   National association of black librarians.   Host annual conference and awards.   Newsletter.   Andrew P. Jackson, President. BCALA, VA State Library, Richmond, Virginia 23219   Phone: (804) 786-2332   Fax: (804) 786-5855   E-mail: **andrew.p.jackson@queenslibrary.org**   Website: **www.bcala.org**

Black College Radio Convention   Annual forum for black college broadcasters, professional broadcasters and members of the music industry.   Lo Jelks, Chairman.   National Association of Black College Broadcasters, Post Office Box 3191, Atlanta, Georgia 30302   Phone: (404) 523-6136 Fax: (404) 523-5467 E-mail: **bcrmail@aol.com** Website: **www.blackcollegeradio.com**

Black Events Central (BEC) Provides information on events for the African-American community ranging from concerts to lectures, networking socials to fundraisers, book signings, festivals.   Contact Black Events Central, 244 5th Avenue, #G282, New York, New York 10001 E-mail: **events@blackeventscentral.com**   Website: **www.blackeventscentral.com**

Black Film & Media Conference   A venue where Black filmmakers can expand and broaden their craft consisting of programs and promotions (film screenings, workshops, expert panels) with insight from both local and national filmmakers, government influences, education, and corporate relationships. BFMC, 923 Spring Garden Street, Suite 300, Philadelphia, Pennsylvania 19123 E-mail: **info@phillybfmc.com** Website: **www.phillybfmc.com/index.html**

Boston Book Bazaar   Nishawanda Ellis, founder.   The Boston Book Bazaar is an annual fair held in August. Kindle Eyes Books Publishing, Post Office Box 692092, Quincy, Massachusetts 02269 E-mail: **nishawnda@kindleeyesbooks.com**   Website: **www.kindleeyesbooks.com**

Indiana Black Expo, Inc. (IBE) Founded in Indianapolis in 1970 by a group of religious and civic leaders. In 1971, the same group created an exposition at the Indiana State Fairgrounds that showcased the achievements of African-Americans in the areas of culture, art, history and economics. Today, Indiana Black Expo, Inc., is a year-round, multifaceted community service organization with 11 chapters around the state of Indiana. Ms. Joyce Rogers, CEO/President. Contact Indiana Black Expo, Inc., 3145 North Meridian Street, Indianapolis, Indiana 46208 Phone: (317) 925-2702 Fax: (317) 925-6624 E-mail: **jrogers@ibeonline.com** Website: **www.indianablackexpo.com**

Independent Black Film Festival Showcases Black cinema during their four (4) day film festival. The IBFF was born from the need to provide platforms to promote and showcase the incredible inventiveness and creativity within the African-American artist community. The IBFF draws attendees and industry delegates from around the world including award-winning film and music producers and directors, screenwriters, animators, film buyers & distributors, and game publishers. Asante Addae, creator and founder of IBFF. Independent Black Film Festival, 949 West Marietta Street, Unit X-109, Atlanta, Georgia 30318 Phone: (404) 249-9529 Fax: (404) 249-9529 E-mail: **info@indieblackfilm.com** Website: **www.indieblackfilm.com**

International Black Women's Film Festival (IBWFF) Festival involves a season of film screenings and activities throughout the spring and summer. Features classic cinema, sneak preview, private, and mini screenings. International Black Women's Film Festival, 155 Tenth Street, San Francisco, California 94103 Fax: (415) 680-2413 E-mail: **ibwff@filmfestivals.net** Website: **www.ibwff.filmfestivals.net**

International Black Writers & Artists (IBWA/LA) Annual conference designed to improve skills, knowledge, and career opportunities for artists of all media. Features workshops, discussions, booksignings and an awards dinner dance banquet. Contact IBWA/LA, Post Office Box 43576, Los Angeles, California 90043 Phone: (323) 964-3721 E-mail: **info@ibwala.org** Website: **www.ibwala.org**.

Juneteenth Celebrated annually, Juneteenth is the oldest known celebration of the ending of slavery. Dating back to 1865, it was on June 19th that the Union soldiers, led by Major General Gordon Granger, landed at Galveston, Texas with news that the war had ended and that all slaves were now free. Author signings. Mr. Ahmud Ward, Birmingham Civil Rights Institute, 520 Sixteenth Street North, Birmingham, Alabama 35203 Phone: (205) 328-9696 Fax: (205) 251-6104 E-mail: **award@bcri.org** Website: **www.bcri.org**

Los Angeles Black Book Expo Itibari M. Zulu, Executive director. Contact Itibari M. Zulu, Amen-Ra Theological Seminary Press, 10920 Wilshire Boulevard., Suite 150-9132, Los Angeles, California 90024 E-mail: **admin@labbx.com** E-mail: **lmz@ucla.edu**

Midwest Regional Black Theatre Festival Held at venues throughout Greater Cincinnati and the surrounding areas, the Festival offers an exhibit of new and established African American plays and musicals; workshops, poetry, music, dance and other activities. Black Theatre Company, 5919 Hamilton Avenue, Cincinnati, Ohio 45224 Phone: (513) 241-6060 Fax: (513) 241-6671 E-mail: **cbtsherman@hotmail.com**

National Association For The Study and Performance Of African American Music (NASPAAM) Newsletter/Professional Organization. The organization serves its members and others by increasing the awareness of Black Music and its contribution to the arts, culture, and society. Frank Suggs, President. NASPAAM, 1201 Mary Jane, Memphis, Tennessee 38116 Phone: (901) 396-2913 E-mail: **fsuggs@midsouth.rr.com** Website: **www.naspaam.org**

National Association Of Black Accountants (NABA) Annual convention. Publishes newsletters and video tapes. Carla Welborn, Director. Contact Gregory Johnson, NABA, 7249-A Hanover Parkway, Greenbelt, Maryland 20770 Phone: (301) 474-6222 Fax: (301) 474-3114 E-mail: **gjohnson@nabainc.org** Website: **www.nabainc.org**

National Association Of Black Owned Broadcasters (NABOB) We host two management conferences annually of African-American owners of radio and television stations across the country. Contact James Winston, NABOB, 1155 Connecticut Avenue, North West, Washington, DC 20036 Phone: (202) 463-8970 E-mail: **info@nabob.org** Website: **www.nabob.org**

National Black Arts Festival Celebrates the arts and culture of people of African descent. Stephanie Hughley, Executive Producer. Contact National Black Arts Festival, 659 Auburn Avenue, #254, Atlanta, Georgia 30312 Phone: (404) 224-3468 Fax: (404) 730-7104 E-mail: **info@nbaf.org** Website: **www.nbaf.org**

National Black Expo Inc. Founded in 1990, by Susan F. Stanley the key mission of National Black Expo Inc., is to improve the economic viability of minority owned business enterprises. Through the exhibition portion of the NBE thousands of small businesses have increased their viability by reaching thousands of new customers. The National Black Expo Inc., 400 West 76th Street #202, Chicago, Illinois 60620 E-mail: **stantley@nationalblackexpo.com** Website: **www.nationalblackexpo.org**

The National Black Theatre Festival The North Carolina Black Repertory Company hosts the famous "The National Black Theatre Festival." A large number of workshops and seminars are available at the Festival. NCBRC, 610 Coliseum Drive, Winston-Salem, North Carolina 27106 Phone: (336) 723-2266 E-mail: **playrite@earthlink.net** Website: **www.nbtf.org**

National Society Of Black Engineers (NSBE) Annual national convention, hosting over 8,000 attendees. Chancee Lundy, National Chairperson. NSBE, 1454 Duke Street, Alexandria, Virginia 22314 Phone: (703) 549-2207 E-Mail: **info@nsbe.org** Website: **www.nsbe.org**

Philadelphia Writers' Conference, Inc. Annual, traditionally held in early June; offers from 14 workshops, seminars, several "manuscript rap." Cash prizes and certificates given plus full tuition to first place winners. Contact D. O. Haggerty, PWC Registrar, 535 Fairview Road, Medford, New Jersey 08055 E-mail: **info@pwcwriters.org** Website: **www.pwcwriters.org**

Romance Slam Jam The conference grew out of an early desire to recognize the authors of this remarkable genre, and to celebrate their craft with their avid fans. Slam Jam, 90-06 Merrick Boulevard, Jamaica, New York 11432 E-mail: **romanceslamjam2005@yahoo.com** Website: **www.romanceslamjam.com**

San Francisco Black Film Festival (SFBFF) Celebration of African American cinema and the African cultural Diaspora. Festival showcases a diverse collection of films - from emerging and established filmmakers - that highlight the beauty and complexity of the African and African American experience. Contact SFBFF, Post Office Box 15490, San Francisco, California 94115 Phone: (415) 771-9271 Fax: (415) 346-9046 E-mail: **info@sfbff.org** Website: **www.sfbff.org**

Urban Network Magazine Annual industry conference. Launched in 1988 by founder, editor, Mary Nichols, aka DJ Fusion, Urban Network Magazine has been serving the music and entertainment industries at large for more than 15 years. A bi-monthly newsletter is sent to several million opt in subscribers at urbannetwork.com/newsletter.html. Contact Mary Nichols, Urban Network Magazine, 14 Easton Avenue, #250 New Brunswick, New Jersey 08901 Phone: (347) 252 4032 E-mail: **djfusion@ureach.com** Website: **www.urbannetwork.com**

Women's Empowerment Expo Created in 1994, in honor of Women's History Month, Women's Empowerment was designed to enhance the lives of African American women by addressing issues that specifically impact their "health, hearts and pocketbooks." Throughout the day, this expo vent offers seminars, workshops, demonstrations, sampling, and shopping. Contact NTR/Special Events, Radio One, Raleigh, 8001 Creedmoor Road, Suite 101 Raleigh, North Carolina 27613 Phone: (919) 848.9736 E-mail: **info@womensempowermentexpo.com** Website: **www.womensempowermentexpo.com**

Women's Leadership Summit Annual, hosted by the National Association of Black Female Executives in Music & Entertainment, Inc. (NABFEME) Founded in 1999 by record industry trailblazer Johnnie Walker, NABFEME supports and empowers professional women of color, executives, managers, and technicians in the music and entertainment industries. More than 2,500 women worldwide have joined this stellar nonprofit organization, whose purpose is to assist with the economic and career development of women in entertainment. NABFEME is comprised of women from many different sectors of the business world and the entertainment industry. The organization's COO and annual Women's Leadership Summit Executive Director is Elektra Entertainment VP, Michelle Madison. Contact NABFEME, 59 Maiden Lane, 27th Floor, New York, New York 10038 Fax: (201) 313-1192 E-mail: **info@NABFEME.org** Website: **www.nabfeme.org**

Gregory J. Reed, Esq.
Author * Agent * Producer

Gregory J. Reed is active in areas of sports, corporate, entertainment, and taxation laws. He is the first African American to receive a Master of Taxation Laws in Michigan. He is the first African American lawyer to Chair a Sports and Entertainment Lawyers Section in the United States. Reed is a producer and represents sports figures, entertainers, firms, and numerous persons from TV to Broadway, including Anita Baker, Wynston Marsalis, The Winans, and First Black Miss USA, Carole Gist and many other artists. He is the only attorney to represent six world champion boxers. He has produced such plays as the Pulitzer Prize winning production, *A Soldier's Play*, which was developed into a screenplay by Columbia Pictures as *A Soldier's Story*, awarded an Oscar. Reed has produced and represented the following Broadway plays: "Ain't Misbehavin"; "For Colored Girls Who Have Considered Suicide When the Rainbow Is Enuf"; "What The Wine Sellers Buy"; "The Wiz"; "Your Arms Too Short To Box With God"; and Rosa Parks "More Than a Bus Story," co-authored with Von Washington. Reed also staged the largest tour entertainment tribute in the U.S. in honor of Dr. Martin Luther King Jr., with Emmy winner Al Eaton in *We Are The Dream*. He produced a documentary of the Last Poets, originators of Rap music, whom he reunited for a national tour.

Author of twelve books, Reed wrote the first exclusive contract negotiating guide explaining tax aspects of entertainment and sports law in the U.S. entitled *Tax Planning and Contract Negotiating Techniques for Creative Persons, Professional Athletes and Entertainers* (1979). His second book, *This Business of Boxing and Its Secrets* (1981) the only book of its kind, made the New York Times bestseller list, and was cited as an international authority on the subject matter. Other releases include *This Business of Entertainment and Its Secrets* (1985) and *Negotiations Behind Closed Doors* (1992). A fifth book, entitled *Economic Empowerment Through The Church* (1994, Zondervan Publishing House, 1994 American Book Awards Winner) is about mass organization, religion, communication, tax planning. Reed's sixth book is *This Business of Celebrity Estates*. Reed is co-author of the book *Quiet Strength* with Mrs. Rosa Parks (Zondervan Publishing House, 1995) and *Dear Mrs. Parks* (1996, Lee & Low Publishing).

In October 1992, Reed purchased the original manuscript on the Autobiography of Malcolm X which included the handwritten notations of both Alex Haley and Malcolm X. He established an exhibition and several media related projects based on the notations. Reed is the founder of the Gregory J. Reed Scholarship Foundation that aids students in the field of arts, engineering and law.

Reed's accomplishments have been cited by the Detroit News as one of the top lawyers in the legal profession, and he is listed in "*Who's Who in Entertainment, Who's Who Among Black Americans, Who's Who Among American Law, and Who's Who in Finance.*" In October 1992 he was inducted into the Black Entertainment and Sports Lawyers Association Hall of Fame.

Consultants

Abdul-Jalil al-Hakim President/CEO of Superstar Management. Mr. Abdul-Jalil al-Hakim negotiates and drafts all agreements for all publishing, merchandising and licensing; commercial advertisements and product endorsements; corporate sponsorships and affiliations; motion picture, television, radio and personal appearances; professional personal services contracts; electronic multimedia, literary, publishing, merchandising, licensing, concerts, tours, broadcasting, and video. He was the first African-American in the field and has taught and lectured Entertainment Law for 30 years. Abdul-Jalil al-Hakim, Superstar Management, 7633 Sunkist Drive, Oakland California 94605 E-mail: (510) 638-0808 Fax: (510) 638-8889 E-mail: **jalil@superstarmanagement.com** Website: **www.superstarmanagement.com**

Carolyn L. Bennett Author, writer, and instructor, Dr. Bennett's essays on current affairs appear regularly in the Dallas Examiner, Buffalo Criterion, Philadelphia New Observer, AIM and About Time magazines. She is a journalist-educator (graduate of Michigan State University, Ph.D. in education; and American University, M.A. in journalism) who has taught editorial and opinion writing, magazine article and feature writing, news writing and editing, journalism issues and ethics at Howard University, the University of Maine, Rowan University and others. She offers writing services and workshops through CMAL Writing Associates. Contact Carolyn L. Bennett, CMAL Writing Associates, 221 Greystone Lane, Rochester, New York 14618 Phone: (585) 442-8507 E-mail: **cwriter85@aol.com** Website: **hometown/cwriter85/index.html**

Ed Bullins Author, playwright, Ed Bullins's latest book is ED BULLINS: 12 Plays and Selected Writings (U of Michigan Press, 2006). Distinguished Artist-in-Residence, Northeastern University. Mr. Bullins is the author of eight books, including <u>Five Plays By Ed Bullins</u>, <u>The Duplex</u>, <u>The Hungered One</u>, <u>Four Dynamite Plays</u>, <u>The Theme is Blackness</u>, and <u>The Reluctant Rapist</u>. He wrote and produced for the theatre several commission works, including *Rainin' Down Stairs* for the 1992 San Francisco Theatre Artaud, and has been editor for a number of theatre magazines and publications. He was producer of *Circles of Times,* Boston's Lyric Theatre in August 2003. Among his awards and grants is three Obie Awards, four Rockefeller Foundation Playwriting Grants, two Guffenheim Playwriting Fellowships, an NEA Playwriting Grant, the AUDELCO Award. Mr. Ed Bullins, 37 Vine Street Roxbury, Massachusetts 02119 Phone: (617) 442-6627 E-mail: **rct9@verizon.net** Website: **www.edbullins.com**

Charrita D. Danley Author and poet and founder of Danley Writing Consultants, offers a wide spectrum of instructional and professional writing and editing services. Dr. Danley has taught English at both the secondary and post-secondary levels. She also teaches college writing courses and conducts presentations, workshops, and seminars related to writing, linguistics and language arts education. She holds a B.A., M.A., and Ph.D., in the field of English, with concentrations in the areas of Composition/Rhetoric, Business Writing, and Linguistics. Dr. Charrita D. Danley, Danley Writing Consultants, 458 Cambridge Court Suite D Riverdale, Georgia 30296 E-mail: **cdanley@danleywriting.com** Website: **www.danleywriting.com**

Tony Darnell Davis Writer, actor, director, and photographer, Mr. Davis works in poetry, short stories, and play writing. He is completing his work on "Black Images in Science Fiction and Fantasy" and will be releasing 12 books of poetry in 2007. Mr. Davis was an Assistant Professor at the University of Cincinnati, teaching Black Drama and Acting workshops. He is currently producing plays for the Free Theatre of Cincinnati and preparing a genealogy book on his family entitled "Pathways to My Past." Tony Darnell Davis, 2511 Essex Place, Studio 111, Cincinnati, Ohio 45206 E-mail: **tony.davis@cchmc.org**

Angela P. Dodson Free-lance editor and writer for magazines, online services, individual authors and book publishers. Dodson has been a consultant, instructor in media studies and public speaking and is the host of a weekly radio program about black Roman Catholics. She is a journalism graduate of Marshall University and has a master's degree in journalism and public affairs from the American University in Washington, D.C. She has led workshops on writing and editing for many organizations. Angela P. Dodson, 324 Hamilton Avenue, Trenton, New Jersey 08609 Phone: (609) 394-7632 Fax: (609) 396-7808 E-mail: **angela4bibr@aol.com**

Latorial Faison Author, poet and instructor, Latorial has taught English and Writing at several colleges and universities including Coker College, Johnson C. Smith University and Central Texas College. She is the founding editor of PoeticallySpeaking.net. She currently teaches for Robert Morris College and ITT and resides in North Chicago. Latorial Faison, Cross Keys Press, Post Office Box 145, Highwood, Illinois 60040   E-mail: **Latorial@PoeticallySpeaking.net** Website: **Latorial@PoeticallySpeaking.net**

Kyra Gaunt Kyra a.k.a. "Professor G" is a singer-songwriter and an associate professor of ethnomusicology at New York University who lectures nationally and internationally on African American music and issues of race, gender and the musical body. Her 2006 book The Games Black Girls Play: Learning the Ropes from Double-Dutch to Hip-hop (NYU Press, 2006) creates a new way of thinking about how black musical style and taste is learned and developed through interactions between the sexes and between genres. Kyra Gaunt, 1 Washington Square Village #5-H, New York, New York 10012 Phone: (646) 831-0615 E-mail: **kyraocity@yahoo.com**

Idris Goodwin Playwright, performer, director, and educator, Idris Goodwin is the recipient of the NEA/TCG Theatre Residency Program for Playwrights for 2004. He holds a BA in Film & Video from Columbia College, Chicago and an MFA in Writing from the School of the Art Institute of Chicago. Since 1999, he has been creating original hip-hop music as a solo artist and in collaboration, releasing CD's independently and for the Chicago based Naiveté Records. As an educator, Goodwin has taught writing and performance workshops all over the city in for numerous programs such as After School Matters, Young Chicago Authors, Perspectives Charter School and Free Street Theater. Idris Goodwin, 1721 West Huron, Apartment 2f, Chicago, Illinois 60622 E-mail: **Idris@hermitsite.com** Website: **www.Idrisgoodwin.com**

International Black Writers & Artists Los Angeles (IBWA/LA) Founded in Los Angeles in 1974 by Mrs. Edna Crutchfield, IBWALA is a network of authors, publishers, visual artists, community and educators dedicated to making sure our writers and artists are published, read, seen, and heard. IBWA/LA, Post Office Box 43576, Los Angeles, California 90043 Phone: (323) 964-3721 E-mail: **info@ibwala.org** Website: **www.ibwala.org**

KHAFRE Writer's colony, now known as: The Harriet Tubman Village, for Writers and Artist is a bed and breakfast facility located in the "Historic South" that provides all the conveniences a writer needs to hone their skills, as an aspiring author. The writers workshops, provided weekly allows each writer to identify and focus on areas of need; and challenges the more established writers to edit their near completed works and submit for publishing consideration, directly to the KHAFRE Publishing. Contact: Sade, KHAFRE, Post Office Box 1134, Ackerman, Mississippi 39735 Phone: (662) 285-9798 E-mail: **khafre@peoplepc.com** Website: **www.khafre.us**

Pat McLean-RaShine A poet and author, Pat presently co-facilitates poetry and creative writing workshops at Temple University's Pan-African Studies Community Education Program (PASCEP) and at Drexel University, both of Philadelphia. She has appeared on several multi media programs, such as "People, Politics & Poetry, Philadelphia Board of Education Public TV and WYBE "Showbiz Rap," to name a few. Recently she was published in "BMa: The Sonia Sanchez Literary Review – Legends and Legacies." "Life Spices From Seasoned Sistahs." And, X-Magazine: A poetry and prose Literary Journal. Pat McLean-RaShine, 632 Elkins Avenue, Philadelphia Pennsylvania 19120 Phone: (215) 683-3620 E-mail: **PMcPoet@aol.com**

Motown Alumni Association, Inc. We help artists, performers, and or musicians to move forward as professional entertainers. Most of our consulting services are free. We deal with amateurs, semi-professionals (wedding bands, and bar bands), and Professional entertainers. Contact Billy Wilson, Motown Alumni Association, Inc., 401 West Michigan Avenue, Suite 616, Ypsilanti, Michigan 48197 Phone: (313) 405-3676 E-mail: **Billy_j_wilson@yahoo.com** Website: **www.motownalumni.com**

Motown Writers Network The largest online organization to network, market, and educate writers on and off the Internet founded by Sylvia Hubbard. Sylvia is webmistress for 4 websites, founder of Write Steps 101, and owner of Hub Books Publishing and she lectures on writing and journalism. She is also a member of The Detroit's Writer's Guild, The Great Lakes Bookseller Associations, and over 30 online and offline literary groups, and has volunteered as a creative writing teacher by being a Writer-In-Residence in Detroit Public Schools for InsideOut. Contact Ms. Sylvia Hubbard, Post Office Box 27310, Detroit, Michigan 48227 Phone: (313) 289-8614 E-mail: **sylviahubbard1@yahoo.com** Website: **www.SylviaHubbard.com**

Daphne Muse Through her more than ten year old editorial service, Daphne Muse works with emerging and established writers to move them from Concept to Manuscript; Fellow at the Women's Leadership Institute (WLI) at Mills College in Oakland, California (1999-2003); Author of four books. Contact Ms. Daphne Muse, 2429 East 23rd Street, Oakland, California 94601 Phone: (510) 436-4716 Fax: (510) 261-6064 E-mail: **msmusewriter@sbcglobal.net** Website: **www.daphnemuse.com**

Carol A. Taylor Former Random House book editor Carol has been in the book publishing business for over 10 years and is a published author, a freelance writer, book editor and an editorial consultant who has worked with book publishers, agents, best selling authors and up and coming writers. For book editing or consulting queries send an e-mail. Ms. Carol A. Taylor, Black Star Consulting, 295 Clinton Avenue #E3, Brooklyn, New York 11205 E-mail: **carol@brownsugarbooks.com** Website: **www.BrownSugarBooks.com**

Garland Lee Thompson, Sr. Co-Founder/Executive Director of The Frank Silvera Writers' Workshop Foundation, Inc., a nonprofit theatre arts organization and playwright development program. The Workshop has earned a well deserved time-honored reputation as a nationally and internationally renowned playwrights' development theatre for emerging playwrights, directors and artists. Garland Thompson, The Frank Silvera Writers' Workshop Foundation, Inc., Post Office Box 1791, Manhattanville Station, New York, New York 10027 Phone: (212) 281-8832 E-mail: **playrite@earthlink.net**   Website: **www.fsww.org**

Ethel Pitts Walker Teaches theatre history and criticism courses with emphasis in multicultural theatre. Also directs productions. Ethel Pitts Walker, San Jose State University, Theatre Arts Department, One Washington Square, San Jose, California 95192 Phone: (408) 924-4586

Gary Watson Specialist in music, motion picture, and television entertainment legal services, Gary has been a guest lecturer for several seminars and conferences, as well as, courses for the University of California. Gary A. Watson, Esq., Gary A. Watson & Associates, 1875 Century Park East, Suite 1000, Los Angeles, California 90067 Phone: (310) 203-8022 Fax: (310) 203-8028 E-mail: **gwatson@garywatsonlaw.com** Website: **www.garywatsonlaw.com**

Kevin Craig West Director, producer and actor working in film, television, radio and stage and also a member of The Barrow Group in NYC, Chair member of Upstate Independents and in addition to being a Voice Acting Teacher and Producer for Voice Coaches, he also works as a Teacher/Artist with Symphony Space. Kevin West, MoBetta Films, Post Office Box 484, Troy, New York 12181 E-mail: **contact@kevincraigwest.com** Website: **www.kevincraigwest.com**

Crystal E. Wilkinson Served as writing mentor and taught creative writing classes for the center at Carnegie Center for Literacy and Learning in Lexington. Also a former chair of the creative writing department for the Kentucky Governor School for the Arts. She has taught creative writing at the University of Kentucky and was recently Writer in Residence/Visiting Professor at Eastern Kentucky University and is now an assistant professor of Creative Writing in Indiana University's MFA program. Member of the faculty in Spalding University's MFA program. Crystal E. Wilkinson, Indiana University, English Department, 442 Ballantine Hall, 1020 Kirkwood Avenue, Bloomington, Indiana 47405 E-mail: **WilkinsonCrystal@aol.com**

Write On! Literary Consortium Company provides literary consulting services. Founder, author, Natasha Brooks-Harris. Contact Write On! Literary Consortium, 297 7th Street, Brooklyn, New York 11215 E-mail: **nabrooks@aol.com**

Write Page Literary Service, Inc. Business and creative writing firm. President and primary consultant, Madge D. Owens is an author and native Atlantan and graduate of Clark College. Ms. Made D. Owens, Write Page Literary Service, Inc., Post Office Box 38288, Atlanta, Georgia 30334 Phone: (404) 280-5029 Fax: (404) 656-0238 E-mail: **writepagemo@yahoo.com**

W.R.A.P. Network, Inc. Writers Group. We share our expertise along with the business and mechanics of writing. Contact Ms. Pamela J. Hudson, M.A., W.R.A.P. Network, Inc., 19785 West 12 Mile Road, Suite 242, Southfield, Michigan 48076 Phone: (313) 283-6089 E-mail: **coaching.acms@yahoo.com** Website: **www.wraponline.net**

Critics/Reviewers

Allbooks Reviews Provides professional book reviews and author promotion at very reasonable fees. We also offer editing, advertising and guest speaking services. Listed in 101 Best Websites for Writers. Allbooks Reviews will review POD as well as traditional. Shirley Roe, Allbooks Review, 6540 Falconer Dr. # 38, Mississauga, Ontario L5N 1M1 Canada Phone: (416) 454-3643 E-mail: **allbookreviews@aol.com**

Edith Y. Billups Free-lance writer and critic for The Washington Informer Newspaper. Edith reviews theater, movies and music, and has written several travel articles for the paper's travel column, "Pack Your Bags." Contact Ms. Edith Y. Billups, The Gabriel Group, Post Office Box 13403, Silver Spring, Maryland 20911 Phone: (301) 562-5460 Fax: (240) 562-5468 E-mail: **eybillups@aol.com**

Black Issues Book Review Founded in 1998 by William E. Cox, President of Cox, Matthews & Associates, Inc., BIBR regular features include Between the Lines, affectionately known as BTL, the inside scoop on what's happening in the publishing industry. BIBR also provides up-to-date news on forthcoming author events, publications, conferences, shows and exhibits. Contact BIBR, Empire State Building, 350 Fifth Avenue, Suite 1522, New York, New York 10118 Phone: (212) 947-8515 Fax: (212) 947-5674 E-mail: **bibredit@cmapublishing** Website: **www.bibookreview.com**

Kenneth (Kanko) Bowens One of the original members of The African American Writers Alliance and part of the African American Online Writers Guild, Mr. Bowens has written reviews for The G.R.I.T.S., an online book review and discussion group. Kenneth Bowens, 1208 Northwest 106th Street, Oklahoma City, Oklahoma 73114 E-mail: **kennethbowens1@cox** Website: **www.kanko.us**

Monique Miles Bruner Graduated from the University of Oklahoma with a Bachelors and Masters degree in Public Administration and a Masters of Human Relations. She has also completed the requirements for her doctoral degree in Adult Education from Oklahoma State University. She writes book reviews for a website that features African American authors at Looseleaves.org. Monique Miles Bruner, 6409 Braniff Drive, Oklahoma City, Oklahoma 73105 Phone: (405) 615-6711 E-mail: **n2delta@yahoo.com**

George E. Curry Former Editor-in-Chief of the National Newspaper Publishers Association News Service. His weekly newspaper column is syndicated by NNPA to more than 200 African-American newspapers. In 2003 the National Association of Black Journalists selected Curry its "Journalist of the Year." Former president of the American Society of Magazine Editors. Former editor of Emerge, and former New York bureau chief for the Chicago Tribune. George E. Curry, National Newspaper Association, 3200 13th Street, North West, Washington, DC 20010 E-mail: **george@georgecurry.com** Website: **www.georgecurry.com**

Anna Dennis Author and book reviewer for The LineUp's Bookworm Column, and co-host of The DR BookChat Radio Show, 97.7 and 88.1 FM (KECG/More Public Radio). She is co-founder of The Bay Area Book Writers Guild (BBWG). Anna Dennis, Apex Publishing, Post Office Box 5077, South San Francisco, California 94083 E-mail: **apexpublishing@aol.com**

Sean Drakes Writer/Correspondent. Drakes specializes in documenting the Caribbean region and has reported on grassroots rituals, celebrated artists, and lifestyle events in the region for inflight magazine like BWIA Caribbean Beat and Air Jamaica's Skywritings. Drakes is a contributor to the lifestyle section of Black Enterprise and MACO magazines and a regular freelance photojournalist with the Atlanta Journal-Constitution, a leading daily newspaper. Travel, daily life, and style are his areas of concentration. E-mail: **contactcoty@hotmail.com**

Sherry Sherrod Dupree Author, historian, instructor and former reference librarian. Reviews manuscripts for secondary school books. Sherry Sherrod Dupree, Santa Fe Community College, 3000 NW 83rd Street, Building S-212, Gainesville, Florida 32606 Phone: (352) 395-5407 E-mail: **sherry.dupree@sfcc.edu**

Daniel Garrett Writer of journalism, fiction, poetry, and drama. Recently he has written a series of in-depth film essays for the web magazine, Offscreen.com, essays that focus on international cultures, philosophy, history, and politics. Previously, Garrett attended Baruch College, where he edited and wrote for The Reporter, before transferring as an undergraduate to the New School for Social Research, where he studied literature, politics, and philosophy and from which he graduated. He edited music interviews for I/Propaganda. He selected poetry for the male feminist magazine Changing Men. His own poetry has been published by AIM/America's Intercultural Magazine, Black American Literature Forum, The City Sun, The Humanist, Illuminations, and a few small book anthologies. (Garrett has written a novel, Heroes and Friends, and three plays, and these await publication). Daniel Garrett, 05-63 135th Street, Richmond Hill, New York 11419 E-mail: **dgarrett31@hotmail.com**

Edward W. Hudlin Jr. Reviews books and films. Teaches and published in all areas of philosophy with specialties in Black Studies, film, and Asian Studies. Director and writer of educational television and radio. Harvard Fellow at the Institute for Afro-American Research. Edward W. Hudlin, Jr., 187 Lake Hillcrest, Glen Carbon, Illinois 62034 Phone: (618) 288-5545

Sharon Hudson Book reviewer. Also, editing provides services for authors - manuscripts, novels, poems, and any literary work. Provides on-line book reviews, critiques of literary events. Contact Sharon Hudson, Loose Leaves Enterprises, Post Office Box 548, Tyrone, Georgia 30290 Phone: (770) 314-5932 E-mail: **akaivyleaf@looseleaves.org** Website: **www.looseleaves.org**

Jacquie Jones An award-winning writer, director and producer of documentary films. In addition to her filmmaking, she is a widely published critic of popular culture and was formerly the editor of the internationally respected journal, Black Film Review. She is also Executive Director of the National Black Programming Consortium (NBPC). Jones holds a BA in English from Howard University and an MA in documentary filmmaking from Stanford University. Jacquie Jones, NBPC, 68 East 131st Street, 7th Floor, Harlem, New York 10037 Phone: (212) 234-8200 Fax: (212) 234-7032 E-mail: **jacquie@nbpc.tv** Website: **www.nbpc.tv**

Joylynn M. Jossel Book reviewer for the Quarterly Review (QBR) out of New York City. Joy is a full-time multi-genre writer who has completed three diaries of poetry. Contact Ms. Joylynn M. Jossel, Post Office Box 298238, Columbus, Ohio 43229 Phone: (614) 284-7933 E-mail: **joylynnjossel@aol.com** Website: **www.joylynnjossel.com**

The Literary Café An online literary magazine featuring book reviews, author and music interviews, Anita Shari Peterson - CEO and President and also webmaster of literarycafe.org, Anita Shari Peterson, PCG Publishing, 5047 West Main Street, #324, Kalamazoo, Michigan 49009 E-mail: **ceo@pcg-publishing.com** Website: **www.pcgpublishing.com**

Winnie MacGregor Writes various articles for the custom car industry. Publishes NationWide Riders 411, a monthly newsletter covering car shows and events and profiles various custom car enthusiasts. Winnie MacGregor, NationWide Riders, LLC, 25422 Trabuco Road #105, Lake Forest, California 92630 Phone: (949) 263-4594 E-mail: **NWRiders@aol.com**

Traci Marquis Published writer. Book and Film Critic for The Grand' Manner Magazine of Connecticut and New York. Contact Ms. Traci Marquis, 1333 Baecher Lane, Norfolk, Virginia 23509 Phone: (757) 353-5450 E-mail: **tbmarquis@hotmail.com**

Daphne Muse Social commentator, and poet, Daphne's commentaries and radio essays have been featured on KTOP-FM, KPFA-FM, KQED-FM and NPR. She has written more than 300 feature articles, essays, reviews and op-ed pieces for major newspapers and academic journals. Ms. Daphne Muse, 2429 East 23rd Street, Oakland, California 94601 Phone: (510) 436-4716 Fax: (510) 261-6064 E-mail: **msmusewriter@sbcglobal.net** Website: **www.daphnemuse.com**

The RAWSISTAZ Reviewers The leading reviewers in the literary industry with a focus on promoting the works of books by and about African-American Authors. The RAWSISTAZ Reviewers, Post Office Box 1362, Duluth, Georgia 30096 Phone: (775) 363-8683 Fax: (775) 416-4540 E-mail: **info@rawsistaz.com** Website: **www.blackbookreviews.net**

Read Zone Book Reviews PR Services. Reviews with a personal touch. We also offer newsletter writing and blog writing services. Post Office Box 145, Whitehall, Pennsylvania 18052 Fax: (530) 504-7094 E-mail: **info@rzbr.com** Website: **www.rzbr.com**

Real Page Turners Provides book reviews for readers. We post book reviews on various online sites, newsletters and online magazines. Monique "Deltareviewer" Bruner, Real Page Turners, Post Office Box 13204, Oklahoma City, Oklahoma 73113 E-mail: **deltareviewer@yahoo.com**

Real Reviewers Submit one review copy (we also accept bound galleys) and press kit to Real Reviewers. Real Reviewers, c/o Jacki Miller, 915 West 86th Street, Chicago, Illinois 60620 E-mail: **jayceemiller@realreviewers.org** Website: **www.realreviewers.org**

Cheryl Robinson Host an internet radio talk show which provides book reviews of the books by interviewed authors. Contact Ms. Cheryl Robinson, Host, Just About Books Talk Show, 1282 Smallwood Drive, West, Suite 116, Waldorf, Maryland 20603 Phone: (301) 643-2077 E-mail: **JustAboutBooks@yahoo.com** Website: **www.JustAboutBookTalkShow.com**

Alvin C. Romer Literary consultant and independent book reviewer. Editor of The Romer Review and Co-Owner of Write On! & Literary Consortium. Alvin C. Romer, Editor, The Romer Review, 415 North West 58th Street, Miami, Florida 33127 Phone: (786) 356-8119 E-mail: **n4wiz51@yahoo.com**

Robert Rosario Music Editor, The Source Magazine. Contact Mr. Robert Rosario, 215 Park Avenue South, 11 Floor, New York, New York 10003 Phone: (212) 253-3700 Fax: (212) 253-9344 E-mail: **boogie@thesource.com**

Wanda Sabir Columnist, and Arts Editor, at the San Francisco Bay View Newspaper. Contact Ms. Wanda Sabir, Post Office Box 30756, Oakland, California 94604 Phone: (510) 261-8436 E-mail: **wsab1@aol.com** Website: **www.wandaspicks.com**

Jeanette Toomer Drama in Education Specialist. MA, Educational Theatre; teacher; curriculum consultant; freelance writer; theatre critic; contributing editor, "Black Mask" contributing writer "Back Stage Weekly" and "NY Amersterdam News." Founder of Drama, Discovery & Learning (DDL), a consulting/training firm. Contact Jeanette Toomer, Post Office Box 1092, Cathedral Station, New York, New York 10025 Phone: (917) 405-1710 E-mail: **nettoomer@yahoo.com**

Ethel Pitts Walker Teaches theatre history and criticism courses with emphasis in multicultural theatre. Also directs productions. Ethel Pitts Walker, San Jose State University, Theatre Arts Department, One Washington Square, San Jose, California 95192 Phone: (408) 924-4586

Jerry W. Ward, Jr. Professor of English at Dillard University, Ward is a poet, literary critic, and editor. He compiled and edited Trouble The Water: 250 Years of African American Poetry (Mentor, 1997). Jerry W. Ward, Jr., Department of English, Dillard University, 2601 Gentilly Boulevard, New Orleans, Louisiana 70122 E-mail: **jerryward31@hotmail.com**

Dera R. Williams Literary columnist - Dera's Den at www.apooo.org. Free lance writer - travel and contributor to literature manual. Contact Dera R. Williams, CocoWriter Book & Tea Parlor, 4316 Rilea Way, Suite #2, Oakland, California 94605 E-mail: **dwillautho@aol.com** Website: **hometown/dwillautho/myhomepage/profile.html**

Monique Baldwin Worrell Founded Flavah Reviewers. Featyres book and author interviews. Monique Baldwin Worrell, 1959 North Peace Haven Road, Suite 205, Winston Salem, North Carolina 27106 E-mail: **anutwist@anutwistaflavah.com** Website: **www.anutwistaflavah.com**

Directories

Access Black Chicago A resource guide to Black cultural, historical and educational points of interest in the City of Chicago, Illinois. Barbara Kensey, co-founder and publisher. Contact Kensey & Kensey Communications, 5212 South Dorchester Avenue, Chicago, Illinois 60615 Phone: (773) 288-8776 Fax: (773) 288-8997 E-mail: **kenseycomm@sbcglobal.net**

African American Yearbook Lists African American organizations, media publications, radio stations and Church resources. Contact TIYM Publishing Company, Inc., 6718 Whittier Avenue, Suite 130, McLean, Virginia 22101 Phone: (703) 734-1632 Fax: (703) 356-0787 E-mail: **tiym@tiym.com** Website: **www.africanamericanyearbook.com**

Arizona's Black Pages A full service advertising agency specializing in reaching the Urban/Black community in Arizona & Nevada. Publishers of Arizona's Black Pages, Neveda's Black Pages (www.nvbp.com) and Arizona Jazz Magazine (www.AZJazz.com). Contact Publisher/CEO, D.A. Peartree. Contact Arizona's Black Pages, 822 East Montecito Avenue, Suite 4, Phoenix, Arizona 85014 E-mail: **editor@AZBP.com** Website: **www.azbp.com**

Black Authors & Published Writers Directory (BAPWD) Directory listing of the Black Literary Market Place: authors, writers, song, film, and playwrights, poets, publishers, producers, agents, bookstores, distributors, librarians, editorial services, columnists, critic reviewers, e-publications, newspapers, magazines, journals, TV news reporters, radio and televison talk shows, voice-over artists, publishing services, audio and video production services, and much more. Grace Adams, founder, editor. Editor and Publisher, Grace Adams. Contact BAPWD c/o The Grace Publishing Company, 829 Langdon Court, Rochester Hills, Michigan 48307 Phone: (248) 651-7758 E-mail: **bapwd@bapwd.com** Website: **www.bapwd.com**

BlackExperts.com A unique online directory that allows African American experts to profile themselves in front of journalists, TV/radio producers, meeting planners, and each other. We are not another speakers bureau, we are a directory! Diversity City Media: 750-Q Cross Pointe Road, Columbus, Ohio 43230 Phone: (866) 910-6277 E-mail: **sales@diversitycity.com** Website: **www.blackexperts.com**

Black History Theme Book and Learning Resource Materials (The) Published by The Association for the Study of African American Life and History (ASALH-The Founders of Black History Month). ASALH was founded by Dr. Carter G. Woodson, the Father of Black History in 1915. In 1926 he celebrated Negro History Week which is now recognized world-wide as Black History Month. ASALH sets the Black History Theme for each year and publishes a theme book which includes essays, articles, selected reading lists, curriculum guides, and more. Contact Dr. Sylvia Cyrus-Albritton, ASALH, CB Powell Building, 525 Bryant Street, North West, Suite C142, Washington, DC 20059 Phone: (202) 865-0053 Fax: (202) 265-7920 E-mail: **executivedirector@asalh.net** Website: **www.asalh.org**

Black Pages USA National Publication. Circulation 50,000. Annually, we will reach all segments of the African-American community including (but not limited to) youth, retirees, and the working class. Contact Gerry McCants, Publisher. Thomas-McCants Media, 355 Crawford Street, #402, Portsmouth, Virginia 23704 Phone: (757) 399-4153 Fax: (757) 399-0969 E-mail: **gerry@blackpagesusa.com** Website: **www.blackpagesusa.com**

Nevada's Black Pages Established in 2003, currently circulating 50,000 copies. Annually. Publisher/CEO, D.A. Peartree. Editor: M. Fitzhugh-Craig. Nevada's Black Pages, 822 East Montecito Avenue, Suite 4, Phoenix, Arizona 85014 E-mail: **editor@AZBP.com** Website: **www.nvbp.com**

Talk of the Town A physical minority business directory interactive website serving business professionals in the state of Kentucky & Southern Indiana. Janeice R. Black, Post Office Box 18088, Louisville, Kentucky 40261 Phone: (502) 287-0278 Fax: (502) 287-0278 E-mail: **talklou@win.net** Website: **www.talkofthetown-lou.com**

The Urban Hollywood Resource Directory National and international directory listings of the African-American film industry. Tanya Kersey, editor and Publisher. Also publishes the Black Talent News Newsletter. Contact Editor, Tanya Kersey, Lacy Street Production Center, 2630 Lacy Street, Los Angeles, California 90031 Phone: (310) 203-1336 Fax: (310) 943-2326 E-mail: **tanya@tanyakersey.com** Website: **www.tanyakersey.com**

Editorial Services

Carolyn L. Bennett Writer-journalist, educator, public affairs columnist since the 1970s, Dr. Bennetts teaching areas and interests: editorial, opinion, feature writing, news writing and reporting, magazine article writing, ethics in journalism, minorities in media, etc. Carolyn L. Bennett, 221 Greystone Lane-16, Rochester, New York 14618 E-mail: **cwriter85@aol.com** Website: **www.hometown.aol.com/cwriter85/index.html**

Better Day Publishing Company Book, brochure and catalog design, copyright application, direct marketing, editorial services, graphic design illustration, material design book publishing. Naresha S. Perry, Publisher. Contact Better Day Publishing Company, 1152 Westheimer, #341, Houston, Texas 77042 Phone: (713) 548-4048 E-mail: **contact@betterdaypublishing.com** Website: **www.betterdaypublishing.com**

Black Star Consulting Former Random House book editor, Carol A.Taylor has been in the book publishing business for over 10 years. She is a published author, a freelance writer, book editor and an editorial consultant who has worked with book publishers, agents, best selling authors and up and coming writers. For book editing or consulting queries send an e-mail. Carol A. Taylor, Black Star Consulting, 295 Clinton Avenue #E3, Brooklyn, New York 11205 E-mail: **carol@brownsugarbooks.com** Website: **www.BrownSugarBooks.com**

Magdalene Breaux Publishing services, technical writing, book production consulting for independent authors and TV production and editing. Contact Ms. Magdalene Breaux, Post Office Box 67, Fairburn, Georgia 30213 Phone: (770) 842-4792 Fax: (770) 964-1875 E-mail: **magbreaux@mindspring.com** Website: **www.familycurse.com**

Into the Spotlight Entertainment Editorial and literary consultants: provides representation and publicity; press kits, press/releases, print advertisement, promotion of events, promotion for tourism, museums, art shows; public relations for businesses. Shonell Bacon, Into the Spotlight Entertainment, 605 Division Street, Lake Charles, Louisiana 70601 Phone: (337) 433-9728 E-mail: **info@intothespotlight-inc.com** Website: **www.intothespotlight-inc.com**

Milligan Literary Agency Editorial consultant and book agent. Ghost writing, book evaluation, book rewriting for mainstream publishing submission; book rewrite when requested by publishing editor. Contact Dr. Rosie Milligan, Milligan Literary Agency, 1425 West Manchester Avenue, Suite C, Los Angeles, California 90047 Phone: (323) 750-3592 Fax: (323) 750-2886 E-mail: **DrRosie@aol.com** Website: **www.milliganbooks.com**

Daphne Muse Through her more than ten year old editorial service, she works with emerging and established writers; move them from Concept to Manuscript. Daphne Muse, 2429 East 23rd Street, Oakland, California 94601 Phone: (510) 436-4716 Fax: (510) 261-6064 E-mail: **msmusewriter@sbcglobal.net** Website: **www.daphnemuse.com**

Novel Ideal Publishing & Editorial Services Company Full service editorial service offering copy editing, content editing and proofreading services. Novel Ideal Publishing & Editorial Services Company, 2274 Salem Road, Suite 106, Post Office Box 173, Conyers, Georgia 30013 E-mail: **novelideal@yahoo.com** Website: **www.electaromeparks.com**

Write On! Literary Consortium Company provides literary consulting services. Founder, Natasha Brooks-Harris is a full-service copy editor, line editor, and proofreader of novel and short fiction manuscripts. She has edited several full-length novels and is working on several more. She has worked in the publishing field since 1987. Currently, Nathasha is the editor of Black Romance and Bronze Thrills magazines. She is the author of Panache, a contemporary romance novel. Contact Ms. Natasha Brooks-Harris, Write On! Literary Consortium, 297 7th Street, Brooklyn, New York 11215 E-mail: **nabrooks@aol.com**

Write Page Literary Service, Inc. An Atlanta-based business and creative writing firm. President and primary consultant, Ms. Madge D. Owens is an author and native Atlantan and graduate of Clark College (now Clark Atlanta University). Contact Ms. Madge D. Owens, Write Page Literary Service, Inc., Post Office Box 38288, Atlanta, Georgia 30334 Phone: (404) 280-5029 Fax: (404) 656-0238 E-mail: **writepagemo@yahoo.com**

Editors

Malaika Adero Senior Editor. Malaika Adero, Atria Books/Simon & Schuster, Simon & Schuster, Inc., 1230 Avenue of the Americas, New York, New York 10020 Phone: 212-698-7000 E-mail: **malaika.adero@simonandschuster.com** Website: **www.simonsays.com**

Carla D. Bluitt Editor and Publisher of Say So! Magazine, a free Christian resource magazine with bi-monthly distribution in the Baltimore/Washington Metropolitan Area. Carla D. Bluitt, Say So! Magazine, 6030 Daybreak Circle, Suite A150/151, Clarksville, Maryland 21029 Phone: (301) 807-5445 E-mail: **cbluitt@saysomagazine.com** Website: **www.saysomagazine.com**

Nathasha Brooks-Harris Editor of Black Romance and Bronze Thrills magazines and the co-owner of Write On! Literary Consortium, a company that provides literary consulting services. Contact Ms. Natasha Brooks-Harris, 297 7th Street, Brooklyn, New York 11215 E-mail: **nabrooks@aol.com**

Caleen Burton-Allen Publisher/Editor-In-Chief of ONYX Style Magazine. Contact Ms. Caleen Burton-Allen, ONYX Style Magazine, 8787 Woodway Drive, Suite 4206, Houston, Texas 77063 Phone: (832) 467-9377 Fax: (832) 467-9378 E-mail: **caleen@onyxstyle.com** Website: **www.onyxstyle.com**

Rakia A. Clark Editor. We do not publish science fiction or fantasy, nor poetry. Interested in literary and contemporary multicultural fiction, especially African American; nonfiction interest, including memoir, history, pop culture, and entertainment. For fiction, send cover letter, first three chapters, and synopsis (no more than five pages). For non-fiction, send cover letter/query, author's qualifications and connections relevant to the book's content and marketing, and summary or outline of the book's content. Rakia A. Clark, Dafina/Kensington/Penguin, Kensington Publishing Corp., 850 Third Avenue, New York, New York 10022 Phone: (877) 422-3665 E-mail: **rclark@kensingtonbooks.com** Website: **www.kensingtonbooks.com**

Dawn Davis Vice President and Executive Editor. Interested in general, non-fiction and fiction related to the Black experience. Contact Ms. Christina Morgan, Assistant, Amistad, HarperCollins Publishers, 10 East 53rd Street, New York, New York 10022 Phone: (212) 207-7000 Website: **www.harpercollins.com**

Algie deWitt Publisher and Editor-in-Chief of MAMi Magazine. Internationally distributed title, Mami Magazine. Algie deWitt, MAMi Magazine, 4408 Aberdeen Lane, Blackwood, New Jersey 08012 E-mail: **algie@mamimagazine.com** Website: **www.mamimagazine.com**

Dawn Fobbs Author and Creative publisher of Stand Magazine for 2 years. Dawn Fobbs, Stand Magazine, Post Office Box 6667, Katy, Texas 77491 Phone: (281) 587-4054 E-mail: **msdawwn@sbcglobal.net** Website: **www.standmagazine.biz**

Michelle Fitzhugh-Craig CEO/Editor-In-Chief, Shades Magazine. Editor of Arizona's Black Pages, a full service advertising agency specializing in reaching the Urban/Black community in Arizona & Nevada. President, Arizona Association of Black Journalists. Contact Michelle Fitzhugh-Craig, Shades Magazine, Post Office Box 46325, Phoenix, Arizona 85063 E-mail: **mcraig@shadesmagazine.com** Website: **www.shadesmagazine.com**

Nancey Flowers Editor-In-Chief of Game Sports Magazine and publisher of Flowers In Bloom Publishing, Inc., Nancey attended Morgan State University in Baltimore, Maryland, where she received her bachelor's degree in mass communications with a minor in journalism. She served as Program Director for The Harlem Book Fair, a contributor to Black Issues Book Review and former Managing Editor of QBR, The Black Book Review. She is a member of Black Americans in Publishing and Delta Sigma Theta Sorority, Incorporated. Contact Ms. Nancey Flowers, Flowers In Bloom Publishing, Post Office Box 473106, Brooklyn, New York 11247 E-mail: **nanceyflowers@msn.com** Website: **www.flowersinbloompublishing.com**

Michelle R. Gipson Publisher of Written Magazine, and former Director of Advertising for Black Issues Book Review and Managing Editor of the Atlanta Daily World's Celebration of Books. She earned both her B.A. in Mass Media and her M.A. in Counseling from Hampton University. She has been published in Jane, Black Issues Book Review, the Atlanta Daily World and Chicken Soup for the African American Soul, and Chicken Soup for the Recovering Soul. Michelle R. Gipson, Written Magazine, Post Office Box 250504, Atlanta, Georgia 30310 Phone: (404) 753-8315 E-mail: **michelle.gipson@writtenmag.com** Website: **www.writtenmag.com**

Melody Guy Senior Editor. Does not accept unsolicited submissions, proposals, manuscripts, or submission queries via e-mail at this time. We recommend you work with an established agency. Ms. Melody Guy, One World/Ballantine/Random, 1745 Broadway, New York, New York 10019 Phone: (212) 782-9000 Website: **www.randomhouse.biz**

Janet Hill Editor. Interested in African American fiction and non-fiction. Contact Christian, Editorial Assistant, Broadway/Harlem Moon/Doubleday, 1745 Broadway, New York, New York 10019 Phone: (212) 782-8724 Website: **www.randomhouse.com/doubleday**

Glenda Howard Editor. Glenda Howard, Kimani Press, 233 Broadway, Suite 1001, New York, New York 10279 Phone: (212) 553 4217 Website: **www.eharlequin.com**

L A Hughes (aka Linda Atkins Hughes) An active member of IBWALA since 1978. She has been associate editor on two IBWALA anthologies and has been the primary editor for several outside projects, fiction and nonfiction. She is editor-in-chief of IBWALA's newsletter / literary magazine, Black Expressions. L A Hughes, International Black Writers & Artists, Los Angeles, Post Office Box 43576, Los Angeles, California 90043 Phone: (323) 964-3721 E-mail: **ahughes@ibwala.org** Website: **www.ibwala.org**.

Roxann Latimer Editor in Chief of the award winning multicultural magazine, Women In Motion. Roxann also works as a television producer with her company WIM Media and as Publisher. Roxann Latimer, WIM Media, 3900 West 22nd Lane #10G, Yuma, Arizona 85364 Phone: (928) 343-9729 E-mail: **wimmedia@yahoo.com** Website: **www.roxannlatimer.com**

Roland S. Martin Nationally award winning journalist and syndicated columnist with Creators Syndicate, the founding editor of BlackAmericaweb.com and currently the executive editor of The Chicago Defender, is a frequent commentator on TV-One, CNN, MSNBC, FOX, and Black Entertainment Television (BET). He is also the author of Speak, Brother! A Black Man's View of America. Contact Monique Smith, WVON 1690AM, 3350 South Kedzie, Chicago, Illinois 60623 Phone: (773) 247-6200 E-mail: **roland@wvon.com** Website: **www.wvon.com**

Erroll McDonald Vice President and Executive Editor. Pantheon/Random Imprints. Interested in adult, fiction and non-fiction books. Contact Mr. Eroll McDonald, Pantheon/Random Imprints, 1745 Broadway, New York, New York 10019 Phone: (212) 572-6030 E-mail: **EMcDonald@randomhouse.com** Website: **www.randomhouse.biz**

Shanté Morgan Editor of Turning Point Magazine, Shanté Morgan has worked for over a decade as a reporter, writing for both newspapers and magazines, covering everything from Hollywood trends to presidential campaigns. Shanté Morgan, Morgan Communications, 1710 North Moorpark Road #163, Thousand Oaks, California 91360 Phone: (310) 594-9890 E-mail: **ShanteMorgan@aol.com**

R. M. Perry Editor/Publisher. The Tennessee Tribune Newspaper, The Tennessee Tribune Building, 1501 Jefferson Street, Nashville, Tennessee 37208 E-mail: **lperry8049@aol.com**

Evette Porter Editor. Imprint Kimani TRU. Interested in young Adult fiction. Manuscript word length approximately 60,000 - 70,000 words. Evette Porter, Editor, Kimani Press, 233 Broadway, Suite 1001, New York, New York 10279 Website: **www.eharlequin.com**

Yvonne Rose Associate Publisher of Amber Communications Group, Inc. (ACGI), the nations largest African-American publisher of self-help books and celebrity biographies in the world. ACGI has partnerships and licensees in the United States, South Africa, Europe, and Asia. ACGI also has a multi-book co-publishing/imprint deal with John Wiley & Sons, Inc., further expanding the Amber/Wiley line of personal finance and beauty books and is recipient of several awards, including: the 2004 Cape Verdean News "Millennium Award for Excellence in Book Publishing. Contact Yvonne Rose, Associate Publisher, Amber Communications Group, Inc., 1334 East Chandler Boulevard, Suite 5-D67, Phoenix, Arizona 85048 Phone: (480) 460-1660 Fax: (480) 283-0991 E-mail: **amberbk@aol.com** Website: **www.amberbooks.com**

Tee C. Royal Senior Editor of BlackBoard Magazine; Books Editor of Mommy Too and TCBW Magazine. Founder of RAWSISTAZ Reviewers, the leading reviewers in the literary industry. Review and promote books by both mainstream and independent authors. Offers literary services to authors, publishers, and the literary community. Contact Ms. Tee C. Royal, Post Office Box 1362, Duluth, Georgia 30096 Phone: (775) 363-8683 Fax: (775) 416-4540 E-mail: **tee@rawsistaz.com** Website: **www.therawreviewers.com**

C. C. Smith Editor/Publisher, Minister of Information, and founder of The Beat Magazine. Has been a radio broadcaster, journalist, photographer, world traveler, and law librarian. C. C. Smith, The Beat Magazine, Post Office Box 65856, Los Angeles, California 90065 Phone: (818) 500-9299 Fax: (818) 500-9454 E-mail: **getthebeat@aol.com** Website: **www.getthebeat.com**

Gina Johnson Smith   Publisher of the Rancho Cucamonga/Ontario community News, Carson/South Bay Community News, and Las Vegas community News. Gina Johnson Smith, Smith Publishing & Media Group, #385 South Lemon Avenue, #E236, Walnut, California 91789 Phone: (909) 987-0433 E-mail: **ginajohnsonsmith@sbcglobal.net**

Dara Stewart Acquisitions Editor, Avery (health) and Viking Studio (illustrated practical non-fiction, imprints of Penguin Group. Dara Stewart, Penguin Group (USA), 375 Hudson Street, New York, New York 10014 E-mail: **dara.stewart@us.penguingroup.com**

L. Marie Wood Editor with Cyber-Pulp Publishing. The author of the Bram Stoker Award recommended novel "Crescendo." Marie's short stories can be found in anthologies such as The Black Spiral and Chimeraworld, as well as in her collection of 35 tales, "Caliginy," also recommended for a Stoker Award in 2003. E-mail: **author@lmariewood.com** Website: **www.lmariewood.com**

ePublications

Africabiz Online Online e-newsletter on investing and trading in Africa. Mr. Khalid Thomas, President. Contact Dynamic Group Ltd, Businessafrica, 1106 Carlyon Road, Cleveland, Ohio 44112 Phone: (347) 534-9329 E-mail: **editor@africabiz.org** Website: **www.africabiz.org**

AACBWI.com The African-American Children's Writers and Illustrators online group is a collective information-sharing forum for children's authors and illustrators, young and old founded by author, Sabra A. Robinson. AACBWI.com, Post Office Box 620324, Charlotte, North Carolina 28262 E-mail: **sabra@sabrarobinson.com** Website: **www.aacbwi.com**

Afropop WorldWide eNewsletter. Premier destination for web denizens interested in contemporary music of Africa and the African Diaspora. Our mission of connecting world class veteran and emerging artists from Africa, the Caribbean and the Americas with music lovers everywhere will find new pathways in the web world. Afropop worldwide producer, Sean Barlow is the Project Director. He edits the weekly Afropop e-Newsletter. Afropop Worldwide, 688 Union Street, Storefront, Brooklyn New York 11215 Website: **www.afropop.org**

AllAfrica Successor to the non-profit Africa News Service, which produced prize-winning print and broadcast reporting for major media such as National Public Radio, the Washington Post and the BBC for two decades, prior to developing an online venture. Reed Kramer, founder, chief executive officer and director. Contact AllAfrica, 920 M. Street, South East, Washington, DC 20002 Phone: (202) 546-0777 Fax: (202) 546-0676 Website: **www.allafrica.com**

BackList Monthly publishing and literary newsletter of African-American interest. Each issue is an intelligent and timely discussion of publishing, writing, and reading trends. Features include: Q&A with Industry Professionals, Book Commentary and Reviews, Publishing News, Author Profiles, Events and Literary Announcements. Read issues online. Galleys, ARC's and press releases, mail to Felicia Pride, Backlist, 55 West 116th Street, Suite 455, New York, New York 10026 E-mail: **felicia@thebacklist.net** Website: **www.thebacklist.net**

Black Book Reviews Leading African American Book Reviews in the industry. Daily newsletter of black book reviews can be found on our site. The RAWSISTAZ Reviewers, Post Office Box 1362, Duluth, Georgia 30096 Phone: (775) 363-8683 Fax: (775) 416-4540 E-mail: **info@rawsistaz.com** Website: **www.blackbookreviews.net**

Black Britain Launched in July 1998 to deliver immediate and regular news and information services to the Black and ethnic minority communities, and to address the shortcomings of mainstream media which continued to cover Black and ethnic minority news interest negatively and/or inadequately. Black Britain c/o The Colourful Network, Suite 5, 2nd Floor, Culvert House, Culvert Road, London SW11 5AP Phone: 08700 76 5656 Fax: 08700 76 5757 Text: 07779 66 5858 E-mail: **publisher@live247.co.uk** Website: **www.live247.co.uk**

Black Coffee Magazine Online magazine, recognize successful African Americans in Business, Entertainment and the Arts. Also a book club and online bookstore. Crystal Cornell, Publisher. Crystallized Publishing, 16208 Eucalyptus Ave #21, Bellflower, California 90706 Phone: (562) 685-4609 E-mail: **crystal@blackcoffeemag.com** Website: **www.blackcoffeemag.com**

Black Collegian Online The electronic version of the national career opportunities magazine. Features commentary by leading African-American writers, lifestyle/entertainment features, general information on college life, and news of what's happening on college campuses today. Black Collegian Online, 140 Carondelet Street, New Orleans, Louisiana 70130 Phone: (832) 615-8871 E-mail: **stewart@imdiversity.com** Website: **www.black-collegian.com**

Black Commentator.com Core audience is African Americans. Features commentary, analysis and investigation, elements of political dialogue that are absolutely essential to the creation of movements for social change. Co-publisher, Peter Gamble. Contact BlackCommentator.com, Suite 473, 93 Old York Road, Jenkintown Pennsylvania 19046 Phone: (202) 318-4032 E-mail: **publisher@blackcommentator.com** Website: **www.blackcommentator.com**

Black Enterprise.co.uk Directory of UK businesses and development / support agencies. BE's mission is to facilitate the development, growth and long-term sustainability of business enterprise. It has the only regular publication of news and information to the African Caribbean business community. Contact Black Enterprise.co.uk c/o The Colourful Network, Suite 5, 2nd Floor, Culvert House, Culvert Road, London SW11 5AP Phone: 08700 76 5656 Fax: 08700 76 5757 Text: 07779 66 5858 E-mail: **publisher@live247.co.uk** Website: **www.live247.co.uk**

Black Literary Players Monthly on-line newsletter update for Black Authors & Published Writers Directory on our website. Features the Black Literary Marketplace: authors, writers, song, film and playwrights, poets, agents, producers, publishers, editors, librarians, bookstores, newspapers, magazines, radio and television stations, talk shows, columnists, critic/reviewers, websites, groups, etc. Grace Adams, Editor. The Grace Company, 829 Langdon Court, #45, Rochester Hills, Michigan 48307 Phone: (248) 651-7758 E-mail: **info@bapwd.com** Website: **www.bapwd.com**

Black Living Network focusing on today's black woman providing news, entertainment, career, health, fitness, beauty, business, personal finance and more! Gloria Sawyers, Publisher. Black Women's Network, 601 E. Palomar, #264, Chula Vista, California 91911 Phone: (619) 254-1704 Fax: (619) 863-5719 E-mail: **editor@blackliving.com** Website: **www.blackliving.com**

Black News Features daily African-American news. The site publishes a weekly e-mail newsletter featuring the top Black news stories of each week. Contact Black News, Diversity City Media, 225 West 3rd Street, Suite #203, Long Beach, California 90802 Phone: (562) 209-0616 E-mail: **support@blacknews.com** Website: **blacknews.com**

Black Students Publishes a weekly e-mail newsletter featuring the latest news, tips, and opportunities for African-American students. Contact Black Students, Diversity City Media, 225 West 3rd Street, Suite #203, Long Beach, California 90802 Phone: (562) 209-0616 E-mail: **support@blackstudents.com** Website: **blackstudents.com**

Black Voices   African-American and Black culture community.   Publication features news, lifestyle, career and entertainment online for African-Americans. Black Voices, Tribune Tower, 435 North Michigan Avenue, Suite LL2, Chicago, Illinois 60611 Phone: (312) 222-4326 Fax: (312) 222-4502 E-mail: **dsquires@corp.blackvoices.com** Website: **www.blackvoices.com**

Center For Communications and Community (C3)   A media institute that helps news organizations develop better connections with the communities they cover. George White is editor of C3 online and assistant director. George White, UCLA Center for Communications, 3701 Stocker Street, Suite 204, Los Angeles, California 90008 Phone: (310) 206-2189 Fax: (310) 206-2972 E-mail: **geowhite@ucla.edu** Website: **www.uclaccc.ucla.edu**

Detroit Gospel A Gospel music and entertainment E-zine providing comprehensive coverage of the Metro-Detroit gospel scene. Daily, breaking news, weekly with new contests and polls, and new featured artists and lifestyle articles. Also maintains database of Detroit's gospel music artists; lists of Detroit's gospel media outlets, record labels, and management companies. Mary Crosby, Editor, Detroit Gospel, 18701 Grand River Avenue, #134, Detroit, Michigan 48223 Phone: (313) 531-1141 E-mail: **editor@detroitgospel.com** Website: **www.detroitgospel.com**

Emerging Minds Online Magazine   Launched in 2003 EM online is a news and cultural magazine for writers of all ages to present their perspectives on the current issues and events. Emerging Minds is a Pan-African news and business magazine that is a distributor (and not a publisher) of content supplied by third parties. Emerging Minds Magazine, 541 Tenth Street, North West, Suite 318, Atlanta, Georgia 30318 E-mail: **emergingminds@emergingminds.org** Website: **www.emergingminds.org**

EXODUS Newsmagazine Published on the internet. Our goal is to bring news from international, national and San Francisco Bay Area perspectives readers find useful and informative. EXODUS Newsmagazine, 1009 East Capitol Exp. #323, San Jose, California 95121 Phone: (408) 821-2916 Fax: (630) 982-3171 E-mail: **hampton@exodusnews.com** Website: **www.exodusnews.com**

Family Digest Online Founded by Darryl L. Mobley, Family Digest Magazine is the leading family magazine in the United States, and the #1 publication for Black families nationwide. Features family and parenting tips and advice, stories, quotes, culture and home, beauty and style, health and fitness. Ms. Susan Benjamin, Editor-in-Chief. Contact Darryl L. Mobley, Family Digest, Post Office Box 342374, Austin, Texas 78734 Fax: (512) 795-2078 E-mail: **editor@familydigest.com** Website: **www.familydigest.com**

Gesica Magazine The Premiere Urban Entertainment Experience. Tonisha Johnson, Editor and Publisher. Gesica Magazine, Post Office. Box 30231, Staten Island, New York 10303 Phone: (718) 216-3530 E-mail: **TonishaJohnson@gmail.com** Website: **www.gesicaonline.com**

Kay3Musik   An Online gospel/Christian music publication serving the mainstream and independent sections of the industry. Resources and inspirational articles, also provides artist promotion. Contact Mr. Robert Kennedy III, Kay3Music, 210 Mill Street, Suite 166, Lancaster, Massachusetts 01523 E-mail: **info@kay3music.com** Website: **www.kay3music.com**

The Literary Café An online literary magazine. Book Reviews, Author Interviews, Music Interviews, much more Anita Shari Peterson - CEO and President. Charles Edward Peterson, Sr., COO and Vice-President. PCG Publishing, 5047 West Main Street, #324, Kalamazoo, Michigan 49009 E-mail: **ceo@pcg-publishing.com** Website: **www.pcgpublishing.com**

Live247 Provides a single point of reference on the internet for multicultural events and entertainment in the UK. Primary target market is the UK urban community - 12 - 29 year olds. Live247.co.uk c/o The Colourful Network, Suite 5, 2nd Floor, Culvert House, Culvert Road, London SW11 5AP Phone: 08700 76 5656 Fax: 08700 76 5757 Text: 07779 66 5858 E-mail: **publisher@live247.co.uk** Website: **www.live247.co.uk**

The Mail & Guardian Online Internet-based news publication in Africa. Launched in early 1994, it is one of South Africa's and Africa's major news publishers and is reputed internationally for its quality content. . The Mail & Guardian Online, Post Office Box 9166, Auckland Park, Johannesburg 2006 South Africa E-mail: **editoronline@mg.co.za** Website: **www.mg.co.za**

Man Up Magazine Publication issued bi-monthly via the internet and targets avid readers and art enthusiast who frequent cultural events. Oasis, author of Push Comes To Shove, is the owner and Editor-In-Chief. Man Up Magazine features the syndicated column Reality On Ice. Its columns range from author features to business and investing. The thing which makes Man Up Magazine unique is that 90% of its contributors are either prisoners or ex-convicts whose life has been changed through adversity and now strives to enhance the quality of life. Oasis Publishing Group c/o Man Up Magazine, Post Office Box 19101, Cleveland, Ohio 44119 Phone: (216) 633-2397 E-mail: **manup@oasisnovels.com** Website: **www.oasisnovels.com**

Memphis Gospel News Gospel music news ezine, featuring upcoming CD releases and artists profiles in the Memphis, Tennessee area. Contact Ms. Tiffany L. Benton, Totally Blessed Music Ministries, 174 Seven Pines Road, Collierville, Tennessee 38017 Phone: (901) 351-1031 E-mail: **memphisgospel@hotmail.com** Website: **www.memphisgospelmusic.com**

Mirror-Gibbs Magazine Weekly on-line magazine with over 300,000 readers a month. Frank Jones is the CEO\publisher of Mirror-Gibbs Publications, a Black Oakland base small press-publishing house. Contact Mr. Frank Jones, Mirror-Gibbs Publication, Post Office Box 6573, Oakland, California 94603 Phone: (510) 409-9571 E-mail: **pinoquit@hotmail.com** Website: **www.gibbsmagazine.com**

MMR e-News E-mail-distributed newswire that features profiles of companies that have expertise in reaching multicultural consumers, conference announcements, press releases and articles on trends in multicultural marketing. Multicultural Marketing Resources, Inc., 286 Spring Street, Suite 201, New York, New York 10013 Phone: (212) 242-3351 Fax: 212) 691-5969 E-mail: **lisa@multicultural.com** Website: **www.multicultural.com**

The National Black News Journal The nation's leading Black-interest E-newsletter. It is distributed weekly to nearly 10,000 subscribers. Robert "Siraj" Taylor, National Black News Journal, 2315 Lincoln Road, North East, #207 Washington, DC 20002 Phone: (202) 486-8103 E-mail: **blacknewsjournal@yahoo.com**

Quarterly Book Review Exclusively dedicated to books about the Africana experience; fiction, nonfiction, poetry, children's books, health and lifestyle management, writers from Africa and the Caribbean. Max Rodriguez, Publisher. Contact QBR, 9 West 126th Street, New York, New York 10027 Phone: (212) 348-1681 Fax: (212) 427-9901 E-mail: **mrodz@qbr.com** Website: **www.qbr.com**

Radio Facts E-zine covers all areas of the industry including: television, music, radio, books, movies, clubs and production from an industry perspective. Contact Mr. Kevin Ross, Radio Facts, 595 Piedmont Avenue North East, Suite 320-314, Atlanta, Georgia 30308 E-mail: **kevin.ross@radiofacts.com** Website: **www.radiofacts.com**

SFBayView Online version of the national Black newspaper San Francisco Bay View is updated weekly; presents perspective from the African American community of San Francisco's Bayview District; weekly events, news, and analysis of local, national, and international issues. San Francisco Bay View, 4917 Third Street, San Francisco, California 94124 Phone: (415) 671-0789 Fax: (415) 671-0316 E-mail: **editor@sfbayview.com** Website: **www.sfbayview.com**

The Talking Drum Yearly publication of academic articles on African and African American Music by a variety of writers published by The National Association for the Study and Performance of African American Music (NASPAAM). Contact Mr. Frank Suggs, President, NASPAAM, 1201 Mary Jane, Memphis, Tennessee 38116 Phone: (901) 396-2913 E-mail: **fsuggs@midsouth.rr.com** Website: **www.naspaam.org**

Talk of the Town A physical minority business directory interactive website serving business professionals in the state of Kentucky & Southern Indiana. Janice R. Black, Post Office Box 18088, Louisville, Kentucky 40261 Phone: (502) 287-0278 Fax: (502) 287-0278 E-mail: **talklou@win.net** Website: **www.talkofthetown-lou.com**

Triangle Offense On-line informative and interactive publication, which promotes the writings of graduate students, employees of community-based organizations, and aspiring journalists and creative writers. La Caille Nous Publishing, Inc., 328 Flatbush Avenue, Suite 240, Brooklyn, New York 11238 Phone: (212) 726-1293 Fax: (212) 591-6465 E-mail: **info@lncpub.com** Website: **www.lcnpub.com**

Urban Network Magazine (UNM) Launched in 1988 by founder, editor, Mary Nichols, aka DJ Fusion, UNM has been serving the music and entertainment industries for more than 15 years. Mary Nichols, UNM, 14 Easton Avenue, #250 New Brunswick, New Jersey 08901 Phone: (347) 252-4032 E-mail: **djfusion@ureach.com** Website: **www.urbannetwork.com**

Women in Focus FORUM Newsletter A professional business network mentoring and supporting women, men and students. Through our triannual printed newsletters and monthly e-newsletters, we provide statistical information, articles, profiles, upcoming events, eduational opportunities and a wealth of other information supporting personal and professional growth. Contact Editor, Women in Focus Forum Newsletter, Post Office Box 1334, Rialto, California 92377 Phone: (909) 873-5055 Fax: (801) 846-0429 E-mail: **Info@wifforum.com** Website: **www.wifforum.com/meetings001.htm**

Tim Greene

Film Actor * Songwriter
Record Producer * Radio & Television Host

D.J. radio personality and film and music video director, Tim Greene is owner of Tim Green Films in Hollywood, California. He is a national Dean's list graduate and Sony Innovators Award finalist of Shaw University with a B.S. Degree in Business Management, with a communications minor. He was heard on L.A.'s top radio station, FM 92 the Beat-KKBT, and FM 102.3 the Rhythm-KJLH, as D.J. "Jammin Jay Williams," where he often took time to speak on the subject of radio and television producing to students. He still enjoys motivating students on the importance of education and positive career endeavors.

As a record producer, Tim has written and produced over 17 national record releases. He managed 68 year-old rap artists, Vivian Smallwod, known as "The Rappin Granny". He was producer, director and host of "Dance City From Hollywood," a television show for the Japanese market and as a regular fundraiser participant in local celebrity tennis tournaments has won over 120 trophies.

Film producer, hip-hop pioneer in four work-filled years, Tim won Best Writer, Producer, Director at the Philadelphia International Film Festival for the parady "Ya Grandma's A Gangsta". Three features, "*Ya Grandma's A Gangsta*", "*Raykwan Cuties*", and *Creepin'*, hundreds of coupons, and thousands of dollars in rebate checks later, Tim Greene has birthed a body of work on which he looks with pride.

Journals

African American Review First published in 1967 as Negro American Literature Forum, and then as Black American Literature Forum, African American Review is published quarterly in March, June, September, and December at Saint Louis University. Each issue averages 176 7x10" pages, and include essays on African-American literature, theatre, film, visual arts, and culture generally; interviews; poetry; fiction; and book reviews. Publications Editor, Joycelyn Moody. Managing Editor, Aileen Keenan. Contact Ms. Joycelyn Moody, African American Review, Saint Louis University, Humanities 317, 3800 Lindell Boulevard, Saint Louis, Missouri 63108 Phone: (314) 977-3688 Fax: (314) 977-1514 E-mail: **moodyjk@slu.edu** Website: **www.aar.slu.edu**

African Journal of Reproductive Health Journal publication provides a forum for African authors as well as others working in Africa, to share findings on all aspects of reproductive health. AJRH, 4 Alofoje Avenue, Off Uwasota Street, Post Office Box 10231, Ugbowo, Benin City, Edo State, Nigeria Phone: 234 52 600151 Fax: 234 52 602334 E-mail: **wharc@hyperia** Website: **www.inasp.uk/ajol/journals/ajrh/about**

African Studies Quarterly Since, 1977, information on authors and a link to the University of Florida. African Studies program, articles, book reviews. ASQ, Post Office Box 115560, 427 Grinter Hall, Gainesville, Florida 32611 Phone: (352) 392-2187 Fax: (352) 392-2435 E-mail: **asq@africa.ufl.edu** Website: **www.web.africa.ufl.edu/asq**

The Afro-Hispanic Review A bilingual journal of Afro-Hispanic literature and culture, is published by the Department of Romance Languages and Literatures of the University of Missouri-Columbia. It appears twice yearly. The Review no longer accepts articles on Afro-Brazilian or Luso-African topics. Palara now handles this field of inquiry. The Afro-Hispanic Review publishes literary criticism, book reviews, translations, creative writing, and relevant developments in the field. Dr. Marvin Lewis, Institute Director. Afro-Romance Institute for Languages & Literatures of the African Diaspora, 318 Arts & Science Building, Columbia, Missouri 65211 Phone: (573) 884-0593 Fax: (573) 884-0595 E-mail: **LewisM@missouri.edu** Website: **www.missouri.edu/~afroroma/index.htm**

Black Business Journal All-business, technology insight and financial information magazine for African-Americans and non-Blacks who do business in the community published twice a month and distributed nationally, The Black Business Journal ncludes diversity features and other business related information. The BBJ focuses on issues with business, financial, public policy and technological implications for African-Americans and others who do business across our communities in the U.S., and in some key issues, internationally. Mr. Chido Nwangwuf, Founder. Black Business Journal, USAfrica Digital Media Networks, 8303 South West Freeway, Suite 100, Houston, Texas 77074 Phone: (713) 270-6500 Fax: 713-270-8131 E-mail: **business@bbjonline.com** Website: **www.bbjonline.com**

Blackfilm.com   Online resource which links the Black film community while cultivating national and international audiences interested in their work. This site provides a forum for filmmakers, scholars and organizations to present information and promote artistic expression. Database of film reviews from African American perspectives. Also features full-length articles, news about video and DVD releases, as well as information about conferences, screenings, and other events. Website: **www.blackfilm.com**

The Black Employment and Entrepreneur Journal   African-American business and career magazine. To request a media kit and/or a copy of the magazine, contact Pamela Burke, Black Employment and Entrepreneur Journal, 22845 Savi Ranch, Suite A, Yorba Linda, California 92887 Phone: (800) 487-5099 Fax: (714) 974-3978 E-mail: **pburke@blackeoejournal.com** Website: **www.blackeoejournal.com**

Black Journalism Review Information, for and about the Black Press in America, BJR, 2062 National Press Building, Washington, DC 20045 Phone: (202) 298-9519 Fax: (202) 234-7437 E-mail: **editor@blackjournalism.com** Website: **www.blackjournalism.com**

The Black Scholar Every issue of the Journal focuses on a subject of major concern in the African American community: education, black political empowerment, social movements, the multicultural debate, black women's activism, the crisis of the black male, the Ebonics debate and more. Features book reviews, announcements, and employment listings by colleges and universities. Robert Chrisman, Editor-in-Chief & Publisher, Robert L. Allen, Senior Editor. The Black Scholar, Post Office Box 22869, Oakland, California 94618 Phone: (510) 547-6633 Fax: (510) 547-6679 E-mail: **BlkSchlr@aol.com** Website: **www.theblackscholar**

Black Tokyo Site for Africans and African-Americans in Tokyo. News, discussions, and many Web sites. Owner, Mr. Craig Nine Designs. Contact Black Tokyo, 3-16-1-2 Takada, Toshima-ku, Tokyo 117-0033   Phone: 011-81-902-338-4435   E-mail: **webmaster@blacktokyo.com** Website: **www.blacktokyo.com**

Callaloo Publishes original works by, and critical studies of, black writers worldwide: fiction, poetry, plays, critical essays, interviews, and annotated bibliographies. The journal offers a rich mixture of fiction, poetry, plays, critical essays, cultural studies, interviews, and visual art, as well as special thematic issues. Contact Journals Manager, Callaloo, The Johns Hopkins University Press, 2715 North Charles Street, Baltimore, Maryland 21218 Phone: (410) 516-6900 E-mail: **webmaster@jhupress.jhu.edu** Website: **www.press.jhu.edu/journals/callaloo**

Context Journal on community issues and news coverage published by the Center for Community and Communications, a journalism, research and training institution working at the intersection of communications, race and community transformation. George White, UCLA Center for Communications, 3701 Stocker Street, Suite 204, Los Angeles, California 90008 Phone: (310) 206-2189   Fax: (310) 206-2972   E-mail: **geowhite@ucla.edu**   Website: **www.uclaccc.ucla.edu**

Good News Journal Journal. Siddeeq Jihad, Publisher. Contact Good News Journal, Post Office Box 43474, Detroit Michigan 48243 Fax: (313) 532-5246 E-mail: **siddeeq@msn.com**

Greater Diversity Free online journal. Journal features employment and business news for minorities. Contact J. Travis Reep, Editor in Chief, Greater Diversity, Post Office Box 2537, Wilmington, North Carolina 28402 Phone: (800) 462-0738 Fax: (910) 763-6304 E-mail: **greater@greaterdiversity.com** Website: **www.greaterdiversity.com**

The Journal of African American History Published quarterly by the founders of Black History Month, The Association for the Study of African American Life and History (ASALH). Formerly The Journal of Negro History. Founded by Carter G. Woodson, January 1, 1916. Sylvia Cyrus, Executive Director. ASALH, CB Powell Building, 525 Bryant Street, North West, Suite C142, Washington, DC 20059 Phone: (202) 865-0053 Fax: (202) 265-7920 E-mail: **executivedirector@asalh.net** Website: **asalh.net**

The Journal of the Afro-American Historical and Genealogical Society Semi-annual publication of the Afro-American Historical and Genealogical Society, Inc. The Journal provides a medium for the publication of original manuscripts, articles, and information on African and African American history and genealogy. Sylvia Polk-Burriss, Editor, AAHGS Journal, 14340 Rosetree Court, Silver Spring, Maryland 20906 E-mail: **spburriss@aol.com** Website: **www.aahgs.org**

The Network Journal Founded in 1993 by Aziz Gueye Adetimirin, the magazine is dedicated to educating and empowering Black professionals and small business owners. The Network Journal, 29 John Street, Suite1402, New York, New York 10038 Phone: (212) 962-3791 Fax: (212) 962-3537 E-mail: **editors@tnj.com**

The North Star Journal of African American religious history. Contact Ms. Judith Weisenfeld, Associate Professor, Department of Religion, Vassar College, Post Office Box 205, 124 Raymond Avenue, Poughkeepsie, New York 12604 E-mail: **juweisenfeld@vassar.edu** Website: **www.northstar.vassar.edu**

Obsidian III: Literature in the African Diaspora Literary journal, biannually. Solicits essays, fiction, poetry, and reviews by creative writers. Obsidian III, English Department, North Carolina State University, Post Office Box 8105, Raleigh, North Carolina 27695 Phone: (919) 515-4153 E-mail: **obsidian@chass.ncsu.edu** Website: **www.ncsu.edu/chass/obsidian**

Palara A multi-lingual journal devoted to African diaspora studies, is housed in the Institute and published annually by the Afro-Romance Institute of the University of Missouri-Columbia, and the Department of African and African American Studies of the Pennsylvania State University. Dr. Marvin Lewis, Institute Director. Palara publishes research. Afro-Romance Institute for Languages & Literatures of the African Diaspora, 318 Arts & Science Building., Columbia, Missouri 65211 Phone: (573) 884-0593 Fax: (573) 884-0595 E-mail: **LewisM@missouri.edu** Website: **www.missouri.edu/~afroroma/index.htm**

Voices: The Wisconsin Review of African Literatures Explores issues of written and oral artistic production in Africa in relationship to the continent of Africa. Mireille A. L. Djenno, Editor. Voices, 1414 Van Hise Hall, 1220 Linden Drive, Madison Wisconsin 53706 E-mail: **madjenno@wisc.edu** Website: **www.african.lss.wisc.edu/all/voices**

Ntozake Shange
Poet * Performance Artist
Playwright * Novelist

Ntozake Shange is a poet, playwright, novelist and performance artist. Her work empowers women to take responsibility for their lives by learning to love themselves and challenge their oppressors. Shange's first choreopoem, and best known work, *for colored girls who have considered suicide, when the rainbow is enuf,* was produced on Broadway and won an Obie Award in 1977. She was born Paulette Williams on October 18, 1948, in Trenton, New Jersey. As a child, family friends who often frequented her home were names like Dizzy Gillespie, Paul Robeson, Walter White, and W.E.B. Dubois. She graduated from Barnard College in 1970, and later earned an MA from the University of Southern California. It was there she changed her name to the Zulu "Ntozake" meaning "she who comes with her own things" and "Shange" meaning "who walks like a lion."

Ntozake Shange is the only poet to have her poetry (*for colorled girls who have considered suicide/when the rainbow is enuf*) translate successfully to Broadway. In 1975, Shange moved to New York. There she started performing the chorepoem in Soho Jazz lofts and later in bars in the lower East Side. Soon, a producer by the name of Woodie King Jr. saw one of these performances. With the help of director Oz Scott, Shange's choreopoem was staged at the New Federal Theatre off-Broadway. In 1976 it was moved to Anspacher Public Theatre, and that same year, it was produced on Broadway at the Booth Theatre. It won several awards including an Outer Circle Award and Tony Award nominations in addition to the Obie Award in 1977. This marked the beginning of Shange's career.

Several other plays and novels followed, including the 2004 children's book, Ellington Was Not a Street (Simon & Schuster, 2004, Coretta Scott King Illustrator Award Winner). Nappy Edges, was published in 1978, featuring fifty poems celebrating the voices of defiantly self - sufficient women. In 1979, chorepoems *Spell #7*, *A Photograph: lovers in motion*, and *Boogie Woogie Landscapes* were published. They comprise the collection Three Pieces, a dramatic trilogy that won the "Los Angeles Time Book Prize for Poetry." In 1982, Shange published her first novel, Sassafrass, Cypress, and Indigo. She continued to publish poetry and write novels. Betsy Brown (1985) is the story of a young girl growing up in St. Louis in the 1950's. Her third novel is Liliane: Resurrection of the Daughter (1994), relates the life of the title character, an artist, from her lovers' perspectives. Liliane uses the information she has within her power as a woman to make her life and the lives of those people around her better.

Shange serves on the faculty in the Department of Drama at the University of Houston and continues to give lectures at various colleges and literary conferences. Her permanent residence is in Philadelphia with her daughter Savannah.

Librarians

Eric Acree Director of African Library, buys. Eric Acree, Cornell University, 309 Uris Library, Ithaca, New York 14853 Phone: (607) 255-1569 Fax: (607) 255-5229 E-mail: **ea18@cornell.edu** Website: **www.cornell.edu**

Jessie B. Arnold Director. J.D. Boyd Library, Alcorn State University, 1000 ASU Drive 539, Alcorn State, Mississippi 39096 Phone: (601) 877-6354 E-mail: **jarnold@lorman.alcorn.edu** Website: **jdboyd.alcorn.edu**

Claudine Ashton Assistant Professor /Acting Head of Reference. Contact Claudine Ashton, Grambling State University, 100 Main Street, Grambling, Louisiana 71245 Phone: (318) 274-2227 E-mail: **ashtonc@gram.edu** Website: **www.gram.edu**

Michael Baker Director. Buys and reviews books. Contact Mr. Michael Baker, Carter G. Woodson Regional Library, 5403 South Aberdeen, Chicago, Illinois 60609 Phone: (312) 747-6900 E-mail: **mbaker@chipublib.org**

Rochelle Ballard Digital Resources Coordinator, Technical Services Department. Princeton University, One Washington Road, Princeton, New Jersey 08544 Phone: (609) 258-7115 Fax: (609) 258-0441 E-mail: **rballard@Princeton.edu**

Roland Barksdale-Hall Managing Editor BCALA Newsletter. Contact Mr. Roland Barksdale-Hall, BCALA, 939 Baldwin Avenue, Suite 1 Sharon, Pennsylvania 16146 Phone: (724) 346-0459 Fax: (724) 342-1808 E-mail: **newsletter@bcala.org**

Rebecca Batson Head Librarian (Acting). Rebecca Batson, William C. Jason Library-Learning Center, Delaware State University, 1200 North DuPont Highway, Dover, Delaware 19901 Phone: (302) 857-6180 Fax: (302) 857-6177 E-mail: **rbatson@desu.edu**

Billy Beal Dean of Learning Resources. Billy Beal, Meridian Community College, 910 Highway 19, North Meridian, Mississippi 39307 E-mail: **bbeal@mcc.cc.ms.us**

Gladys Smiley Bell Reference Librarian. Ms. Gladys Smiley Bell, Hampton University, 130 East Tyler Street, Hampton, Virginia 23668 Phone: (757) 727-5371 Fax: (757) 727-5952 E-mail: **gladys.bell@hamptonu.edu** Website: **www.hamptonu.edu**

Valerie Bell Supervising Librarian-Branch Coordinator. Contact Ms. Valerie Bell, Ocean County Library, 101 Washington Street, Toms River, New Jersey 08753 Phone: (732) 349-6200 E-mail: **bell_v@oceancounty.lib.nj.us**

Stanton F. Biddle Librarian. Stanton Biddle, Baruch College, 17 Lexington Avenue, New York, New York 10010 Phone: (646) 312-1653 E-mail: **Stanton_Biddle@baruch.cuny.edu**

Richard Bradberry　Library Dean. Richard Bradberry, Ph.D., Thurgood Marshall Library, Bowie State University, 14000 Jericho Park Road, Bowie, Maryland 20715　Fax: (301) 860-3848　E-mail: **rbradberry@bowiestate.edu**

Jean Currie Church　Chief librarian. Certified Archivist, Society of American Archivists.　Jean Currie Church, Moorland-Spingarn Research Center, Howard University, 500 Howard Place, North West, Washington, DC 20059　Phone: (202) 806-7497　E-mail: **jchurch@howard.edu**

Regina Clark　Librarian.　Assistant Head of Media Services. Contact Ms. Regina Clark, Emerson College, 120 Boylston Street, Boston, Massachusetts 02116　Phone: (617) 824-8409　E-mail: **regina_clark@emerson.edu**

Rudolph Clay　Head of Reference.　Rudolph Clay, Washington University Libraries, Campus Box 1061, One Brookings Drive, Saint Louis, Missouri 63130　Phone: (314) 935-5059　E-mail: **rudolphc@wustl.edu**

Erin Daix　M.L.S. Associate Librarian Reference Department.　Contact Erin Daix, University of Delaware Library, Newark, Delaware 19717　Phone: (302) 831-6943　Fax: (302) 831-1046　E-mail: **daix@udel.edu**

Trevor A. Dawes　Circulation Services Director.　Trevor A. Davis, Princeton University Library, One Washington Road Princeton, New Jersey 08544　Phone: (609) 258-3231　Fax: (609) 258-0441　E-mail: **tdawes@Princeton.edu**

Rose T. Dawson　Deputy Director.　Contact Ms. Rose T. Dawson, Alexandria Library, 5005 Duke Street, Alexandria, Virginia 22304　Phone: (703) 519-5905　Fax: (703) 519-5916　E-mail: **rdawson@alexandria.lib.va.us**

Bobbie P. Fells　Acquisitions Librarian. Mr. Bobby Fells, J.D. Boyd Library, Alcorn State University, 1000 Alcorn State University Drive 539, Alcorn State, Mississippi 39096　Phone: (601) 877-6354　E-mail: **bpfells@lorman.alcorn.edu**　Website: **jdboyd.alcorn.edu**

Janice Franklin　Library Director. Contact Ms. Janice Franklin, PhD, Alabama State University Library, 915 South Jackson Street, Montgomery, Alabama 36104　Phone: (334) 229-6890　E-mail: **nfoulger@alafu.edu**　Website: **www.lib.alasu.edu**

Marilyn Pringle Gibbs　Head librarian.　Contact Marilyn Pringle Gibbs, Claflin University, 400 Magnolia Street, Orangeburg, South Carolina 29115　Phone: (803) 535-5309　Fax: (803) 535-5091　E-mail: **mpringle@claflin.edu**　Website: **www.claflin.edu**

George C. Grant　Dean of Library and Information Resources.　George C. Grant, PhD., Arkansas State University, Post Office Box 2040, State University, Arizona 72467　Phone: (870) 972-3099　E-mail: **ggrant@astate.edu**

Valerie Griffith　Librarian.　Valerie Griffith, Greenburg Public Library, 300 Tarrytown Road, Elmsford, New York 10523　Phone: (914) 993-1600　E-mail: **vgriffith@greenburghlibrary.org**

S.D. Harris Interim Editor BCALA Newsletter. S.D. Harris, BCALA, Post Office Box 1288, Norwalk, Connecticut 06856 Phone: (203) 299-1226 E-mail: **sdh.newsletter@bcala.org**

Ernestine L. Hawkins Deputy Director. Ms. Ernestine L. Hawkins, East Cleveland Public Library, 14101 Euclid Avenue, East Cleveland, Ohio 44112 Phone: (216) 541-4128 E-mail: **ernestine.hawkins@ecpl.lib.oh.us**

Allene Hayes Digital Projects Coordinator. Acquisitions and Bibliographic Access Directorate. Contact Allene Hayes, Library of Congress, Washington, DC 20540 Phone: (202) 707-1499 Fax: (202) 707-7161 E-mail: **ahay@loc.gov**

Bobby R. Henderson Library Director. Carl S. Swisher Library, Bethune Cookman College, 640 Dr. Mary McLeod Bethune Boulevard, Daytona Beach, Florida 32114 Phone: (386) 481-2187 E-mail: **hendersb@cookman.edu** Website: **www.cookman.edu/library/index**

Jos N. Holman County Librarian. Jos N. Holman, Tippecanoe County Public Library, 627 South Street, Lafayette, Indiana 47901 Phone: (765) 429-0118 E-mail: **jholman@tcpl.lib.in.us** Website: **www.bcala.org/association/exec_board.htm**

Ernestine Holmes Librarian. Acquisitions Department. Contacct Ernestine Holmes, Florida A & M University Libraries, G7 Coleman Library, Tallahassee, Florida 32307 Phone: (850) 599-3969 Fax: (850) 599-8157 E-mail: **ernestine.holmes@famu.edu**

Gerald Holmes Librarian. Reference Department. Gerald Holmes, Jackson Library, UNCG Post Office Box 26170, Greensboro, North Carolina 27402 Phone: (336) 256-0273 Fax: (336) 334-5097 E-mail: **gerald_holmes@uncg.edu**

Brenda Hunter Collection Development Manager. Brenda Hunter, Atlanta-Fulton Public Library 1 Margaret Mitchell Square, North West Atlanta, Georgia 30303 Phone: (404) 730-1714 E-mail: **bhunter@af.public.lib.ga.us**

Julie Hunter Director of the African American Research Library and Cultural Center. Julie Hunter, Director, AARLCC, 2650 Sistrunk Boulevard, Fort Lauderdale, Florida 33311 Phone: (954) 625-2800 E-mail: **jhunter@browardlibrary.org** Website: **www.broward/aarlcc**

Andrew P. Jackson Librarian. Mr. Andrew P. Jackson, Langston Hughes Community Library Cultural Center, Queens Borough Public Library, 100-01 Northern Boulevard, Corona, New York 11368 Phone: (718) 651-1100 E-mail: **andrew.p.jackson@queenslibrary.org**

James B. Jones Coordinator, Acquisitions. James B. Jones, Robert W. Woodruff Library, Clark Atlanta University, Atlanta University Center, 111 James P. Brawley Drive, South West, Atlanta, Georgia 30314 Phone: (404) 522-8980 E-mail: **jbjones@auctr.edu**

Cecy Keller System Director of the Chester County Library System. Ms. Cecy Keller, 413 Valley Avenue, Atglen, Pennsylvania 19310 Phone: (610) 280-2600 E-mail: **ckeller@ccls.org** Website: **www.ccls.org**

Carol King Senior Library Associate, Collection Management Cataloging. Carol King, DeWitt Wallace Library, 1600 Grand Avenue, Saint Paul, Minneapolis 55105 Phone: (651) 696-6000 E-mail: **king@macalester.edu**

Em Claire Knowles Assistant Director, Graduate School of Library and Information Science, Em Claire Knowles, Simmons College, 300 The Fenway, Boston, Massachusetts 02115 Phone: (617) 521-2798 Fax: (617) 521-3192 E-mail: **knowles@simmons.edu**

LeRoy (Lee) LaFleur Liaison Librarian for Public Policy & Management. Contact Leroy Lafleur, Arlington Campus Library, George Mason University, 3401 North Fairfax Drive, Arlington, Virginia 22201 Phone: (703) 993-8268 E-mail: **llafleur@gmu.edu**

Rhea Brown Lawson Director. Nominated as the sixth director in the 101-year history of the Houston Public Library, Texas, she has served as deputy director of the Detroit Public Library, since 2003. Chief of the Central Library, Brooklyn Public Library from 1999 to 2003. MLIS, University of Maryland; Ph.D., Library and Information Studies, University of Wisconsin. Dr. Rhea Lawson, Director, Houston Public Library, 500 McKinney Street Houston, Texas 77002 Phone: (832) 393-1300 Fax: (832) 393-1324 E-mail: **library.director@cityofhouston.net** Website: **www.hpl.lib.tx.us**

Christopher Lee Librarian. Christopher Lee, MLIS, Walsh Library, Seton Hall University, 400 South Orange, New Jersey 07079 Phone: (973) 275-2059 E-mail: **leechria@shu.edu**

Tabitha Lee Interlibrary Loan/ Document Delivery Supervisor. Contact Ms. Tabitha Lee, Emerson College 120 Boylston Street, Boston, Massachusetts 02116 Phone: (617) 824-8333 E-mail: **tabitha_lee@emerson.edu**

Veronica Lee Librarian. Veronica Lee, African American Museum and Library at Oakland, Oakland Public Library, 659 Fourteenth Street, Oakland, California 94612 Phone: (510) 637-0203 Website: **www.oaklandlibrary.org/AAMLO/index.html**

Karen Lemmons Library Media Specialist. Contact Ms. Karen Lemmons, Howe Elementary School, 2600 Garland, Detroit, Michigan 48214 Phone: (313) 642-4801 Fax: (313) 642-4802 E-mail: **camaraife@aol.com**

Jane Moore McGinn Associate Professor, Information and Library Science. Contact Ms. Jane McGinn, PhD., Southern Connecticut State University, 501 Crescent Street, New Haven, Connecticut 06515 Phone: (203) 392-5781 E-mail: **mcginnj1@southernct.edu**

Dianna McKellar M.L.S. Senior Assistant Librarian Reference Department. Dianna McKellar, University of Delaware Library Newark, Delaware 19717 Phone: (302) 831-0790 Fax: (302) 831-1046 E-mail: **mckellar@udel.edu**

Gennette McLaurin Associate Chief Librarian. Gennette McLaurin, Schomburg Center for Research in Black Culture, 515 Malcolm X Boulevard, New York, New York 10037 Phone: (212) 491-2200 E-mail: **gmclaurin@nypl.org** Website: **www.nypl/research/sc/sc**

R. Meeker Director. R. Meeker, Paul and Emily Douglas Library, Chicago State University, 9501 South Martin Luther King Drive, Chicago, Illinois 60628 E-mail: **R-Meeker@csu.edu** Website: **www.csu.edu/Library**

Rosemary Mokia Assistant Professor. Director of Library Services. Dr. Rosemary Mokia, Grambling State University, 100 Main Street, Grambling, Louisiana 71245 Phone: (318) 274-6122 E-mail: **mokiar@gram.edu** Website: **www.gram.edu**

Sibyl E. Moses Reference Specialist, African American History and Culture Humanities and Social Sciences Division. Sibyl E. Moses, Ph.D., The Library of Congress, 101 Independence Avenue, South East, Washington, DC 20540 Phone: (202) 707-0940 E-mail: **smos@loc.gov**

James Murray Librarian/Archivist. Buys, reviews. Contact Mr. James Murray, NAACP. Henry Lee Moon Library, 4805 Mt. Hope Drive, Baltimore, Maryland 21215 Phone: (410) 580-5767 E-mail: **jmurray@naacpnet.org**

Charleszine Nelson Special collection and community resource manager. Blair-Caldwell African American Research Library, 2401 Welton Street Denver, Colorado 80205 Phone: (720) 865-2401 E-mail: **tnelson@denverlibrary.org** Website: **www.aarl.denverlibrary.org**

Lut Nero Dean of Library & Media Services. Lut Nero, The Leslie Pinckney Hill Library, Cheyney University, 1837 University Circle, Post Office Box 200, Cheyney, Pennsylvania 19319 Phone: (610) 399-2069 E-mail: **lnero@cheyney.edu** Website: **www.cheyney.edu**

Carolyn Norman Coordinator, Library and Learning Resources Programs. C. Norman, 1102 Q Street Sacramento, California 95814 E-mail: **cnorman@cccco.edu**

John Page Associate Dean, University of the District of Columbia Learning Resources Division, 4200 Connecticut Avenue Washington, DC 20008 Phone: (202) 274-6030 Fax: (202) 274-6012 E-mail: **jpage@wlrc.org**

Robert Parker Director. Robert Parker, Bishop State Community College Library, 351 North Broad Street, Mobile, Alabama 36603 Phone: (251) 690-6867 E-mail: **rparker@bishop.edu**

Lorna Peterson Library Science Educator. Contact Ms. Lorna Peterson, Sunny-Buffalo Sils University Library, 534 Baldy Hall, Buffalo, New York 14260 Phone: (716) 645-2412 ext. 1165 E-mail: **lpeterso@buffalo.edu**

Bobby Player Head, Acquisitions Department. Bobby, Player, Howard University Libraries, Washington, DC 20059 Phone: (202) 806-7255 E-mail: **bplayer@howard.edu**

Bobbie Pollard Librarian. Stanton Biddle, Baruch College, 17 Lexington Avenue, New York, New York 10010 Phone: (646) 312-1619 E-mail: **bobbie_pollard@baruch.cuny.edu**

Jocelyn Poole Librarian. Jocelyn Poole, Zach Henderson Library, Georgia Southern University, Statesboro, Georgia 30460 Phone: (912) 486-7818 E-mail: **jpoole@georgiasouthern.edu**

Kevin Pothier Head of Acquisitions. Contact Mr. Kevin Pothier, Thurgood Marshall Library. Bowie State University, 14000 Jericho Park Road, Bowie, Maryland 20715 Phone: (301) 860-3994 E-mail: **Kpothier@bowiestate.edu** Website: **www.bowiestate.edu**

Ellen Renaud Academic librarian. Contact Ms. Ellen Renaud, Hudson County Community College, 900 Bergen Avenue, Jersey City, New Jersey 07306 Phone: (201) 714-2229 E-mail: **erenaud@hccc.edu**

Ira Revels Instruction Librarian. Ira Revels, Cornell University, 309 Uris Library, Ithaca, New York 14853 Phone: (607) 255-1569 Fax: (607) 255-7922 E-mail: **ir33@cornell.edu**

LeRoy Robinson Manager/Librarian. Leroy Robinson, Houston Public Library, 7200 Keller, Houston, Texas 77012 Phone: (832) 393-2480 E-mail: **leroy.robinson@cityofhouston.net**

C. P. Roddey Director. Dr. C. P. Roddey, Richard L. Fisher Memorial Library, Clinton Junior College, 1029 Crawford Road, Rock Hill, South Carolina 29730 Phone: (803) 327-7402 E-mail: **cproddey@comporium.net**

Mae L. Rodney Director. Dr. Mae L. Rodney, PhD, C. G. O'Kelly Library, Winston Salem University, Campus Box 19543, Winston Salem, North Carolina 27110 Phone: (336) 750-2440 E-mail: **rodneyml@wssu.edu** Website: **www.wssu.edu/library/librarians/rodney.asp**

Cynthia Rollins Acquisitions librarian. Cynthia Rollins, Schomburg Center for Research in Black Culture, 515 Malcolm X Boulevard, New York, New York 10037 Phone: (212) 491-2254 E-mail: **crollins@nypl.org** Website: **www.nypl/research/sc/sc**

Carol A. Rudisell Librarian. Carol A. Rudisell, Reference Department, Morris Library, Room 117A, 181 South College Avenue, University of Delaware, Newark, Delaware 19717 Phone: (302) 831-6942 Fax: (302) 831-1631 E-mail: **Rudisell@udel.edu**

Lauren Sapp Director. Lauren Sapp, Ph.D., Florida A& M University Libraries, 307 Coleman Library, Tallahassee, Florida 32307 Phone: (850) 599-3370 E-mail: **lauren.sapp@famu.edu**

Ronald Shelton Libriarian. Ronald Shelton, L. Douglas Wilder Library, 1500 North Lombardy Street, Richmond, Virginia 23220 Phone: (804) 257-5721 E-mail: **RShelton@vuu.edu**

W. Ruth Sims Librarian. W. Ruth Sims, Nathan W. Collier Library, 15800 North West 42nd Avenue, Miami, Florida 33054 Phone: (305) 626-3786 E-mail: **rsims@fmc.edu**

Robert Skinner Library Director. Robert Skinner, Xavier University Library Resource Center, Library Post Office Box 1, Drexel Drive, New Orleans, Louisiana 70125 E-mail: **rskinner@xula.edu** Website: **www.xula.edu/Library_Services**

Sylvia Sprinkle-Hamlin Library Director. Sylvia Sprinkle-Hamlin, Forsyth County Public Library, 660 West Fifth Street, Winston-Salem, North Carolina 27101 Phone: (336) 703-3016 Fax: (336) 727-2549 E-mail: **hamlinss@forsythlibrary.org**

Joanna Thompson   Director of Library Services.   Joanna Thompson, Bluefield Campus, Bluefield State College, 219 Rock Street, Bluefield, West Virginia 24701 Phone: (304) 327-4050 E-mail: **jthompson@bluefieldstate.edu** Website: **www.bluefield.wvnet.edu**

Karolyn S. Thompson   Interlibrary Loan Coordinator. Cook Memorial Library, University of Southern Mississippi, Post Office Box 5053, Hattiesburg, Mississippi 39406 Phone: (601) 266-5111 Fax: (601) 266-4410 E-mail: **karolyn.thompson@usm.edu**

Deborah J. Tucker   Librarian.   Deborah J. Tucker, Wayne State University, 213 Kresge, Detroit, Michigan 48202 Phone: (313) 577-2005 E-mail: **deborah.tucker@wayne.edu**

Laura Turner Librarian. Branch Manager. Laura Turner, 4215 Medgar Evers Blvd, Jackson, Mississippi 39213 E-mail: **lturner@jhlibrary.com**

Danny Walker Senior librarian. Contact Mr. Danny Walker, Blair-Caldwell African American Research Library, 2401 Welton Street Denver, Colorado 80205 Phone: (720) 865-2401 E-mail: **dwalker@denver.lib.co.us** Website: **www.aarl.denverlibrary.org**

Michael C. Walker Associate Librarian for Public Services. Michael C. Walker, James Hugo Johnston Memorial Library, Virginia State University, 1 Hayden Drive, Post Office Box 9406, Petersburg, Virginia 23806 Phone: (804) 524-6946 E-mail: **mcwalker@vsu.edu**

Roberta V. Webb District Chief. Roberta V. Webb, Chicago Public Library, South District Office, 2107 West 95th Street, Chicago, Illinois 60643 Phone: (312) 747-0171 Fax: (312) 745-4974 E-mail: **rwebb@chipublib.org**

Lainey Westbrooks Technology Operations Manager. Lainey Westbrooks, East Cleveland Public Library, 15300 Terrace Road, East Cleveland, Ohio 44112 Phone: (216) 541-4128 E-mail: **lainey.westbrooks@ecjpl.oh.us**

Joel White Youth Library Service Coordinator. Joel White, Forsyth County Public Library, 660 West 5th Street, Winston Salem, North Carolina 27101 Phone: (336) 703-3041 Fax: (336) 727-2549 E-mail: **whitejw@forsythlibrary.org**

C. Michael Williams Assistant Librarian. Michael Williams, New River Community/Technical College, 101 Church Street, Lewisburg, West Virginia 24901 Phone: (304) 647-6574 E-mail: **cwilliam@access.k12.wv.us**

Lois Williams Librarian. Lois Williams, Vance H. Chavis Library 900 South Benbow Road, Greensboro, North Carolina 27406 Fax: (336) 412-5960 E-mail: **ann81@hotmail.com**

H. Jamane Yeager Librarian. H. Jamane Yeager, Belk Library, Elon University, Elon, North Carolina 27244 Phone: (336) 278-6576 Fax: (336) 278-6639 E-mail: **jyeager@elon.edu**

Marlene Connor Lynch
Author * Literary Agent

Marlene Connor Lynch began her literary agency in New York City in the mid eighties before moving, in 1995, to the Twin Cities. An accomplished literary agent and former Editor for The Literary Guild of America, Simon and Schuster Publishing Company and, in her first position, Random House, Marlene and The Connor Agency represents books  being published by Clarkson Potter, HarperCollins, Warner Books, Crown, John Wiley and Sons, Sourcebooks, Simon and Schuster, Penguin Putnam and others. The Agency has also served as a consultant and agent for such corporations as Essence Communications, publishers of Essence Magazine and the Simplicity Pattern Company. Marlene's recently published and upcoming titles represented by the agency include: Projects in development include MO' BETTER SOUL a wonderful cookbook by local chef phenom Eric Austin, "The Big E," CAUTION! SNAKE OIL: A Survival Guide to a World Filled With Misinformation About our Health by Heinz Kohler, Willard Long Thorp Professor of Economics, Emeritus, Amherst College, THE WIFE OF JOHN THE BAPTIST by Katherine Ford, a literary novel, MEMOIRS DE LA SOUL: Fantasy Worlds Inspired by Women We Know, a gift book featuring lavish photos of Barbie dolls by Robin Hickman, and many more. Books already available include: THE BLACK WOMAN'S GUIDE TO BEAUTIFUL HAIR by Lisa Akbari, the #1 selling book on hair for black women; HOW TO LOVE A BLACK MAN by Dr. Ronn Elmore (Warner Books), a perennial bestseller by the minister and frequent guest columnist for Essence Magazine; TWELVE MONTHS OF KNITTING by Joanne Yordanou, a soon-to-be-published highly visual knitting book from the new company, Potter Style; SIMPLICITY'S SIMPLY THE BEST SEWING BOOK (Simon and Schuster), nearly a million seller with several book clubs; and many more.

Marlene is cofounder of "Free Spirit," a multicultural literary magazine which still exists at Trinity College and is a frequent reviewer. She is a graduate of Trinity College and the Radcliffe Publishing Procedures Course. She has served as panelist for several conferences including the Howard University Press Publishing Institute, and received certificates of completion from the City University of New York Literary Agent Course and the Direct Mail Marketing Association. Although the agency started and grew in New York City, it is now located in Minneapolis, Minnesota.

Author of two books, Ms. Connor's latest book is WELCOME TO THE FAMILY: Memories of the Past for a Bright Future, published January 2006 by Broadway/Doubleday. Her first book is WHAT IS COOL? Understanding Black Manhood in America (AGATE and Crown publishers for paperback and hardcover respectively).

Magazines

African Voices Magazine   Poetry magazine featuring book reviews and profiles.   African Voices Communications, Inc., 270 West 96th Street, New York, New York 10025 Phone: (212) 865-2982 E-mail: **africanvoices@aol.com**   Website: **www.africanvoices.com**

Afrique Magazine   Monthly French magazine that features current news about popular African entertainment stars and celebrities, interviews, health, beauty, fashion culture, music, tourism and sports.   E-mail: **afriquemagazine@cba.fr** Website: **www.afriquemagazine.com**

Arizona Jazz Magazine (AZJM)   Produced quarterly and covers information on the Arizona jazz scene. Pick up your FREE copy for the Fallat all Borders Bookstores in AZ. Each quarter AZJM covers something fresh and exciting in the local jazz market. Reviews of CD's Select AZ jazz artists with newly released CD creations. Who is going to review it? Our line up of music critics are selected from jazz music aficionados of Arizona. Are you one of them? Read the opinions of people who really buy the music. Opinion is provided as a team review, so there is sometimes conflicting views but always an opinion. Contact Publisher/CEO, D.A. Peartree. Contact Arizona's Black Pages, 822 East Montecito Avenue, Suite 4, Phoenix, Arizona 85014 Phone: (602) 230-8161 E-mail: **editor@azjzz.com** Website: **www.AZJazz.com**

Awareness Magazine (AMAG)   Bi-monthly publication chocked full of Features, On The Rise, The Reading Room, Health and Finance, Poetic Justice, If You Don't Know, Now You Know, and so much more. AMAG, Inc. brings you the voice of the African-American and Latino communities and highlights the heart of those who not only are making it and give back to the community. Contact AMAG, Inc., 175 Park Avenue, Brooklyn, New York 11205 Phone: (718) 699-7707 E-mail: **james@awarenessmagazine.net** Website: **awarenessmagazine.net**

Beat Magazine Bi-monthly publication of reggae, African, Caribbean and world music, information, news, reviews, interviews, discographies and cultural features to an international audience of avid music fans. Now celebrating its 21th anniversary, The Beat features the work of top writers and photographers. Mr. Roger Steffens is founding editor. C. C. Smith, Editor/Publisher. Contact The Beat Magazine, Post Office Box 65856, Los Angeles, California 90065 Phone: (818) 500-9299 Fax: (818) 500-9299 E-mail: **getthebeat@aol.com** Website: **www.getthebeat.com**

Black and Single Magazine   Bi-monthly magazine distributed in Houston. Circulation is 15,000. Black and Single Magazine provides a forum to promote intelligent discussion and understanding among the single community. The reader is the author/writer of the majority of the content in the magazine. We deal with many issues of importance, from health, physical or emotional, to trends in fashion and style, as well as finances. Lynn Jones, Black and Single Magazine, 1924 Calumet, Suite 200, Houston, Texas 77004 Phone: (713) 522-1200 Fax: (713) 522-2808 E-mail: **info@blackandsinglemag.com** Website: **www.blackandsinglemag.com**

Black Collegian Magazine Founded, 1970. BCM is a career and self-development magazine targeted to African-American students seeking information on careers, job opportunities, graduate/professional school, internships/co-ops, and study abroad programs.distributed on over 800 campuses nationwide. Contact The Black Collegian Magazine, IMDiversity, 140 Carondelet Street, New Orleans, Lousiana 70130 Phone: (832) 615-8871 E-mail: **sales@imdiversity.com** Website: **www.blackcollegian.com**

Black Enterprise Magazine Founded in 1968 by Earl G. Graves, Sr. Magazine serves to seek out, analyze and disseminate information that is helpful to African American business people. Black Enterprise Magazine, 130 Fifth Avenue, 10th Floor, New York, New York 10011 Phone: (212) 242-8000 E-mail: **beeditors@blackenterprise.com** Website: **www.blackenterprise.com**

Black History Bulletin A Black History Magazine, published twice a year. Sylvia Cyrus-Albritton, Executive Director. Published by the Association for the Study of African American Life and History (ASALH - The Founder's of Black History Month). ASALH, CB Powell Building, 525 Bryant Street, North West, Suite C142, Washington, DC 20059 Phone: (202) 865-0053 Fax: (202) 265-7920 E-mail: **executivedirector@asalh.net** Website: **asalh.net**

Black Issues Book Review From celebrity author spotlights to analyzing trends in publishing, an insider's view of the world of literature. Angela P. Dodson, Executive Editor. Contact Black Issues Book Review 350 Fifth Avenue, Suite 1522, New York, New York 10118 Phone: (212) 947-8515 E-mail: **Angela4bibr@aol.com** Website: **www.bibookreview.com**

Black Issues In Higher Education Magazine covering issues affecting African Americans and other minorities and underrepresented groups in our nation's colleges and universities. Book reviews. Publisher, Frank L. Matthews. Cox, Matthews & Associates, 10520 Warwick Avenue, Suite B-8, Fairfax, Virginia 22030 Phone: (800) 783-3199 Fax: (703) 385-1839 E-mail: **editor@cmapublishing.com** Website: **www.blackissues.com**

Black MBA Magazine Official publication of the National Black MBA Association. Contact Robin Melton, NBMBA, 180 North Michigan Avenue, #1400, Chicago, Illinois 60601 Phone: (312) 236-2622 Fax: (312) 236-0390 E-mail: **mail@nbmbaa.org** Website: **www.nbmbaa.org**

Black Noir Magazine TonyaSue Carther, Associate Editor. Contact Black Noir Magazine, 100 Park Avenue South, Suite 1600, New York, New York 10017 Phone: (201) 408-4306 E-mail: **Gigone2112@cs.com** Website: **www.floanthonysblacknoir.com**

Black Outdoorsman Magazine highlights outdoor recreational activities of Black men and women; salt/freshwater fishing, boating, scuba diving, biking, climbing, backpacking, and skiing. Contact Charles, K. West, Founder/Publisher. E-mail: **editor@blackoutdoorsman.com** Website: **www.blackoutdoorsman.com**

Black Voices Quarterly Magazine Quarterly publication for alumni, administrators, students and supporters of historically black colleges and universities. Black Voices, Tribune Tower, 435 North Michigan Avenue, Suite LL2, Chicago, Illinois 60611 Phone: (312) 222-4326 Fax: (312) 222-4502 E-mail: **dsquires@corp.blackvoices.com** Website: **www.blackvoices.com**

Booking Matters Magazine Contact Ms. Kendra Norman-Bellamy, Post Office Box 54491, Atlanta, Georgia 30308 Phone: (937) 304- 9473 E-mail: **kendra_bellamy@hotmail.com** Website: **www.knb-publications.com**

Books2Mention Magazine Our mission is to provide our readers with knowledge about all genres in the literary world. B2M will feature articles on authors, conduct author interviews, provide book reviews, display newly released books and discuss up-coming. Contact Editorial Staff, Books2Mention Magazine, 2260 Talbot Ridge, Jonesboro, Georgia 30236 E-mail: **Info@Books2Mention.com** Website: **www.Books2Mention.com**

Business in Africa Africa's leading finance publication aimed at increasing awareness of investment opportunities on the continent. Peter Griffiths Business in Africa Group, Manta House, Norbuy Office Park, 372 Rivonia Boulevard, Rivonia 2128, South Africa Phone: +27 (0)11 807 0948 Fax: +27 (0)11 807 0919 E-mail: **peter@businessinafrica.co.za** Website: **www.businessafrica.net**

CityFlight Publication covering issues facing African Americans locally and nationally with a readership of over 40,000 throughout the San Francisco Bay Area. John Hilton President and CEO, City Flight Media Network, Post Office Box 1484, San Jose, California 95109 Phone: (510) 986-9390 E-mail: **publisher@cityflight.com** Website: **www.cityflight.com**

Class Magazine The social events and profiles glossy magazine for Africans in the United States and North America. Chido Nwangwuf, Founder. Class Magazine, USAfrica Digital Media Networks, 8303 Southwest Freeway, Suite 100, Houston, Texas 77074 Phone: (713) 270-5500 Fax: (713) 270-8131 E-mail: **class@classmagazine.tv** Website: **www.Classmagazine.tv**

Con Brio The official voice of the National Association for the Study and Performance of African American Music (NASPAAM). It publishes articles on African American music, educators, performers and composers. Frank Suggs, President. Contact NASPAAM, 1201 Mary Jane, Memphis, Tennessee 38116 Phone: (901) 396-2913 E-mail: **fsuggs@midsouth.rr.com** Website: **www.naspaam.org**

Crisis Magazine One of the oldest Black periodicals in America.   A bi-monthly publication Crisis Magazine is dedicated to being an open and honest forum for discussing critical issues confronting people of color, American society and the world in addition to highlighting the historical and cultural achievements of these diverse peoples. Founded in 1910 by Founding Editor, W.E.B. Du Bois as the premier crusading voice for civil rights. Contact The Crisis Magazine, 4805 Mount Hope Drive, Baltimore, Maryland 21215 Phone: (866) 636-2227 E-mail: **thecrisiseditorial@naacpnet** Website: **www.thecrisismagazine.com**

Ebony World's largest Black-owned publishing company is the home of Ebony and Jet magazines. Also parts of the company are Fashion Fair Cosmetics, Supreme Beauty Products, EBONY Fashion Fair and Johnson Publishing Company Book Division. The late John H. Johnson, who founded the privately-held company in November 1942 with Negro Digest, was Publisher and Chairman. Ebony Editorial, 820 South Michigan Avenue, Chicago, Illinois 60605 Website: **www.ebony.com**

The Ebony Cactus Magazine Published twice a month, The Ebony Cactus is a full color magazine distributed free by subscription over the Internet. The Ebony Cactus showcases new and established businesses in Arizona, Nevada and Southern California. Contact The Ebony Cactus Magazine, Post Office Box 24982, Tempe, Arizona 85285 Phone: (602) 821-8191 Fax: (602) 437-8852 E-mail: **Publisher@theebonycactus.com**

Essence Magazine The magazine for African-American and Caribbean women. Features personal-growth articles, celebrity profiles, and well-reported pieces on political and social issues. We are also looking for how-to pieces on careers, money, health and fitness, and relationships. Word length is given upon assignment. Please send a query letter rather than submitting a completed manuscript. Contact Editor, Essence, 1500 Broadway, 6th Floor, New York, New York 10036 Phone: (212) 642-0600 E-mail: **webeditor@essence.com** Website: **www.essence.com**

Everybody's General interest Caribbean-American magazine, (music and entertainment, theater, travel, politics, current trends) published 10 times per year. Established in January, 1977, Everybody's serves Caribbean-American consumers from Alaska to Louisiana to New York. Everybody's covers performing arts and concerts, politics, sports, technology, music, fashion, food and restaurants, theater reviews and more. Everybody's has a readership of affluent consumers. Herman Hall Communications, Inc., 1630 Nostrand Avenue, Brooklyn, New York 11226 Phone: (718) 941-1879 Fax: (718) 941-1886 E-mail: **everybodys@msn.com** Website: **www.everybodysmag.com**

Focus Magazine Since 1972, Focus magazine has provided coverage of national issues to a leadership audience. Over 18,000 readers, nearly half of whom are black elected officials, value the magazine for its in-depth, yet straightforward features on politics as well as a broad range of economic and social concerns affecting African Americans and the nation at-large. Focus Magazine, Joint Center For Political and Economic Studies, 1090 Vermont Avenue, North West, Suite 1100, Washington, DC 20005 Phone: (202) 789-3500 Fax: (202) 789-6390 E-mail: **jjoyner@jointcenter.org** Website: **www.jointcenter.org**

Footsteps Magazine celebrating African American heritage and achievement for grades 4 and up. It is an excellent classroom resource for teachers, a valuable research tool for students. Winner of a 2000 Parents' Choice Gold Award and the 1999 Parent's Guide Children's Media Award! Contact Footsteps Magazine, Cobblestone Publishing, 30 Grove Street, Suite C, Peterborough, New Hampshire 03458 Phone: (800) 821-0115 Fax: (603) 924-7380 E-mail: **custsvc@cobblestone.mv.com** Website: **www.footstepsmagazine.com**

Jolie Magazine Magazine. Contact Jolie Magazine, LLC 535 West 34th Street, Suite 411, New York, New York 10001 Phone: (646) 792-2926 E-mail: **info@marclacy.com** Website: **www.jolie-magazine.com**

MAMi Magazine Internationally distributed title, Mami Magazine focuses on latino and black women with such issues as fashion, music, culture and arts. Algie deWitt currently publisher and Editor in Chief of MAMi Magazine. MAMi Magazine, 4408 Aberdeen Lane, Blackwood, New Jersey 08012 E-mail: **algie@mamimagazine.com** Website: **www.mamimagazine.com**

MBE Magazine Published bi-monthly by Minority Business Entrepreneur (MBE) and serves as a nationwide forum for minority and women business owners, corporations and government agencies concerned with minority enterprise development. Examines affirmative action and procurement programs in the public and private sectors. Ginger Conrad, MBE, 3528 Torrance Boulevard, Suite 101 Torrance, California 90503 Phone: (310) 540-9398 Fax: (310) 792-8263 E-mail: **gconrad@mbemag.com** Website: **www.mbemag.com**

Mosaic Books Launched in 1998, with a desire to showcase and honestly critique African American and Hispanic literature, Mosaic has established itself as an important voice on the literary landscape. Ron Kavanaugh, Publisher/Editor in Chief. Ms. Deatra Haime, Reviews Editor. Contact Mosaic Books, 314 West 231 Suite #470, Bronx, New York 10463 E-mail: **listing@mosaicbooks.com**   Website: **www.mosaicbooks.com**

ONYX Style Magazine Caleen Burton-Allen, Publisher/Editor-In-Chief. Contact Onyx Style Magazine, 8787 Woodway Drive, Suite 4206, Houston, Texas 77063 Phone: (832) 467-9377 Fax: (832) 467-9378 E-mail: **caleen@onyxstyle.com** Website: **www.onyxstyle.com**

Shades Magazine Michelle Fitzhugh-Craig, Editor. News, lifestyle, health, mind and body, book reviews, voices. Contact Shades Magazine, Post Office Box 46325, Phoenix, Arizona 85063 E-mail: **mcraig@shadesmagazine.com** Website: **shadesmagazine.com**

Sister 2 Sister Magazine National consumer magazine marketed toward Black women. Editor, Sister 2 Sister Magazine, 6930 Carroll Avenue, Suite 200, Takoma Park, Maryland 20912 Phone: (301) 270-5999 Fax: (301) 270-0085 E-mail: **s2smagazine@aol.com**   Website: **www.s2smagazine.com**

Say So! Magazine A free Christian resource magazine with bi-monthly distribution in the Baltimore/Washington Metropolitan Area. Carla D. Bluitt, Editor and Publisher. Say So! Magazine, 6030 Daybreak Circle, Suite A150/151, Clarksville, Maryland 21029 Phone: (301) 807-5445 E-mail: **cbluitt@saysomagazine.com** Website: **www.saysomagazine.com**

SpokenVizions Magazine   Evolution, the recurring monthly segment of SpokenVizions Magazine is dedicated to publishing poetry from students ranging from 10 to 17 years of age. Poetry submissions must be submitted through school teachers, counselors, by instructors of youth programs. Forward all inquiries to the attention of Tracie Berry-McGhee. Floyd Bokins, Jr., SpokenVizions Entertainment Group, Post Office Box 373, Florissant, Missouri 63032 Phone: (314) 517-8764 E-mail: **www.spokenvizions.com**

Stand Magazine The magazine for make it happen entrepreneurs. Dawn Fobbs, Creative publisher. Dawn Fobbs, Stand Magazine, Post Office Box 6667, Katy, Texas 77491 Phone: (281) 587-4054 E-mail: **msdawwn@sbcglobal.net** Website: **www.standmagazine.biz**

Strong G Island Biz SGB is the world first Urban bilingual music magazine. Gerard Mcleod, Editor-in-Chief. Contact Strong G Island Biz (SGIB), Post Office Box 1244, Bay Shore, New York 11706 Phone: (631) 969-3676 Fax: (631) 666-2444 E-mail: **SGIBmagazine@aol.com** Website: **www.sgibmagazine.com**

Turning Point Bi-monthly. Each Issue, offers insight into those companies that partner with us to provide quality information and programs for our readers. Contact Ms. Patricia A. Means, publisher, Turning Point Communications, Post Office Box 91889, Los Angeles, California 90009 Phone: (310) 821-6910 Fax: (310) 305-8401 E-mail: **info@turningpointmagazine.com** Website: **turningpointmagazine.com**

Upscale Magazine Contact Editorial Office, Upscale Magazine, 600 Bronner Brothers Way, South West, Atlanta, Georgia 30310 Phone: (404) 758-7467 E-mail: **letters@upscalemag.com** Website: **www.upscalemagazine.com**

Women In Motion An award winning multicultural magazine. Ms. Roxann Latimer, Publisher and Editor in Chief. Contact Ms. Roxann Latimer, WIM Media, 3900 West 22nd Lane #10G, Yuma, Arizona 85364 Phone: (928) 343-9729 E-mail: **wimmedia@yahoo.com** Website: **www.roxannlatimer.com**

Written Magazine Created in 2006, Written Magazine is a publication whose mission is to celebrate the reader and to celebrate the word. Written is a nationally syndicated as an insert to African American newspapers. Written is a lifestyle publication. Within Written reviews and critiques books, movies music...any thing with a written component. Written is a bi-monthly publication. Subscriptions are $8 for one year and $15 for two. Publisher, Michelle R. Gipson is the former Director of Advertising for Black Issues Book Review and Managing Editor of the Atlanta Daily World's Celebration of Books. Ms. Michelle R. Gipson, Publisher, Written Magazine, Post Office Box 250504, Atlanta, Georgia 30310 Phone: (404) 753-8315 E-mail: **michelle.gipson@writtenmag.com** Website: **www.writtenmag.com**

Management Companies

Big Fish Productions, Inc Artists Management/Indielabel/Productions. We do any/everything from Artist Management to Director of Events. James Carter, President. Carter Management, Big Fish Productions, Inc., Post Office Box 782. Bronx, New York 10462 Phone: (212) 860-3639 E-mail: **jcarter891@aol.com** Website: **www.bigfishproductionsinc.com**

Capital Entertainment Bil Carpenter runs Capital Entertainment, a small public relations company that has worked extensively with gospel artists such as Vickie Winans, Bishop T.D. Jakes, CeCe Winans, and Donald Lawrence & the Tri-City Singers, among many others. Carpenter's "Did You Know" trivia segments can also be heard weekly on "The BeBe Winans Radio Show" that is syndicated to over 100 radio stations throughout the USA. Bil has written liner note essays for various CD compilations for Sony/BMG Music, and Warner Bros. Bil Carpenter, Capital Entertainment, 217 Seaton Place North East, Washington, D.C. 20002 Phone: (202) 636-7028 E-mail: **carpbil@aol.com** Website: **www.bilcarpenter.com**

Emtro Music Production Artist Itinerary Management. Our session musicians are amongst the finest to be found anywhere. Other services we provide include: Publishing, Mastering, Marketing and Promotions, Shopping Your Artist Project to Record Labels, Remote and Live Recording Services, Radio and Retail Support, Manufacturing, Tour Support, Graphic Design and Photography. Welcomes all songwriters to submit copy written material to be considered for future projects. Emtro Music Production, Post Office Box 12760, Jacksonville, Florida 32209 E-mail: **kishia@theintegritysolution.com** Website: **www.emtro.com**

Herman Hall Communications Producer/Promoter of Caribbean plays, calypso & soca concerts, in the U.S. Also agent for soca/calypso artists to perform anywhere in the U.S. and Canada. We provide management for calypso star, Shadow. Contact Mr. Herman Hall Communications, Inc., 1630 Nostrand Avenue, Brooklyn, New York 11226 Phone: (718) 941-1879 E-mail: **everybodys@msn.com** Website: **www.everybodysmag.com**

Hy'Tara Entertainment Troy Buckner is Founder/CEO of Hy'Tara. She has managed and co-produced Gospel Renown Artist and Stella Award Winner, Kenny Smith and Vernessa Mitchell from the Motown's Grammy Award winning R & B Group, 'Hi-Energy'. Ms. Buckner is currently writing, managing, and producing several upcoming artists. Troy Buckner, Hy'tara Entertainment, Post Office Box 19049, Anaheim, California 92817 Phone: (714) 227-5000 E-mail: **birdinflight@aol.com** Website: **www.abirdinflight.com**

JFK Entertainment & Sports Management Company Provides company management for all types of theatrical productions, represent playwrights, actors, producers and publishers. Contact John F.Kilgore, JFK Entertainment & Sports Management Company, 2266 5th Avenue #77, New York, New York 10037 Phone: (917) 309-4415 Fax: (201) 487-7818 E-mail: **jfkentertainment@yahoo.com**

Major Money Entertainment Music/entertainment company founded by Terry McGill. Artist management; marketing and promotional strategies, including videos, radios, and street promotions, video and movie scripts. All artist and actor negotiations; negotiate distribution agreements. Marketing strategies, (Including local & national publicity, radio promotions, Street promotions, night club promotions, video and retail promotions). Smokey Robinson, The Boys, Today, Good Girls, Temptations, Johnny Gill, Boyz II Men, Stacy Lattisaw, Stevie Wonder, Gerald Alston, Spike Lee/Do The Right Thing Soundtrack, Diana Ross. Current projects include: Pimpsta, Tony Terry, Khia, Don Vito, Atlanta Based Producer/ Business Partner Production and remix credits include: Lil' Jon, Paster Troy, Lil' Scrappy, Blu Cantrell, Mya, Sole`, OutKast, and Ghetto Mafia. Joint venture with Dallas based entertainment company and recording studio, Koast to Koast. Contact Terry McGill, CEO, Major Money Entertainment, 908 Audelia Road, Suite 200, #229, Richardson, Texas 75081 Phone: (972) 675-5242 Fax: (516) 908-3743 E-mail: **majormoney@earthlink.net** Website: **www.majormoneyentertainment.com**

Marshalen Martin & Associates Booking firm. President Marshalen Martin is a professional Radio broadcaster since 1980, and one of the most recognized names in Bay Area gospel radio. Each week she plays the best of Bay Area and nationally known artists, features interviews with a veritable who's who of the gospel world and takes your requests. Contact Marshalen Martin, Marshalen Martin & Associates, 3260 Blume Drive, Suite 520, Richmond, California 94806 Phone: (510) 222-4242 Fax: (510) 262-9054 Website: **www.gospel1190.net**

SpokenVizions Entertainment Group, LLC Contact Quashana Foster, SpokenVizions Entertainment Group, LLC, Post Office Box 373, Florissant, Missouri 63032 Phone: (847) 414-1710 E-mail: **QuashanaFoster@spokenvizions.com**

Terrie Williams Agency Founded 1988, a management entertainment company and consultant: executive coaching, marketing and communications advice, public relations, individual and corporate counseling. Over the years founder and author, Terrie Williams has handled the biggest names in entertainment, sports, business and politics. Companies and organizations also have realized the need for new marketing strategies, and the likes of Revlon, The National Basketball Association, The National Hockey League and Nickelodeon have sought out Terrie to provide them with the proper tools to promote their programs. Terrie Williams, Terrie Williams Agency, 382 Central Park West, Suite 7R, New York, New York 10025 Phone: (212) 316-0305 Fax: (212) 749-8867 E-mail: **tmwms@terriewilliams.com** Website: **www.terriewilliams.com**

Tim Greene Films Film, song and music producer. Management and production company; entertainment acts and rappers, etc. As a record producer, Tim has written and produced over 17 national record releases with such acts as "Soft Touch." Producer, Tim Greene. Tim Greene Films, Post Office Box 20554, Philadelphia, Pennsylvania 19138 Phone: (213) 368-8100 E-mail: **Tim@TimGreeneFilms.com** Website: **www.timgreenefilms.com**

Untamed Entertainment The Untamed Tongues are always in search of poets and recording artists to feature on the Now World Famous Untamed Tongues Poetry Lounge Platform. Send 4 professional quality audio CD's, along with press kits to Untaimed Entertainment, c/o Warrick Roundtree, 7575 West Washington Avenue, Suite 127-171, Las Vegas, Nevada 89128 E-mail: **untamedtongues@yahoo.com** Website: **www.untamedtongues.com**

Museums

A. Phillip Randolph Pullman Porter Museum Information, African American, labor history museum. Gift shop. Randolph Pullman Porter Museum, Post Office Box 6276, Chicago, Illinois 60680 Phone: (773) 928-3935 Fax: (773) 928-8372 E-mail: **blhmuseum-website@yahoo.com** Website: **aphiliprandolphmuseum.com**

African American Museum Cleveland Ohio, preservation, information, of African descent. Contact AAM, 1765 Crawford Road, Cleveland, Ohio 44106 Phone: (216) 791-1700 Fax: (216) 791-1774 E-mail: **ourstory@aamcleveland.org** Website: **www.aamcleveland.org**

African American Museum Dallas. The only museum in the Southwestern United States devoted to the preservation and display of African American artistic, cultural and historical materials. It also has one of the largest African American folk art collections in the United States. The African American Museum incorporates a wide variety of visual art forms and historical documents that portray the African American experience in the United States, Southwest, and Dallas. Contact African American Museum Dallas, 3536 Grand Avenue, Dallas, Texas 75210 Phone: (214) 565-9026 Website: **www.aamdallas.org**

African American Museum and Library at Oakland Research library. Contains materials on the Northern California African American community, with an emphasis on the East Bay. AAMLO features exhibitions and programs. Goal is to reach out and educate the community. Rick Moss, Branch Manager, African American Museum and Library at Oakland, Oakland Public Library, 659 Fourteenth Street, Oakland, California 94612 Phone: (510) 637-0200 E-mail: **rmoss@oaklandlibrary.org** Website: **www.oaklandlibrary.org/AAMLO/index.html**

African American Museum in Phillidelphia Exhibits, events, educational programs, membership, general information. AAMP, 701 Arch Street, Philadelphia, Pennsylvania 19106 Phone: (215) 574-0380 Fax: (215) 574-3110 Website: **www.aampmuseum.org**

African American Research Library and Cultural Center The AARLCC has displayed over 38 major exhibits and offered 184 cultural programs to over 895,000 customer, celebrities, noted authors and international speakers who have made AARLCC a thriving center, a vital component of our community. The AARLCC also offers classes in computer technology and educational, recreational, and cultural programs on a regular basis. Contact AARLCC, Broward County Library, 2650 Sistrunk Boulevard, Fort Lauderdale, Florida 33311 Phone: (954) 625-2800 Website: **www.broward.org/library/aarlcc.htm**

Anacostia Museum The Smithsonian Institution's museum of African American history and culture Explores American history, society, and creative expression. Anacostia Museum, 1901 Fort Place South East, Washington, DC 20020 Phone: (202) 287-3306 E-mail: **AMinfo@si.edu** Website: **www.si.edu/anacostia**

Arna Bontemps African American Museum and Cultural Arts Center   The restored childhood home of Arna Bontemps - poet, author, anthologist, and librarian - who was considered the leading authority of the Harlem Renaissance. The period - sometimes referred to as the "New Negro" movement - is when young Black writers went to Harlem to share the Black experience through their writing. ABAAM, 1327 Third Street, Alexandria, Louisiana 71301 Phone: (318) 473-4692 Fax: (318) 473-4675 Website: **www.arnabontempsmuseum.com**

Birmingham Civil Rights Institute   Our mission is to encourage communication and reconciliation of human rights issues worldwide, and to serve as a depository for civil rights archives and documents. Annual Events, Exhibitions, Archives, Online Resource Gallery. BCRI, 520 Sixteenth Street North, Birmingham, Alabama 35203 Phone: (205) 328-9696 Fax: (205) 251-6104 E-mail: **bcri@bcri.org** Website: **bcri.bham.al.us**

Black American West Museum and Heritage Center   Tells the forgotten story of the African American pioneers who helped to shape the West. This small musuem is housed in the former home of Dr. Justina Ford, Colorado's first African American female doctor. BAWMHC, 3091 California Street, Denver Colorado 80205 Phone: (303) 292-2566 Fax: (303) 382-1981 E-mail: **director1@blackamericanwest.org** Website:**www.blackamericanwest.org**

Boston African American National Historic Site Includes 15 pre-Civil War structures relating to the history of Boston's 19th century African-American community, including the African Meeting House, the oldest standing African-American church in the United States. Boston African American National Historic Site, 14 Beacon Street, Suite 503, Boston, Massachusetts 02108 Phone: (617) 742-5415 Fax: (617) 720-0848 Website: **www.nps.gov/boaf**

California African American Museum The Museum contains African American art, history, and culture. The mission of the California African American Museum is to research, collect, preserve and interpret for public enrichment, the history, art and culture of African Americans with emphasis on California and the western United States. Ms. Charmaine Jefferson, Executive Director. Contact California African American Museum, 600 State Drive, Exposition Park, Los Angeles, California 90037 Phone: (213) 744-2060 E-mail: **info@caamuseum.org** Website: **www.caamuseum.org**

Central Pennsylvania African American Museum Artifacts, arts, papers, books, photographs, describe history, culture, African Americans. Old Bethel African Methodist Episcopal Church, 119 North Tenth Street, Reading, Pennsylvania 19601 Phone: (610) 371-8713 Fax: (610) 371-8739 Website: **www.homestead/cpaam/index**

Charles H. Wright Museum of African American History Founded, 1965 by Dr. Charles Wright. The museum exists to serve Metropolitan Detroit and national communities by providing exceptional exhibitions and programs. Three major exhibitions were added, A is for Africa, a hands-on exhibit for children; Without Sanctuary: Lynching Photography in America; and the new blockbuster core exhibition, And Still We Rise: Our Journey Through African American History and Culture.Charles H. Wright Museum of African American History, 315 East Warren Avenue, Detroit, Michigan 48201 Phone: (313) 494-5800 Fax: (313) 494-5855 E-mail: **wphillip@maah-detroit.org** Website: **www.maah-detroit.org**

Chattanooga African American Museum Collection, multi-media presentations, rare artifacts, African Art, original sculptures, paintings, musical recordings, Black newspapers. Chattanooga African American Museum, 200 East Martin Luther King Boulevard, Chattanooga, Tennessee 37403 Phone: (423) 266-8658 Fax: (423) 267-1076 Website: **www.caamhistory.com**

Dunbar House State Historic Site Permanent exhibit, writer's life, young poet, national spokesman. Dunbar House, Post Office Box 1872, Dayton, Ohio 45401 Phone: (937) 224-7061 E-mail: **lwf@coax.net** Website: **www.coax.net/people/lwf/dunbar.htm**

DuSable Museum of African American History Founded in 1957, Dr. Margaret T. and Charles G. Burroughs, Chicago. DuSable Museum of African American History, 740 East 56th Place, Chicago, Illinois 60637 Phone: (773) 947-0600 Website: **www.dusablemuseum.org**

Museum For African Art We present major exhibitions in our Main Gallery, and smaller changing exhibitions in our Focus Gallery. In addition, we maintain a lively calendar of events for visitors of all ages and a Museum Store. Contact Museum For African Art, 36-01 43rd Avenue at 36th Street, Long Island City, New York 11101 Phone: (718) 784-7700 Fax: (718) 784-7718 E-mail: **museum@africanart.org** Website: **www.africanart.org**

Museum of Afro American History Boston. Dedicated to preserving the contributions of African-Americans. Museum of Afro American History, Administrative Office, 14 Beacon Street, Suite 719, Boston, Massachusetts 02108 Phone: (617) 725-0022 Fax: (617) 720-5225 E-mail: **history@afroammuseum.org** Website: **www.afroammuseum.org**

Museum of the African Diaspora MoAD's goal is to foster a greater understanding of human history and promote cross-cultural communication. As a first voice museum, MoAD will capture the essence of the African Diaspora experiences. V. Denise Bradley, Executive Director. Museum of the African Diaspora, 685 Mission Street, San Francisco, California 94105 Phone: (415) 358-7200 Fax: (415) 358-7252 E-mail: **vdb@moadsf.org** Website: **www.moadsf.org**

National Afro-American Museum and Cultural Center Dayton Ohio, national 1950's exhibition From Victory To Freedom. Michael L. Sampson, Afro-American Museum, 1350 Brush Row Road, Post Office Box 578, Wilberforce, Ohio 45384 Phone: (937) 376-4944 E-mail: **naamcc@erinet.com** Website: **http://ohsweb.ohiohistory.org/places/sw13/index.shtml**

National Civil Rights Museum Located at the Lorraine Motel, the site of Dr. Martin Luther King's assassination, chronicles key episodes of the American civil rights movement and the legacy of this movement to inspire participation in civil and human rights efforts globally, through our collections, exhibitions, and educational programs. Contact National Civil Rights Museum, 450 Mulberry Street, Memphis, Tennessee 38103 Phone: (901) 521-9699 Fax: (901) 521-9740 E-mail: **contact@civilrightsmuseum.org** Website: **www.civilrightsmuseum.org**

National Museum Of African Art Center for the visual arts of Africa, exhibitions, collections, research, and public programs. NMAfASI, MRC 708, Post Office Box 37012, Washington, DC.20013 Phone: (202) 633-1000 Fax: (202) 357-4879 E-mail: **nmafaweb@nmafa.si.edu** Website: **www.nmafa.si.edu/geninfo/geninfo.htm**

October Gallery Founded July 1985, October Gallery has sponsored hundreds of traveling art shows. Produced and sponsored by October Gallery these shows were "Black Art Shows" held in Atlanta, Chicago, New York, Los Angeles, Oakland, Jacksonville, Sarasota, Washington DC, Baltimore, Montreal, Detroit, and a host of other cities. Contact October Gallery, 68 North 2nd Street, Philadelphia, Pennsylvania 19106 Phone: (215) 629-3939 Fax: (215) 923-4737 E-mail: **customerservice@octobergallery.com** Website: **www.octobergallery.com**

San Francisco African American Museum Presents select exhibits on African and/or African American artists. SFAAHCS, Fort Mason Center, Building C, San Francisco, California 94123 Phone: (415) 441-0640

Tubman African American Museum Art, history, and culture. Contact Tubman African American Museum, 340 Walnut Street, Macon, Georgia 31201 Phone: (478) 743-8544 Fax: (478) 743-9063 E-mail: **adra@tubmanmuseum.com** Website: **www.tubmanmuseum.com**

Newsletters

Black Alumni Network Newsletter Published monthly by Columbia University Journalism Alumni. Editor Wayne Dawkins. Black Alumni Network Newsletter, 108 Terrell Road, Box 6693, Newport News, Virginia 23606 Phone: (757) 591-2371 E-mail: **wdawk69643@aol.com**

BCALA Newsletter The BCALA Newsletter goes to all of the approximately 1,000 members of the Black Caucus of the American Library Association 6 times a year. BCALA, Post Office Box 1738, Hampton, Virginia 23669 Phone: (804) 786-2332 Fax: (804) 786-5855 E-mail: **newsletter@bcala.org** Website: **www.bcala.org**

Black Congressional Monitor Published twice-monthly newsletter covering the US Federal Government. Reports on available grant awards, contract and subcontract opportunities, small business set-asides, scholarships, fellowships, internships, Government publications, reports to and by Congress, public notices and meetings. Founding editor and publisher, Lenora Moragne. Len Mor Publications, Post Office Box 75035, Washington, DC 20013 Phone: (202) 488-8879 Fax: (202) 554-3116 Website: **www.bcmonitor.com**

Black Excel Quarterly Newsletter. Since its founding in 1988, Black Excel has helped young people and their parents all across the country to navigate the difficult college admission process. Black Excel services have expanded over the years to include an updated 350+ Scholarship List; a personalized College Help Package; a reference guide to 143 Historically Black Colleges, detailed profiles of individual schools; and a Medical School Help Package. Founder Isaac J. Black. Contact Black Excel, 244 Fifth Avenue, Post Office Box H281, New York, New York 10001 Phone: (212) 591-1936 E-mail: **ijblack@blackexcel.org** Website: **www.blackexcel.org**

Black, Indian, Hispanic, and Asian Women In Action Newsletter (BIHA)   Established in 1983, BIHA serves as a forum for translating current concerns (family violence, racism, ageism, AIDS, chemical abuse) within communities of color. Published Quarterly. Circulation of 1,000. Provides education, information and advocacy for and by Communities of Color. Alice O. Lynch, Executive Director. BIHA, 1830 James Avenue North, Minneapolis, Minnesota 55417 Phone: (612) 521-2986 Fax: (612) 529-6745 E-mail: **info@biha.org** Website: **www.biha.org**

Black Students Quarterly print newsletter featuring the latest news, tips, and opportunities for African-American students. Contact Diversity City Media, 225 West. 3rd Street, Suite #203, Long Beach, California 90802 Phone: (562) 209-0616 E-mail: **support@blackstudents.com** Website: **blackstudents.com**

National Black MBA Association Newsletter Circulation 3,500. Quarterly and one special edition. National Black MBA Association, 180 North Michigan Avenue, Suite 1820, Chicago, Illinois 60601 Phone: (312) 236-2622 Fax: (312) 236-4131 E-mail: **mail@nbmbaa.org** Website: **www.nbmbaa.org**

News Plus National Association of Black Accountants publication. Contact NABA, 7249-A Hanover Parkway, Greenbelt, Maryland 20770   Phone: (301) 474-6222 Fax: (301) 474-3114 Website: **www.nabainc.org**

Statement Newsletter focuses on current National Coalition of One Hundred Black Women (NCBW), issues and devotes attention to (NCBW) programs. Published twice a year. Contact NCBW, 38 West 32nd Street, Suite 1610, New York, New York 10001 Phone: (212) 947-2196 Fax: (212) 947-2477 E-mail: **NC100BW@aol.com** Website: **www.ncbw.org**

Voices in Black Studies Ohio State University National Council for Black Studies. Circulation 1,500. Advertising accepted. Contact Mr. James Devers, Voices in Black Studies, Ohio State University, 1030 Lincoln Tower, Columbus, Ohio 48210 Phone: (614) 292-3922

Newspapers

African-American News & Issues Since 1996. Targeting African-American, readers weekly delivered to more than 100,000 homes and available at more than 5,000 locations. AANI, 6130 Wheatley Street, Houston, Texas, 77091 Phone: (713) 692-1288 Fax: (713) 692-1183 E-mail: **news@aframnews.com** Website: **www.aframnews.com**

Afro-American Newspapers Leading news provider for African-Americans in the Baltimore/Washington, DC metropolitan area and longest running African-American, family-owned newspaper in the nation. Chairman of the Board/Publisher, John J. Oliver Jr. Contact AAN, 2519 North Charles Street, Baltimore Maryland 21218 Phone: (410) 554-8200 Fax: (877) 570-9297 Website: **www.afro.com**

Amsterdam News Unwavering voice of the Black constituency. National, international and New York news, politics and business information. Contact Editor, Amsterdam News, 3200 13th Street, North West, Washington, DC 20010 E-mail: **info@amsterdamnews.com** Website: **www.amsterdamnews.org**

Arizona Informant Local newspaper published weekly covering news worthy events affecting the Arizona African American Community. Arizona Informant, 1746 East Madison, Suite 2, Phoenix, Arizona 85034 Phone: (602) 257-9300 E-mail: **azinformantnews@earthlink.net** Website: **www.arizonainformantnewspaper.com**

Atlanta Tribune The Magazine Black Atlanta's leading source for relevant, thought-provoking news and information on business, careers, technology, wealth-building, politics and education. Pat Lottier, Publisher. Contact Atlanta Tribune, 875 Old Roswell Road, Suite C-100, Roswell, Georgia 30076 Phone: (770) 587-0501 Fax: (770) 642-6501 E-mail: **info@atlantatribune.com** Website: **www.atlantatribune.com**

Baltimore Times Fridays. Circulation 32,000. 10,000 in the Baltimore County, 5,000 in the Prince George County Times, and 5,000 in The Annapolis Times. Publisher, Joye Bramble, Editor, Dena Wane. Baltimore Times, 2513 North Charles, Baltimore, Maryland 21218 Phone: (410) 366-3900 Fax: (410) 243-1627 E-mail: **dwane@btimes.com** Website: **www.btimes.com**

Birmingham Times Circulation 16,500. Weekly publication. Thursday. Contact Mr. James E. Lewis, Publisher, Birmingham Times, 115 Third Avenue West, Birmingham, Alabama 35204 Phone: (205) 251-5158 Fax: (205) 323-2294 E-mail: **jlewis@birminghamtimes.com** Website: **www.thebirminghamtimes.com**

BlackPressUSA National website features news exclusively from African-American journalists and Black community publications. BlackPressUSA, 3200 13th Street North West, Washington, DC 20010 E-mail: **info@blackpressusa.com** Website: **www.BlackPressUSA.com**

Black Reign News Weekly New York City-based award-winning African American newspaper. Reviews books. Contact Tonisha Johnson, Blackreign News, Post Office Box 30231, Staten Island, New York 10303 Phone: (718) 216-3530 E-mail: **tonishajohnson@hotmail.com**

The Black Voice News Established 1972. Weekly newspaper published on Thursdays. Reviews books, films, plays, concerts. Cheryl and Hardy L. Brown, Publishers. Contact Brown Publishing Company, Post Office Box 1581, Riverside, California 92502 Phone: (909) 682-6070 E-mail: **hardybrown@blackvoicenews.com** Website: **www.blackvoicenews.com**

Capitol Outlook Weekly, Thursdays. Circulation 12,500. Reviews books, movies, plays, and songs, advertising. Publisher, Roosevelt Wilson. Capital Outlook, 602 North Adams Street, Tallahassee Florida 32301 E-mail: **coutlook@aol.com** Website: **www.capitaloutlook.com**

Carson/South Bay Community News Ms. Gina Johnson Smith, Publisher. Contact Smith Publishing & Media Group, #385 South Lemon Avenue, #E236, Walnut, California 91789 Phone: (909) 987-0433 E-mail: **ginajohnsonsmith@sbcglobal.net**

Dallas Examiner Published Thursdays; total readership of 100,000. Sample distribution/drop-off points: Churches, high schools and colleges, banks, etc. Mollie Finch Belt, Publisher. Dallas Examiner, 1516 Corinth Street, Dallas, Texas 75215 Phone: (214) 428-3446 Fax: (214) 428-3451 E-mail: **mbelt@dallasexaminer.com** Website: **www.dallasexaminer.com**

Dallas Post Tribune Published Thursdays. Circulation 18,100. T.R. Lee Jr., Publisher/Owner. Dallas Post Tribune, Post Office Box 763939, Dallas, Texas 75376 Phone: (214) 946-7678 Fax: (214) 946-6823 E-mail: **posttrib@airmail.net** Website: **www.dallaspost.com**

Final Call Founded in the 1930s as the Final Call to Islam, the newspaper evolved into Muhammad Speaks in the 1960s and boasted a circulation of 900,000 a week, with monthly circulation of 2.5 million. Today, the weekly Final Call Newspaper serves a readership of diverse economic and educational backgrounds, including circulation in North America, Europe, Africa and the Caribbean. Final Call Publishing, 236 Massachusetts Avenue North East, Suite 610, Washington, DC 20002 Phone: (202) 543-7796 Website: **www.finalcall.com**

Florida Dollar Stretcher Newspaper Serving the African-American communities of Tampa and Plant City, Florida since October 1971. Free. Circulation, 125,000 weekly readers. Sabrina Anette Barnes, Florida Dollar Stretcher, 2002 West Busch Boulevard, Suite C, Tampa, Florida 33612 Phone: (813) 930-9599 Fax: (813) 930-9698 E-mail: **dollarstretcher1@aol.com**

Freedom Socialist Newspaper Quarterly. Luma Nichol, Organizer. Socialist Feminist political party dedicated to eradicating injustice and inequality. Freedom Socialist Newspaper, 5018 Rainier Avenue South, Seattle, Washington 98118 Phone: (206) 722-2453 Fax: (206) 722-2453 E-mail: **fspseattle@mindspring.com** Website: **www.socialism.com**

Frost Illustrated Weekly African American newspaper established in 1968. Editor, Fort Wayne. Contact Frost Illustrated, 3121 South Calhoun Street, Fort Wayne Indiana 46806 Phone: (260) 745-0552 E-mail: **frostnews@aol.com** Website: **www.frostillustrated.com**

Grand Rapids Times Published weekly. Circulation 6,000. Issues that pertain to the African American community. Dr. Patricia Pulliam, Owner/Editor. Contact Grand Rapids Times, 2016 Eastern, Grand Rapids, Michigan 49510 Phone: (616) 245-8737 E-mail: **staff@grtimes.com**

Green County Democrat An African-American oriented newspaper. Published weekly on Wednesdays. Circulation 3,500. We also review books, plays, movies. Contact John Zippert, Publisher, Green County Democrat, Post Office Box 598, Eutaw, Alabama 35462 Phone: (205) 372-3373 Fax: (205) 372-2243 E-mail: **jzippert@aol.com**

Haitian Times Covers Haitian and Haitian-American news: Arts & leisure: entertainment, reviews, profiles, social events, business. Sports: Haitian and American soccer, basketball, tennis. Columns: news from Boston, New York, Miami, and Haiti. The Haitian Times, Inc., 610 Vanderbilt Avenue, Brooklyn, New York, 11238 Phone: (718) 230-8700 Fax: (718) 230-7172 E-mail: **info-ht@haitiantimes.com** Website: **www.haitiantimes.com**

Ink Northeast Indiana's premier Newspaper delivering information, news and knowledge for and about local African Americans. Since, October 2001. Vince Robinson, Publisher. Contact Ink, 1301 Lafayette Street, Suite 202, Fort Wayne, Indiana 46802 Phone: (260) 420-3200 Fax: (260) 420-3210 E-mail: **editor@inknewsonline.com** Website: **www.inknewsonline.com**

The Inland Valley News Since 1992. We service portions of over thirteen cities in the heart of the Inland Valley. Readership in excess of 45,000. Co-Publishers, Gloria Morrow and Tommy Morrow. Shining Glory Publications, Inc., 2249 North Garey Avenue, Pomona, California 91767 Fax: (909) 392-6917 E-mail: **IVNews@aol.com** Website: **www.inlandvalleynews.com**

Insider News Bi-weekly. Circulation 10,000. Contact Ken Lumpkin, Publisher. Insider News, 1661 Douglas Avenue, Racine, Wisconsin 53404 Phone: (262) 632-9370 Fax: (262) 619-3135 E-mail: **insider@wi.net**

Las Vegas Community News Gina Johnson Smith Publisher. Contact Smith Publishing & Media Group, #385 South Lemon Avenue, #E236, Walnut, California 91789 Phone: (909) 987-0433 E-mail: **ginajohnsonsmith@sbcglobal.net**

Long Beach Times Newspaper serving Long Beach, Carson, Compton and surrounding communities; estimated weekly readership 33,000. Richard A. Love, Publisher/Editor. Long Beach Times, 121 Linden Avenue #105, Long Beach, California 90802 Phone: (562) 436-9221 E-mail: **lbtimes@aol.com** Website: **www.lbtimes.net**

Los Angeles Sentinel Largest Black-owned newspaper in the West. Thursdays. Circulation, 125,000. Danny Bakewell, Executive Publisher. Los Angeles Sentinel, 38 Crenshaw Boulevard, Los Angeles, California 90008 Phone: (323) 299-3800 Fax: (323) 299-3896 Website: **www.losangelessentinel.com**

Los Angeles Wave African American newspaper. Contact Editor, The Los Angeles Wave, 4201 Wilshire Boulevard, Suite 600, Los Angeles, California 90010 Phone: (323) 556-5720 Fax: (323) 556-5704 Website: **www.wavenewspapers.com**

Milwaukee Community Journal Weekender   Published weekly. Patricia O'Flynn Pattillo, Publisher/CEO. Milwaukee Community Journal Weekender, 3612 North Martin Luther King Drive, Milwaukee, Wisconsin 53212 Phone: (414) 265-5300 Fax: (414) 265-1536 E-mail: **editorial@communityjournal.net** Website: **www.communityjournal.net**

Milwaukee Times Weekly Circulation 15,000. Contact The Milwaukee Times Weekly, 1938 Martin Luther King Drive, Milwaukee, Wisconsin 53212 Phone: (414) 263-5088 E-mail: **miltimes@execpc.com** Website: **www.themilwaukeetimesweekly.com**

The Mississippi Link Weekly publication. L. Socrates Garrett, Publisher. Nikki Burns, Editor. The Mississippi Link, 2659 Livingston Road, Jackson, Mississippi 39213 Phone: (601) 355-9103 Fax: (601) 355-9105 E-mail: **mslink@misnet.com** Website: **www.mississippilink.com**

The New York Beacon Walter Smith Jr., Publisher. The New York Beacon, Smith Haj Group Inc., 341 West 38th Street, Suite 8R, New York, New York 10018 Phone: (212) 213-8585 Fax: (212) 213-6291 E-mail: **newyorkbeacon@yahoo.com** Website: **www.newyorkbeacon.com**

The Old Gold & Black The student newspaper of Wake Forest University. Published Thursdays during the school year. Old Gold & Black, Post Office Box 7569, Winston-Salem, North Carolina 27109 Phone: (336) 758-5279 Fax: (336) 758-4561 Send guest editorials to: E-mail: **business@ofh.wfu.edu** Website: **www.ogb.wfu.edu**

The Pasadena/San Gabriel Valley Journal News Since 1989, serving Altadena, Pasadena, Monrovia and Duarte and surrounding cities in the west San Gabriel Valley area. Joe C. Hopkins, publisher. The Pasadena/San Gabriel Valley Journal News, 1541 North Lake Avenue, Suite A, Pasadena, California 91104 Phone: (626) 798-3972 Fax: (626) 798-3282 E-mail: **pasjour@pacbell.net** Website: **www.pasadenajournal.com**

Rancho Cucamonga/Ontario Community News Gina Johnson Smith, Publisher. Contact Smith Publishing & Media Group, #385 South Lemon Avenue, #E236, Walnut, California 91789 Phone: (909) 987-0433 E-mail: **ginajohnsonsmith@sbcglobal.net**

The Sacramento Observer Founded, 1962. Dr. William H. Lee, founder and publisher. Contact Publisher, Observer Newspapers, 2330 Alhambra Boulevard, Sacramento, California 95817 Phone: (916) 452-4781 Fax: (916) 452-7744 E-mail: **whlee@sacobserver.com** Website: **www.SacObserver.com**

San Francisco Bay View National Black newspaper. San Francisco Bay View, 4917 Third Street, San Francisco, California 94124 Phone: (415) 671-0789 Fax: (415) 671-0316 E-mail: **editor@sfbayview.com** Website: **www.sfbayview.com**

The Seattle Medium Circulation exceeds 91,000 with a combined readership of more than 321,000 weekly. Radio stations include KRIZ 1420, KZIZ 1560, KYIZ 1620, Seattle/Tacoma and KBMS 1480 - Portland, Oregon. Publisher, Chris B. Bennett. Contact The Seattle Medium Newspaper Group, 2600 South Jackson Street, Seattle, Washington 98144 Phone: (206) 323-3070 E-mail: **mediumnews@aol.com** Website: **www.seattlemedium.com**

Organizations

African American Atelier, Inc. A non-profit, fine arts gallery organization whose mission is promoting an awareness, appreciation and sensitivity to the visual arts and culture of African Americans and working in harmony with other ethnic groups. Celebrating the contributions of past, present and emerging African American and ethnic artists, Atelier was conceived by Alma Adams and the late Eva Hamlin Miller, who were joined by six local artists and community patrons and chartered in 1990. The gallery opened to the public on January 13, 1991 in the Greensboro Cultural. Alma Adams, The African American Atelier, 200 North Davie Street, Box 14, Greensboro, North Carolina 27401 Phone: (336) 333-6885 Fax: (336) 373-4826 E-mail: **info@africanamericanatelier.org** Website: **www.africanamericanatelier.org**

African American Research Library and Cultural Center (AARLCC) Von D. Mizell Branch Library is a research library and cultural center for scholars, students and the general public. The library contains more than 75,000 books, documents, artifacts and related materials that focus on the experiences of people of African descent. AARLCC, 2650 Sistrunk Boulevard, Fort Lauderdale, Florida 33311 Phone: (954) 625-2800 E-mail: **aarlcc@browardlibrary.org** Website: **www.broward.org/aarlcc**

African American Women in Cinema (AAWC) A non profit organization whose mission is to support minority women filmmakers by providing resources in the film industry. Incorporated by the organization's president, Terra Renee in 2000. Contact AAWC, 545 Eighth Avenue, Suite 401, New York, New York 10018 Phone: (212) 769-7949 Fax: (212) 871-2074 E-mail: **info@aawic.org** Website: **www.aawic.org**

African Voices Communications, Inc. Founded 1992. Non profit cultural arts organization. Sponsors literary readings, art exhibitions, writing workshops and other programs. Publishes literary magazine African Voices. Layding Kaliba, Managing Director. Contact Layding Kaliba, African Voices, 270 West 96th Street, New York, New York 10025 Phone: (212) 865-2982 E-mail: **africanvoices@aol.com** Website: **www.africanvoices.com**

Afro-American Cultural Center Organization purpose is to develops processes, functions and attributes throughout Yale and the city of New Haven that are reciprocal and interactive, resulting in a sense of community, cultural vision, competence, efficacy permanence, spiritual well-being, and integrity. Contact Pamela George, Director. Afro-American Cultural Center, 211 Park Steet, New Haven, Connecticut 06520 Phone: (203) 432-4132

Afro-American Historical and Genealogical Society, Inc. AAHGS is non-profit, membership organization committed to the preservation of the history, genealogy, and culture of the African-Ancestored populations of the local, national, and international community. Contact Afro-American Historical and Genealogical Society, Inc., Post Office Box 73067, Washington, DC 20056 Phone: (202) 234-5350 E-mail: **info@aahgs.org** Website: **www.aahgs.org**

Afro-Lousiana Historical & Genealogical Society An organization dedicated to expanding the knowledge base, sources, community consciousness, and education regarding the historical, cultural, and genealogical heritage of African-Americans in general and Louisianans in particular. Mrs. Edna Jordan Smith, founder. African American Historical & Genealogical Society, Post Office Box 2123, Baton Rouge, Louisiana 70821 Phone: (225) 387-1370 E-mail: **info@alhgs.com** Website: **www.alhgs.com**

Birmingham Civil Rights Institute The Birmingham Civil Rights Institute is a multi-media facility that houses exhibitions devoted to highlighting the American Civil Rights Movement (particularly in Birmingham, Alabama) and the Human Rights Movement worldwide. BCRI provides the community with scores of educational programs and special events and houses an archival department that has been used by researchers across the world. Birmingham Civil Rights Institute, 520 16th Street North, Birmingham, Alabama 35203 Phone: (866) 328-9696 Fax: (205) 251-6104 E-mail: **Lpijeaux@bcri.org** Website: **www.bcri.org**

100 Black Men of Greater Cleveland, Inc. Mentoring, education, health and wellness, economic development. Contact 100 Black Men of Greater Cleveland, Inc., 4415 Euclid Avenue, Suite 331, Cleveland, Ohio 44103 Phone: (216) 361-9146 Fax: (216) 361-9148 E-mail: **info@100blackmencleveland.org** Website: **www.100blackmencleveland.org**

Black Broadcasters Alliance National organization of Black broadcasters. The BBC is comprised of owners and professionals who want to see equality and real opportunity for African Americans employed in the broadcasting industry and or who are in pursuit of ownership. The BBC is comprised of broadcasters representing television, radio and cable who are employed or operating in major markets across the United States. Mr. Eddie Edwards, Sr., Chairman. Black Broadcasters Alliance, 711 West 40th Street, Suite 330, Baltimore, Maryland 21211 Fax: (410) 662-0816 E-mail: **e-mail@thebba.org** Website: **www.thebba.org**

Black College Radio and Television Organization Provides an annual forum for black college broadcasters, professional broadcasters and members of the music industry to meet and discuss ways and means to increase minority participation in the broadcasting industry. Lo Jelks, Chairman. Contact BCR, Post Office Box 3191, Atlanta, Georgia 30302 Phone: (404) 523-6136 Fax: (404) 523-5467 E-mail: **bcrmail@aol.com** Website: **www.blackcollegeradio.com**

Black Filmmakers Hall Of Fame Inc. Founded in 1973. Features film presentations and festivals of works by independent black filmmakers. Annual film, video and screenplay competition for independent, Black filmmakers. Also, publishes an annual catalogue featuring biographical material about filmmakers being inducted into the Black filmmakers Hall Of Fame. Felix Curtis, Executive Director, BFHFI, 410 14th Street, Oakland, California 94612 Fax: (510) 839-9858 E-mail: **bfhfinc@aol.com**

Black Press International Non-profit communications and research think tank organization incorporated to mobilize and motivate interest in government and public policies that have direct impact on African-American society. William Reed, President, Black Press International, 405 16th Street, Southeast, Washington, DC 20003 Phone: (202) 547-4125 Fax: (202) 592-1997 E-mail: **wreed@blackpressinternational.com** Website: **www.blackpressinternational.com**

Black Speakers Online A division of Speakers Etc., a Black woman owned speakers bureau initiated in 1996, is the brainchild of Norma Thompson Hollis. BSO offers a directory of Black speakers from a wide range of budgets, geographical areas, topics, talents and entertainments. We provide meeting planners the opportunity to connect with Black speakers and talent while providing Black speakers the opportunity to increase their exposure. Norma Thompson, Black Speakers Online, 11965 Venice Boulevard, Suite 202, Los Angeles, California 90066 Fax: (310) 279-4179 E-mail: **denise@blackspeakers.net** Website: **www.blackspeakersonline.com**

The Black World Today We are a collective of journalists, writers, artists, communicators and entrepreneurs who have banded together to use the information revolution as one means towards the overall empowerment of Black people in the United States and around the world. Our main purpose is to chronicle the daily social, political, cultural and economic realities of Black communities and countries. Our correspondents and columnists will both report and interpret the news that these realities generate. We will focus both on news and features about blacks and general news of value and interest to blacks. Contact Herb Boyd, Managing Editor, The Black World Today, Post Office Box 328, Randallstown, Maryland 21133 Phone: (410) 659-8298 Fax: (410) 521-9993 Website: **www.tbwt.org**

Center for Black Music Research (CBMR) A research unit of Columbia College Chicago devoted to research, preservation, and dissemination of information about the history of black music on a global scale. Contact CBMR, Columbia College Chicago, 600 South Michigan Avenue, Chicago, Illinois, 60605 Phone: (312) 344-7559 Fax: (312) 344-8029 E-mail: **contact@cbmr.colum.edu** Website: **www.cbmr.colum.edu**

The Centre for the Study of Black Cultures in Canada Endeavours to serve as a stimulus to and focal point for faculty, graduate and undergraduate students, as well as independent scholars who are pursuing research in African Canadian Studies, at York University, and elsewhere. The Centre sponsors conferences and other events, and on-going research projects. The website which began in 1998 provides information on African Canadian artists and their work Contact Professor Leslie Sanders, The Centre for the Study of Black Cultures in Canada, York University, 4700 Keele Street, Toronto, ON M3J 1P3 Phone: (416) 736-2100 E-mail: **leslie@yorku.ca** Website: **www.yorku.ca/aconline/index.html**

Charlotte African-American Writers Group The group is comprised of male and female writers who possess volumes of writing experience that we are willing to share with other writers. We represent a diverse and talented group of individuals that express a keen interest in the development of our writing skills. Clayton F. Brown, Founder/President. Contact Charlotte African-American Writers Group, Post Office Box 29155, Charlotte, North Carolina 28229 E-mail: **claytonfbrown@msn.com** Website: **www.caawnc.net**

Coffee Chatter, Inc. Motto: "Chatting With Showbiz Pros." Coffee Chatter provides professionals from the entertainment industry to come and speak for informative purposes only to aspiring actors. Past Guest have included; Actress Anne Marie Johnson, Actress Nicey Nash (From Reno 911), Actor Joseph Marcell, (From TV series Fresh Prince Of Bel Air), and many others. Founder: Actress Lynne Burnett. Coffee Chatter, Inc., 16420 Stagecoach Avenue, Palmdale, California 93591 Phone: (661) 264-4696 E-mail: **coffeechatter1@cs.com**

The Color Of Film Collaborative Non-profit organization that works to support media makers of color and others who have an interest in creating and developing new and diverse images of people of color in film, video and performing arts. TCOF sponsors film screenings and work-in-progress previews annually and throughout the year. Ms. Lisa Simmons, Executive Director. Contact The Color of Film Collaborative, Post Office Box 191901, Roxbury, Massachusetts 02119 Phone: (617) 445-6051 E-mail: **info@coloroffilm.com** Website: **www.coloroffilm.com**

The Dayton Christian Writer's Guild Inc. Organized in September 1993, under the leadership of Ms. Tina Toles. Contact Ms. Tina Toles, Post Office Box 251, Englewood, Ohio 45322 Phone: (937) 836-6600 E-mail: **daytonwriters@ureach.com**

Focus: Joint Center For Political and Economic Studies National nonprofit research and public policy institution founded in 1970 by black intellectuals professionals to provide training and technical assistance to newly elected black officials. Vice President for Communications and Policy and Chief of Staff, Janice F. Joyner. Contact Focus, 1090 Vermont Avenue, North West, Suite 1100, Washington, DC 20005 Phone: (202) 789-3500 Fax: (202) 789-6390 E-mail: **jjoyner@jointcenter.org** Website: **www.jointcenter.org**

International Black Writers & Artists Los Angeles (IBWALA) A 501 (c) 3 grassroots, nonprofit organization dedicated to supporting, motivating, educating and inspiring artists, writers and performers. Founded in Los Angeles in 1974 by Mrs. Edna Crutchfield and other black writers, IBWALA is a network of authors, publishers, visual artists, educators and community members dedicated to making sure our writers and artists are published, read, seen, and heard. IBWALA provides workshops and conferences, information and resources as well as cultural outlets, scholarships, publishing opportunities and more. Ms. Linda A. Hughes, Board Member and Co-conference Planner. Zerline Jennings, publicist and web master. IBWALA, Post Office Box 43576, Los Angeles, California 90043 Phone: (323) 964-3721 E-mail: **info@ibwala.org** Website: **www.ibwala.org**

KHAFRE Writer's colony, now known as: The Harriet Tubman Village, for Writers and Artist is a bed and breakfast facility located in the "Historic South" that provides all the conveniences a writer needs to hone their skills, as an aspiring author. The writers workshops, provided weekly allows each writer to identify and focus on areas of need; and challenges the more established writers to edit their near completed works and submit for publishing consideration, directly to the KHAFRE Publishing. The Harriet Tubman Village for Writers and Artists is "a peaceful place to create a dream." Contact: Sade, KHAFRE, Post Office Box 1134, Ackerman, Mississippi 39735 Phone: (662) 285-9798 E-mail: **khafre@peoplepc.com** Website: **www.khafre.us**

Langston Hughes Community Library and Cultural Center Public Library and Cultural Center. Home of the Black Heritage Reference Center of Queens County, housing over 45,000 volumes of print and non-print circulating items, books and audio-visual materials, on the Black Experience. Special collections: Over 1,000 circulating theses and dissertations on Black Literature. Over 1,000 circulating VHS and DVDs on the Black Experience. Andrew P. Jackson, (Sekou Molefi Baako), Langston Hughes Community Library and Cultural Center, Queens Library, 100-01 Northern Boulevard, Corona, New York 11368 Phone: (718) 651-1100 E-mail: **andrew.p.jackson@queenslibrary.org** Website: **www.queenslibrary.org**

Moorland-Spingarn Research Center One of the world's largest and most comprehensive repositories for the documentation of the history and culture of people of African descent in Africa, the Americas, and other parts of the world. As one of Howard University's major research facilities, the MSRC collects, preserves, and makes available for research a wide range of resources chronicling the Black experience. Dr. Thomas C. Battle, Director. Jean Currie Church, Chief Librarian. Howard University, 500 Howard Place, North West, Washington, DC 20059 Phone: (202) 806-7240 Fax: (202) 806-6405 E-mail: **Jchurch@howard.edu** Website: **www.founders.howard.edu/moorland-spingarn/default.htm**

Motown Writers Network A 4 year old literary organization for Michigan writers founded by Sylvia Hubbard. Mission: Impact the literary community by bringing readers in touch with local writers. With 300 members strong, offers a monthly newsletter, website promotion. Motown Writers Network, Post Office Box 27310, Detroit, Michigan 48227 Phone: (313) 289-8614 E-mail: **motownwriters@yahoo.com** Website: **www.MotownWriters.homestead.com**

Multicultural Marketing Resources President, Editor and Publisher, Ms. Lisa Skriloff. Multicultural Marketing Resources, 101 5th Avenue Suite 10B, New York, New York 10003 Phone: (212) 242-3351 Fax: (212) 691-5969 E-mail: **lisa@multicultural.com** Website: **www.multicultural.com**

MVP Speakers US Sports, the parent company of MVPspeakers.com, was founded in November 1988. US Sports branched out to create MVPspeakers.com, providing more exposure for our renowned speakers and celebrities via the internet. Contact MVP Speakers, Post Office Box 2037, Indian Trail, North Carolina 28079 Phone: (704) 821-2940 Fax: (704) 821-2669 E-mail: **rwussports@aol.com** Website: **www.mvpspeakers.com**

The National Black Programming Consortium (NBPC) Non-profit national media arts organization committed to the presentation, funding, promotion, distribution and preservation of positive images of African Americans and the African Diaspora. Sets the standard and one of the leading providers of historically accurate programming about the African American experience on public television. Jacquie Jones, Executive Director. Mable Haddock, Member and Founding Director. NBPC, 68 East 131st Street, 7th Floor, Harlem, New York 10037 Phone: (212) 234-8200 Fax: (212) 234-7032 E-mail: **info@nbpc.tv** Website: **www.nbpc.tv**

National Coalition Of One Hundred Black Women (NCBW) Founded 1981, NCBW is a nonprofit organization with approximately 7,500 members in 62 chapters in 25 states and the District of Columbia. Annual Candace Award ceremony. Jewell Jackson McCabe, Founder and Chair. Leslie A. Mays, President. National Coalition of One Hundred Black Women, 38 West 32nd Street, Suite 1610, New York, New York 10001 Phone: (212) 947-2196 Fax: (212) 947-2477 E-mail: **NC100BW@aol.com** Website: **www.ncbw.org**

National Council Of Negro Women (NCNW) Founded in 1935 by Dr. Mary Mcleod Bethune with the goal of improving the lives of black women and their families NCNW acts as central source for planning and seeks to fill the gaps that exist in our communities. Dr. Dorothy I. Height, Chair. Contact NCNW, 633 Pennsylvania Avenue, North West, Washington, DC 20004 Phone: (202) 737-0120 Fax: (202) 737-0476 Website: **www.ncnw.org**

National Society Of Black Engineers (NSBE)   Offers academic excellence programs, scholarships, leadership training, professional development and access to career opportunities for thousands of members annually. 10,000 members. Annual National Convention, hosting over 8,000 attendees. Chancee` Lundy, National Chairperson. Contact NSBE, World Headquarters, 1454 Duke Street, Alexandria, Virginia 22314 Phone: (703) 549-2207 Fax: (703) 683-5312 E-mail: **info@nsbe.org** Website: **www.nsbe.org**

National Urban League, Inc. The nation's oldest and largest community-based movement empowering African Americans to enter the economic and social mainstream. E-store and annual conference. Scholarship program. President and CEO, Marc Morial. The National Urban League, Inc., 120 Wall Street, New York, New York 10005 Phone: (212) 558-5300 Fax: (212) 344-5332 E-mail: **info@nul.org** Website: **www.nul.org**

The Organization of Black Screenwriters, Inc. (OBS)   Began in 1988 to support Black screenwriters. "Our primary function is to assist screenwriters in the creation of works for film and television." Sylvia Franklin, president. Contact The Organization of Black Screenwriters, Inc., 1968 Adams Boulevard, Los Angeles, California 90018 Phone: (323) 735-2050 E-mail: **sfranklin@obswriter.com** Website: **www.obswriter.com**

Ralph J. Bunche Center for African American Studies at UCLA Darnell Hunt, Interim IDP Chair. Contact Darnell Hunt, Ralph J. Bunche Center for African-American Studies, UCLA, 160 Haines Hall, Box 951545, Los Angeles, California 90095 Phone: (310) 825-7403 E-mail: **lbritton@bunche.ucla.edu** Website: **www.bunchecenter.ucla.edu**

The RAWSISTAZ Reviewers (TRR)   Founded in September 2000 by Tee C. Royal, the Rawsistaz Reviewers are the leading reviewers in the literary industry with a focus on promoting the works of books by and about African-American Authors. Daily newsletter of black book reviews can be found on our site. The RAWSISTAZ Reviewers, Post Office Box 1362, Duluth, Georgia 30096 Phone: (775) 363-8683 Fax: (775) 416-4540 E-mail: **info@rawsistaz.com** Website: **www.blackbookreviews.net**

Schomburg Center for Research in Black Culture National research library devoted to collecting and documenting the experiences of peoples of African descent throughout the world. Gennette McLaurin, Associate Chief Librarian. Schomburg Center for Research in Black Culture, 515 Malcolm X Boulevard, New York, New York 10037 Phone: (212) 491-2200 E-mail: **gmclaurin@nypl.org** Website: **www.nypl/research/sc/sc**

UNITY: Journalists of Color, Inc.   A strategic alliance advocating news coverage about people of color and aggressively challenging its organizations at all levels to reflect the nation's diversity by modeling how different segments of our diverse country can participate equally in shaping the future. Unity, representing more than 10,000 journalists of color, is comprised of four national associations: Asian American Journalists Association, National Association of Black Journalists, the National Association of Hispanic Journalists, and the Native American Journalists Association. Contact Anna M. Lopez, Executive Director, Unity Journalists of Color, Inc., 1601 North Kent Street, Suite 1003, Arlington, Virginia 22209 Phone: (703) 469-2100 Fax: (703) 469-2108 E-mail: **info@unityjournalists.org** Website: **www.unityjournalists.org**

The Writer's Block, Inc. (WBI) Non-profit organization of African-American writers/authors, aspiring and published, of all genres, who are dedicated to the growth and advancement of its members. WBI also promotes African-American literary events, literature and authors. We support young African-American writers through a scholarship fund. Black Writers Group, The Writer's Block, Inc., Post Office Box 170875, Dallas, Texas 75217 Phone: (972) 223-3074 Fax: (972) 223-3075 E-mail: **afields121@yahoo.com** Website: **www.writersblockinc.org**

Writers Resource Center (WRC) A 501(3)c non-profit writers organization. Janie P. Bess, Founder. WRC, 1500 Oliver Road, Suite K, PMB 265, Fairfield, California 94534 Phone: (707) 399-9169 E-mail: **jpbrites2@sbcglobal.net** Website: **www.writersresourcecenter.com**

Charles W. Cherry II, Esq.
Broadcaster * Publisher * Author * Attorney

A native of Daytona Beach, Florida, Media Mogul, Cherry W. Cherry II, Esq., is a former prosecutor as well as practicing trial attorney in his own firm in Fort Lauderdale, Florida. He is a 1978 honors graduate of Morehouse College, Atlanta Georgia. On December 18, 1982, he was the second African-American student to be simultaneously awarded both the juris Doctor and Master of Business Administration degrees from the University of Florida.

Mr. Charles Cherry II has more than 25 years of media management experience when he began as the publisher of his family-owned weekly newspaper, the Daytona Times, a weekly community newspaper that recently celebrated its 25th anniversary. Cherry served as the General Manager of WPUL-AM since 2000. He has also served a General Manager of WCSZ-AM from 1998 to 2000. He has been on the lecture circuit for over 15 years. His most recent publication is entitled <u>Excellence Without Excuse: The Black Student's Guide to Academic Excellence</u> (International Scholastic Press, 1994)

Currently, Cherry is Vice President/General Counsel and principal shareholder of Tama Broadcasting, Inc., the largest privately Black owned media company in the State of Florida. Tama Broadcasting (Tama) was founded in 2001, by his father the late civil rights activist, Dr. Glen W. Cherry. Tama has holdings that include two newspapers and nine radio stations. Mr. Cherry resides in Plantation, Florida with his family.

Photographers

AUniQue Publishing Company Not only do we aid in entrepreneurial publishing we also offer the services of expression within photography. AUniQue Publishing Company, Post Office Box 184, Fort Worth, Texas 76101 Phone: (817) 320-6123 E-mail: **info@auniquepc.com**

Cliff Chandler Award winning author of three mystery novels. Worked as a professional photographer - German School of Photography, jazz musician - The Muse, and as an editorial writer for a local newspaper. His accomplishments include: Poetry and Short Story Awards, Marquis Who's Who In The East, and the JADA Award Mystery Novel Of The Year 2004. Education: BFA, Pratt Institute, New York; Masters Writing courses at New York University, and editing classes at The New School. Mr. Cliff Chandler, 2492 Tredway Drive, Macon, Georgia 31211 E-mail: **CDuke23@aol.com** Website: **www.authorsden.com/cliffchandler**

Lynisha O. Childers Photographer, poet and author. Lynisha O. Childers Founder/CEO, GreekWorks Entertainment and Infinite Greek Appeal, 550 Palisades Drive South, #102, Birmingham, Alabama 35209 Phone: (205) 940-7566 E-mail: **lynisha_childers@hotmail.com**

Tony Darnell Davis Writer, actor, director, and photographer, with an emphasis on romance, science fiction, and fantasy, he works in poetry, short stories, and play writing. Tony Darnell Davis, 2511 Essex Place, Studio 111, Cincinnati, Ohio 45206 E-mail: **tony.davis@cchmc.org**

Algie deWitt Creative writer, photographer and web/graphics designer. Contact Mr. Algie deWitt, MAMi Magazine, 4408 Aberdeen Lane, Blackwood, New Jersey 08012 E-mail: **algie@mamimagazine.com** Website: **www.mamimagazine.com**

Gloria Dulan-Wilson A freelance writer/photographer, screenwriter and public speaker, Ms. Wilson is a seasoned photo-journalist and public speaker who has covered the Black political arena of New York and Northern New Jersey. Ms. Dulan-Wilson has interviewed and profiled such luminaries as Ossie Davis, Min. Louis Farrakhan, Cong. Charles Rangel, Floyd Flake, Kweisi Mfume, interviewed Diana Ross, Don King, the late Johnnie Cochran, Rosa Parks, the late Mrs. Coretta Scott King, among others. Gloria Dulan-Wilson, 90 Church Street, Suite 3343, New York City, New York 10008 E-mail: **geemomadee@yahoo.com**

C.D. Grant Writer, poet and journalist whose work has appeared in Essence Magazine (for which he was Music Editor for 5 Quindaro (Kansas), Suburban Styles (Westchester, New York), and numerous other periodicals. Mr. Grant completed a course in professional photography with the New York Institute of Photography and is a member of National Press Photographers Association and the International Freelance Photographers Organization. Grant is currently editing a collection of short stories, writing a novel. Mr. C.D. Grant, Publisher, Blind Beggar Press, Post Office Box 437, Bronx, New York 10467 Phone: (914) 683-6792 E-mail: **blindbeggar1@juno.com** Website: **www.blindbeggarpress.com**

Joaquin M. Holloway Jr.   Artistic photographer. The collection of color photographs (all matted and framed) has been shown in many galleries throughout the state of Alabama. Contact Mr. Joaquin M. Holloway Jr., 2206 De Kruif Court, Mobile, Alabama 36617 Phone: (251) 478-5525 E-mail: **joaquinholloway@aol.com**

Gerard McLeod CEO of P.B.G.'s Productions (Photos by Gerard), and Editor-in-Chief of Long Island's first bi-lingual urban music magazine called Strong G Island Biz (SGIB). As a freelance publicity photographer for over 25 years McLeod has supplied photos to and has written for a variety of publications including Where It's At Magazine and Jet Magazine, among others. Internationally, his work has also appeared in Big Daddy from the UK.   He had the pleasure of photographing Richard Burton, James Brown, Crystal Gayle, Chuck Berry, Sylvester Stallone, Destiny's Child, Francesco Scavullo; cover photographer for "Cosmopolitan" magazine. Gerard Mcleod, Post Office Box 1244, Bay Shore, New York 11706 Phone: (631) 969-3676 Fax: (631) 666-2444 E-mail: **SGIBmagazine@aol.com**   Website: **www.sgibmagazine.com**

Monica Morgan Freelance Photographer. Monica runs a full-service photography studio. She is a photojournalist who contributes to Newsweek, Jet, the Detroiter and the Associated Press. Rosa Parks commissioned Monica to do the cover for her current best seller book, Quiet Strength. Ms. Monica Morgan, Monica Morgan Photography, 1301 West Lafayette, Suite 101, Detroit, Michigan 48226 Phone: (313) 963-9402 E-mail: **mmpdet@aol.com**

Jay Nelson Photographer. Host of The Beat website. Jay Nelson, The Beat Magazine, Post Office Box 65856, Los Angeles, California 90065 Phone: (818) 500-9299 Fax: (818) 500-9454 E-mail: **jay@afropulse.com** Website: **www.afropulse.com**

Keith Saunders Marion Designs founder, Keith Saunders, received a Bachelor of Fine Arts degree from American Intercontinental University, a private art school in Atlanta, Georgia. He has been in the design and photography industry for over 5 years. The company designs book covers, business cards, posters, postcards, marketing materials, and logo design. Several of our book covers have made the Essence best seller list and are featured on Black Expressions. Marion Designs has also performed work for top names such as Cingular wireless, AT&T, Simon & Schuster, Random House Publishing, Kensington publishing, La-Z-Boy furniture, Nissan automotive, Fox studios (Garfield movie promotions). Marion Designs, 225 Sunderland Way, Suite # U, Stockbridge, Georgia 30281 Phone: (678) 641-8689 Phone: (678) 641-8689 E-mail: **mariondesigns@bellsouth.net** Website: **www.mariondesigns.com**

Raymond Tyler Freelance Writer/Photographer, Essence Magazine, The Source, and Vibe magazines. Columnist, About Time, Black Men in America.com, and Literafeelya Magazine. Talk Show Host/Producer, Atlantic City Shines (Public Access Channel Two). Contact Mr. Raymond Tyler, Dark Seed Communications, 6701 Black Horse Pike, Suite A-4, EHT, New Jersey 08234 Phone: (609) 677-0168 E-mail: **Darkseedac@aol.com**

Samuel F. Yette Photo-journalist whose works have appeared in National Geographic, People Magazine, Jet Magazine and the movie, "Kiss the Girls" (Paramount), starring Morgan Freeman. Mr. Samuel F. Yette, Cottage Books, 4000 Deerfield Road, Knoxville, Tennessee 37921 Phone: (865) 384-0581 E-mail: **cottagebooks@comcast.net**

Playwrights

Y. Jamal Ali An eclectic blend of artist, scientist, historian and esotericist. Author of over six hundred fifty poems, in addition to numerous essays, articles, short stories and plays, Jamal has been writing seriously for over 25 years. Y. Jamal Ali, Post Office Box 301, Venice, California 90291 Phone: (818) 989-1328 E-mail: **fakoyade@yahoo.com**

Franklin J. Anderson Playwright, screenwriter, Mr. Andersons' play CLASS ran Off-Broadway at Tribeca Theatre in New York in 1994. Co-writer of screenplay Street Tales of Terror. Contact Mr. Franklin J. Anderson, 2610 Harvest Moon, Missouri City, Texas 77489 Phone: (281) 438-1062 E-mail: **f_anderso@hotmail.com**

Stanley Bois Screen writer currently writing for Roc Box Films. My current play is titled Innocence Lost, a stop the violence script dealing with black on black crimes. Contact Mr. Stanley Bois, 1207 SE Curry Street, Port St. Lucie, Florida 34983 Phone: (772) 634-4838 E-mail: **stanleybois@hotmail.com**

Kenneth Bowens Author and playwright and an improv artist and actor, Kanko has written and produced three plays. Education: B.A. in psychology at Central State University (Edmond Oklahoma); Associates degree in electronic design/computer technology. Contact Mr. Kenneth (Kanko) Bowens, 1208 Northwest 106th Street, Oklahoma City, Oklahoma 73114 E-mail: **kennethbowens1@cox.net** Website: **www.Kanko.us**

Michael Antonio Brown Wrote his first script "Cultivated" which is a hip hop drama based loosely on his life as an independent hip hop artist in Seattle. He is producing it independently. Michael Antonio Brown, 27111 167th Place, South East, Suite 105-16, Covington, Washington 98042 E-mail: **admin@cultivatedflix.com** Website: **www.cultivatedflix.com**

Ed Bullins Author, playwright, Ed Bullins's latest book is ED BULLINS: 12 Plays and Selected Writings (U of Michigan Press, 2006). Artist-in-Residence, Northeastern University. Mr. Bullins is the author of six books, including Five Plays By Ed Bullins, The Duplex, The Hungered One, Four Dynamite Plays, The Theme is Blackness, and The Reluctant Rapist. He wrote and produced for the theatre several commission works, including *Rainin' Down Stairs* for the 1992 San Francisco Theatre Artaud, and has been editor for a number of theatre magazines and publications. He was producer of *Circles of Times,* Boston's Lyric Theatre in August 2003. Among his awards and grants is three Obie Awards, four Rockefeller Foundation Playwriting Grants, two Guffenheim Playwriting Fellowships, an NEA Playwriting Grant, the AUDELCO Award, the New York Drama Critics Circle Award for Best American Play of 1974 -75, the National Black Theatre Festival Living Legend Award, and the OTTO Award in 2004. The Ed Bullins Reader will soon be published by Michigan University Press. It will contain plays, prose, interviews, etc., by Mr. Bullins. Ed Bullins, 37 Vine Street, #1, Roxbury, Massachusetts 02119 Phone: (617) 442-6627 E-mail: **rct9@verizon.net** Website: **www.edbullins.com**

L Guy Burton Published writer of a non-fiction book Follow The Right Leader published by Quill Publishers, copyright, 1991, novels Jack In The Pulpit, Xlibris, copyright 2004, and Come Die With Me, PublishAmerica, copyright 2006, magazine articles, poetry, and a movie script. My articles and poetry have appeared in Interrace magazine, and my screenplay Latent Blood—which won honorable mention in a Writer's Digest contest—was represented by The Berzon Agency of Glendale, California. As founder and Director of The Warwick Valley Writers' Association, I have, through this local writers' group, been able to polish, complete and promote several Works in various genres, as well as help others to do the same. L Guy Burton, The Warwick Valley Writers' Association, 12 Burton Lane, Warwick, New York 10990 E-mail: **booknook1@hotmail.com**

Stanley Bennett Clay Author of two novels, Diva (Holloway House) and In Search of Pretty Black Men (Atria Books), Mr. Clay is also author of the stagplays Lovers and Ritual. He wrote the book, music, and lyrics for the stage musical Looking For God. He co-wrote music and lyrics for the stage musical Why Do Fools Fall In Love. He wrote and directed the film Ritual (Urbanworks Entertainment). Recipient: NAACP Image Award, 3 NAACP Theatre Awards, 3 Drama-logue Awards. Stanley Bennett Clay, 1155 4th Avenue, Los Angeles, California 90019 E-mail: **sbcpublishers@earthlink.net**

Ebony Rose Custis A poet working in various mediums including fiction and dramatic writing. Ebony is the author of two collections of poetry: My Moments, and Defining the Color of Ebony. She is author of an award winning one-act drama 'Strange Reflections' and one full length drama 'Taylor's Gift.' Ebony also won First Prize in the Dramatic Writing division of the Margaret Walker College Language Association writing competition for her short play 'Strange Reflections.' She has studied creative writing at the University of Ghana under the instruction of Kofi Awoonor and Kofi Anyidaho. Ms. Ebony Rose Custis, 13211 Vanessa Avenue, Bowie, Maryland 20720 Phone: (301) 602 5918 E-mail: **ebony.custis@gmail.com**

Jackie Daughtry Pseudonyms: Ayani_Meli Journey Shanise Rhodes is an accomplished poet and playwright, as well as a digital storyteller. After graduating from Davidson College, she served for several years as a web manager for an organization promoting healthy children and families in Georgia. She also taught drama at Talbot Academy, an alternative school in Savannah serving the needs of behaviorally challenged youth. Ms. Jackie Daughtry, Post Office Box 32, Sylvania, Georgia 30467 Phone: (912) 687-5546 E-mail: **ayani.meli@gmail.com**

Tony Darnell Davis Writer, actor, director, and photographer. With an emphasis on romance, science fiction, and fantasy, Mr. Davis works in poetry, short stories, and play writing. He is completing his work on "Black Images in Science Fiction and Fantasy" and will be releasing 12 books of poetry in 2007 with his company Birthmark Expressions Unlimited(BEU. Mr. Davis was an Assistant Professor at the University of Cincinnati, teaching Black Drama and Acting workshops. He is currently producing plays for the Free Theatre of Cincinnati and preparing a genealogy book on his family entitled "Pathways to My Past." Tony Darnell Davis, 2511 Essex Place, Studio 111, Cincinnati, Ohio 45206 E-mail: **tony.davis@cchmc.org**

Gerri DeWitt Screenwriter. Contact Gerri DeWitt, The Corporate Catalysts, 590 Means Street, Suite 200, Atlanta, Georgia 30318 Phone: (404) 223-2438 E-mail: **gerri@corpcatalysts.com**

Penelope Flynn Author and Screenwriter of Erotica, Science Fiction, Fantasy, Sensual Romance, Paranormal Romance, Legal comedy and drama and Horror. Penelope Flynn, 824 North Marsalis Avenue, Suite C, Dallas, Texas 75203 Phone: (214) 371-7366 Fax: (214) 942-0980 E-mail: **penelope@penelopeflynn.com**

Darnella Ford Author journalist, Darnella Ford began writing at the age of nine. At the age of 21, she moved to Los Angeles and began writing screenplays and teleplays; selected as a National Walt Disney Fellowship Finalist. Darnella is also a competing Slam Poet who performs regularly throughout the Los Angeles area. Ms. Darnella Ford Phone: (818) 458-2062 E-mail: **dapoet@netscape.com** Website: **www.darnella.com**

Papi Kymone Freeman Writer/producer, playwright and poet, Papi Kymone Freeman is the founder of the National Black LUV Festival which was a Mayor's Art Award Finalist for Excellence in Service to the Arts in 2006, and is currently a board member for Words Beats & Life. He is the subject of one chapter of the book, Beat of A Different Drum: The Untold Stories of African Americans Forging Their Own Paths in Work and Life (Hyperion). In addition, he is the author of a book of poetry entitled, Blood Sweat & Tears. He is a founding member with Genesis Poets and has studied under the tutelage of the legendary independent filmmaker Haile Gerima. Freeman is set to produce his screenplay, Starrchildren in 2007. In 2005, Prison Poetry was awarded the 22nd Annual Larry Neal Award for Drama. Contact Papi Kymone Freeman, Frederick Douglas Station, Post Office Box 31243, Banneker City, Washington, DC 20030 Phone: (202) 547-2459 Fax: (301) 768-4007 E-mail: **kymone@prisonpoetry-theplay.com** Website: **www.prisonpoetry-theplay.com**

Sandra Peoples-Gates Author, award winning poet, playwright, motivational speaker and instructor, Ms. Peoples is owner of BlackBerry Literary Services. She specializes is all aspects of writing, publication and promotion of fiction and non-fiction, poetry, and children's books. Sandra Peoples, BlackBerry Literary Services, 2956 Mackin Road, Flint, Michigan 48504 Phone: (810) 234-0899 E-mail: **bblit@hotmail.com**

Nancy M. Gilliam Author, playwright, Nancy has authored numerous plays, poems and songs including the Billboard Top Twenty hit Take A Chance" by Nuance featuring Vicki Love. Nancy Gilliam, Pen & Sword Publishing, Post Office Box 1952, Philadelphia, Pennsylvania 19105 Phone: (267) 847-5110 E-mail: **melodicg2003@hotmail.com**

Idris Goodwin Playwright, performer, director, and educator, Idris Goodwin is the recipient of the NEA/TCG Theatre Residency Program for Playwrights for 2004. He holds a BA in Film & Video from Columbia College, Chicago and an MFA in Writing from the School of the Art Institute of Chicago. Co-founder of Hermit Arts where he has coordinated events that showcase a variety of musical and spoken word performers, and written and co-produced eight full-length plays in venues such as Chicago Cultural Center, Property Theater, and Curious Theater Branch. He was ecently commissioned to adapt Ira Berkow's Book Maxwell Street: Survival in a Bazaar for a series of outdoor theater performances (2004). Since 1999, Idris has been creating original hip-hop music as a solo artist and in collaboration, releasing CD's independently and for the Chicago based Naiveté records. Idris Goodwin, 1721 West Huron, Apartment 2f, Chicago, Illinois 60622 E-mail: **Idris@hermitsite.com** Website: **www.Idrisgoodwin.com**

Forest Hairston　Songwriter-music producer, screenwriter and poet, Forest Hairston, ForGen Productions, 3654 Barham Boulevard, Suite Q301, Los Angeles, California Phone: (323) 851-1225 E-mail: **fgprod@forgen.com** Website: **www.forgen.com**

William Hairston　Author, playwright and poet, his produced plays include: Walk In Darkness (NYC); Swansong Of The 11th Dawn (NYC); Ira Aldridge (The London Conflict), the winner of the Group Theatre's Playwriting Award, (Seattle, WA, 1987-1988); Double Dare (Theatre Festival, Washington, DC); Black Antigone (NC). He wrote movie and TV scripts for the U.S. Information Agency, including; Apollo-11 Man On The Moon. He is the recipient of a National Endowment for the Arts Literary Grant and a Ford Foundation Theatre Fellowship. He graduated from the University of Northern Colorado, BA, (Greeley), and took additional writing courses at Columbia and New York Universities. William Hairston, 5501 Seminary Road, Falls Church, Virginia 22041 Phone: (703) 845-1281 E-mail: **WilliamRHairston1@msn.com**

Robyn Maria Hamlin　Author/Screenwriter. NOVELS "The Zone of Danger Test" is my breakout novel. I have 3 other working novels in progress. "Shades of Gray" and "Zone of Danger" are my only two registered screenplays to date. I have 4 other working screenplays in progress. Poetry, "The Red Flag," "Bread Crumbs," "The Teamplayer," "A Hand for ME," and "There Is A River" are a few of my poems that have been published to date. My writings have also been featured in both EBONY (October 2005) and ESSENCE (January 2006) magazines. Robyn Maria Hamlin, 1900 Wesleyan Drive, #2807, Macon, Georgia 31210 Phone: (478) 476-8776 E-mail: **hampretired@aol.com**

Leslie Harris　Born and raised in Detroit, Michigan. Received B.S. from Michigan State University and J.D. from University of Detroit Mercy School of Law. Author of 18 manuscripts of poetry. Individual works have been publsihed in various magazines and ezines (Facets Magazine, FRESH! Literary Magazine, Skyline Magazine, Fort Worth Poe, Sentinel Online Magazine and others). Also a songwriter (in various genres). Member of the songwriting team known as Infectious Grooves. E-mail: **quality6287@aol.com**

Rochell D. Hart　The first black woman from Oregon ever chosen to represent the state at the 10th Annual National Poetry Slam (1999 Chicago, IL), Rochell D. "Ro Deezy" Hart is a legend of her own time. The author of six published books, Hart's second title "A Black Girl's Song", was considered for the Oregon Book Award – the highest literary award in the state. A revolutionary, visionary and activist, Ro Deezy has brought her message of Black Power and Man Loving Feministic Pride to audiences across the country. She's had solicited appearances from agencies ranging from NIKE to the Urban League and has shared the stage with a myriad of other influential figures including Nikki Giovanni, Dead Prez and The Roots. Ro Deezy made her acting debut in the nationally acclaimed "first activist film", Turn Off Channel Zero which also featured Professor Griff (of Public Enemy), The Last Poets and more. Rochell D. "Ro Deezy" Hart, Post Office Box 20511, Portland, Oregon 97294 E-mail: **rodeezy@rodeezy.com** Website: **www.rodeezy.com**

Edwardo Jackson　Author, screenwriter and actor. Edwardo Jackson, JCM Books, 15228-B Hawthorne Blvd., Suite 203, Lawndale, California 90260 Phone: (310) 349-3309 Fax: (310) 370-6098 E-mail: **EverAfterANovel@aol.com**

Terence E. Jackson Singer, playwright, poet, and novelist of the controversial novel Nigger's Heaven, Mr. Jackson was born on May 1, 1964 in Detroit, Michigan. Contact Mr. Terence E. Jackson, 690 Durant Place, North East, Suite #2, Atlanta, Georgia 30308   E-mail: **terenceejackson@uspacegallery.com** Website: **www.uspacegallery.com**

Roland S. Jefferson Born: 05-16-39. Author and playwright, Mr. Jefferson is the author of 5 published novels: THE SCHOOL ON 103RD STREET (1976); A CARD FOR THE PLAYERS (1978); 559 TO DAMASCUS (1985); DAMAGED GOODS (2005); ONE NIGHT STAND (2006). Roland Jefferson is a graduate of Howard University Medical School and is now semi-retired from a career as a forensic psychiatrist. Living in Los Angeles, he pursues writing crime fiction novel on a full time basis. He has written four screenplays. He received the NAACP Image Award for Writing (1979); NAACP Special Award of Merit by Black American Cinema Society (1990); 1st Place Award For Drama by Black Filmmakers Hall of Fame (1979). Mr. Roland S. Jefferson, 3870 Crenshaw Boulelvard. #215, Los Angeles, California 90008   Phone: (310) 285-3325 E-mail: **rsjeff@hotmail.com** Website: **www.rolandsjefferson.com**

Melvin Ishmael Johnson Screenwriter and a playwright. Director of Dramastage Qumran Community Theater Workshop. Dramastage Qumran Community Theater, 733 South Hindry Avenue, Inglewood, California 90301 Phone: (310) 348-9853 Fax: (310) 348-9619 E-mail: **bymel2004@yahoo.com**

Ralph P.J. Johnson Has written and directed several screenplays. My company also offers website and software development, video/film productions, and music production. Ralph P.J. Johnson, President, Hi-Tech Media Corp., RR11 Box 11005, Stroudsburg, Pennsylvania 18360 E-mail: **pj@htechmedia.com** Website: **www.htechmedia.com**

Mateen Kemet A former Wall Street bond trader, current English teacher, lifelong martial arts practitioner, aspiring film director and certifiable Bronx New Yorker. A filmmaker since 1997, Mateen, has written and directed 6 short films, 1 music video, and several screenplays. In 1998, he won the prestigious Marion Knott Fellowship which allowed him to work under the auspices of noted Film and Theater Director, Arthur Hiller. In 2002 he received a student filmmaker award from the Directors Guild of America and also placed 2nd at the Black Filmmakers Hall of Fame for his MFA Thesis short, silence. In 2003, silence continues to be recognized, screening in over 65 festivals world wide, and winning 15 awards. These include, The Harvard Black Arts Festival – Grand Prize, Cinematic Images – Grand Prize, and lasty The Urban American Filmmakers Workshop where his Grand Prize entered him into Fox Studio's Searchlab Program with an attached first-look deal. His other notable works -- a Music Video for Oyendasola, an accomplished Opera star, and his first film "Who's the Mack", a 10 minute erotic dramedy that delves into politics of sex in romantic relationships -- have been exhibited at the EMP Rock and Roll Museum in Seattle, and the U.S. festival circuit, respectively. Currently, he is working on a animation project about animal conservation, while writing 2 shorts—The Fillmore Flower and Dinner With Friends which he will direct later this year. One of which will be directed for the Fox Searchlab program. Lastly, Mateen currently is working on the feature version of his short film "silence" and teaches English and Special Education in the Long Beach Unified School District. Contact Mr. Mateen Kemet Phone: (323) 646-4118 E-mail: **nucinema@yahoo.com** Website: **www.runawayfilmworX.com**

Barbara Kensey   Work has also been produced on stage to critical acclaim by several Chicago theater companies. Barbara Kensey, 5212 South Dorchester Avenue, Chicago, Illinois 60615 Phone: (713) 288-8776 Fax: (713) 288-8997 E-mail: **bkencomm@aol.com**

Nwenna Kai   Writer & Film Producer. Contact Ms. Nwenna Kai, Full Moon Productions, 311 San Pascual, Los Angeles, California 90042 Phone: (323) 337-7381 Fax: (323) 936-5691 E-mail: **nwenna@excite.com**

Darryl D'Wayne Lassiter   PAY THE PRICE, Mr. Lassiter's first full-length feature as writer/producer/director won for him the first-place prize "Best Family Drama," New York International Film Festival. He has written screenplays to Dead End Street and the remake of Bill Cosby and Sidney Poitier's Uptown Saturday Night. In development now is the movie, REVENGE. Darryl has written features for Upscale Magazine, Urban Network Magazine, Gospel Today and American News Weekly. He was sports and entertainment editor for the Atlanta Daily World and a contributing writer for the Atlanta Tribune. His film career began in 1991 working on the set of CBS' In The Heat Of The Night. He began his career in television and radio as an announcer and program director in 1985 working at the CBS and ABC network affiliates in Montgomery, Alabama and Atlanta, Georgia. He has produced and directed nearly 50 music videos. He recently was given a proclamation from the mayor of his hometown, inducted into the National Black College Alumni Distinction Hall Of Fame a Lifetime Achievement Literacy Classic Award 2003 and the coveted Stellar Award 2004 for "Video Of The Year." Darryl D'Wayne Lassiter, Post Office Box 50374, Atlanta, Georgia 30302 E-mail: **darryl@ddlentertainment.net** Website: **www.ddlentertainment.net**

Tracey Michae'l Lewis   Author, poet, screenwriter, and playwright, Ms. Lewis has spent a lifetime cultivating poetry, short stories, and plays devoted to examining the human search for Spirit. Lewis has completed work on several screenplays, and the critically acclaimed stage play, KHEPERA, which ran off-Broadway in 2002. She is a professor of English at New Jersey City University and Essex County College. Ms. Tracey Michae'l Lewis, 1845 West Superior, #1R, Chicago, Illinois 60622 E-mail: **traceylewis33@yahoo.com**

Charles E McClinon   Author, playwright, singer and songwriter. Enjoys writing fiction, drama and musicals. Charles E. McClinon, 8307 Mayfair Street, Cincinnati, Ohio Phone: (513) 417-9465 E-mail: **cmcclinon@yahoo.com**

Garry Moore   Chicago native, Garry is a news anchor and senior producer of News 25 Today, Central Illinois' first and highest rated morning news show. After graduating from Bradley University, Garry started his reporting career as a reporter and eventual news director for WXCL-AM in Peoria, a country/western radio station. Garry's journalism and musical career have taken him to South Africa, Ghana, Senegal, The Gambia, The Dominican Republic, Cuba, Brazil, and Haiti. A highly regarded storyteller, drummer, and cultural arts presenter, Garry has appeared at central Ilinois schools, camps, workshops, businesses, and prisons. He is a writer and producer of several successful theatre arts productions, including "Black to the Future," "Dancing My Sisters Back Home," and "The Ghosts of Haiti." Gary Moore, WEEK-TV, 2907 Springfield Road, East Peoria, Illinois 61611 Phone: (309) 698-2525 Fax: (309) 698-9335 E-mail: **gmoore@week.com** Website: **www.week.com**

MWALIM Considered by critics and peers alike to be one of the true modern masters of the oral tradition, Mwalim is a multifaceted performing artist, writer, filmmaker and educator. He has distinguished himself as a playwright, director, actor and teacher. Receiving his formal training from New African Company in Boston, Mwalim's work has been presented throughout the United States and Canada, including his award-winning plays, "Look At My Shorts: An Evening of Short Plays"; "A Party at the Crossroads"; and "OM!: A Street Corner Griot's Comedy." His performance piece "Backwoods People" was presented at the 1999 National Black Drama Festival in Winston Salem, North Carolina. He is a published author of one book, A Mixed Medicine Bag: 7 Original Black Wampanoag Folk-tales, several poems and short stories appearing in numerous anthologies; a recipient of the Martin Luther King, Jr. Artists Grant, New England Broadcasting Association Fellowship, and a three-time recipient of the Ira Aldridge Fellowship. Mwalim, English Department, University of Massachusetts, Dartmouth, 285 Old Westport Road, North Dartmouth, Massachusetts 02747 Phone: (508) 999-8304 Fax: (508) 999-9235 E-mail: **mwalim@gmail.com**

William Pleasant Author, Publisher, Playwright and Documentary Film Maker, William Pleasant is among America's most provocative journalists and playwrights. He has had 13 drama works staged in the past 18 years for the New York City and European stages. His 1991 SKINSHOW was featured in the Vienna Festival. His 1992 controversial adaptation of Jura Soyfer's BROADWAY MELODY 1492 was selected by the U.S. Quintcentennial Committee as an official event. William Pleasant, 22 West Bryan Street, Suite 172, Savannah, Georgia 31401 Phone: (866) 237-7563 E-mail: **yamacrawpress@lycos.com**

Emma E. Pullen Writer/producer/director of four short films, "Marching Into the Millennium," which is narrated by Nichelle Nichols (Lt. Uhura of "Star Trek") and winner of the US International Film and Video Festival's "Certificate for Creative Excellence" for "Documentary, Current Events, Special Events" 1999; "Upon The Shoulders Of Our Ancestors"; "South Los Angeles"; and "Black Hollywood 2000." She also produced a 30-minute video tribute to the late Academy Award nominated actress Beah Richards. Richards co-starred with Danny Glover in Pullen's first television script, a PBS Wonderworks episode, "And The Children Shall Lead" which was nominated for an NAACP Image Award. It moved to The Disney Channel, international market and is now on VHS. Ms. Emma E. Pullen, 1339 North Odgen Drive, Los Angeles, California 90046 E-mail: **eepblackseeds@sbcglobal.net**

Crystal Rhodes Honed her craft after moving to the San Francisco Bay Area where she worked as a reporter, a reviewer, columnist and an entertainment editor. She is author of the critically acclaimed novel, Sin. She co-wrote her latest novel Grandmothers, Incorporated with L. Barnett Evans. "I've written hundreds of articles, profiles and interviews for both newspapers and magazines. I also served as the producer and writer of a weekly cable television series, "Getting By" as well as served as the producer and hostess of my own Bay area radio show titled "Bay Arts Beat" I've written 21 plays, 19 of which have been produced in theatres throughout the United States. My play, The Trip, has been published in two play anthologies: Center Stage: An Anthology of 21 Contemporary Black Playwrights (University of Illinois Press) and Black Women's Blues: A Literary Anthology, 1934-Present (G.K. Hall & Co.). Ms. Crystal Rhodes, Crystal Ink Publishing, Post Office Box 53511, Indianapolis, Indiana 46253 E-mail: **writetome@crystalrhodes.com** Website: **www.crystalrhodes.com**

Evie Rhodes Fiction Author. Writes feature short stories for The Gospel Magazine, Inc. Evie is also the writer for the "Standing In Da Sprit" album, which won a Canadian Music Award for Best Gospel Album, and the scriptwriter for Changed, which won for Best Gospel Music Video. She is the author of four books, The Forgotten Spirit, Expired, Criss Cross, and Out A Order. Contact Ms. Evie Rhodes, Post Office Box 320503, Hartford, Connecticut 06132 Phone: (212) 633-3315 E-mail: **evierhodes@evierhodes.com** Website: **www.evierhodes.com**

Alan Sharpe HIV+ playwright/screenwriter. Body of work focused primarily on contemporary African-American Gay and Lesbian life and culture. Author of plays including, "Auld Lang Syne", "BrotherHOODs", "Christmas Gifts", "Chump Changes", "Family Business", "HeartBeats", "Storm Signals" and the film, "Party." Artistic Director of African-American Collective Theater (ACT) based in Washington, DC. Alan Sharpe, 1848 Columbia Road, North West, #24, Washington, DC 20009 Phone: (202) 745-3662 E-mail: **asharpebgm@msn.com** Website: **www.alansharpe.org**

Tristan Spirit Writes original movie scripts and consults for independent television and independent films. Tristan Spirit, Spiritstyle Enterprises, Inc., 651 West 188th Street, Suite 1-H, New York, New York 10040 Phone: (212) 414-5426 E-mail: **badassclothes@yahoo.com**

Timothy N. Stelly, Sr. Author of three novels: "Tempest In The Stone," "The Malice of Cain," and "Like A Straight-Up Sucka." He is also a frequent contributor to e-zines useless-knowledge.com and e-zinearticles.com. Mr. Stelly has penned more than thirty screenplays, including "Twangbangers." Timothy N. Stelly, Sr., Post Office Box 1264, Pittsburg, California 94565 Phone: (925) 473-0741 E-mail: **stellbread@yahoo.com**

Antoinette Oglesby Taylor Playwright/Writer. I have 6 plays that have been stage read in Louisville Kentucky. I have been writing for 20 plus years and have done greeting cards and poems and short stories. Antoinette Oglesby Taylor, 6411 Shirley Avenue, Prospect, Kentucky 40059 Fax: (502) 228-9775 Phone: (502) 228-4573 E-mail: **jtnursing@aol.com**

Jackie Taylor Founder, Producer, Actor and the Executive Director of the Black Ensemble Theater Company in Chicago, Illinois, Ms. Jackie Taylor has written more than 100 plays including the nationally renowned "The Jackie Wilson Story", "Doo Wop Shoo Bop" and "The Other Cinderella." Jackie Taylor, Executive Director, Black Ensemble Theater Corporation, 4520 North Beacon Street, Chicago, Illinois 60640 Phone: (773) 769-4451 Fax: (773) 769-4533 E-mail: **BlackEnsemble@aol.com**   Website: **www.blackensembletheater.org**

T. Tara Turk Graduated from Eugene Lang at The New School in New York and went on to get her MFA from Sarah Lawrence College in 1998. She was a Van Lier Fellow at New York Theatre Workshop in 2001. Her plays have been read at such esteemed institutions as Ensemble Studio Theatre, New Federal Theatre, New York Theatre Workshop and Frederick Douglas Creative Arts Center. Her plays include Grim Foster's Love Song, FAM, Indigos, Sistaz On The DL, Newly Dead, Thistory, If Eve Left..., east outer drive, the collaborative piece Bryant Park, Garbage in Eden and Vist or Days. She has just recently finished her novel, Things Fall Together, and a screenplay, Smoke and Mirrors. T. Tara Turk, 4970 Fountain Avenue, Los Angeles, California 90029 E-mail: **scruffdiva@yahoo.com**

Van Whitfield Award-winning author. Also writes the BET hit profile show, TurnStyle and is currently writing the authorized biography of former DC mayor, Marion Barry.   He also writes scripts for UPN's hit sitcom, EVE. Mr. Van Whitfield, Post Office Box 941, Lanham, Maryland 20706 E-mail: **vanwhitfield@vanwhitfield.com** Website: **www.vanwhitfield.com**

Jessica Nyel Willis Writer/Author. Experience: articles for magazines, short stories, film script, teleplays, sitcom and drama scripts, as well as novels for young adults and adults. Contact Ms. Jessica Nyel Willis, 8629 144th Street, #2, Jamaica, New York 11435 Phone: (646) 207-1877 E-mail: **JessicaNyelWillis@hotmail.com**

Gloria Dulan-Wilson Freelance writer/photographer, screenwriter and public speaker, Dulan-Wilson has recently taken her 9 years experience in television situation comedy and penned three screenplays, while working with Columbia University and Writers Guild East Black Writers Fellowship program.   She is currently in the process of fine tuning them: "Her Own True Love(c)," "The First Wife(c)" and "The Perpetrators(c)." Ms. Gloria Dulan Wilson, 90 Church Street, Suite 3343, New York City, New York 10008 E-mail: **geemomadee@yahoo.com**

David D. Wright Author/Theatre Company/Producer. Orisha Tales Repertory Radio Theatre Company, 133 East 96th Street, Brooklyn, New York 11212 Phone: (718) 735-8905 E-mail: **osungumi@aim.com**

Alecia Goodlow-Young Author, screenwriter, poet, columnist, and a freelance writer. I write for a newspaper, a magazine, a union organization. Currently with The National Writer's Union/UAW. I hold the position of Co-chair of The National Diversity Committee, A Delegate at the Delegate's Assembly and a Southeast Michigan Steering Committee member. I was also with The Detroit Writer's Guild for a few years. I write in many different genres. Alecia Goodlow-Young, 28490 Tavistock Trail, Southfield, Michigan 48034 Phone: (313) 796-7949 Fax: (313) 541-6638 E-mail: **aleciawrites@sbcglobal.net**

Les Brown

Author * Air Personality
Motivational & Public Speaker

Les Brown, a public speaker who has risen to national prominence, delivers a high-energy message, urging people to "shake off mediocrity and live up" to their greatness. His passion to learn and his hunger to realize greatness in himself has helped him in his career. He rose from a hip-talking morning dee-jay to broadcast manager, from community activist to community leader, from political commentator to 3-term legislator, and from banquet and nightclub emcee to premier keynote speaker on a national and international scale.

In 1989, Les Brown was the recipient of the National Speakers Association's highest honor and the Council of Peers Award of Excellence. He has been featured in *Ebony* and *Essence* magazines and many of the nation's leading newspapers due to his rising prominence and impact of his speaking and training. He was selected one of America's Top Five Speakers for 1992 by Toastmasters International. Brown has appeared on Robert Schuller's *Hour of Power* program and the *Sally Jessy Rapheal Show*.

In 1990, Les recorded his first in a series of speech presentations for the Public Broadcast System. In 1991 the program, *You Deserve with Les Brown* was awarded a Chicago-area Emmy and became the leading program for pledges to PBS stations in their fundraising efforts nationwide. In October 1992, Brown published <u>Live Your Dreams,</u> a book outlining how to maximize human potential, using in part his own story as testimony to the possibilities for the reader. He has produced a six-cassette audio "seminar", *The Courage To Live Your Dreams* in which he demonstrates visualization and self-affirmation techniques designed to motivate and inspire. A 20 minute VHS videocassette program, *How To Keep The Dream Alive* is also available. In September 1993, *King World* presented The Les Brown Show on national Television.

Today Les Brown conducts seminars and motivational speeches for Fortune 500 companies and organizations. He can be heard every Sunday morning on *Les Live* (V103.com).

Poets

Octavia McBride-Ahebee Writer of poetry, short stories and plays. A native of Philadelphia, Pennsylvania, Octavia McBride-Ahebee lived for nine years in Cote d'Ivoire, West Africa. Ms. McBride-Ahebee's newest collection of poetry, Assuming Voices, is published by Lit Pot Press. Her poetry gives voice to women who historically have not been heard; African women, women in refugee camps, and women who are victims of civil war, women who are new immigrants and rural women battling such health issues as breast cancer and obstetric fistula. Ms. McBride-Ahebee, Lit Pot Press, 3909 Reche Road, Suite 96, Fallbrook, California 92028 Phone: (215) 877-2502 E-mail: **obmcbride@hotmail.com** Website: **www.mysite.verizon.net/vze1j2qg**

Y. Jamal Ali An eclectic blend of artist, scientist, historian and esotericist. Author of over six hundred fifty poems, in addition to numerous essays, articles, short stories and plays, Jamal has been writing seriously for over 25 years. Y. Jamal Ali, Post Office Box 301, Venice, California 90291 Phone: (818) 989-1328 E-mail: **fakoyade@yahoo.com**

Paul Alleyne A published writer, (poetry and fiction), as well as a visual artist. He is author of Whatever It Takes (2005), and These Are Our Stories (2007). Contact Mr. Paul Alleyne, 2643 Bridgewater Drive, Grand Prairie, Texas 75054 Phone: (323) 230-9336 Website: **www.redbubble.com/people/bambooo**

Michele Barkley Author of the book Wayfaring Stranger-Poems and producer of the videopoem In View Of A Cup Half-Full. Ms. Barkley is also a visual artist. Ms. Michele Barkley, PMB 88, 3703 South Edmunds Street, Seattle, Washington 98118 Phone: (206) 818-1091 E-mail: **artuncommon@yahoo.com**

Jillina "J-Bax" Baxter Website Journalist – The Hive/Blaze 1 Radio at blaze1graphixs.com in Atlanta, Georgia. J-Bax has written a catalog close to 300 consisting of Rap & R&B songs and poetry pieces. Other projects include working on a number of books (poetry "Vision Though Verses", semi-autobiography "Web Celeb", a fictional novel "The Strangers We Call Friends" and a coffee table book "A Pictorial Purpose". Jillina "J-Bax" Baxter, 184 Second Avenue, Albany, New York 12202 Phone: (518) 210-3518 E-mail: **jbmeow@yahoo.com**

Rose Jackson-Beavers Chief Executive Officer of Prioritybooks Publications grew up in East St. Louis, Illinois and received her Bachelor and Master degrees from Illinois State and Southern Illinois Universities. She has worked as a Freelance writer for the A-Magazine, a St. Louis Publication and as an Opinion Shaper for the North County Journal Newspaper. She currently writes as a columnist for the Spanish Word, a local community newspaper. Published books: "Back Room Confessions" (2004), "Summin to Say, "a book of poems and Essays about everyday life (2001-2002), and "Quilt Designs and Poetry Rhymes" was co-written with nationally known fabric artist, Edna Patterson-Petty. Rose Jackson-Beavers, Post Office Box 2535, Florissant, Missouri 63032 Phone: (314) 741-6789 E-mail: **rosbeav03@yahoo.com**

Gayle Bell Poet. Gayle Bell, 17617 Midway Road #134, Dallas, Texas 75287 Phone: (214) 440-8125 E-mail: **linnbell2002@yahoo.com**

Jennifer Elaine Black Author of several poetry books including "Issues of Life" and "The Healing Tree for all Nations." She is a speaker and instructor for The End Times Arts Movement International founded by herself. She teaches youth to be empowered through the use of their own creativity. She teaches acting, praise dance, writing, and music workshops. She is also a writer for Gatekeeper magazine and Virtuous Woman magazine. Jennifer Elaine Black, The End Times Arts Movement International, Inc., Post Office Box 56394, Little Rock, Arkansas 72215 Phone: (501) 859-0841 E-mail: **booking@thepropheticartist.com**

Kennedy Brazier Author of published Poetry Collection, When The June Bugs Come Out in August (Publish America, 2007). Currently seeking representation for 2 novels. Education: Masters in English/Communications, also a fitness model. Contact Mr. Kennedy Brazier, 4387 Brookmere Drive, Kentwood, Michigan 49512 Phone: (616) 956-9597 E-mail: **Kennedy-lynne@hotmail.com**

Traci Brooks Poet, public speaker and writer, Stepping Into Womanhood is Ms. Brooks' first published work.   Since graduating from San Francisco State University in 1991, she has continued to seek knowledge and understanding of self in order to learn, grow and teach. She is dedicated to the empowerment and uplifting of Black people and seeks to express that spirit in her poetry. Currently she is at work on her second title. Ms. Traci Brooks, Black Buttafly Publishing, Post Office Box 200251, San Antonio, Texas 78220 Phone: (877) 679-2755 E-mail: **yalonna@swbell.net** Website: **www.blackbuttafly.com**

Gregory Bryant Author, writer Gregory Bryant was born and raised in Atlantic City, New Jersey. He attended Atlantic City High School where he graduated in 1981. He also attended Taylor Business Institute in Pomona, New Jersey for accounting. In 1984 he entered the United States Air Force and was stationed at Norton Air Force Base in San Bernardino, California. He received an honorable discharge in 1988 and moved to Greensboro, North Carolina where he works for the United States Postal Service. He has been writing poetry as a hobby from his service days but now writes on a regular basis. He released his first book called "Poems of the Heart" in 2002 with his sophomore effort "Visions" being released in 2003. He has established his own publishing company called Feel the Flow Publishing to provide other poets information on publishing. His company has released 4 books with the 2004 release of "From the Hearts of Women" and His present book "Diary of an Open Mind" released April 2006. He is a member of the North Carolina Poetry Society and the Academy of American Poets. Gregory W. Bryant, Feel the Flow Publishing, 2319 Pinecroft Road, Greensboro, North Carolina 27407 Phone: (336) 601-0954 E-mail: **gb_xpress@yahoo.com** Website: **www.feeltheflowpublishing.com**

Jacquelyn A. Bryant Holds an AAS in Early Childhood Education. I have a story that will be featured in Zane's Choc Flava 2 scheduled out in August 07. I currently have a book of poetry published it is titled, "Love Sweet Love." I have several other books of poetry along with a novel and a book of erotic short stories all to be published at a later date. Jacquelyn A. Bryant, 1821 Foulkrod Place, Philadelphia, Pennsylvania 19124 Phone: (267) 971-6093 E-mail: **mslovelieladie@yahoo.com**

L Guy Burton Published writer of a non-fiction book Follow The Right Leader published by Quill Publishers, copyright, 1991, novels Jack In The Pulpit, Xlibris, copyright 2004, and Come Die With Me, PublishAmerica, copyright 2006, magazine articles, poetry, and a movie script. My articles and poetry have appeared in Interrace magazine, and my screenplay Latent Blood—which won honorable mention in a Writer's Digest contest—was represented by The Berzon Agency of Glendale, California. As founder and Director of The Warwick Valley Writers' Association, I have, through this local writers' group, been able to polish, complete and promote several Works in various genres, as well as help others to do the same. L Guy Burton, The Warwick Valley Writers' Association, 12 Burton Lane, Warwick, New York 10990 E-mail: **booknook1@hotmail.com**

Eileen Carole Founder/Director of The Writers Corner (poetry group). She is an author of two volumes of poetry and co-author/publisher of six anthologies. Her published books are "If Ever You Have Loved", "On A Musical Note," "Hair Stories," "Peace Pages," and "Renaissance Pages." Ms. Carole is also a book producer and graphic artist. Eileen Carole, 1151 Morning View Drive, Unit 110, Escondido, California 92026 E-mail: **eileencarole@sbcglobal.net**

Cliff Chandler Award winning author of three mystery novels: "The Paragons, Vengeance Is mine, and Devastated." Devastated was chosen as "Mystery Novel of the Year" by JADA Press. Former host of "Art With A Capital" WGNM TV64, Macon, Georgia, and editorial writer for a local newspaper. Birth Place: New York, New York USA. Cliff Chandlers accomplishments include Poetry Awards, Short Story Awards, Marquis Who's Who In The East, and the JADA Award Mystery Novel Of The Year 2004. Education: BFA, Pratt Institute, Brooklyn, New York, Masters Writing courses at New York University, and editing classes at The New School. Cliff Chandler, 2492 Tredway Drive, Macon, Georgia 31211 E-mail: **CDuke23@aol.com** Website: **www.authorsden.com/cliffchandler**

Charles L. Chatmon Freelance writer, author/poet of The Depths of My Soul The Voices of South Central, two books of poems about love, social issues, tales of despair and hope. Also a member of the California Writers Collective, a local group of authors. Charles L. Chatmon, Post Office Box 2503, Inglewood, California 90305 E-mail: **chatwrites2@yahoo.com**

James E. Cherry A nationally and internationally published poet and fiction writer whose work has been featured in Callaloo, African American Review, Crab Orchard Review, The Other Half, Sable, Crossroads, Bum Rush the Page (Crown), Beyond the Frontier (Black Classic Press), Roll Call (Third World Press) and others. James E Cherry, Post Office Box 614, Jackson, Tennessee 38302 Phone: (731) 422-2524 E-mail: **monksdream@hotmail.com**

Lynisha O. Childers A poet, photographer, and an aspiring attorney, Ms. Lynisha O. Childers received her Bachelor of Arts in Political Science from Georgia State University. Currently, she is a law student at Birmingham School of Law specializing in Child Advocacy. Lynisha is the author of the 1995 publication, Woman I Am and the 2003 poetry book, The Key to My Diary: Caught Between Happiness and Pain, A Collection of Poems and Thoughts. She is also Founder/CEO, of GreekWorks Entertainment and Infinite Greek Appeal. Contact Ms. Lynisha O. Childers, 550 Palisades Drive South, #102, Birmingham, Alabama 35209 Phone: (205) 940-7566 E-mail: **lynisha_childers@hotmail.com**

Wanda Coleman Winner of the prestigious Lenore Marshall prize in 1999 for Bathwater Wine, Coleman continues to prove herself one of the more innovative poets writing today. If Coleman's love of language were not so apparent on every page, her major theme - birth and femininity, slavery and history - might well get lost in mundane polemics. She is the author of Mad Dog Black Lady (1983, 1987), Imagoes (1989), A War of Eyes and Other Stories (October, 1989, Black Sparrow Press), Mambo Hips and Make Believe (1999), and Mercurochrome (National Book Awards Nomination 2001). Her book Ostinato Vamps was published by the University of Pittsburg Press in 2003. A former medical secretary, magazine editor, journalist and scriptwriter, Coleman has received fellowships from the National Endowment for the Arts and the Guggenheim Foundation for her poetry. Wanda Coleman, GuyJoyee Productions, Post Office Box 451621, Los Angeles, California 90045 E-mail: **GuyJ@comcast.net**

Anthony Carlton Cooke The author's fiction and poetry have appeared in the anthologies, "Bardic Tales and Sage Advice: An Anthology of Fantasy, Horror, and Science Fiction" (winner and honorable mention in the 2005 Bards and Sages Writing Contest), "Gathering of the Minds," as well as the journal, "Cherry Bleeds." His work is also scheduled to appear in the anthology, "In Their Own Words: A Generation Defining Itself, Vol.7," due out late 2007. He lived in San Francisco for twelve years, where he was a featured reader at the Art and Divinity Poetry Series, the North Beach Poetry Festival, and read at many other venues while completing "Symmetry," an experimental speculative fiction novel. Currently, Anthony lives in New York, where he is working on a second novel while pursuing his degree in English Literature and Africana Studies. Mr. Anthony Cooke, 450 Circle Road, Building A, Apt. 101A, Stony Brook, New York 11790 Phone: (718) 869-3708 E-mail: **cooke_ac@hotmail.com**

Heather Covington Poet. Ms. Heather Covington, Disilgold, Post Office Box 652, Baychester Station, Bronx, New York 10469 Phone: (718) 547-0499 E-mail: **disilgold@aol.com** Website: **www.disilgold.com**

Nandi SoJourn Asantewaa Crosby   Poet and dramatic reader, Nandi is the first Women's Studies hire in the history of CSU, Chico. She completed her B.A. in Psychology from St. Mary's College of Maryland, an M.A. in Africana Women's Studies at Clark Atlanta University with a thesis called Black Lesbian Feminist Theory or How to Start a Black Women's (R)Evolution. She received her Ph.D. in Sociology from Georgia State University with a dissertation on The Souls of Black Men: Male Discourse and Critical Implications for Rethinking Black Feminist Thought. Nandi is a poet and performance artist who has won more than 50 awards for her performances. Most recently she shared the stage with Saul Williams in a Spoken Word event in Harlen Adams Theatre. Nandi Crosby, Assistant Professor in Women's Studies and Sociology, California State University, Chico, Center for Multicultural and Gender Studies, Butte 611, Chico, California 95929 Phone: (530) 898-5249 Fax: (530) 898-5986

Ebony Rose Custis A poet working in various mediums including fiction and dramatic writing and author of two collections of poetry: My Moments, and Defining the Color of Ebony. She is also author of an award winning one-act drama 'Strange Reflections' and one full length drama "Taylor's Gift." Ebony is presently touring with her second book, Defining the Color of Ebony. Contact Ms. Ebony Rose Custis, 13211 Vanessa Avenue, Bowie, Maryland 20720 Phone: (301) 602 5918 E-mail: **ebony.custis@gmail.com** Website: **www.roseprose.com**

Dahveed Born in Greensboro, North Carolina, Dahveed's first book of poetry and prose is "Through The Eyes of A Foster Child: A Poetic Journey." He served several years in the United States Marine Corps before pursuing a career in the field of Mental Health. Through his work with foster children and the mentally ill population he created Dahveed's Voice and Vision and worked as a freelance consultant which allows him to speak with other children through various organizations. Contact Dahveed, Post Office Box 881403, San Diego, California 92168 E-mail: **dvv@dahveed.com** Website: **www.dahveed.com**

Kolade Daniel Poet, Songwriter, Scriptwriter. 17 Igun Street, Itire Surulere, Lagos 23401 Nigeria Phone: 23 480 66506 72 E-mail: **koladedaniel@praize.com**

Charrita D. Danley Writer and poet, Dr. Charrita D. Danleys' first novel, Through the Crack, was self-published in 2004 through her company, Chideria Publishing, Inc. Set in the South, the novel explores a family's journey from addiction to recovery, exposing the physical, mental, and emotional struggles experienced along the way. She is a member of many professional and educational organizations as well as a member of Delta Sigma Theta Sorority, Inc. Charrita D. Danley, PhD., Danley Writing Consultants, 458 Cambridge Court, Suite D, Riverdale, Georgia 30296 E-mail: **cdanley@danleywriting.com** Website: **www.danleywriting.com**

Jackie Daughtry Pseudonyms: Ayani_Meli Journey Shanise Rhodes is an accomplished poet and playwright, as well as a digital storyteller. She is working on a novel, a book of poetry and several plays. Jackie Daughtry, Post Office Box 32, Sylvania, Georgia 30467 Phone: (912) 687-5546 E-mail: **ayani.meli@gmail.com** Website: **www.newbirthpowercenter.com**

Tony Darnell Davis Writer, actor, director, and photographer. With an emphasis on romance, science fiction, and fantasy, Mr. Davis works in poetry, short stories, and play writing. He is completing his work on "Black Images in Science Fiction and Fantasy" and will be releasing 12 books of poetry in 2007 with his company Birthmark Expressions Unlimited(BEU. Mr. Davis was an Assistant Professor at the University of Cincinnati, teaching Black Drama and Acting workshops. He is currently producing plays for the Free Theatre of Cincinnati and preparing a genealogy book on his family entitled "Pathways to My Past." Tony Darnell Davis, 2511 Essex Place, Studio 111, Cincinnati, Ohio 45206 E-mail: **tony.davis@cchmc.org**

Vernon J. Davis Jr. His first book,"LOVE, IS, THE BEAUTIFUL BLACK WOMAN" is a tribute to all Black Women. Vernon's first published poem, "Beautiful Black Woman", the basis for his book came out in 1978 in a magazine called Black Forum. More poetry followed in other magazines like SoulWord and Dawn, a magazine supplement to the Los Angeles Sentinel. He has also taught Creative Writing. Mr. Vernon J. Davis, Jr., 3993 Spring Mountain Road #160, Las Vegas, Nevada 89102 Phone: (702) 812-5221 E-mail: **vernjdavis@yahoo.com** Website: **www.loveisthebeautifulblackwoman.com**

Deborah Day A Bay Area poet, Deborah is the author of the Mindful Messages Healing Thoughts for the Hip and Hop Descendants from the Motherland and is the creator of the Mindful Messages Mentoring Program. Contact Ms. Deborah Day, Ashay by the Bay, Post Office Box 2394, Union City, California 94587 Phone: (510) 520-2742 Fax: (510) 477-0967 E-mail: **poetashay@aol.com** Website: **www.ashaybythebay.com**

Don P. Demyers Professor of Biology at the University of the District of Columbia in Washington, D.C. I am a poet and writer. I have written over 100 poems. My poem, "I Think" won an Editors choice award from the International Society of Poets. In addition, I have been awarded the Outstanding Achievement in Poetry Award, Merit Silver Award Bowl, Who's Who in Poetry Award and the Bronze Commemorative Award Medallion as a member of the International Society of Poets. Don P. Demyers, Ph.D., 12007 Fort Washington Road, Fort Washington, Maryland 20744 Phone: (301) 203-9166 E-mail: **ddem776975@aol.com**

Rita Frances Dove African-American writer and teacher who was poet laureate of the United States in 1993-95. Pulitzer Prize for Poetry, 1987. Fulbright, Guggenheim Fellowships, 2 National Endowment For The Arts Grants, Professor of English at the University of Virginia Member of PEN Club; Literary Lion of New York Public Library. Contact Ms. Rita Frances Dove, University of Virginia, Post Office Box 400121, Charlottesville, Virginia 22903 Phone: (434) 924-6618 Fax: (434) 924-1478 E-mail: **rfd4b@virginia.edu**

John D. Evans National award winning poet and author. John D. Evans, TEPC, Inc., Post Office Box 2177 Oak Park, Illinois 60303 Phone: (708) 214-0706 Fax: (708) 383-1336 E-mail: **jdpoetry1@aol.com**

Latorial Faison Her poetry has been published in various literary magazines, journals, and poetry sites. She is author of Secrets of My Soul (2001) and Immaculate Perceptions (2003, CK Press). A native of Courtland, Virginia, she studied English at the University of Virginia, and Virginia Tech. Latorial Faison, Cross Keys Press, Post Office Box 145, Highwood, Illinois 60040 E-mail: **Latorial@PoeticallySpeaking.net** Website: **Latorial@PoeticallySpeaking.net**

Naomi F. Faust Author of four books, three books of poetry and a scholarly book entitled Discipline and the Classroom Teacher (1977). Her published books of poems are Speaking In Verse (1974), All Beautiful Things (1983) and And I Travel by Rhythms and Words (1990). Some of Faust's poems have been widely anthologized and others have appeared in magazines and newspapers, including the New York Voice, and Essence Magazine. The International Poets Academy conferred on Dr. Faust the award of International Eminent Poet. Former professor at Queen's College of the City University of New York. She was named Teacher/Author of the Year by a national journal for her book Discipline and the Classroom Teacher. Naomi Flowe Faust, 112-01 175th Street, Jamaica, New York 11433 Phone: (718) 291-5338

Peggy M. Fisher Holds an MA from Teachers College, Columbia University. Retired, Ms. Fisher is the author of "Lifting Voices: Voices of the Collective Struggle" (1999). Her poems have appeared in several anthologies including Commemorating Excellence: the 1998 Presidential Awards. She is one of the featured authors in an anthology of essays, The Story That Must Be Told, published by Loving Healing Press in June 2007. She has completed a memoir, tentatively titled, Journey to the Jewels Within. She has participated in many conferences and workshops including Hurston-Wright in 1999, The Philadelphia Black Writers' Conference past four years, NJ Council of Arts Writers Program July 2002, 2003, Goucher College 2004, Cave Canem March 2006. Ms. Fisher published "Search Lights for My Soul," in March 2006. Peggy Fisher, Post Office Box 2775, Camden, New Jersey 08101 E-mail: **pyramidcl@cs.com** Website: **www.pmmfisher.com**

Rebera Elliott Foston Author, poet, Dr Foston has published an inspirational journal entitled Peace on Earth, and 20 books of poetry which include No Stoppin' Sense, The Parade and In God's Time. You Don't Live On My Street, the signature volume of this collection was first published in 1991 and remains a favorite because of her sassy poem, "You Don't Live On My Street." When her poem "You Don't Live On My Street" was played on a radio show in Washington, DC, it was the most requested "song" of the day She has brought all of the compassion to her writing that she expressed as a Doctor of Medicine for thirty years. She completed her residency in Family Practice and became Board Certified and a Post Doctoral fellowship in teaching Family Medicine at Michigan State University in East Lansing, Michigan, 1984. Master of theological studies, Foston has examined healing from four different disciplines and shares her insights through her powerful poetry. Her other signature poems are "Annie's Baby" and "Not My Chile." She has performed on BET, and cable markets in New York and Chicago. Rebera Elliott Foston, M.D., DMin, Post Office Box 726, Clarksville, Tennessee 37041 Phone: (800) 418-0374 Fax: (931) 645-3500 E-mail: **minfoston@aol.com** Website: **www.drfoston.com**

Delores King-Freeman Poet, author, producer and host, Dee Freeman has published well received books of poetry entitled "Oceans of Love: To Us From Us" and Poetry She Wrote I: Oh, Magnify Him." She has had a number of poems appear in magazines, anthologies and new papers where some have been recognized with awards for their inspirational, even motivational message. She was presented with a commendation for the City and City Council during Black History Month in 2005. She continues to provide the Lansing State Journal with an article, book review or word of inspiration on a monthly basis. She co-hosts "poetry slams" held at various locations throughout the Greater Lansing area. Freeman looks forward to expanding her Poetree-N-Motion TV program which shares information of community events, history tidbits, book reviews and has guests with current community issues. Freeman is also a talented musical lyricist. Presently, she is in the completion stage of her first fiction novel-a project in conjunction with a movie producer. This novel "Wild, Untamed Michigan: The Way It Was" is scheduled to hit the stores in early or mid 2006, with the second of the "Poetry, She Wrote" series following close behind. Alumnus of Northwood University of Midland and former financial analyst for General Motors. Dee Freeman, 1127 Alexandria Drive, Lansing, Michigan 48917 Phone: (517) 321-3122 Fax: (517) 321-3122 E-mail: **deekfreeman@yahoo.com** Website: **www.deepoette.com**

Papi Kymone Freeman Writer/producer, playwright and poet, Papi Kymone Freeman is the founder of the National Black LUV Festival which was a Mayor's Art Award Finalist for Excellence in Service to the Arts in 2006, and is currently a board member for Words Beats & Life. He is the subject of one chapter of the book, Beat of A Different Drum: The Untold Stories of African Americans Forging Their Own Paths in Work and Life (Hyperion). In addition, he is the author of a book of poetry entitled, Blood Sweat & Tears. He is a founding member with Genesis Poets and has studied under the tutelage of the legendary independent filmmaker Haile Gerima. Freeman is set to produce his screenplay, Starrchildren in 2007. In 2005, Prison Poetry was awarded the 22nd Annual Larry Neal Award for Drama. Contact Papi Kymone Freeman, Frederick Douglas Station, Post Office Box 31243, Banneker City, Washington, DC 20030 Phone: (202) 547-2459 Fax: (301) 768-4007 E-mail: **kymone@prisonpoetry-theplay.com** Website: **www.prisonpoetry-theplay.com**

Andrea Gager Poet and an author Andrea has written one book of poetry, a play and is currently working on a second one. Andrea Gager, 830 Amsterdam Avemue, #8C, New York, New York 10025 Phone: (917) 392-0202 E-mail: **Pastrel1@aol.com**

Daniel Garrett Writer of journalism, fiction, poetry, and drama Garretts book reviews have appeared in American Book Review, The Quarterly Black Review of Books, Rain Taxi, The Review of Contemporary Fiction, and World Literature Today. He selected poetry for the male feminist magazine Changing Men. His own poetry has been published by AIM/America's Intercultural Magazine, Black American Literature Forum, The City Sun, Red River Review, UnlikelyStories.org, and a few small book anthologies. Garrett's essay "The Inner Life and the Social World in the Work of James Baldwin" was published by IdentityTheory.com. He has written a novel, Heroes and Friends, and three plays, Lessons in Demonology, The Art of Losing and An Enemy of the President: and these await publication. Daniel Garrett, 05-63 135th Street, Richmond Hill, New York 11419 E-mail: **dgarrett31@hotmail.com**

Carolyn Gibson A native of Boston, Massachusetts, and a Simmons College graduate, Gibson is author of a novel, "Repairman Jones" and a collection of 60 poems titled "Urban Poetry." Ms. Carolyn Gibson, Carolyn's Corner, Post Office Box 300160, Jamaica Plain, Massachusetts 02130 Phone: (617) 298-7484 Fax: (617) 298-1018 E-mail: **Carolynscorner@aol.com** Website: **www.Carolynscorner.com**

Richard Charles Gibson The authors first book of short stories Life Lessons was published in 2003. Contact Mr. Richard Charles Gibson, 2517 West Harrison Street, Chicago, Illinois 60612 Phone: (312) 243-5343 E-mail: **gibsonsnoopy@aol.com**

Michael Glover Born and raised in St. Matthews, South Carolina, Michael is the author of My Soul Speaks Wisdom: A Collection of Life, Love and Inspirational Poems for Everyday Living. He received a music scholarship to Johnson C. Smith University to play the snare drum where he majored in History and aspired to become a teacher, but instead became an actor. He was encouraged by friends and family to pursue acting because of his comedic talent. Michael started his career in North Carolina at the John Casablancas Modeling and Career Center. In New York, he studied and completed training at The American Academy of Dramatic Arts. Michael has appeared in numerous films, TV shows, and commercials. In addition, he has performed in Off Off Broadway shows in New York City; one notable show was "One Flew over the Cuckoo's Nest". Contact Mr. Michael Glover, 599 Franklin Avenue, #4R,Brooklyn, New York 11238 E-mail: **mysoulspeakswisdom@gmail.com**

C.D. Grant A nationally-published, versatile writer, poet and journalist since 1970 whose work has appeared in Essence Magazine (for which he was Music Editor for 5 Quindaro (Kansas), Suburban Styles (Westchester, New York), and numerous other periodicals. He is also a scholarly writer who has presented papers at Howard University, Pace University and Berkeley and an article has been included in the Educational Resource Information Center (ERIC) of Columbia University as a reference for African and African American music. He has two published books of poetry Keeping Time and Images in a Shaded Light. C.D. Grant, Publisher, Blind Beggar Press, Post Office Box 437, Bronx, New York 10467 Phone: (914) 683-6792 E-mail: **blindbeggar1@juno.com**   Website: **www.blindbeggarpress.com**

Bettye A. Gaines Poems, Poetry, Prose Food for the Soul. Evangelist Bettye Gaines, Women of Excellence Ministries, Post Office Box 21651, Columbia, South Carolina 29221 Phone: (803) 409-8712

Tania Guerrera Author of the book Thoughts and Transformations. The book contains poetry, art and essays all dealing with love, social issues, justice and spirituality from the point of view of an Afro-Puertorican and Native American (Arawak/Taino) woman. Tania Guerrera, Post Office Box 67, Spring Valley, New York 10977 E-mail: **theartist@taniaguerrera.com**

William Hairston Author, playwright and poet, William Hairston has had poems published in anthologies and magazines. He developed, published and edited the DC Pipeline (Washington, DC Government employees' newspaper, 40,000 monthly circulation); National Radio News Editor and Correspondent for the DNC Presidential Campaign of 1968 - Nation Wide). Mr. Hairston's books include: "The World of Carlos" (novel) "Sex and Conflict" (novel) "History of The National Capital Area Council/Boy Scouts of America" "Spaced Out" (space adventure) "Showdown At Sundown" (western novel)" Ira Frederick Aldridge" (The London Conflict) (Play, non-fiction). Contact William Hairston, 5501 Seminary Road, Falls Church, Virginia 22041 Phone: (703) 845-1281 E-mail: **WilliamRHairston1@msn.com**

Evelyn D. Hall Self-published author, residing in, Atlanta, Georgia, Ms. Hall has published three books, Enter Eve's Poetic Paradise, Dontay's Poetic Playground and Dontay's Alphabet Book of Color. Evelyn D. Hall, Post Office Box 1775, Mableton, Georgia 30126 E-mail: **lilpoet2you@aol.com** Website: **www.publish.bluesky40.com**

Robyn Maria Hamlin Author and Screenwriter. Novels, "The Zone of Danger Test" is my breakout novel. I have 3 other working novels in progress. "Shades of Gray" and "Zone of Danger" are my only two registered screenplays to date. I have 4 other working screenplays in progress. Poetry, "The Red Flag," "Bread Crumbs," "The Teamplayer," "A Hand for ME," and "There Is A River" are a few of my poems that have been published to date. My writings have also been featured in both EBONY (October 2005) and ESSENCE (January 2006) magazines. Contact Ms. Robyn Maria Hamlin, 1900 Wesleyan Drive, #2807, Macon, Georgia 31210 Phone: (478) 476-8776 E-mail: **weeda5weeda@aol.com**

Leslie Harris Born and raised in Detroit, Michgan. Married with two children. Received B.S. from Michigan State University and J.D. from University of Detroit Mercy School of Law. Author of 18 manuscripts of poetry. Individual works have been publsihed in various magazines and ezines (Facets Magazine, FRESH! Literary Magazine, Skyline Magazine, Fort Worth Poe, Sentinel Online Magazine and others). Currently working with an agent to secure first publishing deal for a full length book. Also a songwriter (in various genres). Member of the songwriting team known as Infectious Grooves. E-mail: **quality6287@aol.com**

Rochell D. (Ro Deezy) Hart Author of four published books, From The Ghettos To The Heavens (1999), A Black Girl's Song (Highbridge Press, NY 2001), Urban Journeys (2002) and the forthcoming Woke Up And Put My Crown On: The Project of 76 Voices. Rochell D. Hart, Post Office Box 20511, Portland, Oregon 97294 E-mail: **poetrybyro2@hotmail** Website: **www.cdbaby/rochelldhart**

Barbara Haskins Born in Hot Springs, Virginia, Barbara Haskins is the eldest daughter of Levi and Julia Haskins. She has been a resident of Queens, New York for over 40 years; where she has had a lasting commitment to uplift and preserve African-American self esteem. She is a poet, public speaker and educator who has professionally interacted with many African-American luminaries; including Media Host Bob Law, Dr. Jawanza Kunjufu, the Rev. Al Sharpton among others. Ms. Haskins, credited for bringing the Kwanzaa holiday celebration to Queens, New York over 25 years ago, has been heralded by legions of cult fans as the 'Nikki Giovanni' of the New Millennium. She began writing poetry approximately 15 years ago as a hobby to privately express her feelings about prevalent social issues; especially in regard to African-American children.   LET A NEW WOMAN RISE is her first published poetry collection. Ms. Haskins (also known as Barbara Scott) is a public speaker and educator and her commitment to preserve African-American self esteem is apparent through her countless array of cumulative, civic and political citations. Her legacy includes two married children and two grandchildren. Contact Ms. Barbara Haskins, 4465 PReSS, 610-A East Battlefield Road, Suite 279, Springfield, Missouri 65807 Phone: (866) 842-1042 Fax: (775) 257-1286 E-mail: **press4465@yahoo.com** Website: **www.4465press.com**

Linda Hayes Born Linda Diane Mayfield, this aspiring African American poetess grew up in the Red Hook housing projects, of Brooklyn, New York. She graduated from Kingsborough Community College with an Associate in Applied Science degree in Data Processing. Author of a self-published poetry chapbook, "Life Is A Roller Coaster." This book is a collection of poems depicting life's ups, downs twists and turns. She covers such topics as the joys of motherhood, the loss of a parent, abortion, college graduation, homelessness, 9/11 to name a few. Ms. Linda Hayes, 31 Palmetto Drive, New Castle, Delaware 19720 E-mail: **ldmhayes@yahoo.com** Website: **www.angelfire.com/mh/blackfaces/RollerCoaster.html**

Janet Marlene Henderson Adjunct English Composition Professor with the City Colleges of Chicago. She has lectured at Chicago State University and East-West University. A writer of romantic fiction, her first novel is LUNCH WITH CASSIE (2005). Her second novel, THE ASSASSIN WHO LOVED HER, will be published in 2007. She has written four other books, which are all based on the contemporary romantic relationships of young, successful African-American females. Ms. Henderson, who has also lived in Virgina, North Carolina, California, Georgia, Hawaii and Washington, D.C., lives on the Southside of Chicago. Ms. Janet M. Henderson, 7837 South Ada Street, Chicago, Illinois 60620 Phone: (773) 873-8298 E-mail: **janhenderson_3@hotmail.com** Website: **www.janethenderson.net**

Kenneth Henry Jr. Owner of Real Ink Publishing and has authored a poetry book entitled Tears That Grip A Whole Nation. Real Ink specializes in poetry, self help, and youth centered books. Kenneth Henry, Jr., Real Ink Publishing, Post Office Box 496, League City, Texas 77574 E-mail: **realinkpub@yahoo.com**

Akua Lezli Hope   Award winning poet, fiction writer, journalist, and essayist. Author of Embouchure, Poems on Jazz and Other Musics; DARK MATTER, (the first!) anthology of African American Science Fiction, Time Warner Books, 2000; THE BLUELIGHT CORNER, edited by Rosemarie Robotham. Akua Lezli Hope, Post Office Box 33, Corning, New York 14830 E-mail: **akua@artfarm.com** Website: **www.artfarm.com**

Renda Horne Best-selling author of "Seven Years in Egypt: Recognizing Your Setbacks as Set-Ups for Your comeback!" and highly sought-after conference speaker, Renda Horne is founder/overseer and president of Woman at the Wail Ministries, Renda Horne Ministries, and Wailing Enterprises. Contact Ms. Renda Horne, Post Office Box 401479, Redford, Michigan 48240 E-mail: **renda@rendahorne.com** Website: **www.rendahorne.com**

Terence E. Jackson Singer, playwright, poet, and novelist of the controversial book "Nigger's Heaven," a novel. Owns fine arts gallery. Terence E. Jackson, 690 Durant Place, North East, #2, Atlanta, Georgia 30308 Phone: (404) 873-1296 E-mail: **terenceejackson@uspacegallery.com** Website: **www.uspacegallery.com**

Gary Johnson Both a writer and poet, Mr. Gary Johnson saw the need to create another, unique vehicle for emerging and established writers/artists of color. In 1977 he co-founded Blind Beggar Press. The title of the company comes from a poem written by Gary Johnson, Blind Beggar Blues, which speaks of a blind beggar who sees many things better than sighted people. Contact Mr. Gary Johnson, Publisher, Blind Beggar Press, Post Office Box 437, Bronx, New York 10467 Phone: (914) 683-6792 E-mail: **blindbeggar@juno.com**

Vanessa Alexander Johnson Author of When Death Comes a Knockin', a self-help, inspirational book about loss and the grief process (unpublished). She is also contributing author of the following anthologies: Down The Cereal Aisle (Daniels House Publications, 2003), Living by Faith (Obadiah Press, 2004), Celebrations Anthologies (Adassa Prendergast Publishers, 2004). Contact Vanessa Johnson, 303 Kennedy Street, Ama, Louisiana 70031 Phone: (504) 431-7360 E-mail: **vjohns1@bellsouth.net**

L. Dranae Jones Author and publisher of Provocative Poetry and Prose: Portraits of Black Love (2003). L. Dranae Jones aka Sardonyx Jade is the owner and operator of Sardonyx Jade Publishing (SJP), operating out of Los Angeles, California. He is a California State University Dominguez Hills graduate with a Bachelor of Arts in Psychology, have been published by Watermark Press, The International Library of Poetry, Poetry.com, Famous Poets Society, Nobel House, UK, Rolling Out Urban Style Weekly and Playgirl Magazine. He has published four calendars of poetry and the chap book Trap'd by Damnyo (2004). Contact Mr. L. Dranae Jones, Sardonyx Jade Publishing, 1401 North La Brea Avenue, Suite 137, Los Angeles, California Phone: (323) 898-7339 Fax: (213) 252-8471 E-mail: **ldjones@sardonyx-jade.com** Website: **www.sardonyx-jade.com**

Ty Granderson Jones Noted poet who has a spoken word band called Coloured Boyz featuring the famed legendary drummer of The Doors....John Densmore. Screenwriter with an MFA in Acting from UCSD in La Jolla, California. Ty Granderson Jones, Creole Celina Films, A division of Creative Quest, Inc., 8306 Wilshire Boulevard. Suite 432, Beverly Hills, California 90211 Phone: (323) 960-1035 E-mail: **tygrandjones@aol.com**

Joylynn M. Jossel Completed three diaries of poetry. Her first completed her first self-published novel, The Root of All Evil, St. Martin's Press picked up and re-released in June 2004. Joylynn M. Jossel, Post Office Box 298238, Columbus, Ohio 43229 Phone: (614) 284-7933 E-mail: **joylynnjossel@aol.com** Website: **www.joylynnjossel.com**

Chris Knight Author of two books of poetry and practical wisdom for everyday living. Her books entitled, Sister To Sister: Dimensions of a Woman and Sister To Brother: From My Heart to Yours, focuses on self empowerment and relationships with self and significant others. Chris is currently working on her third book of poetry and practical wisdom for young people due out in early spring. She also is writing her first novel that should be completed in the fall. Her forthcoming CD entitled 4YoMind to be released in the spring. Contact Chris Knight, Post Office Box 245457, Brooklyn, New York 11224 E-mail: **Mindgear@Hotmail.com** Website: **www.4YoMind.com**

Melvin Lars Born in Shreveport, Louisiana, May 11,1953. 1975 graduate (BS/Health and English) Louisiana Tech University. Extended matriculation (MA) Texas Southern University 1983, Eastern Michigan University, Saginaw Valley State University, Centenary College (Administrative certification), and Youngstown State University. Occupation: Principal; Woodrow Wilson High School, Youngstown, Ohio. Pastor/founder: Genesis Christian Life Ministries. Publications: Two (2) books of Poetry; "Painted Images", "Reflections of Life". One (1) Educational offering; "Dare To Be Positive/Slammin' Limitations". Honors: Golden Gloves/Heavyweight bosing champion (1975); All (MVSU) SWAC off. guard, NFL free-agent 1975. Greek affiliation: Kappa Alpha Psi Fraternity, Inc. Civic duties: Big Brothers/Big Sisters - others; too numerous to list. Contact Mr. Melvin Lars, 2032 East Reserve Circle, Avon, Ohio 44011 Phone: (440) 934-8032 Fax: (440) 934-8033 E-mail: **larschief@yahoo.com**

Suzanne B. Lester Author of "Expressions from a Jar of Clay" which is her first published book of inspirational/religious poetry. The author currently resides in Athens, Georgia and is employed at Athens Technical College. She is an active member of Timothy Baptist Church under the leadership of the infamous Bishop Jerry F. Hutchins of Jerry F. Hutchins Ministries. In addition to publishing her first book, the author writes and sells specialty poetry. She is also a contributing writer to Reflect-A-Moment newsletter which is a web newsletter by Margie Epps and is also a kingdom poet of the site. Suzanne B. Lester, 151 Sweetgum Way, Athens, Georgia 30601 Phone: (706) 353-3738 E-mail: **poetrylady3@yahoo.com**

Cassie A. Levy Author and poet Ms. Cassie A. Levy is a contributing author to "Delta Girls, Stories of Sisterhood" her story is entitled "Where's the 1st Aid Kit?"; contributing poet to "Violets, Inspirational Poems by Women of Delta Sigma Theta Sorority, Inc." (multiple poems); Poem entitled "Late at Night" accepted for publication by the American Poets Society, Poem entitled "Echo My Blessings" in recognition of Nikki Giovanni placed 1st runner-up in contest sponsored by the Writers of the Wood in Houston, Texas. Pending publications include: The Essence of My Soul (manuscript submitted for consideration for the Walt Whitman Award), article- "Sexual Harassment: Behind the Veil in the 21st Century" and poem - "In My Closet." Cassie Levy, 4950 Sugar Grove #2105, Stafford, Texas 77477 Phone: (832) 465-4064 E-mail: **essence4thesoul@yahoo.com**

Pamela deLeon-Lewis A motivational speaker and poet, Ms. deLeon- Lewis, (a breast cancer survivor), has authored ' Smiling Thru the Tears- a Breast Cancer Survivor Odyssey, her first book of motivational and inspirational poetry that empowers the survivors of cancer. Pamela deleon-Lewis, Post Office Box 101041, Brooklyn, New York 11210 Phone: (917) 673-6350 E-mail: **pamela.deleonlewis@gmail.com**

Tracey Michae'l Lewis As a writer, Lewis' collection of poetry, Collapsed on the Wings of a Sigh: a Poetic Journey won 2002 Best Poetry Book by the SCBC Independent Publishers Awards. She is also the author of the new collection, Divine Nepotism. Dubbed as a young Nikki Giovanni, Divine Nepotism was recently endorsed by the legendary poet/writer. Lewis has completed work on several screenplays, and the critically acclaimed stage play, KHEPERA, which ran off-Broadway in 2002. Tracey Michae'l Lewis, 1845 West Superior, Apartment #1R, Chicago, Illinois 60622 E-mail: **traceylewis33@yahoo.com**

Craigal R. Lindo Author of Heart's Glory. I write poems to help you express your feelings and emotions to that special someone in your life. Craigal R. Lindo, Heart Writer, LLC, 2551 NW 41st Avenue, Suite 405, Lauderhill, Florida 33313 E-mail: **Heartwriter14@aol.com** Website: **www.heartsglory.com**

Haki R. Madhubuti Poetry has been widely anthologized, Mr. Madhubuti has given readings and workshops at over 1,000 colleges, universities and community centers in Africa, Asia, South America, the Caribbean and the United States. He has been a contributing editor of Black Scholar, Cololines, GRIO', and The Zora Neale Hurston Forum. He received the 1991 American Book Award and was named Author of the Year by the Illinois Association of Teachers of English in 1991. Haki R. Madhubuti, Third World Press, 7822 South Dobson Street, Chicago, Illinois 60619   Phone: (773) 651-0700 Fax: (773) 651-7286   E-mail: **twpress3@aol.com** Website: **www.thirdworldpressinc.com**

Maxine Malone A native Californian who now resides in Georgia, the author holds a doctoral degree in Special Education. She currently has poetic work published international and national. Askthlogical Views of the Tigress is her latest work. Maxine Malone, 175 Melrose Creek Drive, Stockbridge, Georgia Phone: (323) 422-0165 E-mail: **Suwynn@charter.net**

Michele Rene Matthews An essayist and poet Michele's work has been published in the Journal of Intergroup Relations and How We Got Over: Testimonies of Faith, Hope and Courage (Reyomi Publishing, June 2003). Her debut novel, Raymond's Daughters was released in September of 2004. Michele Rene Matthews, 5706 Earnhardt Street, Virginia Beach, Virginia 23464 Phone: (757) 420-9119 E-mail: **chele_rene@hotmail.com**

Janie McGee Published writer and storytelling through performance poetry; creative historical novels, short stories, and articles with a Christian base and reflection of black history; artbooks, journals, and prayer books self published and handmade by artist with inspirational themes. Janie McGee, Vintage Coffee Press, 2406 Forest Edge Court, Suite 302B, Odenton, Maryland 21113 E-mail: **vintagecoffeepress@hotmail.com** Website: **www.sundaymorninz.com**

Karen McMeo Her poetry has appeared in ABAFAZI, the Simmons College Journal of Women of African Descent. She holds a Bachelor of Arts in English from the University of Massachusetts at Boston and a Master of Arts in English from Northeastern University. She has worked as a college English instructor, freelance writer, proofreader/copyeditor, public relations assistant, and as a staff reporter. She works as a manuscripts coordinator and is completing Holy Ghost Stories. Karen McMeo, Post Office Box 6382, Woodbridge, Virginia 22195 E-mail: **karenmcmeo@hotmail.com** Website: **www.perfectpathpublishing.com**

Renée McRae Author of the inspirational book of poetry entitled Truth In Rhyme, a textbook for NYC Board of Education. Keynote speaker, workshop facilitator and performance poet, her award-winning poetry has been published in seven anthologies of the National Library of Poetry, and is also displayed on poetry.com. She is currently facilitating on-going workshops with New York City Board of Education and Mental Health Association of NYC, Inc. Renée McRae, Poetic Motivations, Post Office Box 230174, Hollis, New York 11423 Phone: (877) 814-9864 Fax: (253) 681-0464 Website: **www.reneemcrae.com**

Michelle Mellon Served as communications consultant for four years before completing her Master's in Liberal Studies and becoming a freelance writer and editor. She has had articles published in Imprint and Blue Planet Quarterly, poetry in journals and anthologies such as Hodgepodge and Seasons of the Heart, and was co-author of a book chapter on professional mentoring. Recently completed articles for the forthcoming Encyclopedia of African American Literature, and is working on a collection of short stories. Michelle Mellon, 2416 Casa Way, Walnut Creek, California 94597 Phone: (925) 876-4121 Fax: (818) 474-7236 E-mail: **michelle@mpmellon.com** Website: **www.mpmellon.com**

Natalie Milton Writer/Poet. Natalie Milton, 320 Oak Park Square, College Park, Georgia 30349 Phone: (404) 761-0484 E-mail: **n1poem@bellsouth.net**

S. Renee Mitchell Author, writer, playwright, poet, columnist, and novelist, Renee is an award-winning newspaper columnist in Portland, Oregon. She tells people that being a columnist is the best job she's ever had.   But what feeds her spirit is writing poetry and advocating for emotionally wounded women. She also is a powerful public speaker, who uses poetry and personal experiences to bring audiences to their feet, as well as touch their hearts. Renee, a survivor of domestic violence and sexual assault, experienced decades of low self-esteem and feelings of unworthiness. Her tireless and creative work in the last few years to support other survivors of domestic violence resulted in her being selected as one of 2006's 21 Leaders of the 21st Century by New York City-based Women eNews, which bestowed Renee with the international Ida B. Wells Award for Bravery in Journalism. She was also nominated for the 2005 Pulitzer Prize for commentary. And in 2004, BrainstormNW magazine, based in Lake Oswego, selected her as one of the "15 Most Interesting People in Oregon." Renee, who has her MBA, is a single mother of three young children. She is an engaging public speaker, a beaded jewelry creator, a graphic designer, a multi-media artist and a frequent public-school volunteer. She has authored three books of poetry and has recorded two spoken word CDs, all with original music. While completing her MBA in 2001, she opened a small business, NappyRoots Press, a creative consulting company. She speaks to groups about diversity, feminism, women's empowerment, self-esteem and getting the media's attention, among other issues. She also publishes work of local poets, designs and sells T-shirts and greeting cards, and plans Self-Pampering events for women. S. Renee Mitchell, 6835 SW Capitol Hill Road #34, Portland, Oregon 97219 Phone: (503) 803-0864 E-mail: **reneemitchellspeaks@yahoo.com** Website: **www.reneemitchellspeaks.com**

Tiffany Mitchell   Also known as Wrythym, I write poetry and spoken word with song. Tiffany Mitchell, 177 Sycamore Drive, Apartnt110, Park Forest, Illinois 60466 Phone: (708) 748-1392 E-mail: **tmitchel214@msn.com**

Linda Everett Moye' Poet and author of four books of poetry, From A Delta's Heart, The Courage to Say It, Where Spirits Dance and Imagine This. She is also publisher, managing editor, and a contributing author of the collective work, Delta Girls Stories of Sisterhood. She is completing her first two novels for publication in 2005, The Pharaoh's Queen and The Pledge. Her work is included in the poetry anthology, Violets and the cookbook, Occasions to Savor. She has served as guest speaker at colleges, universities, churches, artistic and literary events. She was inducted into the San Antonio Women's Hall of Fame, 2001 in the Creative Arts category for her writing accomplishments. Linda Everett Moye', LEJ Poetic Expressions, Post Office Box 301973, San Antonio, Texas 78703 Phone: (210) 643-43657 Fax: (512) 482-8454 E-mail: **lindamoye@aol.com**   Website: **www.lindamoye.com**

Anthony Jerome Mungin Born in Charleston, South Carolina on April 15, 1965, Mr. Mungin has been writing for over 15 years. He recently published a book of poetry called Conceptions of the Heart and Mind, and Completed a novel called Same Sins Separate Paths. He has started another novel Ungodly Promises, a mystery/drama bringing to light one man's fear about the consequences of not paying homage to God. He holds a bachelors degree in Business as well as a M.B.A., both of which he considers major accomplishments, given the many obstacles. Contact Mr. Anthony J. Mungin, Post Office Box 42087, Houston, Texas 77242   E-mail: **ajmungin@houston.rr.com** Website: **www.conceptionsoftheheartandmind.com**

Daphne Muse Writer, social commentator, and poet, Daphne has written more than 300 feature articles, essays, reviews and op-ed pieces for major newspapers, academic journals and on-line zines. Daphne Muse, 2429 East 23rd Street, Oakland, California 94601 Phone: (510) 436-4716 Fax: (510) 261-6064 E-mail: **msmusewriter@sbcglobal.net**

Ngoma Performance poet, multi-instrumentalist, singer/songwriter and paradigm shifter, who for over 40 years has used culture as a tool to raise sociopolitical and spiritual consciousness through work that encourages critical thought. A former member of the Spirit House Movers and Players with Amiri Baraka and the Contemporary Freedom Song Duo, SERIOUS BIZNESS, Ngoma weaves poetry and song that raises contradictions and searches for a solution for a just and peaceful world.   He was the Prop Slam winner of the 1997 National Poetry Slam Competition in Middletown, Connecticut and was published in African Voices Magazine, Long Shot Anthology, The Underwood Review, Signifyin' Harlem Review and 'Bum Rush The Page/Def Poetry Jam Anthology & Poems on the Road To Peace (Volumes 1, 2 &3, Yale Press). He was featured in the PBS Spoken Word Documentary, "The Apro-Poets" with Allen Ginsberg. He has hosted the slam at the Dr. Martin Luther King Festival of Social and Environmental Justice Festival (Yale University-New Haven, Connecticut) for the past 10 years. His CD's are Movie Documentary "Ngoma: Alive and In Your Face from NYC", "Digitation: Solo Didgeridoo Musik for Meditation" and "Ancient Future Meditational Musik," and Reflections (!964 - 2006). Ngoma, 1845 Adam Clayton Powell Boulevard, #3D, New York, New York Phone: (212) 663-2591 E-mail: **Ngomazworld@aol.com** Website: **www.Ngomazworld.com**

Pam Osbey Author, spoken word artist, and teacher she recently published two books, A Love Story (November 2003), and her first novel, Cause I Can was released in 2004. Pam Osbey, Osbey Books', 7465 South Shore Drive, Chicago, Illinois 60649 Phone: (773) 342-4694 E-mail: **osbeybooks@sbcglobal.net** Website: **www.mochasistah.com**

Frances Callaway Parks Author, poet, seminar leader, speaker, Ms. Parks is the author of several titles. Her latest is a book of inspirational poetry " From the Depths of Silence" released September 2004. Parks is a professor at Chicago State University and publishes under her own company, Victory Services Ink. Contact Frances Callaway Park, Victory Services Ink, 3473 King Drive #333, Chicago, Illinois Phone: (312) 326-2530 Fax: (312) 326-1047 E-mail: **fcparks@sbcglobal.net** Website: **www.wordstransformimgworlds.com**

Richard A. Parks Jr. A 27 year old poet/author who has self published two works, Someone Is Sleeping In My Head and Lost In A Mellow Rain. His book Someone Is Sleeping In My Head which was introduced to the poetry world in December of 2000, was nominated for a Golden Pen Award for poetry collection of the year by the Black Writer's Alliance. His work has appeared on Timbooktu, Mental Satin, The Writeous, Poetry.com, Black Writer's Alliance, Nubian Chronicles and many various newspapers and editorials throughout the southeast. He is a member of the Black Writer's Alliance, The International Society of Poets, and The National Library of Poetry. He is the founder of his own company Nusawf Inc., to promote his own work as well as others. Richard A, Parks Jr., Post Office Box 23901, Alexandria, Virginia 22304 Fax: (703) 614-1663 E-mail: **rip@richardparksjr.com** Website: **www.richardparksjr.com**

Sandra Peoples Author, award winning poet, playwright, motivational speaker and instructor Sandra is owner of BlackBerry Literary Services, a company that exists to help writers become authors in all aspects of writing; publication and promotion of the authors she works with, fiction and non-fiction, poetry, and children's books. Sandra Peoples, BlackBerry Literary Services, 2956 Mackin Road, Flint, Michigan 48504 Phone: (810) 234-0899 E-mail: **bblit@hotmail.com**

Queen Esther Franks Phillips A licensed minister of the gospel of Jesus Christ, freelance writer, author, poet, motivational speaker, public administrator, and mother of three. Ms. Phillips is the founder of Majestic Publications, a Christian online writing ministry. Queen Esther Phillips, Post Office Box 980372, Houston, Texas 77098 Phone: (713) 866-7768 E-mail: **qfphillips@majesticpublications.com**

Marcia Denrique Preudhomme Published a collection of poetry, Reflections of Realism, a collection of short fiction, Stranger Than Fiction, and completed a booklet of poems, The Heart of Truth. She has also received the Editor's Choice Award for Outstanding Achievement in Poetry from the International Library of Poetry, and has been selected for inclusion in the 59th Edition of Marquis Who's Who in America. Contact Marcia Denrique Preudhomme, c/o Teresa R Martin, Esq., Law Offices of Teresa R Martin, P.C., 67 Wall Street, Suite #2211, New York, New York 10005 Phone: (212) 709-8224 E-mail: **denriquebooks@aol.com** Website: **www.denrique.com**

Stephanie M. Pruitt Voted 2004 Poet of the Year by SpokenVizions Magazine, Stephanie is the author of "I AM: A Poetic Journey Towards Self Definition" (2002), and she released her first spoken word CD entitled Choice Words, which is poetry, prose, music, storytelling and much more! She co-hosts a social commentary radio talk show and travels nationwide conducting poetry readings, performances and workshops. Contact Ms. Stephanie M. Pruitt, 1708 21st Avenue South, Suite #149, Nashville, Tennessee 37212 Phone: (615) 545-8018 E-mail: **SPruitt@StephaniePruitt.com** Website: **www.StephaniePruitt.com**

Darren B. Rankins Poet and author of two books of poetry. Christian T-shirt ministry. Darren B. Rankins, 117 Winsford Court Murfreesboro, Tennessee 31730 Phone: (615) 898-0471 E-mail: **Darren_Rankins@yahoo.com** Website: **www.purethoughts.net**

F. B. Rasheed Born, October 14, 1946, Arcadia, Oklahoma, grew up in Guthrie, Oklahoma. Attended and Graduated from the Historically Black, Langston University in 1969, with a degree in Math Education. Taught ninth grade math classes at John F. Kennedy Jr. High School in Oklahoma City before being drafted into the US Army. Served in Viet Nam one year, discharged in December 1970. Graduated from University of Oklahoma in 1972 with MRCPL. 1000's of poems and some short stories to credit with 2 self publish books of poems, "Some Sum Words" and "Read Qur'an the Message You Can Depend Upon.". Contact Mr. F. B. Rasheed, 1621 South West Pennsylvania Avenue, Lawton, Oklahoma 73501 Phone: (580) 678-4993 E-mail: **fbrasheed1@aol.com**

Pat McLean RaShine A Philadelphia Pennsylvania poet and author, Ms. Pat Mclean-Rashine has two books, "HEALING HER HURTS: A collection of short stories that speaks to the soul of a woman," and "Ain't Gonna Bite My Tongue NO More. She is the recipient of several awards, including 1st place for the Sonia Sanchez/Audre Lorde Poetry Competition and second place for Judith Stark Creative Writing Competition at Community College of Philadelphia. Pat presently co-facilitates poetry and creative writing workshops Temple University's Pan-African Studies Community Education Program (PASCEP) and at Drexel University, both of Philadelphia. She has appeared on several multi media programs, such as WUSL Power 99 FM, WHAT AM "Etches", Politics & Poetry, Philadelphia Board of Education Public TV and WYBE "Showbiz Rap," to name a few. Recently she was published in "BMa: The Sonia Sanchez Literary Review – Legends and Legacies." "Life Spices From Seasoned Sistahs." and, X-Magazine. Pat McLean RaShine, 632 Elkins Avenue, Philadelphia Pennsylvania 19120 Phone: (215) 683-3620 E-mail: **PMcPoet@aol.com**

Darlene Mai Roberts Poet/Author of Erotica Escapades. Contact Ms. Darlene Mai Roberts, 451 Robinson Drive, Dunleith Estates, Wilmington, Delaware 19801 Phone: (302) 573-5115 E-mail: **ladydigsu2003@yahoo.com**

Janeen Robichaud Author of two erotic/romance books entitled "Candy" and "Candy2, The Sequel" and "They Killed Me." Janeen Robichaud, 7000 Donald Street, Millville, New Jersey 08332 E-mail: **candyjaneen@aol.com** Website: **www.geocities.com/candyjaneen**

Tina Denise Rodgers Published poet Tina is a graduate from East Carolina University with a BSW in Social Work and trained CPS. She is a motivational speaker for African-American women and youth, and has published a book of poems Expressions of the Heart about real life situations. Tina Denise Rodgers, Post Office Box 1236, Williamston North Carolina, 27892 Phone: (252) 217-9806 E-mail: **tdrjames@yahoo.com**

Christopher Donshale Sims Poet, spoken word artists and author of three chapbooks of poetry: Super Lyrical (2003), Knowledge Manifest: A Book of Life, Community and Culture (2006), and most recently, Barefoot On Wooden Floors (2006). Christopher Sims, 312 Adams Street, Rockford, Illinois 61107 E-mail: **universoulove@yahoo.com**

TyQucondra Smith Senior English major at the University of Central Oklahoma. Member of the Society of Urban Poets (S.O.U.P.) in Oklahoma City. My self-published book of poetry is called Kingdom Poetry. I have a CD to accompany the book where I am ministering the spoken word with music in the background. I opened for world renowned Gospel artist Shirley Caesar in concert in 2005. I opened for Martin Luther King III with a poem from my book when he came to speak at my University (2006). Ty Smith, 1201 North Fretz, #79, Edmond, Oklahoma 73003 E-mail: **kami7910@yahoo.com** Website: **http://speaklife2day.tripod.com**

R. Spirit Received Editor's Choice Award for poem "Dancing Home." Author of new book, The special extended-edition of Dancing Home, A Story of Ancient Vibrations, Published 2007. The original shorter version of the story was published in 2005, and is now out-of-print. R. Spirit is the pen-name of an African American Woman born in the Central Valley of California and raised in the Bay Area, California. She has a degree in Economics which gave her the research skills needed to prepare for her book. She also completed a news writing and reporting course at Stanford University and experience as a religion and education journalist which gave her the writing skill needed to complete her book. R. Spirit, SkyPoint, Ltd., Post Office Box 148, Pleasanton, California 94566 Phone: (925) 426-1120 E-mail: **gina@dancinghometravel.com** Website: **www.dancinghometravel.com**

Cheryl Samuel Stover Dr. Stover is the owner of Academic Connections, a growing consulting business offering customized services to meet your organization's educational and training needs. She has three books available for purchase, From the Inside Out: How to Transform Your School to Increase Student Achievement, Elementary Basic Skills Through Black History; and Walk Out of the Shadows: Poetry to Inspire and Encourage Youth in the 21st Century. This book was written to give our young people a sense of self-worth, hope, and faith to look forward to a successful life. The book was inspired by Dr. Stover's many years of working with disadvantaged and incarcerated youth who faced daily challenges because of poverty, malfunctioning homes, emotional problems, academic difficulties and a variety of other adversities. Dr. Cheryl Samuel Stover, 3516 John G. Richards Road, Post Office Box 153, Liberty Hill, South Carolina 29074 Phone: (803) 273-3772 E-mail: **chrylstover@yahoo.com** Website: **www.wastelandpress.net**

George Edward Tait Born in Oakland and raised in Harlem, George graduated from Pace University in 1968 with a B.A. in English Language and Literature and a minor in French Language and Literature after being a member of the literary society and The Pace Press. From 1968-1972, he taught and tutored English at Queens College while conducting Creative Writing workshops. Defining music as the poetry of sound, Tait became a bandleader and from 1972 to 1975 spearheaded a group called Black Massical Music. He founded The Society of Afrikan Poets and produced a seven year series of weekly poetry readings entitled Black Words for a Wednesday Night. While teaching at Malcolm-King College (1981-1986), his first volume of poetry At Warwas published in 1983, the same year he was named The Poet Laureate of Afrikan Nationalism by leaders of the nationalist community. Several of Tait's poems and articles were published by the New York Amsterdam News. At Arms was published in 1992 in addition to his work being included in the landmark anthology Brotherman; The Odyssey of Black Men in America (1995). George Edward Tait, Post Office Box 1305, New York, New York 10035 E-mail: **georgeedwardtait@msn.com** Website: **www.georgeedwardtait.org**

Jarvis Talley Author of the debut book, No Candles. He began his literary journey as a spoken word artist and performer who has been highlighted at the Showtime at Apollo, BET, and venues across the nation. His work has been highlighted in Ebony, Consciousness and Noire Magazines and featured on many literary sites including, Trimaxx Publishers, The Writers Inn, and Black Men In America. He is writing his second book, 7 Troubles, "Journey to the Green Eyes Beneath the Fedora", slated for publication in 2007. Jarvis Talley, Post Office Box 1265, Austell, Georgia 30012 E-mail: **mrtalley@gmail.com** Website: **www.mrtalley.com**

Antoinette Oglesby Taylor Playwright/Writer of greeting cards, poems and short stories. I have 5 plays that have been stage read in Louisville, Kentucky. Antoinette Oglesby Taylor, 6411 Shirley Avenue, Prospect, Kentucky 40059 E-mail: **jtnursing@aol.com**

Saundra Lee Taylor I'm a young 55 year Black Female from the midwest. I've written some poety over the years, and one is published. My frist love is the theatre. I have written and directed 6 plays. (all Christian base). I believe in God and I trust that my future is a bright one. Saundra Lee Taylor, 1117 North 24th Street, Saint Joseph, Missouri 64506 Phone: (816) 244-7099 Fax: (816) 232-7435 E-mail: **still_i_rise2@yahoo.com**

Juanita Torrence-Thompson The authors 5th poetry book, New York and African Tapestries (Fly By Night Press) is Small Press Review "pick". As Editor/Publisher of non-profit Mobius, The Poetry Magazine since 2006, she has 2 acclaimed issues with award-winning poets: Rita Dove, Nikki Giovanni, Marge Piercy, Diane Wakoski, Robert Bly, Samuel Menashe, Colette Inez, Toi Derricotte, Daniela Gioseffi, Louis Reyes Rivera, Hal Sirowitz, & Mobius 25th anniversary gala. Juanita has read on TV & radio & widely at U.S. colleges, schools, libraries, stores and South Africa, Singapore & Switzerland. Featured speaker Nati Federation of State Poetry Societies convention San Antonio, AAUW, etc. Read at Queensboro President Helen Marshall events, Queens Theatre, Queens Botanical Garden, New Years Marathon Reading, New York Summer Festival, etc. Published in Europe, Canada, Australia, widely in U.S. journals. Poetry columns in New York and Massachusetts papers. 2nd prize spoken word. Juanita Thompson, Torderwarz Publishing Company, Post Office Box 751205, Forest Hills, New York 11375 E-mail: **poetrytown@earthlink.net** Website: **www.mobiuspoetry.com**

Juanita Torrence Thompson Freelance writer and poet, her first book of poetry was Wings Span to Eternity, then Spanning the Years, which was endorsed by poets Rochelle Ratner, Maria Mazziotti Gillan as well as EBONY and Newsday. Celebrating a Tapestry of Life, her third book, was endorsed by Gordon Parks, Nikki Giovanni, as well as Merle English of Newsday. She is currently writing a book about her mother, a noted Baha'i and humanitarian. Eductaion: M.A. in Communications from Fordham University and B.S. in Business and Communications from SUNY, Empire State College. She holds past and present memberships in The Poetry Society of America, the Society of Children's Book Writers and Illustrators, and the American Association of University Women. She is listed in A Directory of American Poets and Fiction Writers, and Who's Who Among African Americans

Maxine E. Thompson Writer, poet and literary agent. Maxine E. Thompson, Black Butterfly Press, Post Office Box 25279, Philadelphia Pennsylvania, 19119 E-mail: **maxtho@aol.com** Website: **www.maxinethompson.com**

Wilbur Thornton Teacher, community worker, actor, instructor, and new author of the book, "The StoryTeller" Uncle Will Tip-Top-Tips, poems, short stories, tips, and fun!. Wilbur "Thorntize" Thornton , Andrew College, 413 College Street, Cuthbert, Georgia 39840 Phone: (229) 209-5218 E-mail: **wilburthornton@andrewcollege.edu**

Brenda M. Tillman The author shares her life experiences – real and imagined, through poetic expression, in her first book, Shades of Mandingo. A native of Hartford, Connecticut, Brenda M. Tillman, who now resides in Atlanta, Georgia, uses the vibrancy and vitality of the metropolitan city as the melting pot to present her talents. Her employment background includes various positions in state government, business and higher education. Through her volunteer efforts, she has been the editor of several newsletters and magazines. She has been writing poetry since her preteen years. She has interviewed several jazz musicians and has been a contributing writer for former Atlanta magazine, Strictly Jazz. Those interviewed include pianist David Beniot, violinist Regina Carter, the late Art Porter, saxophonist, and vocalist Dianne Reeves. She has also written book reviews for Black Issues Book Review Magazine and contributed scriptural-based messages in religious booklets. She is a member of the African Methodist Episcopal Church and Delta Sigma Theta Sorority, Inc. Brenda M. Tillman, Jobrelika Enterprises International, LLC, Post Office Box 311223, Atlanta, Georgia 31131 Phone: (404) 556-7534 E-mail: **shadesofmandingo@yahoo.com**

toniwo Through her poetry, toniwo made people look at their situations and laugh at them. THAT'S WHAT YOU GET FOR RUNNING WITH SCISSORS came from toniwo's inability to contain her observations to a few verses. Some of her creative work has been featured in Black & Single Magazine, Honey Magazine, an upcoming poem featured in Essence Magazine and several national anthologies. toniwo has also been featured on ArtistFirst radio show. toniwo, Blacklight Productions, 2410 South Kirkwood, Suite 136, Houston, Texas 77077 Phone: (713) 591-6610 Fax: (281) 870-1633 E-mail: **toni@toniwo.com** Website: **www.toniwo.com**

Kendal S. Turner Author and Poet, Kendal has written Broken: Yet Sustained By God and the book Anatomy Of The Soul; revealing in more depth the struggles of her past, the redemptive power of Christ and the peace, prosperity and pleasures of Kingdom living. She has done radio interviews on 1140am in Oklahoma. Kendal S. Turner, Post Office Box 32713, Oklahoma City, Oklahoma 73123 E-mail: **contact@kendalsturner.com**

Vincent Tyler Author, Mr. Vincent Tyler has performed at a variety of venues, including poetry sets, book clubs and book signings but it is the way he brings his writing to life during a performance that often first captures what becomes loyal readers. Mr. Tyler's well recognized piece, "Chocolate Cookies" is a story about a man who's life drastically changes after meeting the woman whom he believes to be his soulmate. Mr. Vincent Tyler, Rose Petals Publishing, Post Office Box 19071, Chicago, Illinois 60619 E-mail: **chccookies@aol.com**   Website: **vtyler@rosepetalspublishing.com**

Carmel S. Victor Author of award-winning novel: "Facing Our Skeletons" and Best Work of Poetry for 2005 "Every Day Again: Real Life through Poetry and Short Stories." Carmel S. Victor, Post Office Box 1132, Union, New Jersey 07083 E-mail: **carmel@carmelsvictor.com** Website: **www.carmelsvictor.com**

Frank X Walker   Author of four collections of poetry, Affrilachia, Black Box, Buffalo Dance and most recent When Winter Come. He is also the editor of Eclipsing a Nappy New Mellinium and America! What's My Name: The Other 'Poets' Unfurl the Flag. Walker is the editor of PLUCK! The Journal of Affrilachian Arts and Culture, a founding member of the Affrilachian Poets and a Cave Canem fellow. He is currently the Writer In Resident at Northern Kentucky University and resides in Cincinnati, Ohio. Frank X Walker, Northern Kentucky University, Department of Literature and Language, 207A Landrum Academic Building, Highland Heights, Kentucky 41099 E-mail: **affrilachia@aol.com**

Tonya M. Evans-Walls   Poet and author of Literary Law Guide for Authors: Copyright, Trademark, and Contracts in Plain Language, Seasons of Her and SHINE! Her short story, Not Tonight appears in a new anthology titled Proverbs for the People, published by Kensington. Tonya M. Evans-Walls, Esq., TME Law, 6703 Germantown Avenue, Suite 200, Philadelphia, Pennsylvania 19119 Phone: (215) 438-0468 Fax: (215) 438-0469 E-mail: **tme@tmelaw.net** Website: **www.tmelaw.net**

Jerry W. Ward, Jr.   Professor of English at Dillard University, Jerry Washington Ward, Jr., is a poet, literary critic, and editor. His current projects include The Richard Wright Encyclopedia and Reading Race, Reading America, a collection of social and literary essays. Contact Jerry W. Ward, Jr., Department of English, Dillard University, 2601 Gentilly Boulevard, New Orleans, Louisiana 70122 E-mail: **jerryward31@hotmail.com**

Nagueyalti Warren   Poet and editor living in Atlanta, Georgia, Ms. Warren has published Lodestar and Other Night Lights, (New York: Mellen Press, 1992, a collection of poems); co-edited Southern Mothers: Fact and Fictions in Southern Women's Writing (Baton Rouge: Louisiana State University Press, 1999); Temba Tupu! (Walking Naked) Africana Women's Poetic Self-Protrait, (The Africa World Press, forthcoming). Contact Nagueyalti Warren, 7469 Asbury Drive, Lithonia, Georgia 30058 Phone: (404) 727-6040 E-mail: **nwarren@emory.edu**

Cecil Washington   Author, Cecil writes science fiction, fantasy and horror, in addition to poetry. Some of his published books include Alien Erotica, A collection of short stories and verses, Walkware, A techno-thriller and Badlands: An Underground Science Fiction Novel. Education: graduated from Bowie State University in 1993 with a degree in Business Administration, and minors in Marketing, Music, Communications and Economics. Worked as a QA Test Analyst. Also founded Brothers Sci-Fi Magazine. Cecil Washington, 5701 Galloway Drive, Oxon Hill, Maryland 20745 E-mail: **cecilwashington@yahoo.com** Website: **www.cecilwashington.com**

K. C. Washington   Novella, "Mourning Becomes Her" was published by the Harlem Writers Guild Press (2006). Over 10 of my articles were published as a contributing writer and editor for The Hill. Most recently, I worked as a freelancer providing proofreading, research, and writing services to clientele as diverse as Cover and Urban Latino Magazines. Published a chapbook of poetry through Ridgeway Press and have recorded a spoken word CD. Featured in The Nubian Gallery, a new anthology of African-American poetry. Bachelor of Arts in English, minor in Journalism. Four-year Ford Foundation Scholarship in Journalism, $24,000. Two-year Mellon Fellowship, $12,000. K. C. Washington, 237 Dekalb Avenue, Brooklyn, New York 11205 Phone: (718) 789-0443 E-mail: **kcwbrooklyn@juno.com** Website: **www.a-dark-lady.com.**

Roberta Sonsaray White   Poet, author, and motivational speaker, her first book entitled "Spiritual Metamorphosis" is a dialogue/poetry text. Her second book is forth coming and is a novel. Contact Ms. Sonsaray White, Emory UMC, 6100 Georgia Avenue North West, Washington, DC 20011 Phone: (202) 538-6238 E-mail: **SM4RSWhite@aol.com**

Hubert P. Williams, Jr.   An anointed singer/songwriter/producer, that also writes poetry and inspirational messages to uplift the Name of the Lord. Hubert P. Williams, Jr., Trinity Music Group, 2907 Kingfisher Drive, Fayetteville, North Carolina. Phone: (910) 977-7354 E-mail: **willi526@earthlink.net** Website: **www.geocities.com/trinitymusicgroup2004**

Jennifer L. Williams   Author of the book My Bowl of Cherries is All Pitts. Jennifer Williams, Gentle Touch Design & Publications, Post Office Box 1757, Clinton, Maryland 20735 E-mail: **info@phraseology.net**

Gloria Dulan-Wilson.   Uses poetry to depict and convey information of importance and concern to African Americasn under her company "Poetic License(c)." Gloria Dulan-Wilson, 90 Church Street, Suite 3343, New York City, New York 10008 E-mail: **geemomadee@yahoo.com**

Larry Winfield   Chicago saloon poet, he began writing in the early 80s and attended his first reading at Weeds in 1990. Over the next twelve years he hosted open mics at The Gallery Cabaret, The Underground Wonder Bar and Yo Ma's, featured at many local poetry venues and festivals, organized the protest poetry reading at the ' 96 Democratic Convention, for two years hosted a weekly poetry and jazz show on pirate station Guerilla Love Radio as DJ Merlot, published the poetry books Rosedust, Erzulie and Wicker Park Sonata and the online/print zines Liquid Glyph and City Table Review, produced short films, and performed in Paris, Berlin, Frankfurt, New York, and with ensemble groups Brothers in Verse and the many versions of his poetry band Brass Orchid. He produced the CD's, "Monkey King" and "Erzulie Freda," hosts the "Sundown Lounge" podcast. Larry Winfield, Post Office Box 812091, Los Angeles, California 90017 E-mail: **lwin@larrywinfield.com** Website: **www.larrywinfield.com**

Fredrick Woodard   Visual artist and a published poet. Fredrick Woodard, 2905 Prairie du Chien Road North East, Iowa City, Iowa 52240 E-mail: **fredrick-woodard@uiowa.edu**

Olu Butterfly Woods   Performance poet and author of The Revenge of Dandelions: a collection of poetry. Also, Director of Poetry for the People, Baltimore, Maryland. Olu Butterfly Woods, 6023 Greenspring Avenue, Baltimore, Maryland 21209 Phone: (410) 358-6484 E-mail: **contactus@blackoutstudios.com** Website: **www.blackoutstudios.com**

Sandra L. West   Author and poet, West's "Wendy, Stand up With Your Proud Hair" was anthologized in Say That The River Turns: The Impact of Gwendolyn Brooks (Third World Press, 1987). Her poetry has been published in many outlets including Essence magazine and The Journal of Black Poetry. Literary journals Obsidian and Savannah Literary Journal have published several of her short stories and poems, most recently "What's in a Name, Ghana Mae Jane" for Obsidian III in 2006, a tongue-in-cheek articles that asks why black parents name their children as they do. Sandra L. West, 177 Camden Street, Newark, New Jersey 07103 Phone: (973) 424-0538 E-mail: **slwest@andromeda.rutgers.edu**

Frances Faye Ward-Worthy Poet. Published works: Broadside Press Anthology. Catfish Poets Society Anthology. Columnist: Power, Money, Influence Magazine. Graduated from the Art Institute of Atlanta. I've had classes at Cranbrook Institute (film & video); scriptwriting with Tim Jeffrey. I've been Producion Assistant on music videos, documentaries and TV productions. Headed the poetry committee of the Romance Writers, Houston chapter. Frances Faye Ward-Worthy, 242 Chalmers Detroit, Michigan 48215 E-mail: **worth23karat@yahoo.com**

Marvin X Author of the following: How To Recover From the Addiction to White Supremacy, (A Pan African 12 Step Model for a Mental Health Peer Group), Beyond Religion, toward Spirituality, essays on consciousness, (2007), Wish I Could Tell You The Truth, essays, (2005), Land of My Daughters, poems, (2005), and In the Crazy House Called America, essays, (2002). Marvin X, Black Bird Press, Post Office Box 1317, Paradise, California 95967 E-mail: **mrvnx@yahoo.com** Website: **www.marvinxwrites.blogspot.com**

Sankofa Camille Yarbrough Author of the children's classic book "Cornrows;" Ms. Yarbrough was a member of the Katherine Dunham Dance Company for five years and taught Dunham Technique at Southern Illinois University; The Association for the Study of Classical African Civilizations (ASCAC); The New School For Social Research (The Journey of the Griots-Souls: Unsold); Kean College (Misuse of the African Image in the Media); The Black Caucus of the American Library Association; The National Black Child Development Institute; Kuntu Writers Workshop - Department of African Studies, University of Pittsburgh, "Our Roots Run Deep" - Atlantic Recording Group. Ms. Sankofa Camille Yarbrough, African American Traditions Workshop, 80 Saint Nicholas Avenue Suite 4G, New York, New York 10026 Phone: (212) 865-7460 E-mail: **Yarbroughchosan@aol.com**

Alecia Goodlow-Young Author, screenwriter, poet, columnist and a freelance writer. I write for a newspaper, a magazine, a union organization. Currently with The National Writer's Union / UAW. I hold the position of Co-chair of The National Diversity Committee, A Delegate at the Delegate's Assembly and a Southeast Michigan Steering Committee member. I was also with The Detroit Writer's Guild for a few years. I write in many different genres. Alecia Goodlow-Young, 28490 Tavistock Trail, Southfield, Michigan 48034 Phone: (313) 796-7949 Fax: (313) 541-6638 E-mail: **aleciawrites@sbcglobal.net**

Jackie Y. Young Author of the provocative poetry collection, "Love's Reparations: the Learning Curve between Heartache & Healing" (2006). Jackie Y. Young, 1st Stream Publishing, Post Office Box 26687, Richmond, Virginia 23261 E-mail: **msjayy@jackieyoungwrites.com** Website: **www.jackieyoungwrites.com**

ZaKiYa Born and reared in Brooklyn, New York, Zakiya sees herself as a citizen of the world. She is a self-published author/poet of Muted Whispers her first book of poetry. Her second book titled, A Letter to a Friend is a compact compilation of thoughts that challenge the reader to think in a different direction than they are probably used to. ZaKiYa is currently working on her first fiction novel. Contact ZaKiYa, Post Office Box 20507, Brooklyn, New York 11202 E-mail: **zakiya@ureach.com** Website: **www.zakiyaonline.com**

Narada Michael Walden
Songwriter * Composer
Producer * Recording Artist

Producer and composer Narada Michael Walden has used his formidable musical knowledge to craft a string of pop smashes that have established him as one of the finest and most successful producers working in the record industry today. Known as the "man who helped the Queen of Soul, Aretha Franklin, land her first platinum album", he has produced and co-written three #1 smash hits for Whitney Houston, established himself as a drumming wunderkind while playing alongside guitar aces Jeff Beck and John McLaughlin and has parlayed a healthy solo career into a writing, producing and performing profession, resulting in over ten solo albums. Walden has been honored by his colleagues with a Grammy Award for Best R&B Song in 1985 (*Freeway of Love*), co-writing and producing two smash hits for Franklin, *Freeway* and *Who's Zoomin' Who?*, which opened the way for Franklin to garner her first platinum record in thirty years of record making. He produced *How Will I Know?* from Whitney Houston's multi-platinum 1985 Arista debut and produced and co-wrote the hits, *I Wanna Dance With Somebody*, *Where Do Broken Hearts Go* and *So Emotional*, from her 1987 follow up, *WHITNEY*. Walden also produced and won a Sports Emmy For Houston's *One Moment In Time*, taken from the 1988 Olympics LP.

Other Walden projects have included the 1987 Aretha/George Michael duet *I knew You Were Waiting*, which followed the Walden-produced, *Nothing's Gonna Stop Us Now* (by Starship) into the #1 slot, and the Aretha/Elton John hit duet *Through The Storm*. Besides establishing a "user friendly" studio in San Rafael, Tarpan Studios, and getting back to being a solo artists, he's enjoying in the success of his four #1 single hits including Mariah Carey's Vision Of Love, and I Don't Wanna Cry, Whitney Houston's *All The Man That I Need*, and Lisa Fischer's *How Can I Ease The Pain*? He has also written and completed a number of projects for such artists as Shanice Wilson, Tevin Campbell and Al Jarreau.

Other Top 10 hits written and/or produced by this very talented musician and composer include *Songbird* (Kenny G); *Baby Come To Me* (Regina Belle); *Put Your Mouth On Me* (Eddie Murphy); and *We Don't Have To Take Our Clothes Off* (Jermaine Stewart); *Kisses In the Moonlight* (from the George Benson album, *While The City Sleeps*); *We're Not Making Love Anymore* (Barbra Streisand's album, *Barbra Streisand's Greatest Hits*); and *I Do* (Natalie Cole's Album, *Good To Be Back*)

Producers

Film, Song and Play

Abdul-Jalil al-Hakim President/CEO of Superstar Management world renowned for unprecedented services for Muhammed Ali, Brian Taylor, U.S. Rep. J.C. Watts, Warner Bros. Records, Deion Sanders, Delvin Williams, Giant Records, Kareem Abdul-Jabbar, M.C. Hammer, Capitol Records, Lyman Bostock, Evander Holyfield, Spencer Haywood, Cliff Robinson, Abbey Lincoln, EMI Records, Emanuel Stewart (Lennox Lewis, Prince Naseem Hamed, Oscar DeLa Hoya), Pebbles, John Carlos, Reggie White, Marvin Gaye, Mos Def, Martin Wyatt, and Leslie Allen. He has produced shows for Disney, ABC-TV and ESPN, events in Japan, Russia, Egypt, Romania, Paris, Europe, Brunei, U.S.; consulted BBDO Worldwide Advertising, Starter, Royal Family of Saudi Arabia, The ESPY'S, National Football League EXPERIENCE- Super Bowl, "90210", Black Entertainment Television (BET), Sega, Independant Film Producers (IFP), Screen Actors Guild (SAG), Producers Guild of America (PGA), and Broadcast Music Inc. (BMI), to name a few. Contact Mr. Abdul-Jalil al-Hakim, Superstar Management, 7633 Sunkist Drive, Oakland California 94605 E-mail: (510) 638-0808 Fax: (510) 638-8889 E-mail: **jalil@superstarmanagement.com** Website: **www.superstarmanagement.com**

Blue Phoenix Films An independent film company that strives to create captivating films that will capture the world's attention with innovative stories of good quality that people will enjoy for years to come. Jacquitta McManus, Blue Phoenix Films, Post Office Box 13491, Atlanta, Georgia 30324 E-mail: **info@bluephoenixfilms.com** Website: **www.BluePhoenixFilms.com**

Troy Buckner CEO for her company, Hy'Tara Entertainment, Buckner was the producer and executive producer for the theatrical production, 'Tell Hell I Aint Comin', starring Tommy Ford and Tony Grant from the Grammy nominated R & B Group, 'Az Yet' on the La Face Record label. She has managed and co-produced Gospel Renown Artist and Stella Award Winner, Kenny Smith and Vernessa Mitchell from the Motown's Grammy Award winning R & B Group, 'Hi-Energy'. She is currently writing, managing, and producing several upcoming artists. Troy Buckner, Hy'tara Entertainment, Post Office Box 19049, Anaheim, California 92817 Phone: (714) 227-5000 E-mail: **birdinflight@aol.com** Website: **www.abirdinflight.com**

Jillian Bullock Award winning writer, director and producer. Credits include: "The Champion Inside", Writer, Producer, Actor, Fight Choreographer (A P in A Pod Productions); "Spirit", Writer, Director, Producer, Actor, Fight Choreographer (Jaguar Productions); "Live In Peace Or Die In Peace", Director, Actor; "A Filmmaker's Personal Journey," Documentary, Writer, Director, Actor, Producer (Jaguar Productions, won the Mickey Michaux award); "Dragon Enterprise", Fight Choreographer; "Up Close", Production Assistant; "Philadelphia"- Production Assistant; "MALCOLM X.", Intern. Also works as a freelance writer, a script doctor and a screenwriting judge. Jillian Bullock, Jaguar Productions, Inc., 311 South Park Way, Suite 308F, Broomall, Pennsylvania 19008 Phone: (484) 682-6932 E-mail: **jaguarpro1161@aol.com**

The Charles Group, Inc. Accepts script submissions for possible production. Seeking feature length or short film scripts that are character driven with an Afro-American or Afro-Caribbean theme preferred. Must be able to be produced as a low budget project. The Charles Group, 478 North Highland, Suite 11, Atlanta, Georgia 30307 E-mail: **cynthia_charles@yahoo.com**

The Color Of Film Collaborative Non-profit organization that works to support media makers of color and others who have an interest in creating and developing new and diverse images of people of color in film, video and performing arts. Lisa Simmons, Executive Director. The Color of Film Collaborative, Post Office Box 191901, Roxbury, Massachusetts 02119 Phone: (617) 445-6051 E-mail: **info@coloroffilm.com** Website: **coloroffilm.com**

Courtesy Is Contagious Productions, Inc Record/film production company. Producer, Tico Wells, "Choir Boy", The Five Heartbeats. The company is available to produce and/or direct projects for film, TV, stage, or provide original music. Courtesy Is Contagious Productions, Inc., 11288 Ventura Boulevard, Suite 401, Studio City, California 91604 Phone: (818) 775-3871

Emtro Music Production Music production company specializing in Gospel music. Welcomes "ALL" songwriters to submit copy written material to be considered for future projects. Emtro Music Production, Post Office Box 12760, Jacksonville, Florida 32209 Fax: (904) 772-1491 E-mail: **kishia@theintegritysolution.com** Website: **www.emtro.com**

Shala Esquire Producer for the Record Label, The Movement. Also art director for Antiart Studio. Shala Esquire, 4023 South Calumet, Box 1N, Chicago, Illinois 60653 Phone: (773) 536-3630 E-mail: **scholaone@yahoo.com**

Face To Face, Inc. Providing songwriting, music production, audio recording, engineering, mixing and mastering of musical content for records, commercials, audio soundtracks for film, television and theatre. The company is headed by President/CEO and Multi-platinum Artist/Producer Fred Hammond whose writing style and production skills have created a demand for his services in both Gospel/Christian and Secular Music. He has worked with some of the industry's most sought after and influential talents from The Winans to James Cleveland, Stevie Wonder to Eric Clapton, American Idol Winner Ruben Studdard to Musiq Soulchild, Quincy Jones to Sean "Diddy" Combs, DreamWorks to ABC Films. Has a music catalog of over 300 songs to his credit and having sold over 7 Million records to date. Kevin Wilson, Face To Face, Inc., 501 North Loop, Cedar Hill, Texas 75104 Phone: (972) 293-2885 Fax: (972) 293-6866 E-mail: **kwilson@fredhammondmusic.com** Website: **www.fredhammondmusic.com**

Faith Filmworks, Inc. Independent motion picture production company. No unsolicited screenplays or extended treatments except through established agents or entertainment attorney. Individuals may submit a short pitch or synopsis no longer than half a page in length. Michael Swanson, Producer, Faith Filmworks, Inc., 859 Hollywood Way, Suite 255, Burbank, California 91505 E-mail: **christine@faithfilmworks.com** Website: **www.faithfilmworks.com**

Fat Boy Hits Music Group Publishing company. Arthur Douse, Vice President, writer, and HipHop artist. Fat Boy Hits Music Group, 1244 Herkamer, Brooklyn, New York 11233 Phone: (718) 216-5334 E-mail: **celsiusbk@aol.com**

Film Life, Inc. A film marketing and distribution company whose mission is to spearhead the commercial development of independent Black films. Mr. Jeff Friday, founder. Film Life, Inc., Post Office Box 688, New York, New York 10012 Phone: (212) 966-2411 Fax: (212) 966-2411 E-mail: **info@thefilmlife.com** Website: **www.thefilmlife.com**

First Lady Productions, Inc Producer. Dr. Vera J. Goodman, First Lady Productions, Inc., 2971 Waller Street, Jacksonville, Florida 32254 Phone: (904) 425-0806 E-mail: **firstladypro@aol.com**

Morgan Freeman Film producer and principal of Revelations Entertainment, an independent production company which specializes in film, television, and digital production. E-mail: **info@revelationsent.com** Website: **www.RevelationsEntertainment.com**

Full Moon Productions Film/TV production and development company. Nwenna Kai, Producer, Full Moon Productions, 311 San Pascual, Los Angeles, California 90042 Phone: (323) 337-7381 Fax: (323) 936-5691 E-mail: **nwenna@excite.com**

Kenneth Gamble Co-founder/Chairman, Gamble-Huff Music. Legends, Kenny Gamble and Leon Huff have been songwriting and producing partners for 30 years. Contact Chuck Gamble, 309 South Broad Street, Philadelphia, Pennsylvania 19107 Phone: (215) 985 0900 Phone: (215) 885-0924 E-mail: **chuckgamblepir@aol.com** Website: **www.gamble-huffmusic.com**

Lou Gossett Jr. Producer/film, production company - motion picture/television. Produce movies, will review agent-submitted scripts, treatments. Producers, Lou Gossett Jr., and Dennis Considine. Logo Entertainment, 301 North Canon Drive, Suite 300, Beverly Hills, California 90210 Phone: (310) 276-6700 E-mail: **lou@louisgossett.com** Website: **www.louisgossett.info**

Michael A. Grant Jr. Music producer. Contact Mr. Michael A. Grant, Jr., Imani Jordan Music, 5716 Malcolm Street, Philadelphia, Pennsylvania 19143 Phone: (215) 316-7269 E-mail: **michaelgrant_2@msn.Com**

Tim Greene Film, and song producer. Tim has written and produced over 17 national record releases with such acts as "Soft Touch." Tim Green, Tim Greene Films, Post Office Box 20554, Philadelphia, Pennsylvania 19138 Phone: (213) 368-8100 Website: **www.timgreenefilms.com**

Eddie Gurren CEO/Owner of Golden Boy Music. Contact Mr. Eddie Gurren, Golden Boy Music, 16311 Askin Drive, Pine Mountain, California 93222 Phone: (661) 242-0125 E-mail: **gbrmusic@frazmtn.com**

Herman Hall Producer/promoter and booking agent. Herman Hall Communications, Inc, 1630 Nostrand Avenue, Brooklyn, New York 11226 Phone: (718) 941-1879 Fax: (718) 941-1886 E-mail: **everybodys@msn.com** Website: **www.everybodysmag.com**

Forest Hairston Songwriter/music producer, screenwriter and poet. Contact Mr. Forest Hairston, ForGen Productions, 3654 Barham Boulevard. Suite Q301, Los Angeles, California Phone: (323) 851-1225 E-mail: **fgprod@forgen.com** Website: **www.forgen.com**

Joseph Harrison   Published songwriter. Demo production/multimedia packages using our original music. Contact Mr. Joseph Harrison, Post Office Box 2742, Prairie View, Texas 77446 E-mail: **Joseph_Harrison@pvamu.edu** Website: **www.GrooveDepot.com**

Hermit Arts A not for profit organization committed to producing new performance work co-founded by playwright, performer, director, and educator, Idris Goodman. Contact Mr. Idris Goodwin, Hermit Arts, 1721 West Huron, Apartment 2f, Chicago, Illinois 60622 E-mail: **Idris@hermitsite.com** Website: **www.Idrisgoodwin.com**

Hi-Tech Media Corp   Having written and directed several screenplays, the company is currently involved in the promotion of their first full feature film release "The Evolution of Honey Girl. Ralph Johnson, President, Hi-Tech Media Corp., RR11, Box 11005, Stroudsburg, Pennsylvania 18360 E-mail: **pj@htechmedia.com**   Website: **www.htechmedia.com**

I'm Ready Productions, Inc. Professional touring production company. Contact Mr. Gary Guidry, Producer, I'm Ready Productions, Post Office Box 10254, Houston, Texas 77206 E-mail: **info@imreadyproductions.com** Website: **www.imreadyproductions.com**

Jamar E. FilmWorks Multimedia company that is parent to FilmTrack Recordings, and The Entertainment Source (TES). J.J.E.F., Post Office Box 2170, Atlanta, Georgia 30301 Phone: (678) 318-3607 E-mail: **info@jjefholdings.com** Website: **www.jjefholdings.com**

Rodney Jenkins Musician, songwriter, producer, and savvy businessman, Rodney Jenkins is President/CEO of Dark Child, Inc., a music and song production company. Dubbed "Hitman" by the music industry, Rodney is one of the most sought after pop, R&B and Gospel music producers in the industry. Grammy (s) Award winner, he has written, produced and co-wrote songs for such artists as N'Sync, Backstreet Boys, Destiny Child, Toni Braxton, Brandy, Jennifer Lopez, Mark Anthony, Kenneth "Babyface" Edmunds, to name a few. Rodney Jenkins, Dark Child, Inc. E-mail: **info@darkchild.com** Website: **www.darkchild.com**

Jacquie Jones An award-winning writer, director and producer of documentary films, Jacquie is also Executive Director of the National Black Programming Consortium (NBPC). Jacquie Jones, NBPC, 68 East 131st Street, 7th Floor, Harlem, New York 10037 Phone: (212) 234-8200 Fax: (212) 234-7032 E-mail: **jacquie@nbpc.tv** Website: **www.nbpc.tv**

Ty Granderson Jones Owns his own production company, Creole Celina Films, and is currently in pursuit of producing several of his original screenplays including The Cool and Creepy (a finalist in the Sundance Feature Film Program), and the Pilot Presentation/Short of his edgy character study, Napoleonic. Ty G. Jones, Creative Quest, Inc./Creole Celina Films, 8306 Wilshire Boulevard., Suite 432, Beverly Hills, California 90211 Phone: (323) 960-1035 E-mail: **tygrandjones@aol.com**

Just Me Productions, Inc. (JMPI) A company whose interest is in theater and film. Produced the award winning short film "A Song for Jade." Contact Shari Lynn, Just Me Productions, Inc., 3748 Kinnear Avenue, Indianapolis, Indiana 46218 Phone: (317) 509-2210   E-mail: **justmeproduction@aol.com**

Darryl D'Wayne Lassiter Atlanta based writer, film and video producer. Producer/director of the motion picture, PAY THE PRICE! Winner, Best Family Drama, New York International Film Festival, 2000. Winner, 2004 Stellar Award for best music video for Vickie Winans, Shook. Contact Mr. Darryl D'Wayne Lassiter, Post Office Box 50374, Atlanta, Georgia 30302 E-mail: **producerdirector@paytheprice.com** Website: **www.paytheprice.com**

Spike Lee Film and movie producer. Spike Lee, Forty Acres & A Mule Filworks, Inc., 124 Dekalb Avenue, Brooklyn, New York 11217 Phone: (718) 624-3703 Fax: (718) 624-2008

L O H Productions Modern music jingles and music production company. Founder, Michelle Hicks. L O H Productions, 420 Polk Avenue, Box 3, Cape Canaveral, Florida 32920 Phone: (321) 205-6555 E-mail: **mhicks@lohproductions.com** Website: **www.lohproductions.com**

Midastouch Productions International Global production company specializing in total film & video production, project packaging, budgeting & marketing of documentaries, features, shorts, commercials & music videos. Credits include: Resurrection: From New York to New Zealand (2004 NZ documentary) and video projects in Paris (France - 1997 & 2005), Fiji Islands (2002), Barcelona (Spain - 2005) and Tokyo (Japan - 2005). Michael Deet, Executive Producer, Midastouch Productions International, 21604 Dumetz Road, Woodland Hills, California 91364 Phone: (818) 674-6490 E-mail: **midastouchintl@yahoo.com**

MoBetta Films Kevin Craig West is director, producer and professional union actor working in film, television, radio and stage. "Let´s make a film," were the only words needed for his company, MoBetta Films, to spring into existence. Project Mo(u)rning, the inaugural project from MoBetta Films, was nominated one of the top five submissions to the San Francisco Black Independent Film Festival. Selected by IFP Rough Cut Lab, Lake Placid Film Forum and Urbanworld VIBE Film Festival is The Assassin, where Kevin served as an Actor, Cinematographer and Producer. Kevin is a member of The Barrow Group in NYC, Chair member of Upstate Independents and in addition to being a Voice Acting Teacher and Producer for Voice Coaches, he also works as a Teacher/Artist with Symphony Space. MoBetta Films, Post Office Box 484, Troy, New York 12181 E-mail: **contact@kevincraigwest.com** Website: **www.kevincraigwest.com**

Multi-Provision Music, Inc. Gospel music recording company. International distribution through Infinity/Central South Distribution, Inc. Current Artist: Kenneth Wilson & the Kenneth Wilson Chorale CD Project - "Lifestyles of Worship." Contact Multi-Provision Music, Inc., Post Office Box 363, St. Clair, Michigan 48079 Phone: (810) 326 1609 E-mail: **multiprovisionmusic@yahoo.com**

National Association of Black Female Executives in Music & Entertainment, Inc. A 501 (c) (6) nonprofit professional organization led by volunteer entertainment executives, NABFEME was launched in February 1999 with a mission to raise the profile and elevate the awareness of Black women in music and entertainment. The organization's COO is Elektra Entertainment Vice President, Michelle Madison. NABFEME, Offices of Padell Nadell Fine Weinberger, 59 Maiden Lane, 27th Floor, New York, New York 10038 Phone: (212) 424-9568 E-mail: **johnnie_walker1@msn.com** Website: **www.nabfeme.org**

The National Black Programming Consortium NBPC is committed to the presentation, funding, promotion, distribution and preservation of positive images of African Americans and the African Diaspora. NBPC accepts proposals for the production, post-production, distribution or acquisition phase of programs suitable for national public television broadcasts. Jacquie Jones, Contact NBPC, 68 East 131st Street, 7th Floor, Harlem, New York 10037 Phone: (212) 234-8200 Fax: (212) 234-7032 E-mail: **info@nbpc.tv** Website: **www.nbpc.tv**

Emma E. Pullen Writer/producer/director. Winner of the US International Film and Video Festival's "Certificate for Creative Excellence" for "Documentary, Current Events, Special Events", 1999. In theater, she was writer/producer/director on "Women Of The Bible," a play with Reverend Della Reese-Lett, 2000. She is associate producer of "Colors Straight Up" which was nominated for an Oscar for "Best Documentary Feature" in 1998. Emma E. Pullen, 1339 North Odgen Drive, Los Angeles, California 90046 E-mail: **eepblackseeds@sbcglobal.net**

Pemon Rami Since the 1960's, Pemon Rami has been involved in the development of television production, films, music concerts, documentaries, plays, and multimedia designs for theatres and medical institutions across the country. He co-founded, Mixed Media Productions in 1987, which produced film projects. He also served as Managing/Artistic Director for the Phoenix Black Theatre Troupe. He produced concerts in Los Angeles at the Marla Gibbs Crossroads Theatre featuring: Nancy Wilson, The Winans, Stevie Wonder and others. A former casting director, Rami provided talent for the highly acclaimed feature films and television movies; "Blues Brothers", Mahogany", " Cooley High", "Welcome to Success", "The Spook Who Sat By The Door", "One In A Million", and "Dummy" He has directed over thirty theatrical productions nationally, including "Madame Lily" starring Gladys Knight and Dorian Harewood. Plays he's directed for regional theaters include: "Miss Dessa," "Thru The Eyes Of Women," "227," and "The Wiz." Pemon Rami, CTO, Masequa Myers & Associates, 6100 South Dorchester Avenue, 1 West, Chicago, Illinois 60637 E-mail: **pemon@sbcglobal.net** Website: **www.masequa.com**

Red Wall Productions We are filmmakers. We write, direct and produce, high-quality, low-cost, digital, multimedia stories. Rosalyn Coleman Williams and Craig T. Williams, CEOs. Red Wall Productions, 400 West 43rd Street, Suite 10L, New York, New York 10036 Phone: (212) 695-6669 E-mail: **info@redwallproductions.com** Website: **www.redwallproductions.com**

Gregory J. Reed, Esq. Author, agent, entertainment attorney, and play producer, Reed represents sports figures, entertainers, firms, and numerous persons from TV to Broadway, including Anita Baker, Wynston Marsalis, The Winans, and First Black Miss USA, Carole Gist and many other artists. He is the only attorney to represent six world champion boxers. He has produced such plays as the Pulitzer Prize winning production, *A Soldier's Play*, which was developed into a screenplay by Columbia Pictures as *A Soldier's Story*, awarded an Oscar. He has produced and represented the following Broadway plays: "Ain't Misbehavin"; "For Colored Girls Who Have Considered Suicide When the Rainbow Is Enuf"; "What The Wine Sellers Buy"; "The Wiz"; "Your Arms Too Short To Box With God"; and Rosa Parks "More Than a Bus Story." He also staged the largest tour entertainment tribute in the U.S. in honor of Dr. Martin Luther King Jr., with Emmy winner Al Eaton in *We Are The Dream*. Gregory J. Reed & Associates, 1201 Bagley, Detroit, Michigan 48226 Phone: (313) 961-3580 Fax: (313) 961-3582 E-mail: **gjrassoc@aol.com** Website: **www.gjreedlaw.com**

Simmons Lathan Media Group Russell Simmons and Stan Lathan, the production team responsible for the Tony-award winning Def Poetry Jam on Broadway, the Peabody-award winning Def Poetry series on HBO and the blockbuster Def Comedy Jam franchise, are looking for up and coming urban filmmakers to submit their completed work for consideration for acquisitions, distribution and our New Def Filmmakers Program. Contact Ms. Alexis Frank, Attn: Film Submission, Simmons Lathan Media Group, 521 Fifth Avenue, 28th Floor, New York, New York 10175 E-mail: **alexis@simmonslathan.com** Website: **simmonslathan.com**

SpokenVizions Entertainment Group, L.L.C. Floyd Boykin Jr., producer. Also publishes SpokenVizions Magazine. Contact SVEG, Post Office Box 373, Florissant, Missouri 63032 Phone: (314) 517-8764 E-mail: **info@spokenvizions.com** Website: **www.spokenvizions.com**

Third Coast Productions Production Services. Melvin Joseph Claverie, Producer/Director. Third Coast Productions, Post Office Box 51072, New Orleans, Louisiana 70150 Phone: (504) 915-1731 E-mail: **themelman99@yahoo.com**

C. Sade Turnipseed Professor and executive producer of: educational and literary concept developments for film, television, radio, live stage events and festivals, Ms. Turnipseed is an international consultant for film festivals and literary performances. Her current projects include: The creation of The Harriet Tubman Village, for Writers and Artists--a bed & breakfast establishment, in the Historic South; FESPACO: Paul Robeson Award Initiative, Burkina Faso, Africa; FESPACO 2005 The Best of the Best, the documentary; Kissin' My Dust: A Collection of Love Notes; No More Space for Anything, But LOVE!; and, Saving Our Babies Anthology: By Writers of the 21st Century. Contact C. Sade Turnipseed, Red Clay Publishing, KHAFRE Prouductions, Post Office Box 1134, Ackerman, Mississippi 39735 Phone: (662) 285-9798 E-mail: **CassieSade@peoplepc.com** Website: **www.khafre.us**

Narada Michael Walden Musician, songwriter, composer and producer. Narada Michael Walden, Tarpan Studios, 1925 East Francisco Boulevard., Suite L, San Rafael, California 94901 Phone: (415) 485-1999 Fax: (415) 459-3234 E-mail: **inquiries@tarpanstudios.com** Website: **www.tarpanstudios.com**

Trey Wilson Producer. Trey Wilson, Superkala Records, 200 South Main Street, Enterprise, Alabama 36330 Phone: (334) 393-7922 E-mail: **trey@superkalarecords.com** Website: **www.superkalarecords.com**

Television & Radio

Magdalene Breaux TV host and producer, Magdalene is also the author of supernatural/paranormal erotic literature; The Family Curse, Imaginary Playmate, John E. Calico, ChD, and Family Secrets. A native of New Orleans and graduate of the University of New Orleans, her publishing services include technical writing, book production consulting for independent authors and TV production and editing. Magdalene Breaux, Post Office Box 67, Fairburn, Georgia 30213 Phone: (770) 842-4792 E-mail: **magbreaux@mindspring.com** Website: **www.familycurse.com**

Denver Entertainment Group A coalition of 15 companies from five countries - including the United Kingdom, Singapore and Japan - that includes all segments of media and entertainment production. DEG is linked directly to actors, musicians, composers, producers and business people - and even a chef host to the stars. Art Thomas, a co-founder of Denver Entertainment Group, is also vice president of program development and acquisitions for CoLours TV. He has a master's degree in International Marketing from Notre Dame de Namur University, International Certification from Metro State College. SoNew Productions, (sonew.tv), invited Thomas to the 2004 Cannes Film Festival to promote their documentary film, Earthlings. Afterward, he went to England to work on his first international collaboration with ACF Productions, entitled, 'The Passerby'. Black Filmmaker magazine featured their collaboration in the August/September 2004 issue. In addition to his work on The Champagne Chef Show, which airs on CoLours TV his other credits include, African-American Voter Information Project (Public Service Announcements in 2004), Bed of Dreams, which he co-produced with Annie Schlax, Fit-Hop, starring Van Prueitt, co-founder of Denver Entertainment Group. Art Thomas, Denver Entertainment Group c/o Main Man Films, LLC Post Office Box 3773 Englewood, Colorado 80155 Phone: (303) 331-0339 Fax: (303) 439-0315 E-mail: **info@mainmanfilms.com** Website: **www.mainmanfilms.com**

Kulcha Shok Muzik (KSM) Produces & promotes everything in Caribbean music, reggae, dancehall, soca and Caribbean music, videos, and programming for radio, satellite, the internet, & the airlines. KSM has programs & music that airs on both Delta & Air Jamaica Airlines, XM & Sirius radio and allover the internet. KSM produces a weekly syndicated entertainment report called 'REGGAE VIBES,' heard on nearly 120 radio stations around the world. Clients have included WQAM, WPOW, Shaggy & MCA Records, & Irie FM Jamaica. Lance-O, Kulcha Shok Muzik, 1218 Drexel Avenue, Suite #203, Miami, Florida 33139 Phone: (305) 534-6110 E-mail: **lanceo@kulchashok.com** Website: **www.kulchashok.com**

Najah Productions Literary based production company. Seeks book submissions for their Books-To-Video (BTV) series in 2005. BTV will secure film rights of African-American novels and bring them to home DVD/Video. Contact Ms. Anita S. Peterson, Najah Productions, 598 Indian Trail Road, Suite #256, Indian Trail, North Carolina 28079 Phone: (704) 821-1786 E-mail: **anita@literarycafe.org** Website: **www.literarycafe.org**

The National Black Programming Consortium (NBPC) Accepts proposals for the production, post-production, distribution or acquisition phase of programs suitable for national public television broadcasts. NBPC, 68 East 131st Street, 7th Floor, Harlem, New York 10037 Phone: (212) 234-8200 E-mail: **info@nbpc.tv** Website: **www.nbpc.tv**

Nelson Davis Television Productions (NDTP) Television program production and marketing. Nelson Davis, NDTP, 5800 Sunset Boulevard, Los Angeles, California 90028 Phone: (323) 460-5253 E-mail: **info@makingittv.com** Website: **www.makingittv.com**

NiteLite Productions A commerical production company, services include editorial/post production; theatrical/television pictures. Producer, NiteLite Productions, 10529 Valparaiso Street, Suite 2, Los Angeles, California 90034 Phone: (310) 839-0707 Fax: (310) 839-0149 E-mail: **harry@nitelite.org** Website: **www.nitelite.org**

Naomi Roberson Organizational psychologist and motivational speaker, Dr. Roberson is also a producer, director, and camera operator. She has produced and directed documentaries, award shows, public service announcements, and interviews for local television and the outlying areas. For the past fifteen years, she has been a volunteer talk show host for Access Television. She has an associate degree in accounting, a bachelor's degree in behavioral science, a master's degree in management and human resources, a doctorate in organizational psychology, and a doctorate in divinity. She is a licensed and ordained minister and a board member for a nonprofit charitable organization. Contact Dr. Naomi Roberson, Post Office Box 557533 Chicago, Illinois 60655 Phone: (773) 573-5805 Fax: (708) 596-0226 E-mail: **username:nrshow@comcast.net**

Star Planet Television Since 1986, full service television production facility that produces talk shows geared to the African American community. W. L. Lillard is Founder and CEO/Senior Executive Producer. Contact Star Planet Television Network, 1140 West 103rd Street, Chicago, Illinois 60643 Phone: (773) 445-7788 Fax: (773) 881-0514 Website: **www.starplanettv.com**

Video

Diasporic Communications A multi-media consulting firm specializing in video production consulting and electronic communications development. Provides consulting services for public relations campaigns, produces personal and corporate videos, and advises on communications technology services involving web site content management, and technology feasibility studies involving teleconferencing, distance learning and communications equipment procurement. President and CEO, Deborah Ray-Sims has served as Television Producer, Writer, and Educator. Credits include former Series Producer/Writer for PBS, and recipient of the International Black Filmmaker Hall of Fame Screenwriting finalist Award for the screenplay Dreammakers. She also served as Educator for the Nigerian Television Authority and TV College (Lagos, Nigeria). Deborah Ray-Sims, Diasporic Communications, 2932 Cinnamon Teal Circle, Elk Grove, California 95757 Phone: (916) 479-1161 E-mail: **diasporic@comcast.net**

Joseph Harrison Demo production/multimedia packages using our original music. Also a songwriter. Contact Mr. Joseph Harrison, Post Office Box 2742, Prairie View, Texas 77446 E-mail: **Joseph_Harrison@pvamu.edu** Website: **www.GrooveDepot.com**

Imaginative Media Concepts Full service multi-media music company specializing in unique and innovative ways to use visual as well as musical mediums to maximize and identify with a project and or product. Anthony S. Murray, Creative Consultant, Imaginative Media Concepts, 56 Dobbs Ferry Road, White Plains, New York 10607 Phone: (914) 562-1774 E-mail: **amurrayw@aol.com**

KDB Productions A cutting edge audio services production company located in Conyers, Georgia founded by air personality and Gospel Light radio talk show host, KD Bowe. Contact Mr. KD Bowe, KDB Productions c/o KDYA, Gospel 1190 AM The Light, 3260 Blume Drive, Suite 520, Richmond, California 94806 Phone: (510) 222-4242 Fax: (510) 262-9054 Website: **www.gospel1190.net**

Midastouch Productions International A global production company specializing in total film & video production, project packaging, budgeting and marketing of documentaries, features, shorts, commercial and music videos. Credits include Hip-Hop Resurrection: From New York to New Zealand (2004 NZ docu). Michael Deet, Executive Producer, Midustouch Productions International, 7957 Nita Avenue, West Hills, California 91304 Phone: (818) 888-6798 Fax: (818) 674-6490 E-mail: **midastouchintl@yahoo.com**

NiteLite Productions Commerical production company; broadcast television spots and theatrical trailers; editorial/post/production, promos, music videos and advertising commercials; theatrical/television pictures. Contact NiteLite Productions, 10529 Valparaiso Street, Suite 2, Los Angeles, California 90034 Phone: (310) 839-0707 Fax: (310) 839-0149 E-mail: **harry@nitelite.org** Website: **www.nitelite.org**

Ron Clowney Design Design company offers both traditional art services in addition to computer graphics design work in the areas of print and animation. The traditional art services are pencil or painted portraits, pencil drawings. We also design and construct websites. Contact Ron Clowney Design, 5513 Adode Falls Road, Unit 10, San Diego, California 92120 Phone: (619) 501-5740 E-mail: **rclowney@cox.net** Website: **www.rclowney.com**

Leo D. Sullivan Animator, writer, publisher, director and producer of videos and books that present positive images for African American children and adults. Leo D. Sullivan, Vignette Multimedia, 1800 South Robertson Boulevard., #286, Los Angeles, California 90035 Phone: (323) 939-4174 E-mail: **lsullassoc@aol.com** Website: **www.afrokids.com**

Public Relations

AQ Public Relations Publicity and public outreach strategies for organizations, creative artists, consumer products, film DVDs, theatrical productions, book authors and non-profits. Local and national newspaper, magazine, television and radio placements. Writing and editing press releases, biographies, feature stories, by-lines, pitching, assembling press kits, and scheduling public appearances. Allison Queen, AQ Public Relations, 13428 Maxella Avenue, #128, Marina del Rey, California 90292 Phone: (310) 621-7266 E-mail: **allisonqueen@sbcglobal.net**

Black Gospel Promo, Inc. Now in its 5th year, BGP is the Worldwide leader in E-Marketing to the Gospel Consumer Market and African American Church quickly approaching the One Hundred Fifty Million (150,000,000) mark in cumulative reach. Reaching 150,000+ Internet users worldwide with each E-mail Blast. BGP has promoted for every major gospel record label, gospel artist, pastor, author, convention and Christian business in the African-American Christian Community. Veda Brown is President of Black Gospel Promo, and has over twenty years experience in the business and entertainment industry. A graduate of Moore College of Art and Design with a Bachelor of Fine Arts, Ms. Brown has extensive additional training in Business Development, Music Management, and Project Management from the University of Arts and Temple University. She has worked for CGI Records, Vickie Winans, Bajada Records and consulted for many Gospel Record labels and artist. Veda Brown, Black Gospel Promo, Inc., 45 East Cityline Avenue, #303, Bala Cynwyd, Pennsylvania 19004 Phone: (215) 883-1000 E-mail: **info@blackgospelpromo.com** Website: **www.blackgospelpromo.com**

Crystal C. Brown CEO and President of Crystal Clear Communications, an award winning public relations and marketing firm in Houston, Texas. Crystal C. Brown, 2470 S. Dairy Ashford #252, Houston, Texas 77077 Phone: (281) 589-2007 Fax: (281) 589-7098 E-mail: **cbrown5530@aol.com** Website: **www.crystalcommunicates.com**

Capital Entertainment Bil Carpenter is CEO of Capital Entertainment, a small public relations company that has worked extensively with gospel artists such as Vickie Winans, Bishop T.D. Jakes, CeCe Winans, and Donald Lawrence & the Tri-City Singers, among many others. Carpenter's "Did You Know" trivia segments can also be heard weekly on "The BeBe Winans Radio Show" that is syndicated to over 100 radio stations throughout the USA. In fall 2006 Carpenter released "An Uncloudy Christmas" CD of new collection of holiday songs recorded by Candi Staton, Pookie Hudson & the Spaniels, and others. Bil holds a B.A. in history from the American University in Washington, D.C. He has worked both as a music journalist and a record label publicist. In addition, he has handled publicity campaigns for such diverse subjects as Aaliyah, various members of the Winans gospel dynasty and Coretta Scott King's 30th anniversary March on Washington. A songwriter, Carpenter's songs have been recorded by Grammy nominees David "Pop" Winans and Candi Staton, among others. Bil Carpenter, Capital Entertainment, 217 Seaton Place North East, Washington, D.C. 20002 Phone: (202) 636-7028 E-mail: **carpbil@aol.com** Website: **www.bilcarpenter.com**

The Cherry Group A professional writing and public relations service. The Cherry Group, Post Office Box 614, Jackson, Tennessee 38302 Phone: (731) 422-2524 Fax: (731) 422-2524 E-mail: **thecherrygroup1@yahoo.com**

Danley Writing Consultants Founded in 1998, by Dr. Charrita D. Danley, offers a wide spectrum of instructional and professional writing and editing services to individual, corporate, and non-profit clients. With more than ten years of experience as a teacher, writer, and researcher, Dr. Danley holds a B.A., M.A. and Ph.D. in the field of English, with concentrations in the areas of Composition/Rhetoric, Business Writing, and Linguistics. Dr. Charrita D. Danley, Danley Writing Consultants, 458 Cambridge Court, Suite D, Riverdale, Georgia 30296 E-mail: **cdanley@danleywriting.com** Website: **www.danleywriting.com**

Diasporic Communications The company provides consulting services for public relations campaigns, produces personal and corporate videos, and advises on communications technology services involving web site content management, and technology feasibility studies involving teleconferencing, distance learning and communications equipment procurement. President of Diasporic Communications, Deborah Ray-Sims is a veteran in the communications field where she has served as Television Producer, Writer, and Educator. Her credits include former Series Producer/Writer for PBS, and recipient of the International Black Filmmaker Hall of Fame Screenwriting finalist Award for the screenplay Dreammakers. She has also served as Educator for the Nigerian Television Authority and TV College (Lagos, Nigeria). Deborah Ray-Sims, Diasporic Communications, 2932 Cinnamon Teal Circle, Elk Grove, California 95757 Phone: (916) 479-1161 E-mail: **diasporic@comcast.net**

Diversity City Media Multicultural marketing, public relations, and retail firm. We produce BlackNews.com, BlackShopping.com, BlackStudents.com, and BlackPr.com, a newswire service which provides press release distribution to the Black media. Contact Diversity City Media, 225 West 3rd Street, Suite #203, Long Beach, California 90802 Phone: (866) 910-6277 E-mail: **sales@diversitycity.com** Website: **www.blackpr.com**

Down to Earth Public Relations Company is committed to delivering top media exposure for publishers, author's and motivational speaker's. Down to Earth Public Relations, c/o Earth O. Jallow, Post Office Box 83442, Columbus, Ohio 43203 Phone: (614) 284-7933 Fax: (614) 372-1755 E-mail: **dwn2earthpr@juno.com** Website: **www.dwn2earthpr.com**

411 Communications Founder, president, Marsha Jones is a graduate of Purdue University and has more than 15 years of public relations and marketing experience. Her works have appeared in such regional publications as about..time magazine, Rochester Business Magazine, Business Strategies, The Scene, The Pride of Rochester, and her weekly 411 column in The Buffalo Challenger. She has interviewed such notables as filmmaker Spike Lee, poets Nikki Giovanni and Sonia Sanchez, musicians Miriam Makeba, Hugh Masekela, authors Maya Angelou and Antowne Fisher, comedians Bernie Mac and Chris Rock, and actors Malik Yoba and Danny Glover. Past president of the Rochester Association of Black Communicators, Marsha serves on the Board of Directors for the High Falls Film Festival. Currently, Marsha is working on two novels, Win-Win and Shorts. Contact Marsha Jones, 411 Communications, 97 Culver Parkway, Rochester, New York 14609 E-mail: **defdefyingmj@yahoo.com**

Fredericks Enterprises, Inc. A multimedia company that specializes in the production and marketing of urban literature (also known as Street Lit). Contact Walter Fredericks Enterprises, Inc, 644 Saint Anns Avenue, Suite #1, Bronx, New York 10455　Phone: (917) 664-4070　Fax: (718) 401-8450　E-mail: **wenterprisesinc@yahoo.com**　Website: **www.walterfredericks.com**

The Gabriel Group A Washington-area firm specializing in media relations, fundraising and event-planning, with emphasis on projects that uplift humanity.　Ms. Edith Billups, president. Edith Billups, The Gabriel Group, 8720 Georgia Avenue, Suite 906, Silver Spring, Maryland 20910　Phone: (301) 562-5460　Fax: (240) 562-5468　E-mail: **eybillups@aol.com**

Into the Spotlight Entertainment Provides representation and superb publicity for artists (writers, musicians, etc.).　Shonell Bacon or Tonya Howard, Into the Spotlight Entertainment, 605 Division Street, Lake Charles, Louisiana 70601　Phone: (337) 433-9728　Fax: (337) 433-9728　E-mail: **info@intothespotlight-inc.com**　Website: **www.intothespotlight-inc.com**

Jusbee Jones Under the pseudonym of Jusbee Jones, sports publicist, LaShirl Smith has been associated with sports most of her life.　Continuing her path through the sports world, Jones has worked with professional athletes for over fifteen years in the capacity of sports public relations and marketing.　She is currently President and CEO of a sports entertainment publicity firm. Jones serves on the Board of Directors for several of her clients charitable organizations, a board member of several sports organization, member of several sports affiliations and contributes to a monthly sports entertainment column.　Contact Ms. Jusbee Jones, Adnor Books, 15030 Ventura Boulevard., Suite 525, Sherman Oaks, California 91403　E-mail: **JusbeeJones@aol.com** Website: **www.confessionsofthe12thman.com**

Kensey & Kensey Communications A public relations firm with a specialty in media relations and event marketing in the arts & entertainment arena.　Founder CEO, Barbara Kensey has worked with numerous national figures, including the Rev. Jesse L. Jackson, astronaut, Dr. Mae Jemison, vocalist Betty Carter and Oscar Brown, Jr., among others.　She is a charter member and former executive vice president of the Black Public Relations Society, member of the Publicity Club of Chicago and the Chicago Association of Black Journalists.　She is a recipient of the Merit Award from the Publicity Club of Chicago.　Contact Ms. Barbara Kensey, Kensey & Kensey Communications, 5212 South Dorchester Avenue, Chicago, Illinois 60615　Phone: (773) 288-8776　Fax: (773) 288-8997　E-mail: **Kenseycomm@sbcglobal.net**

Marc Curtis Little Public relations counselor who coordinates publicity for authors in the Southeast United States, especially in Florida and Georgia.　Mr. Little has been a public relations counselor since 1984 and has worked with Benilde Little, author of Good Hair, The Itch and Acting Out, all with Simon and Shuster.　Contact Mr. Marc Curtis Little, 8070 Wakefield Avenue, Jacksonville, Florida 32208　Phone: (904) 924-0303　E-mail: **marc@marcpr.com** Website: **www.marcpr.com**

Mays Media Company creates marketing materials including press releases, sell sheets, e-mail flyers and more.　Contact Ms. Shetia Mays, Mays Media, 5456 Peachtree Industrial Boulevard, #457, Atlanta, Georgia 30341　Phone: (770) 256-8710　E-mail: **smmays@maysmediainc.com** Website: **www.maysmediainc.com**

Denise Meridith A New York City native Ms. Meridith has a BS from Cornell University and a MPA from the University of Southern California. She was the first female professional hired by the US Bureau of Land Management, a natural resource agency, and went on to an illustrious 29 career that took her to six states and the District of Columbia, where she served as the Deputy Director of the agency of 200 offices and 10,000 employees. She retired early in 2002 and has her own public and community relations firm. Since 1998, she has been a regular columnist with the Phoenix Business Journal and was a finalist in the 2004 National Association of Black Journalists' excellence awards. Also a popular speaker on everything from human resources management to environmental justice. Currently, she is completing two books. Denise Meridith Consultants Inc, 5515 North 7th Street, Suite 5, Phoenix, Arizona 85014 Phone: (602) 763-9900 Fax: (602) 222-9072 E-mail: **denisemeridithconsultants@cox.net**

Ministry Marketing Solutions Inc. A Chritian marketing firm. Markets inspiring promotions, products, people and publications. Pam Perry, publicist. Contact Ministry Marketing Solutions Inc., 33011 Tall Oaks, Farmington Hills, Michigan 48336 Phone: (248) 426-2300 E-mail: **pamperry@ministrymarketingsolutions.com**   Website: **ministrymarketingsolutions.com**

Morgan Communications Full-service communications company. Founder, Shanté Morgan, has worked for over a decade as a reporter, writing for both newspapers and magazines, covering everything from Hollywood trends to presidential campaigns. She freelances as a copyeditor and proofreader. She has also worked as a college instructor teaching journalism. Shanté Morgan, Morgan Communications, 1710 North Moorpark Road #163, Thousand Oaks, California 91360 Phone: 310-594-9890 E-mail: **ShanteMorgan@aol.com**

Multicultural Marketing Resources, Inc. (MMR) Established in 1994, is a public relations and marketing company representing minority and women owned businesses and specializing in promoting multicultural marketing & diversity news. We represent the nation's leading experts in marketing to Hispanic, Asian American, African American, and other multicultural consumers. President, Editor and Publisher, Ms. Lisa Skriloff. Multicultural Marketing Resources, 101 5th Avenue Suite 10B, New York, New York 10003 Phone: (212) 242-3351 Fax: (212) 691-5969 E-mail: **lisa@multicultural.com**   Website: **www.multicultural.com**

Nina Denny Public Relations A boutique sized firm that specializes in music and entertainment and offers pr with a personal touch. Contact Nina Denny, Nina Denny Public Relations, Post Office Box 1248, Ogdensburg, New York 13669 Phone: (315) 323-1058 Fax: (877) 349-0225 E-mail: **ndenny@ninadenny.com**   Website: **www.ninadenny.com**

PA Public Relations Company PA Public Relations is a New York based Public Relations Company. Mr. Phil Andrews, CEO. PA Public Relations Company, 158-13 72nd Avenue, Suite 5B, Fresh Meadows, New York 11365 Phone: (718) 380-2062 E-mail: E-mail: **phil.andrews@papublicrelations.com**   Website: **www.papublicrelations.com**

PCG Literary Marketing A full service public relations and marketing firm specializing in literary marketing, publicity and much, much more. Contact Ms. Anita Shari Peterson, PCG Literary Marketing, 1250 Powder Springs Road #1607, Marietta, Georgia 30064   E-mail: **publicist@pcgliterary.com** Website: **www.pcgliterary.com**

PowerFlow Media Cutting edge public relations - We offer complete marketing solutions for emerging and established businesses. Fourth Quarter 2005: Events featuring PowerFlow Media clients, Descending Dove Productions (The Last Adam), author and journalist, Farai Chideya (NPR's News & Notes with Ed Gordon, PopandPolitics.com), ArtsTalk, Call To Womanhood, Heart & Soul Editorial Director Yanick Rice Lamb (Rise and Fly: Tall Tales and Mostly True Rules of Bid Whist), Lori Robinson (I Will Survive: The African-American Guide to Healing from Sexual Assault and Abuse), and Evelyn Coleman (Born In Sin). Contact Ms. Joyce E. Davis, PowerFlow Media, 5157 Seashell Lane, Atlanta, Georgia 30349 Phone: (404) 209-9021 E-mail: **jdavis@powerflowmedia.com** Website: **www.powerflowmedia.com**

Read Zone Book Reviews PR Services. Reviews with a personal touch. We also offer newsletter writing and blog writing services. Post Office Box 145, Whitehall, Pennsylvania 18052 Fax: (530) 504-7094 E-mail: **info@rzbr.com** Website: **www.rzbr.com**

Right Hand Concepts Founder, Ms. Vonetta Booker-Brown has over eight years of experience as an administrative assistant, writer, editor, web designer and graphic artist. Her client roster includes CB Commercial, UBS Warburg, Pitney Bowes, Southern Connecticut State University, Weekly Reader Corporation, Essence Communications, Daymon Worldwide and PH Factor Productions. She is also an accomplished journalist and writer who has contributed to various publications including Stamford Advocate, Fairfield County Weekly, New Haven Register, MediaBistro.com, HealthQuest, Essence, Vibe, Honey and XXL. Vonetta Booker-Brown, Right Hand Concepts, 2020 Pennsylvania Avenue, North West, #341, Washington, DC 20006 E-mail: **chiefelement@gmail.com** Website: **www.righthandconcepts.com**

The Signals Agency A public marketing and management relations firm that represents independent and major record labels, platinum producers and clothing enterprises, including Interscope Records, Loud Records, Indefinite Designs and others. Founder and president, Yasmin Shiraz is former president of College Entertainment Inc., a marketing company whose clients included: Luster Products, Universal Music Group, Motown Records, Reebok, Def Jam Music Group, Virgin Records, and others. Yasmin Shiraz, Post Office Box 220053, Chantilly, Virginia 20153 Phone: (703) 542-5072 Fax: (703) 542-5073 E-mail: **yasminshiraz@aol.com**

Terrie Williams Agency Founded by CEO Terrie Williams in 1988; management entertainment company and consultant: executive coaching, marketing and communications advice, public relations, individual and corporate counseling. Terrie Williams Agency, 382 Central Park West, Suite 7R, New York, New York 10023 Phone: (212) 316-0305 Fax: (212) 749-8867 E-mail: **tmwms@terriewilliams.com** Website: **terriewilliams.com**

Totally Blessed Productions & Promotions Provides music production and promotion services to various artists and businesses. We also conduct workshops, conferences, and present musical events to the public. Ms. Tiffany Benton-Bailey, Totally Blessed Productions & Promotions, 9913 Maury Cove, Olive Branch, Mississippi 38654 Phone: (662) 893-0760 E-mail: **totallyblessedgospel@hotmail.com**

Ed Bullins
Author * Playwright
Lecturer * Instructor

Ed Bullins is currently the Distinguished Artist-in-Residence at Northeastern University in Boston. He earned his MFA in playwriting from San Francisco State University in California. His teaching interests include playwriting, scriptwriting, Afro-American literature, Black History, acting, and directing, and African-American Cultural expressions, i.e. music, film, thought.

He is author of seven books, including <u>Five Plays By Ed Bullins</u>, <u>The Duplex</u>, <u>The Hungered One</u>, <u>Four Dynamite Plays</u>, <u>The Theme is Blackness</u>, and <u>The Reluctant Rapist</u>. His latest book is ED BULLINS: 12 Plays and Selected Writings (U of Michigan Press, 2006). He wrote and produced for the theatre several commission works, including *Rainin' Down Stairs* for the 1992 San Francisco Theatre Artaud, and has been editor for a number of theatre magazines and publications. He was producer of *Circles of Times,* Boston's Lyric Theatre in August 2003.

Among his awards and grants is three Obie Awards, four Rockefeller Foundation Playwriting Grants, two Guffenheim Playwriting Fellowships, an NEA Playwriting Grant, the AUDELCO Award, the New York Drama Critics Circle Award for Best American Play of 1974 -75, the National Black Theatre Festival Living Legend Award, and the OTTO Award in 2004.

Mr. Bullins is an active member of the ACT Roxbury Consortium. His professional affiliations include PEN American Center, The Dramatists Guild, WGAe, and the Modern Language Association.

Publishers

Africa World Press and The Red Sea Press Sister presses" based in Lawrenceville, New Jersey, and dedicated to the publication and distribution of books on the African World and fulfilling a great demand for "non-mainstream" academic texts, poetry, short stories and children's books. Africa World Press Inc., & The Red Sea Press Inc., 541 West Ingham Avenue, Suite B, Trenton, New Jersey 08638 Phone: (609) 695-3200 Fax: (609) 695-6466 E-mail: **senaitkassahun@verizon.net** Website: **africanworld.com**

African American Images Publishes and distributes books of an Africentric nature that promote self-esteem, collective values, liberation, and skill development. We have one of the largest black-owned bookstores in the country, with over 10,000 square feet of space and over 4,000 titles. Owner, President and Publisher, Dr. Jawanza Kunjufu. African American Images, 1909 West 95th Street, Chicago, Illinois 60643 Phone: (312) 445-0322 E-mail: **aarcher@africanamericanimages.com** Website: **www.africanamericanimages.com**

Africana Homestead Legacy Publishers We welcome book proposals of scholarly work from all individuals. The work must document and analyze aspects of the lives of people of African descent throughout the diaspora. We have a special interest in these academic disciplines: African Studies; African American Studies; African Canadian Studies; Art; Anthropology; Biography; Caribbean and Latin American Studies; Communications; Conflict Studies; Culture; Cultural Anthropology; Economics; Education; History; International Relations; Mass Media; Pan-African Studies; Performing Arts; Political Science; Philosophy; Psychology; Public Health; Literature and Fiction; Language; Law; Medicine; Music; Science; Sociology; Women's Studies. We also will re-publish titles that are out of print, and for which the publishing rights are held solely by the author (s). Africana Homestead Legacy Publishers, Post Office Box 2957, Cherry Hill, New Jersey 08034 Phone: (856) 662-9858 Fax: (856) 662-9516 E-mail: **editors@ahlpub.com** Website: **www.ahlpub.com**

Amber Communications Group, Inc. Publisher is the recipient of several awards, including: the Chicago Black Book Fair and Conference Independent Publisher/Press Award, the 2003 BlackBoard Bestseller's African-American Publisher of the Year Award, the 2003 American Library Association Reluctant Reader Award, the 2004 Cape Verdean News Millennium Award for Excellence in Book Publishing and the 2004 1st YOUnity and Disilgold Soul Magazine. Co-Founder of the African American Publisher's Pavilion at Book Expo America. The Company continues to expand with Amber Books, its self-help imprint, Busta Books, its celebrity bio imprint; Colossus Books, the imprint for international personalities and topics; Ambrosia Books, the imprint for literature, fiction and non-fiction; Amber Books for in-general specialty books, and Amber/Wiley Books, its co-publishing/imprint with John Wiley & Sons, Inc. Tony Rose, Publisher. Amber Communications Group, Inc., 1334 East Chandler Boulevard, Suite 5-D67, Phoenix, Arizona 85048 Phone: (480) 460-1660 Fax: (480) 283-0991 **amberbk@aol.com** Website: **www.amberbooks.com**

August Press The company was founded in October 1992 in New Jersey by Wayne Dawkins, president and chief executive officer. August Press has published seven books, all trade paperbacks. Manuscript submissions must include a stamped, self-addressed envelope and a cover letter. Please allow six to eight weeks for a reply. Contact August Press, 108 Terrell Road, Post Office Box 6693, Newport News, Virginia 23606 Phone: (800) 268-4338 Fax: (757) 591-2371 E-mail: **wdawk69643@aol.com** Website: **www.augustpress.net**

Better Day Publishing Founded by Naresha S. Perry. Better Day has provided quality child book publishing and illustration services in the Houston Metro area since April 2001. We also accept finished adult and fictions manuscripts from many genres including science fiction, mystery, and adventure. Contact Ms. Naresha S. Perry, Better Day Publishing Company, 11152 Westheimer, #341, Houston, Texas 77042 Phone: (713) 548-4048 E-mail: **contact@betterdaypublishing.com** Website: **www.betterdaypublishing.com**

Black Classic Press Devoted to publishing obscure and significant works by and about people of African descent. We specialize in republishing works that are out of print. W. Paul Coates, Founder. Contact Editor, Black Classic Press, Post Office Box 13414, Baltimore, Maryland 21203 Phone: (410) 358-0980 Fax: (410) 358-0987 E-mail: **bcp@charm.net** Website: **www.blackclassicbooks.com**

Blind Beggar Press A publishing company owned and operated by People of Colour, and based in the Bronx in New York City, New York. It was founded in 1977 by Gary Johnson and C.D. Grant, both writers and poets who saw the need to create another, unique vehicle for emerging and established writers/artists of color. We have approximately 25 books in print. Blind Beggar Press, Post Office Box 437, Bronx, New York 10467 Phone: (914) 683-6792 E-mail: **blindbeggar1@juno.com** Website: **www.blindbeggarpress.org**

Books for Black Children, Inc. African American children's book publisher. Contact Books For Black Children, Inc., Post Office Box 13261, Reading, Pennsylvania 19612 E-mail: **bbc-inc@att.net**

Clarity Press, Inc. Publishes books on the human dimension of current issues; human rights and social justice. Send query letter first, with c.v., table of contents and synopsis. Contact Editor, Clarity Press, Inc., Suite 469, 3277 Roswell Road, North East, Atlanta, Georgia 30305 Phone: (877) 613-1495 Fax: (877) 613-7868 E-mail: **clarity@islandnet.com** Website: **www.claritypress.com**

Divine Truth Press Publisher of books and ebooks in a keeping-it-real Christian style. D. S. White Publisher. Contact D. S. White, Divine Truth Press, Post Office Box 145, Whitehall, Pennsylvania 18052 Fax: (530) 504-7094 E-mail: **info@divinetruthpress.com** Website: **www.divinetruthpress.com**

Disilgold Small Bronx press founded in 2001. Publishes new books and anthologies via various genres. Publisher, Heather Covington, Disilgold, Post Office Box 652, Baychester Station, Bronx, New York 10469 Phone: (718) 547-0499 E-mail: **disilgold@aol.com** Website: **www.disilgold.com**

Dreams Publishing company Publishes books that promote faith, kindness, honesty, loyalty, and virtue that is well-written, persuasive, and interesting. We want authors that have a different kind of story to tell. We want Authors who want to be published in electronic and print media and who are willing to promote their books worldwide. Please inquire before sending a manuscript. Teresa Rhodes, Acquisition Director. Dreams Publishing Company, Post Office Box 4731, Rocky Mount, North Carolina 27803 Phone: (877) 209-5200 E-mail: **Books@DreamsPublishing.com** Website: **www.dreamspublishing.com**

Eschar Publications African-American book publisher. Contact Ms. Vivian Owens, Eschar Publications, Post Office Box 1194, Mount Dora, Florida 32756 Phone: (352) 455-3554 E-mail: **escharpub@earthlink.net**

First Scribe Books An independently-owned publishing company committed to bringing quality writings expressing the vast dimensions of the Black experience to the world. Contact Publisher, First Scribe Books, Post Office Box 62, Fort Lauderdale, Florida 33302 E-mail: **Firstscribebooks@yahoo.com** Website: **www.firstscribebooks.com**

4465 PReSS A new and popular, online publisher of multicultural fiction and non-fiction book titles. The focus of 4465 PReSS is to deploy and achieve the singular mission of multicentric-representational, publishing excellence. 4465 PReSS is a wholly owned subsidiary of barrendau LLC and 4465 Media. Contact Ms. Deidra Scott Wilson, Associate Publisher, 4465 PReSS, 610-A East Battlefield Road, Suite 279, Springfield, Missouri 65807 Phone: (866) 842-1042 Fax: (775) 257-1286 E-mail: **press4465@yahoo.com** Website: **www.4465press.com**

Fredericks Enterprises, Inc. A multimedia company that specializes in the production and marketing of urban literature (also known as Street Lit). Contact Walter Fredericks Enterprises, Inc, 644 Saint Anns Avenue, Suite #1, Bronx, New York 10455 Phone: (917) 664-4070 Fax: (718) 401-8450 E-mail: **wenterprisesinc@yahoo.com** Website: **www.walterfredericks.com**

Genesis Press, Inc. America's largetst privately owned African-American book publisher. Founded in Columbus, Mississippi in 1993 by attorneys Wilbur and Dorothy Colom. We do accept unagented material and multiple submissions. When submitting, include a query letter, a 2-3 page (and no longer) synopsis of the entire manuscript, and the first three chapters. Acquisitions Editor, Genesis Press, Inc., Post Office Box 101, Columbus, Mississippi 39701 Phone: (662) 329-9927 Fax: (662) 329-9399 E-mail: **customerservice@genesis-press.com** Website: **www.genesis-press.com**

Greene Bark Press Inc. A children's book publishing company and distributor of educational toys and games. Mr. Thomas J. Greene, Publisher. Contact Greene Bark Press Inc, Post Office Box 1108, Bridgeport, Connecticut 06601 Phone: (610) 434-2802 Fax: (610) 434-2803 E-mail: **greenebark@aol.com** Website: **www.greenebarkpress.com**

Gumbs & Thomas Publishers, Inc. Specializing in Kwanzaa books, teachers' guides, cards, posters, children's books & travel guides. Gumbs & Thomas Publishers Inc., Post Office Box 381, New York, New York 10039 Phone: (212) 694-0602 E-mail: **ragumb@aol.com**

Just Us Books Independent publishing company specializing in books and learning materials for children and young people. It focuses on Black history, Black culture and Black experiences. Founded by Wade Hudson and Cheryl Willis Hudson in 1988, this innovative company is now considered one of the leading publishers of Black interest titles for young people. Just Us Books has had a major impact on the publishing industry from its inception. When the company released its first title, AFRO-BETS® ABC Book there were very few Black interest books being published and widely distributed. The pioneering efforts of the Hudsons have helped to demonstrate that there is a viable market for Black interest books. Today, more Black interest books for children and young people are published annually, and more of these books find their way onto the shelves of book stores and retail outlets. In October 1997, Income Opportunities magazine named the couple "Small Business Pioneers of the Year" for the success they have achieved with Just Us Books, Inc., from its meager beginnings to a million-dollar publishing company." We are looking for chapter-book manuscripts of 2,500 to 5,000 words targeted to middle readers (ages 8 to 11) and young adult manuscripts of more than 5,000 words for readers aged 12-16. Wade and Cheryl Willis Hudson, Publishers. Contact Mr. Willie Hudson, Just Us Books, 356 Glenwood Avenue, East Orange, New Jersey 07017 Phone: (973) 672-7701 E-mail: **justusbooks@mindspring.com** Website: **www.justusbooks.com**

KHAFRE Writer's colony. The writers workshops, provided weekly allows each writer to identify and focus on areas of need; and challenges the more established writers to edit their near completed works and submit for publishing consideration, directly to the KHAFRE Publishing. Contact: Sade, KHAFRE, Post Office Box 1134, Ackerman, Mississippi 39735 Phone: (662) 285-9798 E-mail: **khafre@peoplepc.com** Website: **www.khafre.us**

Kings Crossing Publishing Award-winning words by award-winning writers. Award-winning independent publishing company serving the LGBT writing community since 2001. Authors in the past have included award-winners, Penny Mickelbury, Robin G. White, Skyy, Abigail Sewell, Talia Kingsbury and C.C. Carter. Anthologized works have included Ami Mattison and Alix Olson to name a few. The company publishes, fiction, non-fiction, self-help, poetry, and memoir. Manuscripts, partial manuscripts or synopsis may be mailed and should not exceed 50 pages in length. King Crossing Publishing, Post Office Box 673121, Atlanta, Georgia 30006 Phone: (770) 640-9963 E-mail: **kingscrossingpub@aol.com** Website: **www.kingscrossingpublishing.com**

Kinship Press Philadelphia-based African-American imprint of Jewell-Jordan Publishing Company. The mission of Kinship Press is to publish stories that celebrate the African-American experience. A portion of the proceeds from the sale of Kinship Press books will benefit non-profit organizations that seek to edify and uplift the African-American family. Valerie, Kinship Press, 7715 Crittenden Street, Suite 308, Philadelphia, Pennsylvania 19118 Phone: (215) 991-5662 E-Mail: **info@kinshippress.com** Website: **www.kinshipppress.com**

La Caille Nous Established October, 1995. La Caille Nous will collaborate with individuals or institutions to publish works that may fall in or out of our specialty Guichard Cadet, La Caille Nous Publishing Company, 328 Flatbush Avenue, Suite 240, Brooklyn, New York 11238 Phone: (212) 726-1293 Fax: (212) 591-6465 E-mail: **inq@lcnpub.com** Website: **www.lcnpub.com**

Milligan Books Since its founding in 1990, Milligan Books has skyrocketed to become the fastest-growing Black female-owned publishing company in America. The company has published more than 100 Black authors. Dr. Rosie Milligan, founder, publisher. Contact Publisher, Milligan Books, Inc., 1425 West Manchester Avenue, Suite C, Los Angeles, California 90047 Phone: (323) 750-3592 Fax: (323) 750-2886 E-mail: **DrRosie@aol.com** Website: **www.milliganbooks.com**

Mirror-Gibbs Publications Frank Jones is the CEO/publisher of Mirror-Gibbs Publications, a Black Oakland base small press-publishing house. Frank A. Jones, Mirror-Gibbs Publication, Post Office Box 6573, Oakland, California 94603 Phone: (510) 409-9571 E-mail: **pinoquit@hotmail.com** Website: **www.gibbsmagazine.com**

Now U No Publishing Company Publisher. Tonya Bratton, Now U No Publishing Company, Post Office Box 9501, Cincinnati Ohio 45209 Phone: (513) 226-6450 E-mail: **tonya.bratton@nowuno-enterprises.com** Website: **www.nowunopublishingco.com**

PCG Publishing We are a family company that specializes in well-written, quality fiction and non-fiction books. Please do not submit poetry, memoirs, auto-biography, comic, time period novels, or erotic books. Please send query letter and author biography with writing credentials to our corporate office. Anita Shari Peterson, President, PCG Publishing, 5047 West Main Street, #324, Kalamazoo, Michigan 49009 E-mail: **ceo@pcg-publishing.com**

Prioritybooks Publications Publisher. Also, supports youths and teens as they pursue writing careers. The owner and staff assists potential writers in finding a voice, consultant on book issues and help securing book signing facilities. Founder, Chief Executive Officer, Ms. Rose Jackson-Beavers. Prioritybooks Publication, Post Office Box 2535, Florissant, Missouri 63033 Phone: (314) 741-6789 E-mail: **rosbeav03@yahoo.com** Website: **www.prioritybooks.com**

Publishing Communications Provides publishing services for the publication of books, magazines, newsletters and various other publications. We welcome Christian and none-Christian publications as well as fiction and non-fiction literary works and are now accepting works from new authors. Publisher, Publishing Communications, Post Office Box 1023, Austell, Georgia 30168 E-mail: **publisher@publishingcomm.com**

Q-Boro Books Founded in 2004 to publish groundbreaking titles encompassing subjects of African-American interest. These subjects include Street Lit /Urban, Erotica, Chick Lit, Relationship/Drama, Suspense Thrillers, Horror, and more. We are actively seeking new, talented authors of all genres. Mr. Mark Anthony, President & Publisher. Q-Boro Books, Post Office Box 310907 Jamaica, New York 11431 Phone: (718) 977-0885 Fax: (718) 977-8548 E-mail: **info@Qborobooks.com** Website: **www.qborobooks.com**

Strebor Books African American publishing company founded in 1999. Strebor has published over 60 authors, produced numerous best sellers and has recently become an official imprint of Simon and Schuster. Contact Publisher, Strebor Books International/Simon and Schuster, Post Office Box 6505, Largo, Maryland 20792 Phone: (301) 583-0616 Fax: (301) 583-0003 E-mail: **streborbooks@aol.com** Website: **www.streborbooks.com**

Third World Press Since 1967, the nation's oldest, continuously running Black-owned press that published books in all genres. In 2006, became the first African American owned book company to have a book listed as a bestseller by the New York Times, "The Covenant with Black America." Haki R. Madhubuti is Publisher. Bennett J. Johnson, Vice President. Third World Press, 7822 Dobson Street, Chicago, Illinois 60619 Phone: (312) 651-0700 Fax: (312) 651-7286 E-mail: **twpress3@aol.com** Website: **www.thirdworldpressinc.com**

Triple Crown Publications Publisher of urban fiction novels. Began in 2001 with the self-publishing of Author Vickie Stringer's debut novel, "Let That Be The Reason." Contact Publisher, Triple Crown Publications, 4449 Easton Way, 2nd Floor, Columbus, Ohio 43219 Phone: (614) 934 1233 Fax: (614) 934 1593 E-mail: **manager@triplecrownpublications.com** Website: **www.triplecrownpublications.com**

Urban Christian The UC Imprint publishes works of fiction that consist of predominately African-American characters and portray life-changing, dramatic, redeeming tales highlighting life, love and intrigue in the Christian community. Urban Christian Writing Guidelines: Genre: Christian/Inspirational fiction Fiction Manuscript word length: Range of approximately 65,000 - 100,000 words. Manuscript pages: Range of approximately 260-350 pages. Contact Urban Christian Submissions, Post Office Box 128, Reynoldsburg, Ohio 43068 E-mail: **urbanchristianinfo@yahoo.com** Website: **www.urbanchristianonline.net**

Urban Lifestyle Press Accepting manuscripts for Urban Fiction must be 80-100k words in length. Advances given 3-5K. Submit first 3 chapters and synopsis only! Contact Kevin Elliott, Urban Lifestyle Press, Post Office Box 12714, Charlotte, North Carolina 28220 E-mail: **kelliott11@carolina.rr.com**

Walk Worthy Press Christian publisher whose ministry is dedicated to showing, through books, how the Word of God in the Bible can be applied to every area of our daily lives. Ms. Denise Stinson, editor and publisher. She is also founder/president, of Stinson Literary Agency. Contact Manuscript Coordinator, Walk Worthy Press, 33290 West Fourteen Mile Road, Suite 482, West Bloomfield, Michigan 48322 E-mail: **editor@walkworthypress.net** Website: **www.walkworthypress.net**

Write The Vision, Inc. Christian publishing company committed to assisting writers to bring forth their creative visions and to prepare them for publication. Write The Vision has published the following books: To Whom Much Is Given by Maurice M. Gray, Jr. (fiction). I Really Didn't Mean To Get HIV by Livingston N. Lee, Jr. as told to Maurice M. Gray, Jr. (nonfiction). Ocean View by Fred Gaines (nonfiction). All Things Work Together by Maurice M. Gray, Jr. (fiction). Owner/operator Maurice M. Gray, Jr. Contact Write The Vision, Inc., Box 12926, Wilmington, Delaware 19850 Phone: (302) 778-2407 E-mail: **writevision2000@yahoo.com** Website: **www.writethevision.biz**

Publishing Services

AUniQue Publishing Company We aid in entrepreneurial publishing by providing the following affordable writing & freelance accommodations: articles, announcements, book reviews--free, critique consultations, data entry, editing, flyers, ghostwriting, newsletters--concept development, press releases, proofreading, speaking engagements. AUniQue Publishing Company, Post Office Box 184, Fort Worth, Texas 76101 Phone: (817) 320-6123 E-mail: **info@auniquepc.com** Website: **www.auniquepc.com**

BCP Digital Printing Print-On-Demand and document processing company. We are proud to be a family-run business committed to caring for our customers, employees and community. BCP Digital Printing, 4701 Mt. Hope Drive, Suite D, Baltimore, Maryland 21215 Phone: (410)358-0980 E-mail: **bcp@charm.net** Website: **www.bcpdigital.com**

Better Day Publishing The company has provided quality child book publishing and child book illustration services in the Houston Metro area since April 2001. The team, led by CEO and author, Naresha S. Perry, delivers imaginative, professional and speedy publishing services. Better Day generates creative solutions ranging from book design, editing services and the production of web-based marketing materials. Working with electronic arts, we produce direct marketing pieces including posters, postcards, sales sheets, consumer catalogs and brochures. Better Day Publishing, 11152 Westheimer #341, Houston, TX. 77042 Phone: (713) 548-4048 E-mail: **contact@betterdaypublishing** Website: **www.betterdaypublishing.com**

Black Star Consulting Former Random House book editor, freelance writer, book editor and editorial consultant who has worked with book publishers, agents, best selling authors and up and coming writers. Contact Ms. Carol A. Taylor, Black Star Consulting, 295 Clinton Avenue #E3, Brooklyn, New York 11205 E-mail: **carol@brownsugarbooks.com** Website: **www.BrownSugarBooks.com**.

BlackBerry Literary Services Specializes is all aspects of writing, publication and promotion of authors of fiction and non-fiction, poetry, and children's books. Contact Ms. Sandra Peoples, BlackBerry Literary Services, 2956 Mackin Road, Flint, Michigan 48504 Phone: (810) 240-4372 E-mail: **bblit@hotmail.com**

Magdalene Breaux Publishing services, technical writing, book production consulting for independent authors and TV production and editing. Contact Magdalene Breaux, Post Office Box 67, Fairburn, Georgia 30213 Phone: (770) 842-4792 Fax: (770) 964-1875 E-mail: **magbreaux@mindspring.com** Website: **www.familycurse.com**

Danley Writing Consultants Professional writing and editing services to individual, corporate, and non-profit clients. Danley Writing Consultants, 458 Cambridge Court, Suite D, Riverdale, Georgia 30296 E-mail: **cdanley@danleywriting.com** Website: **www.danleywriting.com**

Patrick PJ Davis Marketing and Web Solutions for authors, entertainers and publishing companies. Patrick PJ Davis, Post Office Box 420725, Houston, Texas 77242 Phone: (713) 866-6548 E-mail: **info@blackcottonworks.net** Website: **www.blackcottonworks.net**

Disilgold Provides writers services: press releases, book marketing resources. Book publisher. Heather Covington, Disilgold, Post Office Box 652, Baychester Station, Bronx, New York 10469 Phone: (718) 547-0499 E-mail: **disilgold@aol.com** Website: **www.disilgold.com**

Docuversion Andrea Hinton, CEO of Docuversion, is dedicated to the advancement of African-American literature and the enhancement of reading experiences with well-edited books. Docuversion is a full-service editing firm that specializes in all genres, but with an emphasis on urban lit. Contact Ms. Andrea Hinton, Post Office Box 19101, Cleveland, Ohio 44119. Phone: (216) 633-2397 E-mail: **andrea@docuversion.com** Website: **www.docuversion.com**

Dreams Publishing Company If you feel you can help us to develop a reputation for quality books send us your completed manuscript. We are accepting fiction and nonfiction manuscripts. Dreams Publishing Company, Post Office Box 4731, Rocky Mount, North Carolina 27803 E-mail: **info@DreamsPublishing.com** Website: **www.dreamspublishing.com**

FountainPenn House of Publishing We offer affordable publishing services. We will proofread your manuscript, help you design your book cover, assist you with marketing your book and much more. Contact Roberto Lee Davis or Danielle-Kim Davis, FountainPenn Enterprise, 120 Franklin Avenue, Suite 186, Scranton, Pennsylvania 18503 Phone: (570) 242-8525 E-mail: **robdani2001@fountainpenn.com** Website: **www.fountainpenn.com**

Fredericks Enterprises, Inc. A multimedia company that specializes in the production and marketing of urban literature (also known as Street Lit). Contact Walter Fredericks Enterprises, Inc, 644 Saint Anns Avenue, Suite #1, Bronx, New York 10455 Phone: (917) 664-4070 Fax: (718) 401-8450 E-mail: **wenterprisesinc@yahoo.com** Website: **www.walterfredericks.com**

God's Chosen Pens Promotes nonfiction Christian authors and their books. Educational seminars on everything authors need to know before and after their books have been published. Frederick L. Anderson, GCP, Post Office Box 4172, Houston, Texas 77210 Phone: (832) 654-9567 E-mail: **godschosenpens@aol.com** Website: **www.godschosenpens.com**

K & K Houston, LLC A services oriented company based out of Northern Virginia, the DC Metro area with affiliations in Los Angeles, California. We work with clients from all over the United States. The services we offer are: Book Publishing and Web Design & Internet Marketing Services. Our Web Design & Internet Marketing services are to help you build a strong and lasting public presence and to help you become a household name (Branding) with consumers. With our Book Publishing, we handle the publishing of authors and writers in the areas of Poetry, Motivational, Inspirational, Self-Help and Romance. We handle all aspects of your publishing projects from book design & layout, typesetting, editing, printing, marketing and distribution. Kevin J Houston, K & K Houston, LLC, Post Office Box 1006, Lorton, Virginia 22199 Phone: (703) 878-1905 Fax: (877) 264-8835 E-mail: **kkhouston@kkhouston.com** Website: **www.kkhouston.com**

Images & Illuminations We specialize in web design and development: book design, logos, brochures, posters, invitations, catalogs and more.   Ms. Cheryl Hanna, Director, Images & Illuminations, 214 Sixth Avenue, Suite 3B, Brooklyn, New York 11215 Phone: (718) 783-0131 E-mail: **imagesandilluminations@earthlink.net** Website: **www.imagesandilluminations.com**

Johnswriteme Professional proofreading, book, manuscript and copyediting, proof and edit web pages. johnswriteme, Post Office Box 40261, Fort Worth, Texas 76140 Phone: (817) 366-9440 E-mail: **johnswriteme@sbcglobal.net** Website: **www.johnswriteme.net**

Loose Leaves Full service editing service for manuscripts, novels, poems and any literary work. Sharon Hudson, Loose Leaves Enterprises, Post Office Box 548, Tyrone, Georgia 30290 Phone: (770) 314-5932 E-mail: **akaivyleaf@looseleaves.org**   Website: **www.looseleaves.org**

Lemrac Books We specialize in author consultations and assistance in writing/editing, printing, promoting, marketing, and distributing their books. Contact Ms. Carmel S. Victor, Lemrac Books, Post Office Box 1132, Union, New Jersey 07083 Phone: (908) 206-0828 E-mail: **carmel@carmelsvictor.com**   Website: **www.carmelsvictor.com**

Marion Designs Book Cover Designs. Several of Marion Designs book covers have made the Essence best seller list and are featured on Black Expressions. Contact Keith Saunders, Marion Designs, 225 Sunderland Way, Suite # U, Stockbridge, Georgia 30281 Phone: (678) 641-8689 E-mail: **mariondesigns@bellsouth.net** Website: **www.mariondesigns.com**

Mays Printing Company has consistently met the challenge of delivering quality printing products to corporations, advertisement agencies, government agencies, educational institutions, publishers, packagers, small businesses in addition to personalized services for each individual customer. Mays Printing Company is a Family owned business. Founded in 1946, we are proud to be one of the Cornerstones of Americas rich heritage of Certified African American Businesses. Mays Printing Company, 15800 Livernois Avenue, Detroit, Michigan 48238 Phone: (313) 861-1900 Fax: (313) 861-5660 E-mail: **contact@maysprinting.com** Website: **www.maysprinting.com**

Ministry Marketing Solutions Marketing consulting and public relations agency that targets the African American Christian market. Pam Perry, publicist. Ministry Marketing Solutions, 21442 Hamilton Avenue, Farmington Hills, Michigan 48336 Phone: (248) 426-2300 E-mail: **pamperry@ministrymarketingsolutions.com**   Website: **ministrymarketingsolutions.com**

Daphne Muse Through her more than ten year old editorial service, she works with emerging and established writers; move them from Concept to Manuscript. Contact Daphne Muse, 2429 East 23rd Street, Oakland, California 94601 Phone: (510) 436-4716 Fax: (510) 261-6064 E-mail: **msmusewriter@aol.com** Website: **www.daphnemuse.com**

Novel Ideal Publishing & Editorial Services Company Full service editorial service offering copy editing, content editing and proofreading services. Novel Ideal Publishing & Editorial Services Company, 2274 Salem Road, Suite 106, PMB 173, Conyers, Georgia 30013 E-mail: **novelideal@aol.com** Website: **www.electaromeparks.com**

Oasis Publishing Group Exists for the purpose of publishing books by authors who strive to champion their genres. It was founded in 2006 by Oasis, author of Push Comes To Shove, and operates out of Cleveland, Ohio. This company only publishes three books annually so that each project will receive special attention. It does not accept unsolicited manuscripts. Authors are required to send a query letter via email or snail mail. Oasis Publishing Group, Post Office Box 19101, Cleveland, Ohio 44119 E-mail: **acquisitions@oasisnovels.com**

PageTurner.net Provides author web site design, internet consulting services and website hosting. Contact Pageturner.net, Post Office Box 120, 2951 Marina Bay Drive, #130, League City, Texas 77573 Phone: (866) 875-1044 E-mail: **pwsquare@pageturner.net** Website: **pageturner.net**

Per-fect Words Publishing A professional typeset and book cover design services company: maunscript editing and distribution, web design. Per-fect Words Publishing, Post Office. Box 170451, San Francisco, California 94117 Phone: (415) 252-0577 E-mail: **regina@per-fectwords.com** Website: **www.per-fectwords.com**

Prioritybooks Publications Assist potential writers in finding a voice; consultant on book issues and help securing book signing facilities. Chief Executive Officer, Rose Jackson-Beavers. Contact Prioritybooks Publication, Post Office Box 2535, Florissant, Missouri 63032 Phone: (314) 741-6789 E-mail: **rosbeav03@yahoo.com** Website: **www.prioritybooks.com**

PriorityONE Publications Since 2001. We endeavor to assist Christian writers in self-publishing. Christina Dixon, PriorityONE Publications, Post Office Box 725, Farmington, Michigan 48332 Phone: (800) 331-8841 E-mail: **cdixon@p1pubs.com**

Prism Pages Literary services and publishing company: copy writing, ghost writing, literary critiques. Ms. Lisette Peterson, Prism Pages, Post Office Box 7189, Hampton, Virginia 23666 Phone: (757) 218-8587 E-mail: **info@prismpages.com** Website: **www.prismpages.com**

Publishing Communications Provides publishing services for the publication of books, magazines, newsletters and various other publications. Publisher, Publishing Communications, Post Office Box 1023, Austell, Georgia 30168 E-mail: **publisher@publishingcomm.com**

Tee C. Royal Senior Editor of BlackBoard Magazine; Books Editor of Mommy Too and TCBW Magazine. Founder of RAWSISTAZ Reviewers, the leading reviewers in the literary industry. Offers literary services to authors, publishers, and the literary community. The RAWSISTAZ Reviewers, Post Office Box 1362, Duluth, Georgia 30096 Phone: (775) 363-8683 Fax: (775) 416-4540 E-mail: **tee@rawsistaz.com** Website: **www.therawreviewers.com**

22nd Century Press Independent publisher for self-published authors. We assist in choosing the right services, technology, marketing methods, and all of the basics needed by self-published authors. Our Black Author Showcase is an on/offline catalyst for new self-published authors to market their books. Contact Ms. Diane Williams, 12138 Central Avenue, 223, Mitchellville, Maryland 20721 Phone: (443) 483-4261 E-mail: **diane@22ndCenturyPress.com** Website: **www.22ndCenturyPress.com**

Same Page Promotions Sets up book signings and various venues for authors to meet their West Coast readers in small informal gatherings. Ms. Christine Battle-Ellington, Same Page Promotions, Post Office Box 3581, San Leandro, California 94578 Phone: (510) 632-1600 E-mail: **christine@samepagepromotions.com**   Website: **www.samepagepromotions.com**

Sardonyx Jade Publishing (SJP) Providing editing and consulting services to new authors. Sardonyx Jade Publishing, 1401 North La Brea Avenue, Suite 137, Los Angeles, California Phone: (323) 898-7339 Fax: (213) 252-8471 E-mail: **ldjones@sardonyx-jade.com** Website: **www.sardonyx-jade.com**

Semaj Publications of Denver Copy editing service. James Allen Nolen, Author/Publisher. Contact Semaj Publications of Denver, 13918 East Mississippi Avenue, Suite 506, Aurora, Colorado 80012 E-mail: **orders@semajpublicationsofdenver.com**

Stuff Happens! Literary, personal and business event planning. Renee Williams, Stuff Happens!, Post Office Box 633, Huntsville, Texas 77340 Phone: (936) 650-3952 E-mail: **stuffhappensep@yahoo.com** Website: **www.stuffhappensep.com**

Nicole Tadgell Children's book illustration. Nicole Tadgell, 14 Sampson Street, Spencer, Massachusetts 01562 Phone: (508) 885-7723 E-mail: **nickietart@yahoo.com** Website: **www.nicoletadgell.com**

Martha "Marti" Tucker Ghost writer for three books. Writer, story editor. Martha Tucker, 6605 Green Valley Circle, Culver City, California 90230 Phone: (310) 337-7008 E-mail: **writelink3@aol.com**

Write Page Literary Service, Inc. Business and creative writing firm. Write Page Literary Service, Inc., Post Office Box 38288, Atlanta, Georgia 30334 Phone: (404) 280-5029 Fax: (404) 656-0238 E-mail: **writepagemo@yahoo.com**

Write The Vision, Inc. Editing, proofreading and some publishing services for Christian authors. Contact Mr. Maurice Gray, Write The Vision, Inc., Post Office Box 12926, Wilmington, Delaware 19850 Phone: (302) 778-2407 E-mail: **writevision2000@yahoo.com** Website: **www.writethevision.biz**

Zhanes' Literary Service ZLS offers publicity services to authors. Kenyatta Ingram, publicist. Zhanes' Literary Service, Post Office Box 15381, Chesapeake, Virginia 23323 Phone: (757) 715-4720 E-mail: **zhanespublicity@hotmail.com** Website: **zhanespublicity.5u.com**

Rodney Saulsberry
Author * Actor * Voice Over Artist

Rodney Saulsberry's distinctive announcers voice is literally everywhere. One of the top voice-over talents in the country movie fans have heard Rodney's voice promoting some of their favorites: Tupac Resurrection, How Stella Got Her Groove Back, Diary of a Mad Black Woman, Friday After Next, Drumline, Undercover Brother, The Best Man, Dumb & Dumberer, Finding Forrester, Soul Food, Hardball, Crooklyn, Bamboozled, Clockers, and many more. Black Enterprise Magazine called Saulsberry: "The voice of choice for behind-the-scenes-narration." Saulsberry first set foot on west coast soil when he came to town with a national touring company of Your Arms Too Short To Box With God after a successful Broadway run. The musical was an instant hit in the Los Angeles area and led to an illustrious television acting career for Rodney that included guest starring roles on Taxi, Mash, Gimme a Break, 227, Hill Street Blues and Dr. Quinn Medicine Woman. He also enjoyed series regular status on the soap opera, Capitol and a recurring role on The Young and the Restless. He has been a voiceover commercial pitchman for Zatarain's, Twix, Toyota Camry, ALPO, Honda Accord, Lincoln LS, Verizon, White Castle, 7UP, Burger King, SBC, and Nestle Crunch. He can also be heard reading Books on Tape, as well as narrating E! Entertainments, True Hollywood Story, about Motown R&B singer, Marvin Gaye. In the summer of 2006 he announced promos for the ABC hit Dancing With The Stars. His voice promoted the ABC critically acclaimed Charlie Brown Christmas Special in 2007. He announced the 34th NAACP Image Awards and the Essence Awards specials on FOX Television, The Grammy Awards and the Country Music Awards for CBS.

Celebrity voice-over artist, Saulsberry is the voice of Joe Robbie Robertson on the hit cartoon series Spider-Man and James Rhodey Rhodes in the new animated feature film, The Invincible Iron Man, Chyron in the Animatrix, Ufwapo on Ahh…Real Monsters, Willy on Xyber 9, and has guest starred on many other Saturday morning cartoons that include Rugrats, Duckman, Static Shock and Minoriteam. Rodney lent his melodious baritone singing voice to a jubilant ensemble of background singers on a spirited recording of Hakuna Matata on The Lion King soundtrack. He continued his animation musical journey singing on two numbers from The Prince of Egypt soundtrack, When You Believe and Playing With The Big Boys. As a soloist, Mr. Saulsberry has recorded two rhythm and blues albums that have produced two Billboard charting singles, I Wonder and Look Whatcha Done Now.

He recently became a published author with the release of his first book, <u>You Can Bank on Your Voice: Your Guide to a Successful Career in Voice-Overs</u>, and his new book, <u>Step Up to the Mic: A Positive Approach to Succeeding in Voice-Overs</u>. Mr. Saulsberry currently resides in Agoura, California.

Radio Stations

Chicago Public Radio Home of numerous Black talk radio programs. Colleen Jungbluth, Marketing Director. CPR, Navy Pier, 848 East Grand Avenue, Chicago, Illinois 60611 Phone: (312) 948-4600 E-mail: **cjungbluth@chicagopulicradio.org** Website: **www.wbez.org**

Gospel Radio 1390-AM Interviews authors. Mike Robinson, Program Director, 1390-AM, 233 North Michigan Avenue, Suite 2800, Chicago, Illinois 60601 Phone: (312) 540-2000 E-mail: **ChurchNews@gospel1390.com** Website: **www.gospel1390.com**

KBLX-FM Contemporary music. Nikki Thomas' show is Bay View. Contact KBLX-FM, 55 Hawthorne Street, Suite 900, San Francisco, California 94105 Phone: (415) 284-1029 Fax: (415) 764-1029 E-mail: **info@kblx.com** Website: **www.kblx.com**

KDYA-AM Gospel 1190-AM The Light. Clifford Brown, Jr., Program Director. KDYA, 3260 Blume Drive, Suite 520, Richmond, California 94806 Phone: (510) 222-4242 Fax: (510) 262-9054 E-mail: **RonJordan@gospel1190.net** Website: **www.gospel1190.net**

KDIA-AM 1640-AM. Operations Manager, Clifford Brown Jr. KDIA, 3260 Blume Drive, Suite 520, Richmond, California 94806 Phone: (510) 222-4242 Fax: (510) 262-9054 E-mail: **RonJordan@gospel1190.net** Website: **www.gospel1190.net**

KJLH 102.3 FM Urban Contemporary. Aundrae Russell, Program Director. Contact Greg Johnson, KJLH, 161 North La Brea Avenue, Inglewood, California 90301 Phone: (310) 330-2200 Fax: (310) 330-5555 E-mail: **keslade@kjlhradio.com** Website: **www.kjlhradio.com**

KKBT 100.3 FM Tom Jones in the Morning. Tia Jones, General Manager. KKBT-FM, 5900 Wilshire Boulevard. 19th Floor, Los Angeles, California 90036 Phone: (323) 634-1800 E-mail: **morningshow@thebeatla.com** Website: **www.thebeat.com**

KZWA 104.9 FM Coverage area includes Southwest Louisiana and Southeast Texas. Faye Blackwell, Owner. KZWA, 305 Enterprise Boulevard, Lake Charles, Louisiana 70601 Phone: (337) 491-9955 E-mail: **FBBkzwa@aol.com** Website: **www.kzwa.com**

Sheridan Gospel Network Gospel music; targets African-American Adults 25-54. Contact Sheridan Gospel Network, 4025 Pleasantdale Road, Suite 240 Atlanta, Georgia 30340 Phone: (770) 416-2200 E-mail: **rchristian@sgnthelight.com** Website: **www.sgnthelight.com**

Tama Broadcasting Inc. Mr. Glenn Cherry, President/CEO. Llargest privately Black owned media company in the State of Florida. WTMP 1150-AM and 96.1 FM, Tama Broadcasting, Inc., 5207 Washington Boulevard, Tampa, Florida 33619 Phone: (813) 620-1300 Fax: (813) 628-0713 E-mail: **info@tamabroadcasting.com** Website: **www.tamabroadcasting.com**

WAJZ-FM   Hip hop and R&B.   Contact Program Manager, Albany Broadcasting, 6 Johnson Road, Latham, New York 12110 Phone: (518) 476-9696   Fax: (518) 786-6696   E-mail: **jschaefer@albanybroadcasting.com**   Website: **www.jamz963.com**

WCLK-FM   Jazz 91.9-FM.   Bill Clark, Programming Director.   Contact WCLK-FM, Clark Atlanta University, 111 James P. Brawley Drive, South West, Atlanta, Georgia 30314   Phone: (404) 880-8273   Fax: (404) 880-8869   E-mail: **wclkfm@cau.edu**   Website: **www.wclk.com**

WCLM 1450 AM   Preston T. Brown, President.   Contact WCLM 1450 AM, 3165 Hull Street, Richmond, Virginia 23224   Phone: (804) 231-2186   Fax: (804) 231-7685   E-mail: **webadmin@Richmond.com**   Website: **www.wclmradio.com**

WDBZ 1230-AM   The Buzz.   J Tolliver, Program Director.   Contact WDBZ-AM, 1 Centennial Plaza, Suite 200, 705 Central Avenue, Cincinnati, Ohio 45202   Phone: (513) 749-1230   Fax: (513) 948-1985   E-mail: **jtolliver@radio-one.com**   Website: **www.1230thebuzz.com**

WEUP-AM/FM   Contact Hundley Batts, Sales Coordinator, WEUP Radio Station, Post Office Box 11398, Huntsville, Alabama 35814   Phone: (256) 837-9387   Fax: (256) 837-9404   E-mail: **hundley@103wcup.com**   Website: **www.103weup.com**

WFDU-FM 89.1   Community owned station.   Christian music.   Floyd A. Cray III, Alternative Gospel Music Director, Gospel Vibrations Inc, 114 Shepard Avenue, Teaneck, New Jersey 07666   Phone: (201) 833-0694   E-mail: **GospelVibrations@aol.com**   Website: **www.wfdu.fm**

WFLM 104.7 The Flame   Hot Talk morning show addresses local and national issues.   Joe Fisher, Operations Director.   WFLM 104.7, 6803 S. Federal Highway, Port SaintLucie, Florida 34952   Phone: (772) 460-9356   E-mail: **jfisher@wflm.cc**   Website: **www.wflm.cc**

WFVS AM/FM   Student operated radio studio.   Shirley Ellis, Radio Manager.   Contact WFVS AM/FM, Fort Valley State University, 1005 State University Drive, Fort Valley, Georgia 31030   Phone: (478) 825-6211   E-mail: **ellis@fvsu.edu**   Website: **www.fvsu.edu**

WFXM-FM   Mike Roberts, President/General Manager.   Contact Roberts Communications, Inc., 6174 Highway 57, Macon, Georgia 31217   Phone: (478) 745-3301   Fax: (478) 742-2293   E-mail: **robertsrci@aol.com**

WGFT/WRBP   General Manager, Chuck Jennings.   WGFT/WRBP, 401 North Blaine, Youngstown, Ohio 44505   Phone: (330) 744-5115   E-mail: **jennings.chuck@gmail.com**

WHUR-FM   Howard University radio.   Adult Contemporary.   Steve Hardy Morning Show and Mike Baisden, Love, Lust and Lies heard daily on 96.3 WHUR-FM.   Contact Mr. Mike Kelsey, Howard University, 529 Bryant Street North West, Washington, DC 20059   Phone: (202) 806-3500   E-mail: **support@broadcasturban.net**   Website: **www.whur.com**

WILA-AM   Lawrence A. Toller, General Manager, Post Office Box 3444, Danville, Virginia 24543   Phone: (434) 792-2133   Fax: (434) 792-2134   E-mail: **wilaradio@gamewood.net**

WJAM-FM   Adult, Urban Contemporary.   Also a Gospel talk show hosted by Sister D interviews authors. Scott Communications, Inc., 273 Persimmon Tree Road., Selma, Alabama 36701 Phone: (334) 875-9360 Fax: (334) 875-1340 E-mail: **walxnews@charterinternet.com**

WJMB 1600-AM Jennings Bernard, President. WJMB, Bernard Broadcasting Company, 5316 Cottonwood Road, Memphis, Tennessee 38118 Phone: (901) 794-0416 Fax: (901) 794-3309 E-mail: **jberna12@memphisrealtalk.com**   Website: **www.memphisrealtalk.com**

WJNZ-AM   Interviews authors. Mike St. Cyr, owner. WJNZ, 3777 44th Street, South East, Grand Rapids, Michigan 49512 Phone: (616) 475-4299 E-mail: **mstcyr@wjnz.com** Website: **www.wjnz.com**

WJYD-FM   Christian radio station. WJYD-FM, 350 East 1st Avenue, Suite 100, Columbus Ohio 43201 Phone: (614) 487-1444 E-mail: **fans@radio1col.com** Website: **www.joy106.com**

WKXI-AM Contact Kevin Webb, General Manager. Contact Inner City Broadcast, 731 S. Pear Orchard Road, Ridgeland, Mississippi 39157 Phone: (601) 957-1300 Fax: (601) 956-0516 E-mail: **kwebb1234@aol.com** Website: **www.wkxi.com**

WMCS-AM Don Rosette, General Manager. Contact Mr. Rosette, WMCS-AM, 4222 West Capitol Drive, Milwaukee, Wisconsin 53216 Phone: (414) 444-1290 Fax: (414) 444-1409 E-mail: **drosette@1290wmcs.com**   Website: **www.1290wmcs.com**

WMMJ-FM   Urban Contemporary. Program Director, Kathy Brown. Contact WMMJ-FM, 5900 Princess Garden Parkway, 8th Floor, Lanham, Maryland 20706 Phone: (301) 306-1111 E-mail: **kb@radio-one.com** Website: **www.radio-one.com**

WOAD 105.9AM FM Praise Early Morning Praise with host Percy Davis.   Inner City Broadcast, 731 South Pear Orchard Road, Suite 27, Ridgeland, Mississippi 39157 Phone: (601) 957-1300 Fax: (601) 956-0516 E-mail: **kwebb1234@aol.com** Website: **www.woad.com**

WQOK K97.5-FM Hip Hop and R&B. Program Director, Cy Young. Contact WQOK-FM, 8001-101 Creedmoor Road, Raleigh, North Carolina 27613 Phone: (919) 848.9736 E-mail: **cyoung@radio-one.com** Website: **www.k975.com**

WRSU   Student-operated radio station. Program Director, Jeff Rose, WRSU-FM, Rutgers Univerisy, 126 College Avenue, New Brunswick New Jersey 08903 Phone: (732) 932-7802 Fax: (732) 932-1768 E-mail: **pd@wrsu.org** Website: **www.wrsu.rutgers.edu**

WSRF MYSTIK 1580 AM Interviews artists and authors. Carl Nelson, President. WSRF, 1580, 4431 Rock Island Road, Fort Lauderdale, Florida 33319 Phone: (954) 731-1855 Fax: (954) 731-1833 E-mail: **ron@mystikradio.com** Website: **www.mystikradio.com**

WVAZ-FM   Music; entertainment personalities. Ms.Angenette Natkowski, General Sales Manager, WVAZ-FM, 233 North Michigan Avenue, Suite 2800, Chicago, Illinois 60601 Phone: (312) 540-2000 E-mail: **angenettenatkowski@clearchannel.com** Website: **www.v103.com**

Ruby Dee
Author * Actor * Playwright

Ruby Dee's career in acting has crossed all major forms of media over a span of eight decades. Although she was born Ruby Ann Wallace in Cleveland, Ohio, Ms. Dee considers herself a product of Harlem, where she grew up and began her career as a member of the American Negro Theatre. She received her B.A. from Hunter College in 1945, with degrees in French and Spanish and later studied acting with Paul Mann, Lloyd Richards and Morris Carnovsky. Some of her favorite roles on stage and screen include Lutiebelle in *Purlie Victorious* (written by her late husband, Ossie Davis); Ruth in A *Raisin in the Sun;* Lena in *Boesman and Lena,* for which she received and Obie and a Drama Desk award; and Mary Tyrone in *A Long Day's Journey Into Night,* for which she received a Cable ACE award. Other notable credits include *Anna Lucasta, Wedding Band, St. Lucy's Eyes, The Jackie Robinson Story, Uptight* (which she co-wrote), *Buck and the Preacher, Countdown at Kusini* (which she co-produced with Delta Sigma Theta sorority), *Do The Right Thing, Jungle Fever, Peyton Place, Go Tell It on the Mountain, The Stand,* and *Having Our Say.* She has received several Emmy nominations, and in 1991, won an Emmy for her performance in *Decoration Day.* She completed work as the lead in Number 2, a New Zealand comedy-drama, and is featured with Julie Harris in the independent drama, *The Way Back Home.* She was also featured in the television production of *Their Eyes Were Watching God* (for which performance she won an Audie Award).

In 1988, Ms. Dee was inducted into the Theatre Hall of Fame. With her late husband, Mr. Davis, she has been inducted into the NAACP Image Award Hall of Fame, awarded the Silver Circle Award by the Academy of Television Arts and Science. In December 2004, Ms. Dee and Mr. Davis were recipients of the John F. Kennedy Center Honors. In 1995, Davis and Dee were celebrated as "national treasures" when they received the National Medal of Arts Honor, and in 2000, they received the Screen Actors Guild's highest honor, the Life Achievement Award. She is a member of Actors' Equity Association, the Screen Actors Guild, the American Federation of Television and Radio Artists, and the Writers Guild.

Ms. Dee is author of children's books, <u>Tower to Heaven and Two Ways to Count to Ten</u>; a book of poetry and short stories, <u>My One Good Nerve</u> (which she has adapted into a solo performance piece); and <u>With Ossie and Ruby: In This Life Together</u>, a joint autobiography co-authored with her late husband. She has also narrated several audio books, including Zora Neale Hurston's Their Eyes Were Watching God.

Radio Talk Shows

African New Dawn Since 1992. Mary Nichols aka DJ Fusion, founder. Features a variety of music as well as various news issues and guests. The show broadcasts on the Rutgers University Radio Station, WRSU 88.7 FM. Contact Ms. Mary Nichols, The FuseBox Radio Broadcast, 14 Easton Avenue, #250 New Brunswick, New Jersey 08901 Phone: (347) 252-4032 E-mail: **djfusion@ureach.com**

Afrikaleidoscope An African public affairs program that focuses on the history, current events and future developments in Africa and the African diaspora, including the United States, the Caribbean, Central and South America, the Pacific Islands and even Europe. Elombe Brath, Host, producer. Contact WBAI Radio, 120 Wall Street, 10th Floor, New York, New York 10005 Phone: (212) 209-2834 E-mail: **ebrath@wbai.org** Website: **www.wbai.org**

Afropop Worldwide Radio program hosted by George Collinet for World Music Productions featuring African and world music. Currently distributed by Public Radio International (PRI) to over 100 stations in the U.S. Contact Mr. George Collinet, Afropop Worldwide, Chicago Public Radio, Navy Pier, 848 East Grand Avenue, Chicago, Illinois 60611 Phone: (312) 948-4600 E-mail: **questions@ChicagoPublicRadio.org** Website: **www.wbez.org**

A Round 2 It Internet radio show at artistfirst.com hosted by Delores Thornton, spotlights African American authors and literary entrepreneurs. Contact Marguerite Press, Post Office Box 53941, Indianapolis, Indiana 46253 Phone: (317) 626-6885 Fax: (317) 298-8889 E-mail: **dthorn4047@aol.com** Website: **www.margueritepress.com**

Bay View Public affairs program. Interviews artists and authors. Host Nikki Thomas. KBLX-FM, 55 Hawthorne Street, Suite 900, San Francisco, California 94105 Phone: (415) 284-1029 Fax: (415) 764-1029 E-mail: **info@kblx.com** Website: **www.kblx.com**

KD Bowe Known nation wide for his comedic, witty, and sometimes controversial radio show, KD Bowe is a recipient of the 1998 Trailblazer Award for excellence in the arena of mass media. Contact Mr. KD Bowe, KDYA, Gospel 1190 AM The Light, 3260 Blume Drive, Suite 520, Richmond, California 94806 Phone: (510) 222-4242 Fax: (510) 262-9054 E-mail: **KDBoweMorningShow@sgnthelight.com** Website: **www.gospel1190.net**

Kevin Brown Morning Show Call in talk show at WOL 1450 and WOL-B 1010 hosted by Kevin Brown. Contact Mr. Kevin Brown, KBLX-FM, Post Office Box 76854, Washington, DC 20013 Phone: (800) 450-7876 E-mail: **kbrown@kblx.com** Website: **www.kblx.com**

Les Brown Live Listen to Les Live on V103.com every Sunday morning from 6-8 AM CST. Les Brown, 233 North Michigan Avenue, Suite 2800, Chicago, Illinois 60601 Phone: (800) 733-4226 E-mail: **lesbrown@lesbrown.com** Website: **www.v103.com/main.html**

Billy Daniels Air personality. Ormond Beach, Florida native Bill Daniels attended Bethune-Cookman College on a music scholarship where he earned a BA in English/Communications. In addition to his on-air duties, Billy is the Creative Director and Writer for the Nationally syndicated show "The Bobby Jones Gospel Countdown." Billy Daniels, KDYA, Gospel 1190 AM The Light, 3260 Blume Drive, Suite 520, Richmond, California 94806 Phone: (510) 222-4242 Fax: (510) 262-9054 Website: **www.gospel1190.net**

BookNook Internet radio show at artistfirst.com hosted by Delores Thornton, author of "Ida Mae," and "Babe." She is a columnist for the Indiana Herald newspaper, and for the HYPE Magazine.   Contact Ms. Delores, Thornton, BookNook, Marguerite Press, Post Office Box 53941, Indianapolis, Indiana 46253 Phone: (317) 626-6885 Fax: (317) 298-8889 E-mail: **dthorn4047@aol.com** Website: **www.margueritepress.com**

Jackie Campbell Air personality. Originally from Detroit, Jackie graduated from Wayne State University with a degree specializing in Radio and Television. She has worked for WTVS-TV 56 and WDIV-TV 4 in Detroit, Michigan and WDTN-TV 2 in Dayton, Ohio, as well as other communication entities. Before coming to the Sheridan Gospel Network, she worked as an Assistant to the President at WPBA-TV 30. Ms. Jackie Campbell, KDYA, Gospel 1190 AM The Light, 3260 Blume Drive, Suite 520, Richmond, California 94806 Phone: (510) 222-4242 Fax: (510) 262-9054 E-mail: **jcampbell@sgnthelight.com** Website: **www.gospel1190.net**

The Caldwell Chronicles A newspaper of the air hosted by Earl Caldwell, features 'the Caldwell conversations' with special guests. Earl Caldwell, Host/Executive Producer. Natalie Burnham: Producer. WBAI Radio, 120 Wall Street, 10th Floor, New York, New York 10005 Phone: (212) 209-2932 E-mail: **EarlCaldwell@wbai.org** Website: **www.wbai.org**

Caribbeanwomentoday A segment on Caribbean Weekly; an informational and community affairs program produced by the Duke of Earle Media Group (Florida/Jamaica) and hosted by Dr. Anita Davis-DeFoe, author of A Woman's Guide to Soulful Living and resident advice guru for She-Caribbean, a St. Lucian magazine that is sold in 20 islands, New York, Atlanta, South Florida, Ghana, London, Germany and Italy. Dr. DeFoe is the host of Soulfully Speaking on CaribVoice Radio and Akeru Radio. Dr. Anita Davis-DeFoe, Post Office Box 451973, Sunrise, Florida 33345 Phone: (954) 816-9462 E-mail: **dranitadavisdefoe@hotmail.com** Website: **www.dranitadavisdefoe.com**

Citizens Report Host, Jetie Wilds. WTMP 1150-AM and 96.1 FM. Tama Broadcasting, Inc., 5207 Washington Boulevard, Tampa, Florida 33619 Phone: (813) 620-1300 Fax: (813) 628-0713 E-mail: **info@tamabroadcasting.com** Website: **www.tamabroadcasting.com**

The Conscious Rasta Report Daily talk radio show hosted by Keidi Obi Awadu on LIBRadio.com and LIBtv.com. Keidi is the author of 18 published books including the latest "The Road to Power: Seven Steps to an African Global Order." He has spoken around the world on well-researched and documented subjects covering health and biology, HIV/AIDS solutions, politics, technology, culture, transformation, global business development, media communications and metaphysics. Keidi Obi Awadu, Black Star Media, 5805 Diamond Street, Palmdale California 93552 E-mail: **keidi@libradio.net** Website: **www.LIBRadio.com**

Conversations With Interviews. Contact Lawrence A. Toller, General Manager. WILA-AM, Post Office Box 3444, Danville, Virginia 24543 Phone: (434) 792-2133 Fax: (434) 792-2134 E-mail: **wilaradio@gamewood.net**

Conversations with C. A. Webb The radio show began in 2003 and is heard on WMPR 90.1 FM in Mississippi, Alabama, Louisiana and Arkansas as well as online worldwide at WMPR901.com. Interviews movers and shakers. Host, Cyrus A. Webb. C.A. Webb, WMPR 90.1, 105 McCornell Circle, Brandon, Mississippi 39042 Phone: (601) 201-8139 E-mail: **cawebb@cawebb.com** Website: **www.cawebbconversations.com**

The Daily Drum Host Yakenda Magahee. Adult Contemporary. Howard University, WHUR-FM, 529 Bryant Street North West, Washington, DC 20059 Phone: (202) 806-3500 E-mail: **support@broadcasturban.net** Website: **www.whur.com**

Daybreak with Anthony McCarthy Live Interviews early mornings with host, Mr. Anthony McCarthy. Contact Anthony McCarthy, WEAA-FM 89.9, 1700 E. Coldspring Lane, Benjamin Banneker Building, Room 401, Baltimore, Maryland 21251 Phone: (443) 885-3564 Fax: (443) 885-8206 E-mail: **anthony@anthonymccarthy.com** Website: **www.weaa.org**

Diasporic Music Call in talk show. Interviews authors, etc. Producer, host, Norman "Otis" Redmond. Diasporic Music, Post Office Box 6777, Station A, Toronto, Canada, MSW 1X5 Phone: (416) 408-2817 E-mail: **norman@ckln.fm** Website: **www.ckln.fm**

Doctor in the House Airs Tuesdays, 12pm-1am. Host, Dr. Terry Mason is on staff at Chicago's Mercy Hospital. His topics range from prostate cancer to holistic health. Medical Degree from University of Illinois, Lincoln School of Medicine, Chicago, Illinois. Board Certified by American Board of Urology. Contact Monique Smith, WVON 1450AM, 3350 South Kedzie, Chicago, Illinois 60623 Phone: (773) 247-6200 E-mail: **monews74@hotmail.com** Website: **www.wvon.com**

The DR BookChat Radio Show Heard on 97.7 and 88.1 FM (KECG/More Public Radio). Anna Dennis is co-host. An author, Anna has written several children's short stories and has had commentary published in Essence Magazine. Her books include: Who Will Hear My Screams, The Purest of Pain, and On the Line, is her third novel. She is co-founder of The Bay Area Book Writers Guild and a book reviewer for The LineUp's Bookworm Column.Contact Anna Dennis, Apex Publishing, Post Office Box 5077, South San Francisco, California 94083 E-mail: **apexpublishing@aol.com**

Firstlight Show airs Monday through Friday, 5am- 6am. Award-winning personality, Sharon K. McGhee is News Director & Host. Sharon launched the first WVON book club, Between the Covers. Contact Monique Smith, WVON 1450AM, 3350 South Kedzie, Chicago, Illinois 60623 Phone: (773) 247-6200 E-mail: **monews74@hotmail.com** Website: **www.wvon.com**

FreeStyle Radio air personality and TV show host on public access. Interviews. Contact Freestyle, KOHT-FM 98.3, 3202 North Oracle Road, Tucson, Arizona 85705 Phone: (520) 618-2100 Fax: (520) 618-2165 E-mail: **yofreestyle@hotmail.com** Website: **www.hot983.com**

From A Different Prospective News magazine show. Shows Third World topics include African music, aids in Africa, sanctions, the Grenada revolutions, news and information. Interviews authors. Producer, host, Norman "Otis" Redmond. Contact Mr. Otis Redmond, From A Different Prospective, Post Office Box 6777, Station A, Toronto, Canada, M5W 1X5   Phone: (416) 408-2817 E-mail: **norman@ckln.fm**   Website: **www.ckln.fm**

Frontpage 102.3-FM radio talk show hosted by Carl Nelson. The show covers topics affecting African Americans locally, nationally and internationally. Interviews authors and other artists. Carl Nelson, Frontpage, KJLH, 161 North La Brea Avenue, Inglewood, California 90301 Phone: (310) 330-2200 Fax: (310) 330-5555 E-mail: **frontpage@kjlhradio.com**   Website: **www.kjlhradio.com**

The FuseBox Syndicated radio broadcast, bringing the absolute BEST of Hip-Hop & R&B Music from all over the world along w/ commentary from DJ Fusion & Jon Judah. Founder, Mary Nichols aka DJ Fusion. Contact The FuseBox Radio Broadcast, 14 Easton Avenue., #250 New Brunswick, New Jersey 08901 Phone: (347) 252-4032 E-mail: **djfusion@ureach.com**

Gospel 1190 The Light Show features Bible trivia, entertainment news, African American history, and gospel music! Jackie Campbell is host. She also does voice-overs, and can be heard on various radio stations across the United States. Jackie Campbell, KDYA Gospel 1190 AM The Light, 3260 Blume Drive, Suite 520, Richmond, California 94806 Phone: (510) 222-4242 Fax: (510) 262-9054 E-mail: **jcampbell@sgnthelight.com** Website: **www.gospel1190.net**

The Gospel Ride Home Talk show hosted by Mike Robinson, also Program Director. WGRB, 233 North Michigan Avenue, Suite 2700 Chicago, Illinois 60601 Phone: (312) 540-2000 E-mail: **mrobinson2@clearchannel.com** Website: **www.gospel1390.com**

Gospel Vibrations WFDU-FM Radio show features the largest variety of contemporary Gospel Music. Interviews. Mr. Floyd Cray, producer and host. WFDU-FM, 114 Shepard Avenue, Teaneck, New Jersey 07666 Phone: (201) 833-0694 E-mail: **gospelvibrations@aol.com** Website: **www.gospelvibrations.cc**

Greatness By Design Talk radio show hosted by Ms. Blanche Williams-Corey, author. Interview authors. Show also airs on XM-Satellite Radio-Channel 169 THE POWER. Contact Ms. Blanche Williams-Corey, WOL-AM, 5900 Princess Garden Parkway, 8th Floor, Lanham, Maryland 20706 Phone: (301) 306-1111 E-mail: **blanche@blanchewilliams.com** Website: **www.1230thebuzz.com**

Doc Hollidae Show airs on WJAM 107.9 FM. Doc Hollidae, Scott Communications, Post Office Box 1150, Selma, Alabama 36702 Phone: (334) 875-9360 Fax: (334) 875-1340 E-mail: **walxnews@charterinternet.com**

Insight Hosted by Yakenda Magahee. Howard University radio. Adult Contemporary. Jim Watkins, General Manager. Contact WHUR-FM, Howard University, 529 Bryant Street North West, Washington, DC 20059 Phone: (202) 806-3500 E-mail: **support@broadcasturban.net** Website: **www.whur.com**

Tom Joyner Morning Show Nationally syndicated radio show. Contact ABC Radio Networks, 13725 Montfort Drive, Dallas, Texas 75240 Phone: (800) JOYNER-1 Fax: (972) 458-1690 E-mail: **cs@tomjoyner.com** Website: **www.blackamericaweb.com**

Just About Books Talk Show An Internet radio talk show with a worldwide audience. Features authors, book reviews, book clubs, and literary events for African American book lovers." Executive Producer and Host, Cheryl Robinson. The show airs "live" on Mondays at 9 pm Eastern Standard Time. Contact Ms.Cheryl Robinson, Just About Books Talk Show, 1282 Smallwood Drive, West, Suite 116, Waldorf, Maryland 20603 Phone: (301) 643-2077 E-mail: **JustAboutBooks@yahoo.com** Website: **www.JustAboutBookTalkShow.com**

Kulcha Shok Muzik (KSM) Weekly syndicated entertainment report called 'REGGAE VIBES,' heard on nearly 120 radio stations around the world. Host, Lance-O. Contact Kulcha Shok Muzik, 1218 Drexel Avenue, Suite #203, Miami, Florida 33139 Phone: (305) 534-6110 E-mail: **lanceo@kulchashok.com** Website: **www.kulchashok.com**

LA Speaks Out Weekly interactive talk show of current topics affecting the African American community in Los Angeles, hosted by Jacquie Stephens, News and Public Affairs Director. KJLH Radio, 161 North La Brea Avenue, Inglewood, California 90301 Phone: (310) 330-2200 Fax: (310) 330-5555 E-mail: **jacquie@kjlhradio.com** Website: **www.kjlhradio.com**

Love Lust & Lies Syndicated drive time radio talk show hosted by best selling author, Michael Baisden. Pamela Yvette Exum, PYE Enterprises, Post Office Box 17266, San Antonio, Texas 78217 Phone: (210) 930-0959 Fax: (210) 655-9311 E-mail: **GPhilip@michaelbaisden.com** Website: **www.michaelbaisden.com**

Marshalen Martin A professional Radio broadcaster since 1980, starting at KEST in San Francisco, then moving to KJAM in Pittsburgh, California, and KDIA in Oakland, California, Marshalen Martin is one of the most recognized names in Bay Area gospel radio. Each week she plays the best of Bay Area and nationally known artists, features interviews with a veritable who's who of the gospel world and takes your requests! Marshalen is the daughter of the late Rev. James S. Taylor. She has been a member of the Bay Area Religious Announcers Guild since 1981, is a long-standing member of the Bay Area Black Media Coalition and was named The Church of God In Christ's Professional Women's Foundation "Woman of the Year" for 2001. Ms. Martin also serves as president of her own booking firm Marshalen Martin & Associates. Contact Ms. Marshalen Martin, KDYA, Gospel 1190 AM The Light, 3260 Blume Drive, Suite 520, Richmond, California 94806 Phone: (510) 222-4242 Fax: (510) 262-9054 Website: **www.gospel1190.net**

Anjali McGuirest Air Personality and mid-day radio show host; interviews. Contact KTTB-FM, Radio One, 5300 Edina Industrial Boulevard, Edina, Minnesota 55439 Phone: (952) 842-7200 Fax: (952) 842-1048 E-mail: **selliot@radio-one.com** Website: **www.b96online.com**

Kim McLaughlin-Smith Mid-day radio air personality. Interviews artists and authors. WBNE 93.7, Sea-Communications Media, 122 Cinema Drive, Wilmington, North Carolina 28403 Phone: (910) 772-6300 x 316 Fax: (910) 772-6337 E-mail: **radiobutter@hotmail.com**

Mo in the Midday Host, Monique Caradine; cultural issues. Contact Monique Caradine, WVON 1450AM, 3350 South Kedzie, Chicago 60623 Phone: (773) 247-6200 Fax: (773) 247-2177 E-mail: **info@wvon.com** Website: **www.wvon.com**

Moment Creole WLIB 1190 Host, Stanley Barbot. Information topics directly related to the French Caribbean speaking community. Contact Stanley Barbot, WLIB 1190, I.C.B.C. Broadcast Holdings, Inc., New York, New York E-mail: **momentcreole@wlib.com** Website: **www.wlib.com**

The Morning Magazine 1290 WMCS-AM News magazine show. Keith Murphy, producer and host. Conceptz Communications, Post Office Box 241311, Milwaukee, Wisconsin 53224 Phone: (414) 357-8129 E-mail: **conceptz@sbcglobal.net** Website: **www.keithmurphy.org**

The Morning Praise Praise Party Host, Paster John Hannah. Gospel Radio 1390-AM, 233 North Michigan Avenue, Suite 2800, Chicago, Illinois 60601 Phone: (312) 540-2000 E-mail: **ChurchNews@gospel1390.com** Website: **www.gospel1390.com**

The New Voice of Praise Covers national and local Gospel music. Host, Kimberly. Call in during show hours. Interviews authors. Kimberly, WCLM 1450 AM, 3165 Hull Street, Richmond, Virginia 23224 Phone: (804) 231-7685 Website: **www.wclmradio.com**

Off The Shelf Internet Radio program hosted by author, Denise Turney. Contact Off The Shelf, Chistell Publishing, 2500 Knights Road, Suite 19-01, Bensalem, Pennsylvania 19020 E-mail: **soulfar@aol.com** Website: **www.blakeradio.com**

On the WAAV Line with Rhonda Belamy Weekday Mornings from 8-10am. Contact Host, Rhonda Bellamy, 980-AM WAAV, 3233 Burnt Mill Road #4, Wilmington, North Carolina 28403 Phone: (910) 763-9977 Fax: (910) 762-0456 E-mail: **rhonda@980waav.com** Website: **www.980waav.com**

The Russ Parr Show A nationally syndicated Morning Show. Russ Parr, host. Interviews authors locally. Contact Russ Parr, WFXM-FM, Roberts Communications, Inc., Route 6, Box 735, Highway 57, Macon, Georgia Phone: (478) 745-3301 Fax: (478) 742-2293 E-mail: **robertsrci@aol.com** Website: **www.uptoparr.com**

The Poets Corner Internet talk show. Host, Jamalo White. WJMB Internet Radio, Bernard Broadcasting Company, 5316 Cottonwood Road, Memphis, Tennessee 38118 Phone: (901) 794-0416 E-mail: **jberna12@memphisrealtalk.com** Website: **www.memphisrealtalk.com**

Positively People Talk show hosted by Bailey Coleman. Interviews. WKKV-FM V100, 12100 West Howard Avenue, Greenfield, Wisconsin 53228 Phone: (414) 321-1007 Fax: (414) 799-8100 E-mail: **doclov@clearchannel.com** Website: **www.v100.com**

Stephanie M. Pruitt Co-hosts a social commentary radio talk show. Stephanie M. Pruitt, 1708 21st Avenue South, Suite #149, Nashville, Tennessee 37212 Phone: (615) 545-8018 E-mail: **SPruitt@StephaniePruitt.com** Website: **www.StephaniePruitt.com**

Pulse Of The City Hosted by Robert S. Interviews authors. Contact Robert S., WJNZ-AM, Goodrich Radio Group, 1919 Eastern, Grand Rapids, Michigan 49507 Phone: (616) 475-4299 E-mail: **mjs@wjnz.com** Website: **www.wjnz.com**

Real Talk Show WJMB Internet Radio show hosted by owner and founder, Jennings Bernard. Contact WJMB, Bernard Broadcasting Company, 5316 Cottonwood Road, Memphis, Tennessee 38118 Phone: (901) 794-0416 Fax: (901) 794-3309 E-mail: **jberna12@memphisrealtalk.com** Website: **www.memphisrealtalk.com**

Real Talk w/K.J. A live internet broadcast show with host and author, Kalico Jones at the website artistfirst.com. Artistfirst World Radio, 1062 Parkside Drive, Alliance, Ohio 44601 Phone: (862) 202-1866 E-mail: **kalicojones@yahoo.com** Website: **www.artistfirst.com**

The Relationship Fitness Show Radio program co-hosted by Cheryl Martin.   In a lively interview format, she and relationship fitness coach Johnny Parker provide practical insights to singles and married couples for building and nurturing strong, lasting relationships. Cheryl serves on the U.S. board of World Vision an organization dedicated to tackling the causes of poverty. Cheryl Martin, Post Office Box 15285, Chevy Chase, Maryland 20825 Phone: (301) 907-8215 E-mail: **info@cherylmartin.org** Website: **www.cherylmartin.org**

Reynolds Rap Show hosted by author and award winning journalist, Dr. Barbara A. Reynolds. Received 1999 Journalist of the Year Award from the National Association of Black Journalists. JFJ Publishing, 4806 Saint Barnabas Road, Suite 598, Temple Hills, Maryland 20757 Phone: (301) 899-1341 E-mail: **reynew@aol.com** Website: **www.reynoldsnews.com**

Richmond is Talking Radio talk show hosted by author, Gloria Taylor Edwards. Interviews authors. Ms. Gloria Taylor Edwards, WCLM 1450 AM, 3165 Hull Street, Richmond, Virginia 23224 Phone: (804) 231-7685 E-mail: **vftdgte@aol.com** Website: **www.wclmradio.com**

Roland S. Martin Show Airs Monday through Friday, 10m-1pm with host Roland S. Martin. Contact Ms. Monique Smith, WVON 1690AM, 3350 South Kedzie, Chicago, Illinois 60623 Phone: (773) 247-6200 E-mail: **roland@wvon.com** Website: **www.wvon.com**

Skip Murphy & The Morning Team Show Host, Skip Murphy and Company is celebrating its 10 year anniversary on K10fFM. Interviews authors and other artists. Contact Skip Murphy, K104, 621 North West 6th Street, Grand Prairie, Texas 75050 Phone: (972) 263-9911 E-mail: **Lizl@K104fm.com** Website: **www.k104fm.com**

Spotlight Host, Carla Rowser Canty at WQTQ 89.9 FM. Poets, authors and musicians are encouraged to showcase their work.   Contact Ms. Carla Rowser Canty, A Blackgurl Production, Post Office Box 843, Hartford, Connecticut 06143 Phone: (860) 983-3257 E-mail: **BlackGurrl@aol.com** Website: **www.wqtqfm.com/wqtq**

Soulfully Speaking On CaribVoice Radio and Akeru Radio. Host, Dr. Anita Davis-DeFoe, The Defoe Group, Post Office Box 451973, Sunrise, Florida 33345 Phone: (954) 816-9462 E-mail: **dranitadavisdefoe@hotmail.com** Website: **www.dranitadavisdefoe.com**

Sugarbear Host of afternoon drive time show 3-7pm EST. Sugarbear, WAJZ-FM, Albany Broadcasting, 6 Johnson Road, Latham, New York 12110 Phone: (518) 786-6677 Fax: (518) 786-6696 E-mail: **sugarbear@albanybroadcasting.com** Website: **www.jamz963.com**

Talk of the Town with Donn Ansell Since 1984, Local Morning News Magazine of the Airwaves weekdays from 5:30am-8am. The show is celebrating its 23rd 23rd year on the air and is the longest running show in the region. Host, Donn Ansell. Contact Donn Ansell, 980-AM WAAV, 3233 Burnt Mill Road #4, Wilmington, North Carolina 28403 Phone: (910) 763-9977 Fax: (910) 762-0456 E-mail: **donn@980waav.com** Website: **www.980waav.com**

The Tavis Smiley Show Two-hour weekly radio show of news and newsmakers in expanded conversations. Tavis Smiley, Host. Contact The Tavis Smiley Show, The Smiley Group, 3870 Crenshaw Boulevard, Suite 391, Los Angeles, California 90008 Phone: (323) 290-3940 E-mail: **tavis@tavistalks.com** Website: **www.tavistalks.com**

Thinking It Through Host, Dr. Carlos E. Russell and his nightly guests. Carlos E. Russell, WLIB 1190, I.C.B.C. Broadcast Holdings, Inc., New York, New York Phone: (212) 889-1190 Fax: (212) 447-5193 E-mail: **think@wlib.com** Website: **www.wlib.com**

Today's Black Woman A Nationally syndicated radio talk show reaching over 500,000 women weekly. Founder/host, Jennifer Kreitt. TBW Radio Show, Post Office Box 440981, Kennesaw, Georgia 30160 Phone: (678) 354-4269 Fax: (678) 354-4334 E-mail: **tbwoman@bellsouth.net** Website: **www.todaysblackwomanradio.com**

Tone E. Fly Show Morning show host, Tone E. Fly. Interviews guests. Call the show every morning at (651) 989-4396. Be an intern for the Tone E. Fly Show. Contact KTTB-FM, Blue Chip Broadcasting, 5300 Edina Industrial Boulevard, Edina, Minnesota 55439 Phone: (952) 842-7200 Fax: (952) 842-1048 E-mail: **fly@fly.com** Website: **www.b96online.com**

The Tree of Life Show Kanya Vashon McGhee is the host of The Tree of Life Show on BlakeRadio.com , Channel 5, an internet radio station, where he features guests and subject matters such as Consciousness; God; Karma; the New Sexuality; Life, Death and Reincarnation; Enlightenment; Astrology; Drugs; Mind Control and a myriad of subject matter to enlighten and influence mankind. Married to his work, Kanya sees his patrons as the children of his mission in life, which is the opening of knowledge within each person. Contact Mr. Kanya Vashon McGhee, 1701 M. L. King Drive SW, Atlanta, Georgia 30314 Phone: (404) 753-5700 E-mail: **drkanya@GMail.com** Website: **www.naturalusa.com/ads/treeoflife.html**

UDC Books African American writers and books. Cheryl Lewis Hawkins, host. UDCBooks, Cable TV 19, University of the District of Columbia, 4200 Connecticut Avenue, North West, Building 41, Room 203, Washington, DC 20008 Phone: (202) 274-5300 Fax: (202) 274-5999 E-mail: **udcbooks@aol.com** E-mail: **cabletv19@udc.edu** Website: **www.udc.com**

Urban Journal 93.3 WJZI-FM Daily radio magazine program produced and hosted by Keith Murphy. Conceptz Communications, Post Office Box 241311, Milwaukee, Wisconsin 53224 Phone: (414) 357-8129 E-mail: **conceptz@sbcglobal.net** Website: **www.keithmurphy.org**

Voices from the Drum (VFTD) Radio talk show hosted by mystery writer and author, Gloria Taylor Edwards. Gloria Taylor Ediwards, VFTD, Post Office Box 27504, Richmond, Virginia 23261 Phone: (804) 323-6441 E-mail: **vftdgte@aol.com** Website: **www.wclmradio.com**

The Lincoln Ware Show Talk show discusses local and national issues, hot topics and opinions. Interviews authors. J Tolliver, Program Director. Contact WDBZ-AM, 1 Centennial Plaza, Suite 200, 705 Central Avenue, Cincinnati, Ohio 45202 Phone: (513) 749-1230 Fax: (513) 948-1985 E-mail: **lware@radio-one.com** Website: **www.1230thebuzz.com**

What's Going On? Community affairs program serving the greater San Francisco Bay Area. Interviews artists and authors. Host Ms. Nikki Thomas. Contact KBLX-FM, 55 Hawthorne Street, Suite 900, San Francisco, California 94105 Phone: (415) 284-1029 Fax: (415) 764-1029 E-mail: **info@kblx.com** Website: **www.kblx.com**

Gary Young Radio air personality on Love 101.1 and Promotion Director for Clear Channel Radio Savannah. Interviews guests. Contact Gary Young, Clear Channel Radio Savannah, 245 Alfred Street, Savannah, Georgia 31408 Phone: (912) 964-7794 E-mail: **gary@love1011.com** Website: **www.love1011.com**

Zannie K Afternoon drive-time radio show host at KTTB-FM; interview authors. Program Director, Sam Elliott. Contact KTTB-FM, Radio One, 5300 Edina Industrial Boulevard, Edina, Minnesota 55439 Phone: (952) 842-7200 Fax: (952) 842-1048 E-mail: **selliot@radio-one.com** Website: **www.b96online.com**

Yolanda Joe
Author * Journalist

Yolanda Joe is a native of Chicago, Illinois. She is an author, and a former producer and writer for CBS News, Chicago where she currently resides. A prolific mystery writer she has authored eight best selling books: <u>Falling Leaves of Ivy</u> (Longmeadow Press, 1992), <u>He Say, She Say</u> (Doubleday, 1997), <u>Bebe's By Golly Wow</u>, (Doubleday, 1998), <u>This Just In</u> (One World/Ballantine, 2001), <u>Details at Ten: A Georgia Barnett Mystery</u> (Pocket, 2002), <u>Hit Time</u> (Simon & Schuster, 2002), <u>The Hatwearer's Lesson</u> (Dutton, 2003), and <u>My Fine Lady</u> (Dutton, 2004). Her new book Video Cowboys: A Georgia Barnett Mystery will be released by Simon & Schuster in June, 2005.

Yolanda earned her B.A. in English literature from Yale University; and her M.A. in Journalism from Columbia University.

Theatres

African Continuum Theatre Company (ACTCO) Since 1989. ActCo is a professional theater company whose mission is to illuminate the human condition through producing and presenting professional theatrical productions. ACTco productions reflect an aesthetic rooted in the African and American-American experience. Contact African Continuum Theatre Company, 3523 12th Street, North East, 2nd Floor, Washington, DC 20017 Fax: (202) 529-5782 E-mail: **info@africancontinuumtheatre.com** Website: **www.africancontinuumtheatre.com**

Alliance Theatre Company Now in its fourth decade, the Alliance Theatre has achieved recognition as one of the country's leading theatres, having premiered such works as Pearl Cleage's, Blues for an Alabama Sky; Elton John and Tim Rice's, Elaborate Lives: The Legend of Aida (in partnership with Disney Theatricals); Sandra Deer's, So Long on Lonely Street, and Alfred Uhry's, The Last Night of Ballyhoo. Artistic Director Susan V. Booth. Managing Director Thomas Pechar. The Alliance Theatre Company, 1280 Peachtree Street, North East, Atlanta, Georgia 30309 Phone: (404) 733-4600 E-mail: **info@alliancetheatre.org** Website: **www.alliancetheatre.org**

Black Ensemble Theater Corporation Organization seeks to produce entertaining, educational and enlightening African American theater of excellence that reaches an interracial audience. Jackie Taylor, founder, producer, executive director. Black Ensemble Theater Corporation, 4520 North Beacon Street, Chicago, Illinois 60640 Phone: (773) 769-4451 Fax: (773) 769-4533 E-mail: **BlackEnsemble@aol.com** Website: **www.blackensembletheater.org**

Castillo Theatre A non-traditional theatrical production house which promotes human development through performance. Dr. Fred Newman is founder and Artistic Director. Contact Castillo Theatre, c/o All Stars Project Inc., 543 West 42nd Street, New York, New York 10036 Phone: (212) 941-9400 E-mail: **rgrunwald@castillo.org** Website: **www.castillo.org**

Cincinnati Black Theatre Company Offers theatrical productions, performance and employment opportunities, children's theatre, educational programs and community outreach in all aspects of theatre arts. CBTC is committed to increasing literacy, promoting diversity and multiculturalism, pursuing collaborations, and providing access to the arts. As a result of successfully producing the Midwest Regional Black Theatre Festival in 1998 and 2000, Cincinnati Black Theatre Company (CBTC) officially became a 501(c) (3) non-profit organization in November 2001. Contact Cincinnati Black Theatre Company, 5919 Hamilton Avenue, Cincinnati, Ohio 45224 Phone: (513) 241-6060 Fax: (513) 241-6671 E-mail: **cbtcsherman@hotmail.com**

Dramastage Qumran Community Theater Melvin Ishmael Johnson, Director. Dramastage Qumran Community Theater, 733 South Hindry Avenue, Inglewood, California 90301 Phone: (310) 348-9853 Fax: (310) 348-9619 E-mail: **bymel2004@yahoo.com**

Frank Silvera Writers' Workshop Foundation, Inc. Celebrating its 32nd Year Anniversary during the 2004-2005 season (September to June), the Frank Silvera Writers' Workshop Foundation, Inc., is a nonprofit theatre arts organization and playwright development program. The FSWW is one of the few Equity approved showcase theatres based in Harlem. It was founded by playwright/director Garland Lee Thompson, Sr., along with actor/director Morgan Freeman, director/actress Billie Allen and journalist Clayton Riley. The Frank Silvera Writers' Workshop Foundation, Inc., Post Office Box 1791, Manhattanville Station, New York, New York 10027   Phone: (212) 281-8832   E-mail: **playrite@earthlink.net**   Website: **www.fsww.org**

New Federal Theatre Specializes in minority dramas by presenting plays to the culturally diverse greater New York area and supports emerging writers by bringing their work to full scale productions; hires directors, actors, designers and playwrights. Workshop classes in acting and playwrights. Woodie King Jr., Director. New Federal Theatre, 466 Grand Street, New York, New York 10003 E-mail: **newfederal@aol.com** Website: **www.newfederaltheatre.org**

North Carolina Black Repertory Company (NCBRC) Host of the "National Black Theatre Festival." A large number of workshops and seminars are available at the National Black Theatre Festival. NCBRC, 610 Coliseum Drive, Winston-Salem, North Carolina 27106 Phone: (336) 723-2266 Fax: (336) 723-2223 E-mail: **llhamlin@bellsouth.net** Website: **www.nbtf.org**

Orisha Tales Repertory Radio Theatre Company The theatre company and it's author/producer, produces and writes dance dramas based on the Yoruba tradition in the Old World and the Diaspora. These productions are also presented as radio dramas. Founder, Producer and Executive Director, David D. Wright. Orisha Tales Repertory Radio Theatre Company, 133 East 96th Street, Brooklyn, New York 11212 Phone: (718) 735-8905 E-mail: **orisatalesradio@aol.com** Website: **www.orishatalesrepertoryradiotheatrecompany.org**

People's Theatre, Inc. Celebrates the diversity of our communities through community service and quality theatre. We are dedicated to a multicultural approach to the artistic and social needs of today. People's Theatre, Inc., Post Office Box 678910, Orlando, Florida 32867 Phone: (407) 426-0545 E-mail: **admin@peoplestheatre.org** Website: **www.peoplestheatre.org**

Theatre Inc. Founder/President, Tony Darnell Davis. Essex Studios, 2511 Essex Place, Cincinnati, Ohio 45206 Phone: (513) 363-7797 E-mail: **davisad@email.uc.edu**

Woodruff Arts Center Named for Atlanta Coca-Cola magnate Robert W. Woodruff whose support helped make the Woodruff Center possible, The Atlanta Memorial Arts Center opened in 1968 to commemorate the 106 Atlanta arts supporters who died in a 1962 plane crash in Paris. In 1985, the Memorial Arts Center became a part of the Robert W. Woodruff Arts Center to include both facilities. Woodruff Arts Center includes: Alliance Theatre Company, Atlanta College of Art, Atlanta Symphony Orchestra, High Downtown Folk Art & Photography Galleries, High Museum of Art, and 14th Street Playhouse. Shelton G. Stanfill, President and C.E.O. Contact Robert W. Woodruff Arts Center, 1280 Peachtree Street North East, Atlanta, Georgia 30309   Phone: (404) 733-5000   E-mail: **info@woodruffcenter.org**   Website: **www.woodruffcenter.org**

TV News Reporters

Cheryl A. Adams News Anchor. Contact Ms. Cheryl Adams, WXIN-TV, 6910 Network Place, Indianapolis, Indiana 46278 Phone: (317) 687-6555 E-mail: **cherylann7@earthlink.net**

Roslyn Anderson Anchor/Reporter. Contact Robin Anderson, WLBT-TV3, Post Box 1712, Jackson, Mississippi 39215 Phone: (601) 948-3333 E-mail: **roslyn@wlbt.com**

Audrey Barnes A frequent substitute anchor, Audrey Barnes joined WUSA 9 as a general assignment reporter in May of 2003. Audrey is a graduate of the University of Maryland College Park and has a degree in Broadcast Journalism. She also has a Master's degree from the Medill School of Journalism at Northwestern University. Prior to coming to WUSA 9, Audrey worked at two other Washington stations. She also spent three years as morning anchor for WBAL-TV in Baltimore where she shared the anchor desk with 9 News Meteorologist Tony Pann. Audrey has also been a reporter and anchor for television stations in Salisbury, Maryland; Jacksonville, Florida; and Charlotte, North Carolina. She was the 6 and 11pm anchor at WJRT-TV in Flint, Michigan before returning home to the Washington area to be near her family. Audrey Barnes, WUSA-TV (Channel 9, CBS) 4100 Wisconsin Avenue, North West, Washington, DC 20016 Phone: (202) 895-5999 E-mail: **abarnes@wusatv9.com** Website: **www.wusatv9.com**

ReShonda Tate Billingsley General assignment reporter for KRIV-TV, the Fox affliate in Houston, Texas. Member of National Association of Black Journalists and Alpha Kappa Alpha Sorority, Inc. E-mail: **ReShondaT@aol.com** Website: **www.reshondatatebillingsley.com**

Christina Brown Anchor/Reporter. Christina Brown, KTNV-TV, 3355 South Valley View Boulevard, Las Vegas, Nevada 89102 Phone: (702) 257-8422 E-mail: **cbrown@ktnv.com**

Regina Carswell News Anchor. Contact WXIX-TV, 635 West Seventh Street, Cincinnati, Ohio 45203 Phone: (513) 421-0119 Fax: (513) 421-3022 E-mail: **rmcarswl@aol.com**

Linda Coles Executive Producer, New Jersey Network, 25 South Stockton Street, Trenton, New Jersey 08625 Phone: (609) 777-5030 E-mail: **lcoles@njn.org** Website: **www.njn.org**

Shelton Green News Reporter. Contact Shelton Green, KVUE News, 3201 Steck Avenue, Austin, Texas 78757 Phone: (512) 459-2086 E-mail: **Sgreen@kvue.com**

Maya Golden News Reporter. Maya joined KLTV in 2004 as a general assignments reporter. Born in Dallas, she grew up in Garland, Texas. She graduated from Texas A&M University in December, 2001 with a Bachelor of Arts in Journalism. Maya came to KLTV from WFAA-TV in Dallas where she worked as a production assistant. She also worked with ESPN Radio 103.3 FM in Dallas, in promotions. Maya Golden, KLTV-7, 105 West Ferguson, Tyler, Texas 75702 Phone: (903) 597-5588 E-mail: **mgolden@kltv.com** Website: **www.kltv.com**

JC Hayward   Anchors WUSA 9 News at noon and 5pm. In 30 years at WUSA 9, JC has consistently been rated one of the top news people in Washington broadcast journalism. In 1976, she won a local Emmy Award in the Best Newscaster category. In 1994, she won a local Emmy Award for her interview with Riddick Bowe. In June 1995, she was awarded the prestigious Board of Governors Award, a local Emmy given for "truly outstanding achievement and unique accomplishment of some duration and durability." Hayward has interviewed many national and international figures, including Nancy Reagan, Maya Angelou, and Luciano Pavarotti. In April 1986, she appeared on CBS-TV's popular daytime soap opera, "Capital." In July 1988, she hosted two WUSA 9 News specials, "JC & Friends." Hayward also covered Nelson Mandela's U.S. visit, reporting from Boston, Atlanta, and Miami. She co-hosted Channel 9's "Every woman," a daily one-hour talk show that was syndicated in four markets. She has produced several award-winning documentaries. The 1972 one-hour program, "Sahel: The Border of Hell," won two local Emmy Awards. In 1977, Hayward traveled to Kenya and Uganda, filming a documentary on Ugandan refugees, "We Shall Return," which earned her a Bronze Medal from the 1980 International Film Festival in New York. And "Somalia: The Silent Tragedy," on the world's largest refugee situation was syndicated by the Public Broadcast System and broadcast in England, Australia and the Caribbean. JC Hayward, WUSA-TV (Channel 9, CBS) 4100 Wisconsin Avenue, North West, Washington, DC 20016 Phone: (202) 895-5999 E-mail: **jhayward@wusatv9.com** Website: **www.wusatv9.com**

Denise Jackson   A native of Peoria, Denise attended Richwoods High and went on to Bradley University, graduating in 1986 with a bachelor's degree in journalism. Denise has been with WEEK since 1999, and is currently a reporter, as well as News 25 Weekend co-anchor. Previously, Denise was a news anchor for WWNY-TV, Watertown, New York.   Denise serves on the board of directors of the Tri-County Urban League and the YMCA Invest in Youth Campaign 2000, and is active in her church. Contact Ms. Denise Jackson, WEEK-TV, 2907 Springfield Road, East Peoria, Illinois 61611 Phone:(309) 698-2525 Fax: (309) 698-9335 E-mail: **djackson@week.com** Website: **www.week.com**

Beverly Mahone A veteran journalist with more than 25 years of experience in radio and television. In May 2006, Ms. Mahone published her first non-fiction book entitled: "Whatever! A Baby Boomer's Journey Into Middle Age." The book resulted from a journal Ms. Mahone was writing about her menopausal experiences and other challenging life issues. Also a motivational speaker she owns a media coaching and consulting business. Contact Ms. Beverly Mahone, Post Office Box 11037, Durham, North Carolina 27703 Phone: (301) 356-6280   E-mail: **bmahone@nc.rr.com** Website: **www.talk2bev.com**

Ray Metoyer News Reporter. Contact Mr. Ray Metoyer, MBC Network, 800 Forrest Street, Atlanta, Georgia 30318 Phone: (404) 350-2509 E-mail: **rmetoyer@mindspring.com**

Garry Moore A Chicago native, Gary is a news anchor and senior producer of News 25 Today. After graduating from Bradley University, he started his reporting career as a reporter and eventual news director for WXCL-AM in Peoria. He is a writer and producer of several successful theatre arts productions, including Black to the Future, Dancing My Sisters Back Home, and The Ghosts of Haiti. Gary Moore, WEEK-TV, 2907 Springfield Road, East Peoria, Illinois 61611 Phone: (309) 698-2525 E-mail: **gmoore@week.com** Website: **www.week.com**

Russell Motley Anchor/Reporter. WTEV-TV, 11700 Central Parkway, Jacksonville, Florida 32224 Phone: (904) 996-0531 Fax: (904) 642-5665 E-mail: **russellomotley@aol.com**

Tracey Neale Six-time Emmy award winner, Tracey Neale, joined the WUSA 9 News anchor team, as a key anchor on the 6pm and 11pm newscasts in August of 2004. In the past three years, Neale won the National Capital/Chesapeake Bay Chapter Emmy award for "Outstanding News Anchor." Tracey has also been awarded the 2003 Associated Press Award and the 2003 Emmy for Investigative Reporting on the Serial Sniper. She won the prestigious Edward R. Murrow Award in 2000 for a documentary on AIDS in Africa. The programs also earned her an Emmy Award; two first place awards from the National Association of Black Journalists and the Associated Press Award for Outstanding Journalism. Additionally, she received the World Health Organization's Pan-American Award for Excellence in International Reporting for her work in Africa. She is a graduate of James Madison University in Harrisonburg, Virginia. Contact Ms. Tracey Neale, WUSA-TV (Channel 9, CBS) 4100 Wisconsin Avenue, North West, Washington, DC 20016 Phone: (202) 895-5999 E-mail: **tneale@wusatv9.com** Website: **www.wusatv9.com**

Christine Nelson Reporter/KLTV 7 News 5 pm News Anchor. Christine comes to Tyler from Greenville, Mississippi where she was the 5, 6 & 10 pm anchor for WABG-TV where she became a Delta favorite most recently being named 2004 Television Personality of the Year by newspaper readers. In 2001, she broke the story on the construction halt of a plant being built in the Delta. It led to a protest by hundreds of residents and her coverage of the story placed in the "Best General News" category in the Mississippi Associated Press Awards. She has interviewed one-on-one state Governors and Congressmen, but she considers her interview with the First Lady of the United States, Laura Bush, her most memorable interview. Christine is a graduate of the University of Georgia. KLTV-7, 105 West Ferguson, Tyler, Texas 75702 Phone: (903) 597-5588 Fax: (903) 753-7111 E-mail: **cnelson@kltv.com** Website: **www.kltv.com**

Jack Noldon News Reporter, weekend anchor. After serving two tours in Vietnam, Jack left the army and moved to California where he graduated with a degree in journalism from California Sate University, Northridge. He interned at KTLA-TV in Hollywood and was hired there as a news writer. In December 1977, Jack accepted a weekend anchor and reporting position at KSEE 24. Jack Noldon, KSEE 24, 5035 East McKinley Avenue, Fresno, California 93727 Phone: (559) 454-2424 E-mail: **jackn@ksee.com** Website: **www.ksee24.com**

Charles Robinson Correspondent. Contact Mr. Charles Robinson, Maryland Public Television, 11767 Owings Mills Boulevard, Owings Mills, Maryland 21117 Phone: (410) 581-4325 E-mail: **crobinson@mail.mpt.org**

Ronda Robinson Investigative News Reporter. Ronda Robinson, WBRC-TV, 1720 Valleyview Drive, Birmingham, Alabama 35209 Phone: (205) 583-8413 E-mail: **rrobinson@wbrc.com** Website: **www.wbrc.com**

Kafi B. Rouse Host/Producer. Kafi B. Rouse, WGNT-TV, 1318 Spratley Street, Portsmouth, Virginia 23704 Phone: (757) 398-3152 Fax: (757) 398-3189 E-mail: **kbrouse@wgnttv.com**

James Tatum
Composer * Musician

Award winning pianist, composer, educator and director of the James Tatum Trio Plus, James Tatum is one of America's leading jazz musicians. His remarkable virtuosity and musicianship have placed him among the most outstanding keyboard artists of this generation. Tatum is a former Detroit School's High School Fine Arts Department Head and has been honored by the Black Jazz Music Caucus of the National Association of Jazz Educators for his outstanding contributions to jazz in education. Named Musician of the Year by the State of Michigan in 1990, he has been recognized by the Michigan Senate and the U.S. House of Representatives for his efforts to make jazz a national American treasure. He has been awarded keys to several cities throughout the United States. His Trio Plus is a regular performer at the Detroit Montreaux Jazz Festival.

In 1987, Tatum and a coalition of concerned educators and civic leaders founded the James Tatum Foundation For the Arts, Inc., a non-profit organization dedicated to serving the needs of artistic youth. The Foundation awards scholarships to deserving talented youth to assist their arts studies beyond high school. The Foundation's primary fundraiser is the presentation of music from Tatum's original composition, *The Contemporary Jazz Mass*, performed annually at Detroit Orchestra Hall, Detroit, Michigan.

James Tatum also presents a unique lecture program designed to enhance music appreciation in the educational setting with special emphasis on jazz music, one of America's richest forms of cultural heritage. His jazz lecture seminar/performance covers such topics as *Jaxx-What Is It?, The History of Jazz, Jazz Artists and Their Styles, and Listening To Jazz Throughout Its History.* The series is designed to encourage audience participation throughout the lecture and appeals to audiences in K-12 and university and adult level.

TV Talk Shows

America's Black Forum Created twenty-eight years ago ABF presents insightful and balanced debate on current and critical issues with top newsmakers from around the world. Contact Nikki Webber, Director of Talent, TVOne, 1010 Wayne Avenue, 10th Floor, Silver Spring, Maryland 20910 Phone: (301) 755-0400 E-mail: **nwebber@tv-one.tv** Website: **www.tv-one.tv**

Atlantic City Shines A public access talk show produced and hosted by columnist and photo journalist, Raymond Tyler. Public Access Channel Two, 6701 Black Horse Pike, Suite A-4, EHT, New Jersey 08234 Phone: (609) 677-0168 E-mail: **troubleman@aolhiphop.com**

Black Accent on LA "For Members Only" TV The longest running locally produced African-American TV program in LA, 24 years running. Tom Reed, Host/Executive Producer. Black Accent on LA, Post Office Box 27487, Los Angeles, California 90027 Phone: (818) 894-8880

B. Smith with Style A nationally televised weekly lifestyle television show featuring numerous celebrity guests. B. Smith, TVOne, 1010 Wayne Avenue, 10th Floor, Silver Spring, Maryland 20910 Phone: (301) 755-0400 E-mail: **feedback@bsmith.com** Website: **www.bsmith.com**

Caribbeanwomentoday A segment on Caribbean Weekly; an informational and community affairs program produced by the Duke of Earle Media Group (Florida/Jamaica) and hosted by Dr. Anita Davis-DeFoe, author of A Woman's Guide to Soulful Living and resident advice guru for She-Caribbean, a St. Lucian magazine that is sold in 20 islands, New York, Atlanta, South Florida, Ghana, London, Germany and Italy. Dr. DeFoe is the host of Soulfully Speaking on CaribVoice Radio and Akeru Radio. Contact The Defoe Group, Post Office Box 451973, Sunrise, Florida 33345 Phone: (954) 816-9462 E-mail: **dranitadavisdefoe@hotmail.com** Website: **www.dranitadavisdefoe.com**

Christian Television Network Founded in 1982 CTN is the nations first African-American Christian television network. The mission of CTN is "To communicate the Gospel of Jesus Christ by producing inspirational engaging interactive Christian programming and wholesome family-oriented entertainment through broadcasting cable casting web casting and worldwide satellite." Founder, President Glenn Plummer. Contact LeJohn Plummer, Christian Television Network, 23705 Plymouth Road, Detroit, Michigan 48239 Phone: (313) 533-1942 E-mail: **ljplummer@ctnusa.org** Website: **www.ctnusa.org**

Colours TV Multicultural television network production of Black Star Communications (BSC), an African American owned, non-profit corporation formed for civic, charitable, and educational purposes. Ms. Tracy Jenkins Winchester, President. Art Thomas, Vice President. Damon Purdy, Manager Post Production. Contact Colours TV, 200 Quebec Street, Building 600, Suite 209, Denver, Colorado 80230 Phone: (303) 326-0088 E-Mail: **info@colourstv.org** Website: **www.colourstv.org**

Community Affairs Hosted by Gilda Stanbery-Cotney. Interviews and Community Affairs. WFVS TV 21, Fort Valley State University, 1005 State University Drive, Fort Valley, Georgia 31030 Phone: (478) 825-6211 Website: **www.fvsu.edu**

CTN Live A daily talk show hosted by Reverend Glenn Plummer featuring interesting people within and without the faith community. Reverend Plummer and guests explores topics that affect the body of Christ. Live with Glenn R. Plummer (cc) airs on Familynet. Contact LeJohn Plummer, Chrisitan Television Network, 23705 Plymouth Road, Detroit, Michigan 48239 Phone: (313) 533-1942 E-mail: **ljplummer@ctnusa.org** Website: **www.ctnusa.org**

Distortion 2 Static (D2S) The D2S crew makes it a point to interview both the best in Bay Area Hip Hop, as well as out-of-town artists visiting the Bay. Host, Mac Mall, aka "the Mac-nificent." Contact Mac Mall, Distortion 2 Static, 570 Beale Street Suite 204, San Francisco, California 94107 E-mail: **holla@distortion2static.com** Website: **www.distortion2static.com**

Express Yourself Literary Café Cable TV show hosted by Dr. Rosie Milligan, founder and director of "Black Writers on Tour," and former columnist for Black Issue Book Review Magazine. Contact Milligan Books, 1425 West Manchester Avenue, Suite C, Los Angeles, California 90047 Phone: (323) 750-3592 Fax: (323) 750-2886 E-mail: **DrRosie@aol.com** Website: **www.milliganbooks.com**

The Grant Salaam Show, On Common Ground Television show hosted by Grant Salaam. Grant Hassan Salaam, Post Office Box 1061, Pine Lake, Georgia 30072 Phone: (877) 376-0776 E-mail: **grantsalaam@yahoo.com** Website: **www.salaamcalligraphy.com**

Inside FVSU Entertaining and informative shows. Interviews. Hosted by Dr. Myldred Hill. Inside FVSU, WFVS TV 21, Fort Valley State University, 1005 State University Drive, Fort Valley, Georgia 31030 Phone: (478) 825-6211 Website: **www.fvsu.edu**

In the Corner TV show features 30-minutes of the hottest music videos and celebrity interviews in Atlanta. Carleen Brown, station manager/adjunct faculty. CAU-TV, Clark Atlanta University, 111 James P. Brawley Drive, South West, Atlanta, Georgia 30314 Phone: (404) 880-6230 Website: **www.cautv.com**

Jericho Broadcasting Organization dedicated to changing the face of the black media by focusing our marketing efforts, and programming directly at African-Americans. President/CEO, Mr. Roy M. Eavins II. Jericho Broadcasting Network, Post Office Box 2468, Eatonville, Florida 32751 Phone: (407) 875-8484 E-mail: **Info@erichobroadcasting.com** Website: **www.jerichobroadcasting.com**

Jewel Daniels Black Business Professionals and Entrepreneurs founder Jewel Daniels, hosts a weekly television show on Comcast. Founded in 2000, each year, the (BBPE), hosts a national conference whose mission to service the minority business community. Jewel Daniels, Black Business Professionals and Entrepreneurs, Post Office Box 60561, Savannah, Georgia 31420 Phone: (912) 354-7400 Fax: (501) 694-9220 E-mail: **jewel@blackbusinessprofessionals.com** Website: **www.blackbusinessprofessionals.com**

The Literary Cafe Author talk show dedicated to promoting and showcasing African-American authors. Contact Ms. Anita Shari Peterson, Najah Productions, Peterson Creative Group, 598 Indian Trail Road, Suite #256, Indian Trail, North Carolina 28079 Phone: (704) 821-1786 E-mail: **anita@literarycafe.org** Website: **www.literarycafe.org**

Live with Glenn R. Plummer (cc) Airs on Familynet. Host, Glenn R. Plummer. Contact LeJohn Plummer, Chrisitan Television Network, 23705 Plymouth Road, Detroit, Michigan 48239 Phone: (313) 533-1942 E-mail: **ljplummer@ctnusa.com** Website: **www.ctnlive.com**

Making It! Minority Success Stories A weekly television program that focuses on minority entrepreneurs hosted by award winning journalist Nelson Davis. Contact Nelson Davis, Making It!, 5800 Sunset Boulevard, Los Angeles, California 90028 Phone: (323) 460-5253 E-mail: **info@makingittv.com** Website: **www.makingittv.com**

The Montel Williams Show Daily talk show with host, Montel Williams. Contact Producer, The Montel Williams Show, 433 West 53rd Street, New York, New York 10019 Phone: (212) 989-8101 Website: **www.montelshow.com**

News 25 Today Central Illinois' first and highest rated morning news show. Interviews guest. Garry Moore, senior producer. Gary Moore, WEEK-TV, 2907 Springfield Road, East Peoria, Illinois 61611 Phone: (309) 698-2525 Fax: (309) 698-9335 E-mail: **gmoore@week.com** Website: **www.week.com**

News & Notes with Ed Gordon Host, Ed Gordon. Contact National Public Radio (NPR), 635 Massachusetts Avenue, North West, Washington, DC 20001 Phone: (202) 513-3232 Fax: (202) 513-3329 Website: **www.npr.org**

Platinum Plus TV Hip Hop driven talk show featuring local young up and coming artists due to air on FOX 54 network in October. Platinum Plus Productions, 301 Converse Court Columbus, Georgia 31907 Phone: (706) 687-4581 E-mail: **platinumplus@peoplepc.com**

Poetree-N-Motion TV program which shares information of community events, history tidbits, book reviews and has guests with current community issues. Hosted by poet, author, and producer, Dee Freeman. Show airs in Lansing, Michigan on Comcast Cable Channel 16 on Thursdays at 3:30PM and East Lansing, Michigan, Channel 30 WELM on Tuesdays at 7:00PM. Dee Freeman, 1127 Alexandria Drive, Lansing, Michigan 48917 Phone: (517) 321-3122 Fax: (517) 321-3122 E-mail: **deekfreeman@yahoo.com** Website: **www.deepoette.com**

Road To Success TV show hosted by Bill McCreary. Contact Quest Media Entertainment, Inc., 1000 Richmond Terrace, Staten Island, New York 10301 Phone: (718) 727-3777 Fax: (718) 727-2132 E-mail: **questmedia@questmedia.net** Website: **www.questmedia.net**

Sayword An entertainment television show hosted by Carla Rowser Canty. Poets, musicians, public speakers, authors, etc., are encouraged to showcase. Contact Ms. Carla Rowser Canty, A Blackgurl Production, Post Office Box 843, Hartford, Connecticut 06143 Phone: (860) 983-3257 E-mail: **BlackGurrl@aol.com** Website: **www.wqtqfm.com/wqtq**

Shades of Opinion Talk show examines breaking news, events, and issues affecting the African American community. Show features leaders who shape the future. Hosted by Christopher. WYBE Public Television, 8200 Ridge Avenue, Philadelphia, Pennsylvania 19128 Phone: (215) 483-3900 Fax: (215) 483-6908 E-mail: **talkshows@wybe.org** Website: **www.wybe.org**

Singletary Says Show series centers around solutions for families with specific financial tribulations hosted by author and syndicated columnist Michelle Singletary. Contact Ms. Nikki Webber, Director of Talent, TVOne, 1010 Wayne Avenue, 10th Floor, Silver Spring, Maryland 20910 Phone: (301) 755-0400 E-mail: **nwebber@tv-one.tv** Website: **www.tv-one.tv**

Straight Talk African American television show hosted by President and CEO of Star Planet Television and Associated Companies, W. L. Lillard. Show airs on channel 25. W. L. Lillard, Star Planet Television Network, 1140 West 103rd Street, Chicago, Illinois 60643 Phone: (773) 445-7788 Fax: (773) 881-0514 Website: **www.starplanettv.com**

Talkin with Da Prez Hosted by FVSU President Kofi Lomotey. Interviews. Contact Talkin with Da Prez, WFVS TV 21, Fort Valley State University, 1005 State University Drive, Fort Valley, Georgia 31030 Phone: (478) 825-6211 Website: **www.fvsu.edu**

Tavis Smiley Presents   Television Talk Show hosted by Tavis Smiley. Contact Producer, KCET & The Smiley Group, 4401 Sunset Boulevard, Los Angeles, California 90027 Phone: (323) 666-6500 E-mail: **tsinfo@kcet.org** Website: **www.pbs.org/kcet/tavissmiley**

Tony Brown's Journal The longest running show on PBS, hosted by Tony Brown. Guests. Tony Brown Productions, 2214 Frederick Douglass Boulevard, Suite 124, New York, New York 10026 Phone: (212) 694-4800 E-mail: **mail@tbol.net** Website: **www.tonybrownsites.com**

TV One on One Host, Cathy Hughes interviews the most influential African American from business leaders, to entertainment gurus to spectacular athletes. Contact Nikki Webber, Director of Talent, TVOne, 1010 Wayne Avenue, 10th Floor, Silver Spring, Maryland 20910 Phone: (301) 755-0400 E-mail: **nwebber@tv-one.tv** Website: **www.tv-one.tv**

Wordz in Motion TV Literary and Entertainment TV on WHPR TV 33 & Comcast Cable 20 & 71. Contact Dynasty Publications Inc, Post Office Box 35274, Detroit, Michigan 48235 Phone: (248) 763-2254 E-mail: **metrodetroitliterarycollective@mllbnetwork.com** Website: **www.dynastypublications.net**

Wright Place™ TV Show Dr. Letitia S. Wright, D.C, host. The only business lifestyle show for women, seen on Southern California Network Television KVMD. The Wright Place™ TV Show, 8300 Utica Avenue, 3rd Floor, Rancho Cucamonga, California 91730 E-mail: **info@wrightplacetv.com** Website: **www.wrightplacetv.com**

The Writer's Network   Cable television program celebrating 27 years.   Interviews contemporary writers, publishers, artists, and musicians. C.D. Grant, host and co-founder of the company. The Writer's Network, Post Office Box 437, Bronx, New York 10467 Phone: (914) 683-6792 E-mail: **blindbeggar1@juno.com** Website: **www.blindbeggarpress.org**

Voice-Over Artists

KD Bowe Born in Norfolk, Virginia, KD Bowe was raised in Currituck County, North Carolina. During his college years, a casual request for the time from his college radio station's general manager began his highly popular career in radio. Known nation wide for his comedic, witty, and sometimes controversial radio show, KD's rich baritone voice has been used on hundreds of commercials, and as the signature voice for radio and TV stations both nationally and abroad. He's been featured on several artists' recording projects and has even recorded his own single that gained national airplay. A recipient of the 1998 Trailblazer Award for excellence in the arena of mass media, KD Bowe is also the CEO of KDB Productions, a cutting edge audio services production company located in Conyers, Georgia. Contact KD Bowe, KDYA, Gospel 1190 AM The Light, 3260 Blume Drive, Suite 520, Richmond, California 94806 Phone: (510) 222-4242 Fax: (510) 262-9054 Website: **www.gospel1190.net**

Jackie Campbell Air personality. Originally from Detroit, Jackie graduated from Wayne State University with a degree specializing in Radio and Television. She has worked for WTVS-TV 56 and WDIV-TV 4 in Detroit, and WDTN-TV 2 in Dayton, Ohio, as well as other communication entities. Before coming to the Sheridan Gospel Network, she worked as an Assistant to the President at WPBA-TV 30, Public Television in Atlanta. Jackie also does voice-overs, and can be heard on several public TV affiliates and various radio stations across the United States. Contact Ms. Jackie Campbell, KDYA, Gospel 1190 AM The Light, 3260 Blume Drive, Suite 520, Richmond, California 94806 Phone: (510) 222-4242 Fax: (510) 262-9054 E-mail: **jcampbell@sgnthelight.com** Website: **www.gospel1190.net**

Vivi Monroe Congress The author of The Bankrupt Spirit Principles for Turning Setbacks into Comebacks, The McMillon Family cookbook: Something to Shout About! and newly released, Manna for Mamma: Wisdom for Women in the Wilderness hold a Bachelor of Arts in Human Relations, a Master of Theological Studies and a Doctor of Ministry degree in Christan Counseling. She creatively couples her formal training in psychology, dance, voice-over and modeling with artistic expressions such as literature, music and meditation (s) to reach those caught up in the struggles of life. Dr. Vivi Monroe Congress, Little Light Productions, LLC, Post Office Box 540741, Grand Prairie, Texas 75054 E-mail: **littlelightprod@aol.com** Website: **www.drvivimonroecontress.com**

Billy Daniels Air personality and Ormond Beach, Florida native Bill Daniels attended Bethune-Cookman College on a music scholarship where he earned a BA in English/Communications. In addition to his on-air duties, Billy is the Creative Director and Writer for the Nationally syndicated show "The Bobby Jones Gospel Countdown." He is also a voice-over talent for commercials and other programming for SPS (Sheridan Production Services). Billy's inspirational booster is "If your vision doesn't cost you something, then it's only a daydream." KDYA, Gospel 1190 AM The Light, 3260 Blume Drive, Suite 520, Richmond, California 94806 Phone: (510) 222-4242 Fax: (510) 262-9054 Website: **www.gospel1190.net**

Lance-O Founder and CEO of Kulcha Shok Musik. The company produces and promotes everything in Caribbean music. KSM specializes in producing reggae music as well as reggae, dancehall, soca & Caribbean music programming for radio, satellite, the internet, & the airlines. KSM has programs & music that airs on both Delta & Air Jamaica Airlines, XM & Sirius radio and allover the internet. KSM produces a weekly syndicated entertainment report called 'REGGAE VIBES,' heard on nearly 120 radio stations around the world. KSM also produces radio & voiceover spots. Clients have included WQAM, WPOW, Shaggy & MCA Records, & Irie FM Jamaica. Contact Mr. Lance-O, Kulcha Shok Muzik, 1218 Drexel Avenue, Suite #203, Miami, Florida 33139 Phone: (305) 534-6110 E-mail: **lanceo@kulchashok.com** Website: **www.kulchashok.com**

Mary T. Sala Actor based in Los Angeles and voice over talent. Mother of two young children. University Professor, real estate investor, singer, voice/speech coach. Film: Light The Flambeau, Production HQ. T.V. and commercials: GM-Pontiac, Visa, Microsoft, My Mylanta, Loving, ABC T.V. Off Broadway: The Caucasian Chalk Circle, Public Theatre, New York, Once in a Lifetime, Samuel Beckett Theatre, New York. Tours: Young Playwrights Festival Tour, Foundation of the Dramatists Guild, New York, Alice in Wonderland, DearKnows Production Company, Lincoln Center, New York. Ms. Mary T. Sala, 2629 Foothill Boulevard, #344, La Crescenta, California 91214 Phone: (818) 541-7675 Fax: (818) 279-0533 E-mail: **marytsala@yahoo.com** Website: **www.marytsala.com**

Rodney Saulsberry This Detroit native and University of Michigan Graduates' distinctive announcers voice is literally everywhere. He records all of the radio and television promos for the Indiana Pacers home basketball games. As one of the top trailer voices in the business, fans have heard his voice promoting some of their favorites: Friday After Next, The Best Man, Soul Food, All About The Benjamin's and many more. He has been a voiceover commercial pitchman for Zatarain's, ALPO, Lincoln LS, Toyota, 7UP, Burger King, and many others. He can also be heard reading narrating E! Entertainments, and True Hollywood Story. Rodney Saulsberry, Post Office Box 1735, Agoura Hills, California 91376 Phone: (818) 207-2682 E-mail: **rodtalks@rodneysaulsberry.com** Website: **www.rodneysaulsberry.com**

Troy Smauldon Voice-over artist. Troy Smauldon, 43393 Eureka Drive, Clinton Township, Michigan 48036 Phone: (586) 260-8915 E-mail: **troyboywonder@msn.com**

TKO Productions Specializes in voiceovers and copywriting. Originated by former female production director, T.K. Jones. TKO Productions, 2637 G Suffolk Avenue, High Point, North Carolina 27265 Phone: (843) 437-6009 E-mail: **tk.jones@citcomm.com** Website: **www.tko-productions.com**

Voice Addict Productions, LLC Voice-over imaging and commercial/promo production company. Contact Mr. Kevin Genus, Voice Addict Productions, 13809 Jefferson Park Drive, Suite 3304, Herndon, Virginia 20171 Phone: (732) 821-8570 E-mail: **kevin@kevingenus.com** Website: **www.kevingenus.com**

Web Designers

Artic Designs, Inc. Web design and hosting company. Contact Mr. Arthur Huntley, Artic Designs, Inc., Post Office Box 44191, Atlanta, Georgia 30336 E-mail: **info@articdesigns.com** Website: **www.articdesigns.com**

Association of African American Web Designers Directory Professional organization AAWDD is an index of black professional web developers located throughout the United States: graphic designers, programmers, writers, system administrators, marketers, e-commerce, flash and network specialist, and other web professionals. AAWDD, Post Office Box 146, Malone, New York 12953 Website: **www.africanamericanwebdesigners.com**

Association of African American Web Developers The Association of African American Web Developers is a vehicle for promoting camaraderie, collaboration, and professional growth among men and women of color in all phases of web development and design, and to demonstrate their talents, skills, creativity, and contributions to the growth of the industry. Wiley Pompey-Kulia, Founder. Website: **www.aaawd.net**

Designs4U Web design and development, hosting. Ms. Kinya, McDowell, Owner, Designs4U, Chicago, Illinois 60649 Phone: (312) 699-9277 E-mail: **kinya@designs4u.net** Website: **www.designs4u.net**

Designing Vision A Christian based professional graphic and web design services company. Contact Designing Vision, 904 Kostner Avenue, Matteson, Illinois 60443 Phone: (708) 747-9733 E-mail: **info@designingvision.com** Website: **www.designingvision.com**

Fruitful Works, Inc. Company dedicated to providing professional high-quality web services to small businesses, entrepreneurial enterprises, community organizations, schools, gospel recording artists, and Christian churches at a reasonable cost. Mary Cosby, FruitfulWorks, Inc., 18701 Grand River, Suite #134, Detroit, Michigan 48223 Phone: (313) 531-1141 E-mail: **webmaster@fruitfulworks.com** Website: **www.fruitfulworks.com**

Images & Illuminations A design studio offering extensive print design services including book design, logos, brochures, posters, invitations, and catalogs. Ms. Cheryl Hanna, Design Director. Contact Images & Illuminations, 214 Sixth Avenue, Suite 3B, Brooklyn, New York 11215 Phone: (718) 783-0131 E-mail: **imagesandilluminations@earthlink.net** Website: **www.imagesandilluminations.com**

Nubonyx.com A minority owned Internet Service Provider founded in 2000, with the idea of creating an independent, entrepreneurial, versatile ISP that would serve a severely neglected segment of American consumers. Nubonyx.com, 1564A Fitzgerald Drive, #133, Pinole, California 94564 E-mail: **service@nubonyx.com** Website: **www.nubonyx.com**

Overjoy Creations Web Design   Founded by Michelle Hammonds in 2003. Although based in Houston, Texas we are able to assist companies all over the United States with their web development needs. OverJOY Creations Web Design, Post Office Box 711117 Houston, Texas 77271 Phone: 713-723-2188 E-mail: **michelle_hammonds@overjoycreations.com** Website: **www.overjoycreations.com**

PageTurner.net   Provides web site design, internet consulting services and website hosting. Contact Pamela Walker-Williams, Pageturner.net, Post Office Box 120, 2951 Marina Bay Drive, #130, League City, Texas 77573 Phone: (866) 875-1044 E-mail: **pwsquare@pageturner.net** Website: **pageturner.net**

Patrick PJ Davis Marketing and web solutions for authors, entertainers and publishing companies. Contact Patrick PJ Davis, Post Office Box 420725, Houston, Texas 77242 Phone: (713) 866-6548 E-mail: **info@blackcottonworks.net** Website: **www.blackcottonworks.net**

Quill Link Website development, flash animation, software and database development. Quill Link, Post Office Box 481616, Charlotte, North Carolina 28269 E-mail: **contacts@quillink.net** Website: **www.quillink.net** Phone: (704) 509-9975 Fax: (508) 300-7713

Right Hand Concepts Web designer. Founder, Vonetta Booker-Brown creates press releases, bios and media kits for artists and small businesses. She is the designer, creator and editor of Triscene.com, an online magazine that covers the New York and Connecticut area. Vonetta Booker- Brown, Right Hand Concepts, 2020 Pennsylvania Avenue, North West, #341, Washington, DC 20006 Phone: (203) 382-0403 E-mail: **chiefelement@gmail.com** Website: **www.righthandconcepts.com**

Ron Clowney Design Founder, Ron Clowney offers both traditional art services in addition to computer graphics design work in the areas of print and animation, pencil or painted portraits, pencil drawings of notable homes that the owner wants drawn and any type of commissioned artwork. Contact Ron Clowney Design, 5513 Adode Falls Road, Unit 10, San Diego, California 92120 Phone: (619) 501-5740 E-mail: **rclowney@cox.net** Website: **www.rclowney.com**

SaveOnHosting.net We offer a variety of low-cost web design & hosting services. We can create a custom website for your business at a price that is fair and affordable. SaveOnHosting.net, 3137 Houston Drive, Columbus, Ohio 43207 Phone: (614) 886-9922 Fax: (614) 497- 0626 E-mail: **sales@saveonhosting.net** Website: **www.saveonhosting.net**

Shilo Web Design Monique Boea is the principal developer for Shilo and has over 8 years experience in designing Web sites for clients across the country. Lee Thomas, President. Shilo Web Design, 619 East College Avenue, Suite C3, Decatur, Georgia 30030 Phone: (404) 371-9355 E-mail: **info@shilowebdesign.net** Website: **www.shilowebdesign.net**

Tek Solutions, Inc An information technology consulting company that develops innovative technology solutions for a wide range of small businesses including web site design and creation and hosting. Tek Solutions, Inc., Post Office Box 6031, Broadview, Illinois 60155 Phone: (708) 223-8401 E-mail: **dkbrown@teksolutionsinc.com** Website: **www.teksolutionsinc.com**

Web Groups

*Listed below are group websites addresses —Do not e-mail always post directly on message boards or e-mail must be from a group subscriber.

AACBWI	**AACBWI@yahoogroups.com**
African American FemalePlaywrights	**Afamfemplaywrights@yahoo.com**
African American Readers	**AfricanAmericanReaders@yahoogroups.com**
African American Media Club	**African_American_Media_Club@yahoogroups.com**
African American Teachers	**Africanamericanteachers@yahoogroups.com**
African American Women in Cinema	**AAWIC_group@yahoo.com**
BAPWD.com	**bapwdcom@yahoogroups.com**
Black Book Reviews	**BlackBookReviews@yahoogroups.com**
Black-Filmmakers	**Black-Filmmakers@yahoogroups.com**
Black Playwrights	**BlackPlaywrghts@yahoogroups.com**
Black Teachers Association	**BlackTeachersAssociation@groups.msn.com**
Black Theatre Productions	**BlackTheatreProductions@yahoogroups.com**
BLNNJ	**BLNNJ@yahoogroups.com**
Brown Bag Entertainment	**Brownbagentertainment@yahoogroups.com**
Doebook Announce	**Doebookannounce@yahoogroups.com**
Ebony Book Luvers	**Ebonybookluvers@yahoogroups.com**
FeatureFilm	**FeatureFilm@yahoogroups.com**
Harambee 2004	**Harambee2004@yahoogroups.com**
The Kalico Jones Project	**Thekalicojonesproject@yahoogroups.com**
Ladies Makin Movies	**Ladiesmakinmovies@yahoogroups.com**
Luv4self_Network	**Lov4self_Network@yahoo.com**
The Making Of A Bestseller	**Themakingofabestseller@yahoogroups.com**
Mixed Minds Book Club	**MixedMindsBookClub@groups.msn.com**
Motown Writers	**Motownwriters@yahoo.com**
MWG_Book Club	**MWG-ABMT-Group@yahoo.com**

Pentouch News	Pentouch-news@yahoo.com
RAWSISTAZ Review	RAWSISTAZ_Review@yahoo.com
Romance Announce	RomanceAnnounce@yahoo.com
Romance Noire Book Club	Romancenoirebookclub@yahoogroups.com
Shenandoah Site	ShenandoahSite@groups.msn.com
SistatoSista Literary Reading Group	SistatoSistaLiteraryReadingGroup@groups.msn.com
Tampa Bay African-American Film	Tampa_Bay_African_American_Film@yahoogroups
Tanya Kersey	Tanyakersey@yahoo.com

Web Sites

Writer's Sites:

Authors Supporting Authors Positively   www.asap-online.org

Black Writer's Alliance   www.blackwriters.org

The Hurston/Wright Foundation   www.hurstonwright.org

Motown Writers Network   www.SylviaHubbard.com

Reader's Sites:

A Place of Our Own (APOOO)   www.apooo.org

Black Book Plus   www.blackbookplus.com

The Black Library   www.theblacklibrary.com

Black Expressions Book Club   www.blackexpressions.com

Book Remarks   www.book-remarks.com

CushCity   www.cushcity.com

The G.R.I.T.S. Reading Group   www.thegrits.com

R.A.W. Sistaz Reading Group   www.Rawsistaz.com

Romance Sites:

Heartrate Reviews   www.heartratereviews.com

Romance in Color   www.romanceincolor.com

The Romance Reader's Connection   www.theromancereadersconnection.com

Literary Sites:

Awareness Magazine	**www.awarenessmagazine.net**
African American Literature Book Club	**www.aalbc.com**
BAPWD.com	**www.bapwd.com**
Diva Tribe	**www.divatribe.com**
Hueman Bookstore On-line	**www.huemanbookstore.com**
Ngoshi Books	**www.nghosibooks.com**
The Romer Review	**www.theromerreview.com**
Shadow Poetry	**www.shadowpoetry.com**
The Star Lite Cafe	**www.thestarlitecafe.com**

Index